IISS

D1794978

THE MILITARY BALANCE 1992-1993

Published by BRASSEY'S for

THE INTERNATIONAL
INSTITUTE FOR
STRATEGIC STUDIES

23 Tavistock Street London WC2E 7NQ

THE MILITARY BALANCE 1992–1993

Published by Brassey's for
The International Institute for Strategic Studies
23 Tavistock Street, London WC2E 7NQ

Director

Dr Bo Huldt

**Assistant Director
for Information**

Col. Andrew Duncan

Information Officers:

Ground Forces
Phillip Mitchell

Aerospace
Wg Cdr Kenneth Petrie RAF

Naval Forces
Cdr Geoffrey Bryant RN

Defence Economist
Nicolas Protonotarios

Editorial/Production:
Victoria Fisher
Clare Wilkes
Rosalind Winton

This publication has been prepared by the Director of the Institute and his Staff, who accept full responsibility for its contents. These do not, and indeed cannot, represent a consensus of views among the worldwide membership of the Institute as a whole.

First published Autumn 1992

ISBN 1 85753 027 6
ISSN 0459-7222

Military Balance (ISSN 0459 7222) is published annually by Brassey's (UK) Ltd, 165 Great Dover Street, London SE1. All orders accompanied with payment should be sent directly to Turpin Distribution Services Ltd, Blackhorse Road, Letchworth, Herts SG6 1HN, UK. 1992 annual subscription rate is UK and overseas £33.50 single copy £35.00, North America $52.50, single copy $55.00. Airfreight and mailing in the USA by Publications Expediting Inc., 200 Meacham Avenue, Elmont, New York 11003, USA.
USA POSTMASTER: send address changes to Military Balance, Publications Expediting Inc., 200 Meacham Avenue, Elmont, New York 11003, USA. Application to mail at second-class postage is pending at Jamaica, New York 11431. All other despatches outside the UK by Printflow Air within Europe and Printflow Airsaver outside Europe.

Printed in the UK by Halstan & Co. Ltd., Amersham, Bucks

CONTENTS

THE MILITARY BALANCE 1992–1993
LAYOUT AND PRINCIPLES OF COMPILATION

The Military Balance is updated each year to provide a timely, quantitative assessment of the military forces and defence expenditures of over 160 countries. This volume contains such data as at 1 June 1992. This chapter explains how *The Military Balance* is structured and outlines the general principles followed. The format for country entries remains the same as in the 1991–92 edition.

The break-up of the Soviet Union has necessitated a re-evaluation of the way in which *The Military Balance* divides the world into geographical sections. Although in mid-1992 the Commonwealth of Independent States (CIS) still controls the nuclear forces and some other military assets (such as Border Troops) of the former Soviet Union, it is not a subject of international law, and therefore does not warrant a separate section (although it does feature in the essay 'Nuclear Developments', see pp. 222–28). Russia is both a European and an Asian state and is given a separate section. *The Military Balance* assumes that Russia has taken on all former USSR overseas deployments unless there is specific evidence to the contrary. The section on 'Non-NATO Europe' has been expanded to include the Baltic Republics, Byelarus, Ukraine, Moldova and the three Trans-Caucasian republics (Azerbaijan, Armenia and Georgia). The latter have been included in Europe as signatories of the Conventional Forces in Europe Treaty (CFE). Bosnia-Herzegovina, Croatia, Macedonia and Slovenia are listed as independent, while Serbia and Montenegro are shown as the follow-on state to the Federal Republic of Yugoslavia. We have decided to divide the Asian and Australasian section in two. 'Central and South Asia' will cover the five Central Asian republics of the former Soviet Union (Kazakhstan, Kyrgyzstan, Tajikistan, Turkmenistan and Uzbekistan), Afghanistan, Bangladesh, India, Myanmar (Burma), Nepal, Pakistan and Sri Lanka. The remaining Asian countries are in the 'East Asia and Australasia' section (with China no longer receiving individual section status). The order in which the regional groupings appear in the book has been altered (see Contents page).

GENERAL ARRANGEMENT

There are two parts to *The Military Balance*. The first comprises national entries grouped by region; the Index on p. 12 gives the page reference for each national entry. Regional groupings are preceded by a short introduction describing significant changes in defence postures, economic status and military aid arrangements of the countries concerned. Inclusion of a country or state in no way implies legal recognition for or IISS approval of it.

The second section contains analytical essays which cover developments in the nuclear forces of the US and former Soviet Union, including both progress in arms-control negotiations and the implications of unilateral declarations, and the conventional forces of the signatories of the CFE Treaty, in the light of published data and arms-control agreements (accompanied by tables showing the relative strengths of the relevant forces). Other tables provide information on nuclear delivery means, and a comparison of defence expenditure and military manpower of all countries listed in *The Military Balance* for which there is sufficient data. A list of military agreements reached at CIS summits, showing which republics signed each, and extracts from the main agreements are included. There is also a summary of the composition of all United Nations and other peacekeeping forces, together with a short description of their missions.

At the back of the book there is a list of the type, name/designation, maker and country of origin of all aircraft and helicopters listed in *The Military Balance*.

A map of the territory of the former Soviet Union and its immediate neighbours is provided as a loose insert. The map illustrates the agreed apportionment of Treaty Limited Equipments (TLE) (under the CFE) between the republics of the former Soviet Union and the current deployment of TLE.

ABBREVIATIONS AND DEFINITIONS

Space limitations necessitate the use of abbreviations, a list of which is on a fold-out sheet at the back of the book. The abbreviation may have both singular or plural meanings, e.g., 'elm' = 'element' or 'elements'. The qualification 'some' means *up to*, whilst 'about' means *the total could be higher than given*. In financial data, the $ sign refers to US dollars unless otherwise stated; the term billion (bn) signifies 1,000 million (m). Footnotes particular to an entry in one country or table are indicated by letters, while those which apply throughout the book are marked by symbols (i.e. * for training aircraft counted by the IISS as combat capable, and † where serviceability of equipment is in doubt).

NATIONAL ENTRIES

Information on each country is given in a format as standard as the available information permits: economic and demographic data, and military data including manpower, length of conscript service, outline organization, number of formations and units, the inventory of major equipments of each service, followed where applicable by a description of their deployment. Details of national forces stationed abroad and of foreign stationed forces are also given.

GENERAL MILITARY DATA

Manpower

The 'Active' total comprises all servicemen and women on full-time duty (including conscripts and long-term assignments from the Reserves). Under the heading 'Terms of service' only the length of conscript service is shown; where service is voluntary, there is no entry.

In *The Military Balance* the term 'Reserve' is used to describe formations and units not fully manned or operational in peacetime, but which can be mobilized by recalling reservists in an emergency. Unless otherwise indicated, the 'Reserves' entry includes all reservists committed to rejoin the armed forces in an emergency, except when national reserve service obligations following conscription last almost a lifetime. Then *The Military Balance* strength estimates of effective reservists are based on the numbers available within five years of completing full-time service, unless there is good evidence that obligations are enforced for longer. Some countries have more than one category of Reserves, often kept at varying degrees of readiness; where possible these differences are denoted using the national descriptive title, but always under the heading of Reserves, so as to distinguish them from full-time active forces.

Stocks of equipment held in reserve and not assigned to either active or reserve units are listed as 'in store'.

Other Forces

Many countries maintain paramilitary forces whose training, organization, equipment and control suggest they may be usable in support, or in lieu, of regular military forces. These are listed and their roles described, after the military forces of each country; their manpower is not normally included in the Armed Forces totals at the start of each entry. Home Guard units are counted as paramilitary. Where paramilitary groups are not on full-time active duty, the suffix (R) is added after the title to indicate that they have reserve status. When internal opposition forces are armed and appear to pose a significant threat to the security of a state, their details are listed separately after national paramilitary forces.

Equipment

Numbers are shown by function and type and represent total holdings, including active and reserve operational and training units and 'in store' stocks. Inventory totals for missile systems (e.g., SSM, SAM, ATGW, etc.) relate to launchers and not to missiles.

Operational Deployments

The Military Balance does not normally list short-term operational deployments, particularly where military operations are in progress. The contribution or deployment of forces on operations are normally covered in the text preceeding each regional section.

GROUND FORCES

The national designation is normally used for army formations. The term 'regiment' can be misleading. In some cases it is essentially a brigade of all arms; in others, a grouping of battalions of a single arm; and lastly (the UK and French usage) a battalion-sized unit. The sense intended is indicated. Where there is no standard organization the intermediate levels of command are shown as HQ, followed by the total numbers of units which could be allocated between them. Where a unit's title overstates its real capability, the title is put in inverted commas, and an estimate of the comparable NATO unit size in parentheses: e.g., 'bde' (coy).

Equipment

The Military Balance uses the same definitions as those agreed to at the Conventional Forces in Europe (CFE) negotiations. These are:

Battle Tanks (MBT): armoured tracked combat vehicles weighing at least 16.5 metric tonnes unladen, armed with a 360° traverse gun of at least 75-mm calibre. Any new wheeled combat vehicles entering service which meet these criteria will be considered to be battle tanks.

Armoured Personnel Carriers (APC): a lightly armoured combat vehicle designed and equipped to transport an infantry squad; may be armed with integral/organic weapons of less than 20-mm calibre. Versions of APC converted for other uses (such as weapons platform, command post, communications terminal) which do not allow the transporting of infantry are considered 'look alikes' and are not regarded as treaty-limited equipment (TLE), but are subject to verification.

Armoured Infantry Fighting Vehicle (AIFV): an armoured combat vehicle designed and equipped to transport an infantry squad, armed with an integral/organic cannon of at least 20-mm calibre.

Heavy Armoured Combat Vehicles (HACV): an armoured combat vehicle weighing more than six metric tonnes unladen, with an integral/organic direct-fire gun of at least 75-mm (which does not fall within the definitions of APC, AIFV or battle tank). *The Military Balance* does not list HACV separately, but under their equipment type (light tank, recce or assault gun), and where appropriate annotates them as HACV.

Artillery: Systems with calibres of 100mm and above, capable of engaging ground targets by delivering primarily indirect fire, namely guns, howitzers, gun/howitzers, multiple rocket launchers (MRL) and mortars.

Weapons with bores of less than 14.5mm are not listed, nor, for major armies, are handheld ATK weapons.

Military Formation Strengths

The table below gives the approximate manpower and major equipment strengths of the main military formations of selected countries.

	Armoured/Tank Division						Mechanized/Motor Rifle/Infantry Division[a]					
	Men[b]	MBT	AIFV[c]	APC[c]	Arty/Mor[d]	ATGW[e]	Men[b]	MBT	AIFV[c]	APC[c]	Arty/Mor[d]	ATGW[e]
US	16,800	348	240[f]	–	111	192	17,100	290	300[f]	–	75	240
Russia[g]	11,100	319	325	22	162	9	13,500	213	215	332	204	39
China	9,900	323	–	–	32	52	13,400	80	–	–	60	54
UK	14,900	285	225[f]	190	72	120	14,000	–	–	129	54	126
Germany	21,250	308	164	–	158	159	21,500	252	190	–	164	189
France	9,000	190	114	140	68	48	7,200	–	–	270	42	96

[a] Type of Division: US Mechanized; Russia Motor Rifle; China, UK, France Infantry; Germany Armoured Infantry.
[b] Manpower is for war establishment.
[c] Incl only basic inf, AIFV/APC, not 'look alikes'.
[d] Incl MRL, SP and towed arty and mor of 100-mm calibre or over.
[e] Figures comprise only those mounted on vehicles with a *primary* ATK role.
[f] When *Bradley/Warrior* issues complete.
[g] Strengths are for traditional divisions (3 tank, 1 MRR or 1 tank, 3 MRR) Divisional holdings vary considerably.

NAVAL FORCES

Categorization is based partly on operational role, partly on weapon fit and partly on displacement. Ship classes are identified by the name of the first ship of that class, except where a class is recognized by another name (e.g. *Krivak, Kotlin* etc.). Where the class is based on a foreign design, the original class name is added in parentheses.

Each class of vessel is given an acronym designator based on the NATO system. All designators are included in the Abbreviations on the fold-out sheet at the end of the book.

The term 'ship' is used to refer to vessels of over both 1,000 tonnes full-load displacement and 60m overall length; vessels of lesser displacement but of 16m or more overall length are termed 'craft'. Vessels of less than 16m length overall have not been included.

The term 'commissioning' has different meanings in a number of navies. In *The Military Balance* we use the term to mean that a ship has completed fitting out, initial sea trials, and has a naval crew; operational training may not have been completed, but in all other respects the ship is available for service. By 'decommissioning', we mean a ship has been removed from operational duty and the bulk of its naval crew transferred. De-storing and dismantling of weapons may not have started.

Classifications and Definitions

To aid comparison between fleets, naval entries have been subdivided into the following categories, which do not necessarily agree with national categorization:

Submarines: Submarines with SLBM are listed separately under 'Strategic Nuclear Forces'.

Principal Surface Combatants: All surface ships with both 1,000 tonnes full-load displacement and a weapons system other than for self-protection. They comprise aircraft carriers (with a flight deck extending beyond two-thirds of the vessel's length), battleships (armour-protected, over 30,000 tonnes, and with armour-protected guns of at least 250-mm bore); cruisers (over 8,000 tonnes) and destroyers (less than 8,000 tonnes), both of which normally have an anti-air warfare role and may also have an anti-submarine capability; and frigates (less than 8,000 tonnes), which normally have an anti-submarine role.

Patrol and Coastal Combatants: All ships and craft whose primary role relates to the protection of the sea approaches and coastline of a state. Included are: corvettes (600–1,000 tonnes and carrying weapons systems other than for self-protection); missile craft (with permanently fitted missile launcher ramps and control equipment); torpedo craft (with an anti-surface-ship capability). Ships and craft which fall outside these definitions are classified 'patrol'.

Mine Warfare: This category covers surface vessels configured primarily for minelaying or mine countermeasures, which can be minehunters, minesweepers or dual-capable vessels.

A further classification divides both coastal and patrol combatants and mine warfare vessels into: offshore (over 600 tonnes), coastal (300–600 tonnes) and inshore (less than 300 tonnes).

Amphibious: Only ships specifically procured and employed to disembark troops and their equipment over unprepared beachheads have been listed. Vessels with an amphibious capability, but which are known not to be assigned to amphibious duties, are not included. Amphibious craft are listed at the end of each entry.

Support and Miscellaneous: This category of essentially non-military vessels provides some indication of the operational sustainability and outreach of the navy concerned.

Weapons Systems: Weapons are listed in the order in which they contribute to the ship's primary operational role. After the word 'plus' are added significant weapons relating to the ship's secondary role. Self-defence weapons are not listed. To merit inclusion, a SAM system must have an anti-missile range of 10km or more, and guns must be of 100-mm bore or greater.

Organizations: Naval groupings such as fleets and squadrons are often temporary and changeable; organization is only shown where it is meaningful.

AIR FORCES

The following remarks refer to aviation units forming an integral part of ground forces, naval forces and (where applicable) Marines, as well as to separate air forces.

The term 'combat aircraft' comprises aircraft normally equipped to deliver ordnance in air-to-air or air-to-surface combat. In previous editions of *The Military Balance* reconnaissance aircraft were not counted as combat but, as the CFE Treaty counts some types as combat capable, we have attempted to differentiate between combat-capable types (Su-24, RF-4 etc.) and non-combat types (TR-1). Most air forces therefore show an increase in the number of combat aircraft held. The 'combat' totals include aircraft in operational conversion units (OCU) whose main role is weapons training, and training aircraft of the same type as those in front-line squadrons and assumed to be available for operations at short notice. (Training aircraft considered to be combat-capable are marked by an asterisk *.)

Air force operational groupings are shown where known. Squadron aircraft strengths vary; attempts have been made to separate total holdings from reported establishment strength.

The number of categories of aircraft listed is kept to a minimum. 'Fighter' is used to denote aircraft with the capability (weapons, avionics, performance) for aerial combat. Dual-capable aircraft are shown as FGA, fighter, etc., according to the role in which they are deployed. Often different countries use the same basic aircraft in different roles; the key to determining these roles lies mainly in aircrew training. For bombers, long-range means having an unrefuelled *radius of action* of over 5,000km, medium-range 1,000–5,000km and short-range less than 1,000km; light bombers are those with a payload of under 10,000kg (which is no greater than the payload of many FGA).

The CFE Treaty lists three types of helicopters: attack (one equipped to employ anti-armour, air-to-ground or air-to-air guided weapons by means of an integrated fire control and aiming system); combat support (which may or may not be armed with self-defence or area suppression weapons, but without a control and guidance system); and unarmed transport helicopters. *The Military Balance* uses the term 'attack' in the CFE sense, and the term 'assault' to describe armed helicopters used to deliver infantry or other troops on the battlefield. Except in the case of CFE signatories, *The Military Balance* continues to employ the term 'armed helicopters' to cover those equipped to deliver ordnance, including ASW ordnance.

ECONOMIC AND DEMOGRAPHIC DATA

Economic Data

Figures for Gross Domestic Product (GDP) are provided, but Gross National Product (GNP) and Net Material Product (NMP) are used when necessary (GNP equals GDP plus net income from abroad; NMP equals GNP minus non-earning state services). GDP figures are quoted at current market prices. Where available, published sources are used, but estimated figures are used when data is incomplete. GDP/GNP growth rates cited are real growth in real terms. Inflation rates are based on available consumer price indices and refer to annual averages. 'Debt' means gross foreign debt and includes all long-, medium- and short-term debt, both publicly and privately owed; no account is taken of similar debt owed to the country in question by others.

Wherever possible, the UN System of National Accounts, based on the latest available International Monetary Fund (IMF) *International Financial Statistics* (*IFS*), has been used. Other sources include the data from *Economic Survey of Europe 1991–1992* (New York: UN, 1992), *World Economic Outlook* (Washington, DC: IMF, 1991), *World Debt Tables (1991–1992): External Debt of Developing Countries* (Washington, DC: World Bank, 1991) and *Key Indicators of Developing Asian and Pacific Countries*, vol XXII, (Asian Development Bank, 1991). For the states of the former Soviet Union we have used IMF Economic Review papers, and for the former states of Yugoslavia, the *Southeastern European Yearbook* (Athens: Hellenic Foundation for Defence and Foreign Policy, 1991).

Defence Expenditure

The latest defence expenditure or budget data available as at 1 June 1992 is quoted. Some countries include internal and border security force expenditures in their defence budgets; where separate budgets exist they are indicated in footnotes. Figures may vary from previous years, often because of updates made by the governments themselves.

NATO uses a 'standard definition' of defence expenditure which includes all spending on regular military forces, military aid (including equipment and training) to other nations, military pensions, host government expenses for NATO tenant forces, NATO infrastructure and civilian staff costs; but excludes spending on paramilitary forces. Both the nationally calculated defence expenditure and the NATO definition are shown.

Foreign Military Assistance (FMA) figures are included, where these exceed $US1m, with other economic data in country entries. The total of FMA received is shown, together with the providing countries. FMA includes both cash grants and credits; it may also include the cost of military training.

Currency Conversion Rates

National currency figures have been converted into $US to permit comparisons. The rate is averaged for the national financial year (for 1992–93 figures, the mid-1992 rate is used). Wherever possible, exchange rates are taken from *IFS*, though they may not be applicable to commercial transactions. Plan Econ PPP (Purchase Power Parity) estimates have been used for some East European economies, and exchange rates have been adjusted accordingly. For the former USSR states, exchange rates are derived from the official exchange rate for 1991 with the $US value of the rouble adjusted according to independent sources from the states themselves. Where appropriate, the interpretation of national currencies has departed significantly from the official one, when this would have resulted in a meaningless figure. In some cases, in an effort to make $US figures more relevant for international comparisons, a different set of exchange rates has been used to calculate national accounts and defence spending, reflecting the differences in Purchase Power Parity terms between the civilian and military sectors.

Population

All population data is taken from the latest census data available in *World Population Projections 1987–88* (Washington, DC: World Bank, 1988) and the *1987 Demographic Yearbook* (New York: UN, 1989), latest national statistics where available, as well as calculated trends and projections.

WARNING

The Military Balance is a quantitative assessment of the personnel strengths and equipment holdings of the world's armed forces. It is in no way an assessment of their capabilities. It does not attempt to evaluate the quality of units or equipment, nor the impact of geography, doctrine, military technology, deployment, training, logistic support, morale, leadership, tactical or strategic initiative, terrain, weather, political will or support from alliance partners.

Nor is the Institute in any position to evaluate and compare directly the performance of items of equipment. Those who wish to do so can use the data provided to construct their own force comparisons. As essays in many editions of *The Military Balance* have made clear, however, such comparisons are replete with difficulties, and their validity and utility cannot but be suspect.

The Military Balance provides the actual numbers of nuclear and conventional forces and weapons based on the most accurate data available, or failing that, on the best estimate that can be made with a reasonable degree of confidence – this is not the number that would be assumed for verification purposes in arms-control agreements (with the sole exception of the CIS–American nuclear strategic balance tables on pp. 227–28).

The data presented each year in *The Military Balance* reflects judgments based on information available to the Director and Staff of the Institute at the time the book is compiled. Information may differ from previous editions for a variety of reasons, generally as a result of substantive changes in national forces, but in some cases as a result of our reassessment of the evidence supporting past entries. Inevitably, over the course of time we have come to believe that some information presented in earlier versions was erroneous, or insufficiently supported by reliable evidence. Hence, it is not always possible to construct valid time series comparisons from information given in successive editions, although we do attempt to distinguish, for significant changes, between new acquisitions and revised assessments in the text which introduces each regional section.

CONCLUSION

The Institute owes no allegiance whatsoever to any government, group of governments, or any political or other organization. Our assessments are our own, based on the material available to us from a wide variety of sources. The cooperation of all governments has been sought and, in many cases, received. Not all countries have been equally cooperative, and some of the figures have necessarily been estimated. We take pains to ensure that these estimates are as professional and as free from bias as possible. The Institute owes a considerable debt to a number of its own members and consultants who have helped in compiling and checking material. The Director and Staff of the Institute assume full responsibility for the facts and judgments contained in this study. We welcome comments and suggestions on the data presented, since we seek to make it as accurate and comprehensive as possible.

Readers may use items of information from *The Military Balance* as required, without applying for permission from the Institute, on condition that the IISS and *The Military Balance* are cited as the source in any published work. However, reproduction of major portions of *The Military Balance* must be approved in writing by the Institute prior to publication.

October 1992

1

COUNTRIES

INDEX

The United States

Nuclear Developments

Strategic Forces

A protocol to the START Treaty was signed on 23 May 1992 by the US and the four nuclear republics of the former Soviet Union: Russia, Byelarus, Ukraine and Kazakhstan. The signatories agreed that: the four republics assumed the obligations of the former USSR under the Treaty; and that they are to make arrangements among themselves to implement the limits and restrictions of the Treaty and to allow the verification provisions to function.

In September 1991 and in his State of the Union address on 28 January 1992, President Bush announced packages of unilateral disarmament measures and proposed other measures which he would be prepared to take if they were agreed to bilaterally. At his meeting with President Yeltsin in Washington on 16 June 1992 it was announced that further deep cuts to strategic nuclear forces would be made. Neither side would deploy ICBM with multiple warheads, and the US committed itself to having only 1,750 warheads on SLBM. The details of the three packages and the responses made by Presidents Gorbachev and Yeltsin are analysed in 'Nuclear Developments' on pp. 222–26.

The *Minuteman* II force of 450 ICBM is due to be eliminated under START. They have been stood down from alert status; the electrical command and controls have been deactivated by inserting keys into the safety control switches. The process of removing the missiles from their silos prior to destruction is reported to have begun. The programmes to develop the rail-mobile version of the MX *Peacekeeper* and the small ICBM (*Midgetman*) have been terminated. No more MX *Peacekeeper* ICBM will be produced.

The ten ballistic missile submarines (SSBN) armed with *Poseidon* C-3 SLBM have been withdrawn from patrol, and all missiles will have been removed from the boats by September 1992. They are no longer considered operational but will still be START-countable until the process of removing the missile launch tube hatches and their associated superstructure fairings required by the Treaty is completed. Nuclear sea-launched cruise missiles (SLCM) have been withdrawn from all ships. Production of the W-88 warhead (which is understood to have a yield of 300–475KT compared to the 100KT yield of the W-76 warhead it would replace) for the *Trident* D-5 SLBM has been stopped. A fifth SSBN armed with *Trident* D-5 SLBM commissioned in June 1992, it is now START-countable but will not join operational patrols until 1993, after a shakedown and training period.

Plans to develop a new short-range attack missile (SRAM II) for the air force have been cancelled. Production of the advanced cruise missile (ACM) is to cease after 640 of the original order for 1,000 missiles has been completed. Under the administration's plans only 20 B-2 bombers are to be procured (instead of the 75 requested in FY1991 and the original programme for 132); however, Congress has only authorized the production of 16 aircraft. A force of 136 B-52Gs and Hs is to be maintained for both nuclear and conventional roles, with the remaining B-52G ALCM-equipped aircraft to be retired by the end of 1993. After the implementation of START there will be 84 B-52H ALCM-capable bombers. Some 281 bombers in store at the elimination centre at Davis-Monathan Air Base are START-countable; ten bombers have been eliminated since the Treaty was signed. There are now four B-2 aircraft under test.

A new command, US Strategic Command (STRATCOM) was formed on 1 June 1992, with responsibility for the targeting and control of strategic nuclear forces (ICBM, SLBM and bombers). Strategic Air Command (SAC) has been disbanded and its assets reassigned to the two new Air Force Commands: Air Combat Command (ACC) and Air Mobility Command (AMC). ACC will be responsible for organizing, training and equipping both missile and bomber units, while their operational use is the task of STRATCOM.

Tactical Nuclear Forces

Both the US and Russia are to withdraw and destroy all warheads for nuclear artillery and short-range surface-to-surface missiles (SSM). The seven *Lance* SSM battalions have been deactivated and 45 launchers eliminated. All naval nuclear warheads (less SLBM but including bombs for both carrier and shore-based naval aircraft) have been withdrawn; about half are to be destroyed. On 17 October 1991 NATO's Nuclear Planning Group (NPG) approved US plans to withdraw about 50% of air-delivered weapons from Europe. It is estimated that about 700 tactical nuclear bombs would remain. All nuclear weapons had been withdrawn from Korea by 18 October 1991, and on 2 July 1992 President Bush announced that all nuclear artillery shells, *Lance* SSM warheads and nuclear depth-bombs had been withdrawn from Europe. At the same time, he said that all tactical nuclear weapons had been withdrawn from US Navy ships.

Strategic Defense Initiative

In November 1991 Congress passed the Warner-Nunn Missile Defense Act which established two goals:

- The provision of advanced Theater Missile Defense (TMD) by the mid-1990s to US forces deployed abroad and to US friends and allies.
- Deployment of a Limited Defense System (LDS), including one or an adequate additional number of ground sites and space-based sensors, capable of providing a highly effective defence of the US against limited attacks of ballistic missiles. As an initial step, the Secretary of Defense was directed to develop a system for deployment at the first site by the earliest date allowed by the availability of appropriate technology or by FY1996.

While the Act restricted ballistic missile defence (BMD) to that permitted by the 1972 ABM Treaty (this allows only one area to be defended by no more than 100 ABM interceptors), it also urged the President to pursue immediate discussions with the (then) Soviets with a view to agreeing amendments to the ABM Treaty to allow:

- Additional Ground Sites and Interceptors
- Increased use of space sensors
- Clarification of development and testing
- Flexibility for advanced ABM technology
- Clarification between TMD and ABM defences.

The FY1993 Budget Request has included $5.4bn for SDI, of which $2.27bn is earmarked for LDS which will comprise the reactivation of the site at Grand Forks, North Dakota for the deployment of Ground-Based Interceptors (GBI). GBI is an exoatmospheric kinetic interceptor with a fly-out speed of 6.5km per second. GBI would be activated by Ground-Based Radar (GBR) located at Grand Forks, unless agreement (in the context of the ABM Treaty) can be reached to allow the deployment of other GBR and the upgrading of existing early-warning radar, in which case GBI would give defence coverage of the whole of the US and Canada, bar North-west Canada and Alaska.

The FY1993 Budget Request also includes $2.1bn (or 37% of the SDI budget) for continued research and development of SDI. Of this, $575.6m is for research on space-based interceptors in the Global Protection Against Limited Strikes (GPALS) concept. In addition to GBI, GPALS would field an exo-endoatmospheric interceptor (E2I), another ground-based missile which could intercept incoming missiles both in space and, primarily, after re-entry into the atmosphere.

$1.06bn has been requested in FY1993 for TMD. In the short term, priority is being given to upgrading *Patriot* to increase its lethality and the area that can be defended. In the longer term, the Theater High Altitude Area Defense (THAAD) system is being designed to have an intercept range of a few hundred kilometres. The first 'prototype' battery for evaluation and assessment purposes will be in place by 1996 and will have an operational capability in an emergency. THAAD is planned to be fully deployed by the turn of the century.

Conventional Forces

US conventional forces have begun a programme of reorganization and reduction to establish 'the base force' needed to meet the demands of deterrence, forward presence, crisis response and reconstitution. By 1997, active manpower strength is to be reduced to 1.6 million. The 1995 force levels are to be: Army: 12 active, six reserve and two cadre divisions; Marines: three expeditionary forces each of one division and an air wing; Air Force: 15 active and 11 reserve fighter wing equivalents, with an aircraft inventory of 5,300; Navy: 12 carriers in a 451 ship fleet.

Ground Forces

The reduction in the number of active formations and units has continued. Virtually all formations deactivated during the year were located in Germany. One Corps HQ, one armoured and one mechanized division, two aviation and two artillery brigades, and an armoured cavalry regiment have been deactivated. Two National Guard divisions, one armoured and one infantry, are being run down in strength prior to deactivation but, as yet, Congress has withheld its approval. Two further active infantry divisions are to be deactivated and two more ARNG divisions are scheduled to become cadre divisions by 1995.

Although the overall total holding of tanks has been reduced, the number of M-1 *Abrams* has been increased by 400. There have been small increases in the number of artillery and MLRS pieces. The ATGW holding has increased substantially with an additional 3,500 *TOW* mounted on Hummer (high mobility vehicle (HMV)) and 400 M-901 (*TOW* cupola mounted on M-113 APC). The *Lance* SSM is being eliminated, only 20 remain on inventory, of which none are located in Europe. Air defence weapons holdings have been increased by 36 M-167 *Vulcan*, 60 *Avengers* (vehicle-mounted *Stinger*) and 130 *Patriot* launchers. Around 50 *Hawk* and 140 *Chaparral* SAM launchers have been withdrawn from Europe. AH-1S attack helicopters have also been withdrawn, but the number of AH-64A has increased by ten. The CH-47 transport helicopter has been retired from service. A large amount of equipment located in Europe is to be transferred to NATO allies in the next 12 months, including 2,000 M-60 MBT, over 200 203mm M-110 SP guns and 600 M-113 APC.

The FY1993 budget request cancelled the Air Defence Anti-Tank System (ADATS) after some $180m had been spent on development. Although funds were added in FY1992 to upgrade the earlier model M-1 tank guns from 105mm to 120mm, none were included in the FY1993 request. In the Armoured Systems Modernization programme the Block III tank has been suspended indefinitely, priority has been given to the Advanced Force Artillery System and the Field Artillery Resupply-Vehicles Ammunition. Important programmes which have not been affected, so far, by budgetary cuts are the *Javelin* (the 'fire and forget' anti-tank weapon which can be operated by only one soldier), and the Advanced Gun System (AGS) – a light tank to replace the airborne forces' elderly *Sheridan* tank.

Air Force

A major reorganization of the main air force commands has taken place. Strategic Air Command (SAC), Tactical Air Command (TAC) and Military Airlift Command (MAC) have been replaced by Air Combat Command (ACC) and Air Mobility Command (AMC). ACC will control ICBM, all combat aircraft, reconnaissance and command-and-control aircraft, and some theatre airlift and tankers. AMC will control all inter-theatre airlift and most theatre airlift and tankers. Both new commands will provide forces to the unified commands (STRATCOM, Central Command etc) as operations require. Both Commands will contain composite air wings containing a range of aircraft types (FGA, air defence, recce, EW, tankers etc.) as well as the traditional single aircraft-type wings.

The air force has already reduced the number of active fighter/attack squadrons from 76 to 57, while reserve squadrons have increased from 49 to 55. The main reductions have been to A-10s (seven squadrons cut and some 130 aircraft less) and F-4 *Wild Weasel* (five squadrons). The Air National Guard has retired its F-4E aircraft. While numbers of active F-15 and F-16 squadrons have been reduced, those in the air reserves have increased. A number of units have been withdrawn from Europe and Asia. In the UK one squadron of F-111E/F has been withdrawn, three more leave in July 1992, and the remaining three should leave in 1993. The EF-111 squadron has returned to the US and three A-10 squadrons have also been withdrawn from the UK. The first of two F-15 squadrons has deployed, and the special operations wing is forming. All F-16 aircraft have now been withdrawn from Spain, but as yet no decision has been made regarding a new base for them in Italy. From Germany one squadron of F-15 and three of F-16 have been withdrawn. A number of aircraft have been withdrawn from Japan (18 F-15, 24 F-16) and South Korea (18 RF-4C).

Although in general most development programmes are to be stretched in time, the F-22 advanced tactical fighter schedule is unchanged and is to enter production in FY1996, notwithstanding the crash of the first prototype. The FY1993 request includes $2.7bn for eight more C-17 strategic transport aircraft. Because of the success of the JSTARS surveillance aircraft in *Operation Desert Storm*, its programme has been accelerated: two production aircraft will be procured in FY1993, one in FY1994 and two in FY1995. A total force of 20 aircraft is planned.

Navy

While 24 combatants have been retired during the year, a number of modern warships have commissioned. Three improved *Los Angeles*-class attack submarines have commissioned and two older types retired (one *Sturgeon* and one *Permit*). The last two battleships have been retired and put into preservation. The last *Midway*-class aircraft carrier has decommissioned and is to be retained in preservation. The *Forrestal* has been reassigned as the training carrier to replace the *Lexington*, which has been struck. A sixth *Nimitz*-class carrier commissioned in July 1992. Two additional cruisers, both *Ticonderoga*-class Baseline 2/3 with the *Aegis* command-and-control system, have commissioned, and a further two *Ticonderoga* will commission before the end of the year. Four destroyers have been retired (one *Coontz*-class and three *Adams*-class). A second *Arleigh Burke*-class will commission in November 1992. Fourteen *Knox*-class frigates have been retired, with five more to go by September 1992. The remaining eight are to be redesignated as training frigates at the end of FY1992. The first *Osprey*-class coastal minehunter will have commissioned by the end of FY1992. Six more are under construction, three more were ordered in FY1992, and funding for two has been requested in FY1993. The *Seawolf*-class attack submarine programme has been cancelled in the FY1993 request and only one boat will be completed. Under pressure from Congress, however, the administration may agree to a second boat being built.

Defence Spending

The Senate House Authorization Conference Committee finally completed the FY1992 defence budget process on 13 November 1991. It authorized $270.9bn against the request for $278.28bn. As usual, there were numerous adjustments made to the request (434 of 2,203 line items were altered). The major cuts made were in respect of B-2 bomber procurement, which received only $1bn instead of the $2.4bn requested, and Congress capped production at 15 operational aircraft, whereas the administration had requested to procure four more aircraft, and the *Peacekeeper* rail-mobile ICBM for which no funding was provided. For the second year running, Congress authorized $790m for the development of the V-22 *Osprey* tilt-rotor aircraft which the DoD did not request.

For FY1993 the administration has requested $281bn (including $12.1bn for Department of Energy defence activities), which represents a decline of 4.5% in real terms compared to FY1992. The administration's long-term aim is to save $50bn in programme costs between FY1993 and FY1997. The main areas of savings being: a reduction in the number of B-2 bombers to be procured ($14.5bn); the termination of the *Seawolf* attack submarine programme ($17.5bn); the modification of the *Comanche* helicopter programme ($3.4bn); the cancellation of the ADATS ($1.7bn); and the small ICBM (*Midgetman*) programme ($1.0bn); and ending production of the ACM ($1.3bn). The President's message notwithstanding ('these cuts are deep . . . this deep, but no deeper'), Congress is likely to look for larger savings than these. The currently projected Budget Request for FY1997 (in FY1993 $) is $251.3bn.

Further savings could come from proposed recisions in the FY1992 authority totalling $7.1bn. These would be made in programmes scheduled for termination, those programmes added by Congress which the DoD did not request (such as the V-2 *Osprey*), and those where the funds authorized have not been spent.

The major items in the FY1993 Budget Request are for air force and navy programmes. For the air force: F-22 Advanced Tactical Fighter development ($2.2bn), B-2 bomber ($3.95bn) for continued development and procurement of four aircraft, C-17 strategic transport ($2.93bn) with procurement of eight aircraft. For the navy: FA-18 ($2.94bn) for development of FA-18E/F and procurement of 48 FA-18C/D aircraft, *Trident* II SLBM ($1.05bn) for procurement of 21 missiles, DDG-51 destroyer ($3.47bn) for procurement of four ships. Naval funding, at $84.6bn, is hardly altered from FY1992 authority, army funding is cut the most; down $4bn (in real terms) to $63.3bn, while the air force receives an additional $3.7bn (in real terms) with $83.9bn.

US Defence Budgets

Explanatory Note:
Each year the US government presents its Defense Budget to Congress for the next two fiscal years, together with a long-term spending plan covering a further three years. Until approved by Congress, the Budget is referred to as the Budget Request, after approval it becomes the Budget Authority (BA), and authorizes funds for immediate and future disbursement. The term Total Obligational Authority (TOA) represents the value of direct defence programmes for each fiscal year regardless of financing (i.e. from previous fiscal years and receipts from earned income or interest). The term 'outlay' represents actual expenditure; each year the government estimates what the outlay will be, the difference between this and the BA providing for contingencies. However, moneys authorized, particularly in the procurement and construction areas, are rarely all spent in the year of authorization, though contracts are signed which commit the government to payment in future years. On average, carried forward authorities constitute some 40% of each year's outlay, while similarly some 40% of each year's BA will be carried forward to future years.

Table I: Selected Budgets 1981–93 ($bn)[a]

FY 1 Oct– 30 Sept	National Defense Function[b] (BA)	(outlay)	Department of Defense (BA)	(outlay)	Atomic Energy Defense Activities (outlay)	International Security Assistance (outlay)	Veterans Administration (outlay)	Total Govt Exp (outlay)	Total Govt Budget Deficit (outlay)
1981	180.001	157.513	176.110	153.868	3.398	5.095	22.991	678.209	78.936
1982	216.547	185.309	211.513	180.741	4.309	5.416	23.958	745.706	127.940
1983	245.043	209.903	238.900	204.410	5.171	6.613	24.846	808.327	202.784
1984	265.16	227.413	258.176	220.928	6.120	7.924	25.614	851.781	185.324
1985	294.656	252.748	286.27	245.154	7.098	9.391	26.292	946.316	212.260
1986	289.146	273.375	281.436	265.480	7.445	10.499	26.356	990.258	221.167
1987	287.427	281.999	279.469	273.966	7.451	7.106	26.782	1,003.830	149.687
1988	292.008	290.361	283.755	281.935	7.913	4.500	29.428	1,064.051	155.090
1989	299.567	303.559	290.837	294.880	8.119	1.467	30.066	1,144.064	153.400
1990	303.263	299.331	292.999	289.755	8.988	8.652	29.112	1,251.778	220.470
1991	303.574	273.292	290.904	262.389	10.004	9.823	31.349	1,323.011	268.746
1992ε	289.170	307.304	276.222	294.639	11.685	7.783	33.819	1,475.439	399.733
(administration request)									
1993	280.972	291.353	267.628	278.273	11.901	7.007	34.383	1,515.307	349.946

[a] Data is from *Historical Tables, Budget of the United States Government – Supplement, Fiscal Year 1993* (Washington, DC: USGPO, 1992), *Budget of the United States Government Fiscal Year 1991* and *Annual Report of the Secretary of Defense to the President and the Congress*, January 1992 (Washington, DC: USGPO, 1992). All categories include off-budget items.
[b] The National Defense budget function includes DoD Military Activities, Department of Energy Atomic Energy Defense Activities, and smaller support agencies such as the Federal Management Agency, the Selective Service System and the General Services Administration Stockpile of Strategic Materials, National Defense Function. International Security Assistance and Veterans Administration are *NOT* included, nor is spending by NASA and the Coast Guard.

Table II: Defense Budget Authorities

	Billion current $ (*Billion constant 1985 $*)						
	FY 1985	1988	1989	1990	1991	1992ε	1993 request
Personnel	67.8 *(67.8)*	76.6 *(69.7)*	78.5 *(68.1)*	78.9 *(65.4)*	84.2 *(66.5)*	79.2 *(61.4)*	77.1
Operations & Maintenance	77.8 *(77.8)*	81.6 *(74.2)*	86.2 *(74.8)*	88.3 *(73.2)*	131.9 *(104.2)*	92.4 *(71.6)*	86.5
Procurement	96.8 *(96.8)*	80.1 *(72.8)*	79.4 *(68.9)*	81.4 *(67.4)*	71.7 *(56.6)*	60.5 *(46.9)*	54.4
RD&TE	31.3 *(31.3)*	36.5 *(33.2)*	37.5 *(32.6)*	36.5 *(30.2)*	36.2 *(28.6)*	36.9 *(28.6)*	38.8
Military construction	5.5 *(5.5)*	5.3 *(4.8)*	5.7 *(4.9)*	5.1 *(4.2)*	5.2 *(4.1)*	4.9 *(3.8)*	6.2
Family	2.9 *(2.9)*	3.2 *(2.9)*	3.3 *(2.9)*	3.1 *(2.6)*	3.3 *(2.7)*	3.7 *(2.9)*	4.0
Other Housing	4.7 *(4.7)*	0.4 *(0.4)*	0.2 *(0.2)*	−0.3 *(−0.2)*	−41.7 *(−33.6)*	−1.5 *(−1.2)*	0.6
Total DoD spending	286.8 *(286.8)*	283.8 *(259.4)*	290.8 *(255.5)*	293.0 *(247.3)*	290.9 *(234.6)*	276.2 *(215.8)*	267.6
Atomic energy	7.3 *(7.3)*	7.7 *(7.0)*	8.3 *(7.3)*	9.7 *(8.2)*	11.6 *(9.3)*	12.0 *(9.4)*	12.1
Other	0.5 *(0.5)*	0.5 *(0.5)*	0.6 *(0.6)*	0.6 *(0.5)*	1.1 *(0.9)*	1.0 *(0.8)*	1.2
TOTAL NATIONAL DEFENSE	294.6 *(294.6)*	292.0 *(266.9)*	299.6 *(263.3)*	303.3 *(255.9)*	303.6 *(244.8)*	289.2 *(225.9)*	281.0

THE UNITED STATES

GDP	1990: $5,513.8bn	
	1991: $5,673.9bn	
Growth	1990: −0.3%	1991: −0.8%
Inflation	1990: 4.8%	1991: 4.3%
Debt	1990: $757.26bn	1991: $828.50bn
Def exp	1991: BA $290.90bn, Outlay $287.45bn	
Def bdgt	1992: BA $270.90bn, Outlay $282.60bn	
Request	1993: BA $267.63bn, Outlay $272.80bn	
NATO defn	1991: $305.59bn	

Population: 251,842,600

	13–17	18–22	23–32
Men	8,730,500	8,826,300	20,404,800
Women	8,401,500	8,506,500	19,888,300

TOTAL ARMED FORCES:
ACTIVE: 1,913,750 (212,600 women) (excl Coast Guard).
RESERVES:
READY RESERVE: 1,784,050. Selected Reserve and Individual Ready Reserve to augment active units and provide reserve formations and units:
NATIONAL GUARD: 561,450. Army (ARNG) 443,150; Air (ANG) 118,300.
RESERVE: 1,222,600. Army 680,900; Navy 266,850; Marines 104,600; Air Force 170,250.

STANDBY RESERVE: 28,700. Trained individuals for mob: Army 1,200; Navy 12,350; Marines 600; Air Force 14,550.
RETIRED RESERVE: 178,700. Trained individuals to augment support and training facilities: Army 88,300; Navy 28,800; Marines 7,200; Air Force 54,400.

US STRATEGIC COMMAND: (US STRATCOM)
HQ Offutt Air Force Base, Nebraska (manpower incl in Navy and Air Force totals).

NAVY: 504 SLBM in 25 SSBN.
SSBN
13 *Ohio* (SSBN-726)
  5 with 24 UGM-133A *Trident* D-5 (120 msl)
  8 with 24 UGM-93A *Trident* C-4 (192 msl)
6 *Franklin* (SSBN-726) with 16 *Trident* C-4 (96 msl)
6 *Madison* (SSBN-627) with 16 *Trident* C-4 (96 msl)
10 *Poseidon* C-3 SSBN have been withdrawn from patrol. Distinction must be drawn between decommissioning and being no longer START-countable. Three have decommissioned, two are to become dry deck shelters. As at 1 June 1992 they all remain

START-countable. 2 *Trident* C-4 SSBN will be retired by the end of FY 1992.

AIR FORCE (from Air Combat Command (ACC)): 2 Air Forces.
ICBM: 1,000. 6 strategic msl wings (2 wings being deactivated) (msl complex) (2 with 20 launcher groups/control centres, 4 with 15):
450 *Minuteman* II (LGM-30F) (undergoing deactivation).
500 *Minuteman* III (LGM-30G).
50 *Peacekeeper* (MX; LGM-118A); in mod *Minuteman* silos.
AIRCRAFT: 268 hy bbr (549 START-countable); 13 bbr wings (9 B-52, 4 B-1B).
BOMBERS:
OPERATIONAL: 270.
4 wings (6 sqn) with 95 B-1B.
5 wings (6 sqn) with 94 B-52H (with AGM-86B ALCM).
4 wings (4 sqn) with 81 B-52G:
2 sqn (40 ac) with ALCM/SRAM.
2 sqn (41 ac) conventional only.
FLIGHT TEST CENTRE: 10: 4 B-52, 2 B-1B, 4 B-2.
AWAITING CONVERSION/ELIMINATION: 281 B-52; -C 29, -D 88; -E 49; -F 52; -G 63 (44 ALCM equipped).

STRATEGIC RECCE/INTELLIGENCE COLLECTION (SATELLITES)
IMAGERY: KH-11: 160–400-mile polar orbit, digital imagery (perhaps 3 operational). KH-12 (*Ikon*): 1 launched 1989. AFP-731: Optical imaging satellite with sensors operating in several wavebands. 203-km orbit, at approx 60° inclination; to replace KH-11. *Lacrosse* radar-imaging satellite.
OCEAN SURVEILLANCE (OSUS): 4 satellite-clusters to detect ships by infra-red and radar.
NAVIGATIONAL SATELLITE TIMING AND RANGING (NAVSTAR): 17 satellites, components of global positioning system (24 by 1993).
ELINT/COMINT: 2 *Chalet* (*Vortex*), 2 *Magnum*, 2 *Jumpseat*; 'Ferrets' (radar-monitoring satellites).
NUCLEAR DETONATION DETECTION SYSTEM: Detects and evaluates nuclear detonations. Sensors to be deployed in NAVSTAR satellites.

STRATEGIC DEFENCES:
US Air Force Space Command: (HQ: Peterson AFB, Colorado).
North American Aerospace Defense Command (NORAD), a combined US–Canadian org (HQ: Peterson AFB, Colorado).

EARLY WARNING:
DEFENCE SUPPORT PROGRAMME (DSP): infra-red surveillance and warning system. Approved

constellation: 3 operational satellites and 1 operational on-orbit spare.
BALLISTIC MISSILE EARLY WARNING SYSTEM (BMEWS): 3 stations: Clear (Alaska); Thule (Greenland); Fylingdales Moor (UK). Primary mission to track ICBMs and SLBMs. Also used to track satellites.
SPACETRACK: USAF radars Pirinclik (Turkey), Shemya (Aleutians), Clear, Thule and Fylingdales; optical tracking systems in New Mexico, Choejong-San (S. Korea), San Vito (Italy), Maui (Hawaii), Diego Garcia (Indian Ocean).
DETECTION AND TRACKING RADARS: at Kwajalein Atoll (Marshall Islands), Saipan, Northern Mariana Islands, Ascension Island (Atlantic), Antigua (Caribbean), Kaena Point (Hawaii), Massachusetts Institute of Technology (Lincoln Laboratory).
USN SPACE SURVEILLANCE SYSTEM (NAVSPASUR): 3 transmitting, 6 receiving sites field stations in south-east US.
PERIMETER ACQUISITION RADAR ATTACK CHARACTERIZATION SYSTEM (PARCS): 1 north-facing phased-array system at Cavalier AFS (N. Dakota); 2,800-km range.
PAVE PAWS: phased-array radars in Massachusetts, Georgia, Texas, California; 5,500-km range.
MISCELLANEOUS RADARS: US Army: Kwajalein Atoll (Pacific). USAF: Ascension Island (Atlantic), Antigua (Caribbean), Kaena Point (Hawaii), MIT Lincoln Laboratory, (Massachusetts).
GROUND-BASED ELECTRO-OPTICAL DEEP SPACE SURVEILLANCE SYSTEM (GEODSS): White Sands (New Mexico), Taegu (S. Korea) and Maui (Hawaii), Diego Garcia (Indian Ocean).

AIR DEFENCE:
RADARS:
OVER-THE-HORIZON-BACKSCATTER RADAR (OTH-B): 1 in Maine (limited operation, mothballed). 1 in Mount Home AFB, Montana, (mothballed). Range 900km (minimum) to 3,300km.
NORTH WARNING SYSTEM: to replace DEW line. 15 automated long-range radar stations now operational. 39 short-range (110–150km) stations due in service by 1992.
DEW LINE: 31 radars: Alaska (7), Canada (20) and Greenland (4) roughly along the 70°N parallel from Point Lay, Alaska to Greenland (system being deactivated, completion by September 1993).
AIRCRAFT:
ACTIVE: 48: 2 Air Force:
2 with 36 F-15C/D (Alaska).
1 with 12 F-15C/D (Iceland).
ANG: 216: 12 sqn:
2 with 36 F-15A/B.
10 with 180 F-16A/B.
Augmentation: ac on call from Navy, Marine Corps and Air Force.

AAM: *Sidewinder, Sparrow,* AMRAAM.

ARMY: 674,800 (77,700 women).

5 Army HQ, 4 Corps HQ (1 AB).
2 armd div (3 bde HQ, 5 tk, 4 mech inf, 3 SP
   arty bn, 1 MLRS bty,[b] 1 AD bn; 1 avn bde)
   (incl 1 ARNG bde in 1 div).
5 mech div (3 bde HQ, 4 tk, 5 mech inf, 3 SP
   arty bn; 1 MLRS bty;[b] 1 AD bn; 1 avn bde)
   (incl 1 ARNG bde in 3 div).
1 inf div (3 bde HQ, 2 air aslt, 4 mech inf, 2
   tk, 3 arty bn, 1 MLRS bty, 1 AD bn; 1 avn
   bde).
4 lt inf div (3 bde HQ, 9 inf, 3 arty, 1 AD bn; 1
   avn bde) (incl 1 ARNG/AR bde in 2 div).
1 air aslt div (3 bde HQ, 9 air aslt, 3 arty bn; avn
   bde (7 hel bn: 3 ATK, 2 aslt, 1 comd, 1 med tpt)).
1 AB div (3 bde HQ, 9 para, 1 lt tk, 3 arty, 1 AD,
   1 cbt avn bn).
2 indep armd bde (2 tk, 1 mech inf, 1 SP arty bn)
   (2–3 ARNG bn).
1 mot inf bde (3 motor, 1 arty bn).
2 inf (theatre def) bde (3 inf, 1 lt arty bn).
1 AB bn gp.
7 avn bde (1 army, 4 corps, 2 trg).
2 armd cav regt.
7 arty bde.
1 theatre AD comd.
9 *Patriot* SAM bn: 3 with 3 bty (all to form 6 bty
   as eqpt becomes available).
8 *HAWK* SAM bn.

READY RESERVE:

ARMY NATIONAL GUARD (ARNG): 443,150
(32,200 women): capable after mob of manning
10 div (2 armd, 2 mech, 5 inf, 1 lt inf); 20 indep
bde (5 armd, 7 mech, 8 inf (3 lt) incl 5
'Roundout' (1 armd, 3 mech, 1 lt inf) for Regular
Army div; 2 armd cav regt; 1 inf gp (Arctic recce:
5 scout bn); 18 fd arty bde HQ. Indep bn: 5 tk, 3
mech, 1 mtn inf, 46 arty, 4 lt ATK (*TOW*), 18
AD (4 *HAWK*, 8 *Chaparral*, 5 *Stinger* SP, 1
Vulcan/Stinger SP), 62 engr.

ARMY RESERVE (AR): 680,900 (121,100 women): 12
trg div, 2 trg bde (no cbt role). 3 indep bde: 1 mech,
1 inf (theatre def), 1 lt inf ('Roundout'); 2 arty bde
HQ, 73 indep bn (1 tk, 2 inf, 16 arty, 56 engr).

EQUIPMENT:

MBT: some 15,629: 896 M-48A5, 2,156
M-60/M-60A1, 5,155 M-60A3, 7,422 M-1/M-1A1
Abrams. (Plus 639 CFE-declared M-47 in store).
LIGHT TANKS: 900 M-551 *Sheridan*.
RECCE: 55 *Fuchs*.
AIFV: 5,371 M-2/-3 *Bradley*.
APC: some 26,480, incl 5,259 M-577, 13,102 M-113.
TOWED ARTY: 2,393:

105mm: 538 M-101, 514 M-102, 164 M-119;
155mm: 550 M-114, 627 M-198.
SP ARTY: 3,471:
155mm: 2,442 M-109A1/A2/A6;
203mm: 1,029 M-110A1/A2.
MRL: 227mm: 435 MLRS incl some 30 ATACMS
capable.
MORTARS: 107mm: 4,536 (incl 1,989 M-106 SP,
2,547 M-30); 120mm: some 63.
SSM: 20 *Lance* launchers (in store).
ATGW: 14,306 *TOW* (incl 101 M-113, 5,776
Hummer, 3,058 M-901, 5,371 M-2/M-3 *Bradley*),
6,140 *Dragon* launchers.
RCL: 1,868 incl 84 mm: 27 *Carl Gustav*; 1,841
90mm and 106mm.
AD GUNS: 20mm: 126 M-167 *Vulcan* towed, 198
M-163 SP.
SAM: FIM-92A *Stinger*, 109 *Avenger* (vehicle-mounted
Stinger), 348 M-54 and M-48 SP *Chaparral*, 394
Improved HAWK, 432 *Patriot* launchers.
AMPHIBIOUS: 29 ships:
5 *Frank Besson* LST: capacity 32 tk.
24 *Runnymede* LCU: capacity 7 tk.
Plus craft: some 125 LCM, 26 ACV.
AVIATION: incl eqpt in store.
  AIRCRAFT: Some 433, incl 74 OV-1D, 30
  RC-12D/G/H/K, 27 RU-21, 17 RV-1D, 120
  C-12D, 16 C-23A/B, 3 DHC-7, 116 U-21, 6
  UV-18A, 2 UV-20A, 22 T-42.
  HELICOPTERS: some 8,010 (1,664 armed hel): 916
  AH-1S, 712 AH-64A, 36 AH-6/MH-6, 2,950
  UH-1 (being replaced), 3 EH-1H (ECM), 1,070
  UH/MH-60A, 66 EH-60A (ECM), 314 CH-47D,
  41 CH-54, 280 OH-6A, 1,622 OH-58A/C/D.

NAVY (USN): 546,650 (55,100 women): 4

Fleets: 2nd (Atlantic), 3rd (Pacific), 6th
(Mediterranean), 7th (W. Pacific).
SUBMARINES: 110:
STRATEGIC SUBMARINES: 25: (see p. 18).
TACTICAL SUBMARINES: 87: (incl about 8 in refit).
  SSGN: 18:
  10 imp *Los Angeles* (SSN-751) with 12 ×
    Tomahawk SLCM (VLS), 533mm TT (Mk
    48 HWT, *Harpoon, Tomahawk*).
  8 mod *Los Angeles* (SSN-719) with 12 ×
    Tomahawk SLCM (VLS); plus 533mm TT
    (Mk 48 HWT, *Harpoon, Tomahawk*).
  SSN: 69:
  31 *Los Angeles* (SSN-688) with Mk 48 HWT,
    plus *Harpoon, Tomahawk* SLCM.
  34 *Sturgeon* (SSN-637) with Mk 48 HWT; plus
    Harpoon, Tomahawk SLCM.
  (Incl 3 capable of special ops).
  3 *Permit* (SSN-594) with Mk 48 HWT, plus
    Harpoon.
  1 *Narwhal* (SSN-671) with Mk 48 HWT,
    Harpoon, Tomahawk SLCM.

SUBMARINES, OTHER ROLES: 1:
1 *Houston* (SSN-609) (special ops).

PRINCIPAL SURFACE COMBATANTS: 188:

AIRCRAFT CARRIERS: 12 (excl 1 in long refit/refuel
and 1 in SLEP).
CVN: 6 (plus *Enterprise* in long refit/refuel)
6 *Nimitz* (CVN-68) (96/102,000t) (incl *G.
Washington* 4 July 1992).
CV: 6 (plus 1 *Kitty Hawk* in SLEP):
2 *Kitty Hawk* (CV-63) (81,000t).
1 *Kennedy* (CV-67) (79,700t).
3 *Forrestal* (CV-59) (79,250/81,100t).
AIR WING: 13: (11 active, 2 reserve). The average
mix of type and numbers of ac assigned to an
Air Wing:
2 ftr sqn with 20 F-14A.
3 FGA/attack sqn:
2 lt with 20 F/A-18A.
1 med with 10 A-6E.
2 ASW sqn:
1 with 6 S-3B ac; 1 with SH-3H hel.
1 ECM sqn with 4 EA-6B.
1 AEW sqn with 4 E-2C; 4 KA-6D tkr.
CRUISERS: 48 (incl some 8 in refit):
CGN: 9:
4 *Virginia* (CGN-38) with 2 × 2 SM-2 MR
SAM/*ASROC* SUGW; plus 2 × 4 *Tomahawk*
SLCM, 2 × 4 *Harpoon*, SH-2F hel (Mk 46
LWT), 2 × 3 ASTT, 2 × 127mm guns.
2 *California* (CGN-36) with 2 × SM-2 MR;
plus 2 × 4 *Harpoon*, 1 × 8 *ASROC*, 2 × 3
ASTT, 2 × 127mm guns.
1 *Truxtun* (CGN-35) with 1 × 2 SM-2 ER
SAM/*ASROC*; plus 2 × 3 ASTT, 1 × SH-2F
hel, 1 × 127mm gun.
1 *Long Beach* (CGN-9) with 2 × 2 SM-2 ER;
plus 2 × 4 *Tomahawk*, 2 × 4 *Harpoon*, 1 × 8
ASROC, 2 × 3 ASTT, 2 × 127mm guns.
1 *Bainbridge* (CGN-25) with 2 × 2 SM-2 ER
plus 2 × 4 *Harpoon*, 1 × 8 *ASROC*, 2 × 3 ASTT.
CG: 39:
21 *Ticonderoga* (CG–47 Aegis):
5 Baseline 1 (CG-47–51) with 2 × 2 SM-2
MR/*ASROC*; plus 2 × 4 *Harpoon*, 2 × 1
127mm guns, 2 × 3 ASTT, 2 × SH-2F or
SH-60B hel.
16 (18 by November 1992) Baseline 2/3,
(CG-52) with 2 × VLS Mk 41 (61 tubes
each) for combination of SM-2 ER, and
Tomahawk. Other weapons as Baseline 1.
9 *Belknap* (CG-26) with 1 × 2 SM-2
ER/*ASROC*; plus 2 × 3 ASTT, 2 × 4
Harpoon, 1 × 127mm gun, 1 × SH-2F hel.
9 *Leahy* (CG-16) with 2 × 2 SM-2 ER/*ASROC*;
plus 2 × 3 ASTT, 2 × 4 *Harpoon*.
DESTROYERS: 45: (incl some 7 in refit).
DDG: 14:
1 (2 by November 1992) *Arleigh Burke*
(DDG-51 *Aegis*) with 2 × VLS Mk 41 (32

tubes fwd, 64 tubes aft) for combination of
Tomahawk, SM-2 ER and *ASROC*; plus 2 ×
4 *Harpoon*, 1 × 127mm gun, 2 × 3 ASTT, 1
× SH-60B hel.
4 *Kidd* (DDG-993) with 2 × 2 SM-2
MR/*ASROC*; plus 2 × 3 ASTT, 2 × SH-2F
hel, 2 × 4 *Harpoon*, 2 × 127mm guns.
4 *Coontz* (DDG-37) with 1 × 2 SM-2 ER; plus
1 × 8 *ASROC*, 2 × 3 ASTT, 1 × 127mm
gun, and with 2 × 4 *Harpoon*.
5 *Adams* (DDG-2) with 1 × SM-1; plus 1 × 8
ASROC, 2 × 3 ASTT, 2 × 127mm guns;
Harpoon SSM.
DD: 31:
31 *Spruance* (DD-963) (ASW):
15 with 1 × 8 *ASROC*, 2 × 3 ASTT, 1 ×
SH-2F hel; plus 2 × 4 *Harpoon*, 2 ×
127mm guns; 7 with 2 × 4 *Tomahawk*.
16 with 1 × VLS Mk 41 (*Tomahawk*), 2 × 3
ASTT, 1 × SH-60B hel; plus 2 × 127mm
guns, 2 × 4 *Harpoon*.
FRIGATES: 83: (incl some 10 in refit).
FFG: 51:
51 *Oliver Hazard Perry* (FFG-7), (18 in NRF)
all with 2 × 3 ASTT; 24 with 2 × SH-60B
hel; 27 with 2 × SH-2F hel; all plus 1 ×
SM-1 MR/*Harpoon*.
FF: 32:
32 *Knox* (FF-1052) (27 by September 1992 of
which 8 will be trg by end FY92) (11 in
NRF) with 1 × 8 *ASROC*, 1 × SH-2F hel, 4
× ASTT; plus *Harpoon* (from *ASROC*
launcher), 1 × 127mm gun.
ADDITIONAL IN STORE: 1 CV, 4 BB, 9 DDG, 14 FF,
5 AO, 1 AR.

PATROL AND COASTAL COMBATANTS: 30:
Note: Mainly responsibility of Coast Guard.
MISSILE CRAFT: 6 *Pegasus* PHM with 2 × 4 *Harpoon*.
PATROL, INSHORE: 24⟨.

MINE WARFARE: 24:
MINELAYERS: None dedicated, but mines can be laid
from attack submarines, aircraft and surface
ships (limited).
MINE COUNTERMEASURES: 24:
1 *Osprey* (MHC-51) MHC.
8 *Avenger* (MCM-1) MCO.
10 *Aggressive* (MSO-422)/*Acme* (MSO-509) MCO
(9 with NRF).
5 MSB-15 MSI⟨.

AMPHIBIOUS: 65:
COMMAND: 2 *Blue Ridge*: capacity 700 tps.
LHA: 6:
1 (2 by September 1992) *Wasp*: capacity 1,900
tps, 60 tk; with 6 AV-8B ac, 12 CH-46, 4
CH-53, 4 UH-1N, 4 AH-1T hel; plus 12
LCM-6 or 3 LCAC.
5 *Tarawa*: capacity 1,700 tps, 100 tk, 4 LCU, 6
AV-8B ac, 12 CH-46, 4 CH-53, 4 UH-1N, 4
AH-1T hel.

LPH: 7 *Iwo Jima*: capacity 1,750 tps, 4 AV-8B ac, 2 CH-46, 10 CH-53, 1 UH-1N hel.
LPD: 12: 11 *Austin*, 1 *Raleigh*: capacity 930 tps, 4 tk.
LSD: 13:
  8 *Whidbey Island* with 4 LCAC or 21 LSM: capacity 450 tps, 40 tk.
  5 *Anchorage* with 4 LCAC or 15 LCM: capacity 350 tps, 38 tk.
LST: 20 *Newport* (3 NRF): capacity 400 tps, 10 tk.
LKA (amph cargo ships): 5 *Charleston*: capacity 360 tps, 10,000 tonnes stores.
CRAFT: some 86:
  33 LCAC: capacity 1 MBT.
  53 LCU-1610: capacity 3 MBT.
  Numerous LCVP, LCU, LCM.

SUPPORT AND MISCELLANEOUS: 162:

(Total includes 72 USN ships, 81 ships of the Military Sealift Command Fleet Auxiliary Force, and 9 AGOR owned by the US Navy, but operated by civil research institutes.)
UNDERWAY SUPPORT: 51:
  AO: 24: 5 *Cimarron*, 7 *Wichita*, 9 *Henry Kaiser*, 3 *Neosho*.
  AOE: 4 *Sacramento*.
  AE: 12: 7 *Butte*, 5 *Suribachi/Nitro*.
  AF: 11: 7 *Mars*, 1 *Rigel*, 3 *Sirius*.
MAINTENANCE AND LOGISTICS: 70:
  9 AD, 8 AS, 1 AR, 12 AT, 14 AOT, 2 AH, 24 salvage/rescue (3 NRF).
SPECIAL PURPOSES: 10:
  1 *Forrestal* avn trg, 2 comd, 7 technical spt.
SURVEY AND RESEARCH: 43:
  18 *Stalwart* AGOS (towed array).
  4 *Victorious* AGOS (SWATH).
  10 AGOR, 11 AGHS.

RESERVES:

NAVAL RESERVE SURFACE FORCES: 44 ships:
  18 FFG, 11 FF, 9 MCMV, 3 amph and 3 spt/misc vessels. Incl in main Navy entry. Crewed by about 70% active USN and 30% NR.
COMBAT SUPPORT FORCES (provision of units for MCM, underwater ops, ashore construction, cargo handling).
AUGMENT FORCES (provision of additional manpower to regular org).

NAVAL AVIATION: (About 87,000) incl 11
carrier air wings.
AIRCRAFT:
FIGHTER: 22 sqn with F-14A.
FGA/ATTACK: 41 sqn:
  16 med with A-6E.
  6 lt with A-7E.
  19 with F/A-18A.
ELINT: 2 sqn with EA-3, EP-3.
ECM: 13 sqn with EA-6B.

MR: 22 land-based sqn with P-3B, P-3C, P-3CIII.
ASW: 6 sqn with S-3A, 6 with S-3B.
AEW: 13 sqn with E-2C.
COMD: 1 sqn with EC-130Q (TACAMO).
OTHER: 14 spt sqn with C-130F, LC-130F/R, EC-130G/Q, C-2A, CT-39, C-131, UC-12B ac; and hel (see below).
TRAINING:
  5 'Aggressor' sqn with F-5E/F, T-38, A-4, F-16N.
  17 trg sqn with T-2B/C, T-34C, T-44, T-45A, T-47 ac and hel (see below).
HELICOPTERS:
ASW: 36 sqn:
  10 with SH-60B (LAMPS Mk III).
  11 (3 NR) with SH-2F (LAMPS Mk I).
  15 with SH-3H (SH-60F to replace).
MCM: 4 sqn: 2 with RH-53D, 2 with MH-53E.
MISC: 6 spt sqn with SH-3, 4 with CH-46, 1 with CH-53E.
TRG: 2 sqn with TH-57A/B/C.

RESERVES: 224 cbt ac; 42 armed hel.
  2 attack carrier wings: 14 sqn:
    4 lt attack (1 with 12 A-7E; 3 with 36 F/A-18).
    2 med attack with 20 A-6E.
    4 ftr with 48 F-14.
    2 AEW with 10 E-2C.
    1 ECM with EA-6A/B.
    1 tkr with KA-6D.
  2 MR wings: 13 sqn with 108 P-3A/B/C.
  1 tac spt wing: 14 sqn:
    2 composite with TA-4F/A-4F.
    1 spt with C-131H.
    11 spt with C-9B.
  1 hel wing: 9 sqn:
    5 ASW (2 with 12 SH-3D, 3 with 24 SH-2F).
    1 lt attack with 6 HH-1K.
    1 MCM with 12 RH-53D.
    2 cbt spt sqn with 16 HH-60.
(To form: aircrew associate units).
EQUIPMENT: (incl NR)
  1,735 cbt ac; 421 armed hel.
AIRCRAFT:
F-14: 423. **-A:** 314 (ftr, incl 48 NR); **-A plus:** 68 (ftr) **-D:** 41 (ftr).
F/A-18: 663. **-A:** 261 (FGA, incl 36 NR); **-B:** 27* (trg); **-C:** 283 (FGA); **-D:** 92* (trg).
F-5E/F/T-38: 40 (trg).
F-16: 26. **-N:** 22 (trg). **TF-16N:** 4 (trg).
A-4: 253 (trg). **-E/-F:** 59 (trg); **TA-4F/J:** 194 (trg).
A-6: 432. **-E:** 299 (FGA, incl 20 NR); **EA-6B:** 113 (ECM, incl 4 NR); **KA-6D:** 20 (tkr incl 8 NR).
E-2C: 92. 82 (AEW, incl 10 NR); **TE-2B:** 10 (trg).
A-3: 10. **EA-3:** 9 (ELINT, incl 4 NR); **KA-3B:** 1 (tkr).
P-3: 334. **-B:** 68 (MR, NR); **-C:** 242 (MR, NR); **EP-3:** 17 (ELINT); **RP-3:** 7.
S-3A/B: 99 (ASW).
C-130: 20. **EC-130Q:** 7 (comd). **-F/LC-130F/R:** 13 (misc).

CT-39: 13 (misc). **C-2A**: 35 (tpt). **C-9B**: 19 (tpt).
T-2B/C: 150 (trg). **US-3**: 5 (tpt). **T-39D/N**: 18 (trg).
TA-7C: 7 (trg). **T-44**: 54 (trg). **T-45**: 16 (trg).
HELICOPTERS:
  HH-1K: 6 (attack, NR).
  RH-53D: 18 (MCM, incl 12 NR); **MH-53E**: 31 (MCM).
  SH-60: 197 **-B**: 137 (ASW); **-F**: 60 (ASW).
  HH-60H: 16 (cbt spt, NR).
  SH2F/G: 98 (ASW, incl 24 NR).
  SH-3D/G/H: 120 (ASW incl 12 NR).
  CH-46: 231 (tpt, trg).
MISSILES:
  AAM: AIM-120 AMRAAM being delivered.
  AIM-7 *Sparrow*, AIM-54A/C *Phoenix*,
  AIM-9 *Sidewinder*.
  ASM: AGM-78D *Standard* ARM, AGM-45
  Shrike, AGM-88A *HARM* (anti-radiation);
  AGM-84 *Harpoon*.

MARINE CORPS: 193,000 (8,800 women).
GROUND: 3 div (3 inf regt (with up to 9 inf, 1
  armd inf bn with LAV-25), 1 arty regt, 1 recce,
  1 tk, 1 cbt engr, 1 aslt amph bn).
3 Force Service Support Groups.
2 bn Marine Corps Security Force (1 each in
  Atlantic and Pacific).
Marine Security Guard Bn (1 HQ, 7 region coy)
RESERVES (MCR):
  1 div: (3 inf (9 bn), 1 arty regt (5 bn); 2 tk, 1
  armd inf (with LAV-25), 1 aslt amph, 1 recce,
  1 cbt engr bn).
1 Force Service Support Group.

EQUIPMENT:
MBT: 125 M-60A1 (plus 591 in store), 221 M-1A1
  Abrams.
LAV: 384 LAV-25 (25mm gun), 335 LAV (variants,
  incl ATGW).
AAV: 1,322 AAV-7A1 (all roles).
TOWED ARTILLERY: 105mm: 335 M-101A1; 155mm:
  566 M-198.
SP ARTILLERY: 155mm: 131 M-109A3.
MORTAR: 81mm: 473.
ATGW: 1,238 *TOW*, 1,218 *Dragon*, 96 LAV-AT (*TOW*).
RCL: 83mm: 1,417.
SAM: 1,929 *Stinger*.

AVIATION: 3 active air wings.
AIR WING: (no standard org but a notional wing is
  shown below): 148 fixed-wing aircraft, 152 hel:
  48 F/A-18, 10 A-6, 60 AV-8B, 6 EA-6B, 12
  OV-10, 12 KC-130, 60 CH-46, 44 CH-53, 24
  AH-1, 24 UH-1.
AIRCRAFT:
FIGHTER/ATTACK: 10 sqn with F-18A/C.
FGA: 9 sqn:
  7 lt with AV-8B.
  2 med with A-6E.

ECM: 4 sqn with 20 EA-6B.
FAC: 2 sqn with 36 OV-10A/D.
COMD: 4 sqn with 48 F/A-18D.
TANKER: 3 sqn with KC-130T.
TRAINING: 2 sqn.
HELICOPTERS: 30 sqn:
ARMED: 6 lt attack/utility sqn with AH-1/UH-1N.
TRANSPORT: 15 med with CH-46E, 9 hy with
  CH-53 (4 with -A/-D, 5 with -E).
TRAINING: 2 sqn.
SAM:
  2 bn with *Improved HAWK*.
  3 bn with *Stinger*.

RESERVES (MCR):
AVIATION: 1 air wing: 84 cbt ac, 24 armed hel.
AIRCRAFT:
FIGHTER/ATTACK: 4 sqn with 24 F-4S; 2 with 36 F-18A.
FGA: 4 sqn with 24 A-4M.
FAC: 1 sqn with 12 OV-10A.
TANKER: 2 tkr/tpt sqn with 18 KC-130T.
HELICOPTERS:
ARMED: 2 attack sqn with 24 AH-1J.
TRANSPORT: 3 sqn (2 med with 24 CH-46E, 1 hy
  with 18 CH-53A).
UTILITY: 3 sqn with 24 UH-1N.
SAM: 1 bn with *HAWK*.

EQUIPMENT: 410 cbt ac (incl 84 MCR); 96 armed
  hel (incl 24 MCR).
AIRCRAFT:
  F-18A/-B/-C/-D: 201 (FGA incl 36 MCR, 33* trg).
  AV-8B: 165. 139 (FGA), 14* (trg); **TAV-8B:** 12* (trg).
  A-4M: 24 (FGA, 24 MCR).
  A-6: 40. **-E:** 20 (attack); **EA-6B:** 20 (ECM);
  OV-10A/D: 48 (FAC, incl 12 MCR).
  F-5E/F: 14 (trg, MCR).
  KC-130: 62. **-F:** 28 (OCU), **-R:** 14, **-T:** 20 (tkr, MRC).
HELICOPTERS:
  AH-1J/T/W: 114. 96 (armed, incl 24 MCR), 18 trg.
  UH-1N: 108 (incl 24 MCR, 12 trg).
  CH-46D/E: 230 (tpt, incl 24 MCR, 6 HMX, 20 trg).
  CH-53-A/-D/-E: 187 (tpt, incl 14 MCR, 22 trg).
  RH-53D: 7 (MCR).
  VH-60A: 9 (VIP tpt).
  VH-3D: 11 (VIP tpt).
MISSILES:
  SAM: *Improved HAWK, Stinger*.
  AAM: *Sparrow, Sidewinder*.
  ASM: *Maverick*.

COAST GUARD (By law a branch of the
  Armed Forces; in peacetime operates under, and
  is funded by, the Department of Transportation.

Budgets are not incl in the figures at pp. 17–18):
Budget 1991: BA $3.43bn.
    1992: BA $3.60bn.
    1993: Request $3.82bn.
Strength: 38,200 (includes 3,000 women).

PATROL VESSELS: 148:
PATROL, OFFSHORE: 48:
12 *Hamilton* high endurance with HH-65A
LAMPS *Dolphin* hel, 2 × 3 ASTT, 4 with 1 ×
76mm gun, 3 with *Harpoon* SSM (4 in refit).
13 *Bear* med endurance with 1 × 76mm gun,
HH-65A hel.
15 *Reliance* med endurance with 1 × 3 inch gun,
hel deck.
8 other med endurance cutters.

PATROL, INSHORE: 100:
49 *Farallon*, 2 *Cape Higgon*, 3 *Sea Hawk* SES, 46
Point Hope⟨.

SUPPORT AND OTHER: 12:
2 icebreakers, 9 icebreaking tugs, 1 trg.

AVIATION: 77 ac, 152 hel.
FIXED WING: 25 HU-25A, 7 HU-25B, 9 HU-25C, 1
EC-130V, 30 HC-130H, 1 CA-21, 2 RG-8A, 1
VC-4A, 1 VC-11.
HELICOPTERS: 36 HH-3F, (being replaced with
HH-60J), 20 HH-60J, 96 HH-65A.

COAST GUARD RESERVE: 19,930.
Selected: 11,600; Ready 7,800; Standby 530.

STRATEGIC SEALIFT:
Military Sealift Command, in addition to the
Fleet Auxiliary Force, operates and administers
strategic sealift resources.

TOTAL SEALIFT SHIPS: 285:
ACTIVE: 68:
  STRATEGIC MOBILITY: 45:
    (15 dry cargo (incl 2 ro-ro veh ships, 4 ro-ro
    container), 22 tankers, 8 fast veh/cargo).
  AFLOAT PREPOSITIONING: 23:
    2 AK, 4 barge lift, 13 Maritime Prepositioning
    (to support MEB), 1 semi-submersible heavy
    lift ship, 3 AOT.
RESERVE: 217: (in preservation in CONUS ports).
  READY RESERVE FORCE (RRF): 107 (19 active;
    remainder at 5 to 20 days' reactivation notice):
    Incl: 48 AK (incl 18 veh carriers), 9 gasoline
    tkr, 1 pax, 8 crane ships, 20 ro-ro, 7 barge lift.
  NATIONAL DEFENSE RESERVE FLEET (NDRF): 110
    (60 to 90 days' reactivation notice, but many
    ships very old and of doubtful serviceability):
    28 dry cargo, 11 tkr, 71 'Victory' WW II cargo.
AUXILIARY STRATEGIC SEALIFT. About a further 350
US-flag and effectively US-controlled ships
potentially available to augment these holdings.

AIR FORCE: 499,300 (71,000 women); 3,485
cbt ac (incl ANG, AFR); plus 1,300+ in store.

STRATEGIC: (organization: see p. 19).
TACTICAL: 30 active cbt wings, comprising some
57 sqn (sqn may be 18 or 24 ac).
FIGHTER/ATTACK: 57 tac ftr sqn:
15 with F-15.
4 with F-15E.
22 with F-16C/D.
8 (2 trg) with F-111.
5 with A-10.
1 *Wild Weasel* with F-4G.
2 with F-117.

SUPPORT:
RECCE: 1 sqn with RF-4C.
3 sqn with U-2R and RC135.
AEW: 1 Airborne Warning and Control wing; 7 sqn
(incl 1 trg) with E-3.
EW: 4 sqn with EC-130, EF-111.
FAC: 8 tac air control sqn:
3 with OA-10A.
4 mixed A-10A/OA-10A.
1 with OA-37B.
SPECIAL OPERATIONS (5,947): 3 wing, 11 sqn (see
pp. 25–26).
TRAINING:
1 'Aggressor' sqn with F-16.
31 trg sqn with F-16, T-37, T-38, T-39, T-41,
T-43, UV-18, Schweizer 2-37, C-5, C-12,
C-130, C-141 ac and HH-60, HH-3, HH-53,
U/TH-1 hel.
TRANSPORT: 34 sqn:
22 strategic: 5 with C-5; 17 with C-141.
12 tac airlift with C-130.
Units with KC-10, C-135, VC-137, C-140, C-9,
C-12, C-20, C-21.
TANKER: 36 sqn:
30 with KC-135, 6 with KC-10A.
SAR: 7 sqn (incl STRATCOM msl spt), HH-3,
HH-1, HH-60 hel.
MEDICAL: 3 medical evacuation sqn with C-9A.
WEATHER RECCE: 1 sqn with WC-135.
TRIALS/weapons trg units with A-10, F-4, F-15,
F-16, F-111, T-38, C-141 ac, UH-1 hel.

EQUIPMENT:
LONG RANGE STRIKE/ATTACK: 276 cbt ac.
  B-52: 175: **-G:** 81 (41 conventional); **-H:** 94 strike
  (with AGM-86 ALCM) (plus in store B-52:
  281† **-C:** 29, **-D:** 88, **-E:** 49, **-F:** 52, **-G:** 63).
  B-1B: 97 (strike, trg, test).
  B-2: 4 (flt testing).
RECCE: U-2R/RT: 16, **RC-135:** 19
COMMAND:
  E-4B: 4, **EC-135:** 11.
TACTICAL: 3,638 cbt ac; (incl 826 ANG, 251 AFR
plus 1,013 in store); no armed hel.
  F-4: 256. **-E:** 34 (FGA), **-G:** 87 (incl 6 ANG (*Wild
  Weasel*)); **RF-4C:** 135 (recce: 28 USAF, 107
  ANG). Plus 772 in store (incl 128 RF-4C).

F-15: 838: **-A/B/C/D:** 98 (ftr, incl 48 ANG); 511 (FGA incl 116 ANG); 122* (OCU); **-E:** 107 (FGA). Plus 12 in store.

F-16: 1,679. 1,152 (FGA; incl 171 AFR, 372 ANG); 288* (OCU); 239 (ftr, ANG).

F-111: 275. **-A:** 2* (OCU); **-D:** 34 (FGA), 24* (OCU); **-E/F:** 160 (FGA); **-G:** 23 (OCU); plus 56 in store, EF-111A: 32 (ECM).

F-117: 55. 46 (FGA), 9* (trg), plus 1 test.

A-7: 162 (ANG); plus 131 in store.

A-10A: 372 (FGA, incl 107 ANG, 80 AFR); 88* (OCU); plus 42 in store.

E-3: 34 (AWACS).

EC-18B: 4 (Advanced Range Instrumentation).

E-8A: 2 (JSTARS ac).

WC-135B: 7 (weather recce).

AC-130: -A: 10 (special ops, AFR); **-H:** 10 (special ops, USAF); **HC-130N/P:** 55 (24 special ops; 31 SAR incl 10 ANG, 11 AFR); **EC-130E/H:** 30 (special ops incl 8 ANG); **MC-130E/H:** 22 (special ops); **WC-130E/H:** 12 (weather recce, AFR).

OA-37B: 33 (FAC, plus 10 in store).

OA-10: 111 (FAC, incl 21 ANG).

TRANSPORT:

C-5: 119. **-A:** 69 (strategic tpt; incl 12 ANG, 32 AFR); **-B:** 50 (incl 6 OCU).

C-141B: 265 (230 strategic tpt, 16 OCU, 10 ANG, 9 AFR).

C-130: 566. 538 (tac tpt, incl 193 ANG, 130 AFR); 28 (trg, incl 8 ANG).

C-135A/B/C/E: 10.

VC-137B/C: 7 (VIP tpt).

C-9A: 23. **-A:** 20 (19 medical, 1 cmd spt); **VC-9C:** 3 (VIP).

C-12: 86 (liaison, incl 13 ANG).

C-17A: 1 (flt test).

C-22A/B: 5 (tpt incl 4 ANG).

C-23A: 3.

VC-25A1: 2. **C-26A:** 17 (tpt incl 13 ANG).

C-27A: 4 (tpt).

C-29A: 6 (cal).

T-43A: 4 (tpt ANG).

TANKERS:

KC-135: 632 (457 USAF, 145 ANG, 30 AFR), plus 12 in store.

KC-10A: 59 tkr/tpt.

TRAINING:

MiG-21: 24. **MiG-23:** 4. **T-37B:** 535 (plus 71 in store). **T-38:** 721 (plus 86 in store).

T-39: 4. **T-41A/C:** 100. **T-43A:** 19. **TC-135S:** 1. **TC-135W:** 1. **UV-18A:** 2. **Schweizer 2-37:** 8. **T-1A:** 4.

HELICOPTERS:

CH/HH-3: 55. 49 (trg, SAR), 6 (special ops).

CH/HH-53: 6 (trg).

MH-53-J: 41 *Pave Low* (special ops), incl 12 on mod programme at any time.

HH/MH-60G: 63. 22 (special ops), 41 (SAR incl 5 ANG).

UH-1H/N: 28: **UH-1H,** 68.

MISSILES:

AAM: AIM-9E/H/J/P *Sidewinder*, AIM-7C/D/E/F/M *Sparrow*, AIM 120.

ASM: 1,300 AGM-69A SRAM; 1,600 AGM-86B ALCM; 21,000+ AGM-65A/B/D/G *Maverick*; 5,500+ AGM-45 *Shrike*; 5,557 AGM-88A/B *HARM*; AGM-78A/D *Standard*; AGM-84A *Harpoon*.

RESERVES:

AIR NATIONAL GUARD (ANG): 118,285 (15,775 women).

24 wings, 99 sqn; 959 cbt ac.

FIGHTER: 216 ac.

12 AD sqn (see pp. 19–20).

FGA: 31 sqn; 636 ac.

1 with 12 A-10, 6 OA-10.

6 with 126 A-7D/K

4 with 72 A-10.

16 with 330 F-16.

4 with 90 F-15A/B.

RECCE: 6 sqn (ACC) with 107 RF-4C.

EW: 1 sqn (AFSOC) with 8 EC-130E.

FAC: 1 sqn with 18 OA-10.

TRANSPORT: 21 sqn:

18 tactical with 173 C-130A/B/E/H.

3 strategic: 1 with 11 C-5; 2 with 12 C-141B.

TANKER: 15 sqn with 148 KC-135E/R.

SAR: 3 sqn with 10 HC-130 ac, 14 MH-60G hel.

TRAINING: 8 sqn with 132 ac.

AIR FORCE RESERVE (AFR):

21 wings, 59 sqn (37 with ac); 237 cbt ac.

FGA: 12 sqn:

7 with 150 F-16; 5 (incl 1 trg) with 87 A-10.

TRANSPORT: 18 sqn:

14 tactical with 124 C-130B/E/H; 1 weather recce with 10 WC-130E/H.

3 strategic: 2 with 28 C-5A, 1 with 8 C-141B.

TANKER: 3 sqn with 30 KC-135E.

SPECIAL OPERATIONS: 2 sqn (AFSOC):

1 with 9 AC-130A.

1 with 5 H/CH-3 hel.

SAR: 3 sqn (AMC) with 9 HC-130H ac, 7 H/CH-3, 8 HH-60 hel.

ASSOCIATE: 21 sqn (personnel only):

4 sqn for C-5, 13 for C-141, 1 aero- medical for C-9. 3 sqn for KC-10.

CIVIL RESERVE AIR FLEET (CRAF): 442 commercial ac (numbers fluctuate):

LONG-RANGE: 406

255 passenger (Boeing 747, L-1011, DC-8/-10), 151 cargo (Boeing 707, 747, DC-8/-10).

SHORT-RANGE: 36 (Boeing 727, 737, 757).

SPECIAL OPERATIONS FORCES:

Units only listed – manpower and eqpt shown in relevant single service section.

ARMY: (4,000):
  5 SF gp (each 3 bn).
  1 Ranger inf regt (3 bn).
  1 avn gp.
  1 Psychological Operations gp (4 bn).
  1 Civil Affairs, 1 sigs, 1 spt bn.
RESERVES:
  2 ARNG SF gp (6 bn).
  1 ARNG avn bn.
  2 AR SF gp (6 bn).
  3 AR Psychological Operations gp.
  12 AR Civil Affairs HQ (3 comd, 5 bde, 4 gp).
  24 AR Civil Affairs coy.

NAVY: (3,360):
  1 Naval Special Warfare Command.
  2 Naval Special Warfare Gps.
  4 Naval Special Warfare units.
  7 Sea-Air-Land (SEAL) teams.
  2 SEAL delivery veh teams.
  3 Special Boat units.
  4 amph tpt submarines.
  6 Drydeck shelters (DDS).
RESERVES: (1,400):
  6 Naval Special Warfare gp det.
  2 Naval Special Warfare unit det.
  5 SEAL team det.
  2 Special Boat sqn.
  4 Special Boat unit.
  1 engr spt unit.
  2 cbt spt special hel sqn.

AIR FORCE: (5,950)
  1 air force HQ, 3 wings, 11 sqn:
    3 with MC-130.
    1 with AC-130.
    3 with HC-130.
    3 with MH-53 hel.
    1 with MH-60 hel.

RESERVES: (1,244)
  3 sqn (AFSOC):
    1 with 9 AC-130A (AFR).
    1 with 5 HH-3 hel (AFR).
    1 with 8 EC-130E (ANG).

DEPLOYMENT:
Commanders' NATO appointments also shown.
(e.g., COMEUCOM is also SACEUR)

EUROPEAN COMMAND (EUCOM): some
  210,100: HQ Stuttgart-Vaihingen (Commander is
  SACEUR).
ARMY: HQ US Army Europe (USAREUR),
  Heidelberg (Commander is COMCENTAG).
NAVY: HQ US Navy Europe (USNAVEUR),
  London (Commander is also CINCAFSOUTH).
AIR FORCE: HQ US Air Force Europe (USAFE),
  Ramstein (Commander is COMAAFCE).

GERMANY:
  ARMY: 117,500 (assigned to CENTAG unless
    shown otherwise).
    V Corps with 1 armd, 1 mech inf div, 1 armd
      cav regt, 4 arty, 1 engr, 2 corps avn bde.
    1 inf bde: (Berlin).
    Army AD Comd (2 bde with 4 bn (16 bty)
      HAWK, 7 bn Patriot (24 bty)).
    1 engr bde.
    Prepositioned equipment (POMCUS) for 2
      armd, 3 mech, 1 lt inf div, 1 armd cav regt.
      Approx 70% stored in Ge.
  EQUIPMENT (incl POMCUS in Ge, Be and Nl):
    Some 4,900 MBT, 1,820 AIFV, 2,200
    arty/MRL/mor, 240 attack hel.
  AIR FORCE: 30,900, 144 cbt ac.
    2 air force HQ: USAFE and 17th Air Force.
    3 tac ftr wings: 7 sqn (2 with 48 F-16C/D, 3 with
      12 F-4G plus 36 F-16C/D, 2 with 48 F-15).
    1 cbt spt wing, 1 tac air control wing.
    1 tac airlift wing: incl 14 C-130E and 4 C-9A.
    1 air base gp.
BELGIUM:
  ARMY: 1,200. Approx 15% of POMCUS stored
    in Be.
  NAVY: 120.
  AIR FORCE: 600.
GREECE:
  ARMY: 50.
  NAVY: 180. Base facilities Soudha Bay. Makri (Crete).
  AIR FORCE: 1,000, 1 air base gp. Facilities at
    Iraklion (Crete).
ITALY:
  ARMY: 3,600. HQ Vicenza. 1 AB bn gp, 1 arty bty.
  NAVY: 6,000. HQ Gaeta, bases at Naples, La
    Maddalena, 1 MR sqn with 9 P-3C at
    Sigonella.
  AIR FORCE: 5,500: 1 ftr wing (ac on det only).
MEDITERRANEAN:
  NAVY: Some 15,500.
    Sixth Fleet: typically 4 SSN, 1 CVBG (1 CV,
    6–8 surface combatants, 2 fast support ships),
    1 URG (4–6 support ships, 2 or 3 escorts), 1
    amph ready gp (3–5 amph ships with 1 MEU
    embarked), 4 depot ships.
NETHERLANDS:
  ARMY: 900. Approx 15% of total POMCUS is
    stored in Nl.
  AIR FORCE: 1,400: 18 cbt ac.
    1 tac ftr gp with 18 F-15A/B.
NORWAY: Prepositioning for 1 MEB (17 tanks, 24
  arty, no aviation assets).
PORTUGAL: (for Azores, see Atlantic Command).
  NAVY: 400.
  AIR FORCE: 1,200.
SPAIN:
  NAVY: 3,400, base at Rota.
    1 MR sqn with 9 P-3C.

TURKEY:
  ARMY: 800.
  NAVY: spt facilities at Iskenderun and Yumurtalik.
  AIR FORCE: 3,600, facilities at Inçirlik.
  1 tac gp, 2 air base gps.
  Installations for SIGINT, space tracking and
    seismic monitoring.
UNITED KINGDOM:
  NAVY: 2,400. HQ London, admin and spt
    facilities, 1 SEAL det.
  AIR FORCE: 17,700: 180 cbt ac.
  1 air force HQ: 3 tac ftr wings, 1 Air Base GP:
    11 sqn (6 with 110 F-111E/F, 3 with 60
    A-10, 1 with 7 U-2R, 1 with 10 F-15E).
  1 special ops wing with 5 MH-53 J, 12 MH-130H.
  1 SAR sqn with 6 HC-130, 5 MH-53.

PACIFIC COMMAND (USPACOM):

HQ: Hawaii.
ALASKA:
  ARMY: 9,500. 1 lt inf div.
  AIR FORCE: 10,300. 1 air force HQ; 3 sqn (2
    with 36 F-15C/D, 1 with 20 F-15E).
HAWAII:
  ARMY: 19,500. HQ US Army Pacific (USARPAC).
    1 lt inf div.
    1 ARNG inf bde.
  AIR FORCE: 5,400. HQ Pacific Air Forces
    (PACAF).
    1 air base wing, 1 tac ftr sqn with 24 F-15A/B
    (ANG), 1 comd/control sqn with 3 EC-135.
  NAVY: ε10,000. HQ US Pacific Fleet. Homeport
    for some 17 submarines, 16 PSC and 10 spt
    and misc ships.
  MARINES: 10,700. 1 MEB (from MEF in
    Okinawa).
PHILIPPINES:
  NAVY: ε1,000. Subic Bay base. Scheduled to close
    by 31 December 1992. Maint and log facilities.
  MARINES: 550.
SINGAPORE:
  NAVY: About 120, log facilities.
  AIR FORCE: 30 det spt sqn.
JAPAN:
  ARMY: 2,200.
    1 corps HQ, base and spt units.
  AIR FORCE: 10,300: 1 air force HQ: 78 cbt ac.
    2 wings (6 sqn) with 36 F-15C/D, 24 F-16, 18
      F-15E, 5 C-12F, 2 C-21A ac, 3 UH-1E/F/N hel.
    1 sqn with 2 E-3 AWACS.
    1 tac tpt gp with 19 C-130 (ANG).
    1 sqn with 8 KC-135 tkr (ANG).
    1 SAR sqn with 2 HC-130 ac, 4 HH-60 hel (ANG).
  NAVY: 5,500: Bases: Yokosuka (HQ 7th Fleet).
    Homeport for 1 CV, 8 surface combatants.
    Sasebo. Homeport for 3 submarines, 3 amph
    ships.
  MARINES: 21,300: 1 MEF (incl Okinawa).

SOUTH KOREA:
  ARMY: 26,500.
    1 Army HQ (UN command).
    1 inf div, 3 arty (1 SP), 1 MLRS, 1 AD bn.
  AIR FORCE: 9,000: 1 air force HQ: 2 wings, 84
    cbt ac.
    3 sqn with 72 F-16.
    1 tac control sqn with 12 OA-10.
    1 SAR sqn with 4 MH-60G hel.
    1 recce det with 3 U-2, 2 C-12.
GUAM:
  AIR FORCE: 3,000: spt facilities:
  NAVY: 4,300, MPS-3 (eqpt for 1 MEB). Naval air
    station, comms and spt facilities.
AUSTRALIA:
  AIR FORCE: 300.
  NAVY: 400: comms facility at NW Cape,
    SEWS/SIGINT station at Pine Gap, and SEWS
    station at Nurrungar.
DIEGO GARCIA:
  NAVY: 900, MPS-2, 5 MPS (eqpt for 1 MEB).
    Naval air station, spt facilities.
US WEST COAST:
  MARINES: 1 MEF.
AT SEA:
  PACIFIC FLEET: (HQ Pearl Harbor).
  Main base: Pearl Harbor.
    Other bases: Bangor (Washington); San Diego
      and Long Beach (California).
    Submarines: 8 *Ohio* SSBN, 4 SSGN, 29 SSN.
    Surface Combatants: 5 CV/CVN, 23
      CG/CGN, 7 DDG, 14 DD, 20 FFG, 16 FF.
    Amphibious: 1 comd, 3 LHA, 3 LPH, 7 LPD,
      6 LSD, 8 LST, 3 LKA.
  Surface Combatants divided among two fleets:
    Third Fleet (HQ San Diego): covers Eastern
      and Central Pacific, Aleutians, Bering Sea,
      etc. Typically 4 CVBG, 4 URG. Amph Gp.
    Seventh Fleet (HQ Yokosuka, Japan): covers
      Western Pacific, Japan, Philippines,
      ANZUS responsibilities, Indian Ocean.
      Typically 1 CVBG, 1 URG, Amph Gp (1
      MEU embarked).
  INDIAN OCEAN: (det from Seventh/Second Fleets).

CENTRAL COMMAND (USCENTCOM):

Takes command of deployed forces in its region.
HQ USCENTCOM. MacDill AFB, Florida.

AT SEA:
Joint Task Force Middle East.
1 comd ship, 1 LPD, 6 PSC, 3 MCO.
1 CVBG in N. Arabian Sea. (1 MEU (SOC) in
  AOR). Forces provided from Atlantic and Pacific.
SAUDI ARABIA:
  AIR FORCE: Units on rotational detachment,
    numbers vary (incl: F-4G, F-15, F-16, F-117,
    C-130, KC-135, U-2, J-STARS). 1 *Patriot* bn.

SOUTHERN COMMAND (USSOUTHCOM):
  HQ USSOUTHCOM: Quarry Heights, Panama.
  HQ US Southern Air Force (12th Air Force):
    Bergstrom, Texas.
PANAMA:
  ARMY: HQ US Army South, Fort Clayton
    Panama: 7,700.
    1 inf bde (2 inf bn, 1 avn bn).
  NAVY: HQ US Naval Forces Southern
    Command, Fort Amador, Panama: 500.
    Special boat unit, fleet support.
  MARINES: 200.
  AIR FORCE: 2,100.
    1 air div: A-7, OA-37, C-130 ac.
HONDURAS:
  ARMY: 800.

ATLANTIC COMMAND (USLANTCOM):
  HQ: Norfolk, Virginia (Commander is
    SACLANT).
US EAST COAST:
  MARINES:
    1 MEF.
    1 Reserve div.
  NAVY:
    MPS-1 ships (eqpt for 1 MEB)
BERMUDA:
  NAVY: 1,100.
CUBA:
  NAVY: 1,900 (Guantánamo).
  MARINES: 400 (Guantánamo).
ICELAND:
  NAVY: 1,800. 1 MR sqn with 9 P-3.
  AIR FORCE: 1,200.
    1 AD sqn with 12 F-15C/D, 1 comd/control
      sqn with 2 E-3, 1 SAR sqn with 4 HH-3.
  MARINES: 100.
PORTUGAL (AZORES):
  NAVY: 400.
    Facilities at Lajes.
    1 MR ac det with 3 P-3C (from Rota).
  AIR FORCE: 1,200.
    1 SAR det.
UK:
  NAVY: ε150.
    Comms and int facilities, Edzell, Thurso.
AT SEA:
  ATLANTIC FLEET: (HQ Norfolk, Virginia).
    Other main bases: Groton (Connecticut);
    Charleston (S. Carolina); King's Bay (Georgia);
    Mayport (Florida).
    Submarines: 5 *Ohio*, 12 other SSBN, 11
      SSGN, 40 SSN.
    Surface Combatants: 6 CV/CVN, 18
      CG/CGN, 7 DDG, 15 DD, 29 FFG, 15 FF.
    Amphibious: 1 LCC, 2 LHA, 4 LPH, 6 LPD,
      5 LSD, 12 LST, 2 LKA.

Surface Forces divided into two Fleets:
Second Fleet (HQ Norfolk): covers Atlantic,
  both north and south. Typically 4–5
  CVBG, Amph Gp, 4 URG.
Sixth Fleet (HQ Gaeta, Italy): Mediterranean.
  Under op comd of EUCOM. See EUCOM
  entry for typical force levels.

UN AND PEACEKEEPING
CAMBODIA (UNTAC): 17 Observers.
EGYPT (MFO): 500, 1 inf bn.
IRAQ/KUWAIT (UNIKOM): 20 Observers.
MIDDLE EAST (UNTSO): 36 Observers.
WESTERN SAHARA (MINURSO): 30 Observers.

CONTINENTAL UNITED STATES
  (CONUS): Major units/formations only listed.

FORCES COMMAND: (FORSCOM): 233,300:
  ARMY: provides general reserve of cbt-ready
    ground forces for other comd.
  Active: 4 Army HQ, 3 Corps HQ, 1 armd,
    4 mech, 2 lt inf, 1 AB, 1 air aslt div; 2 armd,
    1 mot inf, 3 arty bde; 1 armd cav regt.
  Reserve: ARNG: 2 armd, 2 mech, 5 inf, 1 lt inf
    div; 20 indep bde, 2 armd cav regt. AR: 3
    indep bde.

US STRATEGIC COMMAND (USSTRATCOM):
  See entry on pp. 18–19.

AIR COMBAT COMMAND (ACC):
  Responsible for provision of strategic AD units
  and of cbt-ready Air Force units for rapid
  deployment.

US SPECIAL OPERATIONS COMMAND
  (USSOCOM): Has under comd all active, reserve
  and National Guard special ops forces of all
  services based in CONUS. See pp. 25–26.

US TRANSPORTATION COMMAND
  (USTRANSCOM): Responsible for providing all
  common-user airlift, sealift and land
  transportation to deploy and maintain US forces
  on a global basis.

AIR MOBILITY COMMAND (AMC):
  Responsible for providing strategic, tac and
  special op airlift, aero-medical evacuation, SAR
  and weather recce.

MILITARY SEALIFT COMMAND
  See entry for Strategic Sealift, p. 24.

PARAMILITARY:
CIVIL AIR PATROL (CAP): 68,000 (27,500 cadets);
  HQ, 8 geographical regions, 52 wings, 1,881
  units, 579 CAP ac, plus 8,465 private ac.

NATO

NATO has continued to develop its plans for the reorganization of its command structure and most NATO countries have begun the draw-down of their armed forces following the disbandment of the Warsaw Pact and the collapse of the Soviet Union. NATO has sought to cooperate with the former members of the Warsaw Pact and with the new republics of the former Soviet Union.

NATO Reorganization

Details of NATO's new strategic concept were announced after the summit meeting in Rome on 7 and 8 November 1991. At the meeting two conclusions were reached: that the new environment does not change the purpose of the Alliance; and that this environment offers NATO opportunities to frame its strategy within a broad approach to security. The report foresaw that reduced armed forces at a lower level of readiness must have enhanced mobility and flexibility. The North Atlantic Council also announced the establishment of an institutional relationship between NATO, the former members of the Warsaw Pact (which at that time included the USSR) and the Baltic republics, to be called the North Atlantic Cooperation Council (NACC). NACC would hold annual meetings at ministerial level and periodic meetings at ambassadorial level. The first meeting of NACC at foreign minister level was held on 20 December 1991. On 10 March 1992 a meeting of ambassadors agreed a plan for dialogue, partnership and cooperation covering a wide range of topics, including defence planning, defence conversion, dissemination of information and air traffic management. By then NACC had been expanded to include the republics of the former Soviet Union. NACC met again at ministerial level in Oslo on 5 June 1992, when the members of NATO, the former members of the Warsaw Pact and the relevant republics of the former Soviet Union signed an agreement reconfirming their commitment to the Conventional Forces in Europe Treaty (CFE).

At the North Atlantic Council meeting on 4 June 1992, the Council, while supporting the proposal at the Helsinki Follow-up Meeting for CSCE to give itself regional status under chapter VIII of the UN Charter, recognized that NATO had the capacity to contribute to CSCE action in respect of crisis management and the settlement of disputes. NATO is therefore now prepared to support peacekeeping activities on a case-by-case basis by making available resources and expertise. Such support does not preclude the involvement of other CSCE countries. This carefully worded statement has been seen as the basis of a new role for NATO in out-of-area peacekeeping missions. It is important to put this development in perspective. First, many NATO nations already take a full part in UN peacekeeping missions, so this is not an entirely new role for NATO forces. Second, NATO must first be requested to provide peacekeeping assistance by the CSCE, where a unanimous vote (bar one) is necessary. Involvement is then subject to a unanimous NATO decision and there is no mandatory requirement for any member to contribute to the force. That said, NATO can play a very positive role in peacekeeping, particularly with regard to planning, movement and logistics, command and control, and joint training and development of operating procedures.

Some, but not all, of the expected changes to NATO's command structure have been announced. The number of Major NATO Commands will be reduced to two, with the abolition of Channel Command. In Allied Command Europe (ACE) there are to be three Major Subordinate Commands: Southern (AF South), Central (AFCENT) and North West; this last is to replace Allied Forces Northern Europe and United Kingdom Air Forces. The new Command's headquarters will be in the UK, and it will have responsibility for the land areas of Norway and the UK, the maritime areas of the Baltic Sea, the Channel, and an as yet undemarcated area of the North Sea. AFCENT will in future include Denmark and Schleswig-Holstein, but will contain only three Subordinate Commands: Allied Land Forces Central Europe, Allied Air Forces Central Europe, and Baltic Approaches (maritime forces allocated to AFNORTHWEST). Northern and Central Army Groups and 2nd and 4th Tactical Air Forces will be disbanded.

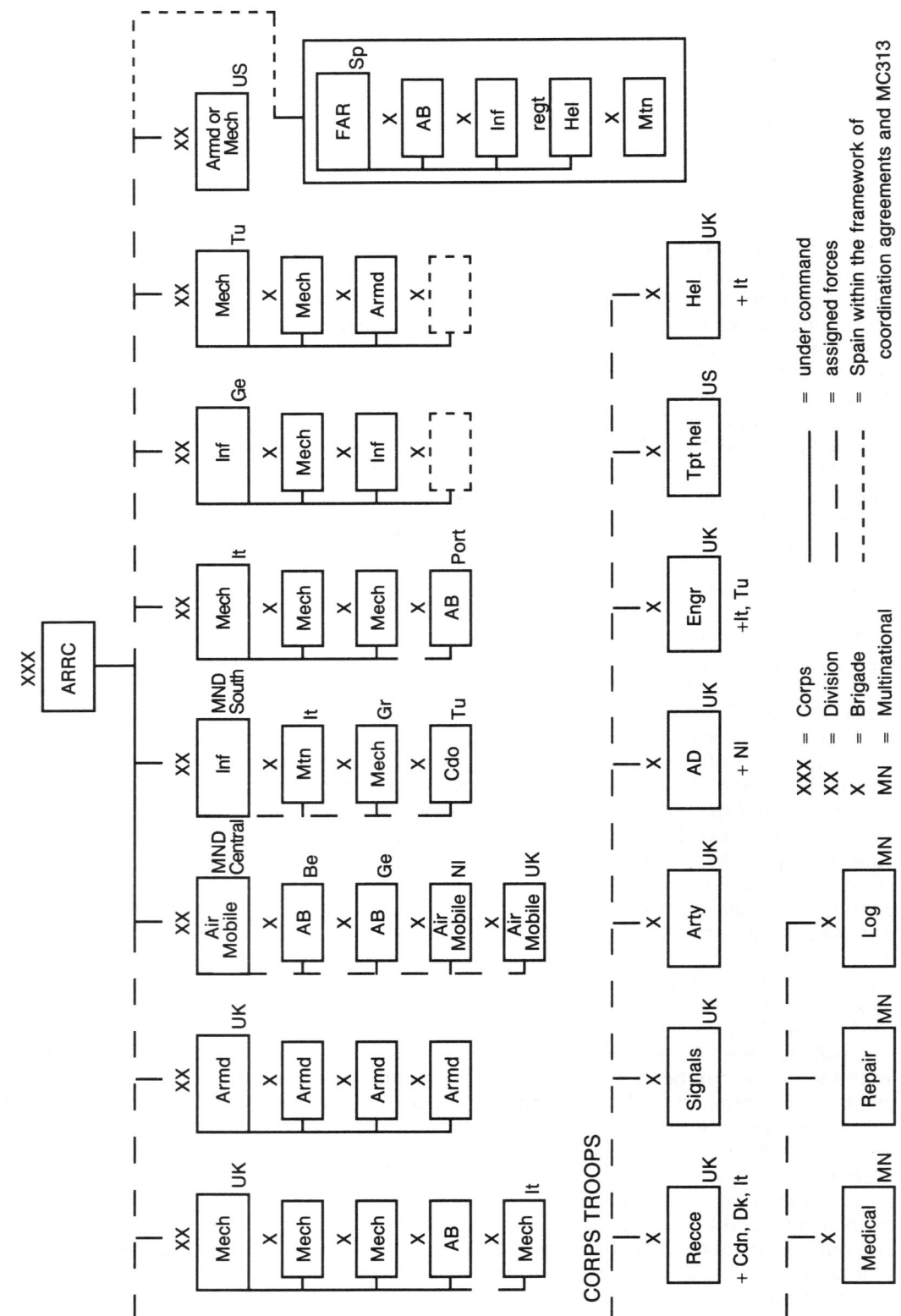

NATO RAPID REACTION FORCES (LAND)

Arrangements for setting up the ACE Rapid Reaction Force (ARRF) are well in hand. It is to be directly subordinate to SACEUR. Only the headquarters of the two multinational divisions will be under operational command of ARRF in peacetime; the other divisions and the brigades of the multinational divisions remain under national command until released to ARRF. HQ ARRF will be the administrative HQ for all British Army units in Germany. The diagram on p. 30 shows the full order of battle of the ARRF, but it is not expected that all eight divisions are ever likely to be deployed together. Assigned forces are more in the nature of items on a menu which can be chosen to suit particular operational situations. The description 'rapid' could be misleading. The force will be at no higher state of readiness than NATO forces were at the height of the Cold War. It has been stated that the force could deploy within 14 days. The force will contain two multinational divisions (MND). MND (Central) is to be an air-mobile division with two airborne brigades (Belgian and German) and two air-mobile brigades (Netherlands and UK). The division will be well supplied with attack helicopters, and its units will often deploy by helicopter. MND (South) will comprise: an Italian mountain brigade, a Greek mechanized brigade and a Turkish Commando Brigade. There is also to be a Rapid Reaction Force (Air) under the command of a German officer. Some 20 squadrons of aircraft and ten surface-to-air-missile (SAM) units have been assigned. Most components of the RRFs have dual roles, the second being with one of NATO's main defence force formations.

No firm details of the organization of NATO's main defence forces have yet been released, but it is widely believed that most corps in the Central Region will be multinational in that each national corps will contain a division from another nationality.

European Pillar

European Union

Opinion was divided on the text of the foreign and security policy section of the Treaty for European Unity, which was signed by the members of the EC at Maastricht in December 1991. The Treaty established a common foreign and security policy and laid down a number of provisions to govern it. As far as security policy is concerned, the Treaty states: 'The common foreign and security policy shall include all questions related to the security of the European Union, including the eventual framing of a common defence policy, which might in time lead to a common defence'. Decisions on security matters can only be made unanimously. The Union requested the Western European Union (WEU) 'to elaborate and implement decisions and actions of the Union which have defence implications'. In a separate declaration the member states of the WEU set out the role of the WEU and its relation to the European Union and to the Atlantic Alliance. The WEU will be developed as the defence component of the European Union and as a means of strengthening the European pillar of the Atlantic Alliance. The primacy of NATO in the defence field was recognized by the statements 'WEU will act in conformity with the positions adopted in the Atlantic Alliance' and 'arrangements aimed at giving WEU a stronger operational role will be fully compatible with the military dispositions necessary to ensure the collective defence of all Allies'.

Western European Union

In the Petersberg Declaration issued following the WEU Council of Ministers on 19 June 1992, it states that: . . . 'Apart from contributing to the common defence in accordance with Article 5 of the Washington Treaty and Article V of the modified Brussels Treaty respectively, military units of WEU member States, acting under the authority of WEU, could be employed for: humanitarian and rescue tasks; peacekeeping tasks; tasks of combat forces in crisis management, including peacemaking.'

The Council decided to establish a Planning Cell from 1 October 1992 located with the Secretariat-General in Brussels. The Planning Cell will be responsible to the WEU Council, and its tasks will be to:

- prepare contingency plans for the employment of forces under WEU auspices;
- prepare recommendations for the necessary command, control and communication arrangements, including standing operating procedures for headquarters which might be selected;
- keep an updated list of units and combinations of units which might be allocated to WEU for specific operations. (Forces can be 'double-hatted' to both NATO and WEU, but their commitment to WEU operations would only be made after consultation with NATO.)

The Planning Cell will not have a command task although, in the case of employment of WEU forces in a crisis, elements of the Planning Cell might team up with the selected headquarters.

When it is fully operational in 1993 the Planning Cell will comprise some 40 officers and NCOs from the nine member countries of WEU. It will have five sections dealing with Coordination, Plans, Operations/Exercises, Logistics/Movements/Finances and Communications. The three services will be represented in each section.

The WEU first discussed the possibility of space cooperation in April 1989 and an ad hoc group prepared a study on the requirement for: the verification of arms-control agreements; the monitoring of crises affecting European security; and the monitoring of environmental hazards. In 1991 it was agreed that a WEU Satellite Centre would be established at Torrejón in Spain, for an experimental period of three years from 1 January 1992 with a budget of £26.8m. During its experimental phase, the Centre will have some 50 staff and will train analysts in the interpretation of imagery using data available from commercial satellites such as SPOT, LANDSAT and ERS. The future of the Centre will be reviewed towards the end of the three-year period. Subsequently, the Centre could become more operational, particularly for crisis monitoring and verification, by using data from satellites with better resolution such as *Hélios* – due to be launched in 1994. In this context, a Memorandum of Understanding has been drawn up under which the *Hélios* partners (France, Italy and Spain) would make data available to the WEU Satellite Centre. This data could then be analysed by the image interpreters who have been trained in the Centre, and the results passed back to national capitals. In its ultimate phase, the Centre could be responsible for operating WEU's autonomous satellite observation capability, currently the subject of a feasibility study by a European industrial consortium led by Dornier, under the auspices of a WEU Study Management Team based in Paris.

In July 1992 the WEU coordinated the deployment of a multinational naval force to the Adriatic Sea to take part in the monitoring of sanctions imposed on Serbia and Montenegro.

Franco-German Corps

At the Franco-German summit in La Rochelle in May 1992, President Mitterrand and Chancellor Kohl revealed their intention to establish a Franco-German force which could form the core of a future European army. The French rationale for the 'Euro-Corps' was that it would be prudent to begin the process of forming a European army well before any decision was taken to withdraw all US troops from Europe. The Germans claim that by going along with the French proposal they would, in effect, bind France closer to NATO's military command and might even achieve French reintegration. An operational Franco-German corps is planned by October 1995; it will comprise a French tank division, stationed at Trier in Germany, and a German contribution of a division or several brigades (no definite commitment has yet been announced). Other West European countries have been invited to take part, and Belgium, Luxembourg and Spain have expressed interest. The role of the Corps has been described as: contributing to the Allies' joint defence; peacekeeping and peacemaking tasks; and humanitarian assignments. The German units earmarked for the Corps will remain assigned to NATO. It is not clear, however, how the Corps could play a part in Allied defence of Western Europe without duplicating NATO's role. The French Defence Minister has said that it would 'operate under the authority of a NATO command in case of aggression', but, presumably, at such a time the German component would be operating with its assigned NATO formation. Nor is a tank division necessarily the best formation to employ in peacekeeping or humanitarian relief. As yet, the problems of the German constitution and the use of German forces outside the NATO area remain unresolved, potentially affecting both Euro-Corps and NATO's ARRF.

Nuclear Forces

Both France and the UK continue to improve their strategic nuclear capability at the same time as they reduce the size of their nuclear forces.

France has two *Triomphant*-class SSBN under construction, the first to be operational in 1995, and two more planned but not yet ordered. The development programme for the M-5 SLBM has been extended, and the missile is now unlikely to be operational until around 2005 and so will have to be retrofitted. One *Le Redoubtable*-class SSBN was retired at the end of 1991. The minimum number of SSBN at sea at any given time is to be two (versus the three since 1983). A decision has been taken not to replace the S-3D IRBM with a new land-based missile, but no decision has been taken as to how long the S-3D will remain in service. Sub-strategic forces are being reduced. The *Hadès* programme for an SSM replacement for *Pluton* has now been cancelled. It had been much reduced from the original planned order of 120 missiles, and those completed were to have been kept in store and not deployed. Now it is understood that no missiles will be kept. Two regiments of *Pluton* SSM have been disbanded and two squadrons of *Jaguar* aircraft re-roled for conventional operations only. Only three as opposed to five squadrons of nuclear-capable *Mirage* 2000N aircraft will be maintained, and only one (instead of two) squadron of *Super Etendard*. In April 1992 France suspended its nuclear tests until the end of the year; the moratorium could be extended if others followed suit. On 3 August 1992 France acceded to the Nuclear Non-Proliferation Treaty (NPT).

The first of the **UK**'s *Vanguard*-class SSBN was launched in March 1992 and is expected to be operational by the end of 1994. Two further boats are under construction and the government formally placed an order for the fourth in July 1992, although work has been in progress for some time and considerable expenditure incurred for long-lead items. The number of nuclear warheads eventually to be deployed in the *Trident*-armed SSBN has not been revealed; the maximum could be 512, compared to the 192 deployed in *Polaris*-armed SSBN. Following the recent arms agreement reached by the US and Russia, which will require US *Trident* SLBM to be downloaded to only four warheads, there could be increased pressure on the British government to commit itself to a smaller number. In this context Prime Minister John Major has said 'we will maintain the minimum necessary' and a Foreign Office Minister remarked 'that may in certain circumstances be substantially less than the maximum'. On the other hand, the possibility of Russia deploying a system similar to the US-planned Limited Defense System (which could intercept up to 200 incoming warheads) could persuade the UK to deploy the full number of warheads. Even so, the *Trident* SLBM of two SSBN would be needed to swamp such a defensive system. The UK followed the US and the Soviet Union in deciding to withdraw all tactical nuclear weapons from naval ships and shore-based maritime air-stations in October 1991. In June 1992 it was announced that these weapons, all nuclear depth-bombs, were to be destroyed. The Defence Secretary has affirmed that the UK still plans to replace its air-delivered free-fall nuclear bombs. One *Polaris* submarine, HMS *Revenge*, has decommissioned. *Lance* SSM are being withdrawn from service and the Missile Regiment will be disbanded.

Conventional Forces

Military Developments

The strength of the **Belgian** armed forces has been reduced by 5,000 men and conscription cut by two months (to ten months, with eight for those stationed in Germany). A mechanized infantry brigade has been withdrawn from Germany and one has been disbanded. A *Gepard*-equipped Air Defence Battalion has also been withdrawn from Germany and transferred to the reserves. One squadron of *Mirage* V FGA aircraft has been disbanded. Six mine countermeasures ships have been retired by the Belgian Navy. **Canada** has withdrawn one squadron of CF-18 FGA aircraft from Germany and disbanded it. Two squadrons of CP-121 maritime reconnaissance aircraft have also been disbanded. All CH-47 helicopters have been retired, but an additional two helicopter squadrons have been formed. One of the four *Iroquois*-

class frigates being upgraded to destroyer is now undergoing sea-trials. One *St Laurent*-class frigate has been retired. The apparent drop in the strength of the army by 13,000 is because the numbers attributed to 'Tri-service' units have been increased by a similar number. The **Danish** Navy has commissioned a third *Tumleren* (which are modified Norwegian *Kobben*-class) submarine. Three *Hvidbjornen*, 1,600-ton, offshore patrol craft have been retired, while two more 3,500-ton *Thetis*-class and two more *Flyvefisken*-class have been commissioned.

The **French** Army has disbanded one armoured division (stationed in Germany) and one combat helicopter regiment. New equipment deliveries include 19 MLRS and 55 *Mistral* SAM launchers. The navy has commissioned one *Rubis*-class submarine and placed one *Daphné*-class in store. Two *Floréal*-class frigates, which are armed with *Exocet* and embark one helicopter, have commissioned, and two frigates have been retired: the *Duperré*-class and one *Commandant Rivière*-class. The navy has taken delivery of six AS-365 SAR helicopters. The air force has re-equipped one squadron of *Mirage* F-1 fighters with *Mirage* 2000 and one squadron of *Mirage* IIIE FGA aircraft with *Mirage* 2000N. The air force has formed four squadrons with *Mistral* SAM.

The **German** armed forces have been reduced in strength by 29,000 men, of which 19,000 were in the army. An additional 60 *Leopard*-2 MBT and 220 Rh-202 20mm air defence guns have been delivered. In the air force, one F-4 wing has been transferred from FGA to the air defence role, and one wing of *Alpha Jet* FGA has been disbanded. Sixteen more *Tornado* ECR aircraft have been delivered, and two *Patriot* SAM wings formed. The navy has retired two Type-205 submarines and 13 mine countermeasures ships of different classes.

The **Greek** Air Force has taken delivery of 24 F-4 fighters provided by the US and also four F-16D FGA/fighters and six *Mirage* 2000E fighters. They expect to receive up to 20 RF-4E from Germany. The Greek Navy has commissioned one destroyer (US *Adams*-class) and two corvettes (German *Thetis*-class). By the end of 1992, three more *Adams* destroyers, three US *Knox*-class frigates and an additional two *Thetis* corvettes will also have entered service. Older ships have been paid off (three US *Fletcher*-class destroyers and two US *Cannon*-class and one German *Rein*-class frigates).

The armed forces in **The Netherlands** have been reduced in strength by 8,000 men, of which 4,000 were in the army. The *Lance* SSM battalion has been disbanded. The air force has taken delivery of seven more F-16 fighter/FGA aircraft, and the navy has commissioned a second *Zeeleeuw*-class submarine and a second *Karel Doorman*-class frigate, while retiring a *Dolfijn*-class submarine.

The **Spanish** armed forces have been reduced in strength by 40,000 men, of which 36,000 were in the army. Conscription has been reduced from one year to nine months. The army has taken delivery of 140 more BMR-600 APC. The reorganization of the air force has been completed with Training Command and Air Force HQ Group being disbanded. Tactical units of Training Command have been transferred to the Gibraltar Strait Air Command, and transport training units with the transport and support squadrons of the HQ Group have been transferred to Central Air Command. The navy has retired its last four *Churruca* (US *Gearing*)-class destroyers. The **Turkish** Army has taken delivery of a number of equipments, most transferred from other forces under the SHAPE 'Harmonization Plan'. These include: 140 *Leopard* MBT 300 BTR-60 APC, 12 M-109 155mm SP guns, eight M-110 203mm SP guns and 14 more MLRS. The air force has taken delivery of 30 more F-16 FGA aircraft, most built under licence in Turkey, and 12 S-2AE anti-submarine warfare aircraft. The navy has retired three *Burakreis* (US *Guppy*)-class submarines. The US Army is transferring a total of 2,000 M-60A1 and A3 MBT, and 240 M-110 203mm SP guns to Greece, Turkey and Spain, but some are going to Portugal (MBT only) and Denmark (M-110 only).

The manpower strength of the **UK** armed forces is reduced by 7,000, of which 4,000 are from the army. The army has taken delivery of 100 more *Warrior* AIFV and 20 more MLRS, one more infantry battalion has been equipped with *Warrior* and one more with *Saxon* wheeled APC. In July 1992 the organization and title of the Ulster Defence Regiment was changed. It is now the Royal Irish Regiment, and will eventually comprise one general service battalion and seven battalions for service in Northern Ireland only (with both full-time and part-time soldiers). The Royal Navy has commissioned a seventh *Trafalgar*-class nuclear-powered submarine and retired one Swiftsure-class. Three *Oberon*-class diesel submarines have been retired and two more *Upholder*-class commissioned. Five *Leander*-class frigates and four mine countermeasures ships (two *Waveney*-class and two *Ton*-class) have been retired, while one more *Norfolk*-class Type 23 frigate and a third *Sandown*-class minehunter have commissioned, and orders for three more Type 23 frigates placed. The assault ship *Intrepid* is now in reserve. The government has announced its plans for the amphibious fleet. A helicopter support ship and two assault ships (to replace *Fearless* and *Intrepid*) will be procured, and three *Sir Lancelot*-class landing ships are to be refitted and modernized. So far only the tender for the helicopter support ship, which would be able to operate 12 *Sea King*-type helicopters and embark an amphibious landing force of some 500 men with vehicles and equipment, has been invited. The air force has withdrawn and disbanded two squadrons of *Tornado* GR-1 FGA aircraft from Germany and placed the aircraft in store. A second reconnaissance squadron with *Tornado* GR-1A has been formed, and a further five *Sentry* E-3D airborne early warning aircraft have been delivered to complete the squadron's inventory of seven aircraft. Five Air Defence squadrons with *Rapier* SAM have been disbanded, and the *Bloodhound* SAM has been withdrawn from service. The United Kingdom Mobile Force, one of whose operational roles was the reinforcement of Jutland and Schleswig-Holstein, has been disbanded.

Future Plans

Last year *The Military Balance* reported the plans to reorganize and reduce the strength of the armed forces of Belgium, Canada, France, The Netherlands and the UK. In July 1992 the **Belgian** government announced its intention to abolish conscription by 1994, and to cut the strength of its armed forces by roughly 50%. From 1 January 1993 the Belgian Air Force will reduce its air combat strength from the present seven squadrons to four. Two dedicated all-weather intercept F-16 squadrons will be disbanded, as well as the remaining *Mirage* 5BR squadron.

Italian Army plans include a reduction in strength of some 25% and the restructuring of formations in terms of readiness. There are to be five brigades, manned by volunteers whose state of readiness will vary between one to ten days. There will be similar all-volunteer naval and air force units. The next group of ten brigades will be composed of both volunteers and conscripts, and will have reaction times of between 30 and 90 days. The last group consists of reserve forces which will take over 90 days to mobilize.

Canada has decided to withdraw all its forces from Europe. The previous plan had been to leave a force of some 1,100 troops in Germany, but this has now been cancelled and the withdrawal will be completed in 1994.

More details of the **British** Army's restructuring plan, 'Options for Change', have been released. There are to be two divisions assigned to ARRF. The armoured division to remain in Germany will have three brigades (existing divisions have only two), each with two tank and two armoured infantry battalions. The other division, based in the UK, will also have three brigades: two mechanized (with one tank, one armoured infantry, two mechanized infantry and one SP artillery battalions); and an airborne brigade with two parachute and two infantry battalions. The UK element of ARRF corps troops will include three armoured reconnaissance regiments, three MLRS regiments and four air defence regiments (two equipped with *Rapier* SAM and two with the High Velocity Missile (HVM)). In addition, the UK will provide one airmobile brigade to the MND (Central), which will comprise two infantry battalions and two aviation regiments.

The **French** 1992–94 three-year defence programme includes: the exploratory development of the *Zenon* ELINT satellite and the *Osiris* radar-imaging satellite. A new ELINT aircraft (*Sarigue*) is to be ordered, as is the *Horizon* helicopter-borne radar system. Army strength is to be reduced to 225,000 (of which 115,000 will be conscripts) by 1997, organized into eight divisions (four armoured and mechanized and four in FAR). The *Leclerc* tank order will be for 800 MBT and the NH-90 helicopter programme has been confirmed. Air force aircraft strength will be cut and orders for the *Rafale* fighter stretched out. A review of reserve forces will be carried out with a view to making service more attractive.

The **German** Army is being reorganized and the number of Field Army brigades reduced. As considerably more warning time will be available in the future, it has been decided to amalgamate the Field and Territorial Armies and to combine their command elements. There are to be three Territorial/Corps HQ and eight Military District/Division HQ. In addition, two purely divisional HQ for short-notice operational tasks will be established. The total number of brigades will be 28 with differing levels of active/reserve components and readiness. Seven brigades are likely to be at full strength and at a high state of readiness. The four divisions to be disbanded are two armoured, one armoured infantry and the airborne division. Germany indicated its intention not to continue in the European Fighter Aircraft (EFA) consortium when the aircraft enters the production phase. It proposes instead that the remaining development funds should be switched to designing a less expensive aircraft, which would therefore be less capable. Supporters of the EFA project maintain that with the growing exports of Russian aircraft, such as MiG-29, Su-27 and in the future MiG-31 and MiG-33, a plane with EFA's capability will still be needed, and that any alternative as capable would be more expensive.

The **Turkish** Army is carrying out a major reorganization due to be completed in 1994. The basic structure of four armies will remain, but with two independent corps. The division level of command (with the exception of one division) is to be removed, with corps commanding brigades directly. It is expected that the final number of brigades will be 32 (14 armoured, 15 mechanized infantry, 1 infantry and 2 commando). The increase in the number of armoured formations will be made possible by the SHAPE 'Harmonization Plan', under which Turkey is receiving over 800 M-60A1/A3 MBT from the US and 236 *Leopard* 1 A1/4 MBT from Germany. Manpower strength is likely to be reduced to 350,000.

A new naval standing force has been established by NATO to operate permanently in the Mediterranean (STANAVFORMED). It will comprise ships from the navies of Germany, Greece, Italy, The Netherlands, Spain, Turkey, the UK and the US. It will replace the Naval on Call Force (NAVOCFORMED). In July 1992 the force deployed to the Adriatic Sea to take part in the monitoring of sanctions imposed on Serbia and Montenegro.

BELGIUM

GDP	1990: fr 6,577bn ($196.81bn)
	1991: fr 6,905bn ($202.21bn)
Growth	1990: 3.4%	1991: 1.4%
Inflation	1990: 3.5%	1991: 3.2%
Debt	1989: $89.77bn	1990: $91.00bn
Def bdgt	1991: fr 102.39bn ($3.00bn)
	1992: fr 101.70bn ($2.97bn)
NATO defn	1991: fr 162.96bn ($4.77bn)
$1 = fr	1989: 39.404	1990: 33.418
	1991: 34.148	1992: 34.250
fr = Belgian francs

Population: 9,856,600

	13–17	*18–22*	*23–32*
Men	312,600	339,200	763,000
Women	299,800	326,000	737,200

TOTAL ARMED FORCES:
ACTIVE: 80,700 (incl 5,000 Medical Service); 2,950 women; 32,300 conscripts.
Terms of service: 8 months in Germany or 10 months in Belgium. To be 8 months for all (1993).

RESERVES: Total Reserve Status: 228,800. With service in past 3 years: ε146,000 (Army 139,100; Medical Service 36,800; Navy 12,400; Air Force 40,500).

ARMY: 54,000 (23,300 conscripts). Both figures incl Medical Service.
1 Corps HQ.
1 armd bde (2 tk, 2 mech inf, 1 SP arty bn, 1 ATK coy).
2 mech inf bde (each 1 tk, 2 mech inf, 1 SP arty bn, 1 ATK coy).
1 para-cdo regt (3 para-cdo bn, armd recce sqn, ATK coy, arty bty).
1 indep recce bn.
2 SP arty bn.
3 AD bn: 2 *HAWK*; 1 *Gepard* AA.
3 engr bn (2 fd, 1 bridge).
3 lt avn sqn.
RESERVES: some on immediate recall status;
1 armd bde (2 tk, 2 mech inf, 1 SP arty bn, 1 ATK coy).
1 mot inf bde (2 mot inf, 1 SP arty bn, 1 ATK coy, 1 recce sqn).
1 para cdo, 1 *Gepard* AA, 1 engr (eqpt) bn.
Territorial defence: 11 lt inf regt, 4 lt inf bn.

EQUIPMENT:
MBT: 334 *Leopard* 1, 25 M-41.
LIGHT TANKS: 133 *Scorpion.*
RECCE: 153 *Scimitar.*
AIFV: 514 AIFV-B.
APC: 1,362: incl 509 M-113, 266 *Spartan,* 510 AMX-VCI, 77 M-75 to be sold/scrapped.
TOTAL ARTY: 376 (60 in store).
    TOWED ARTY: 105mm: 21 M-101.
    SP ARTY: 207: 105mm: 28 M-108; 155mm: 41 M-109A3, 127 M-109A2; 203mm: 11 M-110.
    MORTARS: 107mm: 130 M-30 (incl some SP); 120mm: 18. Plus 81mm: 285.
SSM: 5 *Lance* launchers (in store).
ATGW: 420 *Milan* (325 veh-mounted), 43 *Striker* AFV with *Swingfire* (in store).
ATK GUNS: 80 JPK-90mm SP (to be scrapped).
AD GUNS: 20mm: 36 HS-804, 100 M-167 *Vulcan;* 35mm: 54 *Gepard* SP.
SAM: 39 Improved *HAWK,* 22 *Mistral.*
AIRCRAFT: 10 BN-2A *Islander.*
HELICOPTERS: 43 SA-318, 6 A-109.

NAVY: 4,400 (1,600 conscripts).
BASES: Ostend, Zeebrugge.
FRIGATES: 4 *Wielingen* with 2 × ASTT (Fr L-5 LWT), 1 × 6 ASW mor; plus 4 × MM-38 *Exocet* SSM, 1 × 100mm gun and 1 × 8 *Sea Sparrow* SAM.
MINE WARFARE: 16 MCMV:
    6 *Van Haverbeke* (US *Aggressive* MSO).
    10 *Aster* (tripartite) MHC.
SUPPORT AND MISCELLANEOUS: 3:
    2 log spt/comd with hel deck, 1 research/ survey.
HELICOPTERS: 3 SA-318.

AIR FORCE: 17,300 (4,300 conscripts).
FGA: 4 sqn with F-16A/B.
FIGHTER: 2 sqn with F-16A/B.
RECCE: 1 sqn with *Mirage* 5BR.
TRANSPORT: 2 sqn: 1 with 12 C-130H; 1 with 2 Boeing 727QC, 3 HS-748, 5 *Merlin* IIIA, 2 *Falcon* 20.
TRAINING: 5 sqn: 3 with *Alpha Jet;* 1 with SF-260, 1 with CM-170.
SAR: 1 sqn with *Sea King* Mk 48.
EQUIPMENT: 122 cbt ac (plus 74 in store), no armed hel.
AIRCRAFT:
    Mirage: 5BR: 15 (recce); plus 47 in store (37-BA, 10-BD).
    F-16: 107: **A/B:** 72 (FGA), 35 (ftr); plus 27 in store.
    C-130: 12 (tpt).
    Boeing 727: 2 (tpt). **HS-748:** 3 (tpt). **CM-170:** 18 (liaison). **SF-260:** 28 (trg). *Alpha Jet:* 31 (trg).
HELICOPTERS:
    Sea King: 5 (SAR).

MISSILES:
    AAM: AIM-9 *Sidewinder.*

FORCES ABROAD:
GERMANY: 19,000;
    1 corps HQ, 1 armd bde; 2 arty, 1 *Gepard* AA, 2 SAM, 2 engr bn; 3 hel sqn.
UN AND PEACEKEEPING:
CAMBODIA (UNTAC): 2 Observers.
CROATIA (UNPROFOR): 510, plus 3 Observers.
INDIA/PAKISTAN (UNMOGIP): 2 Observers.
MIDDLE EAST (UNTSO): 4 Observers.

FOREIGN FORCES:
NATO:
    HQ NATO Brussels.
    HQ SHAPE Mons.
WEU:
    Military Planning Cell (from October 1992).
US:
    Some 1,900, Army (1,200); Navy (100+); Air (600).

CANADA

GDP	1990: $C 671.58bn ($US 575.57bn)		
	1991: $C 679.20bn ($US 592.83bn)		
Growth	1990: 0.5%	1991:	−1.5%
Inflation	1990: 4.8%	1991:	5.6%
Debt	1989: $US 238.86bn		
	1990: $US 266.29bn		
Def bdgt	1991: $C 13.20bn ($US 11.52bn)		
	1992: $C 12.42bn ($US 10.35bn)		
NATO defn[a]	1991: $C 14.00bn ($US 12.22bn)		
$ 1 = $C	1989: 1.1840	1990:	1.1668
	1991: 1.1457	1992:	1.2000

Population: 27,016,600

	13–17	18–22	23–32
Men	947,400	978,000	2,336,400
Women	906,600	936,000	2,245,400

[a] Canadian fiscal year is 1 April–31 March. NATO data refer to calendar year.

Canadian Armed Forces are unified and are organized in functional commands. Mobile Command commands land combat forces, and Maritime Command all naval forces. Air Command commands all air forces, but Maritime Command has operational control of maritime air forces. Mobile Command has operational control of TAG. HQ 4 ATAF in Europe has operational control of 1 Canadian Air Division.
This entry is set out in the traditional single service manner.

TOTAL ARMED FORCES:
ACTIVE: 84,000; 9,400 women; of the total
strength some 22,600 are not identified by service.
RESERVES: Primary 29,700. Army (Militia) (incl
comms) 24,500; Navy 3,600; Air 1,600.
Supplementary 35,300.

ARMY (Land Forces): 22,000.
1 Task Force HQ:
1 mech bde gp with 1 armd regt, 2 mech inf
bn, 1 arty, 1 engr regt.
3 inf bde gp, 2 with 1 armd regt, 3 mech inf
bn, 1 arty, 1 engr regt. 1 with 1 armd regt, 1
inf bn, 1 AB, 1 arty, 1 engr regt.
1 AD regt (4 bty); 1 indep AD bty.
1 indep engr spt regt.
RESERVES: Militia: 18 armd, 18 arty, 52 inf, 11
engr, 20 spt bn level units, 12 med coy.
Canadian Rangers: Northern region: 1,220: 54
patrols. Atlantic region: 1,017: 30 patrols.
Pacific region: 280: 10 patrols.
EQUIPMENT:
MBT: 114 *Leopard* C-1.
RECCE: 174 *Lynx*, 195 *Cougar*.
APC: 1,404: 881 M-113 A2 (136 in store), 55
M-577, 269 *Grizzly*, 199 *Bison*.
TOWED ARTY: 255: 105mm: 12 Model 44 (L-5) pack,
189 C1 (M-101); 155mm: 54 M-114 (in store).
SP ARTY: 155mm: 76 M-109.
MORTARS: 81mm: 150.
ATGW: 150 *TOW* (incl 64 M-113 SP).
RCL: 84mm: 780 *Carl Gustav*.
AD GUNS: 35mm: 20 GDF-005; 40mm: 57 L40/60.
SAM: 21 ADATS, 111 *Blowpipe*, 14 *Javelin*.

NAVY (Maritime Forces): 17,000.
SUBMARINES: 3 *Ojibwa* (UK *Oberon*) SS with Mk
48 HWT; plus *Harpoon* USGW.
PRINCIPAL SURFACE COMBATANTS: 18:
DESTROYERS: 4
DDG: 4 *Iroquois* ex-FFH (in conversion refit/post
refit trials) with 1 × Mk-41 VLS for 29 SM-2
MR, 2 CH-124 *Sea King* ASW hel (Mk 46
LWT), 2 × 3 ASTT, plus 1 × 76mm gun.
FRIGATES: 14:
FFH: 6:
1 *Halifax* with 1 CH-124A *Sea King* ASW (or 1
EH-101) hel (Mk 46 LWT), 2 × 2 ASTT; plus 2
× 4 *Harpoon* and 2 × 8 *Sea Sparrow* SAM
(without full ASW system).
2 *Annapolis*, 3 *St Laurent* with 1 *Sea King* hel, 2
× 3 ASTT, 1 × 3 ASW mor; plus 2 × 76mm gun.
FF: 8:
4 Improved *Restigouche* with 1 × 8 *ASROC*, 2 ×
3 ASTT, 1 × 3 ASW mor.
4 *Mackenzie* with 2 × 3 ASTT, 2 × 3 ASW mor,
plus 4 × 76mm gun.

PATROL AND COASTAL COMBATANTS: 12:
6 *Fundy* (ex MSC) PCC (trg).
5 *Porte St Jean* PCC, 1 PCI⟨ (reserve trg).
MINE WARFARE: 2:
2 *Anticosti* MSO (converted offshore spt vessels)
(reserve trg).
SUPPORT AND MISCELLANEOUS: 8:
2 *Protecteur* AO with 3 *Sea King*, 1 *Provider* AO
with 2 *Sea King*, 1 AO, 3 AGOR, 1 diving spt.

DEPLOYMENT AND BASES:
ATLANTIC: Halifax (HQ) (Maritime Commander is
also COMCANLANT): 3 SS, 2 DDG, 5 FF, 2
AGOR. 2 MR sqn each with 7 CP-140, 3 ASW
hel sqn with 32 CH-124 hel.
PACIFIC: Esquimalt (HQ): 7 FF, 1 AGOR, 6 PCC.
1 MR sqn with 4 CP-140.
RESERVES: 4,400 in 24 divisions: Patrol craft,
MCM, Naval Control of Shipping, augmentation
of regular units.

AIR FORCE: 22,400.
CANADIAN AIR DIVISION (Lahr AB, Germany):
1 sqn with CF-18; plus 1 NATO-assigned
reinforcement sqn with CF-18 based in Canada.
FIGHTER GROUP:
FIGHTER: 5 sqn (1 trg) with CF-18.
1 sqn with CF-5.
EW: 1 trg sqn with CE-144 (CL-601), CT-133.
EARLY WARNING: Canadian NORAD Regional
Headquarters at North Bay. 47 North Warning
radar sites: 11 long-range, 36 short-range; Region
Operational Control Centre (ROCC), (2 Sector
Operational Control Centres SOCC).
4 Coastal Radars and 2 Transportable Radars.
MARITIME AIR GROUP:
MR: 4 sqn (1 trg) with CP-140 *Aurora*;
ASW: 3 hel sqn (1 trg) with CH-124, *Sea King*.
LIAISON: 2 utility sqn with T-33.
TACTICAL AIR GROUP (TAG):
HELICOPTERS: 13 sqn: 5 with CH-135, 4 with
CH-136; 4 reserve sqn with CH-136.
AIR TRANSPORT GROUP:
TRANSPORT: 6 sqn:
4 (1 trg) with CC-130E/H *Hercules*.
1 with CC-137 (Boeing 707).
1 with CC-109, CC-144.
SAR: 4 tpt/SAR sqn (1 with twinned reserve sqn) with
CC-115, CC-130, CC-138 ac; CH-113/-113A hel.
LIAISON: 3 base hel flt with CH-118, CH-135.
TRAINING: (reports direct to HQ Air Comd).
2 flying schools with CF-116, CT-133, CT-114,
CC/CT-142 ac; CH-139 hel.
1 demonstration sqn with CT-114.
EQUIPMENT: 198 cbt ac (plus 62 in store); 131
armed hel.
AIRCRAFT:
CF-18: 123 **-A:** 84; **-B:** 39 (plus **-A:** 2 in store).

CF-5: 57 **-A:** 26; **-D:** 31 (plus **-A:** 55, **-D:** 5 in store).
CP-140: 18 (MR).
CC-130E/H: 31 (26 tpt, 5 AAR/tpt).
CC-137: 5 (3 tpt, 2 tkr/ tpt).
CC-109: 7 (tpt). **CC/E-144:** 16 (6 EW trg, 3 coastal patrol, 7 VIP/tpt). **CC-138:** 7 (SAR/tpt). **CC-115:** 10 (SAR/tpt). **CT-133:** 51 (EW trg/tpt plus 9 in store). **CT-114:** 108 (trg). **CC/T-142:** 8 (2 tpt, 6 trg).

HELICOPTERS:
CH-124: 32 (ASW, afloat); plus 3 in store.
CH-135: 44 (37 tac, 7 SAR/liaison). **CH-136:** 64 (62 tac, 2 test/trg). **CH-113:** 14 (SAR/tpt).
CH-118: 9 (liaison). **CH-139:** 14 (trg).

FORCES ABROAD:
GERMANY:
1 mech bde gp (3,600) (assigned to CENTAG); 1 air div: (1,500) 1 FGA sqn.
NORWAY: prepositioned TLE: 6 arty, 14 ACV.
UN AND PEACEKEEPING:
ANGOLA (UNAVEM II): 15 Observers.
CAMBODIA (UNTAC): 208.
CROATIA (UNPROFOR): 1,200: 1 inf bn, 1 engr coy, 12 Observers.
CYPRUS (UNFICYP): 576: 1 inf bn.
EGYPT (MFO): 24.
EL SALVADOR (ONUSAL): 17.
IRAQ/KUWAIT (UNIKOM): 50; engr sub-unit.
MIDDLE EAST (UNTSO): 16.
SYRIA/ISRAEL (UNDOF): 216 (log).
WESTERN SAHARA (MINURSO): 34.

PARAMILITARY:
COAST GUARD: 6,400 (civilian-manned); some 89 vessels including: 1 heavy icebreaker/cable ship, 7 heavy, 6 medium and 5 light icebreakers; 14 large SAR cutters/tenders; plus 2 DHC-7R ac, 37 hel, 5 hovercraft.

DENMARK

GDP	1990:	kr 800.00bn ($129.26bn)	
	1991	kr 832.00bn ($130.10bn)	
Growth	1990:	1.8%	1991: 1.6%
Inflation	1990:	2.6%	1991: 2.4%
Debt	1990:	$133.30bn	1991: $141.18bn
Def bdgt	1991:	kr 16.73bn ($2.61bn);	
	1992:	kr 16.85bn ($2.59bn)	
NATO defn	1991:	kr 17.10bn ($2.67bn)	
$1 = kr	1989:	7.310	1990: 6.189
	1991:	6.396	1992: 6.500
kr = Danish kroner			

Population: 5,075,600

	13–17	18–22	23–32
Men	165,000	186,500	393,400
Women	158,000	173,300	377,400

TOTAL ARMED FORCES:
ACTIVE: 29,200 (10,100 conscripts, 980 women).
Terms of service: 9–12 months (up to 27 months in certain ranks).
RESERVES: 72,500: Army 54,600; Navy 5,800; Air Force 12,100. Home Guard (*Hjemmevaernet*) (volunteers to age 50): Army 54,500; Naval 4,000; Air Force 10,700.

ARMY: some 17,300 (8,500 conscripts, 400 women):
Covering Force (peacetime units requiring some reinforcement to be combat ready and mob of some reserve units):
1 corps HQ, 1 div HQ.
5 mech inf bde, each with 1 tk, 2 mech (incl 1 Reserve), 1 arty bn, spt units.
6 regt cbt gp.
2 recce bn.
1 avn unit, some 8 pl.
Regional Defence (cadre basis until mob):
7 Regional HQ.
4 regt cbt gp (each 2–3 inf bn, 1 arty bn, 1 tk coy).
1 inf bn (UN).
EQUIPMENT:
MBT: 499: 230 *Leopard* 1A3/4, 216 *Centurion*, 53 M-41DK-1.
APC: 643 M-113.
TOTAL ARTY: 553.
  TOWED ARTY: 317: 105mm: 184 M-101; 155mm: 24 M-59, 97 M-114/39; 203mm: 12 M-115.
  SP ARTY: 155mm: 76 M-109.
  MORTARS: 120mm: 160 Brandt. Plus 81mm: 388 (incl 55 M-106/-125).
ATGW: 140 *TOW* (incl 56 SP).
RCL: 84mm: 1,117 *Carl Gustav*; 106mm: 150 M-40.
AD GUNS: 40mm: 36 L/60.
SAM: *Hamlet* (*Redeye*).
AIRCRAFT: 8 SAAB T-17.
HELICOPTERS: 13 Hughes 500M/OH-6, 12 AS-550C2.

NAVY: 4,900 (incl 200 women, 800 conscripts).
BASES: Copenhagen, Korsør, Frederikshavn.
SUBMARINES: 5:
  3 *Tumleren* (mod No *Kobben*) SSC with Sw FFV Type 61 HWT.
  2 *Narhvalen*, SSC with FFV Type 61 and 41 HWT.
FRIGATES: 3:
  3 *Niels Juel* with 2 × 4 *Harpoon* SSM.
PATROL AND COASTAL COMBATANTS: 33:
MISSILE CRAFT: 10 *Willemoes* PFM with 2 × 4 *Harpoon*.

PATROL: 23:
  OFFSHORE: 4:
    1 *Beskytteren*, 3 *Thetis* PCO all with 1 *Lynx* hel.
  COASTAL: 9:
    6 (7 by end of 1992) *Flyvefisken* (Stanflex 300) PFC.
    3 *Agdlek* PCC.
  INSHORE: 10: 9 *Barsø*, 1⟨.
MINE WARFARE: 9:
  MINELAYERS: 6: 4 *Falster* (400 mines), 2 *Lindormen*
  (50 mines).
MCMV: 3 *Alssund* (US MSC-128) MSC.
SUPPORT AND MISCELLANEOUS: 7:
  2 AOT (small), 4 icebreakers (civilian-manned), 1
  Royal Yacht.
HELICOPTERS: 8 *Lynx* (up to 4 embarked).

COAST DEFENCE: 2 coastal fortresses; 150mm
  guns; 40mm AA guns. Coastal radar.
RESERVES (Home Guard): 37 inshore patrol
  craft.

AIR FORCE: 7,000 (800 conscripts, 400 women).
TACTICAL AIR COMMAND:
FGA/FIGHTER: 5 sqn: 4 with F-16A/B;
  1 with F-35 *Draken*.
FGA/RECCE: 1 sqn with RF-35 *Draken*.
TRANSPORT: 1 sqn with C-130H, *Gulfstream* III,
  SAAB T-17.
SAR: 1 sqn with S-61A hel.
TRAINING: 1 flying school with T-17.
AIR DEFENCE GROUP:
AD: 2 SAM bn: 8 bty with *Improved HAWK*, 129 40
  mm L/60, 28 40 mm/L70.
CONTROL/REPORTING GROUP: 5 radar
  stations.
EQUIPMENT: 106 cbt ac, no armed hel.
AIRCRAFT:
  F-16A/B: 63 (FGA/ftr).
  F-35: 43. 16 (FGA/ftr); **RF-35:** 18* (FGA/recce);
  TF-35: 9* (trg).
  C-130H: 3 (tpt). *Gulfstream* **III:** 3 (tpt). **SAAB**
  T-17: 29 (6 liaison, 23 trg).
HELICOPTERS:
  S-61: 8 (SAR).
MISSILES:
  ASM: AGM-12 *Bullpup*.
  AAM: AIM-9 *Sidewinder*.
  SAM: 36 *Improved HAWK*.

FORCES ABROAD:
UN AND PEACEKEEPING:
CROATIA (UNPROFOR): 860: 1 inf bn, 150
  Observers (EEC).
CYPRUS (UNFICYP): 1 bn: 350.
INDIA/PAKISTAN (UNMOGIP): 6 Observers.
IRAQ/KUWAIT (UNIKOM): 7 Observers, 45 spt
  personnel.
MIDDLE EAST (UNTSO): 11 Observers.

FOREIGN FORCES:
NATO:
  HQ Allied Forces Baltic Approaches (BALTAP).

FRANCE

GDP	1990:	fr 6,484.60bn ($1,190.86bn)		
	1991:	fr 6,842.40bn ($1,212.74bn)		
Growth	1990:	2.9%	1991:	1.8%
Inflation	1990:	3.4%	1991:	3.1%
Debt	1989:	$146.00bn		
Def bdgt	1991:	fr 194.55bn ($34.48bn);		
	1992:	fr 195.48bn ($34.91bn)		
NATO defn	1991:	fr 239.17bn ($42.39bn)		
$1 = fr	1989:	6.3801	1990:	5.4453
	1991:	5.6420	1992:	5.6000

Population: 56,897,600

	13–17	18–22	23–32
Men	1,994,500	2,088,100	4,336,400
Women	1,907,800	2,002,500	4,184,500

TOTAL ARMED FORCES:
ACTIVE: some 431,700 (14,000 women, 210,800
  conscripts) incl 5,200 Central Staff, 8,600 (2,300
  conscripts) Service de santé, 400 Service des
  essences not listed below.
  Terms of service: 10 months (can be voluntarily
  extended to 18–24 months).
RESERVES: Earmarked for mob: 374,000;
  Army 280,000, Navy 24,000, Air 70,000.
  Potential: 1,314,500; Army 915,000, Navy
  220,000, Air 179,500.

STRATEGIC NUCLEAR FORCES:
(17,000; some 1,700 Army, 5,000 Navy, 9,700
  Air Force, 600 Gendarmerie).

NAVY: 64 SLBM in 4 SSBN.
SSBN: 4:
  1 *L'Inflexible* with 16 M-4/TN-70 or -71; plus
  SM-39 *Exocet* USGW.
  3 mod *Le Redoutable* with 16 M-4; plus SM-39.
  Not included: 1 *Le Redoutable* (S-610) in long
  refit and conversion to M-4.

AIR FORCE:
IRBM: 18 SSBS S-3D/TN-61 msl in 2 sqn. (Test
  centre: 4 silos.)
BOMBERS: 2 sqn with 15 *Mirage IVP* (*ASMP*:
  Air-Sol, Moyenne-Porteé nuclear ASM), plus 13 in
  store, 3 sqn with 45 *Mirage* 2000N (ASMP)

TRAINING: 5 *Mirage* IIIB, 1 *Mystère-Falcon* 20P, 4 *Alpha Jet*.
TANKERS: 1 wing:
3 sqn with 11 C-135FR.
COMMUNICATIONS: 4 C-160 *ASTARTE* airborne comms centres.
RECCE: 3 *Mirage* IVP.

'PRESTRATEGIC' NUCLEAR FORCES: (8,450).

ARMY (6,100): 24 *Pluton* SSM launchers.
NAVY (190): 38 *Super Etendard* strike ac (*ASMP* nuc ASM); plus 19 in store.
Eqpt also listed with Service sections.

ARMY: 260,900, (6,000 women, 156,400 conscripts).

Note: regiments are normally of bn size.
1 army (continental ops).
2 corps each with 2 armd, 1 mot inf div.
Summary div combat units:

12 armd regt	2 armd recce regt
8 mech inf regt	6 mot inf regt
7 arty regt	5 ATK sqn.

Army/corps units: 2 armd recce, 1 para (special ops), 1 inf, 5 arty (incl 1 MLRS), 3 SSM with *Pluton* (each of 3 bty, 2 launchers each), 4 *Roland* SAM (each of 4 bty), 3 *HAWK* SAM regt (incl 1 trg), 2 cbt hel (each 30 SA-330, 20 SA-341/-342 ATK, 15 SA-341 gunships), 5 engr, 1 EW regt.
Rapid Action Force (FAR: 47,300).
1 para div: 6 para inf, 1 armd cavalry, 1 arty regt.
1 air portable marine div: 3 inf, 2 lt armd, 1 arty regt, 2 engr coy.
1 lt armd div: 2 armd cavalry, 2 APC inf, 1 arty, 1 engr regt.
1 mtn div: 5 mtn inf, 1 lt armd, 1 arty regt; 1 engr bn.
1 air-mobile div: 1 inf, 3 cbt, 1 comd, 1 spt hel regt. (Total 274 hel: 80 SA-330, 90 SA-342/*HOT*, 94 SA-341 (30 gun, 74 recce/liaison).)
1 Franco/German bde (2,100: Fr units incl 1 lt armd, 1 mot inf regt; 1 recce sqn).
Foreign Legion (8,500):
1 armd, 1 para, 6 inf, 1 engr regt.
11 Marine inf regt (overseas).

RESERVES:

2 lt armd div (based on inf and armd schools): cbt units: 3 tk, 3 inf, 1 arty, 1 engr regt.
1 territorial div (Rhine) (active: 1 engr regt; reserve: 5 engr, 1 AD regt, 3 inf bn).
Individual reinforcements for 1st Army and FAR (101,000).
3 Defence Zone, 1 indep region; 5 defence district; 7 regional defence bde (each 2 inf, 1 armd regt: AML-90, *Milan*, 120mm mor), 22 combined arms regt.

1 inf div (def of Strategic Nuclear Forces);
6 frontier inf regt.
EQUIPMENT:
MBT: 1,343 AMX-30 (658 -B2).
LIGHT TANKS: 143 AMX-13.
RECCE: 325 AMX-10RC, 192 ERC-90F4 *Sagaïe*, 588 AML-60/-90 (perhaps 300 in store), 240 VBL M-11.
AIFV: 816 AMX-10P/PC.
APC: 124 AMX-13 VTT, 3,840 VAB.
TOTAL ARTY: 1,436.
TOWED ARTY: 415: 105mm: 149 HM-2; 155mm: 206 BF-50 (40 in store), some 60 TR-F-1.
SP ARTY: 371: 155mm: 253 AU-F-1, 118 F-3 (94 in store).
MRL: 227mm: 30 MLRS.
MORTARS: 120mm: 364 RT-F1, 256 M-51.
SSM: 24 *Pluton* launchers.
ATGW: 1,400 *Milan*, *HOT* (incl 135 VAB SP).
RL: 89mm: 11,200; 112mm: *APILAS*.
AD GUNS: 1,242: 20mm: 105 53T1, 775 53T2; 30mm: 362 towed.
SAM: 399: 69 *HAWK*, 180 *Roland* I/II, 150 *Mistral*.
HELICOPTERS 682: 22 AS-332M, 123 SA-313/-318, 4 AS-555, 63 SA-316/-319, 133 SA-330, 153 SA-341F/M (16 with *HOT*, 67 gun-armed, 70 utility), 184 SA-342M (154 with *HOT*, 30 utility).
AIRCRAFT: 5 MH-1521, 3 Reims-Cessna 406.

NAVY: 64,900 incl 11,000 Naval Air, 3,100 Marines (2,500 women; 19,000 conscripts).

COMMANDS: 1 strategic sub (ALFOST), 2 home (CECLANT, CECMED), 2 overseas: Indian Ocean (ALINDIEN), Pacific Ocean (ALPACI).
BASES: *France:* Cherbourg, Brest (HQ), Lorient, Toulon (HQ). *Overseas:* Papeete (HQ) (Tahiti); La Réunion; Nouméa (New Caledonia); Fort de France (Martinique).
SUBMARINES: 17.
STRATEGIC SUBMARINES: 4 SSBN (see p. 40).
TACTICAL SUBMARINES: 13:
SSN: 5 *Rubis* ASW/ASUW with F-17 HWT, L-5 LWT and SM-39 *Exocet* USGW.
SS: 8:
4 *Agosta* with F-17 HWT and L-5 LWT; plus *Exocet* USGW.
4 *Daphné*, with E-15 HWT and L-5 LWT; (plus 4 in store).
PRINCIPAL SURFACE COMBATANTS: 41:
CARRIERS: 2:
2 *Clémenceau* CVS, (33,300t) capacity 40 ac (typically 2 flt with 16 *Super Etendard*, 1 with 6 *Alizé*; 1 det with 2 *Etendard* IVP, 2 *Super Frelon*, 2 *Dauphin* hel.
CRUISERS: 1:
1 *Jeanne d'Arc* CCH (trg/ASW) with 6 MM-38 *Exocet* SSM, 4 × 100mm guns, capacity 8 × *Lynx* hel.
DESTROYERS: 4 DDG:

2 *Cassard* with 1 × 1 *Standard* SM-1 MR; plus 8 × MM-40 *Exocet*, 1 × 100mm gun, 2 × ASTT, 1 *Lynx* hel (ASW/OTHT).

2 *Suffren* with 1 × 2 *Masurca* SAM; plus 1 *Malafon* SUGW, 4 ASTT, 4 MM-38 *Exocet*, 2 × 100mm guns.

FRIGATES: 34:

2 *Floréal* with 2 MM-38 *Exocet*, 1 AS-365 hel and 1 × 100mm gun.

7 *Georges Leygues* with 2 *Lynx* hel (Mk 46 LWT), 2 × ASTT; plus 5 with 8 MM-40, 2 with 4 MM-38 *Exocet*, all with 1 × 100mm gun.

3 *Tourville* with 2 × *Lynx* hel, 1 *Malafon* SUGW, 2 × ASTT; plus 6 × MM-38 *Exocet*, 2 × 100mm guns.

1 *Aconit* with *Malafon*, 2 × ASTT; plus 8 MM-38 *Exocet*, 2 × 100mm guns.

4 *Commandant Rivière* with 2 × 3 ASTT, 1 × 12 ASW mor; plus 3 with 4 × MM-38 *Exocet*, all with 2 × 100mm guns.

17 *D'Estienne d'Orves* with 4 × ASTT, 1 × 6 ASW mor; plus 6 with 2 × MM-38, 6 with 4 × MM-40 *Exocet*, all with 1 × 100mm gun.

PATROL AND COASTAL COMBATANTS: 23:

COASTAL: 21:

10 *L'Audacieuse*.

8 *Léopard* PCC (trg).

1 *Sterne*, 1 *Grebe* and 1 *Phenix* PCC (Public Service Force).

INSHORE: 2 *Athos* PCI.

MINE WARFARE: 21: (2 *Athos*)

MINELAYERS: Nil, but submarines and *Thetis* (trials ship) have capability.

MINE COUNTERMEASURES: 21:

9 *Eridan* tripartite MHC.

5 *Circé* MHC.

3 *Ouistreham* (US *Aggressive*) MSO.

4 *Vulcain* MCM diver spt.

AMPHIBIOUS: 9:

1 *Foudre* LPD, capacity 450 tps, 30 tk, 4 *Super Puma* hel, 2 CDIC LCT or 10 LCM.

2 *Ouragan* LPD: capacity 350 tps, 25 tk, 2 *Super Frelon* hel.

1 *Bougainville* LSD: capacity 500 tps, 6 tk, 2 AS-332 hel: (assigned to spt DIRCEN nuclear test centre South Pacific).

5 *Champlain* LSM (*BATRAL*): capacity 140 tps, 7 tk.

Plus craft: 7 LCT, 26 LCM.

SUPPORT AND MISCELLANEOUS: 37:

UNDERWAY SUPPORT: 5:

5 *Durance* AO.

MAINTENANCE/LOGISTIC: 21:

1 AOT, 1 *Jules Verne* AK with 2 SA-319 hel, 4 *Rhin* depot/spt, 1 *Rance* med and trg spt, all with hel; 8 tpt, 6 ocean tugs (3 civil charter).

SPECIAL PURPOSES: 5:

2 msl trials, 1 sonar trials, 1 mine warfare trials, 1 underwater trials.

SURVEY/RESEARCH: 6: 5 AGHS, 1 AGOR

NAVAL AIR FORCE: (11,000). 145 cbt ac; 52 armed hel.

NUCLEAR STRIKE: 3 flt with *Super Etendard* (AN-52 nuclear weapons).

FIGHTER: 1 flt with F-8E (FN) *Crusader*, undergoing SLEP.

ASW: 2 flt with *Alizé*.

MR: 6 flt, 4 with *Atlantic*, 2 with *Gardian*.

RECCE: 1 flt with *Etendard* IVP.

OCU: *Etendard* IVM; *Alizé*; *Zéphir*.

TRAINING: 5 units with N-262 *Frégate*, Piper *Navajo*, EMB-121 *Xingu*, MS-760 *Paris*, *Falcon* 10MER, *Rallye* 880, CAP 10, *Zéphyr*.

MISCELLANEOUS: 4 comms/liaison units (1 VIP) with *Falcon* 10MER, *Alizé*, N-262, EMB 121, *Xingu, Navajo*.

1 trial unit with *Atlantique* 2, MS-760 *Paris*.

2 lt ac units with 12 *Rallye* 880, 6 CAP-10.

ASW: 2 sqn with *Lynx*.

COMMANDO: 2 aslt sqn with SA-321.

TRAINING: SA-316.

MISCELLANEOUS: 2 comms/SAR units with SE-3130, SA-316, 1 trials unit with SE-3130, SA-319, *Lynx*, SA-321.

EQUIPMENT: 102 cbt ac (plus 43 in store); 38 armed hel (plus 14 in store).

AIRCRAFT:

Super Etendard: 38 (strike); plus 19 in store. Total of 48 to be mod for *ASMP*.

Etendard: 18. **IVP:** 8 (recce); **IVM:** 10 (trg). Plus 7 in store.

Crusader: 12 (ftr) plus 7 in store. 18 of these undergoing SLEP.

Alizé: 25 (17 ASW, 8 trg) plus 6 in store.

Atlantic: 24 (MR), plus 12 in store.

Atlantique: 6 (MR).

Gardian: 5 (MR).

Zéphyr: 14 (trg). **Nord 262:** 25 (15 MR trg, 10 misc). **Navajo:** 11 (2 trg, 9 misc). **Xingu:** 18 (11 trg, 7 misc). **Rallye 880:** 16 (4 trg, 12 misc). **CAP-10:** 8 (misc). **MS-760:** 8 (trg). *Falcon* **10MER:** 5 (3 trg, 2 misc).

HELICOPTERS:

Lynx: 35 (ASW).

SA-321: 12 (12 ASW) plus 5 in store.

SA-313: 16 (4 trg, 12 misc).

SA-316/-319: 32 (15 trg, 17 misc).

AS-365: 6 (SAR).

MISSILES:

ASM: AS-12/-20/-30, *Martel* AS-37, *Exocet* AM-39.

AAM: R-530, R-550 *Magic*, AIM-9 *Sidewinder*.

MARINES: (3,100) (Fusiliers-Marins).

COMMANDO UNITS: (600).

4 Assault gp.

1 Attack Swimmer unit.
1 HQ section.
NAVAL BASE PROTECTION: (2,000).

PUBLIC SERVICE FORCE: Naval personnel, performing general coast guard, fishery, SAR and traffic surveillance duties; 1 *Sterne*, 1 *Grebe*, 1 *Phenix* PCC, 3 N-262 ac, 3 SA-360 hel (ships included in naval patrol and coastal totals). Command exercised through 'Maritime Prefectures': No. 1 at Cherbourg, No. 2 at Brest, No. 3 at Toulon.

AIR FORCE: 91,700 (5,500 women, 35,400 conscripts), incl strategic and prestrategic forces.
AIR DEFENCE COMMAND (CAFDA):
FIGHTER: 4 wing, 11 sqn:
  5 with *Mirage* F-1C;
  6 with *Mirage* 2000C.
TRAINING: 4 flt with CM-170
CONTROL: automatic *STRIDA* II, 10 radar stations, 1 wing with 4 E3F.
SAM: 12 sqn (1 trg) with 24 *Crotale* bty (48 fire, 24 radar units).
  4 sqn *Mistral*.
AA GUNS: 300 bty (20mm).
TACTICAL AIR FORCE (FATAC):
  6 wing, 2 sqn.
FGA: 12 sqn:
  1 sqn with *Mirage* 2000N.
  2 sqn with *Mirage* IIIE;
  3 sqn with *Mirage* III/*Mirage* VF;
  6 sqn with *Jaguar* A.
RECCE: 1 wing, 3 sqn with *Mirage* F-1CR.
TRAINING: 1 OCU sqn with *Jaguar* A/E;
  1 OCU sqn with *Jaguar* A/E.
  1 OCU sqn with F1 C/B,
  1 OCU sqn with *Mirage* 2000/BC.
(Attached to Air Transport Command – see below):
EW: 2 sqn: 1 with C-160 ELINT/ESM ac, AS-330 hel; 1 with DC-8 ELINT.
HELICOPTERS: 1 sqn with SA-313, SA-319.
AIR TRANSPORT COMMAND (COTAM):
TRANSPORT: 19 sqn:
  1 hy with DC-8F;
  5 tac with C-160/-160NG/C-130H;
  13 lt tpt/trg/SAR with C-160, DH-6, EMB-121, *Falcon* 20, *Falcon* 50, *Falcon* 900, MS-760, N-262.
TRAINING: 1 OCU with N-262, C-160.
HELICOPTERS: 5 sqn with AS-332, AS-355, SA-313/-316/-319, SA-365.
TRAINING: 1 OCU with SA-313/-316, SA-330.
TRAINING COMMAND (CEAA): (5,000).
TRAINING: *Alpha Jet*, CAP-10B/-20, CM-170, EMB-121, TB-30.
EQUIPMENT: 808 cbt ac, no armed hel.

AIRCRAFT:
  Mirage: 496: **F-1B:** 19 (OCU); **F-1C:** 120 (ftr);
    F-1CR: 53 (recce); **IIIE:** 45 (FGA); **IIIB/BE:** 17* (trg); **-5F:** 39 (FGA); **IVP:** 19 (bbr); **-2000B/C:** 120 (97 -C, 23 -B); **-2000N:** 64.
  Jaguar: 153: **-A:** 119 (FGA, trg); **-E:** 34* (trg).
  Alpha Jet: 159* (trg).
  DC-8: 4.
  C-130: 12. **-H:** 3 (tpt); **-H-30:** 9 (tpt).
  C-135F/FR: 11 (tkr).
  C-160: 77 (2 *Gabriel* ELINT/ESM, 4 *ASTARTE* comms, 40 tac tpt, 9 OCU, 22 -NG tac tpt).
  CN-235M: 2 (tpt).
  N-262: 24 (21 lt tpt, 2 trg, 1 trials).
  C-212: 5 (Flt Test Centre spt).
  Falcon: 20: **-20:** 14 (7 tpt, 7 misc), **-50:** 4 (tpt), **-900:** 2 (tpt). **MS-760:** 40 (misc). **DHC-6:** 10 (tpt). **EMB-121:** 25 (4 tpt, 21 trg). **TB-30:** 148 (trg): **CAP-10B/230:** 53 (trg).
HELICOPTERS:
  SA-313: 20 (incl 9 OCU) (*Alouette* II).
  SA-319: 35 (*Alouette* III).
  SA-330: 28 (25 tpt, 3 OCU) (*Puma*).
  AS-332: 6 (tpt) (*Super Puma*).
  SA-365: 1 (tpt) (*Dauphin*).
    2 (tpt) (*Cougar*).
  AS-350: 6 (*Ecureuil*).
  AS-355: 34 (tpt) (*Fennec*).
MISSILES:
  ASM: AS-30/-30L, *Martel* AS-37.
  AAM: *Super* 530F/D, R-550 *Magic* 1/11.

DEPLOYMENT:
NAVY:
Atlantic Fleet: (HQ, Brest): 4 SSBN, 6 SS, 1 CCH, 2 DDG, 11 FF, 9 MCM, 2 amph.
Channel Flotilla: (HQ, Cherbourg): 3 FF, 5 MCMV.
Mediterranean Fleet: (HQ, Toulon): 5 SSN, 2 SS, 2 CV, 4 DDG, 10 FF, 3 MCMV, 1 amph.

FORCES ABROAD:
GERMANY: 16,000; 1 corps HQ, 1 armd div. Berlin: (2,700); 1 armd regt, 1 mot inf regt.
ANTILLES-GUYANA: (HQ Cayenne): 8,200; 2 marine inf, 1 Foreign Legion regt, 4 ships (incl 1 tpt), 1 *Atlantic* ac (Dakar, Senegal), 1 air tpt unit (1 C-160 ac, 4 SA-330, 1 SA-316, 6 AS-350, 1 AS-550C2 hel).
INDIAN OCEAN (Mayotte, La Réunion): 3,400; incl 1 marine inf regt, 1 spt bn, 1 Foreign Legion coy, 1 air tpt unit (1 C-160 ac, 3 SA-319 hel).
NAVY: Indian Ocean Squadron, Comd ALINDIEN (HQ afloat): (1,400); 4 FF, 3 patrol combatants, 1 amph, 3 spt (1 comd), 1 *Atlantic* ac.
NEW CALEDONIA (HQ Nouméa): 3,700; 1 marine inf regt; some 10 AML recce, 5 105mm arty; 1 air tpt unit, 1 ALAT det (1 C-160, 1 *Gardian* MR

ac, SA-319, 7 SA-330 hel). Navy: 2 P-400 PCC. Gendarmerie (1,100).

POLYNESIA (HQ Papeete): 4,000 (incl Centre d'Experimentations du Pacifique); 1 marine, 1 Foreign Legion regt, 1 air tpt unit (3 SE-210, *Gardian* ac; 3 AS-332, 3 SA-319 hel), Gendarmerie.

PACIFIC NAVAL SQUADRON (comd, ALPACI, HQ Papeete) (700); 3 FF, 5 patrol and coastal, 3 amph, 5 *Gardian* MR ac.

CENTRAL AFRICAN REPUBLIC: 1,200:
  GARRISON: 1bn gp incl 1 motor coy; 1 pl AML armd cars (6); spt coy with O-1E lt ac, 120mm mor, *Milan* ATGW.
  FROM FRANCE: 1 AML armd car sqn and 1 tp (10 AML), 2 inf coy, 1 arty bty (105mm), 1 avn det (4 SA-330 hel); air elm with 5 *Jaguar*, 3 C-160 ac.

CHAD: 750; 2 inf coy; AA arty units; 3 C-160 ac, 2 SA-330 hel.

COTE D'IVOIRE: 500; 1 marine inf regt (10 AML-60/-90, 5 AMX-13); 1 AS-350 hel.

DJIBOUTI: 4,000; 1 marine inf, 1 Foreign Legion regt; 36 ERC-90 recce, 5 155mm arty, 16 AA arty; 3 amph craft, 1 ALAT det (5 SA-330 hel); 1 sqn with 10 *Mirage* F-1C, 1 C-160 ac, 2 SA-316, 1 SA-319 hel.

GABON: 500; 1 marine inf regt (5 AML-60); 1 C-160, *Atlantic* ac, 1 SA-319 hel.

RWANDA: 200; 1 para coy.

SENEGAL: 1,200; 1 marine inf regt (10 AML-60/-90); *Atlantic* MR ac; 1 air tpt unit (1 C-160 tpt ac; 2 SA-316/-319 hel).

TURKEY: 150; 1 air unit with 8 *Mirage* F-1CR, 1 C-135.

UN AND PEACEKEEPING:

CAMBODIA (UNTAC): 1,400; 1 mot inf bn, 6 C-160 ac, 6 SA-330 hel.

CROATIA (UNPROFOR): 2,900; 2 inf bn, 1 log bn.

EGYPT (MFO): 40; incl 1 DHC-6.

IRAQ/KUWAIT (UNIKOM): 17 Observers.

LEBANON (UNIFIL): 800; 1 log bn, 1 coy Gendarmerie.

MIDDLE EAST (UNTSO): 21 Observers.

WESTERN SAHARA (MINURSO): 5 Observers.

PARAMILITARY:

GENDARMERIE: 94,600 (1,400 women, 10,900 conscripts, plus 990 civilians); incl: *Territorial* (57,200); *Mobile* (17,100); *Schools* (5,300); *Republican Guard* (3,100); *Overseas* (3,400); *Maritime* (1,200); *Air* (1,100); *Air Tpt* (1,100); *Arsenals* (400); *Administration* (4,700); *Reserves* (130,000).

EQUIPMENT: 121 AML, 28 VBC-90 armd cars; 33 AMX-VTT, 155 VBRG-170 APC; 288 81mm mor; 15 PCI; 6 Cessna 206C ac; 3 SE-3130, 3 SA-316, 9 SA-319, 29 AS-350 hel.

GERMANY

GDP	1990: DM 2,403.40bn ($1,487.53bn)	
	1991: DM 2,782.4bn ($1,676.65bn)	
Growth[a]	1990: 4.7%	1991: 3.2% [0.1%]
Inflation[a]	1990: 2.7%	1991: 3.5% [4.7%]
Debt	1990: $415.55bn	1991: $405.78bn
Def bdgt	1991: [DM 53.61bn ($32.30bn)];	
	1992: [DM 52.13bn ($31.03bn)]	
NATO defn	1991: [DM 66.18bn ($39.88bn)]	
$1 = DM	1989: 1.8800	1990: 1.6157
	1991: 1.6595	1992: 1.6800

DM = Deutschmark

Population:[a] [79,753,000]

	13–17	18–22	23–32
Men	[2,090,000]	[3,011,000]	[6,858,000]
Women	[1,979,000]	[2,874,000]	[6,458,000]

[a] Figures in [ ] denote combined East and West German economic and demographic data.

TOTAL ARMED FORCES:

ACTIVE: 447,000 (201,700 conscripts; 3,000 active Reserve trg posts, all Services. *Terms of service:* 12 months.

RESERVES: 904,700 (men to age 45, officers/NCO to 60): Army 770,200, Navy 21,600, Air 112,900.

ARMY: 316,000 (163,800 conscripts); and 7,600 staff not listed below.

FIELD ARMY: (203,400) 3 Corps, 12 div.
  I Corps (NORTHAG):
    3 armd, 1 armd inf div.
  II Corps (CENTAG):
    1 armd, 1 armd inf, 1 AB, 1 mtn div.
  III Corps (CENTAG):
    2 armd, 1 armd inf div.
  1 armd inf div (LANDJUT).
  (Armd div with 2 armd and 1 armd inf bde; armd inf div with 2 armd inf and 1 armd bde; mtn div with 1 armd, 1 armd inf and 1 mtn bde; all with 1 armd recce bn, 1 arty regt (1 bn each: 18 FH-70, 18 203mm, 16 110mm MRL), 1 AD regt (with 35mm *Gepard*), 1 avn sqn; AB div with 3 AB bde.)
  Corps Tps: 4 SSM bn each with 6 *Lance*; 3 AD comd (each 1 regt with 36 *Roland*).
  1 *Roland* SAM bn.
  1 AD arty bn with *Gepard* 35mm.
  3 avn comd each 1 lt (48 UH-1D), 1 med tpt (32 CH-539), 1 ATGW hel (56 Bo-105 *HOT*) regt.

TERRITORIAL ARMY (cadre: 64,000 in peacetime);
  Command Structure: 3 Territorial Comd (linked with NATO cmd), 5 Military Districts, 28

Military Regions, 76 Sub-regions: Units (eqpt holding only unless stated).

10 Home Defence bde, 5 with 2 armd, 2 armd inf, 1 arty bn plus full log spt (at 50–60% in peacetime) (two assigned to field army div). 5 with 1 armd, 2 armd inf, 1 arty bn.

1 German/French bde (Ge units incl 1 mech inf, 1 arty bn; 1 SP ATK coy).

15 Home Defence regt with 3 mot inf bn, 18 120mm mor.

150 Home Defence coy, 300 Security pl.

EASTERN COMMAND (41,000):

1 Corps/Territorial Cmd HQ, 2 Military Districts/div HQ, 14 Military Regions, 45 Sub-Regions.

6 Home Defence bde; 3 inf, 4 arty bn.

EQUIPMENT:

MBT: 7,090: 649 M-48A2G (Territorial bn), 2,084 *Leopard* 1A1 (1,258 to be upgraded to A5), 2,083 *Leopard* 2 (700 to be upgraded), 1,725 T-54/-55, 549 T-72M.

LIGHT TANKS: 143 PT-76.

RECCE: 408 SPz-2 *Luchs*, 52 TPz-1 *Fuchs* (NBC), 118 *Wiesel*, 1,262 BRDM-1/-2.

AIFV: 3,250: 2,100 *Marder* A1/A2 (to upgrade to A3), 1,150 BMP-1/-2.

APC: 10,955: 891 TPz-1 *Fuchs*, 2,682 M-113, 220 M-577, 2,115 BTR-40, 293 BTR-50, 2,165 BTR-60, 1,175 BTR-70, 685 BTR-152, 729 MT-LB.

TOTAL ARTY: 4,592.

  TOWED ARTY: 1,499: 105mm: 44 M-56, 195 M-101; 122mm: 335 D-30, 397 M-1938 (M-30); 130mm: 175 M-46; 152mm: 137 D-20; 155mm: 216 FH-70.

  SP ARTY: 1,263: 122mm: 374 2S1; 152mm: 95 2S3; 155mm: 573 M-109A3G; 203mm: 221 M-110A2.

  MRL: 556: 110mm: 204 *LARS*; 122mm: 260 Cz RM-70, 59 BM-21, 227mm: 33 MLRS.

  MORTARS: 1,274: 120mm: 490 Brandt, 499 Tampella on M-113, 210 M-120, 75 2B11.

SSM: 26 *Lance* launchers (incl 2 in store).

ATGW: 1,975 *Milan*, 207 *TOW*, 316 RJPz-(*HOT*) *Jaguar* 1, 162 RJPz-(*TOW*) SP, AT-3 *Sagger* (incl BRDM-2SP), AT-4 *Spigot*, AT-5 *Spandrel*.

RCL: 106mm: 99 (in store).

ATK GUNS: 85mm: 64 D-48; 90mm: 121 JPz-4-5 SP; 100mm: 267 T-12.

AD GUNS: 3,295: 20mm: 1,989 Rh 202 towed; 23mm: 295 ZU-23, 131 ZSU-23-4 SP; 35mm: 432 *Gepard* SP; 40mm: 204 L/70; 57mm: 244 S-60.

SAM: 658 *Fliegerfaust* 1 (*Redeye*), SA-7, 226 SA-4/-6/-8/-9, 143 *Roland* SP.

HELICOPTERS: 205 PAH-1 (Bo-105 with *HOT*), 184 UH-1D, 110 CH-53G, 97 Bo-105M, 141 SA-313, 10 SA-318, 8 Mi-2, 29 Mi-8 (T/TB), 7 Mi-9, 49 Mi-24.

MARINE: (River Engineers): 36 LCM, 12 PCI (river)〈.

NAVY: 35,200 (1,900 Eastern Command) incl naval air, 8,900 conscripts.

BASES: Glücksburg (Maritime HQ) and four main bases: Wilhelmshaven, Kiel, Olpenitz and Warnemünde. Other bases with limited support facilities: Baltic: Eckernförde, Flensburg, Neustadt, Peenemünde. North Sea: Borkum, Bremerhaven, Emden.

SUBMARINES: 22:

18 Type 206/206A SSC with *Seeaal* DM2 533mm HWT (12 conversions to T-206A complete).

4 Type 205 SSC with DM3 HWT.

PRINCIPAL SURFACE COMBATANTS: 14:

DESTROYERS: 6:

DDG: 3 *Lütjens* (mod US *Adams*) with 1 × 1 SM-1 MR SAM/*Harpoon* SSM launcher, 2 × 127mm guns; plus 1 × 8 *ASROC* (Mk 46 LWT), 2 × 3 ASTT.

DD: 3 *Hamburg* (ASUW) with 2 × 2 MM-38 *Exocet*, 4 × 533mm TT (SUT), 3 × 100mm guns.

FRIGATES: 8:

8 *Bremen* with 2 *Lynx* hel (ASW/OTHT), 2 × 2 ASTT; plus 2 × 4 *Harpoon*.

PATROL AND COASTAL COMBATANTS: 43:

CORVETTES: 3:

3 *Thetis* (ASW) with 1 × 4 ASW RL, 4 × 533mm TT.

MISSILE CRAFT: 40:

10 *Albatros* (Type 143) PFM with 2 × 2 *Exocet*, and 2 × 533mm TT.

10 *Gepard* (T-143A) PFM with 2 × 2 *Exocet*.

20 *Tiger* (Type 148) PFM with 2 × 2 *Exocet*.

MINE WARFARE: 40:

MINELAYERS: 1 *Sachsenwald* (600+ mines).

MINE COUNTERMEASURES: 39:

10 *Hameln* (T-343) comb ML/MCC.

6 *Lindau Troika* MSC control and guidance, each with 3 unmanned sweep craft.

10 converted *Lindau* (T-331) MHC.

2 *Schütze* (T-340/-341) comb ML/MSC.

10 *Ariadne*/*Frauenlob* MSI.

1 MCM diver spt ship.

AMPHIBIOUS: Craft only: some 11 LCU.

SUPPORT AND MISCELLANEOUS: 42:

UNDERWAY SUPPORT: 2:

2 *Spessart* AO.

MAINTENANCE/LOGISTIC: 27:

4 *Rhein* SS/MCMV spt, 5 small (2,000t) AOT, 6 *Lüneburg* log spt, 2 AE, 8 tugs, 2 icebreakers (civil).

SPECIAL PURPOSE: 9:

3 AGI, 2 trials, 3 multi-purpose (T-748), 1 trg.

RESEARCH AND SURVEY: 4:

1 AGOR, 3 AGHS (civil-manned for Ministry of Transport).

NAVAL AIR ARM:

4 wings, 8 sqn:

2 wings with *Tornado*.

1 MR/ASW wing with *Atlantic*, *Lynx*.

1 SAR/liaison wing with Do-28, *Sea King*.

FGA: 2 sqn with *Tornado*.

FGA/RECCE: 1 sqn with *Tornado*.
MR/ELINT: 2 sqn with *Atlantic*.
LIAISON: 1 sqn with Do-28/Do-228.
ASW: 1 sqn with *Sea Lynx* Mk 88 hel.
SAR: 1 sqn with *Sea King* Mk 41 hel.
EQUIPMENT: 118 cbt ac, 19 armed hel.
AIRCRAFT:
  Tornado: 102 (91 FGA, 11* trg) plus 3 in store.
  Atlantic: 19 (14 MR, 5 ELINT).
  Do-28: 18 (16 SAR, liaison; 2 environmental
    protection).
  Do-228: LM: 1 (environmental monitoring).
HELICOPTERS:
  Sea Lynx Mk 88: 19 (ASW).
  Sea King Mk 41: 22 (SAR).
MISSILES:
  ASM: AS-12/-20/-30, *Kormoran, Sea Eagle*.
  AAM: AIM-9 *Sidewinder*.

AIR FORCE: 95,800 (9,300 Eastern Command) (29,000 conscripts).
TACTICAL COMMAND (GAFTAC).
5 air div: 1 tac, 2 AD, 2 mixed Eastern Division.
FGA: 9 wings, 18 sqn:
  5 wings with *Tornado*.
  1 with F-4F.
  3 with *Alpha Jet*.
FIGHTER: 3 wings with F-4F (6 sqn).
RECCE: 2 wings with RF-4E (3 sqn).
EW: 1 trg sqn with HFB-320 *Hansa Jet*.
SAM: 6 wings (each 6 sqn) *Patriot*; 6 wings (each 6
  sqn) *HAWK*; 14 sqn *Roland*, 1 wing (2 sqn) SA-5.
RADAR: 2 tac Air Control Commands:
  10 sites; 3 remote radars.
  3 sites; 12 remote radars in Eastern division.
AAM: *Sidewinder*.
ASM: AS-20.
TRANSPORT COMMAND (GAFTC).
TRANSPORT: 3 wings: 4 sqn with Transall C-160,
  incl 1 (OCU) with C-160, Do-28.
  1 special air mission wing with Boeing 707-320C,
  Airbus A-310, VFW-614, CL-601, Do-28 ac;
  UH-1D hel (VIP).
HELICOPTERS: 1 wing: 3 sqn; plus 1 det with
  UH-1D (liaison/SAR).
ADDITIONAL FORCES: 1 special mission sqn with
  Il-62, Tu-154, L-410S, Mi-83, 1 tpt sqn with
  An-26, 1 tpt/SAR sqn with Mi-8T/mil.
TRAINING COMMAND:
FGA: 1 det (Cottesmore, UK) with *Tornado*;
  1 OCU (Beja, Portugal) with *Alpha Jet*.
FIGHTER: OCU (George AFB, Alabama) with F-4E.
TRAINING: NATO joint pilot trg (Sheppard AFB,
  Texas) with T-37B, T-38A; primary trg sqn
  with Beech-Bonanza.
LIAISON: base flt with Do-28D.
EQUIPMENT: 653 cbt ac (42 trg (overseas)); plus
  336 for disposal, no attack hel.

AIRCRAFT:
  F-4: 230. **-F:** 152 (FGA, ftr); **-E:** 7 (OCU, in US);
    RF-4E: 71* (recce).
  Tornado: 236 (161 FGA, 35* ECR, 23* OCU,
    17* in tri-national trg sqn (in UK)).
  MiG-29: 20 (ftr), **-UB:** 4 (trg).
  Alpha Jet: 163 (145 FGA, 18* wpn trg in Portugal).
  Transall C-160: 85 (tpt, trg).
  Boeing 707: 4 (VIP). **CL-601:** 7 (VIP). **Do-28-D2:**
    54 (6 VIP, 48 tpt/liaison). **Do-228:** 1 (tpt).
  HFB-320: 7 (tpt). **Il-62:** 3 (tpt). **L-410-S:** 4
    (VIP). **T-37B:** 35. **T-38A:** 41. **Tu-154:** 2 (tpt).
  VFW-614: 3 (VIP), **AN-26:** 9.
HELICOPTERS:
  UH-1D: 109 (105 SAR, tpt, liaison; 4 VIP).
  Mi-8T: 40 (SAR tpt).
  Mi-8S: 6 (VIP).
  Mi-2: 20 (civil rescue).
MISSILES:
  ASM: AS-20, AGM-65 *Maverick*.
  AAM: AIM-9 *Sidewinder*.
  SAM: 216 *Hawk* launchers; 95 *Roland* launchers.
    288 *Patriot* launchers, 12 SA-5 launchers.
AIRCRAFT OF FORMER GDR AIR FORCE:
(not being operated)
FIGHTER: MiG-21: 251; MiG-23: 63; Su-22: 54; (all
  TLE will be disposed of in accordance with CFE).
TRANSPORT: Tu-134: 3; An-26: 3; L-410T: 8; L-39: 52.
HELICOPTERS: Mi-2: 5 (20 in use for civilian rescue);
  Mi-9: 1; Mi-14: 14; Mi-24: 2.

DEPLOYMENT:
NAVY: 1 FF with STANAVFORMED and 1 DDG,
  1 FF, 1 AO in Mediterranean on 3-month
  roulement with some gaps (about 50% cover).
UN AND PEACEKEEPING:
CAMBODIA (UNTAC): 144 medical staff.

PARAMILITARY:
FEDERAL BORDER GUARD (Ministry of Interior):
  24,900; 5 cmd (constitutionally has no cbt
  status). Eqpt: 300 MOWAG SW-3/-4 APC; 2
  P-149D, 1 Do-27 ac; Bo-105M, 32 SA-318C, 13
  UH-1D, 8 Bell 212, 22 SA-330, 3 SA-332L hel.
  Some 13 patrol craft: 1 PCO, 12 PCC plus boats.
COAST GUARD: 535; some 8 PCI, 1 inshore tug,
  plus boats.

FOREIGN FORCES:
NATO:
  HQ Northern Army Gp (NORTHAG).
  HQ Central Army Gp (CENTAG).
  HQ Allied Air Forces Central Europe.
  HQ Allied Land Forces Jutland and
    Schleswig-Holstein (LANDJUT).
  HQ Allied Command Europe Mobile Force (AMF).

HQ 2 Allied Tactical Air Force (2 ATAF).
HQ 4 Allied Tactical Air Force (4 ATAF).
BELGIUM: 19,000; 1 corps HQ, 1 armd bde, 2 arty, 1 AA, 2 SAM, 2 engr bn (NORTHAG).
CANADA: 5,100; 1 mech bde gp (1bn with UNPROFOR).
1 air div with 1 FGA sqn (CENTAG/4 ATAF).
FRANCE: 16,000; 1 corps HQ, 1 armd div.
Berlin: (2,700), 1 armd, 1 inf regt.
NETHERLANDS: 4,700; 1 armd bde (NORTHAG).
UNITED KINGDOM: 62,800; 1 corps HQ, 3 armd div, 6 ac sqn, 1 hel sqn (NORTHAG/2 ATAF).
Berlin: (2,800), 1 inf bde.
US: 148,400. 1 army HQ, 1 corps HQ; 1 armd, 1 mech div; 2 air force HQ; with 7 sqn FGA/ftr, 1 cbt spt wing, 1 tac airlift wing, (CENTAG/4 ATAF).
Berlin: (4,300), 1 inf bde.
RUSSIA: 177,000. Army: 1 Gp, 4 Army HQ, 3 TD, 3 MRD. Air: 1 Air Army HQ; 6 FGA, 7 ftr regt.

GREECE

GDP	1990: dr 10,455.00bn ($65.96bn)	
	1991: dr 12,337.80bn ($67.69bn)	
Growth	1990: −0.2%	1991: 1.3%
Inflation	1990: 20.4%	1991: 19.5%
Debt	1991: $22.00bn	
Def bdgt	1991: dr 726.23bn ($3.98bn)	
	1992ε: dr 838.80bn ($4.30bn)	
NATO defn	1991: dr 711.22bn ($3.90bn)	
FMA	1992: $350.5m	
$1 = dr	1989: 162.42	1990: 158.51
	1991: 182.27	1992: 195.00
dr = drachmas		

Population: 10,209,800

	13–17	*18–22*	*23–32*
Men	369,500	381,000	766,200
Women	349,000	360,000	730,200

TOTAL ARMED FORCES:
ACTIVE: 159,300 (125,800 conscripts, 4,200 women).
Terms of service: Army up to 19, Navy up to 23, Air Force up to 21 months.
RESERVES: some 406,000 (to age 50). Army some 350,000 (Field Army 230,000, Territorial Army/National Guard 120,000); Navy about 24,000; Air about 32,000.

ARMY: 113,000 (100,000 conscripts, 2,200 women).
FIELD ARMY (82,000): 3 Military Regions.
1 Army, 4 corps HQ.
2 div HQ (1 armd, 1 mech).

9 inf div (3 inf, 1 arty regt, 1 armd bn) 2 Cat A, 3 Cat B, 4 Cat C.
5 indep armd bde (each 2 armd, 1 mech inf, 1 SP arty bn) Cat A.
1 indep mech bde (2 mech, 1 armd, 1 SP arty bn), Cat A.
2 inf bde.
1 marine bde (3 inf, 1 lt arty bn, 1 armd sqn) Cat A.
1 cdo, 1 raider regt.
4 recce bn.
10 fd arty bn.
6 AD arty bn.
2 SAM bn with *Improved HAWK*.
2 army avn bn.
1 indep avn coy.
Units are manned at 3 different levels: Cat A 85% fully ready; Cat B 60% ready in 24 hours; Cat C 20% ready in 48 hours.
TERRITORIAL DEFENCE: (31,000):
Higher Mil Comd of Interior and Islands HQ.
4 Mil Comd HQ (incl Athens).
1 inf div.
1 para regt.
8 fd arty bn.
4 AD arty bn.
1 army avn bn.
RESERVES (National Guard): 34,000. Role: internal security.
EQUIPMENT:
MBT: 1,879 (154 in store): 396 M-47, 1,220 M-48 (299, 110 A2, 212 A3, 599 A5), 154 AMX-30, 109 *Leopard* 1A3.
LIGHT TANKS: 198 M-24.
RECCE: 48 M-8.
AIFV: 96 AMX-10P.
APC: 1,995 (517 in store): 110 *Leonidas*, 114 M-2, 403 M-3 half-track, 372 M-59, 996 M-113.
TOTAL ARTY: 1,908.
> **TOWED ARTY:** 875: 105mm: 18 M-56, 469 M-101; 140mm: 32 5.5-in; 155mm: 271 M-114; 203mm: 85 M-115.
> **SP ARTY:** 299: 105mm: 76 M-52; 155mm: 48 M-44A1, 51 M-109A1, 84 M-109A2; 175mm: 12 M-107; 203mm: 28 M-110A2.
> **MORTARS:** 107mm: 602 M-30, 132 M-106 SP. Plus 81mm: 690.
ATGW: 394: *Milan, TOW* (incl 36 SP).
RCL: 90mm: 1,057 EM-67; 106mm: 763 M-40A1.
AD GUNS: 20mm: 101 Rh-202 twin; 30mm: 24 *Artemis* 30 twin; 40mm: 227 M-1, 95 M-42A twin SP.
SAM: 42 *Improved HAWK, Redeye*.
AIRCRAFT: 3 *Aero Commander*, 2 *Super King Air*, 20 U-17A.
HELICOPTERS: 9 CH-47C1, 85 UH-1D/H/AB-205, 1 AB-212, 15 AB-206, 10 Bell 47G, 30 Hughes 300C.

NAVY: 19,500 (ε11,400 conscripts, ε9,000 women);
BASES: Salamis, Patras, Soudha Bay.

SUBMARINES: 10:
8 *Glavkos* (Ge T-209/1100) with 533mm TT (trg).
2 *Katsonis* (US *Guppy*) with 533mm TT.

PRINCIPAL SURFACE COMBATANTS: 13:

DESTROYERS: 9:
1 ex-USN *Adams* (DDG-2) with 1 × SM-1; plus 1 × 8 *ASROC*, 2 × 3 ASTT, 2 × 127mm guns, *Harpoon* SSM.
7 *Themistocles* (US *Gearing*) (ASW) with 1 × 8 *ASROC*, 2 × 3 ASTT, 1 with AB-212 hel; plus 3 × 2 127mm guns, 4 with 2 × 4 *Harpoon* SSM.
1 *Miaoulis* (US *Sumner*) with AB-212 hel, 2 × 3 ASTT; plus 3 × 2 127mm guns.

FRIGATES: 4:
2 *Elli* (Nl *Kortenaer*) with 2 AB-212 hel, 2 × 3 ASTT; plus 2 × 4 *Harpoon*
2 *Aetos* (US *Cannon*) with 2 × 3 ASTT.
Plus 3 ex-USN *Knox* (FF-1052) (on loan) with 1 × 8 *ASROC*, 1 × SH-2F hel, 4 × ASTT; plus *Harpoon* (from *ASROC* launcher) 1 × 127mm gun by end 1992.

PATROL AND COASTAL COMBATANTS: 37:

CORVETTES: 2:
2 ex-Ge *Thetis* (ASW) with 1 × 4 ASW RL, 4 × 533mm TT (5 by end of 1992).

MISSILE CRAFT: 16:
14 *Laskos* (Fr *Combattante*) PFM, 8 with 4 × MM-38 *Exocet*, 6 with 6 *Penguin* 2 SSM, all with 2 × 533mm TT.
2 *Stamou*, with 4 × SS-12 SSM.

TORPEDO CRAFT: 10:
6 *Hesperos* (Ge *Jaguar*) PFT with 4 × 533mm TT.
4 No '*Nasty*' PFT⟨ with 4 × 533mm TT.

PATROL: 9:
COASTAL: 2 *Armatolos* (Dk *Osprey*) PCC.
INSHORE: 7: 2 *Tolmi*, 5 PCI⟨.

MINE WARFARE: 16:
MINELAYERS: 2 *Aktion* (US LSM-1) (100–130 mines).
MINE COUNTERMEASURES: 14:
9 *Alkyon* (US MSC-294) MSC.
5 *Atalanti* (US *Adjutant*) MSC.

AMPHIBIOUS: 12:
1 *Chios* LST with hel deck: capacity 300 tps, 16 tk.
1 *Nafkratoussa* (US *Cabildo*) LSD: capacity 200 tps, 18 tk, 1 hel.
2 *Inouse* (US *County*) LST: capacity 400 tps, 18 tk.
4 *Ikaria* (US LST-510): capacity 200 tps, 16 tk.
4 *Ipopliarhos Grigoropoulos* (US LSM-1) LSM, capacity 50 tps, 4 tk.
Plus about 66 craft: 2 LCT, 8 LCU, 22 LCM, some 34 LCVP.

SUPPORT AND MISCELLANEOUS: 14:
2 AOT, 4 AOT (small), 1 ex-Ge *Lüneburg* log spt, 1 trg, 1 AE, 5 AGHS.

NAVAL AIR: 15 armed hel.
ASW: 1 hel div: 3 sqn:
2 with 11 AB-212 (ASW);
1 with 4 SA-319 (with ASM).

AIR FORCE: 26,800 (14,400 conscripts, 1,100 women).
TACTICAL AIR FORCE: 8 cbt wings, 1 tpt wing.
FGA: 9 sqn:
3 with A-7H.
2 with F-104G.
2 with F-16.
2 with F-4E.
FIGHTER: 9 sqn:
2 with F-4E.
3 with F-5A/B.
1 with RF-5A.
2 with *Mirage* F-1CG.
1 with *Mirage* 2000E/D.
RECCE: 2 sqn:
1 with RF-4E.
1 with RF-104.
MR: 1 sqn with HU-16B.
TRANSPORT: 3 sqn with C-130H, YS-11, C-47, Do-28, *Gulfstream*.
LIAISON: T-33A.
HELICOPTERS: 3 sqn with AB-205A, AB-206A, Bell 47G/OH-13H, AB-212.
AD: 1 bn with *Nike Hercules* SAM (36 launchers).
12 bty with *Skyguard/Sparrow* SAM, twin 35mm guns.

AIR TRAINING COMMAND:
TRAINING: 4 sqn:
1 with T-41A; 1 with T-37B/C; 2 with T-2E.
EQUIPMENT: 381 cbt ac (plus 77 in store), no armed hel.
AIRCRAFT:
A-7H: 44. 39 (FGA); plus 6 in store; **TA-7H:** 5 (FGA).
F-104: 62. **F-104G:** 40 (FGA), plus 20 in store; **TF-104G:** 8* (FGA); **RF-104G:** 14 (recce), plus 4 in store.
F-5: 81. **-A:** 64, plus 10 in store; **-B:** 8, plus 1 in store. **RF-5A:** 9, plus 3 in store.
F-4: 59. **-E:** 54, plus 19 in store; **RF-4E:** 5 (recce).
F-16: 40. **-C:** 36 (FGA/ftr), plus 4 in store; **-D:** 4.
Mirage **F-1:** CG: 25 (ftr), plus 5 in store.
Mirage **2000:** 34. **-E:** 30 (ftr); **BG:** 4* (trg), plus 5 in store.
HU-16B: 8 (MR). **C-47:** 8 (tpt). **C-130H:** 11 (tpt).
CL-215: 14 (tpt, fire-fighting). **Do-28:** 12 (lt tpt).
Gulfstream **I:** 1 (VIP tpt). **T-2:** 36* (trg). **T-33A:** 40 (liaison). **T-37:** 29 (trg). **T-41:** 19 (trg).
YS-11-200: 6 (tpt).
HELICOPTERS:
AB-205A: 14 (tpt). **AB-206A:** 2 (tpt). **AB-212:** 3 (tpt). **Bell 47G:** 5 (liaison).
MISSILES:
ASM: AGM-12 *Bullpup*, AGM-65 *Maverick*.
AAM: AIM-7 *Sparrow*, AIM-9 *Sidewinder*, R-550 *Magic*.
SAM: 36 *Nike Hercules*, 40 *Sparrow*.

FORCES ABROAD:
CYPRUS: 2,250. 2 inf bn and officers/NCO seconded to Greek-Cypriot forces.
UN AND PEACEKEEPING
IRAQ/KUWAIT (UNIKOM): 7 Observers.
WESTERN SAHARA (MINURSO): 1 Observer.

PARAMILITARY:
GENDARMERIE: 26,500; MOWAG *Roland*, 15 UR-416 APC, 6 NH-300 hel.
COAST GUARD AND CUSTOMS: 4,000; some 100 patrol craft, 2 Cessna *Cutlass*, 2 TB-20 *Trinidad* ac.

FOREIGN FORCES:
US: 1,250+. Army (50); Navy (200) facilities at Soudha Bay. Air (1,000) 2 air base gp.

ICELAND

GDP	1990:	K 350.46bn ($6.01bn)		
	1991:	K 382.51bn ($6.48bn)		
Growth	1990:	0.5%	1991:	1.3%
Inflation	1990:	15.5%	1991:	6.8%
Debt	1991:	$3.52bn		
$1 = K	1989:	57.042	1990:	58.284
	1991:	58.996	1992:	60.000

K = Kronur

Population: 259,800

	13–17	18–22	23–32
Men	11,000	11,000	22,800
Women	10,200	10,000	20,900

ARMED FORCES: None.

PARAMILITARY: 130
COAST GUARD: 130:
BASE: Reykjavik
PATROL CRAFT: 3:
  2 *Aegir*, 1 *Odinn* PCO with hel deck.
AVIATION: 1 F-27 ac, 1 SA-360.

FOREIGN FORCES:
NATO: Island Commander Iceland (ISCOMICE, responsible to CINCEASTLANT).
US:
  NAVY: 1,800: **MR:** 1 sqn with 9 P-3C.
  AIR FORCE: 1,200: 1 sqn with 18 F-15 plus AEW, tkr and SAR ac and hel.

NETHERLANDS:
NAVY: 30, 1 P-3C.

ITALY

GDP	1990:	L 1,306,833bn ($1,090.75bn)	
	1991:	L 1,406,875bn ($1,134.03bn)	
Growth	1990:	2.0%	1991: 1.0%
Inflation	1990:	6.4%	1991: 6.4%
Debt	1989:	$203.45bn	
Def bdgt[a]	1991:	L 24,465.90bn ($19.72bn)	
	1992:	L 26,500.00bn ($21.20bn)	
NATO defn	1991:	L 29,267.00bn ($23.59bn)	
$1 = L	1989:	1,372.1	1990: 1,198.1
	1991:	1,240.6	1992: 1,250.0

L = lire
[a] Excl budget for Carabinieri.

Population: 57,345,000

	13–17	18–22	23–32
Men	1,940,500	2,182,500	4,512,400
Women	1,843,900	2,078,800	4,330,800

TOTAL ARMED FORCES:
ACTIVE: 354,000 (211,000 conscripts).
  Terms of service: All services 12 months
RESERVES: 584,000. Army 520,000 (obligation to age 45), immediate mob 240,000.
  Navy 36,000 (to age 39 for men, variable for officers to 73). Air 28,000 (to age 25 or 45 (specialists)).

ARMY: 230,000 (167,000 conscripts).
FIELD ARMY:
  3 Corps HQ (1 mtn):
    1 with 1 mech, 1 armd bde, 1 armd cav bn, 1 arty regt.
    1 with 3 mech, 1 armd bde, 1 amph (2 bn), 2 arty regt, 1 avn gp.
    1 with 4 mtn bde, 1 avn gp, 1 armd cav bn, 3 hy arty bn.
  1 AD comd: 2 *HAWK* SAM, 1 AA regt.
  1 avn gp (1 sqn AB-412, 2 sqn CH-47).
TERRITORIAL DEFENCE:
  7 Military Regions.
  7 indep mech bde.
  Rapid Intervention Force (*FIR*):
    1 AB bde (incl 1 SF bn),
    1 mech bde, 1 Marine bn (see Navy), 1 hel unit (Army), 1 air tpt unit (Air Force).
  2 armd cav regt (1 recce).
  2 inf regt (1 mot).
  1 hy arty regt.
  2 engr regt.
  5 avn units.

RESERVES: On mob: 1 armd, 1 mech, 1 mtn bde.
EQUIPMENT:
MBT: 1,220: 300 M-60A1, 920 *Leopard*
RECCE: 6 *Centauro* B-1 (trials).
APC: 3,879: 2,183 M-113, 1,667 VCC1/-2, 14 Fiat 6614, 15 LVTP-7.
TOTAL ARTY: 1,952 (101 in store).
   TOWED ARTY: 967: 105mm: 357 Model 56 pack; 155mm: 164 FH-70, 423 M-114; 203mm: 23 M-115.
   SP ARTY: 283: 155mm: 260 M-109G/-L; 203mm: 23 M-110A2.
   MRL: 227mm: 2 MLRS.
   MORTARS: 120mm: 700. Plus 81mm: 1,205.
SSM: 6 *Lance* launchers.
ATGW: 432 *TOW* (incl 270 SP), 1,000 *Milan*.
RL: 1,000 *APILAS*.
RCL: 80mm: 720 *Folgore*.
AD GUNS: 25mm: 50 SIDAM SP; 40mm: 252.
SAM: 126 *HAWK*, 145 *Stinger*.
AIRCRAFT: 60: 48 SM-1019, 12 O-1E (target acquisition/utility).
HELICOPTERS: 28 A-109, 6 A-129, 92 AB-205A, 136 AB-206 (observation), 14 AB-212, 17 AB-412, 30 CH-47C.

NAVY: 48,000 incl 1,500 air arm, 600 special forces and 800 marines; (19,000 conscripts).
   5 Main Commands: Fleet (Commander also COMEDCENT); Upper Tyrrhenian; Adriatic; Lower Tyrrhenian; Ionian and Strait of Otranto.
BASES: La Spezia (HQ), Taranto (HQ), Ancona (HQ), Brindisi, Augusta, Messina, La Maddalena, Cagliari, Naples (HQ), Venice.
SUBMARINES: 8:
   2 *Pelosi* (imp *Sauro*) with Type 184 HWT.
   4 *Sauro* with Type 184 HWT.
   2 *Toti* SSC with Type 184 HWT.
PRINCIPAL SURFACE COMBATANTS: 29:
CARRIER: 1:
   1 *G. Garibaldi* CVV with 16 SH-3 *Sea King* hel, 4 *Teseo* SSM, 2 × 3 ASTT (has capability to operate V/STOL ac acquisition in progress).
CRUISERS: 1:
   1 *Vittorio Veneto* CGH with 1 × 2 SM-1 MR SAM, 6 AB-212 ASW hel (Mk 46 LWT); plus 4 *Teseo* SSM, 2 × 3 ASTT.
DESTROYERS: 3:
   1 *Luigi Durand de la Penne* (ex-*Animoso*) DDG with 1 × SM-1 MR SAM, 2 × 4 *Teseo* SSM, plus 2 × AB-2/2 hel, 1 × 127mm gun, 2 × ASTT.
   2 *Audace* DDGH, with 1 × SM-1 MR SAM, 4 *Teseo* SSM, plus 2 × AB-212 hel, 1 × 127mm gun, 2 × 3 ASTT.
FRIGATES: 24:
   8 *Maestrale* FFH with 2 AB-212 hel, 2 × 533mm DP TT; plus 4 *Teseo* SSM, 1 × 127mm gun.
   4 *Lupo* FF with 1 AB-212 hel, 2 × 3 ASTT; plus 8 *Teseo* SSM, 1 × 127mm gun. (Note: 4

additional *Lupo* FF built for Iraq likely to be taken into service by end of 1992.)
   1 *Alpino* with 1 AB-212 hel, 2 × 3 ASTT, 1 × ASW mor.
   8 *Minerva* with 2 × 3 ASTT.
   3 *De Cristofaro* with 2 × 3 ASTT, 1 ASW mor.
ADDITIONAL IN STORE: 2 CGH, 1 DDG, 1 SSC.
PATROL AND COASTAL COMBATANTS: 15:
CORVETTES: 1:
   1 *Albatros* with 2 × 3 ASTT.
MISSILE CRAFT: 6 *Sparviero* PHM with 2 *Teseo* SSM.
PATROL OFFSHORE: 4 *Cassiopea* with 1 AB-212 hel.
COASTAL: 4 *Bambu* (ex-MSC) PCC assigned MFO.
MINE WARFARE: 12:
MCMV: 12:
   2 *Storione* (US *Aggressive*) MSO.
   5 *Lerici* MHC.
   5 *Castagno* (US *Adjutant*) MHC.
AMPHIBIOUS: 2:
   2 *San Giorgio* LPD: capacity 350 tps, 30 trucks, 2 SH-3D or CH-47 hel, 7 craft.
   Plus some 40 craft: about 4 LCU, 22 LCM and 14 LCVP.
SUPPORT AND MISCELLANEOUS: 34:
   2 *Stromboli* AO, 2 tugs, 11 coastal tugs, 4 water tankers, 3 trials, 2 trg, 3 AGOR, 6 tpt, 1 salvage.
SPECIAL FORCES (600) (*Comando Subacquei Incursori* – COMSUBIN):
   6 gp; 2 assigned aslt swimmer craft; 2 raiding ops; 1 underwater ops; 1 SF; 1 school; 1 research.
MARINES (San Marco gp) (800):
   1 bn gp.
   1 trg gp.
   1 log gp.
EQUIPMENT: 30 VCC-1, 10 LVTP-7 APC, 16 81mm mor, 8 106mm RCL, 6 *Milan* ATGW.

NAVAL AIR ARM (1,500); 2 cbt ac, 36 armed hel.
FGA: 2* TAV-8B.
ASW: 5 hel sqn with 36 SH-3D, 60 AB-212.
ASM: *Marte* Mk 2.

AIR FORCE: 76,000 (25,000 conscripts).
FGA: 6 FGA/recce sqn:
   3 with *Tornado*;
   1 with F-104S (being modernized);
   2 with G-91Y.
CAS: 3 sqn:
   3 with AMX.
   1 lt attack with MB-339.
FIGHTER: 7 sqn with F-104S.
RECCE: 1 sqn with F/RF-104G.
MR: 2 sqn with *Atlantic* (Navy-assigned; to be modernized).
EW: 1 ECM/recce sqn with G-222VS, PD-808.
CALIBRATION: 1 navigation-aid calibration sqn with G-222RM, PD-808, MB-339.

TRANSPORT: 3 sqn: 2 with G-222; 1 with C-130H.
COMMUNICATIONS: 1 sqn with *Gulfstream* III, *Falcon* 50, P-166M, SIAI-208M, PD-808, MB-326, DC-9 ac; SH-3D hel.
TRAINING: 1 OCU with TF-104G;
1 det (Cottesmore, UK) with *Tornado*;
6 sqn with G-91T, MB-326, MB-339A, SF-260M ac; AB-47G, NH-500 hel.
SAR: 1 sqn and 3 det with HH-3F.
6 det with AB-212.
AD: 8 SAM gp with *Nike Hercules*;
12 SAM bty with *Spada*.
EQUIPMENT: 449 cbt ac (plus 88 store), no armed hel.
AIRCRAFT:
Tornado: 80 (70 FGA, 10* in tri-national trg sqn), plus 15 in store.
F-104: 164. **-S:** 126 (18 FGA, 84 ftr, 24* trg), plus 20 in store; **RF-104G:** 18 (recce), plus 16 in store; **TF104G:** 20 (OCU).
AMX: 52. 49 (FGA); **-T:** 3* (trg).
G-91: 99. **-Y:** 40 (FGA), plus 15 in store; **-T:** 59* (trg); plus 9 in store.
MB-339: 85 (15 tac, 65 (incl 50*) trg, 5 calibration), plus 7 in store.
Atlantic: 18 (MR).
MB-326: 56 (liaison).
Boeing-707: 1 (tkr/tpt). **C-130H:** 12 (tpt). **G-222:** 42 (38 tpt, 4 calibration), plus **-GE:** 1 (ECM).
DC9-32: 2 (VIP). *Gulfstream* **III:** 2 (VIP).
Falcon **50:** 4 (VIP). **P-166:** 17: (**-M:** 11, DL3: 6 liaison and trg). **PD-808:** 18 (ECM, calibration, VIP tpt); **SF-260M:** 39 (trg). **SIAI-208:** 36 (liaison).
HELICOPTERS:
HH-3F: 19 (SAR).
SH-3D: 2 (liaison).
AB-212: 35 (SAR).
AB-412: 4.
AB-47G: 19 (trg).
NH-500D: 50 (trg).
MISSILES:
ASM: AS-20, *Kormoran*, AGM-65 *Maverick*.
AAM: AIM-7E *Sparrow*, AIM-9B/L *Sidewinder*, *Aspide*.
SAM: 96 *Nike Hercules*, 7 bty *Spada*.

FORCES ABROAD:
UN AND PEACEKEEPING:
EGYPT (MFO): 90; 4 PCC.
INDIA/PAKISTAN (UNMOGIP): 7 Observers.
IRAQ/KUWAIT (UNIKOM): 6 Observers.
LEBANON (UNIFIL): 52. Hel unit.
MIDDLE EAST (UNTSO): 9 Observers.
WESTERN SAHARA (MINURSO): 6 Observers.

PARAMILITARY:
CARABINIERI (Ministry of Defence) 111,400:
Territorial: 9 bde, 24 regt, 101 gp. Trg: 1 bde.

Mobile def: 2 bde, 1 cav regt, 13 mobile bn, 1 AB bn, avn and naval units.
EQUIPMENT: 48 Fiat 6616 armd cars; 92 VCC2, 119 M-113, 24 M-106 APC; 22 A-109, 4 AB-205, 40 AB-206, 9 AB-412 hel.
PUBLIC SECURITY GUARD (Ministry of Interior): 80,400: 11 mobile units; 40 Fiat 6614 APC, 3 P-64B, 5 P-68 ac; 12 A-109, 20 AB-206, 9 AB-212 hel.
FINANCE GUARDS (Treasury Department): 53,000; 13 Zones, 20 Legions, 128 Gps; 13 A-109, 68 Nardi-Hughes (40 NH-500C, 16 -D, 12 -M) hel; 3 PCI, 65⟨; plus 309 boats.
HARBOUR CONTROL (*Capitanerie di Porto*) (Subordinated to Navy in emergencies): Some 25 PCI⟨, 100+ boats.

FOREIGN FORCES:
NATO:
HQ Allied Forces Southern Europe (AFSOUTH).
HQ 5 Allied Tactical Air Force (5 ATAF).
US: 15,100. Army (3,600); 1 AB bn gp; Navy (6,000); Air (5,500); 1 ftr wing.

LUXEMBOURG

GDP	1990: fr 291.50bn ($8.72bn)	
	1991: fr 306.08bn ($8.96bn)	
Growth	1990: 2.3%	1991: 2.5%
Inflation	1990: 3.7%	1991: 3.1%
Debt	1989: $552m	1990: $421m
Def bdgt	1991: fr 3.61bn ($105.72m)	
	1992: fr 3.88bn ($107.83m)	
NATO defn	1990: fr 3.23bn ($96.74m)	
	1991: fr 3.61bn ($105.57m)	
$1 = fr	1989: 39.404	1990: 33.418
	1991: 34.148	1992: 36.000

fr = Luxembourg francs

Population: 364,600 (104,000 foreign citizens)

	13–17	*18–22*	*23–32*
Men	11,000	12,100	27,900
Women	10,400	11,600	27,200

TOTAL ARMED FORCES:
ACTIVE: 800.

ARMY: 800.
1 lt inf bn.
EQUIPMENT:
APC: 5 *Commando*.
ATGW: *TOW* some 6 SP (*Hummer*).
RL: *LAW*.

AIR FORCE: (None, but for legal purposes NATO's E-3A AEW ac have Luxembourg registration.)
1 sqn with 18 E-3A *Sentry* (NATO Standard), 2 Boeing 707 (trg).

FORCES ABROAD:
UN AND PEACEKEEPING:
CROATIA (UNPROFOR): 40.

PARAMILITARY:
GENDARMERIE: 560.

NETHERLANDS

GDP	1990: gld 504.20bn ($276.90bn)	
	1991: gld 530.57bn ($283.77bn)	
Growth	1990: 3.5%	1991: 2.2%
Inflation	1990: 2.5%	1991: 3.9%
Debt	1990: $75.00bn	
Def bdgt	1991: gld 14.12bn ($7.55bn)	
	1992: gld 14.08bn ($7.41bn)	
NATO defn	1991: gld 13.54bn ($7.24bn)	
$1 = gld	1989: 2.1207	1990: 1.8209
	1991: 1.8697	1992: 1.9000
gld = guilders		

Population: 14,855,600

	13–17	18–22	23–32
Men	483,500	559,300	1,261,400
Women	463,200	536,400	1,206,700

TOTAL ARMED FORCES:
ACTIVE: 93,000 (incl 3,900 Royal Military Constabulary, 800 Inter-Service Organization); 2,600 women; 43,500 conscripts.
Terms of service: Army and Air Force 12 months, Navy 12–15 months.
RESERVES: 144,300 (men to age 35, NCO to 40, officers to 45). Army 125,300 (some – at the end of their conscription period – on short leave, immediate recall), Navy some 9,000 (7,000 on immediate recall); Air Force 10,000 (immediate recall).

ARMY: 60,800 (38,000 conscripts).
1 Corps HQ, 3 mech div HQ.
3 armd bde (incl 1 cadre).
6 mech inf bde (incl 2 cadre).
1 indep inf bde (cadre).
3 fd arty, 1 AD gp.
1 army avn wing.

Summary Combat Arm Units:

17 mech inf bn.	13 arty bn.
2 inf bn.	4 AD bn.
12 tk bn.	3 hel sqn (Air
4 recce bn.	Force-manned).

RESERVES: cadre bde and corps tps completed by call-up of reservists.
Territorial Command (40,500 on mob): 2 inf bde, 4 bn, spt units, could be mob for territorial defence.
Home Guard: 3 sectors; inf weapons.
EQUIPMENT:
MBT: 913 (incl 163 in store): 468 *Leopard* 1A4, 445 *Leopard* 2.
AIFV: 984 (incl 142 in store): 718 YPR-765, 266 M-113C/-R all with 25mm.
APC: 2,204: 476 M-113, 1,120 YPR-765, 608 YP-408 (in store).
TOTAL ARTY: 824.
    TOWED ARTY: 165: 105mm: 42 M-101 (in store); 155mm: 123 M-114.
    SP ARTY: 298: 155mm: 222 M-109A3; 203mm: 76 M-110 (in store).
    MRL: 227mm: 22 MLRS.
    MORTARS: 107mm: 141 M-30, 53 M-106 SP (in store); 120mm: 145 (incl 10 in store).
    SSM: 7 *Lance* launchers (in store).
ATGW: 753 (incl 135 in store): 427 *Dragon*, 326 (incl 302 YPR-765) *TOW*.
RL: 84mm: *Carl Gustav*.
RCL: 106mm: 185 M-40.
AD GUNS: 35mm: 95 *Gepard* SP; 40mm: 131 L/70 towed.
SAM: 474 *Stinger*.
HELICOPTERS: 62 SA-316 (to be replaced), 28 Bo-105 (Air Force-manned).
MARINE: 1 tk tpt, 3 coastal, 15 river patrol boats.

NAVY: 15,500, incl naval air arm (900) and marines (2,400) (1,600 conscripts).
BASES: Netherlands: Den Helder (HQ); Vlissingen. Overseas: Willemstad (Curaçao), Oranjestad (Aruba).
SUBMARINES: 5:
    2 *Zeeleeuw* with Mk 48 HWT; plus *Harpoon* USGW.
    2 *Zwaardvis* with Mk 37 HWT.
    1 *Dolfijn* with Mk 37 HWT.
PRINCIPAL SURFACE COMBATANTS: 16:
DESTROYERS: 4 DDG (NL desig = FFG):
    2 *Tromp* with 1 SM-1 MR SAM; plus 2 × 4 *Harpoon* SSM, 1 × 2 120mm guns, 1 *Lynx* hel (ASW/OTHT), 2 × 3 ASTT (Mk 46 LWT).
    2 *Van Heemskerck* with 1 SM-1 MR SAM; plus 2 × 4 *Harpoon*, 2 × 2 ASTT.
FRIGATES: 12:
FF: 12
    2 *Karel Doorman* with 2 × 4 *Harpoon* SSM, plus 2 × 2 ASTT; 1 *Lynx* (ASW/OTHT) hel.

10 *Kortenaer* with 2 *Lynx* (ASW/OTHT) hel, 2 × 2 ASTT; plus 2 × 4 *Harpoon*.

MINE WARFARE: 26:

MINELAYERS: none, but *Mercuur*, listed under spt and misc, has capability.

MINE COUNTERMEASURES: 26:
15 *Alkmaar* (tripartite) MHC (6 in reserve).
11 *Dokkum* MSC (5 in reserve).

AMPHIBIOUS: craft only; about 12 LCA.

SUPPORT AND MISCELLANEOUS: 9:
2 *Poolster* AOR (1–3 *Lynx* hel), 3 survey, 1 *Mercuur* torpedo tender, 2 trg, 1 aux.

NAVAL AIR ARM: (900);

MR: 1 sqn with F-27M (see Air Force).

MR/ASW: 2 sqn (1 trg) with P-3C.

ASW/SAR: 2 sqn with *Lynx* hel.

EQUIPMENT: 13 cbt ac, 22 armed hel.

AIRCRAFT:

P-3C: 13 (MR).

HELICOPTERS:

Lynx: 22 (ASW, SAR).

MARINES: (2,400).
3 marine bn (1 cadre).
1 spt bn.

RESERVE: 1 marine bn†.

AIR FORCE: 12,000 (3,500 conscripts).

FGA: 4 sqn with F-16A/B;

FIGHTER: 4 sqn with F-16A/B (3 ftr/FGA, 1 ftr).

RECCE: 1 sqn with F-16A.

MR: 2 F-27M (assigned to Navy).

TRANSPORT: 1 sqn with F-27.

TRAINING: 1 sqn with PC7.

OCU: 1 sqn with F-16B (temporarily integrated with 1 F-16A ftr sqn).

SAR: 1 flt with SA-319.

AD: 8 bty with *HAWK* SAM (4 in Ge).
4 bty with *Patriot* SAM (in Ge).

EQUIPMENT: 188 cbt ac, no armed hel.

AIRCRAFT:

F-16: 188. **-A:** 153 (125 FGA/ftr, 20 recce, 8* trg);
-B: 35 (32 FGA/ftr, 3* trg).

F-27: 14 (12 tpt, 2 MR).

PC7: 10 (trg).

HELICOPTERS:

SA-316: 4 (SAR).

MISSILES:

AAM: AIM-9/L/N *Sidewinder*.

SAM: 48 *HAWK*, 20 *Patriot*, 100 *Stinger*.

AD: GUNS: 25 VL 4/41 *Flycatcher* radar, 75 L/70 40mm systems.

FORCES ABROAD:

GERMANY: 4,700. 1 armd bde (2 armd inf, 1 tk bn), 1 recce bn, 1 engr bn, spt elm, 4 *HAWK*, 4 *Patriot* bty.

NETHERLANDS ANTILLES: 1 frigate, 1 amph cbt det, 1 MR det with 2 F-27MPA ac.

ICELAND: 30: 1 P-3C (at Keflavik).

UN AND PEACEKEEPING:

ANGOLA (UNAVEM II): 15 Observers.

CAMBODIA (UNTAC): 415, 1 marine bn, 1 engr unit; 3 F-27 ac, 3 SA-316 hel.

CROATIA (UNPROFOR): 324: 1 sigs bn.

EGYPT (MFO): 105: 5 sigs det.

MIDDLE EAST (UNTSO): 15 Observers.

PARAMILITARY:

ROYAL MILITARY CONSTABULARY:
(*Koninklijke Marechaussee*): 3,900 (400 conscripts); 3 'div' comprising 10 districts with 72 'bde'.

FOREIGN FORCES:

NATO:
HQ Allied Forces Central Europe (AFCENT).

US: 2,300. Army 900; Air 1,400, 1 tac ftr gp.

NORWAY

GDP	1990:	kr 662.44bn ($105.83bn)		
	1991:	kr 690.22bn ($106.47bn)		
Growth	1990:	1.8%	1991:	1.6%
Inflation	1990:	4.2%	1991:	3.4%
Debt	1989:	$75.61bn	1990:	$80.14bn
Def bdgt	1991:	kr 22.43bn ($3.46bn)		
	1992:	kr 23.16bn ($3.51bn)		
NATO defn	1991:	kr 22.63bn ($3.49bn)		
$1 = kr	1989:	6.9045	1990:	6.2597
	1991:	6.4829	1992:	6.6000

kr = kroner

Population: 4,215,600

	13–17	18–22	23–32
Men	144,000	161,300	333,600
Women	137,000	153,000	315,500

TOTAL ARMED FORCES:

ACTIVE: some 32,700 (22,800 conscripts) incl 400 Joint Services org, 500 Home Guard permanent staff.
Terms of service: Army, Navy coast arty, Air Force, 12 months plus 4 to 5 refresher trg periods; Navy 15 months.

RESERVES: 285,000 mobilizable in 24–72 hours; obligation to 44 (conscripts remain with fd army units to age 35; officers to age 55; regulars: 60). Army: 159,000; Navy: 26,000; Air: 28,000.

Home Guard: War some 85,000.
Second-line reserves: 60,000 (all services).

ARMY: 15,900 (13,000 conscripts).
2 Commands, 5 district comd, 1 div, 16 subordinate comd.
STANDING FORCES:
North Norway:
1 reinforced mech bde: 2 inf, 1 tk, 1 SP fd arty, 1 engr bn, 1 AD bty, spt units.
1 border garrison bn.
1 reinforced inf bn task force: inf, tk coy, fd arty, AD bty.
South Norway:
1 inf bn (Royal Guard).
Indep units.
RESERVES: cadre units for mob: 3 div HQ, 3 armd, 4 mech, 6 lt inf bde, 5 mech, 23 inf, 7 arty bn; 60 indep inf coy, tk sqn, arty bty, engr coy, sigs units, spt.
LAND HOME GUARD: 80,000
18 districts each divided into 2–6 sub-districts and some 470 sub-units (pl).
EQUIPMENT:
MBT: 211: 78 *Leopard* 1, 55 M-48A5, 78 NM-116 (M-24/90).
AIFV: 53 NM-135 (M-113/20mm).
APC: 150 M-113.
TOTAL ARTY: 527.
  TOWED ARTY: 105mm: 228 M-101; 155mm: 48 M-114.
  SP ARTY: 155mm: 126 M-109A3GN SP.
  MORTARS: 107mm: 97 M-30F1, 28 M-106A1 SP. Plus 81mm.
ATGW: *TOW*-1/-2, 97 NM-142 (M-113/*TOW*-2).
RCL: 57mm: M-18; 84mm: *Carl Gustav*; 106mm: M-40A1.
AD GUNS: 20mm: Rh-202; 40mm: L/60 and L/70.
SAM: 108 RBS-70.

NAVY: 7,300, incl 2,000 coastal artillery (4,500 conscripts).
8 Naval/Coast defence comd.
BASES: Horten, Haakonsvern (Bergen), Ramsund, Olavsvern (Tromsø).
SUBMARINES: 11:
5 *Ula* with Ge *Seeaal* DM2A3 HWT.
6 *Kobben* SSC (with Swe T-612) HWT.
FRIGATES: 5 *Oslo* with 2 × 3 ASTT, 1 × 6 *Terne* ASW RL; plus 6 × *Penguin* 2 SSM.
PATROL AND COASTAL COMBATANTS: 35:
MISSILE CRAFT: 35:
14 *Hauk* PFM with 6 × *Penguin* 2, 2 × 533mm TT.
15 *Storm* PFM with 6 × *Penguin* 2.
6 *Snøgg* PFM with 4 × *Penguin* 2, 4 × 533mm TT.
MINE WARFARE: 8:
MINELAYERS: 2:

2 *Vidar*, coastal (300–400 mines).
Note: Amph craft also fitted for minelaying.
MINE COUNTERMEASURES: 6:
3 *Sauda* MSC, 1 *Tana* MHC.
2 diver spt.
AMPHIBIOUS: craft only; 5 LCT
SUPPORT AND MISCELLANEOUS: 2:
1 *Horten* sub/patrol craft depot ship.
1 Royal Yacht.
ADDITIONAL IN STORE: 3 SS, 2 corvettes, 1 MSC, 3 PFM.
NAVAL HOME GUARD: 7,000. On mob assigned to 8 naval/coast defence comd.
7 *Tjeld* PFT, 2 LCT, some 400 fishing craft.
COAST DEFENCE: 32 fortresses:
34 arty bty: 75mm; 105mm; 120mm; 127mm; 150mm guns.
Some cable mine and torpedo bty.

AIR FORCE: 9,500 (5,300 conscripts).
FGA: 4 sqn with F-16 (incl 1 OCU).
FIGHTER: 1 trg sqn with F-5A/B (has AD role).
MR: 1 sqn with P-3C/N *Orion* (2 assigned to coast guard).
TRANSPORT: 3 sqn:
1 with C-130.
1 with *Falcon* 20 (tpt, EW).
1 with DHC-6.
TRAINING: MFI-15.
SAR: 1 sqn with *Sea King* Mk 43.
COAST GUARD: 1 sqn with *Lynx* Mk 86.
TAC HEL: 2 sqn:
2 with Bell 412 SP.
AD: 22 lt AA arty bty.
(Being delivered: 6 bty NOAH SAM, 10 bty RB-70).
EQUIPMENT: 85 cbt ac (plus 9 in store), no armed hel.
AIRCRAFT:
  F-5A/B: 20 (ftr/trg); plus 9 in store.
  F-16: 61. -A: 49 (FGA), -B: 12 (FGA).
  P-3: -C: 4 (MR); -N: 2 (coast guard).
  C-130H: 6 (tpt).
  Falcon 20C: 3 (EW/tpt).
  DHC-6: 3 (tpt); MFI-15: 18 (trg).
HELICOPTERS:
  Bell 412 SP: 17 (tpt).
  Lynx Mk 86: 6 (coast guard).
  Sea King Mk 43: 10 (SAR).
MISSILES:
  ASM: *Penguin* Mk-3.
  AAM: AIM-9L/N *Sidewinder*.
AD:
  GUNS: 40mm: 32 L/60, 64 L/70.
  SAM: NOAH (Norwegian-adapted *HAWK*).
ANTI-AIRCRAFT HOME GUARD (on mob under comd of Air Force): 3,000; 2bn (9 bty) lt AA; some Rh-202 20mm, 72 L/60 40mm guns (being replaced by Rh-202).

FORCES ABROAD:
UN AND PEACEKEEPING:
ANGOLA (UNAVEM II): 15 Observers.
EGYPT (MFO): Staff Officers.
INDIA/PAKISTAN (UNMOGIP): 7 Observers.
IRAQ/KUWAIT (UNIKOM): 8 Observers, medical unit (20).
LEBANON (UNIFIL): 900; 1 inf bn, 1 service coy, plus HQ personnel.
MIDDLE EAST (UNTSO): 17 Observers.

PARAMILITARY:
COAST GUARD: 680:
PATROL OFFSHORE: 13:
  3 *Nordkapp* with 1 × *Lynx* hel (SAR/recce), 2 × 3 ASTT, fitted for 6 *Penguin* Mk 2 SSM.
  1 *Nornen*, 2 *Farm*, 7 chartered.
AIRCRAFT: 2 P-3N *Orion* ac, 6 *Lynx* hel (Air Force-manned).

FOREIGN FORCES:
NATO:
  HQ Allied Forces Northern Europe (HQ AFNORTH).
US: Prepositioned eqpt for 1 MEB.

PORTUGAL

GDP	1990:	esc 8,529.80bn ($59.84bn)	
	1991:	esc 8,553.40bn ($66.12bn)	
Growth	1990:	4.2%	1991: 2.7%
Inflation	1990:	14.3%	1991: 11.4%
Debt	1991:	$35.00bn	
Def bdgt	1991:	esc 206.80bn ($1.43bn)	
	1992:	esc 215.50bn ($1.48bn)	
NATO defn	1991:	esc 289.59bn ($2.00bn)	
FMA[a]	1992:	$167.8m	
$1 = esc	1989:	157.46	1990: 142.55
	1991:	144.48	1992: 146.00

esc = escudos
[a] Incl $40m as Economic Support.

4Population: 10,618,400

	13–17	18–22	23–32
Men	418,600	428,800	873,800
Women	407,900	416,200	853,200

TOTAL ARMED FORCES:
ACTIVE: 58,300 (32,800 conscripts).
Terms of service: All services 8–12 months.
RESERVES: 190,000 (all services) (obligation: men to age 35; officers to 65).

ARMY: 32,700 (24,800 conscripts).
  6 Territorial Commands (4 military regions, 2 military zones).
  1 composite bde (1 mech, 2 mot inf, 1 tk, 1 fd arty bn).
  3 inf bde.
  1 SF bde (2 SF, 1 arty, 1 log bn).
  3 cav regt.
  15 inf regt, each 1 armd, 3 inf bn.
  3 fd, 1 AD, 1 coast arty regt.
  2 engr regt.
EQUIPMENT:
MBT: 129+: 43 M-47, 86 M-48A5.
RECCE: 8 *Saladin*, 40 AML-60, 15 V-150, 21 EBR-75, 8 ULTRAV M-11, 30 *Ferret* Mk 4.
APC: 253: 172 M-113, 79 V-200 *Chaimite*, 2 EBR.
TOTAL ARTY: 306 incl:
  TOWED ARTY: 142: 105mm: 54 M-101, 24 M-56; 140mm: 24 5.5-in; 155mm: 40 M-114A1.
  SP ARTY: 155mm: 6 M-109A2.
  MORTARS: 158: 107mm: 58 M-30 (incl 14 SP); 120mm: 100 Tampella.
COAST ARTY: 150mm: 15; 152mm: 6; 234mm: 6.
ATGW: 48 *TOW* (incl 18 M-113, 4 M-901), 31 SS-11 (incl 22 V-200 *Chaimite*), 45 *Milan* (incl 6 ULTRAV M-11).
RCL: 240: 90mm: 112; 106mm: 128 M-40.
AD GUNS: 105 incl 20mm: M-163A1 *Vulcan* SP; 40mm: L/60.
SAM: 12 *Blowpipe*, 5 *Chaparral*.

DEPLOYMENT:
  Azores and Madeira: 2,000. 3 inf regt, 2 coast arty bn, 2 AA bty.

NAVY: 15,300 incl 2,500 marines (5,000 conscripts) 3 comd: Continental, Azores, Madeira.
BASES: Lisbon (Alfeite), Portimão (HQ Continental comd), Ponta Delgada (HQ Azores), Funchal (HQ Madeira).
SUBMARINES: 3:
  3 *Albacora* (Fr *Daphné*) SS with EL-5 HWT.
FRIGATES: 11:
  3 *Vasco Da Gama* (Meko 200) with 2 × 3 ASTT (US Mk-32), 2 × *Super Lynx* hel (not yet acquired), plus 2 × 4 *Harpoon* SSM, 1 × 8 *Sea Sparrow* SAM, 1 × 100mm gun.
  4 *Commandante João Belo* (Fr *Cdt Rivière*) with 2 × 3 ASTT, 1 × 4 ASW mor; plus 3 × 100mm gun.
  4 *Baptista de Andrade* with 2 × 3 ASTT; plus 1 × 100mm gun.
PATROL AND COASTAL COMBATANTS: 29:
PATROL OFFSHORE: 6:
  6 *João Coutinho* PCO.
PATROL COASTAL: 10:
  10 *Cacine*.
INSHORE: 12⟨: 5 ARGOS⟨, 7⟨.

RIVERINE: 1 *Rio Minho*⟨.
AMPHIBIOUS: Craft only; 3 LCU, 13 LCM
SUPPORT AND MISCELLANEOUS: 11:
1 AO, 3 AOT (small), 1 AK, 3 AGHS, 2 trg,
1 tug.

MARINES: (2,500) (1,300 conscripts).
3 bn (2 inf, 1 police), spt units.
EQUIPMENT: *Chaimite* APC, mor, 7 LCM.

AIR FORCE: 10,300 (3,000 conscripts) incl
2,200 AB tps listed with Army.
1 operational air command (COFA).
FGA: 3 sqn:
2 with A-7P;
1 with G-91R3/T1;
SURVEY: 1 sqn with C-212B.
MR: 1 sqn with P-3P.
TRANSPORT: 6 sqn:
1 with C-130;
2 with C-212;
1 with *Falcon* 20 and *Falcon* 50.
2 with SA-316 hel.
SAR: 2 sqn with SA-330 hel.
LIAISON: 1 sqn with Reims-Cessna FTB-337G.
TRAINING: 4 sqn:
1 with C-212 ac, SA-316 hel;
1 with T-38.
1 with T-37C;
1 with SOCATA TB-30 *Epsilon*
EQUIPMENT: 83 cbt ac, no attack hel.
AIRCRAFT:
Alpha Jet: 10 (FGA).
A-7: 38. **-7P:** 32 (FGA); **TA-7P:** 6* (trg).
G-91: 29. **-R3:** 24 (FGA); **-T1:** 5* (trg).
P-3P: 6 (MR).
C-130H: 6 (SAR, tpt).
C-212: 26. **-A:** 22 (16 tpt/SAR, 4 OCU, 2 ECM
trg); **-B:** 4 (survey).
Cessna 337: 12 (liaison).
Falcon 20: 3 (tpt, calibration).
Falcon 50: 3 (tpt).
RF-10: 2 (trg).
T-37: 23 (trg).
T-38: 12 (trg).
Epsilon: 17 (trg).
HELICOPTERS:
SA-330: 10 (SAR/tpt).
SA-316: 35 (trg, utility).

FORCES ABROAD:
CROATIA (UNPROFOR): 3 Observers.

PARAMILITARY:
NATIONAL REPUBLICAN GUARD: 20,900;
Commando Mk III APC, 7 SA-313 hel .

PUBLIC SECURITY POLICE: 20,000.
BORDER SECURITY GUARD: 8,900.

FOREIGN FORCES:
NATO:
NATO HQ for IBERLANT area at Lisbon (Oeiras).
US: 1,600. Navy (400). Air (1,200) (incl Azores).
GERMANY: Air. OCU (Beja) with 18 *Alpha Jet*.

SPAIN

GDP	1990: pts 50,087.0bn ($491.39bn)	
	1991: pts 54,775.0bn ($527.14bn)	
Growth	1990: 3.8%	1991: 2.5%
Inflation	1990: 6.7%	1991: 5.9%
Debt	1990: $100.45bn	1991: $113.00bn
Def bdgt	1991: pts 858.33bn ($8.26bn)	
	1992: pts 785.88bn ($7.41bn)	
NATO defn	1991: pts 938.81bn ($9.03bn)	
FMA	1990: $2.1m (US)	
$1 = pts	1989: 118.38	1990: 101.93
	1991: 103.91	1992: 106.00

pts = pesetas

Population: 40,307,800

	13–17	*18–22*	*23–32*
Men	1,652,600	1,683,900	3,207,800
Women	1,565,900	1,606,400	3,096,200

TOTAL ARMED FORCES:
ACTIVE: 217,000 (158,100 conscripts (to be
reduced), some 200 women) .
Terms of service: 9 months.
RESERVES: 498,000 (all services to age 38);
Immediate Reserve: 140,000:
Army 122,000; Navy 10,000; Air Force 8,000.

ARMY: 146,000 (118,000 conscripts);
8 Regional Operational Commands incl
2 Overseas:
1 armd div (1 armd inf, 1 mech bde, 1 arty, 1
lt armd cav, 1 engr regt).
1 mech div (2 mech bde, 1 arty, 1 lt armd
cav, 1 engr regt).
1 mot div (2 mot, 1 mech bde, 1 arty, 1 lt
armd cav, 1 engr regt).
2 mtn div (each 2 bde, 1 arty, 1 engr regt).
2 armd cav bde (each 1 armd, 2 lt armd cav,
1 arty regt).
1 air portable bde.
5 island garrison (bde).
6 special ops bn.
5 regional engr units.

General Reserve Force:
1 Rapid Action Force (FAR) HQ.
  1 Spanish Legion (6,400): 4 regt;
    2 with 1 mech, 1 mot bn, 1 ATK coy;
    1 with 2 mot bn; 1 lt inf bn.
    1 with 1 mot bn, 1 special ops bn.
  1 AB bde (3 bn).
  1 AD comd (6 AD regt incl 1 *HAWK* SAM bn,
    1 composite *Aspide* bn, 1 *Roland* bn).
  1 fd arty comd (1 fd, 1 locating, 1 MRL regt).
  1 engr comd (3 engr regt).
Army Aviation (FAMET) with:
  1 attack hel bn.
  1 tpt bn (1 med, 1 hy coy).
  4 utility units.
1 Coast Arty Comd (6 mixed arty regt; 1 coast
  arty gp).

EQUIPMENT:
MBT: 838 (84 in store): 299 AMX-30 (60-EM2), 329
  M-47E1, 46 M-47E2, 164 M-48A5E.
RECCE: 340 BMR-VEC, 100 BMR-625.
APC: 1,900: 1,213 M-113, 687 BMR-600.
TOTAL ARTY: 1,355.
  TOWED ARTY: 722: 105mm: 284 M-26, 170 M-56
    pack; 122mm: 160 390-1; 155mm: 84 M-114;
    203mm: 24 M-115.
  SP ARTY: 156: 105mm: 48 M-108; 155mm: 96
    M-109A1; 203mm: 12 M-110A2.
  MRL: 140mm: 12 *Teruel*.
  MORTARS: 120mm: 265 M-40, 192 M-106 SP, 8
    BMR SP. Plus 81mm: 1,200 (incl 187 SP).
COAST ARTY: 6-in: 117; 305mm: 16; 381mm: 17.
ATGW: 442 *Milan*, 28 *HOT*.
RCL: 106mm: 654.
AD GUNS: 20mm: 329 GAI-BO1; 35mm: 92
  GDF-002 twin; 40mm: 274 L/70.
SAM: 24 *Improved HAWK*, 18 *Roland*, 13
  Skyguard/Aspide.
HELICOPTERS: 189 (28 attack): 3 HU-8, 59 HU-10B,
  68 HA-15 (31 with 20mm guns, 28 with *HOT*, 9
  trg), 6 HU-18, 17 HR-12B, 18 HT-21, 18 HT-17.

DEPLOYMENT:
CEUTA AND MELILLA: 15,800;
  2 armd cav, 2 Spanish Legion, 2 mixed arty regt;
  2 lt AD bn, 2 engr, 1 coast arty gp.
BALEARIC ISLANDS: 5,000;
  1 inf regt: 2 mot bn. 1 arty regt: 2 fd arty, 1 coast
  arty; 1 engr bn, 1 special ops coy.
CANARY ISLANDS: 8,500;
  2 inf bn, 1 Spanish Legion, 2 coast arty regt, 2
  engr bn, 2 special ops coy.

NAVY: 36,000, incl marines (21,900 conscripts).
5 Commands (Fleet, plus 4 Naval Regions:
  Cantabria (Atlantic), Mediterranean, Straits,
  Canaries).
BASES: Ferrol (HQ Cantabria), Cadiz (HQ Straits
  and Rota (HQ Fleet)), Cartagena (HQ
  Mediterranean and submarine base), Palma de
  Mallorca, Mahón, Las Palmas (HQ Canaries).

SUBMARINES: 8:
4 *Galerna* (Fr *Agosta*) with F-17 and L-5 HWT
  plus possibly *Exocet* USGW.
4 *Delfin* (Fr *Daphné*) with F-17 and L-5 HWT.

PRINCIPAL SURFACE COMBATANTS: 16:
CARRIERS: 1 (CVV):
  1 *Príncipe de Asturias* (16,200t). Air gp: typically
    6 AV-8B, 5 *Sea King* (Mk 46 LWT), 2 AB-212
    (1 SAR, 1 tpt), 2 *Sea King* AEW.
FRIGATES: 15:
  FFG: 9 (AAW/ASW):
    4 *Santa Maria* (US *Perry*) with 1 × 1 SM-1
      MR/*Harpoon* launcher, 1 × SH-60B hel, 2 ×
      3 ASTT.
    5 *Baleares* with 1 × 1 SM-1 MR SAM, 1 × 8
      ASROC, 2 × 533mm, 4 × 324mm ASTT;
      plus 2 × 4 *Harpoon*, 1 × 127mm gun.
  FF: 6 *Descubierta* with 2 × 3 ASTT, 1 × 2 ASW
    RL; plus 2 × 2 *Harpoon* SSM.
PATROL AND COASTAL COMBATANTS: 39:
PATROL OFFSHORE: 4: 4 *Serviola*.
COASTAL: 20:
  1 *Cormoran*, 6 *Lazaga* PFC, 10 *Anaga*, 3 *Nalón*
  (ex MSC) PCC.
INSHORE: 15:
  6 *Barceló* PFI; 9 PCI⟨ (plus some 58 boats).
MINE WARFARE: 12:
MCMV: 12:
  4 *Guadalete* (US *Aggressive*) MSO.
  8 *Júcar* (US *Adjutant*) MSC.
AMPHIBIOUS: 4:
  2 *Castilla* (US *Paul Revere*) amph tpt, capacity:
    1,400 tps.
  2 *Velasco* (US *Terrebonne Parish*) LST, capacity:
    300 tps, 18 tk.
Plus 13 craft: 3 LCT, 2 LCU, 8 LCM.
SUPPORT AND MISCELLANEOUS: 27:
  1 AOR, 1 tpt, 5 ocean tugs, 2 diver spt, 6 water
  carriers, 7 AGHS, 4 trg, 1 sub salvage.

NAVAL AIR:
FGA: 2 sqn:
  1 with AV-8S *Matador* (*Harrier*), TAV-8S.
  1 with AV-8B.
LIAISON: 1 sqn with 3 *Comanche*, 3 *Citation*.
HELICOPTERS: 4 sqn:
  ASW: 2 sqn:
    1 with SH-3D/G *Sea King* (mod to SH-3H
      standard).
    1 with SH-60B (LAMPS-III fit).
  AEW: 1 flt with SH-3D (*Searchwater* radar).
  COMMAND/TRANSPORT: 1 sqn with AB-212.
  TRAINING: 1 sqn with Hughes 500.
EQUIPMENT: 21 cbt ac, 28 armed hel.
AIRCRAFT:
  AV-8: 21. **-S:** 8 (FGA); **-B:** 11 (FGA); **TAV-8S:** 2*
    (trg).
  Comanche: 1 (liaison). ***Citation* II:** 3 (liaison).

HELICOPTERS:
  AB-212: 10 (ASW/SAR).
  SH-3: 12 (9 -**H** ASW, 3 -**D** AEW).
  Hughes 500: 10 (trg).
  SH-60B: 6 (ASW).

MARINES: (7,000). (5,500 conscripts)
  1 marine regt (3,500): 2 inf, 1 spt bn; 3 arty bty.
  5 marine garrison gp.
EQUIPMENT:
MBT: 17 M-48E.
AFV: 17 *Scorpion* lt tk, 19 LVTP-7 amph, 35 BLR.
TOWED ARTY: 105mm: 12 Oto Melara M-56 pack.
SP ARTY: 155mm: 6 M-109A.
ATGW: 12 *TOW*, 18 *Dragon*.
RL: 90mm: C-90C.
RCL: 106mm: 52.
SAM: 12 *Mistral*.

AIR FORCE: 35,000 (18,200 conscripts).
CENTRAL AIR COMMAND (MACEN): 4 wings.
FIGHTER: 3 sqn:
  2 with EF-18 (F-18 *Hornet*);
  1 with RF-4C;
TRANSPORT: 7 sqn.
  2 sqn with C-212.
  2 sqn with CN-235, C-212.
  1 sqn with Boeing 707.
  1 sqn with *Falcon* (20, 50, 900).
  1 sqn with AS-332 (tpt).
SUPPORT: 4 sqn
  1 sqn with CL-215.
  1 sqn with C-212 (EW).
  1 sqn with C-212AAC, AS-332 (SAR).
  1 sqn with C-212.
TRAINING: 4 sqn.
  1 sqn with C-212.
  1 sqn with C-101.
  1 sqn with Beech (*Baron*).
  1 sqn with Beech (*Bonanza*).
EASTERN AIR COMMAND (MALEV): 2 wings.
FIGHTER: 3 sqn:
  2 with EF-18 (F-18 *Hornet*)
  1 with *Mirage* III EE/ED.
TRANSPORT: 2 sqn:
  1 sqn with C-130H.
  1 sqn tkr/tpt with KC-130H
SUPPORT: 1 sqn with C-212 ac, hel (SAR) AS-332.
GIBRALTAR STRAIT AIR COMMAND
  (MAEST): 5 wings
FIGHTER: 2 sqn with *Mirage* F-1 CE/BE.
FGA: 4 sqn
  1 sqn with F-5A.
  1 sqn with RF-5A.
  2 sqn with F-5B (OCU).
MR: 1 sqn with P-3A/B.

TRAINING: 6 sqn
  2 hel sqn with AB-205, SA-330 *Hughes* 300C, S-76C.
  1 sqn with C-212.
  1 sqn with E-26 (*Tamiz*)
  1 sqn with C-101.
  1 sqn with C-212.
LIAISON: 1 sqn with Do-27/CASA C-127.
CANARY ISLANDS, AIR COMMAND
  (MACAN): 1 wing.
FGA: 1 sqn with *Mirage* F-1EE.
TRANSPORT: 1 sqn with C-212.
SAR: 1 sqn with F-27 ac, AS-332 hel (SAR).
LOGISTIC SUPPORT COMMAND (MALOG):
  1 sqn.
  1 trials sqn with C-101, C-212 E-26, EF-18, *Mirage* F-1.
EQUIPMENT: 207 cbt ac, no armed hel.
AIRCRAFT:
  EF-18 A/B: 70 (ftr, OCU).
  F-5: 46. -**A:** 12 (FGA); -**B:** 22 (OCU);
    RF-5A: 12 (recce).
  Mirage: 76. **F-1CE:** 33 (FGA); **F-1BE:** 4 (ftr);
    F-1EE: 17 (ftr); **IIIEE:** 17 (ftr); **IIIDE:** 5 (ftr).
  RF-4C: 8 (recce).
  P-3: 7. -**A:** 2 (MR); -**B:** 5 (MR).
  Boeing 707: 3 (tkr/tpt).
  C-130H: 12. 7 (tpt); **KC-130H:** 5 (tkr).
  C-212: 78. (24 tpt, 9 SAR, 8 recce, 9 survey, 26 trg, 2 EW).
  C-101: 82 (trg).
  CL-215: 21 (spt).
  ***Falcon* 20:** 5 (VIP tpt); ***Falcon* 50:** 1 (VIP tpt);
    ***Falcon* 900:** 2 (VIP tpt).
  F-27: 3 (SAR).
  Do-27/CASA C-127: 46 (liaison).
  E-26: 39 (trg).
  Other: 32: **E-20** (*Baron*) 5 trg, **E-24** (*Bonanza*) 27, trg: **CN-235:** 12 tpt.
HELICOPTERS:
  AB-205/UH-1H: 7 (trg). **SA-330:** 5 (trg), **AS-332:** 13 (SAR tpt), **Hughes 300C:** 17 (trg), **S-76C:** 2 (trg).
MISSILES:
  AAM: AIM-7 *Sparrow*, AIM-9 *Sidewinder*.

FORCES ABROAD:
UN AND PEACEKEEPING:
ANGOLA (UNAVEM II): 20 Observers.
EL SALVADOR (ONUSAL): 124 Observers.

PARAMILITARY:
GUARDIA CIVIL: 64,600 (3,000 conscripts); 20 inf *tercios* (regt) with 56 rural bn, 6 traffic security gp, rural special ops gp; 22 BLR APC, 17 BO-105, 6 BK-117 hel; 3 patrol vessels.

FOREIGN FORCES:
US: 3,400. Navy (3,400).

TURKEY

GDP	1990: TL 283,187.0bn ($108.56bn)
	1991: TL 481,100.0bn ($115.32bn)
Growth	1990: 9.1% 1991: 0.3%
Inflation	1990: 60.2% 1991: 68%
Debt	1990: $48.00bn 1991: $49.21bn
Def bdgt[a]	1991: TL 14,970.04bn ($3.59bn)
	1992: TL 28,443.00bn ($4.18bn)
NATO defn	1991: TL 20,887.83bn ($5.01bn)
FMA[b]	1992: $703.5m (US)
$1 = TL	1989: 2,121.7 1990: 2,608.6
	1991: 4,171.8 1992: 6,800.0

TL = Turkish liras

[a] Incl budget for Gendarmerie.
[b] Incl $75m as Economic Support.
An additional $4bn will benefit the national defence fund agreed by Saudi Arabia, Kuwait, UAE, US within the next five years.

Population: 58,103,600

	13–17	18–22	23–32
Men	3,005,000	2,867,600	5,031,800
Women	2,944,300	2,776,800	4,838,500

TOTAL ARMED FORCES:
ACTIVE: 560,300 (481,000 conscripts).
Terms of service: 18 months.
RESERVES: 1,107,000 to age 46 (all). Army 950,000, Navy 84,000, Air 73,000.

ARMY: 450,000 (410,000 conscripts).
4 army HQ: 10 corps HQ.
1 mech div (3 mech regt, 1 arty, 1 recce bn).
14 inf div (10 with 2 inf regt, 1 arty bn; 4 with 2 inf, 1 armd regt, 1 arty bn).
1 inf trg div (with 2 inf trg, 2 arty trg bde)
7 armd bde (each 2 armd, 2 mech inf, 2 arty bn).
4 mech bde (each 1 armd, 1 mech inf, 1 arty regt, 1 recce sqn).
1 mot inf bde.
9 inf bde (each 2 inf, 1 arty regt, 1 recce sqn).
1 indep inf trg bde.
1 indep arty trg bde.
1 AB bde (3 AB, 1 mtn arty bn).
2 cdo bde (each 3 cdo, 1 arty bn).
1 armd regt.
1 Presidential Guard regt.
5 coastal def bn.
Corps units: 10 tk, 50 (30 fd, 20 AD) arty bn.
Note: some div and bde may be understrength.
RESERVES: 1 armd, 1 inf bde.

EQUIPMENT:
MBT: some 3,928: 523 M-47 (in store), 1,130 M-48A1/A2 (to be -A5), 1,980 M-48A5 T1/T2, some 295 *Leopard* 1A3.
LIGHT TANKS: 114 M-24 (in store).
RECCE: M-8 (in store).
AIFV: 80 AIFV.
APC: 3,860: 500 M-59 (in store), 2,460 M-113, 600 M-2/-3 (in store), 300 BTR-60.
TOTAL ARTY: 4,235.
  TOWED ARTY: 1,740: 105mm: 830 M-101A1; 150mm: 104 Skoda; 155mm: 500 M-114A1, 150 M-59; 203mm: 156 M-115.
  SP ARTY: 546: 105mm: 300 M-52, 26 M-108; 155mm: 162 M-109; 175mm: 34 M-107; 203mm: 24 M-110.
  MRL: 227mm: 20 MLRS; plus 70mm: 20 RA-7040 40 tube, towed.
  MORTARS: 1,929: 107mm: 1,250 M-30, 179 M-106 SP 120mm: 500. Plus 81mm: 1,500 incl SP.
COAST ARTY: 240mm: 20.
ATGW: 400 *Cobra*, 300 SS-11, 516 *TOW* SP, 392 *Milan*.
RL: M-72.
RCL: 57mm: 1,631 M-18; 106mm: 2,300 M-40A1.
AD GUNS: 1,285: 20mm: 200 GAI-DO1; 35mm: 260 GDF-003; 40mm: 725 L60/70, 100 M-42A1.
SAM: 12 *Rapier*, 150 *Stinger*, *Redeye*.
AIRCRAFT: 163: 8 Cessna 206, 4 -421, 1 *Cherokee*, 40 *Citabria*, 1 DHC-2, 5 Do-27A, 19 -28D, 50 O-1E, 15 T-42A, 20 U-17.
HELICOPTERS: 323: 5 AH-1, 20 AB-204, 130 AB-205, 20 AB-206A, 3 AB-212, 30 OH-13H, 70 TH-55, 30 UH-1D, 15 UH-1H.

NAVY: 52,300, incl marines (ε40,000 conscripts).
BASES: Ankara (Navy HQ and COMEDNOREAST), Gölcük (HQ Fleet), Istanbul (HQ Northern area and Bosphorus), Izmir, (HQ Southern area and Aegean), Eregli (HQ Black Sea), Iskenderun, Aksaz Bay, Mersin (HQ Mediterranean).
SUBMARINES: 12 SS:
  6 *Atilay* (Ge Type 209/1200) with SST-4 HWT.
  4 *Burakreis*† (plus 2 non op) (US *Guppy*) with Mk 37 HWT.
  2 *Hizirreis* (US *Tang*) with Mk 37 HWT.
PRINCIPAL SURFACE COMBATANTS: 20:
DESTROYERS: 12:
  8 *Yücetepe* (US *Gearing*) (ASW/ASUW) with 2 × 3 ASTT (Mk 46 LWT); 5 with 1 × 8 *ASROC*, 2 with *Harpoon* SSM, all with 2 × 2 127mm guns.
  2 *Alcitepe* (US *Carpenter*) with 1 × 8 *ASROC*, 2 × 3 ASTT, 1 × 2 127mm guns.
  1 *Zafer* (US *Sumner*) with 2 × 3 ASTT, 3 × 2 127mm guns.
  1 *Muavenet* (mod *Sumner*), weapons as *Zafer*; plus 80 mines.
FRIGATES: 8:

4 *Yavuz* (Ge *MEKO* 200) with 1 × AB-212 hel (ASW/OTHT), 2 × 3 ASTT; plus 2 × 4 *Harpoon* SSM, 1 × 127mm gun.

2 *Gelibolu* (Ge T-120 *Köln*) with 4 × 533mm ASTT, 2 × 4 ASW mor; plus 2 × 100mm gun.

2 *Berk* with 2 × 3 ASTT, 2 Mk 11 *Hedgehog*.

PATROL AND COASTAL COMBATANTS: 47:
MISSILE CRAFT: 16:
8 *Doğan* (Ge Lürssen-57) PFM with 2 × 4 *Harpoon* SSM.

8 *Kartal* (Ge *Jaguar*) PFM with 4 × *Penguin* 2 SSM, 2 × 533mm TT.

TORPEDO CRAFT: 2:
2 *Turfan* (Ge *Jaguar*) PFT with 4 × 533mm TT.
PATROL: 29:
COASTAL: 7: 1 *Girne* PFC, 6 *Sultanhisar* PCC.

INSHORE: 22: 1 *Bora* (US *Asheville*) PFI, 12 AB-25 PCI, 4 AB-21, 5⟨.

MINE WARFARE: 37:
MINELAYERS: 4:
1 *Nusret* (400 mines).

3 *Mordoğan* (US LSM) coastal (400 mines).

Note: *Gelibolu* FF, *Bayraktar*, *Sarucabey* and *Çakabey* LST and *Turfan* PFT have minelaying capability.

MINE COUNTERMEASURES: 33:
12 *Seymen* (US *Adjutant*) MSC.

4 *Trabzon* (Cdn *Bay*) MSC.

6 *Karamürsel* (Ge *Vegesack*) MSC.

4 *Foça* (US *Cape*) MSI.

7 MCM base ships⟨.

AMPHIBIOUS: 7 LST:
2 *Ertuğrul* (US *Terrebonne Parish*): capacity 400 tps, 18 tk.

2 *Bayraktar* (US LST-512): capacity 200 tps, 16 tk.

2 *Sarucabey*: capacity 600 tps, 11 tk.

1 *Çakabey*: capacity 400 tps, 9 tk.

Plus about 62 craft: 34 LCT, 5 LCU, 23 LCM.

SUPPORT AND MISCELLANEOUS: 28:
1 *Akar* AO, 5 spt tankers, 3 depot ships, 3 salvage/rescue, 2 survey, 4 tpt, 5 tugs, 2 repair, 1 div spt, 2 trg.

NAVAL AVIATION: 22 combat ac, 15 armed hel.

ASW: 1 sqn with 22 S-2A/E/TS-2A *Tracker* ac (Air Force aircraft, Air Force and Navy crews); 3 AB-204AS, 12 AB-212 ASW hel.

MARINES: 1 regt (4,000).
HQ, 3 bn, 1 arty bn (18 guns), spt units.

AIR FORCE: 58,000 (31,000 conscripts).
2 tac air forces, 1 tpt, 1 air trg comd.

FGA: 17 sqn:
5 (1 OCU) with F-5A/B (1 incl RF-5A, RT-33A recce);

4 (1 OCU) with F-4E (1 incl RF-4E recce);

3 with F-16 (1 OCU, 1 converting)

5 (1 OCU) with F/TF-104G.

FIGHTER: 2 sqn with F-104S/G, TF-104G.

RECCE: RF-5A, RF-4E (see FGA, above).

ASW: 1 sqn with S-2A/E *Tracker* (see Navy).

TRANSPORT: 4 sqn:
1 with C-130H and C-47;

1 with C-160D;

2 with C-47 (1 ECM/ELINT/SAR/calibration);

2 VIP tpt units with *Viscount* 794, C-47.

LIAISON:
3 HQ flt with C-47, AT-11, T-33 ac; UH-1H hel;

10 base flt with C-47, T-33 ac; UH-1H, UH-19B (Sikorsky S-55) hel.

TRAINING: 3 sqn: 1 with T-34, T-41; 1 with T-33, T-38; 1 with T-37; trg schools with C-47 ac, UH-1H hel.

SAM: 8 sqn with *Nike Hercules*; 2 *Rapier* sqn.

EQUIPMENT: 573 cbt ac (plus 167 in store), no attack hel.

AIRCRAFT:
F-16C/D: 100 (92 FGA, 8* -D trg).

F-5: 136. **-A:** 48 (FGA); **-B:** 10 (6 FGA, 4 recce); **RF-5A:** 18 (recce); **NF-5A/B:** 60 (FGA); plus some 44 in store.

F-4E: 143. 105 (FGA); 30 (OCU); **RF-4E:** 8 (recce); plus 30 in store.

F-104: 161. **-G:** 129 (FGA); **TF-104G:** 12 (10 FGA, 2 ftr); **-S:** 20 (ftr); plus 90 in store.

S-2A/E *Tracker*: 34.

C-130: 9 (tpt). **C-160D:** 20 (tpt). **Viscount:** 3 (VIP). **C-47:** 54 (38 tpt, 6 VIP, 10 trg). **Citation:** -11: 4, -111: 3. **CN-235:** 2 (tpt). **SF-260D:** 15 (trg) (VIP tpt). **BN-2A:** 2 (obs) **T-33:** 95 (60 trg/OCU, 30 liaison/OCU, 5 recce). **T-34:** 12 (trg). **T-37:** 30 trg; plus 12 in store. **T-38:** 28 (trg). **T-41:** 18 (trg).

HELICOPTERS:
UH-1H: 45+ (tpt, liaison, base flt, trg schools).

AS-330: 4.

SAM: 128 *Nike Hercules*, 24 *Rapier*.

DEPLOYMENT:
ARMY:

1st Army: HQ *Istanbul*: 4 Corps with 1 mech, 7 inf div; 5 armd, 2 inf bde, 1 armd regt.

2nd Army: HQ *Malatya*: (mainly located in Zone excluded from CFE): 2 Corps with 1 armd, 2 mech, 2 inf, 1 AB, 2 cdo bde.

3rd Army: HQ *Erzincan*: 2 Corps with 4 inf div; 2 armd (1 reserve), 2 mech, 4 inf bde (1 reserve).

4th Army: HQ *Izmir*: 1 inf trg div; 2 inf bde.

Force Tps: 1 Corps (Ankara) with 1 inf div; 1 mot inf, 1 inf trg, 1 arty trg bde; 1 Presidential guard regt. 1 Corps of 2 inf div (see Forces Abroad).

FORCES ABROAD:
CYPRUS: 1 corps of 2 inf div, (30,000); 300 M-48A5 MBT; 100 M-113, 100 M-59 APC; 144 105mm, 36 155mm, 8 203mm towed; 18

105mm, 6 155mm SP; 114 107mm mor; 84 40mm AA guns; 8 ac, 12 hel.

UN AND PEACEKEEPING
IRAQ/KUWAIT (UNIKOM): 7 Observers.

PARAMILITARY:
GENDARMERIE/NATIONAL GUARD: (Ministry of Interior, Ministry of Defence in war) 70,000 active, 50,000 reserve (being reorganized).
COAST GUARD: 1,100: 28 PCI, 8 PCI⟨, plus boats, 4 tpt.

FOREIGN FORCES:
NATO:
HQ Allied Land Forces South Eastern Europe (LANDSOUTHEAST).
HQ 6 Allied Tactical Air Force (6 ATAF).
US: 4,400. Army (800). Air (3,600): 1 tac, 1 air base gp. EC-111, F-111, A-10 at Inçirlik.
UK: Air (180): 8 *Jaguar*, 2 VC-10 Ac at Inçirlik.
FRANCE: Air (150): 8 *Mirage* F-1CR, 1C-135.

UNITED KINGDOM

GDP	1990:	£549.51bn ($980.74bn)	
	1991:	£575.36bn ($1,017.98bn)	
Growth	1990:	1.0%	1991: −2.1%
Inflation	1990:	9.5%	1991: 5.9%
Debt	1989:	$325.30bn	
Def exp	1990:	£21.80bn ($38.91bn)	
	1991:	£22.85bn ($40.43bn)	
Def bdgt	1991:	£24.42bn ($43.21bn);	
	1992:	£24.24bn ($41.20bn)	
NATO defn	1990:	£24.65bn ($43.61bn)	
$1 = £	1989:	0.6099	1990: 0.5603
	1991:	0.5652	1992: 0.5882

Population: 56,696,600

	13–17	*18–22*	*23–32*
Men	1,833,500	2,041,800	4,430,600
Women	1,744,300	1,942,300	4,253,900

TOTAL ARMED FORCES:
ACTIVE: 293,500 (incl 19,100 women and some 9,000 enlisted outside the UK).
RESERVES: 353,000.
Army: 268,800: Regular 188,600; Territorial Army (TA) 71,300; Home Service Force some 2,900. R Irish Regt 6,000 (3,000 part time).
Navy: 33,300: Regular 27,500; Volunteers and Auxiliary Service 5,800.
Marines: 3,900: Regular 2,700; Volunteers and Auxiliary Forces 1,200.
Air Force: 47,000: Regular 44,800; Volunteers and Auxiliary Forces 2,200.

STRATEGIC FORCES: (1,900).
SLBM: 32 msl in 2 SSBN:
2 *Resolution* SSBN each with 16 *Polaris* A-3TK msl. (Plus 1 in extended refit.)
Ballistic Missile Early Warning System (BMEWS) station at Fylingdales (to be upgraded).

ARMY: 145,400 (incl 7,800 women and 8,700 enlisted outside the UK, of whom some 7,300 are Gurkhas.)
(Note: regt are normally of bn size).
5 Military Districts, 1 corps HQ.
3 armd div (2 with 3 armd bde, 1 with 2 armd, 1 mech bde (*Saxon* in UK), all 3 arty, 1 engr, 1 avn regt, 1 AD bty).
corps tps: 1 arty bde (1 SSM, 3 hy, 2 AD regt), 2 armd recce, 4 engr regt.
1 mech bde (*Saxon*).
1 air mobile bde.
1 AB bde.
5 inf bde (2 reserve).
11 inf bde HQ (3 control ops in N. Ireland, remainder mixed regular and TA for trg/administrative purposes only).
3 engr bde HQ.
1 inf regt (2 active bn; 7 reserve bn with internal sy role in N. Ireland only).
Summary Combat Arm Units:
14 armd regt (incl 1 trg regt).
5 armd recce regt.
15 mech inf bn (7 FV 432, 8 *Saxon*).
6 armd inf bn (*Warrior*).
31 inf bn (incl 5 Gurkha).
3 AB bn (2 only in para role).
1 SF (SAS) regt.
19 arty regt (3 hy (incl 1 MLRS) 1 SSM with 12 *Lance* launchers; nuclear warheads withdrawn, 8 SP, 6 fd (incl 1 cdo, 1 AB), 1 locating).
3 AD regt (*Rapier*).
13 engr regt (incl 1 Gurkha, 1 amph, 1 armd).
5 avn regt (plus 1 forming).

RESERVES:
Territorial Army: 2 armd recce, 3 lt recce regt, 41 inf bn, 2 SF (SAS), 2 fd, 1 arty recce, 4 AD (*Blowpipe/Javelin*), 11 engr regt, 1 avn sqn.
Hong Kong Regiment. Gibraltar Regiment.

EQUIPMENT:
MBT: 1,318: 426 *Challenger*, some 850 *Chieftain*, 42 *Centurion*.
LIGHT TANKS: some 275 FV 101 *Scorpion*.
RECCE: some 315 FV 107 *Scimitar*, some 1,000 *Ferret*, some 350 *Fox*, 13 FV 601 *Saladin*, 11 *Fuchs*.
AIFV: some 605 *Warrior* (MCV-80), 13 FV 432 *Rarden*.
APC: 3,501: some 2,000 FV 432, some 250 FV 603 *Saracen*, some 411 FV 103 *Spartan*, some 527 AT-105 *Saxon*, 313 Humber.
TOTAL ARTY: 762.
TOWED ARTY: 345: 105mm: 212 L-118, 52 M-56; 140mm: 9 5.5-in; 155mm: 72 FH-70.

SP ARTY: 370: 105mm: 200 FV 433 *Abbot;*
155mm: 111 M-109A1, 3 SP-70 (trials); 175mm:
40 M-107; 203mm: 16 M-110 (to be withdrawn).
MRL: 227mm: some 47 MLRS.
MORTARS: 81mm: some 500 (incl 110 SP).
SSM: 14 *Lance* launchers (in store).
ATGW: ε1,100 *Milan* (incl 72 FV 103 *Spartan* SP),
87 *Swingfire* (FV 102 *Striker* SP), *TOW.*
RCL: 84mm: *Carl Gustav.*
SAM: *Blowpipe, Javelin* (incl 93 SP), *Starburst;* 120
Rapier (some 50 SP).
AIRCRAFT: 5 BN-2, 21 *Chipmunk* trg.
HELICOPTERS: 30 *Scout,* 159 SA-341, 138 *Lynx*
AH-1/-7/-9, 4 A-109.
LANDING CRAFT: 2 *Ardennes,* 9 *Arromanches* log; 4
Avon, LCVP⟨; 3 tugs, 28 other service vessels.

NAVY (RN): 62,100 (incl 6,100 Air, 7,600
Marines, 4,000 women and 300 enlisted outside
the UK).
ROYAL FLEET AUXILIARY (RFA): (2,550
civilians) man major spt vessels.
ROYAL MARITIME AUXILIARY SERVICE (RMAS):
(2,100 civilians) provides harbour/coastal services.
RESERVES:
ROYAL FLEET RESERVE: (20,300) Ex-regulars, no
trg commitment.
ROYAL NAVAL RESERVE (RNR): (4,700) 6 HQ
units, 11 Sea Trg Centres (STC), 12 Comms Trg
Centres (CTC), 1 MCM sqn: 10 MCMV, 19 PCI.
ROYAL NAVAL AUXILIARY SERVICE (RNXS):
(3,200) 72 auxiliary service units; Port HQ,
patrols, etc.
BASES: UK: Northwood (HQ Fleet, CINCHAN/
CINCEASTLANT), Devonport (HQ), Faslane,
Portland, Portsmouth, Rosyth (HQ). Overseas:
Gibraltar, Hong Kong.
SUBMARINES: 21:
STRATEGIC SUBMARINES: 2 SSBN (plus 1 in long
refit) (see p. 61).
TACTICAL SUBMARINES: 19:
SSN: 13 (incl 1 in refit):
7 *Trafalgar,* 5 *Swiftsure* all with Mk 24 HWT
and *Harpoon* USGW.
1 *Valiant* with Mk 24 HWT and *Harpoon .*
SS: 6:
3 *Upholder†* (incl 1 in refit) with Mk 24 HWT
and *Harpoon.*
3 *Oberon* with Mk 24 HWT.
PRINCIPAL SURFACE COMBATANTS: 43:
CARRIERS: 2 *Invincible* CVV (plus 1 in long refit);
each with **ac:** 8 *Sea Harrier* V/STOL; **hel:** 12 *Sea
King:* up to 9 ASW, 3 AEW; plus 1 × 2 *Sea Dart*
SAM.
DESTROYERS: 12 DDG (incl 1 in refit and 1
undergoing modernization):
12 *Birmingham* with 1 × 2 *Sea Dart* SAM; plus
1 *Lynx* hel, 2 × 3 ASTT, 1 × 114mm gun.

FRIGATES: 29 (incl 1 in refit):
4 *Cornwall* (Type 22 Batch 3) with 1 *Sea King* hel
(*Sting Ray* LWT), 2 × 3 ASTT; plus 2 × 4
Harpoon SSM, 1 × 114mm gun.
10 *Broadsword* (Type 22 Batch 1/2) with 2 *Lynx*
hel (2 with 1 × *Sea King*), 2 × 3 ASTT; plus 4
× MM-38 *Exocet* SSM (4 Batch 1 trg).
4 *Norfolk* (Type 23) with 1 × *Lynx* hel, 2 × 2
ASTT, plus 2 × 4 *Harpoon* SSM, 1 × 114mm gun.
6 *Amazon* with 1 *Lynx* hel, 2 × 3 ASTT; plus 4 ×
MM-38 *Exocet,* 1 × 114mm gun.
5 *Leander:*
4 (Batch 2/3A) with 1 *Lynx* hel, 2 × 3 ASTT;
plus 4 × MM-38 *Exocet.*
1 (Batch 2) trg with 2 × 3 ASTT.
PATROL AND COASTAL COMBATANTS: 27:
OFFSHORE: 13 PCO: 1 *Polar Circle,* 2 *Castle,* 7
Jersey, 3 *Peacock.*
INSHORE: 14 PCI: 3 *Kingfisher,* 1 *Manly* (trg), 10⟨.
MINE WARFARE: 32:
MINELAYER: No dedicated minelayer, but all
submarines have limited minelaying capability.
MINE COUNTERMEASURES: 32:
13 *Brecon* MCO.   5 *Ton* MHC.
3 *Sandown* MHC.   1 *Wilton* MHC, trg.
10 *Waveney* MSO (with RNR).
AMPHIBIOUS: 6:
1 *Fearless* LPD with 4 LCU, 4 LCVP; capacity
400 tps, 15 tk, 3 hel.
1 *Sir Galahad,* 4 *Sir Lancelot* LST: capacity 340
tps, 16 tk (*Sir G.* 18), 1 hel (RFA manned).
Plus 32 craft: 15 LCU, 17 LCVP.
Note: See Army for additional amph lift capability.
SUPPORT AND MISCELLANEOUS: 32:
UNDERWAY SUPPORT: 10:
3 *Olwen,* 4 *Green Rover* AO, 2 *Fort Grange,* 1
Resource AEF.
MAINTENANCE/LOGISTIC: 11:
1 AR, 4 AOT, 3 AE, 3 AT.
SPECIAL PURPOSE: 6:
1 AVT, 1 trg (chartered), 3 trials/research,
1 Royal Yacht.
SURVEY: 5 AGHS.
(26 of above civilian manned, either RFA or RMAS).
In store (not counted above): 1 LPD, 2 MSO, 1 AEF.

FLEET AIR ARM (FAA): 6,100
FIGHTER/ATTACK: 3 ac sqn with *Sea Harrier* FRS-1.
ASW: 6 hel sqn with *Sea King* HAS-5;
ASW/ATTACK: 2 sqn with *Lynx* HAS-2/-3 (in indep flt).
AEW: 1 hel sqn with *Sea King* AEW-2, 1 sqn with
Sea King Mk5.
COMMANDO SUPPORT: 3 hel sqn with *Sea King* HC-4.
SAR: 1 hel sqn with *Sea King* HC-4.
TRAINING: 2 sqn: 1 with *Jetstream* ac; 1 with SA-341
Gazelle HT-2 hel.
FLEET SUPPORT: *Canberra* T-18/-22, *Hunter* T-7/-8,
GA-11, PR-11, 3 *Mystère-Falcon* 20 (civil
registration, operated under contract).

LIAISON: HS-125 (VIP, operated by RAF), *Sea Heron, Sea Devon.*
EQUIPMENT: 45 cbt ac, 153 armed hel.
AIRCRAFT:
Sea Harrier/Harrier: 45. *Sea Harrier* **FRS-1:** 40 (some being mod to FRS-2). **T-4N:** 5* (trg).
Canberra: 2 (spt). 3 in store.
Hunter: 19 (spt, trg), (plus 12 in store).
HS-125: 2 (VIP tpt); *Mystère-Falcon 20:* 11 (spt);
Jetstream: 19. **T-2:** 15 (trg); **T-3:** 4 (trg);
Chipmunk: 14 (trg plus 2 in store).
HELICOPTERS:
Sea King: 120. **HAS-5:** 76 (51 ASW, 25* trg). **HC-4:** 34 (cdo). **AEW-2:** 10.
Lynx: 77. **HAS-2:** 55. **HAS-3:** 22.
Gazelle **HT-2/-3:** 26 (trg plus 5 in store).
MISSILES:
ASM: *Sea Skua, Sea Eagle.*
AAM: AIM-9 *Sidewinder.*

MARINES (RM): (7,600).

1 cdo bde: 3 cdo; 1 cdo arty regt (Army) + 1 bty (TA); 2 cdo engr sqn (1 Army, 1 TA), 1 log regt (joint Service); 1 lt hel sqn.
1 mtn and arctic warfare cadre.
Special Boat Service (SF): HQ: 5 sqn.
1 aslt sqn (6 landing craft).
1 gp *(Commachio).*
EQUIPMENT:
ATGW: *Milan.*
SAM: *Javelin, Blowpipe.*
HELICOPTERS: 8 SA-341, 6 *Lynx* AH-1.

AIR FORCE (RAF): 86,000 (incl 7,300 women).
FGA/BOMBER: 9 sqn: (nuclear capable)
7 with *Tornado* GR-1;
2 with *Buccaneer* S-2A/B (maritime strike, with *Sea Eagle* ASM).
FGA: 5 sqn:
3 with *Harrier*; GR-5/-7.
2 with *Jaguar.*
FIGHTER: 9 sqn, plus 1 flt:
2 with *Phantom*; plus 1 flt (Falklands).
7 with *Tornado* F-3.
RECCE: 2 sqn with *Tornado* GR-1A; 1 photo-recce unit with *Canberra* PR-9, 1 sqn with *Jaguar.*
MR: 4 sqn with *Nimrod* MR-2.
AEW: 1 sqn with 7 *Sentry* E-3D.
ECM/ELINT: 2 sqn: 1 ECM with *Canberra*, 1 ELINT with *Nimrod* R-1.
TANKER: 3 sqn: 1 with *Victor* K-2; 1 with VC-10 K-2/-3; 1 with *Tristar* K-1/KC-1 (tkr/tpt).
TRANSPORT: 5 sqn:
1 strategic with VC-10 C-1.
4 tac with *Hercules* C-1/-1K/-1P/-3P.
LIAISON: 1 comms sqn with HS-125, *Andover* ac; SA-341E hel.
Queen's Flt: BAe -146-100, *Wessex* hel.
CALIBRATION: 2 sqn: 1 with *Andover* E-3/-3A (Airborne Radio Relay);

1 cal/target facility with *Canberra* B-2/E-15/T-4/TT-18.
OCU: 7: *Tornado* GR-1, *Tornado* F-3, *Jaguar* GR-1A/T2A, *Harrier* GR-3/5, *Canberra* B-2/T-4, *Hercules*, SA-330/CH-47.
1 wpn conversion unit with *Tornado* GR-1.
2 tac wpn units with *Hawk* T-1A.
TRAINING: *Hawk* T-1A, *Jet Provost, Jetstream* T-1, *Bulldog* T-1, *Chipmunk* T-10, HS-125 *Dominie* T-1, *Tucano* T-1.
TACTICAL HELICOPTERS: 6 sqn: 1 with CH-47; 1 with CH-47 and SA-330; 2 with *Wessex* HC-2; 2 with SA-330.
SAR: 2 hel sqn; 9 flt: 4 with *Wessex* HC-2; 5 with *Sea King* HAR-3.
TRAINING: *Wessex*, SA-341.
EQUIPMENT: 466 cbt ac (plus 273 in store), no armed hel.
AIRCRAFT:
Tornado: 198: **GR-1:** 120 (72 strike, 6 recce, 18* in tri-national trg sqn (Cottesmore), 24* in wpn conversion unit); **F-2/3:** 78 (60 ftr, 18* OCU); plus 112 in store (29 F-2/-3, 83 GR-1).
Buccaneer: 23, plus 38 in store.
Jaguar: 53 (43 FGA, 10* OCU); plus 32 in store.
Harrier: 66. **GR-3/-5/-7:** 57 (43 FGA, 14* OCU); **T-4:** 9, 3* (on sqns), 6* (OCU); plus 61 in store.
Phantom: **FGR-2:** 26; plus 30 in store.
Hawk: 144 (70* tac weapons unit (*Sidewinder*-capable), 74 trg).
Canberra: 20. **T-4:** 3 (trg); **PR-7:** 2 (trg); **PR-9:** 5 (recce); **T-17:** 10 (ECM); plus 8 in store.
Nimrod: 33. **R-1:** 3 (ECM); **MR-2:** 30* (MR); plus 3 MR-2 in store.
Sentry (E-3D): 7 (AEW).
Victor: 8 (tanker) plus 3 in store.
Tristar: 8. **K-1:** 2 (tanker/tpt); **KC-1:** 4 (tanker/cgo); **C-2:** 2 (tpt) plus 1 in store.
VC-10: 19. **C-1:** 10 (strategic tpt to be mod to tanker/tpt); **K-2:** 5 (tanker); **K-3:** 4 (tanker) plus 9 in store.
Hercules: 54. **C-1:** 5 (OCU); **C-1K:** 6; **C-1/-3:** 43, plus 8 in store.
Andover: 16 (8 cal, 8 liaison).
HS-125: 24; **T-1:** 12 (trg); **CC-1/-2/-3:** 12 (liaison) plus 7 in store.
BAe-146: 3 (VIP tpt).
Jet Provost: 70 (trg) plus 35 in store.
Tucano: 100 (trg).
Jetstream: 10 (trg) plus 1 in store.
Bulldog: 117 (trg).
Chipmunk: 66 (trg) plus 12 in store.
HELICOPTERS:
Wessex: 64 (36 tac tpt, 11 SAR, 15 OCU, 2 VIP).
CH-47: 31 (25 tac tpt, 6 OCU) plus 3 in store.
SA-330: 42 (37 tac tpt, 5 OCU) plus 1 in store.
Sea King: 17 (15 SAR, 2 OCU) plus 2 in store.
SA-341: 28 (liaison, trg) plus 2 in store.

MISSILES:
ASM: *Martel*, AGM-84A *Harpoon*, *Sea Eagle*.
AAM: AIM-9B/D/G *Sidewinder*, AIM-7E *Sparrow*,
Sky Flash.
ARM: ALARM.

ROYAL AIR FORCE REGIMENT:

2 wing HQ.	2 fd sqn.
3 lt armd sqn.	5 SAM sqn (*Rapier*).

EQUIPMENT:
37 *Scorpion* lt tk; 114 *Spartan* APC, 13 *Saracen*
APC, 80 *Rapier* SAM.
RESERVES (Royal Auxiliary Air Force Regiment):
6 fd def sqn; 2 lt AA gun sqn with 12 × twin
35mm *Oerlikon* and *Skyguard*.

DEPLOYMENT:
ARMY:
United Kingdom Land Forces (UKLF):
Reinforcements for 1 (BR) Corps (declared to
NORTHAG).
   regular: 1 air-mobile bde, 1 arty regt, 1
     avn sqn. TA: 2 inf bde, 2 arty regt.
   1 mech bde (for armd div).
   Additional TA units incl 18 inf bn, 2 SAS, 1 arty
     recce, 4 AD (*Blowpipe*) regt.
Allied Command Europe Mobile Force (*Land*)
(AMF(L)): (some 2,300): UK contribution: 1 inf
bn, 1 arty bty, 1 sigs sqn, 1 log bn.
HQ Northern Ireland: (some 12,000 plus 6,000
(incl part time) for service in Northern Ireland
only): 3 inf bde HQ, up to 12 major units in inf
role (6 resident, 6 roulement inf bn), 1 engr sqn,
1 avn regt. 7 inf bn (service in NI only).
Remainder of Army regular and TA units for
Home Defence.
NAVY:
FLEET: (CinC is also CINCEASTLANT).
   Regular Forces, with the exception of most Patrol
   and Coastal Combatants, Mine Warfare and
   Support forces are declared to NATO or
   EASTLANT.
MARINES: 1 cdo bde (declared to AFNORTH).
AIR FORCE:
STRIKE COMMAND: (CinC is also CINCUKAIR).
   Commands all combat air operations other than
   for RAF (Germany), Belize and Falklands: 3
   Groups: No. 1 (Strike, Attack, Transport), No
   11 (Air Defence), No 18 (Maritime).
SUPPORT COMMAND: trg, supply and maint spt
   of other comds.

OVERSEAS:
ANTARCTICA: 1 ice patrol ship (in summer).
ASCENSION ISLAND: RAF: *Hercules* C-1K det.
BELIZE: 1,500. Army: some 1,200; 1 inf bn, 1
armd recce tp, 1 fd arty bty, 1 engr sqn, 1 hel flt
(3 *Gazelle* AH-1). RAF: 300; 1 flt (4 *Harrier*

GR-3 FGA, 4 *Puma* hel), 1 *Rapier* AD det (4 fire
units) RAF Regt.
BRUNEI: Army: some 800: 1 Gurkha inf bn, 1 hel
flt (3 hel).
CANADA: Army: trg and liaison unit. RAF:
Tornado det.
CYPRUS: 4,200. Army: 2,700.
2 inf bn, 1 armd recce, 1 engr spt sqn, 1 hel flt.
Navy: 2 PCI.
RAF: 1,500: 1 hel sqn (*Wessex*), det of *Phantom*,
Tornado ac, 1 lt armd sqn RAF Regt.
FALKLAND ISLANDS: some 1,600. Army: 1 inf coy
gp, 1 engr sqn (fd, plant). RN: 1 DD/FF, 1
patrol, 1 AO, 1 AR. RAF: 1 *Phantom* flt, 6
Hercules C-1K, 3 *Sea King* HAR-3, 6 CH-47 hel,
1 sqn RAF regt (*Rapier* SAM).
(Garrison may vary throughout the year.)
GERMANY: 62,800. Army (BAOR declared to
NORTHAG): 50,000; 1 corps HQ; 3 armd div; 1
arty bde, 2 armd recce, 7 engr regt. Berlin Inf
Bde: 2,800; 3 inf bn, 1 armd, 1 engr sqn. RAF:
10,000 (declared to 2 ATAF); 6 ac sqn, 1 hel sqn:
4 *Tornado*, 2 *Harrier*, (1 SA-330/CH-47 (tpt)).
RAF regt: 1 Wing HQ; 2 *Rapier* SAM, 1 lt armd
sqn. Berlin: (700).
GIBRALTAR: 1,000. Army: 100; Gibraltar regt
(400). Navy/Marines: 500; 2 PCI, Marine det, 2
twin *Exocet* launchers (coast defence), base unit.
RAF: 400; periodic *Jaguar* ac det.
MEDITERRANEAN: 1 FF/DD STANAVFORMED.
HONG KONG: 6,500. Army: 5,700 (British 1,600,
Gurkha 4,100). Gurkha inf bde with 1 UK, 3
Gurkha inf bn, 1 Gurkha engr regt, 1 hel sqn (−)
with 10 *Scout* AH-1, 3 small landing craft, 3 other
vessels. Navy/Marines: 500 (300 locally enlisted);
3 *Peacock* PCC, (12 patrol boats in local service).
RAF: 300; 1 *Wessex* hel sqn (10 HC-2) (until
1997). Reserves: Hong Kong regt (1,200).
INDIAN OCEAN (Operation Armilla): 2 DD/FF, 1
spt ship. Diego Garcia: 1 naval party, 1 Marine det.
NEPAL: Army: 1,200 (Gurkha trg org).
TURKEY: (Incirlic). Army: 30. RAF: 150; 8 *Jaguar*,
2 VC-10.
WEST INDIES (see also Belize): 1 DD/FF.
MILITARY ADVISERS: 455 in 30 countries.

UN AND PEACEKEEPING:
CAMBODIA (UNTAC): 38 Observers, 70 naval, 13
mine clearance.
CROATIA (UNPROFOR) 263: 3 Observers, 1
medical unit.
CYPRUS (UNFICYP): 789: 1 inf bn(-), 1 armd recce
sqn, 1 hel flt, engr and log spt (incl spt for UNIFIL).
EGYPT (MFO): 31 admin and spt.
IRAQ/KUWAIT (UNIKOM): 15 Observers.
WESTERN SAHARA (MINURSO): 15 Observers.

FOREIGN FORCES:
US: 20,100. Navy (2,400). Air (17,700):
1 Air Force HQ, 180 cbt ac trg.
GERMANY/ITALY: Tri-national *Tornado* trg sqn.

Non-NATO Europe

Political Developments

The three Baltic republics: **Estonia, Latvia** and **Lithuania** declared their independence on 20 August 1991, and this was recognized by the European Community on 27 August and by the USSR on 1 September. The USSR itself broke up in December 1991, shortly after Ukraine's referendum vote in favour of independence. By 18 December Gorbachev had acknowledged the end of the Soviet Union, and on 21 December the republics of the former USSR, with the exception of Georgia, agreed to form the 'Commonwealth of Independent States' (CIS). All of the republics of the former USSR have been admitted to the United Nations, and have joined the Conference for Security and Cooperation in Europe (CSCE) and the North Atlantic Cooperation Council (NACC). The armed forces of Armenia, Azerbaijan, Byelarus, Georgia, Moldova and Ukraine are covered in this section.

Yugoslavia began to disintegrate in 1991 and the process worsened in 1992. Slovenia, Croatia and Bosnia-Herzegovina have been recognized as independent states by the US, the EC and others, and were admitted to the United Nations on 22 May 1992. In mid-1992, however, recognition of Macedonia's independence was still being withheld as a result of Greek reservations. A United Nations peacekeeping force (UNPROFOR) has been deployed to Croatia following the establishment of a cease-fire by the EC monitoring teams, coupled with successful negotiations by Lord Carrington, the Chairman of the EC-sponsored peace conference. The UN force originally had no mandate to operate in Bosnia, although it had planned to base its HQ in Sarajevo. In June 1992, however, the mandate was enlarged to allow UNPROFOR to supervise the withdrawal of anti-aircraft and heavy weapons in order to reopen the airport. The intensity of the fighting there has led to the temporary withdrawal of the EC monitoring teams. The Federal Republic of Yugoslavia (FRY), comprising **Serbia** and **Montenegro** was established on 27 April 1992. On 30 May the UN Security Council adopted Resolution 757, which imposed a number of mandatory sanctions on the FRY concerning trade, economic cooperation, movement of aircraft, sport and diplomatic representation. A naval monitoring force coordinated by the WEU was established on 10 July 1992.

Russia has agreed to the withdrawal from **Poland** of all troops by 15 November 1992, bar a small group to coordinate the transit of troops from Germany. No agreement has been reached yet on a programme of withdrawal of forces from the Baltic States. Russia is still insisting that this must wait until after the withdrawal from Germany, due to be completed in 1994.

The fourth CSCE follow-up meeting began in Helsinki on 24 March 1992.

Albania joined NACC on 5 June 1992. It was the first country to join which was neither a member of NATO, nor a member of the Warsaw Pact at the time of its dissolution, nor a republic of the former Soviet Union. Finland attended the June meeting as an observer.

The dissolution of the **Czechoslovakian** Federation, which was heralded by the overwhelming majority won by the Movement for Democratic Slovakia in the Slovak elections, is scheduled to take place by 30 September 1992, by which time the Federal Assembly is expected to have passed the necessary constitutional law. Discussions on the future of the armed forces are taking place; the Eastern Military District could form the basis for Slovak armed forces. The Czechoslovak Defence Minister has given assurances that until two separate armies are operationally ready, the armed forces will remain under joint command.

Arms Control

Byelarus and **Ukraine**, together with Kazakhstan, Russia and the US, signed a protocol to the START Treaty in Madrid on 23 May 1992, in which the republics of the former USSR committed themselves to assuming the obligations of the former USSR. Byelarus and Ukraine further committed themselves to adhere to the Treaty on the Non-Proliferation of Nuclear Weapons as non-nuclear weapon states in the shortest possible time. All tactical nuclear weapons had been withdrawn from Byelarus by 28 April 1992 and from Ukraine by 5 May 1992.

At Tashkent on 15 May 1992, Armenia, Azerbaijan, Byelarus, Georgia, Kazakhstan, Moldova, Russia and Ukraine signed a Joint Declaration in connection with the Treaty on Conventional Armed Forces in Europe (CFE). In this they committed themselves to fulfil the obligations of the Treaty as successor states of the USSR. They agreed on apportionment of treaty limited equipment (TLE) between them in conformity with the geographical sub-limits imposed by CFE. Items which were the subject of protocols to CFE were also apportioned: land-based naval aircraft, Mi-24 helicopters not subject to the limits on attack helicopters, TLE held by Coastal Defence, Naval Infantry and Strategic Rocket Forces.

It has been agreed that the territory of the Baltic states does not form part of the Atlantic to the Urals (ATTU) zone. Russia agreed at Tashkent to fulfil the obligations of CFE in regard to forces and TLE stationed in the Baltic states, and also in Germany and Poland.

Details of the apportionment are set out in the essay on 'Conventional Forces in Europe' on pp. 237–44. On 5 June 1992, the 16 NATO and five East European states along with eight republics of the former USSR, re-signed CFE. NACC called on all states to ratify the Treaty so that it could come into force by the Helsinki summit meeting of the CSCE on 9–10 July 1992.

Military Developments

There have been few significant changes to the order of battle and equipment holdings of the non-NATO European countries. The former members of the Warsaw Pact await the ratification of CFE before embarking on the destruction of surplus equipment; some effort has been made to sell surplus armaments before treaty ratification ends that as a means of disposal. They continue to plan and implement the reorganization and relocation of their forces in the changed strategic situation in which they find themselves.

The opening up of **Albania** has provided improved information. The armed forces have some 8,000 fewer men than previously reported; there are seven more infantry brigades but these are cadre formations. Tank holdings are much larger at 590, as against the 190 listed in *The Military Balance 1991–1992*; they are all T-34 or T-54. The navy has over 20 more fast inshore patrol craft, and the air force 20 more J-6 fighters than previously listed.

In **Bulgaria** four motor rifle divisions have been converted into Regional Training Centres, presumably on the Soviet model and with a mobilization role. *The Military Balance* incorrectly showed a drop in the number of *Poti*-class ASW corvettes last year; the correct holding is six, one more than listed in 1990–91. **Czechoslovak** Army manpower has been reduced by 15,000 men. There are now three, as opposed to two, ground force regional commands. A reorganization of divisions has taken place; there are three tank (previously five), and four mechanized (five MRD) active divisions with the ability to mobilize seven more (four mechanized and three infantry). Three SSM brigades have been disbanded and all *Scud* and *FROG* SSM put into store. There is now one SSM regiment equipped with eight SS-21. The MiG-21 aircraft shown as trainers in *The Military Balance 1991–1992* have been formed into an operational squadron. The main part of the armed forces are still located in the Czech-lands; the two tank training divisions in Slovakia have been converted to active divisions, one tank and one mechanized. From 1 October 1992 conscripts will only serve in units located in their parent republic. There has been a reduction of 6,000 men in the strength of the **Hungarian** Army. The Corps have been renamed Military Districts. The manpower of the **Polish** armed forces has been reduced by 45,000 men (39,000 army, 6,000 air force). A fourth Military District, the Krakow, has been formed, covering the southern part of the Warsaw Military District. One mobilization division has been upgraded. A small number of army equipment increases have been noted (17 more *Dana* 155mm SP guns, 16 2S12 120mm SP mortars, and 4 SS-21 SSM, the first in Polish units). The navy has sold 14 *Polnocny* LSM, leaving only one still in service. The air force has transferred some 30 MiG-21 fighters to naval aviation, giving the navy its first fixed-wing aircraft. The **Romanian** Army has disbanded two airborne brigades. Some 400 TABC-79 locally-produced armoured reconnaissance vehicles are now in service and 16 more Model 89 122mm SP guns have been acquired. The navy has commissioned one more *Tetal*-class frigate. In mid-1991 a mechanized division was converted to a naval infantry force comprising an infantry division and a tank regiment. It is some 5,000-men strong, with around 300 tanks, 100mm, 122mm and 152mm towed artillery and 122mm MRL.

The situation regarding the armed forces of the former Soviet Union differs from republic to republic. In **Byelarus** and **Ukraine** it is clear that, with the exception of the strategic nuclear forces, all armed forces have been taken over by the republics. A decision has been made to split the Black Sea Fleet between Georgia, Russia and Ukraine, but the details have not been agreed. However, the Tashkent Declaration shows that Naval Aviation, Naval Infantry and Coastal Defence Troops will belong to Ukraine. In **Moldova** a proportion of the troops are being transferred. Those subordinate to the 14th army, however (mainly based in the Dnestr province) will not be transferred and will be withdrawn to Russia, but not for some years. The former Soviet Army has not become involved in the fighting in Georgia, or between Armenia and Azerbaijan, and is considered to be under the jurisdiction of Russia. All three Transcaucasian Republics are establishing their own armed forces. In general, these are lightly armed, but with some heavy weapons, including tanks, artillery and MRL, either stolen from or perhaps handed over by army units, as has recently been reported.

In **Cyprus** the National Guard has added a number of items to its weapons inventory: 12 more AMX-30B-2 MBT, 36 more 105mm towed artillery pieces, nine 155mm TR-F1 guns, their first SP artillery – 12 F3 155mm guns, and 114 RT61 120mm mortars. The armed forces of **Malta** have been reorganized; there are now three regiments. The first has been converted to the equivalent of a standard infantry battalion, the second contains the air, air defence and maritime units, and the third or 'depot' regiment contains logistic and administrative elements.

Finnish armed forces have received some new equipment. The army has an additional 50 A-180 *Sisu* APCs and has acquired its first SP artillery – 18 2S5 152mm guns. The navy has commissioned two more *Rauma*-class fast patrol craft armed with RBS-15SF SSM, with a fourth craft to become operational before the end of 1992. Two new minelayers have also commissioned: the *Hämeenmaa* is a 1,000-ton ship, capable of laying 120 mines; the *Pansio* is the first of a class of three, has strengthened ramps fore and aft and so can also be used as a landing craft. Its capacity is 50 mines or 100 tons of vehicles and cargo. Finland is to buy 64 F/A-18 *Hornet* fighter-attack aircraft, with delivery commencing in 1995.

The **Swedish** Navy has also commissioned two more *Göteburg*-class fast missile craft armed with eight RBS-15 SSM; a fourth ship in the class will become available in 1993. The air force has increased from 105 to 140 its holdings of SK-60 trainers, which also have a light-attack/reconnaissance capability. The **Swiss** Army has increased its holding of *Leopard* 2 MBT (Swiss designation Pz-87) from 180 to 275 and has retired some hundred *Centurions* (Pz-55/-57). A further 140 MOWAG *Piranha* with *TOW*-2 ATGW have been delivered. The air force has retired over 40 *Hunter* FGA aircraft. Parliament has approved the principle of purchasing 34 F/A-18 aircraft, but no action will be taken until the result of the referendum to be held in July 1993 is known. A plan, *Army* 95, to reduce the army's mobilizable strength from 625,000 to 400,000 has been announced. Recruit training will be cut from 17 to 15 weeks, and reservist refresher training will be standardized at 19 days every second year over a 20-year period.

The situation regarding armed forces in the territory that was **Yugoslavia** is less than clear. FRY forces – the Yugoslav National Army (JNA) – remain loyal to the Federal President and, in effect, to Serbia. The JNA has withdrawn all its forces from Croatia, Slovenia, Macedonia and most, if not all, from Bosnia, although individual soldiers may well have been detached to join their local militia. The air force appears still to be totally under JNA control, while the navy has split between **Croatia** where most of the naval facilities were located and JNA/Serbia operating out of Montenegran ports. The independent republics have few tanks, artillery or other heavy weapons. Their forces are to a large extent based on the former Territorial Defence organization.

This section now includes **Estonia**, **Latvia** and **Lithuania**. They are all forming their own defence forces, which will be modest in size and armament. Priority is being given to Border Troops. Progress in establishing forces has been slow due mainly to lack of finance, but also to a lack of the necessary expertise, to a general reluctance to volunteer for service, and to the exemptions from conscript service (given in Latvia to students, farm workers and 'sole providers').

ALBANIA

GNP	1989ε:	lekë 24.40bn ($3.80bn)
	1990ε:	lekë 28.10bn ($3.24bn)
Growth	1990ε:	−13%	1991ε:	−35%
Inflation	1990ε:	30%	1991ε:	100%
Debt	1990ε:	$350m	1991ε:	$500m
Def bdgt[a]	1990ε:	lekë 1.030bn ($160.29m)
	1991ε:	lekë 950m ($103.19m)
$1 = lekë	1988:	5.50	1989:	5.63
	1990:	6.42	1991ε:	25.0

[a] Dollar values are estimated.

Population: 3,417,000

	13–17	18–22	23–32
Men	176,900	165,900	302,100
Women	170,000	158,400	291,400

TOTAL ARMED FORCES:
ACTIVE: 40,000 (22,400 conscripts).
Terms of service: 18 months.
RESERVES: 155,000 (to age 56): Army 150,000, Navy/Air Force 5,000.

ARMY: 27,000 (20,000 conscripts).
4 Military Districts.
1 tk bde.
11 inf bde (7 cadre).
3 arty regt.
6 lt coastal arty bn.
1 engr regt.
EQUIPMENT:†
MBT: 597: 229 T-34, 368 T-54/-59. (ε only 70 T-34, 30 T-54/-59 op)
RECCE: 15 BRDM-1.
APC: 150: BTR-40/-50/-152, Ch Type-531, 46 Ch Type-77-1. (ε 80 op)
TOWED ARTY: 122mm: M-1931/37, 120 M-1938, Ch Type-60; 130mm: Ch Type-59-1;
152mm: M-1937, 90 Ch Type-66, D-1.
MRL: 107mm: Ch Type-63.
MORTARS: 82mm: 259; 120mm: 58; 160mm: 64.
RCL: 82mm: T-21.
ATK GUNS: 45mm: M-1942; 57mm: M-1943;
85mm: 61 D-44, Ch Type-56; 100mm: 34 Type-86.
AD GUNS: 23mm: 12 ZU-23-2/ZPU-1; 37mm: 140 M-1939; 57mm: 82 S-60; 85mm: 30 KS-12; 100mm: 56.

NAVY: ε2,000 (ε1,000 conscripts). Additional 400 may serve in coast defence.†
BASES: Durrës, Vlorë, Sazan Island.
SUBMARINES: 2 Sov *Whiskey* with 533mm TT (plus 1 trg, unserviceable).

PATROL AND COASTAL COMBATANTS: 60:
TORPEDO CRAFT: 30 Ch *Huchwan* PHT with 2 × 533mm TT.
PATROL: 30:
3 Sov *Kronshtadt* PCO; 12 P4 PFI⟨, 6 Ch *Shanghai*-II and some 9 Sov PO-2 PFI⟨ (border guards).
MINE WARFARE: 4 Sov T-301 MSI;
SUPPORT: 1 Sov *Khobi* harbour tanker.

AIR FORCE: 11,000 (1,400 conscripts);
112 cbt ac†, no armed hel.
FGA: 3 sqn:
1 with 10 J-2;
2 with 12 J-4, 20 J-6.
FIGHTER: 3 sqn:
2 with 50 J-6;
1 with 20 J-7.
TRANSPORT: 1 sqn with 10 C-5 (An-2), 3 Il-14M, 6 Li-2.
HELICOPTERS: 2 sqn with 28 Ch Z-5.
TRAINING: 8 CJ-5, 10 MiG-15UTI, 6 Yak-11.
SAM:† some 4 SA-2 sites, 22 launchers.

PARAMILITARY: 16,000.
INTERNAL SECURITY FORCE: (5,000).
PEOPLE'S MILITIA: (3,500).

ARMENIA

GDP	1991:	r 15.7bn ($9.22bn)
Growth	1991:	−19%
Inflation[a]	1991:	100%
Debt	1991:	$750m
Def bdgt[b]	1992:	r 250m
$1 = r	1991:	1.70

Population: 3,293,000 (1.5% Russian)

13–17	18–22	23–32
309,100	279,900	428,100

[a] Year average
[b] Provisional draft budget; 1991 roubles

TOTAL ARMED FORCES:
Terms of service: conscription,
RESERVES: Some mobilization reported, possibly 300,000 with military service within 15 years.

ARMY: Armed forces of up to 50,000 reported incl 2 MRD.

PARAMILITARY:
Military: ε30,000.

FOREIGN FORCES:
RUSSIA (Trans-Caucasus MD)
Army: 23,000: 1 army HQ, 4 MRD, 2 arty regt, 250 MBT, 350 AIFV, 350 arty/MRL/mors, 7 attack hel. Air Defence: 80 SAM.

AUSTRIA

GDP	1990: OS 1,792.30bn ($157.63bn)	
	1991ε: OS 1,926.60bn ($165.01bn)	
Growth	1990: 4.6%	1991ε: 3.6%
Inflation	1990: 3.2%	1991: 3.3%
Debt	1990: $32bn	
Def bdgt	1991: OS 19.60bn ($1.68bn)	
	1992ε: OS 19.86bn ($1.70bn)	
$1 = OS	1990: 11.370	1991: 11.676
	1992: 11.700	

OS = schilling

Population: 7,544,400

	13–17	18–22	23–32
Men	235,000	269,700	620,600
Women	224,900	258,700	600,800

TOTAL ARMED FORCES: (Air Service
forms part of the Army):
ACTIVE: some 52,000 (ε22,400 conscripts; some 66,000 reservists a year undergo refresher training, a proportion at a time).
Terms of service: 6 months recruit trg, 60 days reservist refresher trg during 15 years (or 8 months trg, no refresher); 60–90 days additional for officers, NCO and specialists.
RESERVES: 200,000 ready (72 hrs) reserves; 960,000 with reserve trg but no commitment, all ranks to age 50.

ARMY: 46,000 (19,500 conscripts).
Field Units:
Corps: 3 HQ, 3 arty (cadre), 1 guard, 1 SF bn, 1 SP ATK, 2 AA (cadre), 2 engr bn (cadre), 2 log regt (cadre).
3 mech bde (each 1 tk, 1 mech inf, 1 SP arty; 2 with 1 SP ATK bn); 1 recce bn (cadre), 1 AA, 1 engr bn.
1 air-mobile, 1 mtn bn.
9 Provincial Commands.
Peacetime: trg and maint.
On mob: equates to div HQ (with 1 inf bde, 1 or more territorial defence regt and indep units).
30 *Landwehrstammregimenter* (trg regt, no war role):
RESERVES:
8 inf bde HQ: with 25 inf, 8 arty bn.

Territorial Tps: (82,000):
25 inf regt, 90 inf coy, 38 guard coy; 18 hy, 14 lt inf, 15 inf/ATK bn, 5 hy arty bty (static), 13 engr, 6 ATK coy.
EQUIPMENT:
MBT: 159 M-60A3.
APC: 460 Saurer 4K4E/F.
TOWED ARTY: 105mm: 108 IFH (M-2A1); 155mm: 24 M-114.
SP ARTY: 155mm: 54 M-109A2.
FORTRESS ARTY: 155mm: 24 SFK M-2.
MRL: 128mm: 18 M-51.
MORTARS: 81mm: 700; 107mm: 82 M-2; 120mm: 240 M-43.
ATGW: 73 RBS-56 *Bill*.
RCL: 74mm: *Miniman*; 84mm: *Carl Gustav*; 106mm: 446 M-40A1.
ATK GUNS:
  SP: 105mm: 225 *Kuerassier* JPz SK.
  TOWED: 85mm: 220 M-52/-55;
  STATIC: 90mm: some 60 M-47 tk turrets; 105mm: some 200 L7A1 (*Centurion* tk);
AD GUNS: 20mm: 560; 35mm: 74 GDF-002 twin towed; 40mm: 38 M-42A1 twin SP.
MARINE WING (under School of Military Engineering): 2 river patrol craft⟨; 10 unarmed boats.

AIR FORCE: 6,000 (2,400 conscripts)
54 cbt ac, no armed hel.
1 air div HQ; 3 air regt; 3 AD bn.
FGA: 1 regt with 30 SAAB 105 Oe.
FIGHTER: 1 regt with 24 J-35Oe.
HELICOPTERS:
  RECCE: 12 OH-58B, 12 AB-206A.
  TRANSPORT: (med): 23 AB-212; (lt): 8 AB-204 (9 in store).
  SAR: 24 A-316 B *Alouette*.
LIAISON: 1 sqn with 2 *Skyvan* 3M, 15 O-1 (10 -A, 5 -E), 11 PC-6B.
TRAINING: 16 PC-7.
AD: 3 bn with 36 20mm, 18 M-65 twin 35mm AA guns; *Super-Bat* and *Skyguard* AD, *Goldhaube*, Selenia MR(S-403) 3-D radar systems.

FORCES ABROAD:
UN AND PEACEKEEPING:
CAMBODIA (UNTAC): 3 Observers.
CYPRUS (UNFICYP): 1 inf bn (409).
IRAQ/KUWAIT (UNIKOM): 7 Observers.
MIDDLE EAST (UNTSO): 14.
SYRIA (UNDOF): 1 inf bn (532).
WESTERN SAHARA (MINURSO): 1 Observer.

AZERBAIJAN

| GDP | 1991: r 22.41bn ($13.18bn) |
| Growth | 1991: −2% |

Inflation[a] 1991: 87.3%
Debt 1991: $1.30bn
Def bdgt 1992: r 2.80bn
$1 = r 1991: 1.70

Population: 7,131,000 (7.9% Russian)

13–17	18–22	23–32
742,600	677,500	884,200

[a] Year average

TOTAL ARMED FORCES:
Terms of service: conscription,
RESERVES: Some mobilized. Possibly over 500,000 with military service within 15 years.
ARMY: National Defence Army: ε5,000. Armed forces of up to 30,000 reported forming.
NAVY: Share of Caspian Flotilla. 5 mine warfare fly Azerbaijan flag.

PARAMILITARY:
Militia (Ministry of Internal Affairs): 20,000+
Popular Front: Karabakh People's Defence: up to 12,000 claimed.

OPPOSITION:
Armed forces of Nagorno-Karabakh: ε30–50,000 incl volunteers from Armenia.

FOREIGN FORCES:
RUSSIA: (Trans-Caucasus MD)
Army: (HQ Yerevan) 62,000.
1 army HQ, 3 MRD, 1 ABD, 2 arty regt, 400 MBT, 800 AIFV, 470 arty/MRL/mors, 14 attack hels. Air Force: 1 bbr regt (30 Su-24), 1 FGA regt (30 Su-25), 1 recce regt (30 MiG-25, Su-24). Air Defence: 1 ftr regt (30 MiG-25), 135 SAM.

BOSNIA-HERZEGOVINA

GDP 1991ε: $10.95bn
Growth 1991ε: –32%

Population: 4,508,000 (39.5% 'Muslims', 32% Serbs, 18.4% Croats)

MILITIAS:
SERB: ε67,000 (incl Serbian Guard, Serbian Volunteer Guard, Chetnick, Beli Orlori).
EQUIPMENT:
MBT: ε300. **APC:** ε180. **Arty:** ε480.
MUSLIM: ε30–50,000 (incl 'Green Beret')
CROAT: ε50,000 (incl Patriotic League, HOS (Croatian Defence Army)).

FOREIGN FORCES:
UN (UNPROFOR): 3 inf bn (Egypt, France, Ukraine).

BULGARIA

GDP	1990ε: leva 45.60bn ($31.63bn)	
	1991ε: leva 138.40bn ($25.72bn)	
Growth	1990ε: –12%	1991: –23%
Inflation	1990ε: 37.7%	1991ε: 400%
Debt	1990: $11.05bn	1991: $12.30bn
Def bdgt[a]	1991: leva 2.84bn ($1.79bn)	
	1992: leva 8.11bn ($1.31bn)	
$1 = leva	1990: 0.80	1991: 16.0
	1992: 23.6	

[a] Dollar values are estimated.

Population: 9,098,000

	13–17	18–22	23–32
Men	334,000	329,100	632,300
Women	319,200	313,600	604,700

TOTAL ARMED FORCES:
ACTIVE: 107,000 (70,000 conscripts). (Excl some 10,000 construction tps.)
Terms of service: 18 months.
RESERVES: 472,500. Army 420,000; Navy (to age 55, officers 60 or 65) 7,500; Air (to age 60) 45,000.

ARMY: 75,000 (49,000 conscripts).
3 Military Districts/Army HQ:
1 with 1 tk bde;
1 with 2 MRD, 2 Regional Training Centre (RTC), 1 tk bde;
1 with 2 MRD, 2 RTC, 2 tk bde;
Army tps: 4 *Scud*, 1 SS-23, 1 SAM bde, 3 arty, 3 AD arty, 1 SAM regt.
1 AB regt (manned by Air Force).
EQUIPMENT:
MBT: 2,100 (450 in store): 590 T-34 (400 in store), 1,200 T-55 (50 in store), 310 T-72.
ASSAULT GUN: 150 SU-100 (CFE HACV).
RECCE: 60 BRDM-1/-2.
AIFV: 29 BMP-1, 94 BMP-23.
APC: 680 BTR-60, 1,100 MT-LB.
TOTAL ARTY: 2,129.
TOWED: 716: 100mm: 15 M-1944 (BS-3); 122mm: 282 M-30, 32 M-1931/37 (A-19); 130mm: 72 M-46; 152mm: 104 M-1937 (ML-20), 211 D-20.
SP: 665: 122mm: 665 2S1.
MRL: 238: 122mm: 214 BM-21; 130mm: 24 RM-130.
MORTARS: 510: 107mm: 63 M-1938; 120mm: 359 *Tundzha* M-1938/43 SP; 160mm: 88 M-160.
SSM: launchers: 28 *FROG*-7, 36 *Scud*, 8 SS-23.

ATGW: 200 AT-3 *Sagger*.
ATK GUNS: 85mm: 150 D-44; 100mm: 200 T-12.
AD GUNS: 400: 23mm: ZU-23, ZSU-23-4 SP;
   57mm: S-60; 85mm: KS-12; 100mm: KS-19.
SAM: 20 SA-3, 27 SA-4, 20 SA-6.

NAVY: ε10,000 (ε5,000 conscripts).
BASES: coastal: Varna (HQ), Atiya, Sozopol,
  Balchik. **Danube:** Vidin (HQ).
SUBMARINES: 3 *Pobeda* (Sov *Romeo*) class with
  533mm TT (1 non-op).
FRIGATES: 2: 1 *Druzki* (Sov *Riga* with 4 × 5 ASW
  RL; plus 3 × 533mm TT, 3 × 100mm guns.
  1 *Smeli* (Sov *Koni*) with 1 × 2 SA-N-4 SAM, 2 ×
  12 ASW RL; plus 2 × 2 76mm guns.
PATROL AND COASTAL COMBATANTS: 27:
CORVETTES: 9: 6 *Poti* ASW with 2 × ASW RL, 4 ×
  ASTT.
  1 *Tarantul II* ASUW with 2 × 2 SS-N-2C *Styx*,
    2 × 4 SA-N-5 *Grail* SAM; plus 1 × 76mm gun.
  2 *Pauk I* with 1 SA-N-5 SAM, 2 × 5 ASW RL;
    plus 4 × 406mm TT.
MISSILE CRAFT: 6 *Osa* PFM with 4 × SS-N-2A/B
  Styx SSM.
TORPEDO CRAFT: 4 *Shershen* PFT with 4 × 533mm TT.
PATROL INSHORE: about 8 *Zhuk* PFI⟨
MINE WARFARE: 35:
MINELAYERS: None but SS and FF have capability.
MCMV: 35:
  4 *Sonya* MSC.
  31 MSI: 6 *Vanya*, 2 *Yevgenya*, 5 *Olya*, 18⟨.
AMPHIBIOUS: 2:
  2 Sov *Polnocny* LSM, capacity 150 tps, 6 tk;
  Plus craft: 10 *Vydra* LCM.
SUPPORT AND MISCELLANEOUS: 9:
  2 AOT, 2 AGOR, 1 AGI, 2 trg, 2 AT.

NAVAL AVIATION: 10 armed hel.
HELICOPTERS: 1 SAR/ASW sqn with 6 Mi-14
  (ASW), 2 Mi-8, 2 Ka-25.

COASTAL ARTY:
  2 regt, 20 bty:
GUNS: 100mm: ε150; 130mm: SM-4-1.
SSM: SS-C-1b *Sepal*, SSC-3 *Styx*.

NAVAL GUARD: 3 coy.

AIR FORCE: 22,000 (16,000 conscripts), incl
  AB regt listed under Army;
  259 cbt ac, 44 attack hel.
2 air div, 1 mixed air corps, 7 cbt regt.
FGA: 1 regt with 39 Su-25.
  1 regt with 18 MiG-23.
FIGHTER: 4 regt with some 36 MiG-23MF B/G; 85
  MiG-21PFM, 18 MiG-29, 2 MiG-29 UB.

RECCE: 1 regt with 19 MiG-21, 21 Su-22.
TRANSPORT: 1 regt with 2 An-2, 3 An-24, 4 An-26,
  6 L-410, 1 Yak-40 (VIP).
SURVEY: 1 An-30.
HELICOPTERS: 2 regt with 12 Mi-2, 25 Mi-8/17, 44
  Mi-24 (attack).
TRAINING: 3 trg regt with 55 L-29, 33 L-39, 21 *MiG-21.
MISSILES:
  ASM: AS-7 *Kerry*.
  AAM: AA-2 *Atoll*, AA-7 *Apex*, AA-8 *Aphid*.
  SAM: SA-2/-3/-5/-10 (20 sites, some 110 launchers).

FORCES ABROAD:
UN AND PEACEKEEPING:
CAMBODIA (UNTAC): 474

PARAMILITARY:
BORDER GUARDS (Ministry of Interior): 12,000;
  12 regt.
SECURITY POLICE: 4,000.
RAILWAY AND CONSTRUCTION TROOPS: 18,000.

BYELARUS

GDP	1991:	r 71.6bn ($42.12bn)	
Growth[a]	1991:	−3%	
Inflation[b]	1991:	80.3%	
Debt	1991:	$3.40bn	
Def bdgt	1992[c]ε:	r 17bn	
$1 = r[d]	1991:	1.70	

Population: 10,259,000 (13.2% Russian)

13–17	*18–22*	*23–32*
767,900	718,100	1,374,800

[a] NMP growth
[b] Year average
[c] Excluding procurement; with arms purchases the
defence budget may be as high as r28bn.
[d] Byelarus is preparing to introduce its own version of
the rouble, the rubel = 10 roubles.

TOTAL ARMED FORCES
ACTIVE: 125,000 (reducing to 90,000 on
  formation of National Armed Forces).
  Terms of service: 18 months.
RESERVES: Some 350,000 with military service
  within 5 years.

STRATEGIC NUCLEAR FORCES:
  (CIS-controlled forces on Byelarus territory).
ICBM: 54
  SS-25 *Sickle* (RS-12m): 80 (mobile, single
  warhead msl; 2 bases with 9 units of 9).

GROUND FORCES: (95,000)
  3 army HQ
  6 TD (1 trg)
  3 MRD
  1 ABD
  1 arty div
  9 arty bde/regt (incl 5 MRL)
  5 SSM bde
  2 ATK bde
  1 *Spetsnaz* bde
  1 AB bde
  5 SAM bde
  2 attack hel regt.

EQUIPMENT:
MBT: 1,850: 20 T-54, 310 T-62, 1,520 T-72.
LIGHT TANKS: 10 PT-76.
AIFV: 2,460: 1,020 BMP-1, 1,000 BMP-2, 130 BRM, 310 BMD.
APC: Some 1,400: 770 BTR-50P/-60P/-70/-80/-152, 100 BTR-D, 500 MT-LB.
TOTAL ARTY: some 1,400 incl:
  TOWED ARTY: 425: 122mm: 180 D-30; 152mm: 60 D-20, 135 2A65, 50 2A36.
  SP ARTY: 510: 122mm: 210 2S1; 152mm: 130 2S3, 120 2S5; 203mm: 50 2S7.
  COMBINED GUN/MORTAR: 120mm: 72 2S9.
MRL: 350: 122mm: 220 BM-21; 220mm: 80 9P140; 300mm: 50 9A52.
  MORTARS: 36: 120mm: 24 2S12, 12 PM-38.
SSM: 60 *Scud*, 36 *FROG*/SS-21.
HELICOPTERS:
  ATTACK: 80 Mi-24;
  SUPPORT: 30 Mi-6, 90 Mi-8, 9 Mi-24K, 6 Mi-24P.
  TRANSPORT: 15 Mi-26, 27 Mi-2.

AIR FORCE: 20,000
  1 air army, 502 cbt ac, no armed hel.
BOMBERS: 3 regt with 25 Tu-16, 65 Tu-22, 40 Tu-26.
FGA/BOMBERS: 1 div, 3 regt with 90 Su-24.
FGA: 3 regt with 90 Su-25.
FIGHTER: 1 regt with 50 MiG-29.
RECCE: 2 regt: 1 with 13 Tu-16, 29 Tu-22. 1 with 15 MiG-21, 30 MiG-25, 5 Su-24.
ECM: 1 regt with 30 MiG-25, 20 Yak-28.
HELICOPTER: 1 regt: 2 Mi-2, 40 Mi-8, 2 Mi-24P.

AIR DEFENCE: 10,000
  1 PVO army, 115 cbt ac.
FIGHTER: 3 regt with 65 MiG-23, 50 MiG-25.
SAM: 650 SAM.

CROATIA

GDP	1991ε:	$22.50bn
Growth	1991ε:	−30%
Debt	1991:	$3.10bn

Population: 4,653,000 (75% Croats, 11% Serb)

TOTAL ARMED FORCES:
ACTIVE: ε105,000
  Terms of service: 10 months.
RESERVES: 100,000

ARMY: 100,000 (incl 50,000 mob reservists).
  2 mech bde.
  1 mot bde.
  5 inf bde.
  1 mtn bde.
  1 arty regt.
  3 ATK regt.
  1 engr regt.
RESERVES:
  Local Defence Force (org on 'bde' basis probably as for former Territorial Defence).
EQUIPMENT
MBT: ε200 incl T-34, T-54.
APC: ε200.
ARTY: ε150 (no further details), plus RCL, AD guns and man-portable SAM.

AIR FORCE: 250: said to be forming, no cbt ac.

AIR DEFENCE: 4,000
  no details available.

NAVY: ε5,000
BASES: Split, Pula, Sibenik, Ploce.
Minor facilities: Lastovo, Vis.
SUBMARINES: 1: *Una* SSI for SF ops.
PATROL AND COASTAL COMBATANTS: some 12:
CORVETTES: 2 *Kobra*-class (unlikely to be fully op).
MISSILE CRAFT: 3:
  1 *Rade Koncar* PFM with 2 × SS-N-2B *Styx*.
  2 *Mitar Acev* (Sov *Osa-I*) PFM with 4 × SS-N-2A.
TORPEDO CRAFT: 2:
  2 *Topcider* (Sov *Shershen*) with 4 × 533mm TT.
PATROL: 5:
  COASTAL: 1 *Mornar* ASW with 4 × ASW RL.
  INSHORE: 4 *Mirna*
MINE WARFARE: 1
MINELAYERS: None, but DTM-211 LCT can lay 100 mines – see amph forces.
MCM: 1:
  1 *Vukov Klanac* MHC†

AMPHIBIOUS: craft only; 11: 3 DTM-211 LCT, about 8 DJC-601 LCM.
SUPPORT AND MISCELLANEOUS: 2:
1 salvage, 1 Sov *Moma* survey.

PARAMILITARY:
Police: 40,000 armed.
HOS (Croatian Defence Army): 10,000.

FOREIGN FORCES:
UN (UNPROFOR): 12 inf bn, plus spt units from 18 countries.

CYPRUS

GDP	1990:	£C 2.52bn ($5.51bn)	
	1991:	£C 2.66bn ($5.61bn)	
Growth	1990:	4.5%	1991: 2.4%
Inflation	1990:	5.8%	1991: 5.1%
Debt	1989:	$1.51bn	1990: $1.90bn
Def exp	1990:	£C 149.90m ($304.10m)	
	1991:	£C 130.0m ($284.50m)	
$1 = £C	1989:	0.493	1990: 0.457
	1991:	0.461	1992: 0.457

Population: 707,400

	13–17	*18–22*	*23–32*
Men	28,100	24,900	55,400
Women	26,500	23,700	52,400

TOTAL ARMED FORCES:
ACTIVE: 8,000 (incl 400 women).
Terms of service: conscription, 26 months, then reserve to age 50 (officers 65).
RESERVE: 88,000: 45,000 first-line (age 20–34); 43,000 second-line (age 35–50).

NATIONAL GUARD: 10,000.
1 Army, 2 div HQ.
2 bde HQ.
1 armd bde (-).
13 inf bn (incl 4 reserve).
1 SF bn.
1 ATK bn.
7 arty bn.
EQUIPMENT:
MBT: 52 AMX-30B-2.
RECCE: 126 EE-9 *Cascavel*, ε36 EE-3 *Jararaca*.
AIFV: 27 VAB-VCI.
APC: 43 *Leonidas*, 116 VAB (incl variants).
TOWED ARTY: 193: 75mm: 4 M-116A1 pack; 76mm: 54 M-42; 88mm: 18 25-pdr; 100mm: 36 M-1944; 105mm: 72 incl M-101, M-56; 155mm: 9 TR F1.

SP: 155mm: 12 F3.
MRL: 128mm: 24 Yug M-63 (YMRL-32).
MORTARS: 81mm: 72 incl SP; 82mm: 80 M-41/-43 some SP; 107mm: 12 M-2; 120mm: 114 RT61.
ATGW: *Milan* (24 on EE-3 *Jararaca*), *HOT* (18 on VAB).
RL: 89mm: 450 M-20.
RCL: 57mm: 216 M-18; 106mm: 144 M-40A1.
AD GUNS: 155: 20mm: M-55; 35mm: 8 GDF-003; 40mm; 94mm: 3.7-in.
SAM: 24 SA-7, 18 *Mistral*.
MARINE: 1 *Salamis* PFI⟨.
AIRCRAFT: 1 BN-2A *Maritime Defender*, 2 PC-9, 1 PA-22.
HELICOPTERS: 2 Bell 206, 4 SA-342 *Gazelle* (with *HOT*).

PARAMILITARY:
ARMED POLICE: 3,700; Shorland armd cars, 2 17m PCI⟨.

FOREIGN FORCES:
GREECE: 950 (ELDYK) (Army) 2 inf bn, plus ε1,300 officers/NCO seconded to Greek-Cypriot National Guard.
UNITED KINGDOM: (in Sovereign Base Areas) 4,200: Army: 2 inf bn, 1 armd recce sqn. Air Force: 1 hel sqn plus ac on det.

UNITED NATIONS:
UNFICYP: some 2,300; 3 inf bn (Austria, Canada, Denmark), 1 inf bn (-), armd recce sqn (UK).

'Turkish Republic of Northern Cyprus'

Data presented here represents the *de facto* situation in the island. It in no way implies recognition, or IISS approval.

Def bdgt	1987ε:	TL 5.20bn ($6.07m)	
	1988:	TL 8.00bn ($5.62m)	
$1 = TL	(1987):	857	(1988): 1,422

TL = Turkish lira

TOTAL ARMED FORCES:
ACTIVE: some 4,000.
Terms of service: conscription, 24 months, then reserve to age 50.
RESERVES: 11,000 first-line; 10,000 second-line; 5,000 third-line.

ARMY:
7 inf bn.
MARITIME: 2 patrol boats.

FOREIGN FORCES:

TURKEY: 30,000; 1 corps of 2 inf div, 300 M-48A5 MBT; 100 M-113, 100 M-59 APC; 144 105mm, 36 155mm, 8 203mm towed; 18 105mm, 6 155mm SP; 114 107mm mor, 84 40mm AA guns; 8 ac, 12 hel.

CZECHOSLOVAKIA

GDP	1990ε: Kcs 818.97bn ($111.90bn)	
	1991ε: Kcs 952.24bn ($98.02bn)	
Growth	1990: −3.1% 1991: −20% (NMP)	
	1991ε: −10% (GDP)	
Inflation	1990: 11.0%	1991ε: 65.0%
Debt	1990: $8.1bn	1991: $9.3bn
Def exp[a]	1989: Kcs 28.40bn ($4.60bn)	
	1990: Kcs 29.70bn ($4.32bn)	
Def bdgt[a]	1991: Kcs 26.50bn ($2.80bn)	
	1992ε: Kcs 26.90bn ($2.45bn)	
$1 = Kcs	1989: 15.050	1990: 17.950
	1991: 29.480	1992: 29.200

Kcs = koruny

[a] Incl police and sy bdgt

Population: 15,788,800

	13–17	18–22	23–32
Men	649,600	612,000	1,111,200
Women	628,200	590,100	1,073,800

TOTAL ARMED FORCES:

ACTIVE: 145,800 (75,000 conscripts) (incl some 29,000 Ministry of Defence staff, centrally controlled units for EW, trg, log and civil defence not listed below).
Terms of service: 18 months.

RESERVES: 495,000. Army 450,000 (1.1m more with residual liability to age 60); Air Force 45,000.

ARMY: 72,000 (57,000 conscripts).
3 Command HQ:
  West with 2 TD, 3 mech div (1 mob), 1 arty, 2 engr bde; 1 ATK bn.
  Centre with 2 mech div (1 mob), 2 inf div (mob), 1 arty bde; 1 ATK bn.
  East with 1 TD, 3 mech div (2 mob), 1 inf div (mob); 1 arty, 1 engr bde; 1 ATK bn.
1 SSM regt; 1 hy arty bn,
1 AB bde.
4 engr (2 bridge, 2 road construction) bde.

EQUIPMENT:

MBT: 3,208 (1,580 in store): 992 T-54, 1,401 T-55, 815 T-72.

RECCE: 450: some 250 BRDM, 201 BPZV.

AIFV: 1,229: 934 BVP-1 (BMP-1), 280 BMP-2, 15 BRM-1K.

APC: 3,057: 442 OT-62A/B, 1,124 OT-64A/C, 532 OT-65, 339 OT-810, 620 OT-90 in store. (plus some 1,387 'look alike' types).

TOTAL ARTY: 3,414 (1,850 in store).

  TOWED: 1,821 (1,361 in store): 100mm: 500 (461) M-53; 122mm: 94 M-1931/37 (A-19), 911 (884) M-1938 (M-30), 260 D-30; 130mm: 12 M-46; 152mm: 44 (16) M-1937 (ML-20).

  SP: 548: 122mm: 148 2S1; 152mm: 388 *Dana* (M-77); 203mm: 12 2S7.

  MRL: 796 (489 in store): 122mm: 471 (243) RM-70; 130mm: 325 (246) RM-130 (M-51)

  MORTARS: 249: 120mm: 241; 240mm: 8 2S4.

SSM: 68 (60 in store) launchers: 26 *FROG*, 8 SS-21, 30 *Scud*, 4 SS-23.

ATGW: AT-3 *Sagger*, AT-5 *Spandrel* (some 1,615 SP).

AD GUNS: 400: 30mm: M-53/-59 SP; 57mm: S-60.

SAM: SA-7, 32 SA-9/-13.

AIR FORCE: 44,800 (18,000 conscripts); 304 cbt ac (98 plus in store (for sale)), 56 attack hel.
3 AD div, 1 mixed air corps, 2 hel regt.

FGA: 4 regt:
  1 with 41 MiG-21.
  1 with 32 MiG-23BN.
  1 with 42 Su-22.
  1 with 38 Su-25.

FIGHTER: 2 regt and 2 sqn.
  2 sqn with 28 MiG-21, 8 L-39.
  1 regt with 33 MiG-23MF/ML.
  1 regt with 20 MiG-21, 20 MiG-29.

RECCE: 1 regt with 4 L-29, 23 MiG-21RF, 15 Su-22.

TRANSPORT: 2 regt with 4 An-24, 5 L-410M (plus 2 with Army), 1 Tu-134, 2 Tu-154, 1 Yak-40.

HELICOPTERS: 2 regt:
  ATTACK: 56 Mi-24.
  ASSAULT TPT: (med) 52 Mi-2, 27 Mi-8, 1 Mi-9, 50 Mi-17.

TRAINING: 3 units: 35 L-29, 44 L-39, 26 MiG-21U/MF.

IN STORE: 98 plus incl Su-7/-20, MiG-21.

AAM: AA-2 *Atoll*, AA-7 *Apex*, AA-8 *Aphid*.

AD: 1 SA-4 bde, 7 SAM regt:
  some 40 sites; 250 SA-2/-3/-4/-5/-6.
  1 bn, 12 SA-10B.

DEPLOYMENT:

CZECH LANDS: 2TD, 5 mech div (2 mob), 2 inf div (mob), 1 AB, 2 arty, 1 SSM bde, 4 FGA, 2 ftr, 2 attack hel regt.

SLOVAKIA: 1 TD, 3 mech div (2 mob), 1 inf div (mob), 1 arty bde, 1 ftr sqn.

FORCES ABROAD:

UN AND PEACEKEEPING:

ANGOLA (UNAVEM II): 16 Observers.

CROATIA (UNPROFOR): 1 inf bn (480), 20 Observers, 8 mil police.

KOREA (NNSC): Staff.

PARAMILITARY:
BORDER GUARDS: 8,000.
INTERNAL SECURITY FORCES: 2,500.
CIVIL DEFENCE TROOPS: 5,000.

ESTONIA

GDP   1991:   r 16.75bn ($9.85bn)
Growth   1991:   −10.8%
Inflation   1991:   211.8%
Debt   1991: $496m
Def bdgt[a] 1992:   r 135m
$1 = r   1991:   1.70
r[b] = rouble
[a] For the first half of 1992.
[b] Estonia is introducing the Kroon to replace the rouble in mid-1992.

Population: 1,583,000

13–17	18–22	23–32
116,200	110,800	212,100

TOTAL ARMED FORCES:
ACTIVE: ε2,000
Terms of service: 15 months.

GROUND FORCES:
Border guard.
Rapid reaction force.
Territorial def unit.

FOREIGN FORCES:
RUSSIA: 23,000
Army: 1 MRD, 1 *Scud*, 1 *Spetsnaz* bde (190 MBT, 160 AIFV, 20 arty/MRL/mor), Air Force: 1 bbr regt (18 cbt ac), Air Defence: 3 ftr regt (120 cbt ac, 250 SAM).

FINLAND

GDP   1990:   m 524.955bn ($137.30bn)
           1991:   m 511.801bn ($126.56bn)
Growth   1990: 0.4%   1991:   −6.1%
Inflation 1990: 6.1%   1991:   4.0%
Debt   1990: $57.66bn   1991: $69.70bn
Def exp   1990: m 7.199bn ($1.88bn)
Def bdgt 1991: m 8.909bn ($2.20bn)
          1992: m 9.087bn ($1.98bn)
$1 = m   1989: 4.2912   1990:   3.8235
         1991: 4.0444   1992:   4.6000
m = markka

Population: 5,036,400

	13–17	18–22	23–32
Men	161,000	165,100	375,800
Women	154,100	158,700	363,000

TOTAL ARMED FORCES:
ACTIVE: 32,800 (24,100 conscripts).
Terms of service: 8–11 months (11 months for officers, NCOs and soldiers with special duties). Some 30,000 a year do conscript service.
RESERVES (all services): some 700,000; some 50,000 reservists a year do refresher trg: total obligation 40 days (75 for NCO, 100 for officers) between conscript service and age 50 (NCO and officers to age 60).
Total strength on mob some 500,000, with 300,000 in general forces (bde etc) and 200,000 in local defence forces, (Army 460,000, Navy 12,000, Air Force 30,000) plus 200,000 unallocated as replacements etc.

ARMY: 27,300 (21,600 conscripts).
7 Military Areas; 23 Military Districts:
   1 armd trg bde (reserve armd bde) (1 armd, 1 mech inf, 1 ATK bn, 1 arty regt, 1 AA bty).
   8 inf trg bde (each 3 inf bn; 3 with 1 arty regt, 1 with 1 arty bn).
   2 indep inf bn.
   1 arty bde.
   Coast arty: 2 regt; 3 indep bn (1 mobile).
   4 AD regt (incl 1 SAM bn with SAM-79).
   2 engr bn.
(All units have a primary trg role).
RESERVES:
2 armd bde.	10 *Jaeger* bde.
14 inf bde.	1 coast bde.
Some 50 indep bn.	200 local defence units.

EQUIPMENT:
MBT: 60 T-55, 63 T-72.
LIGHT TANKS: 15 PT-76.
AIFV: 40 BMP-1, 32 BMP-2.
APC: 31 BTR-50P, 87 BTR-60, 2 BTR-80, 220 A-180 *Sisu*, 213 MT-LB.
TOWED ARTY: 105mm: 252 M-37/-61; 122mm: 276 H-63 (D-30); 152mm: 72 M-38, K-89; 155mm: 36 M-74 (K-83).
SP ARTY: 152mm: 18 2S5.
COAST ARTY: 100mm: D-10T (tank turrets); 122mm: M-60; 130mm: 170 M-54; 152mm: 240.
COAST SSM: some RBS-15.
MRL: 122mm: M-76 (BM-21).
MORTARS: 81mm: 880; 120mm: 614.
ATGW: 24 M-82 (AT-4 *Spigot*), 12 M-83 (BGM-71C *Improved TOW*), AT-5 *Spandrel*.
RL: 112mm: *APILAS*.
RCL: 55mm: M-55; 66mm: 66 KES, 75 (M-72A3); 95mm: 100 SM-58-61.

AD GUNS: 23mm: 100+ ZU-23; 30mm; 35mm: GDF-005, *Marksman* GDF-005 SP; 57mm: 12 S-60 towed, 12 ZSU-57-2 SP.
SAM: SAM-79 (SA-3), SAM-78 (SA-7), SAM-86 (SA-16), SAM-90 (*Crotale* NG).

NAVY: 2,500 (1,000 conscripts).
BASES: Upinniemi (Helsinki), Turku.
4 functional sqn (gunboat, missile, patrol, mine warfare). Approx 50% of units kept fully manned. Others in short-notice storage, rotated regularly.
PATROL AND COASTAL COMBATANTS: 23:
CORVETTES: 2 *Turunmaa* with 1 × 120mm gun, 2 × 5 ASW RL.
MISSILE CRAFT: 11:
  4 *Helsinki* PFM with 4 × 2 MTO-85 (Sw RBS-15SF) SSM.
  4 *Tuima* (Sov *Osa-II*) with 4 MTO-66 (Sov SS-N-2B) SSM.
  3 *Rauma* PFM with 2 × 2 and 2 × 1 MTO-85 (Sw RBS-15SF) SSM.
PATROL CRAFT: inshore: 10:
  2 *Rihtniemi* with 2 ASW RL.
  3 *Ruissalo* with 2 ASW RL.
  5 *Nuoli* PFI‹.
MINE WARFARE: 10:
MINELAYERS: 4
  1 *Hämeenmaa*, 120 mines.
  1 *Pohjanmaa* (trg), 120 mines; plus 1 × 120mm gun.
  1 *Keihässalmi*, 100 mines.
  1 *Pansio* aux minelayer, 50 mines.
MCM: 6 *Kuha* MSI‹.
AMPHIBIOUS: craft only; 3 *Kampela* LCU tpt, 5 *Kala* LCU.
SUPPORT AND MISCELLANEOUS: 17:
  5 *Valas* coastal tpt (can be used for minelaying).
  1 *Aranda* AGOR (civil, Min of Trade control).
  2 *Hylje* PCO (Min of Environment, manned by navy).
  9 icebreakers (civil, Board of Navigation control).

AIR FORCE: 3,000 (1,500 conscripts);
116 cbt ac, no armed hel.
3 AD areas: 3 fighter wings.
FIGHTER: 3 wings:
  1 with 16 MiG-21bis; 10 *Hawk* Mk 51.
  2 with 41 J-35, 20 *Hawk* Mk 51.
OCU: 4* MiG-21U/UM, 5* SAAB SK-35C.
RECCE: some *Hawk* Mk 51 and MiG-21 bis (incl in fighter sqn).
SURVEY: 3 *Learjet* 35A (survey, ECM trg, target-towing).
TRANSPORT: 1 ac sqn with 3 F-27.
1 hel flt with 2 Hughes 500, 7 Mi-8 (tpt/SAR).
TRAINING: 20 *Hawk** Mk 51, 28 L-70 *Vinka*.

LIAISON: 15 Piper (9 *Cherokee Arrow*, 6 *Chieftain*), 1 L-90 *Redigo*.
AAM: AA-2 *Atoll*, AIM-9 *Sidewinder*, RB-27, RB-28 (*Falcon*), MATRA *Mistral*.

FORCES ABROAD:
UN AND PEACEKEEPING:
CROATIA (UNPROFOR): 300.
CYPRUS (UNFICYP): 7.
INDIA/PAKISTAN (UNMOGIP): 5.
IRAQ/KUWAIT (UNIKOM): 7.
LEBANON (UNIFIL): 1 inf bn (572).
MIDDLE EAST (UNTSO): 22.
SYRIA (UNDOF): 1 inf bn (396).

PARAMILITARY:
FRONTIER GUARD (Ministry of Interior): 4,400 (on mob 24,000); 4 frontier, 3 coast guard districts, 1 air comd; 2 offshore, 3 coastal, 10 inshore patrol craft; 3 Mi-8 (SAR), 2 AS-332, 3 AB-412, 7 AB-206 hel; 4 lt ac.

GEORGIA

(Not a member of the Commonwealth of Independent States)

GDP	1991:	r 23.47bn ($13.81bn)
Growth[a]	1991:	−25%
Inflation[b]	1991:	80%
Debt	1991:	$1.30bn
Def bdgt	1992:	r 6bn
$1 = r	1991:	1.70

Population: 5,456,000 (12.8% Russian)

13–17	*18–22*	*23–32*
440,400	409,200	720,200

[a] NMP growth.
[b] Year average.

TOTAL ARMED FORCES:
Terms of service: conscription, 18 months.
RESERVES: Possibly up to 500,000 with military service in last 15 years.

ARMY: Armed forces of up to 20,000 planned incl:-
  2 Corps HQ.
  1 mech bde.
  Border tps.

PARAMILITARY:
National Guard (Ministry of Interior): ε3,000 (to be 13,000)

OPPOSITION FORCES:
SOUTH OSSETIA: No details known.

FOREIGN FORCES:
RUSSIA (Trans-Caucasus MD):
Army: 20,000, 1 MD HQ, 1 Corps HQ, 4 MRD (1 trg), 1 AB bde, 1 ATK regt, 1 attack hel regt, 1 hel unit (40 Mi-8, 25 Mi-26), 850 MBT, 680 AIFV, 370 arty/MRL/mors, 48 attack hel. Air Force: 1 air army HQ, 1 bbr div HQ, 2 regt: (60 Su-24), 1 ftr div, 2 regt; (80 MiG-23, MiG-29), 1 recce regt: (30 Su-17). Air Defence: 2 ftr regt (40 Su-15, 30 Su-27, 175 SAM).
PEACEKEEPING: 1 AB bn (Russia).

HUNGARY

GDP	1990: f 2,080.90bn ($59.30bn)		
	1991ε: f 2,880.00bn ($53.90bn)		
Growth	1990: −3.9%	1991ε: −6.0%	
Inflation	1990: 28.2%	1991: 36%	
Debt	1990: $20.27bn	1991: $21.47bn	
Def exp[a]	1989: f 47.76bn ($1.81bn)		
	1990: f 52.00bn ($1.45bn)		
Def bdgt[a]	1991: f 54.40bn ($1.23bn)		
	1992[b]: f 59.60bn ($1.16bn)		
$1 = f	1989: 59.066	1990: 63.206	
	1991: 74.735	1992: 80.000	

f = forint
[a] Incl. internal police and sy budget.
[b] Does not incl costs incurred by Yugoslav crisis est at f150–200m a month.

Population: 10,543,800

	13–17	18–22	23–32
Men	399,400	391,700	708,800
Women	380,800	371,800	676,900

TOTAL ARMED FORCES:
ACTIVE: 80,800 (53,900 conscripts).
Terms of service: 12 months.
RESERVES: 192,000: Army: 180,600; Air: 11,400 (to age 50).

LAND FORCES: 63,500 (41,900 conscripts).
4 Military District Corps/HQ:
  1 with 2 tk, 2 mech bde, 1 MRL, 1 ATK, 1 AD arty, 1 engr regt.
  1 with 1 tk, 3 mech, 2 arty, 1 ATK bde, 1 ATK, 1 engr regt.
  1 with 4 mech, 1 arty, 1 AD arty, 1 engr bde, 1 engr regt.
  1 (Budapest) with 1 guard, 1 engr regt, 1 rivercraft bde.

EQUIPMENT:
MBT: 1,357 (439 in store): 72 T-34 (in store), 58 T-54 (44 in store), 1,090 T-55 (323 in store), 137 T-72.
LIGHT TANKS: 7 PT-76.
RECCE: 190: some 150 BRDM-2, 40 FUG D-442.
AIFV: 493 BMP-1, 7 BRM-1K.
APC: 1,302: 42 BTR-50, 66 BTR-60, 148 BTR-80, 997 PSZH D-944, 49 MT-LB. (Plus some 836 'look alike' types).
TOTAL ARTY: 1,040:
  TOWED: 574: 122mm: 230 M-1938 (M-30) (147 in store); 152mm: 49 M-1943 (D-1), 295 D-20 (6 in store).
  SP: 156: 122mm: 151 2S1 (3 in store); 152mm: 5 2S3.
  MRL: 122mm: 58 BM-21.
  MORTARS: 120mm: 3 2S12, 249 M-120.
ATGW: 329: 117 AT-3 *Sagger*, 30 AT-4 *Spigot* (incl BRDM-2 SP), 182 AT-5 *Spandrel*.
ATK GUNS: 85mm: 69 D-44; 100mm: 101 MT-12.
AD GUNS: 23mm: 14 ZSU-23-4 SP; 57mm: 144 S-60.
SAM: 240 SA-7, 54 SA-14.
Rivercraft bde:
MCMV: 6 Nestin⟨ MSI (riverine); 45 mine disposal/patrol boats.

AIR FORCE: 17,300 (12,000 conscripts);
91 cbt ac plus 43 in store, 39 attack hel.
2 air corps:
FIGHTER:
  2 regt with 50 MiG-21bis/MF, 9 MiG-23MF. (Plus 43 MiG-21 bis/MF in store.)
RECCE: 1 sqn with 11 Su-22.
TRANSPORT: 2 An-24, 9 An-26, 3 L-410.
HELICOPTERS: 3 regt.
  1 ATK/tpt.
    2 sqn with 39 Mi-24.
    1 sqn with 23 Mi-8/-17;
  1 tpt with 25 Mi-8
  1 liaison with 34 Mi-2
TRAINING: 15 *MiG-21U, 3 *MiG-23, 3 *Su-22.
AAM: AA-2 *Atoll*.
AD: some 16 sites
  1 bde: 18 SA-4
  5 regt: 82 SA-2/-3/-5, 40 SA-6, 28 SA-9, 4 SA-13.

FORCES ABROAD:
UN AND PEACEKEEPING:
ANGOLA (UNAVEM II): 15 Observers.
IRAQ/KUWAIT (UNIKOM): 7 Observers.
MIDDLE EAST (UNTSO): 2 Observers.

PARAMILITARY:
BORDER GUARDS: (Ministry of Interior) 20,000 (14,500 conscripts); 11 districts.
CONSTRUCTION TROOPS: (Ministry of Defence) 750 (675 conscripts).

CIVIL DEFENCE TROOPS: 2,000.
INTERNAL SECURITY TROOPS: 1,500.

IRELAND

GDP	1990: £I 25.69bn ($42.61bn)	
	1991ε: £I 26.72bn ($43.17bn)	
Growth	1990: 7.1%	1991: 1.5%
Inflation	1990: 3.3%	1991: 3.2%
Debt	1989: $28.90bn	1990: $28.60bn
Def exp	1989: £I 264.80m ($375.76m)	
	1990: £I 306.00m ($507.50m)	
Def bdgt	1990: £I 292.00m ($484.29m)	
	1991: £I 317.00m ($552.60m)	
$1 = £I	1989: 0.7047	1990: 0.6030
	1991: 0.5737	1992: 0.6061

Population: 3,769,000

	13–17	18–22	23–32
Men	174,600	175,000	320,200
Women	166,900	168,400	308,100

TOTAL ARMED FORCES:
ACTIVE: 13,000 incl 100 women.
Terms of service: voluntary, 3-year terms to age 60, officers 56–65.
RESERVES: 16,100 (obligation to age 60, officers 57–65). Army: first-line 1,000, second-line 14,800. Navy 350.

ARMY: 11,200.
4 Territorial Commands.
1 inf force (2 inf bn).
4 inf bde:
2 with 2 inf bn, 1 with 3, all with 1 fd arty regt, 1 cav recce sqn, 1 engr coy;
1 with 2 inf bn, 1 armd recce sqn, 1 fd arty bty.
Army tps: 1 lt tk sqn, 1 AD regt, 1 Ranger coy.
(Total units: 11 inf bn; 1 UNIFIL bn *ad hoc* with elm from other bn, 1 tk sqn, 4 recce sqn (1 armd), 3 fd arty regt (each of 2 bty); 1 indep bty, 1 AD regt (1 regular, 3 reserve bty), 3 fd engr coy, 1 Ranger coy).
RESERVES:
4 Army Gp (garrisons), 18 inf bn, 6 fd arty regt, 3 cav sqn, 3 engr sqn, 3 AA bty.
EQUIPMENT:
LIGHT TANKS: 14 *Scorpion*.
RECCE: 19 AML-90, 32 AML-60.
APC: 60 Panhard VTT/M3, 10 *Timoney*, 2 A-180 *Sisu*.
TOWED ARTY: 88mm: 48 25-pdr; 105mm: 12 lt.
MORTARS: 81mm: 400; 120mm: 72.
ATGW: 21 *Milan*.
RCL: 84mm: 444 *Carl Gustav*; 90mm: 96 PV-1110.

AD GUNS: 40mm: 24 L/60, 2 L/70.
SAM: 7 RBS-70.

NAVY: 1,000.
BASE: Cork.
PATROL AND COASTAL COMBATANTS: 7:
7 PCO:
1 *Eithne* with 1 *Dauphin* hel;
3 *Emer*, 1 *Deirdre*.
2 *Orla* (UK *Peacock*).

AIR FORCE: 800.
16 cbt ac, 15 armed hel.
3 wings (1 trg):
COIN: 1 sqn with 5 CM-170-2 *Super Magister*.
COIN/TRAINING: 1 sqn with 7 SF-260WE,
1 SF-260 MC ac, 2 SA-342L trg hel.
MR: 2 *Super King Air* 200, 1 CASA 235.
TRANSPORT: 1 HS-125, 1 *Super King Air* 200, 1 *Gulfstream* IV.
LIAISON: 1 sqn with 6 Reims Cessna F-172H, 1 F-172K.
HELICOPTERS: 3 sqn.
1 Army spt with 8 SA-316B.
1 Navy spt with 2 SA-365.
1 SAR with 5 SA-365.

FORCES ABROAD:
UN AND PEACEKEEPING:
ANGOLA (UNAVEM II): 15 Observers.
CAMBODIA (UNTAC): 17 Observers.
CROATIA (UNPROFOR): 4.
CYPRUS (UNFICYP): 8.
EL SALVADOR (ONUSAL): 4 Observers.
IRAQ/KUWAIT (UNIKOM): 7.
LEBANON (UNIFIL): HQ (100), 1 bn+ (770); 4 AML-90 armd cars, 10 *Sisu* APC, 4 120mm mor.
MIDDLE EAST (UNTSO): 20.
WESTERN SAHARA (MINURSO): 6.

LATVIA

GDP	1991: r 22.31bn ($13.12bn)
Growth	1991: −8%
Inflation	1991: 172.2%
Debt	1991: $912m
Def bdgt[a]	1992: r 257.4m
$1 = r	1991: 1.70

r[b] = roubles

[a] For the first half of 1992; fiscal year in Latvia consists of 2 periods: 1 Jan–30 June, 1 July–30 Dec.
[b] Latvia is planning to introduce the Lat to replace the rouble in 1992.

Population: 2,687,000

13–17	18–22	23–32
193,500	188,100	360,000

TOTAL ARMED FORCES:
ACTIVE: 2,550 (1,950 conscripts)
Terms of service: 18 months.

GROUND FORCES:
1 border guard bde (8 bn).
1 rapid reaction bn.
1 coast def unit.
NAVY:
1 Coast Guard div.

PARAMILITARY:
HOME GUARD: 12,000 (on mob).

FOREIGN FORCES:
RUSSIA: 40,000
Army: 1 TD (trg), 1 attack hel regt, (130 MBT, 80 AIFV, 80 arty/MRL/mor, 24 attack hel), Air Force: 1 FGA, 1 recce regt (90 cbt ac), 1 tpt hel regt (20 Mi-8), Air Defence: 1 ftr regt (40 cbt ac, 250 SAM).

LITHUANIA

GDP	1991: r 32.81bn ($19.30bn)		
Growth*a*	1991: −12.8%		
Inflation	1991: 216.4%		
Debt	1991: $1.13bn		
Def bdgt	1992: r 1bn		
$1 = r	1991: 1.70		

r*b* = rouble
a NMP growth
b Lithuania is planning to introduce the Lita = r10, to replace the rouble in 1992.

Population: 3,723,000

	13–17	18–22	23–32
	289,900	279,300	491,400

TOTAL ARMED FORCES:
ACTIVE: 7,000.
Terms of service: Conscription authorized.
RESERVES: National Guard: 12,500.

GROUND FORCES:
Border guard.
Rapid reaction force.
Territorial def force.

FOREIGN FORCES:
RUSSIA: 43,000

Army: 1 MRD, 2 ABD (1 trg), 2 arty bde, 1 attack hel regt, (180 MBT, 780 AIFV, 260 arty/MRL/mor, 4 *FROG*/SS-21), Air Force: 1 FGA regt (50 cbt ac), Air Defence: (125 SAM).

MACEDONIA

Macedonia considers itself independent.

GDP   1991ε: $5.06bn

Population: 2,124,500 (67% Macedonians, 20% Albanians, 4.5% Turks, 2% Serbs, 2% 'Muslims', 2.4% Gypsies).

TOTAL ARMED FORCES
ACTIVE: ε20,000.
RESERVES: 80,000 planned.

ARMY: 20,000
3 divisions planned.
EQUIPMENT: No heavy weapons, former Territorial Defence Force: Mors, RCL, AD guns, man-portable SAM.
AIR FORCE: 50: no ac. only hels planned.

MALTA

GDP	1990: LM 785.4m ($2.47bn)		
	1991ε: LM 832.5m ($2.58bn)		
Growth	1990: 6.3%	1991:	5.8%
Inflation	1990: 3.0%	1991:	2.6%
Debt	1990: $141.7m	1991:	$146.1m
Def exp	1989: LM 7.52m ($21.59m)		
	1990: LM 6.72m ($21.19m)		
Def bdgt	1991: LM 7.51m ($23.28m)		
	1992: LM 9.11m ($27.70m)		
$1 = LM	1989: 0.3483	1990:	0.3172
	1991: 0.3226	1992:	0.3289

LM = lira

Population: 355,300

	13–17	18–22	23–32
Men	13,900	13,000	26,900
Women	12,900	12,000	24,100

TOTAL ARMED FORCES:
ACTIVE: 1,650.

'ARMED FORCES OF MALTA':
Comd HQ, spt tps.

No. 1 Regt (inf bn) with:
  3 rifle, 1 spt coy.
No. 2 Regt (composite regt):
  1 air sqn with 3 SA-316, 2 Breda Nardi
    Hughes, 1 AB-206A, 3 AB-47G, 1 Bell 47G
    hel and 5 O-1 (*Bird Dog*) ac.
  1 maritime sqn with some:
  2 ex-GDR *Kondor* II PCC, 3 PCI, 2 PCI⟨
    plus boats.
1 AD bty; 14.5mm: 50 ZPU-4; 40mm: 40 Bofors.
No. 3 Regt (Depot Regt) with:
  1 engr sqn.
  1 workshop, 1 ordnance, 1 airport coy.

MOLDOVA

GDP	1991:	r 22.25bn ($13.09bn)
Growth[a]	1991:	−11.9%
Inflation[b]	1991:	98%
Debt	1991:	$1.10bn
Def bdgt[c]	1992:	r 4.1bn
$1 = r	1991:	1.70

Population: 4,362,000 (12.8% Russian)
13–17	*18–22*	*23–32*
357,700	305,300	558,300

[a] NMP growth.
[b] Year average.
[c] Incl national security.

TOTAL ARMED FORCES:
Terms of service: conscription,
RESERVES: some mob, possibly 300,000 with
military service within 15 years.

ARMY: 12,000.
Armed Forces planned to incl 1 inf bde, 1 AA
bde, 1 air force bde.

AIR FORCE:
1 ftr regt with 30 MiG-29

AIR DEFENCE:
80 SAM.

PARAMILITARY:
National Guard (Ministry of Interior): ε4,000.

OPPOSITION FORCES:
Dnestr: ε15,000.
Dnestr bn, Cossack force, Republican Guard

FOREIGN FORCES
RUSSIA (14th Army)
1 army HQ (Dnestr), 2 MRD (Dnestr, Ukraine), 2
arty bde (Moldova), 2 SSM bde (Moldova), 1
SAM bde, 1 attack hel regt (Ukraine), 1 hel unit
(Dnestr), 230 MBT, 70 AIFV, 330 arty/MRL/
mors, 24 *Scud*, 40 attack hel.
PEACEKEEPING: 6 AB bn (Russia), 2 inf bn
(Ukraine), 2 bn (Moldova).

POLAND

GDP	1990ε:	z 828,233.0bn ($124.60bn)
	1991ε:	z 1,391,431.4bn ($102.40bn)
Inflation	1990:	680%	1991ε: 70%
Growth	1990:	−12%	1991ε: −8%
Debt	1990:	$45.8bn	1991: $45.0bn
Def exp[a]	1989:	z 2,214.0bn ($3.23bn)
	1990:	z 14,954.0bn ($2.54bn)
Def bdgt[a]	1991:	z 23,274.70bn ($2.61bn)
	1992ε:	z 38,450.00bn ($2.44bn)
$1 = z	1989:	1,420.86	1990: 9,500.0
	1991:	10,576	1992: 15,000

z = zlotys
[a] Dollar values are estimated.

Population: 38,207,000
	13–17	*18–22*	*23–32*
Men	1,548,700	1,386,000	2,764,000
Women	1,487,400	1,329,000	2,646,000

TOTAL ARMED FORCES:
ACTIVE: 296,500 (167,400 conscripts).
Terms of service: All services 18 months.
RESERVES: 435,200. Army 352,000; Navy
18,700 (to age 50); Air Force 64,500 (to age 60).

ARMY: 194,200 (109,800 conscripts) (incl
centrally controlled staffs (2,900); trg (25,900)
and log units (28,100)).
3 Military Districts/Army HQ (1 forming):
  1 (Pomerania) with 3 mech div, 1 coast def, 1
    arty, 1 *Scud*, 1 engr bde, 1 SA-6 regt.
  1 (Silesia) with 4 mech div, 2 arty, 1 *Scud*, 2
    engr, 2 SA-4 bde, 2 ATK, 1 SA-6 regt.
  1 (Warsaw) with 2 mech div, 1 engr bde, 3 guard
    (ceremonial), 1 arty, 1 SA-6 regt.
  1 (Krakow) forming with 2 mech div, 1 air aslt,
    1 mtn inf bde.
Div tps: 3 SA-6, 2 SA-8 regt.
RESERVES: 1 mob mech div.
EQUIPMENT:
MBT: 2,850: 2,065 T-55, 785 T-72.
LIGHT TANKS: 30 PT-76.

RECCE: 685 FUG/BRDM-2.
AIFV: 1,409 BMP-1, 62 BMP-2.
APC: 752: 692 OT-64, 60 OT-62, plus some 900 'look alike' types.
TOTAL ARTY: 2,316:
  TOWED: 883: 122mm: 715 M-1938 (M-30); 152mm: 166 D-20, 2 D-1.
  SP: 617: 122mm: 498 2S1; 152mm: 111 *Dana* (M-77); 203mm: 8 2S7.
  MRL: 262: 122mm: 232 BM-21, 30 RM-70.
  MORTARS: 120mm: 554 M-120.
SSM: launchers: 40 *FROG*, 25 *Scud* B.
ATGW: 411: 271 AT-3, 115 AT-4 *Spigot*, 18 AT-5 *Spandrel*, 7 AT-6 *Spiral*.
ATK GUNS: 85mm: 722 D-44.
AD GUNS: 945: 23mm: ZU-23-2, ZSU-23-4 SP; 57mm: S-60.
SAM: 260: SA-6/-7/-8/-9/-13.

NAVY: 19,300 incl Naval Aviation. (10,600 conscripts).
BASES: Gdynia, Hel, Swinoujscie; Kolobrzeg (border/coast guard).
SUBMARINES: 3:
  1 *Orzel* SS (Sov *Kilo*) with 533mm TT.
  2 *Wilk* (Sov *Foxtrot*) with 533mm TT.
PRINCIPAL SURFACE COMBATANTS: 2:
DESTROYERS: 1 *Warszawa* DDG (Sov mod *Kashin*) with 2 × 2 SA-N-1 *Goa* SAM, 4 × SS-N-2C *Styx* SSM, 5 × 533mm TT, 2 × ASW RL.
FRIGATES: 1 *Kaszub* with 2 × ASW RL, 4 × 533mm TT, 76mm gun.
PATROL AND COASTAL COMBATANTS: 20:
CORVETTES: 4 *Gornik* (Sov *Tarantul I*) with 2 × 2 SS-N-2C *Styx* SSM.
MISSILE CRAFT: 8 Sov *Osa*-I PFM with 4 SS-N-2A SSM.
PATROL: 8:
  8 *Obluze* PCI
MINE WARFARE: 24:
MINELAYERS: None, but submarines *Krogulec* MSC and *Lublin* LSM have capability.
MINE COUNTERMEASURES: 24:
  8 *Krogulec* MSC.
  14 *Notec* MSI.
  2 *Leniwka* MSI.
AMPHIBIOUS: 6:
  5 *Lublin* LSM, capacity 130 tps, 8 tk.
  1 *Polnocny* LSM, capacity 180 tps, 6 tk, with 2 × 140mm MRL (used as comd ship).
  Plus craft: 3 *Deba* LCU.
(None of the above are employed in amph role.)
SUPPORT AND MISCELLANEOUS: 10:
  2 AGI, 4 spt tankers, 2 survey, 2 trg.

NAVAL AVIATION: 1 div (2,300);
  38 cbt ac, 4 armed hel.
  1 ftr regt with 38 MiG-21.

1 sqn SAR/liaison with: 3 Mi-8, 2 An-28, 2 AN-2, 9 Mi-2, 4 TS-11, 3 W-3 Sokol.
1 Special Naval regt with 12 TS-11, 10 AN-2, 1 ASW/SAR regt with 8 Mi-2, 1 Mi-8, 15 Mi-14 (4 ASW).

COAST DEFENCE: (4,200).
  6 arty bn with M-1937 152mm.
  3 SSM bn with SS-C-2B.

AIR FORCE: 83,000 (incl AD tps) (47,000 conscripts);
  423 cbt ac, (plus 86 in store for sale), 31 attack hel.
  2 air div:
FGA: 4 regt:
  4 with 20 Su-20, 104 Su-22.
RECCE: 24 MiG-17, 8 Su-20.
FIGHTER: 3 Air Defence Corps: 8 regt with 221 MiG-21/U; 37 MiG-23MF; 9 MiG-29.
RECCE: 24 MiG-21RU.
TRANSPORT: 2 regt with: Ac: 10 An-2, 1 An-12, 11 An-26, 10 Yak-40, 1 Tu-154, 3 Il-14. Hel: 4 Mi-8, 1 Bell 412.
HELICOPTERS: 3 attack regt: 30 Mi-24 (attack), 130 Mi-2 and 21 Mi-8 (assault), 3 Mi-17.
TRAINING: 18 *Su-22.
IN STORE: 33 MiG-21, 7 MiG-21R, 24 MiG-17, 22 MiG-15 U7.
AAM: AA-2 *Atoll*, AA-8 *Aphid*.
ASM: AS-7 *Kerry*.
SAM: 4 bde; 1 indep regt with 45 sites with 250 SA-2/-3/-5.

FORCES ABROAD:
UN AND PEACEKEEPING:
CAMBODIA (UNTAC): 176.
CROATIA (UNPROFOR): 1 bn (899).
IRAQ/KUWAIT (UNIKOM): 7.
KOREA (NNSC): Staff.
LEBANON (UNIFIL): 84.
SYRIA (UNDOF): 159. Log spt.
WESTERN SAHARA (MINURSO): 2 Observers.

PARAMILITARY:
BORDER GUARDS (Ministry of Interior): 20,000:
  14 Provincial Comd: 14 units; 18 PCI: 5 *Obluze*, 2 *Gdansk*, 11 *Pilica*.
PREVENTION UNITS OF CITIZENS MILITIA: (OPOMO): 18,000 (13,000 conscripts).

FOREIGN FORCES:

RUSSIA: Northern Group of Forces: 16,000: Army: 1 Gp HQ; 1 elm, 1 TD, 1 MRD, 1 attack hel regt (220 MBT, 600 ACV, 120 arty/MRL/mor, 50 attack hel). Air Force: 1 air army 1 bbr div, 1 ftr div, 1 recce regt, 1 attack hel regt (155 cbt ac, 20 attack hel). (All cbt tps to have withdrawn by 15 November 1992.)

ROMANIA

GNP	1990: lei 671.50bn ($44.60bn)	
	1991ε: lei 2,100.00bn ($37.10bn)	
Growth	1990: −11.0%	1991ε: −13.5%
Inflation	1990: 15.3%	1991ε: 165.5%
Debt	1990: $3.55bn	1991: $2.50bn
Def exp*a*	1990: lei 29.80bn ($1.33bn)	
	1991ε: lei 32.30bn ($1.01bn)	
Def bdgt*a*	1991: lei 85.1bn ($1.15bn)	
	1992ε: lei 173.7bn ($0.96bn)	
$1 = lei	1989: 14.922	1990: 29.400
	1991: 80.130	1992: 225.000

---

a Dollar values are estimated.

Population: 22,749,000

	13–17	18–22	23–32
Men	945,600	955,200	1,621,200
Women	914,500	917,800	1,563,800

TOTAL ARMED FORCES:

ACTIVE: 200,000 (126,700 conscripts).

Terms of service: Army, Air Force: 12 months; Navy: 18 months.

RESERVES: 593,000: Army 565,000; Navy 7,000; Air 21,000.

ARMY: 161,000 (105,000 conscripts).

4 Army Areas:
1 with 1 TD, 1 MRD, 1 mtn bde, 1 AB regt;
1 with 2 MRD, 1 mtn, 1 AD bde, 1 AB, 1 arty, 1 ATK regt.
1 with 2 MRD, 1 tk, 1 mtn, 1 AD bde, 1 AB, 1 arty, 1 ATK regt.
1 with 1 TD, 2 MRD, 2 mtn, 1 AD bde, 1 AB, 1 arty, 1 ATK regt.

MOD tps:
2 *Scud*, 2 arty bde; 2 AA regt.

EQUIPMENT:

MBT: 2,875 incl 1,059 T-34, 756 T-55, 30 T-72, 456 TR-85, 413 TR-580.

ASSAULT GUN: 412: 326 SU-76, 66 SU-100, 20 ISU-152.

RECCE: 139 BRDM-2, 8 TAB-80.

AIFV: 156 MLI-84.

APC: 2,638 incl variants: 28 BTR-40, 35 BTR-50, 50 BTR-60, 155 TAB-77, 441 TABC-79, 1,872 TAB-71, 57 MLVM (MT-LB).

TOTAL ARTY: 3,707.

TOWED: 1,546: 100mm: 267 Skoda (various models); 105mm: 87 Schneider; 122mm: 458 M-1938 (M-30), 2 M-1931/37 (A-19); 130mm: 144 Gun 82; 150mm: 128 Skoda (Model 1934), 6 Ceh (Model 1937); 152mm: 84 D-20, 54 Gun-How 85, 61 Model 1938, 255 Model 81.

SP: 48: 122mm: 6 2S1, 42 Model 89.

MRL: 446: 122mm: 116 APR-21, 294 APR-40; 130mm: 36 R-2.

MORTARS: 1,667: 120mm: 1,002 M-120, 603 Model 1982; 160mm: 50 M-160; 240mm: 12 M-240.

SSM: launchers: 13 *Scud*, 12 *FROG*.

ATGW: 534: AT-1 *Snapper*, AT-3 *Sagger* (incl BRDM-2).

ATK GUNS: 1,450: 57mm: M-1943; 85mm: D-44; 100mm: 829 Gun 77, 75 Gun 75.

AD GUNS: 1,118: 30mm; 37mm; 57mm; 85mm; 100mm.

SAM: 62 SA-6/-7.

NAVY: 19,000 (10,000 conscripts). 1 maritime div, 1 patrol boat bde, 1 river bde, 1 maritime/river bde, 1 nav inf div.

BASES: Coastal: Mangalia, Constanţa; **Danube:** Braila, Giurgiu, Tulcea.

SUBMARINE: 1 Sov *Kilo* SS with 533mm TT.

PRINCIPAL SURFACE COMBATANTS: 6:

DESTROYER: 1 *Muntenia* DDG with 4 × 2 SS-N-2C *Styx* SSM, plus SA-N-5 *Grail* SAM, 2 IAR-316 hel, 2 × 3 533mm TT.

FRIGATES: 5 *Tetal* with 2 × ASW RL, 4 × ASTT.

PATROL AND COASTAL COMBATANTS: 90:

CORVETTES: 6: 3 Sov *Poti* ASW with 2 × ASW RL, 3 × 533mm TT.
3 *Tarantul I* with 2 × 2 SS-N-2C *Styx*, 1 × 4 SA-N-5 *Grail* SAM; plus 1 × 76mm gun.

MISSILE CRAFT: 6 Sov *Osa* PFM with 4 × SS-N-2A *Styx*.

TORPEDO: 38:
12 *Epitrop* PFT with 4 × 533mm TT.
26 Ch *Huchuan* PHT with 2 × 533mm TT (incl ε8 non-op).

PATROL: 40:
OFFSHORE: 4 *Democratia* (GDR M-40) PCO.
COASTAL: 2 Sov *Kronshtadt* PCC.
INSHORE: 8: 4 Ch *Shanghai* PFI, 4 Ch *Huchuan*.
RIVERINE: 26: 4 *Brutar* with 1 × 100mm gun, 22⟨.

MINE WARFARE: 34:

MINELAYERS: 2 *Cosar*, capacity 100 mines.

MCM: 32:
4 *Musca* MSC.
3 T.301 MSI (plus some 9 non-op).
25 VD141 MSI⟨.

SUPPORT AND MISCELLANEOUS: 10:
2 'Croitor' log spt/tenders (hel deck), 3 spt tankers, 2 AGOR, 1 trg, 2 tugs.
HELICOPTERS: 2 1AR-316.

NAVAL INFANTRY: (Marines): (some 5,000).
1 inf div (3 inf, 1 arty regt).
1 indep tk regt.
EQUIPMENT:
MBT: 294: 107 T-34, 187 TR-580.
ASSAULT GUN: 36 SUC-76, 20 ISU-152.
APC: 193 TAB-71, 46 TABC-79, 8 TAB-77, 3 TAB-80, 5 BTR-50.
TOWED ARTY: 100mm: 54 Gun 77; 122mm: 36 M-1938 (M-30), 152mm: 36 Model 81.
MRL: 122mm: 18 APR-21, 18 APR-40.
MORTARS: 120mm: 36 Model 1982, 104 M-120.

COASTAL DEFENCE (1,000): HQ Constanţa.
4 sectors:
4 coastal arty bty with 32 130mm.
10 AA arty bty.
3 with 18 30mm.
5 with 30 37mm.
2 with 12 57mm

AIR FORCE: 20,000 (10,700 conscripts);
486 cbt ac, 220 armed hel (attack hel).
Air Force comd plus 2 air div: 8 cbt regt.
FGA: 2 regt with 19 MiG-17, 59 IAR-93, 72 MiG-15.
FIGHTER: 19 sqn regt with 189 MiG-21, 36 MiG-23, 12 MiG-29.
RECCE: 2 sqn: 1 with 14 Il-28 (recce/ECM), 1 with 10 MiG-21.
TRANSPORT: 1 regt with 9 An-24, 14 An-26, 2 Il-18, 2 Boeing 707, 1 Rombac 1-11, 10 1AR-316B, 7 Mi-8.
SURVEY: 3 An-30.
HELICOPTERS: 5 regt plus 2 sqn with 104 IAR-316B, 82 IAR-330-H, 28 Mi-8, 2 Mi-17, 4 SA-365N.
TRAINING: 32 IAR-823, 10 IAR28, 14 *IAR-93, 45 L-29, 32 L-39, 18* MiG-15, 29 *MiG-21, *2 MiG-29UB, *6 1AR-99. *6 MiG-23DC, 17 An-2, 13 YAK-5.
AAM: AA-2 Atoll, AA-7 Apex.
AD: 1 div: 20 SAM sites with 120 SA-2.

FORCES ABROAD:
UN AND PEACEKEEPING:
IRAQ/KUWAIT (UNIKOM): 7 Observers.

PARAMILITARY:
BORDER GUARDS: (Ministry of Interior): 15,000 (11,700 conscripts: 6 bde, 7 naval gp; 20 Ch Shanghai II PFI).
GENDARMERIE (Ministry of Interior): 34,800: 8 bde; some APC.
NATIONAL GUARD: in process of being reorganized.
CONSTRUCTION TROOPS: 25,000.

SLOVENIA

GDP	1991ε: $19.04bn
Growth	1991ε: −20%
Debt	1991: $1.66bn
Def bdgt	1992: $170m

Population 1,927,000 (90% Slovenes)

TOTAL ARMED FORCES:
ACTIVE: 15,000
Terms of service: 7 months.
RESERVES: ε85,000.

ARMY: 15,000 (20,000 planned)
7 Military District.
1 inf bde.
1 ATK bde.
1 AD bde.
EQUIPMENT
MBT: ε120 T-55
APC: ε20 plus arty, RCL, AD guns and man-portable SAM.

PARAMILITARY
Police: 4,500 armed (plus 5,000 reserve).

SWEDEN

GDP	1990:	S kr 1,340.15bn ($226.42bn)	
	1991:	S kr 1,431.60bn ($236.73bn)	
Growth	1990:	0.3%	1991: −1.2%
Inflation	1990:	10.4%	1991: 9.5%
Debt	1990:	$167.0bn	1991: $172.0bn
Def bdgt	1991:	S kr 35.454bn ($5.86bn)	
	1992:	S kr 37.784bn ($6.19bn)	
$1 = kr	1989:	6.4469	1990: 5.9188
	1991:	6.0475	1992: 6.1000
kr = kronor			

Population: 8,336,400

	13–17	18–22	23–32
Men	263,000	286,800	589,900
Women	250,500	273,000	562,700

TOTAL ARMED FORCES:
ACTIVE: 60,500 (38,800 conscripts);
Terms of service: Army and Navy 7½–15 months, Air Force 8–12 months.
RESERVES[a] (obligation to age 47): 709,000:
Army (incl Local Defence and Home Guard) 550,000; Navy 102,000; Air Force 57,000.

ARMY: 43,500 (27,000 conscripts).
3 Military comd; 26 Defence districts (*Laens*).
PEACE ESTABLISHMENT:
41 armd, cav, inf, arty, AA, engr, sig, spt regt (local defence, cadre for mob, basic conscript plus refresher trg).
WAR ESTABLISHMENT: (700,000 on mob)
Field Army: (350,000).
4 armd bde.
2 mech bde (incl *Gotland* bde).
10 inf, 5 *Norrland* bde.
100 indep armd, inf, arty and AA arty bn.
1 avn bn.
6 arty avn pl.
Local Defence Units: (230,000)
60 indep bn, 400–500 indep coy.
Home Guard: (125,000)
incl inf, arty, static arty, AD
EQUIPMENT:
MBT: 340 Strv-101, 110 Strv-102/-104 (*Centurion*), 335 Strv-103B.
LIGHT TANKS: ε250 Ikv-91.
APC: 600 Pbv-302.
TOWED ARTY: 105mm: 550 Type-40; 155mm: 300 FH-77A/-B.
SP ARTY: 155mm: 30 BK-1A.
MORTARS: 81mm: 1,000; 120mm: ε600.
ATGW: RB-55 (*TOW*, incl Pvrbv 551 SP), RB-56 *Bill*.
RCL: 84mm: AT-4, *Carl Gustav*; 90mm: PV-1110.
AD GUNS: 40mm: 600.
SAM: RBS-70 (incl Lvrbv SP), RB-77 (*Improved HAWK*).
AIRCRAFT: 17 SK-61C (BAe *Bulldog*) observation, 2 Dornier Do-27 tpt.
HELICOPTERS: 20 Hkp-9A ATK, 16 Hkp-3 tpt, 26 Hkp-5B trg, 19 Hkp-6A utility.

NAVY: 9,500, incl coast defence and naval air (5,950 conscripts).
BASES: Muskö, Karlskrona, Härnösand, Göteborg (spt only).
SUBMARINES: 12:
4 *Västergötland* with TP-617 HWT and TP-42 LWT.
1 modernized *Näcken* (AIP) with TP-617 and TP-42.
2 *Näcken*, 5 *Sjöormen*, with TP-61 and TP-42.
PATROL AND COASTAL COMBATANTS: 41:
MISSILE CRAFT: 33 PFM:
3 *Göteborg* with 4 × 2 RBS-15 SSM; plus
2 × 533mm or 4 × 400mm TT, 4 × ASW mor.
2 *Stockholm* with 4 × 2 RBS-15 SSM; plus
2 × 533mm or 4 × 400mm TT, 4 × ASW mor.
16 *Hugin* with 6 RB-12 (No *Penguin*) SSM; plus
4 ASW mor.
12 *Norrköping* with 4 × 2 RBS-15 SSM or up to 6 × 533mm TT.
PATROL: 8:
1 PCI, 7 PCI⟨.
MINE WARFARE: 28:

MINELAYERS: 3:
1 *Carlskrona* (200 mines), trg.
2 *Älvsborg* (200 mines).
(mines can be laid by all SS classes).
MINE COUNTERMEASURES: 25:
1 *Uto* MCMV spt.
7 *Landsort* MCC.
3 *Arkö* MSC.
10 MSI, 4 MSI⟨.
AMPHIBIOUS: craft only; 12 LCM.
SUPPORT AND MISCELLANEOUS: 11:
1 AGI, 1 salvage ship, 1 survey, 6 icebreakers, 2 tugs.

COAST DEFENCE:
6 coast arty bde: 12 mobile, 53 static units incl
2 amph defence bn, arty, barrier bn, minelayer sqn.
EQUIPMENT:
GUNS: 40mm incl L/70 AA, 75mm, 120mm incl
CD-80 *Karin* (mobile); 75mm, 120mm *Ersta* (static).
MORTARS: 81mm.
SSM: RBS-17 *Hellfire*, RBS-08A, RBS-15KA, RB-52.
MINELAYERS: 13 coastal, 16 inshore.
PATROL CRAFT: 18 PCI⟨.
AMPHIBIOUS: 16 LCM, 80 LCU, about 60 LCA.

NAVAL AIR: 1 cbt ac, 14 armed hel.
ASW: 1 C-212 ac.
HELICOPTERS: 3 sqn with 14 Hkp-4B/C ASW, 10 Hkp-6 liaison.

AIR FORCE: 7,500 (5,500 conscripts);
499 cbt ac, no armed hel.
1 attack staff.
4 AD districts.
FGA: 6 sqn:
5 with 79 AJ-37;
1 (OCU) with 18 SK-37.
FIGHTER: 11 sqn:
3 with 65 J-35, 11 SK-35C;
8 with 138 JA-37.
RECCE: 3 sqn with *48 SH/SF-37.
ECM: 2 *Caravelle* (ECM/ELINT).
TRANSPORT: 1 sqn with 8 C-130E/H, 3 *King Air*
200, 2 *Metro* III (VIP), 16 SK-60E, 1 SAAB 340B.
TRAINING: 22 J-32D/E (14 -E ECM trg; 8 -D
target-towing), 30 SK-50, 140 *SK-60 (also have
lt attack/recce role), 50 SK-61.
SAR: 10 Hkp, 10 *Super Puma*.
3 Hkp 9B (Bo-105 CBS).
UTILITY: 6 Hkp-3, 2 Hkp-10 hel.
AAM: RB-24 (AIM-9B/3 *Sidewinder*), RB-27
(*Falcon*), RB-28 (*Improved Falcon*), RB-71
(*Skyflash*), RB-74 AIM 91 (*Sidewinder*).
ASM: RB-04E, RB-05A, RB-15F, RB-75 (*Maverick*).
AD: Semi-automatic control and surveillance
system, *Stril* 60, co-ordinates all AD components.

FORCES ABROAD:
UN AND PEACEKEEPING:
ANGOLA (UNAVEM II): 15 Observers, 10 civilian police.
CROATIA (UNPROFOR): 106 incl 34 Observers, 6 mil police, 1 inf coy.
CYPRUS (UNFICYP): 8.
EL SALVADOR (ONUSAL): 4 Observers.
INDIA/PAKISTAN (UNMOGIP): 8 Observers.
IRAQ/KUWAIT (UNIKOM): 7 Observers.
KOREA (NNSC): Staff.
LEBANON (UNIFIL): 548: 1 log bn.
MIDDLE EAST (UNTSO): 36 Observers.

PARAMILITARY:
COAST GUARD: (600); 1 *Gotland* PCO and 1 Kbv-171 PCC (fishery protection), 70 PCI‹; Air Arm: 3 C-212 MR, 1 Cessna 337G, 1 402C ac.
CIVIL DEFENCE: shelters for 6,300,000. All between age 16–25 liable for civil defence duty.
VOLUNTARY AUXILIARY ORGANIZATIONS: Some 35,000 volunteers for army units from: Motor Cycle Corps, Radio Organization, Women's Motor Transport Corps, Women's Auxiliary Defence Services, Red Cross, Swedish Women's Voluntary Defence Service.

a Each year some 100,000 reservists carry out refresher trg; length of trg depends on rank (officers up to 31 days, NCO and specialists, 24 days, others 17 days). Commitment is 5 exercises during reserve service period, plus mob call-outs.

SWITZERLAND

GDP	1990:	fr 312.40bn ($224.90bn)	
	1991:	fr 327.00bn ($228.03bn)	
Growth	1990:	2.2%	1991: −0.5%
Inflation	1990:	5.4%	1991: 5.8%
Debt	1990:	$341bn	
Def bdgt	1991:	fr 5.454bn ($3.80bn)	
	1992:	fr 5.548bn ($3.65bn)	
$1 = fr	1989:	1.6359	1990: 1.3892
	1991:	1.4340	1992: 1.5200
fr = francs			

Population: 6,508,600

	13–17	18–22	23–32
Men	194,000	221,700	498,200
Women	184,500	210,200	479,000

TOTAL ARMED FORCES: (Air Corps forms part of the Army):
ACTIVE: about 1,600 regular, plus recruits (2 intakes of 18,000 each for 17 weeks only).
Terms of service: 17 weeks compulsory recruit trg at age 19–20, followed by reservist refresher trg of 3 weeks over an 8-year period between ages 20–32 for *Auszug* (call out), 39 days over a 3-year period (33–42) for *Landwehr* (militia). some 390,000 attend trg each year.
RESERVES (all services): 625,000.

ARMY: 565,000 on mob.
3 corps, each 1 mech, 2 inf div, 1 inf, 1 cyclist, 1 SAM, 1 engr regt, 1 arty bn, 1 hel sqn, 1 lt ac flt.
1 mtn corps with 3 mtn div (each 1 inf, 1 fortification, 1 redoubt bde), 1 mtn, 7 inf, 1 engr, 5 pack horse bn, 1 hel sqn.
Corps Tps:
6 Territorial Zones: each with log, medical and civil defence regt.
11 border bde.
Army Tps:
1 inf, 3 engr regt, 3 sigs (EW) bn.
1 airport guard regt, 1 indep airport bn.
20 fortress guard coy.
EQUIPMENT:
MBT: some 812: some 275 Pz-87 (*Leopard* 2), 43 Pz-55 (*Centurion*), 143 Pz-61, 195 Pz-68, 156 Pz-68/75.
AIFV: 480 M-63/-73 (M-113 with 20mm).
APC: 709 M-63/-73 (M-113) incl variants.
TOWED ARTY: 105mm: some 288 Model-35, 420 Model-46.
SP ARTY: 155mm: 468 PzHb-66/-74 (M-109U).
MORTARS: 2,000: 81mm: M-33, M-72; 120mm: 300 (incl 120 SP) M-64/-74.
ATGW: 180 MOWAG *Piranha* with *TOW*-2; 2,700 B/B-65 (*Bantam*), B/B-77 (*Dragon*).
RL: 83mm: 20,000 M-80.
RCL: 106mm: 600 M-58.
ATK GUNS: 90mm: 850 Model-50/-57; 106mm: 150 M-58.
AD GUNS: 20mm: 1,700; 35mm: 260 GDF-002.
SAM: 60 B/L-84 (*Rapier*).
MARINE: 12 *Aquarius* patrol boats.

AIR CORPS: 60,000 on mob (incl military airfield guard units).
242 cbt ac, no armed hel.
The Air Corp is an integral part of the Army, structured in 1 Air Force, 1 AD, 1 airbase and 1 bde Comd and control.
FGA: 6 sqn with 80 *Hunter* F-58, 7 T-68.
FIGHTER: 8 sqn:
6 with 91 *Tiger* II/F-5E, 12 *Tiger* II/F-5F;
2 with 30 *Mirage* IIIS, 4 -III BS.
RECCE: 1 sqn with 18 *Mirage* IIIRS.
LIAISON/SAR: 1 sqn with 18 PC-6, 2 *Learjet* 36.
HELICOPTERS: 7 sqn with 9 AS-332 M-1, 5 SA-316.
TRAINING: 19 *Hawk* Mk 66, 28 P-3, 39 PC-7, 8 PC-9.
ASM: AGM-65A/B *Maverick*.
AAM: AIM-9 *Sidewinder*, AIM-26 *Falcon*.
1 airbase bde:
3 regt × 4 bn, each with 4 bty of 20mm and twin 35mm guns with *Skyguard* fire-control radar.

1 AD bde:
  1 SAM regt (2 bn, each of 2 bty; 64 *Bloodhound*);
  7 AD arty regt (each with 2 bn of 3 bty; 35mm guns, *Skyguard* fire control).

FORCES ABROAD:
UN AND PEACEKEEPING:
CROATIA (UNPROFOR): 4 Observers.
KOREA (NNSC): 4 Staff.
MIDDLE EAST (UNTSO): 5 Observers, fixed wing air sp.
WESTERN SAHARA (MINURSO): 1 med unit (60).

PARAMILITARY:
CIVIL DEFENCE: 480,000 (300,000 fully trained). Shelter programme for 5,500,000; emergency supplies and medical facilities.

UKRAINE

GDP	1991:	r 234.0bn ($137.65bn)
Growth[a]	1991:	−9.6%
Inflation[b]	1991:	84.20%
Debt	1991:	$13.40bn
Def bdgt	1992:	r 116bn
$1 = r	1991:	1.70

Population: 51,839,000 (20.3% Russian)

13–17	18–22	23–32
3,651,000	3,369,500	6,842,800

[a] NMP growth.
[b] Year average.

TOTAL ARMED FORCES:
ACTIVE 230,000 (excl strategic Nuclear Forces and Black Sea Fleet)
Terms of service: 18 months.
RESERVES Some 1m with military service within 5 years.
Forming independent armed forces to include a navy based on former Soviet Union forces. Two year transition period.

STRATEGIC NUCLEAR FORCES:
(CIS-controlled forces on Ukraine territory)
ICBM: 176
  SS-19 *Stiletto* (RS-18): 130 (at two sites).
  SS-24 *Scalpel* (RS-22): 46 (silo-based, one site co-located with SS-19).
BOMBERS: 41 (plus 2 in store), 21 Tu-95H (ALCM-equipped plus 2-A/-B in store), 20 Tu-160 (ALCM-equipped).

TANKERS: 20 Il-78.

GROUND FORCES: 150,000
(former Carpathian, Kiev and Odessa MDs)
6 Army HQ
1 Corps HQ
1 arty corps HQ
4 TD (2 trg)
14 MRD (2 trg)
1 ABD
2 AB bde
1 *Spetsnaz* bde
3 arty div
8 arty bde/regt, (incl 3 MRL)
7 ATK bde
12 SSM bde
9 SAM bde
7 attack hel regt.
EQUIPMENT:
MBT: 6,300: 2,700 T-54/-55, 200 T-62, 2,100 T-64, 1,000 T-72, 300 T-80.
LIGHT TANKS: 180 PT-76.
AIFV: 3,686: 1,770 BMP-1, 1,250 BMP-2, 6 BMP-3, 350 BRM, 310 BMD.
APC: 2,200 BTR-50P/-60P/-70/-80/-152, 100 BTR-D, 1,500 MT-LB plus 4,500 'look alikes'.
TOWED ARTY: 830: 122mm: 250 D-30; 152mm: 250 D-20, 110 2A65, 220 2A36.
SP ARTY: 1,165: 122mm: 520 2S1; 152mm: 510 2S3, 25 2S5, 10 2S19, 203mm: 100 2S7.
COMBINED GUN/MORTAR: 120mm: 80 2S9.
MRL: 531: 122mm: 310 BM-21, 18 9P138; 132mm: 3 BM-13; 220mm: 150 9P140; 300mm: 50 9A52.
MORTARS: 470: 120mm: 210 2S12, 260 PM-38.
SSM: 132 *Scud*, 72 *FROG*/SS-21.
HELICOPTERS:
  ATTACK: 240 Mi-24.
  SUPPORT: 60 Mi-6, 280 Mi-8, 8 Mi-24K, 5 Mi-24P.
  TRANSPORT: 20 Mi-26, 80 Mi-2.

AIR FORCE: 50,000
3 air army, some 1,100 cbt ac.
BOMBERS: 2 div HQ, 3 regt (1 trg) with 30 Tu-16, 30 Tu-22, 36 Tu-26.
FGA/BOMBER: 2 div, 5 regt with 150 Su-24.
FGA: 2 regt with 60 Su-24, 30 Su-25.
FIGHTER: 2 div, 8 regt with 80 MiG-23, 220 MiG-29, 40 Su-27.
RECCE: 3 regt with 30 Tu-22, 15 MiG-25, 30 Su-17, 12 Su-24.
ECM: 1 regt with 35 Yak-28.
TRAINING: 4 centres with 240 MiG-21, 60 Su-24, 550 L-39/L-29.

AIR DEFENCE: ε30,000
1 PVO Army, 270 cbt ac.

FIGHTER: 7 regt: 80 Su-15, 110 MiG-23, 80 MiG-25.
SAM: 2,400.

NAVY
BLACK SEA FLEET: (HQ Sevastopol)
(Ukraine). To be divided between Russia,
Ukraine, and Georgia. Details not yet decided.
BASES: Sevastopol, Odessa (Ukraine), Poti
(Georgia), .
SUBMARINES: 18: tactical 16: 2 SSG, 14 SS; other
roles: 2.
PRINCIPAL SURFACE COMBATANTS: 39: 1 CGH, 5
cruisers, 7 destroyers, 26 frigates.
OTHER SURFACE SHIPS: 60 patrol and coastal
combatants, 30 mine warfare, 16 amph, some
140 spt and misc.
NAVAL AVIATION: 5,300[a].
some 163 cbt ac (plus 215 in store); 85 cbt hel.
BOMBERS: 2 regt, 2 sqn with 45 Tu-26 (Tu-22M); 10
Tu-16, 10 Tu-22; plus ε50 Tu-16 in store.
FGA: 40 Su-17; plus 170 Su-17, Su-25 in store.
FIGHTER: 1 regt, 35 MiG-29.
ASW:
  AIRCRAFT: 23 Be-12.
  HELICOPTERS: 85: 31 Mi-14, 49 Ka-25, 5 Ka-27.
MR/EW:
  AIRCRAFT: 21: 2 An-12, 12 Tu-16, 6 Tu-22, 1 Il-20.
  HELICOPTERS: 5 Ka-25.
MCM: 5 Mi-14 hel.
TANKERS: 3 Tu-16.
NAVAL INFANTRY:[a]
1 bde: (265 APC, 60 arty/MRL).
COASTAL DEFENCE:[a] 2,300
1 Coast Defence div (270 MBT, 320 AIFV, 160
arty/MRL).
1 arty bde (120 arty).

FORCES ABROAD
BOSNIA-HERZEGOVINA (UNPROFOR): 1 inf bn.

PARAMILITARY FORCES
National Guard: 6,000 (to be 30,000; former MVD
eqpt in service).

[a] Allotted to Ukraine under CFE protocol.

+--+
| 'Federal Republic of |
| Yugoslavia': |
| **SERBIA/MONTENEGRO** |
+--+

GDP[a]	1990:	ND 1,428.34bn ($54.37bn)
	1991ε:	ND 5,712.00bn ($18.75bn)
Growth	1990: −9.0%	1991ε: −20%
Inflation	1990: 180%	1991ε: 300%
Debt	1990: $17.60bn	1991: $16.40bn

Def bdgt[a]	1991ε:	ND 135.00bn ($3.49bn)
	1992ε:	ND 245.00bn ($3.76bn)
$1 = ND[a]	1989: 2.876	1990: 11.318
	1991: 37.850	1992: 70.000

ND = New Dinar
[a] Dollar values are estimated.

Population: Serbia 9,893,000 (incl 65% Serbs).
Montenegro 643,000 (incl 68% Montenegrins,
13.5% Muslims). A further 2,032,000 Serbs were
living in the other Yugoslav Republics before the
civil war began.

TOTAL ARMED FORCES:
ACTIVE: 135,000 (44,500 conscripts).
Terms of service: 12 months.
RESERVES: some 400,000 (former Territorial
Defence Force).

ARMY: (JNA) some 100,000 (ε37,000 conscripts);
1 mech inf div HQ.

3 tk bde.	1 mech bde.
14 mot inf bde.	4 mtn bde.
2 inf bde.	1 SSM (*FROG*) bde.
1 arty bde.	8 arty regt.
1 ATK arty bde.	5 ATK arty regt.
9 AD regt.	1 SAM-6 regt.

RESERVES:
6 partisan 'div' (former Territorial Defence).
EQUIPMENT:
MBT: 1,000: 800 T-54/-55, some 200 M-84 (T-74;
mod T-72) and T-72.
LIGHT TANKS: 13 PT-76.
RECCE: 92 M-3A1, 18 M-8, some 130 BRDM-2.
AIFV: 952 M-80.
APC: 143 M-60P.
TOWED ARTY: 1,364: 105mm: 334 M-56; 122mm: 24
M-1931/37, 216 M-1938, 251 D-30; 130mm: 159
M-46; 152mm: 12 M-1937, 11 D-20, 72 M-84;
155mm: 201 M-59, 84 M-65.
SP ARTY: 105mm: M-7; 122mm: 84 2S1.
MRL: 128mm: 55 M-77, 132 M-63.
MORTARS:[c] 82mm: 3,400; 120mm: 3,000.
SSM: 10 *FROG*-7.
ATGW: 282 AT-3 *Sagger* incl SP (BOV-1, BRDM-1/2).
RCL:[c] 57mm: 1,550; 82mm: 2,000 M-60PB SP;
105mm: 650 M-65.
ATK GUNS:[c] 75mm: 748: M-1943, Pak 40; 90mm: 80
M-36B2 (incl SP); 100mm: 511 T-12.
AD GUNS:[c] 20mm: 166 M-55/-75, 29 BOV-3 SP
triple; 30mm: 174 M-53, M-53/-59, 8 BOV-3 SP;
57mm: 20 ZSU-57-2 SP.
SAM: 60 SA-6, 140 SA-7, 42 SA-9.

NAVY: ε6,000 (4,500 conscripts).
BASE: Kotor. (Most former Yug bases are now in
Croatian hands.)

SUBMARINES: 5:
2 *Sava* SS with 533mm TT
3 *Heroj* SS with 533mm TT
(Plus 5 *Una* SSI for SF ops).

FRIGATES: 4:
2 *Kotor* with 4 × SS-N-2B *Styx* SSM, 2 × 12 ASW RL, 2 × 3 ASTT.
2 *Split* (Sov *Koni*) with 4 SS-N-2B *Styx* SSM, 2 × 12 ASW RL.

PATROL AND COASTAL COMBATANTS: 54:
MISSILE CRAFT: 12:
5 *Rade Koncar* PFM with 2 × SS-N-2B *Styx*.
7 *Mitar Acev* (Sov *Osa-I*) PFM with 4 × SS-N-2A.
TORPEDO CRAFT: 12:
12 *Topcider* (Sov *Shershen*) with 4 × 533mm TT.
PATROL: 30:
COASTAL: 1 *Mornar* ASW with 4 × ASW RL.
INSHORE: 6 *Mirna*
RIVERINE: some 23.
MINE WARFARE: 13
MINELAYERS: None, but DTM-211 LCT can lay 100 mines – see amph forces.
MCM: 13:
3 *Vukov Klanac* MHC
4 UK *Ham* MSI.
6 *M-117* MSI.
(plus some 13 riverine MSI⟨⟩).
AMPHIBIOUS: craft only; 33: 11 DTM-211 LCT, 22 DJC-601 LCM.
SUPPORT AND MISCELLANEOUS: 5:
3 PO-91 *Lubin* tpt, 1 trg, 1 river flagship.

MARINES: (900)
2 marine bde (2 regt each of 2 bn).

AIR FORCE: 29,000 (3,000 conscripts);
480 cbt ac, 136 armed hel.
3 air corps each 1 AD div, incl ac, AD arty, SAM.
FGA: 12 sqn with 69 P-2 *Kraguj*, 50 *Jastreb*, 25 *Super Galeb*, 69 *Orao*-2.
FIGHTER: 8 sqn with 98 MiG-21F/PF/M/bis, 10 MiG-21U, 18 MiG-29 (16 -A, 2 -UB).
RECCE: 4 sqn with 12 *Galeb*, 20 *Jastreb* RJ-1, 25 *Orao*-1, 14 MiG-21.
ARMED HEL: 36 Mi-8 (aslt); 100 *Gazela* (attack).
ASW: 1 hel sqn with 4 Mi-14, 4 Ka-25, 2 Ka-27.
TRANSPORT: 2 ac sqn with 2 An-12, 15 An-26, 4 CL-215 (SAR, fire-fighting), 2 *Falcon* 50 (VIP), 2 *Learjet* 25, 6 PC-6, 6 Yak-40.
LIAISON: 46 UTVA-66 ac, 14 *Partizan* hel.
TRAINING: ac: 70 **Super Galeb/Jastreb*, 100 UTVA-75/-76;
hel: 20 *Gazela*.
AAM: AA-2 *Atoll*, AA-8 *Aphid*, AA-10 *Alamo*, AA-11 *Archer*.
ASM: AGM-65 *Maverick*, AS-7 *Kerry*.
AD: 8 SAM bn, 8 sites with 24 SA-2, 16 SA-3. 15 regt AD arty.

FORCES ABROAD:
UN AND PEACEKEEPING:
ANGOLA (UNAVEM II): 11 Observers.

---

c A number of these weapons have been taken over by Bosnia-Herzegovina, Croatia, Macedonia and Slovenia.

Russia

Last year's edition of *The Military Balance* went to press just after the attempted coup against President Gorbachev became known and before his return to Moscow. Since then the Soviet Union has broken up and the eventual size, shape and degree of cooperation of the armed forces of the newly independent republics remain in a state of flux.

President Gorbachev's last contribution to nuclear disarmament was to announce in October 1991 (in response to President Bush's earlier announcement) the Soviet Union's intention: to withdraw and destroy all warheads for artillery and short-range surface-to-surface missiles, to withdraw nuclear weapons (other than SLBM) from naval ships and maritime shore air stations, to withdraw anti-aircraft nuclear warheads and to destroy atomic demolition mines. The details of this announcement and those made later by President Yeltsin, who signed a joint understanding with the US on further substantial reductions in strategic offensive arms, are analysed in 'Nuclear Developments' on pp. 222–28.

At first it looked as though the Commonwealth of Independent States (CIS), formed in Minsk in December 1991 by the four nuclear-armed republics and joined later that month in Alma-Ata by all the republics of the former Soviet Union, except Georgia (and the three Baltic states), might keep control of all of the armed forces. Shortly afterwards it was proposed that the forces might split into three components. The first component, which would be under direct CIS command, would comprise all nuclear forces, anti-ballistic missile (ABM) and air defence forces, airborne troops, the Border Command and probably the navy. The second component would consist of ground forces and their supporting air forces, to be known as general-purpose forces, which, while being administered by the republics, would be considered as joint forces intended to ensure the security of all CIS members. The third component would be republican paramilitary forces such as national guards. The last Defence Minister of the USSR, Marshal of the Air Force, Yevgeniy Shaposhnikov was appointed Supreme Commander of the CIS armed forces in December 1991. Later, in March 1992, a commander was appointed for CIS general-purpose forces. A number of agreements, covering a wide range of subjects, were reached at each of the CIS summit meetings (a full list of those involving defence and security matters is shown at p. 245). Amongst those covering military matters were agreements on: Peacekeeping, the Status of General Purpose Forces, Maintenance of Supplies, Recruitment and Joint Command of Border Troops. However, not all agreements were signed by all 11 CIS republics.

On 15 May 1992, Armenia, Azerbaijan, Byelarus, Georgia, Kazakhstan, Moldova, Russia and Ukraine signed a Joint Declaration with the aim of furthering the implementation of the Treaty on Conventional Armed Forces in Europe which included agreement on how the quotas for Treaty Limited Equipments (TLE) of the former Soviet Union would be shared between them without violating the provisions of CFE. On 23 May, Byelarus, Kazakhstan, Ukraine and Russia, together with the US, signed a protocol to the START Treaty; it was agreed that the four republics, as successor states, would assume the obligations of the former USSR under the Treaty.

Once it had become clear that Ukraine, and possibly other republics, were determined to form their own independent armed forces and so undermine the concept of joint general-purpose forces, President Yeltsin issued in May 1992 a decree establishing Russian Armed Forces and setting up a Ministry of Defence. Russia then took control of all armed forces in the Groups of Forces (in Germany, Poland and the Baltic republics) and also of the 14th Army (mainly based in Moldova), and the former Soviet units still in the Trans-Caucasus republics. There have been reports that some units in the Trans-Caucasus have been transferred to Armenia and Azerbaijan. Forces in the Central Asian republics currently remain under joint control of Russia and the republic concerned. Already Turkmenistan has signed a protocol with Russia to set up national armed forces under joint command; air defence is to be a Russian responsibility. In this section we list: all forces under CIS control; the navy, including the Black Sea Fleet which is to be divided between Russia, Ukraine and Georgia in three years, but no details of the split are available (the Black Sea Fleet is listed again under Ukraine); Ground, Air and Air Defence forces, including those located in the Groups of Forces, the 14th Army and in the republics of the Trans-Caucasus (these forces are also shown under the country in which they are deployed as Foreign Forces). Forces in the Central Asian republics are listed under both the relevant republic and Russia.

By June 1992 the armed forces of the CIS had been reduced to the Strategic Deterrent Forces (ICBM, SLBM and bombers (as yet it is unclear whether medium bombers, which are not START-countable but which formed part of the long-range air force, are subordinate to the CIS or not)), ABM defence, Space and Border Troops (although here a number of republics are forming their own border troops to police the borders between republics of the former USSR). The CIS will also oversee the destruction of nuclear weapons.

Nuclear Forces

Strategic Systems

The development of rail-mobile SS-24 has been completed, with three more launchers added. There are now more than 340 road-mobile SS-25 deployed, an increase of about 80, of which some 50 are deployed in Russia. SS-25 production may continue, as it is the most modern single-warhead ICBM in the Russian inventory. Older ICBM continue to be withdrawn; in the last 12 months 46 SS-11 and seven SS-17 have been eliminated. No new SSBN have become operational, while five *Yankee-I*, armed with single-warhead SS-N-6 have been retired. There has been virtually no change to the strategic bomber force, although the numbers attributed to training and test roles have been altered.

Short-Range Nuclear Forces

With the decision to destroy all SSM and artillery nuclear warheads, it is possible that most SSM will be withdrawn from service and units disbanded. So far, five *Scud* and one SS-21-armed SSM brigades have been withdrawn from the Western Group of Forces (WGF). About two-thirds of the Tu-16 medium bombers have been withdrawn from units and placed in store. All nuclear warheads for tactical nuclear weapons are now located on Russian territory.

Conventional Forces

Withdrawal from Eastern Europe and Mongolia

The withdrawal from eastern Germany continues according to schedule; one army has completely withdrawn, although some of its formations have been resubordinated to other armies still in Germany. Two armies have only one division left in Germany; in total there are now only ten divisions there (six tank, three motor rifle and one artillery). Initially, divisions were withdrawn and redeployed elsewhere; now it is usual for them to be disbanded while still in Germany and their armaments back-loaded to stores or destroyed *in situ*. Whether surplus manpower is reallocated to understrength units still in Germany is not known, nor whether back-loaded equipment is being kept as mobilization packs. A number of air force units have withdrawn and the aircraft inventory in the WGF is some 200 lower than 12 months ago. Withdrawal of the Northern Group of Forces from Poland has been speeded up and is now due to be completed by the end of 1992. About half the force, which includes the separate Air Army Legnica which used to be controlled at Theatre of Operations level, has now left Poland. There is little information available as to where withdrawn units and equipments have been relocated. The withdrawal from Mongolia will be completed in 1992; only 3,000 administrative troops now remain.

Ground Forces

Shortly after the Baltic states achieved independence, the Baltic Military District was re-designated the North-Western Group of Forces. Russia had maintained that it did not intend to withdraw its troops from the Baltic states until the withdrawal from Germany and

Poland had been completed; more recently there have been talks on speeding up the withdrawal, but no firm schedule has been agreed. There have been complaints that new recruits have been sent to units in the Baltic states contrary to an agreement that there would be no reinforcement. However, if troop rotation is not allowed, units in the Baltic states will only have their regular cadre of officers and *praporshchiks* (long-service warrant officers) by the time they come to withdraw in 1994. Also, the airborne training division is located in Lithuania; we may see this unit redeploy shortly if it cannot continue to train new parachutists.

All ground force units must be suffering severe manpower shortages, not just because call-up orders are being widely ignored but because most republics now restrict their men to serving only on their own territory. While the number of tank and motor rifle divisions are being reduced as these are disbanded, the size of the airborne forces has increased. The division resubordinated to the Ministry of Interior troops has been returned to the Ministry of Defence, and there is also an eighth division not previously listed in *The Military Balance*; it is located in Uzbekistan. There are also three more airborne brigades; it is not known when these previously unlisted units were formed.

Production of the more modern equipment types continues. To the combined inventories of Russia, Byelarus and Ukraine have been added: 200 T-80 and over 4,000 T-72 MBT (this last figure is a reassessment, however, and not a true increase achieved in the last 12 months), 90 203mm 2S7 and 130 152mm 2S19 SP guns, 40 300mm *Smerch* 9A52 and around 900 220mm 9P140 MRL. The number of Mi-24 attack helicopters has risen by about 100.

Units of the Russian Army are taking part in peacekeeping operations for the first time. An airborne battalion has deployed to Croatia as part of UNPROFOR. Regional peacekeeping forces have been established to provide buffer zones between: Moldova and the breakaway province of Dnestr; Georgia and South Ossetia, which is attempting to split from Georgia and join the North Ossetian autonomous republic of Russia. Six battalions have deployed to Moldova and two to South Ossetia.

Naval Forces

The Russian Navy has been hard hit by the economic measures imposed over the last 12 months and before. Manpower has been substantially reduced, sea-time has been drastically cut and no warships are deployed in the Mediterranean, Persian Gulf or Indian Ocean. No new construction has been started in 1992 and work on about half the 130 ships under construction has been halted. A large number of older ships have been taken out of service; a few new ships have commissioned.

One *Oscar*-class SSGN has commissioned, while one *Echo*-class SSGN and one *Victor*-class SSN have been retired. All six high-speed, titanium-hulled *Alfa*-class SSN have been prematurely retired after only 15 years service. Seven *Juliet*-class and the last 20 *Whiskey*-class diesel-powered submarines have also been paid off. Virtually all non-nuclear submarines kept in store have been sold off for scrap.

The *Kuznetsov* (originally named *Tbilisi*) aircraft carrier, which commissioned in late 1990, was transferred from the Black Sea to the Northern Fleet in December 1991. The carrier *Kiev* has been prematurely retired from the Pacific Fleet and a second carrier of the class is in long refit. Two large carriers are under construction in the Nikolayev South shipyard in Ukraine. It appears that work on fitting-out the *Varyag* (launched in late 1988) has been suspended awaiting funds from a hypothetical foreign sale; work on the larger *Ulyanovsk* (laid down in 1988) has stopped and dismantling has commenced. All *Yak*-38 V/STOL aircraft have been withdrawn from service, leaving the *Kuznetsov* as the only carrier capable of operating fixed-wing aircraft.

More than 30 other surface combatants have been retired, including one *Moskva*-class, one *Admiral Zozulya*-class and three *Kronshtadt*-class cruisers, plus six destroyers and 20 frigates. A small number of ships have commissioned: notably one *Udaloy*-class guided-missile cruiser (but one will probably be scrapped after a serious fire), a seventh *Krivak*-III large patrol vessel for service with the Border Forces and two more *Ropucha*-class LST. *The Military Balance 1991–92* incorrectly deleted a *Grozny*-class destroyer.

Air Forces

It is considered that sufficient funds will be available to allow the core development programmes in the military aircraft industry to continue, despite the state of the Russian economy and the general reduction in funds for research and development. The Aviation Department of the Ministry of Industry has established a defence sales organization and it can be expected to market Russian fighter aircraft aggressively. Although production of MiG-29 for the Russian Air Force has stopped, export models are still being produced; over 300 MiG-29 aircraft have been sold to ten countries. The MiG-33, one of a number of new fighter aircraft types that are undergoing flight-testing, is a highly developed version of the MiG-29. It has more powerful engines, a new radar, a new infra-red search system and fly-by-wire controls. China is the first export customer for the agile Su-27, which has a 'look down-shoot down' capability. An improved version of the Su-27 is undergoing development trials and will provide the air force with an interim long-range multirole aircraft. It is expected that the Russian equivalent of the US F-22 (advanced tactical fighter), the first Russian plane to incorporate 'stealth' technology, will soon make its maiden flight.

Some aircraft have been added to the inventory; the numbers held by Russia, Byelarus and Ukraine have increased by some 50 Su-25, 20 Su-27 and 60 MiG-31 fighters. There have been suggestions that the air force and the Aviation of Air Defence may be combined in one force.

RUSSIA

FORMER SOVIET UNION

NMP	1989:	r 675.0bn 1990: r 975.0bn
GNP	1990ε:	r 1,234.0bn ($2,042.70bn)
	1991:	r 1,891.1bn ($1,112.4bn)
Growth	1990ε:	–4.0% 1991: –17%
Inflation	1991:	89%
Debt[a]	1989:	$49.50bn 1990: $54.00bn
		Official data
Def exp	1989:	r 77.300bn ($119.44bn)
	1990:	r 77.800bn ($128.79bn)
Def bdgt	1990:	r 70.500bn ($116.70bn)
	1991:	r 96.560bn ($133.70bn)
		Estimated[b]
Def bdgt	1990:	r 136.15bn ($225.38bn)
	1991:	r 171.88bn ($237.99bn)
$1 = r	1989:	0.6472 1990: 0.6041
	1991:	1.70

r = roubles

[a] Foreign debt was officially limited to r 39bn in convertable currency.

[b] Def bdgt estimates are based on a re-evaluation of costs by function. Soviet published data has been used throughout, including official exchange rates.

RUSSIA

GDP	1991:	r 1,130.0bn ($664.71bn)
Growth	1991:	–9%
Inflation[a]	1991:	90%
Debt	1991:	$49.8bn

Def bdgt	1991:	r 89.27bn ($52.51bn)
	1992:	r 411.30bn
$1 = r	1991:	1.70

[a] Year average

Population: 148,041,000 (82% Russian)

13–17	18–22	23–32
10,637,800	9,622,700	19,837,500

TOTAL ARMED FORCES:

ACTIVE: some 2,720,000 (over 1,500,000 conscripts) incl about 200,000 Ministry of Defence staff, centrally controlled units for EW, trg, rear services, but excl 700,000 railway and construction tp.

Terms of service: 18 months. Women with medical and other special skills may volunteer.

RESERVES: some 3,000,000 with service within last 5 years: Reserve obligation to age 50; total: some 20,000,000.

COMMONWEALTH OF INDEPENDENT STATES CENTRALLY CONTROLLED FORCES:

STRATEGIC DETERRENT FORCES:

181,000 (incl 38,000 assigned from Air and Navy).

NAVY: (12,000). 832 msl in 55 SSBN.
SSBN: 55: (all based in Russian ports)

6 *Typhoon* with 20 SS-N-20 *Sturgeon*	(120 msl).
7 *Delta-IV* with 16 SS-N-23 *Skiff*	(112 msl).
14 *Delta-III* with 16 SS-N-18 *Stingray*	(224 msl).
4 *Delta-II* with 16 SS-N-8 *Sawfly*	(64 msl).
18 *Delta-I* with 12 SS-N-8 *Sawfly*	(216 msl).
6 *Yankee-I* with 16 SS-N-6 *Serb*	(96 msl).

STRATEGIC ROCKET FORCES: (144,000 incl 70,000 conscripts): 5 rocket armies, org in div, regt, bn and bty, 126 launcher groups, normally 10 silos (6 for SS-18) and one control centre; SS-25 units each 9 launchers; 12 SS-24 trains each 3 launchers, 2 msl test centres.
ICBM: 1,400.
SS-11 *Sego*: 280 mod 2/3 (at 6 fields; all in Russia).
SS-13 *Savage* (RS-12): 40 (at 1 field, all in Russia).
SS-17 *Spanker* (RS-16): 40 (at 1 field; mod 3/4 MIRV; all in Russia).
SS-18 *Satan* (RS-20): 308 (at 6 fields; mostly mod 4/5, 10 MIRV; 204 Russia, 104 Kazakhstan).
SS-19 *Stiletto* (RS-18): 300 (at 4 fields; mostly mod 3, 6 MIRV; 170 Russia, 130 Ukraine).
SS-24 *Scalpel* (RS-22): 92 (deployment complete; 56 silo-based and 36 rail-mobile, 10 MIRV; 10 silo, 36 train Russia, 46 silo Ukraine).
SS-25 *Sickle* (RS-12M): 340+ (mobile, single-warhead msl; 9 bases with some 37 units of 9; 260+ Russia, 80 Byelarus).
GROUND DEFENCE: some 1,700 APC, 140 Mi-8 hel declared under CFE. (APC: Russia (West of Urals) 700, Ukraine 416, Byelarus 585).

STRATEGIC AVIATION: (25,000)
Long-Range Forces (Moscow).
Western CIS: 1 air army (Smolensk).
Far East: 1 air army (Irkutsk).
BOMBERS: 581 (251 START-countable).
LONG-RANGE: 170, plus 8 test ac.
150 Tu-95 (45 B/G with AS-4 ASM, 84 H with AS-15/-16 ALCM, 20 T (trg)) plus 8 test ac.
20 Tu-160 (ALCM-capable).
MEDIUM-RANGE:[c] 320 (CFE-countable).
50 Tu-16 (AS-6 ASM), plus 100 in store.
80 Tu-22.
190 Tu-26 (Tu-22m) (AS-4 ASM) (incl 20 trg).
RECCE/ECM: 83 (CFE-countable).
13 Tu-16, 60 Tu-22, 10 Il-20/-22.
TANKERS: 75:
25 Mya-4, 10 Tu-16, 40 Il-78.
[c] It is not clear whether medium-range bombers will remain under CIS control.

DEPLOYMENT:
RUSSIA:
Moscow MD: 20 Tu-95T, 20 Tu-26 (trg).

Leningrad MD: 20 Tu-26. North Caucasus MD: 22 Tu-95H-16, 25 Mya-4 tankers. Far East MD: 45 Tu-95B/G, 50 Tu-16, 60 Tu-26. Plus 45 Tu-16 in store.
BYELARUS: 13 Tu-16 (recce), 50 Tu-22, 30 Tu-22 (recce), 36 Tu-26, plus 25 Tu-16 in store.
UKRAINE: 22 Tu-95H-16, 20 Tu-160, 30 Tu-22, 30 Tu-22 (recce), 36 Tu-26, plus 30 Tu-16 in store.
KAZAKHSTAN: 40 Tu-95H/6/16
ESTONIA: 18 Tu-26

STRATEGIC DEFENCE:
ABM: 100: ABM-1B *Galosh*, SH-11 (mod *Galosh*), SH-08 *Gazelle* (Russia).
WARNING SYSTEMS:
SATELLITES: 9 with ICBM/SLBM launch detection capability. Others incl 2 photo-recce, 11 ELINT, 3 recce.
RADARS:
OVER-THE-HORIZON-BACKSCATTER (OTH-B): 3: 2 near Kiev and Komsomolsk (Ukraine), covering US and polar areas; 1 near Nikolayevsk-na-Amure, covering China.
LONG-RANGE EARLY-WARNING:
ABM-ASSOCIATED:
8 long-range phased-array systems at Baranovichi, Skrunda (Byelarus), Mukachevo (Ukraine), Olnegorsk (Kola), Lyaki (Azerbaijan), Sary-Shagan (Kazakhstan), Pechora (Urals), Mishelevka (Irkutsk).
11 *Hen House*-series; range 6,000km, 6 locations covering approaches from the west and south-west, north-east and south-east and (partially) south.
Engagement, guidance, battle management: 1 *Pillbox* phased-array at Pushkino (Moscow).

NAVY: 320,000, (ε 200,000 conscripts), incl 12,000 Strategic forces, 62,000 naval air, 29,500 coastal defence, coastal arty, naval infantry.
SUBMARINES: 250:
STRATEGIC SUBMARINES: 55 (see p. 92).
TACTICAL SUBMARINES: 183:
SSGN: 36:
9 *Oscar* with 24 × SS-N-19 *Shipwreck* USGW (VLS); plus T-65 HWT.
5 *Charlie-II* with 8 × SS-N-9 *Siren* USGW, plus T-53 HWT.
7 *Charlie-I* with 8 × SS-N-7 *Starbright* USGW; plus T-53 HWT.
11 *Echo-II* ε3 with 8 × SS-N-3A *Shaddock*, ε15 with SS-N-12 *Sandbox* SSM; plus T-53 HWT.
3 *Yankee* '*Notch*' with 20+ SS-N-21 *Sampson* SLCM.
1 *Yankee* (trials) with SS-NX-24 SLCM.

SSN: 59:

8 *Akula* with T-65 HWT; plus SS-N-21.

3 *Sierra* with T-65 HWT; plus SS-N-21.

26 *Victor-III* with T-65 HWT; plus SS-N-15 or -16.

7 *Victor-II* with T-53 HWT; plus SS-N-15 or -16.

15 *Victor-I* with T-53 HWT.

SSG: 8 *Juliet* with 4 × SS-N-3A *Shaddock* SSM.

SS: 80 (all with T-53 HWT): 21 *Kilo*, 18 *Tango*, 38 *Foxtrot*, 3 *Romeo*.

OTHER ROLES: 12:

SSN: 2 *Uniform* experimental/trials.

SS: 10: 1 *Beluga*, 4 *Bravo* wpn targets, 1 *Golf-I* research, 1 *Lima*, 2 *India* rescue, 1 *X-Ray* trials.

IN STORE: 3: 3 *Foxtrot* (not counted in totals).

PRINCIPAL SURFACE COMBATANTS: 192:

CARRIERS: 4:

1 *Kuznetsov* (ex-*Tbilisi*) CVV (65,000t) capacity 25–30 fixed wing ac and 8–10 ASW hel with 12 SS-N-19 *Shipwreck* SSM, 4 × 6 SA-N-9 SAM, 8 CADS-1, 2 RBU-12 (not fully op).

1 *Gorshkov* (ex *Baku*) (CVV) (38,000t) capacity 15 V/STOL ac, 16 Ka-25/-27 hel (ASW with E-45/-75 LWT/AEW/OTHT/SAR); plus 6 × 2 SS-N-12 *Sandbox* SSM, 4 × 8 SA-N-6 *Grumble* SAM. 2 × 100mm guns.

2 *Kiev* (CVV) (38,000t) (incl *Kiev* in refit) capacity 15 V/STOL ac, 16 Ka-25/-27 hel; plus 4 × 2 SS-N-12 *Sandbox* SSM, 2 × 2 SA-N-3 SAM, 1 × 2 SUW-N-1.

CRUISERS: 33:

CGN: 3 *Admiral Ushakov* (ex *Kirov*) (AAW/ASUW) with 12 × 8 SA-N-6 *Grumble*, 20 SS-N-19 *Shipwreck* SSM, 3 Ka-25/-27 hel for OTHT/AEW/ASW; plus 1 with 1 × 2 130mm guns, 1 with 1 × 2 SS-N-14 *Silex* SUGW (LWT or nuc payload), 10 × 533mm TT.

CG: 30:

1 *Moskva* (CGH) (ASW) with 18 Ka-25 hel (E45-75 LWT), 1 × 2 SUW-N-1; plus 2 × 2 SA-N-3 SAM.

3 *Slava* (AAW/ASUW) with 8 × 8 SA-N-6 *Grumble*, 8 × 2 SS-N-12 *Sandbox* SSM, 1 Ka-25/-27 hel; (AEW/ASW); plus 8 × 533mm TT, 1 × 2 130mm guns.

11 *Udaloy* (ASW) with 2 × 4 SS-N-14 *Silex* SUGW, 2 × 12 ASW RL, 8 × 533mm TT, 2 Ka-27 hel; plus 2 × 100mm guns.

7 *Nikolayev* (*Kara*) (ASW) with 2 × 4 SS-N-14 *Silex* SUGW, 10 × 533mm TT, 1 Ka-25 hel; plus 2 × 2 SA-N-3 *Goblet*; (1 (*Azov*) with 3 × 8 SA-N-6, only 1 × SA-N-3 and other differences).

7 *Kronshtadt* (*Kresta-II*) (ASW) with 2 × 4 SS-N-14 SUGW, 1 Ka-25 hel, 10 × 533mm TT; plus 2 × 2 SA-N-3 SAM.

1 *Admiral Zozulya* (*Kresta-I*) (ASUW/ASW) with 2 × 2 SS-N-3b *Shaddock* SSM, 1 Ka-25 hel (OTHT), 10 × 533mm TT.

DESTROYERS: 26:

DDG: 26:

AAW/ASUW: 20:

15 *Sovremennyy* with 2 × 4 SS-N-22 *Sunburn* SSM, 2 × 1 SA-N-7 *Gadfly* SAM, 2 × 2 130mm guns, 1 Ka-25 (B) hel (OTHT); plus 4 × 533mm TT.

3 *Grozny* (*Kynda*) (ASUW) with 2 × 4 SS-N-3b; plus 1 × 2 SA-N-1 *Goa* SAM, 6 × 533mm TT.

2 *Sderzhannyy* (mod *Kashin*) with 4 SS-N-2C *Styx* SSM, 2 × 2 SA-N-1 SAM; plus 5 × 533mm TT.

ASW: 6:

6 *Komsomolets Ukrainyy* (*Kashin*) with 2 × 12 ASW RL, 5 × 533mm TT; plus 2 × 2 SA-N-1 SAM, (1 with trials fit 1 × SA-N-7).

FRIGATES: 129:

11 *Rezvyy* (*Krivak-II*) with 1 × 4 SS-N-14 *Silex* SUGW, 8 × 533mm TT, 2 × 12 ASW RL; plus 2 × 100mm guns.

21 *Bditelnyy* (*Krivak-I*) (weapons as *Rezvyy* but with 2 × twin 76mm guns).

1 *Neustrashimyy* with 2 × 12 ASW RL.

1 '*Riga*' with 2 × 16 ASW RL, 2 or 3 × 533mm TT, 3 × 100mm guns.

(*Note:* Frigates listed below lie between 1,000 and 1,200 tonnes full-load displacement and are not counted in official releases.)

67 '*Grisha-I, -III, -V*', with 2 × 12 ASW RL, 4 × 533mm TT.

12 '*Parchim-II*' (ASW) with 2 × 12 ASW RL, 4 × 406mm ASTT.

3 '*Mirka-I, -II*', with 4 × 12 ASW RL, 5 or 10 × 406mm ASTT.

13 '*Petya*' with ASW RL, 5 or 10 × 406mm ASTT.

PATROL AND COASTAL COMBATANTS: 305:

CORVETTES: 76:

40 *Tarantul* (ASUW), 2 -*I*, 18–*II* both with 2 × 2 SS-N-2C *Styx*; 20 -*III* with 2 × 2 SS-N-22 *Sunburn*.

36 *Nanuchka* (ASUW) -*I*, -*III* and -*IV* with 2 × 3 SS-N-9 *Siren*.

MISSILE CRAFT: 40:

26 *Osa* PFM with 4 × SS-N-2C.

14 *Matka* PHM with 2 × 1 SS-N-2C.

TORPEDO CRAFT: 29:

29 *Turya* PHT with 4 × 533mm TT.

PATROL CRAFT: 160:

OFFSHORE: 10 T-58/-43.

COASTAL: 10:

7 *Pauk* PFC (ASW) with 2 × ASW RL, 4 × ASTT.

2 *Poti* PFC (ASW) with 2 × ASW RL, 4 × ASTT.

1 *Babochka* PHT (ASW) with 8 × ASTT.

INSHORE: 5: SO-1 with 2 × ASTT.

RIVERINE AND CASPIAN: 135: (probably with Border Troops)

21 *Yaz* with 2 × 115mm gun.

10 *Piyavka*, 8 *Vosh*, 96 misc⟨.

MINE WARFARE: About 218:
MINELAYERS: 3 *Pripyat* (*Alesha*), capacity 300 mines. (*Note:* All submarines and many surface combatants are equipped for minelaying.)

MINE COUNTERMEASURES: About 215:
OFFSHORE: 45:
1 *Gorya* MCO.
35 *Natya-I* and *-II* MSO.
9 T-43 MSO.
COASTAL: About 100:
28 *Yurka* MSC.
2 *Andryusha* MSC (trials).
About 70 *Sonya* MSC
INSHORE: About 70:
20 *Vanya*, about 50 MSI⟨.

AMPHIBIOUS: 80:
LPD: 3 *Ivan Rogov* with 4–5 Ka-27 hel: capacity 520 tps, 20 tk;
LST: 41:
27 *Ropucha*: capacity 225 tps, 9 tk.
14 *Alligator*: capacity 300 tps, 20 tk.
LSM: 36 *Polnocny* (3 types): capacity 180 tps, 6 tk: (some adapted for mine warfare but retain amph primary role).
Plus CRAFT: about 100:
LCU: 9 *Vydra*.
LCM: About 26 *Ondatra*.
LCAC and SES: about 65: incl 6 *Pomornik*, 18 *Aist*, 7 *Tsaplya*, 19 *Lebed*, 2 *Utenok*, 10 *Gus*.
3 *Orlan* 'wing-in-ground-effect' (WIG) experimental.

SUPPORT AND MISCELLANEOUS: about 685:
UNDERWAY SUPPORT: 30:
1 *Berezina*, 6 *Chilikin*, 23 other AO.
MAINTENANCE AND LOGISTICS: about 262:
18 AS, 40 AR, 12 general maint/spt, 27 AOT, 18 missile spt/resupply, 80 tugs, 14 special liquid carriers, 13 water carriers, 40 AK.
SPECIAL PURPOSES: about 142:
60 AGI (some armed), 5 msl range instrumentation, 8 trg, about 65 icebreakers (civil manned), 4 AH.
SURVEY/RESEARCH: about 251:
40 naval, 60 civil AGOR.
100 naval, 40 civil AGHS.
11 space-associated ships (civil manned).
MERCHANT FLEET (auxiliary/augmentation):
2,800 ocean-going vessels (17 in Arctic service), incl 125 ramp-fitted and roll-on/roll-off (ro-ro), some with rails for rolling stock, 3 roll-on/float-off, 14 barge carriers, 48 passenger liners, 500 coastal and river ships.

NAVAL AVIATION: (60,000).
Some 1,100 cbt ac; 290 armed hel.

Four Fleet Air Forces; org in air div, each with 2–3 regt of HQ elm and 2 sqn of 9–10 ac each; recce, ASW, tpt/utility org in indep regt or sqn.
BOMBERS: some 235:
7 regt with some 155 Tu-26 (Tu-22M), (AS-4 ASM).
2 regt with some 70 Tu-16 (AS-5/-6 ASM), 10 Tu-22.
FGA: 350:
165 Su-17.
100 Su-24.
55 Su-25.
30 MiG-27.
FIGHTERS: 35 MiG-29.
TRAINING: Some 300: Tu-16*, Tu-26*, Tu-95*, Su-25*, Su-27*, MiG-29*.
ASW: 191 ac, 264 hel:
AIRCRAFT: 58 Tu-142, 41 Il-38, 92 Be-12.
HELICOPTERS: 69 Mi-14, 85 Ka-25, 110 Ka-27.
MR/EW: some 90 ac, 25 hel:
AIRCRAFT: incl 24 Tu-95, 39 Tu-16 MR/ECM, 5 Tu-22, 12 Su-24, 8 An-12, 2 Il-20.
HELICOPTERS: 25 Ka-25.
MCM: 25 Mi-14 hel.
CBT ASLT: 25 Ka-27 hel.
TANKERS: 18 Tu-16.
TRANSPORT:
AIRCRAFT: 26 An-12, 8 An-24, 7 Il-14.
HELICOPTERS: 17 Mi-6/-8.
ASM: AS-2 *Kipper*, AS-4 *Kitchen*, AS-5 *Kelt*, AS-6 *Kingfish*, AS-7 *Kerry*, AS-10 *Karen*, AS-11 *Kilter*, AS-12 *Kegler*, AS-13 *Kingbolt*, AS-14 *Kedge*.

COASTAL DEFENCE FORCES (incl Naval Infantry, Coastal Artillery and Rocket Troops, Coastal Defence Troops):

NAVAL INFANTRY (Marines): (some 12,000).
1 inf div (7,000: 3 inf, 1 tk, 1 arty regt).
4 indep bde (1 reserve) (type: 3,000: 4 inf, 1 tk, 1 arty, 1 MRL, 1 ATK bn.
4 fleet SF bde: 2–3 underwater, 1 para bn, spt elm.
EQUIPMENT:
MBT: 240 T-55.
LIGHT TANKS: 100 PT-76.
RECCE: 60 BRDM-2/*Sagger* ATGW.
APC: some 2,000: BTR-60/-70, some 400 MT-LB.
SP ARTY: 120mm: 160 2S9; 122mm: 144 2S1.
MRL: 122mm: 90 9P138.
COMBINED GUN/MORTAR: 120mm: 160 2S9 SP.
ATGW: 50 AT-3/-5.
AD GUNS: 23mm: 60 ZSU-23-4 SP.
SAM: 250 SA-7, 10 SA-8, 35 SA-9/-13.

COASTAL ARTILLERY AND ROCKET TROOPS: (4,500).
1 coastal arty div (role: protects approaches to naval bases and major ports).
EQUIPMENT:
ARTY: incl SM-4-1 130mm.

SSM: 40 SS-C-1b *Sepal* (similar to SS-N-3), SS-C-3, *Styx*, SS-C-4 reported.

COASTAL DEFENCE TROOPS: (13,000)
4 Coast Defence div.
2 arty regt.
1 MG/arty bn.
EQUIPMENT:
MBT: 1,080 T-80.
AIFV: 960 BMP.
APC: 480 BTR-60/-70, 790 MT-LB.
TOTAL ARTY: 992.
   TOWED ARTY: 872. 100mm: 12 BS-3; 122mm: 290
     D-30; 152mm: 144 D-20, 330 2A65, 96 2A36.
   SP ARTY: 152mm: 48 2S5.
   MRL: 122mm: 72 BM-21.

DEPLOYMENT:

NORTHERN FLEET: (Arctic and Atlantic) (HQ
   Severomorsk) (Russia):
   BASES: Kola Inlet, Motovskiy Gulf, Gremikha,
     Polyarnyy, Litsa Gulf.
SUBMARINES: 126: strategic: 34 SSBN; tactical: 85:
   21 SSGN, 38 SSN, 2 SSG, 24 SS. (2–3 were
   normally deployed to Mediterranean.) 7 other roles.
PRINCIPAL SURFACE COMBATANTS: 61: 3 CVV, 11
   cruisers, 9 destroyers, 38 frigates.
OTHER SURFACE SHIPS: 25 patrol and coastal
   combatants, 40 mine warfare, 12 amph, some
   190 spt and misc.
NAVAL AVIATION:
   218 cbt ac; 70 armed hel.
BOMBERS: 70: 30 Tu-16, 40 Tu-26.
FIGHTER/FGA: 70: 30 MiG-27, 40 Su-25.
ASW:
   AIRCRAFT: 78: 38 Tu-142, 16 Il-38, 24 Be-12;
   HELICOPTERS: 55: (afloat): 10 Ka-25, 45 Ka-27.
MR/EW:
   AIRCRAFT: 30: 2 An-12, 12 Tu-16, 14 Tu-95, 2 Il-20.
   HELICOPTERS: 5 Ka-25.
MCM: 8 Mi-14 hel.
CBT ASLT HEL: 10 Ka-27.
COMMUNICATIONS: 6 Tu-142.
TANKERS: 5 Tu-16.
NAVAL INFANTRY:
   2 bde (80 MBT, 110 arty).
COASTAL DEFENCE:
   1 Coast Defence div (270 MBT, 790 MT-LB,
     150 arty),
   1 arty regt (120 arty).

BALTIC FLEET: (HQ Kaliningrad):
   BASES: Kronshtadt (Russia), Liepaja (Latvia),
     Baltiysk (Russia), Tallinn (Estonia).
SUBMARINES: 20: strategic: nil; tactical: 19: 2 SSG,
   17 SS; other roles: 1 SS.
PRINCIPAL SURFACE COMBATANTS: 39: 4 cruisers, 3
   destroyers, 32 frigates.

OTHER SURFACE SHIPS: 140 patrol and coastal
   combatants, 60 mine warfare, 21 amph, some
   120 spt and misc.
NAVAL AVIATION:
   212 cbt ac, 45 armed hel.
FGA: 180: 5 regts: 80 Su-17, 100 Su-24.
ASW:
   AIRCRAFT: 20: 10 Il-38, 10 Be-12;
   HELICOPTERS: 35: 3 Ka-25, 22 Ka-27, 10 Mi-14.
MR/EW:
   AIRCRAFT 14: 2 An-12, 12 Su-24.
   HELICOPTERS: 5 Ka-25.
MCM: 5 Mi-14 hel.
CBT ASLT HEL: 5 Ka-29.
NAVAL INFANTRY:
   1 bde, (40 MBT, 60 arty/MRL) (Russia).
COAST DEFENCE:
1 Coast Defence div (270 MBT, 320 AIFV, 160
   arty) (Lithuania) 1 arty regt (120 arty) (Russia).
1 SSM regt: some 8 SS-C-1b *Sepal*.

BLACK SEA FLEET: (HQ Sevastopol)
(Ukraine). To remain under joint command for 3
years, then to be divided between Russia,
Ukraine, and Georgia.
   BASES: Sevastopol, Odessa (Ukraine), Poti (Georgia).
SUBMARINES: 18: tactical 16: 2 SSG, 14 SS; other
   roles: 2.
PRINCIPAL SURFACE COMBATANTS: 36: 2 CGH, 3
   cruisers, 7 destroyers, 24 frigates.
OTHER SURFACE SHIPS: 60 patrol and coastal
   combatants, 30 mine warfare, 16 amph, some
   140 spt and misc.
NAVAL AVIATION:[d]
   163 cbt ac, plus 220 in store; 85 cbt hel.
BOMBERS: 65: 2 regt, 2 sqn with 45 Tu-26 (Tu-22M);
   10 Tu-16; 10 Tu-22, plus ε50 Tu-16 in store.
FGA: 40: Su-17, plus 140 Su-17, 30 Su-25 in store.
FIGHTER: 35: MiG-29.
ASW:
   AIRCRAFT: 23 Be-12.
   HELICOPTERS: 85: 31 Mi-14, 49 Ka-25, 5 Ka-27.
MR/EW:
   AIRCRAFT: 21: 2 An-12, 12 Tu-16, 6 Tu-22, 1 Il-20.
   HELICOPTERS: 5 Ka-25.
MCM: 5 Mi-14 hel.
TANKERS: 3 Tu-16.
NAVAL INFANTRY:[e]
   1 bde: (265 APC, 60 arty/MRL) (Ukraine).
COASTAL DEFENCE:[e]
1 Coast Defence div (270 MBT, 320 AIFV, 160
   arty/MRL) (Ukraine).
1 arty bde (120 arty) (Ukraine).
[d] Shore-based aircraft allotted to Ukraine.
[e] Allotted to Ukraine under CFE protocol.

CASPIAN FLOTILLA (HQ Baku):
   To be divided between Azerbaijan, Russia and
   Turkmenistan.

PRINCIPAL SURFACE COMBATANTS: 2 frigates.
OTHER SURFACE SHIPS: 25 patrol and coastal combatants, 10 mine warfare, 10 amph, 10 spt.

PACIFIC FLEET (Indian Ocean) (HQ Vladivostok) (Russia):
BASES: Vladivostok, Petropavlovsk, Kamchatskiy, Magadan, Sovetskaya Gavan; abroad: Aden (South Yemen).
SUBMARINES: 86: strategic: 21 SSBN; tactical: 63: 15 SSGN, 2˙ SSN, 2 SSG, 25 SS; other roles: 2 SS.
PRINCIPAL SURFACE COMBATANTS: 54: 1 carrier, 13 cruisers, 7 destroyers, 33 frigates.
OTHER SURFACE SHIPS: 55 patrol and coastal combatants, 78 mine warfare, 21 amph, some 225 spt and misc.
NAVAL AIR (Pacific Fleet Air Force) (HQ Vladivostok): 220 cbt ac, 99 cbt hel.
BOMBERS: 100: 2 regt with 70 Tu-26, 1 with 30 Tu-16 *Badger* C/G.
FGA: 50: 1 regt with 35 Su-17, 15 Su-24.
ASW:
   AIRCRAFT 70: 20 Tu-142, 15 Il-38, 35 Be-12.
   HELICOPTERS: 89: (afloat): 23 Ka-25, 38 Ka-27; (ashore): 28 Mi-14.
MR/EW:
   AIRCRAFT: 62: 2 An-12, 50 Tu-16, 10 Tu-95.
   HELICOPTERS: 10 Ka-25.
MCM: 6 Mi-14 hel.
CBT ASLT HEL: 10 Ka-27.
COMMUNICATION: 7 Tu-142.
TANKERS: 10 Tu-16.
NAVAL INFANTRY:
   1 div HQ, 3 inf, 1 tk and 1 arty regt:
COAST DEFENCE:
   1 Coast Defence div.

GENERAL PURPOSE FORCES:
(incl all units and eqpt in Russia, Groups of Forces, 14th Army (Moldova) Trans-Caucasus MD and jointly controlled forces in Central Asian republics).
GROUND FORCES: 1,400,000 (about 1,000,000 conscripts).
8 Military Districts (MD) plus Trans-Caucasus, 3 Groups of Forces
19 Army HQ, 7 Corps HQ.
22 TD (incl 5 trg) (3 tk, 1 motor rifle, 1 arty, 1 SAM regt; 1 armd recce bn; spt units).
81 MRD (incl 9 trg) (3 motor rifle, 1 arty, 1 SAM regt; 1 indep tk, 1 ATK, 1 armd recce bn; spt units).
6 ABD (incl 1 trg) (each 3 para, 1 arty regt; 1 AA bn).
8 MG/arty div.
8 arty div incl 1 trg: (no standard org: perhaps 4 bde (12 bn): 152mm SP, 152mm towed and MRL: some will have older eqpt).

Some 48 arty bde/regt. No standard org: perhaps 4 bn: 2 each of 24 152mm towed guns, 2 each of 24 152mm SP guns. 7 hy arty bde (with 4 bn of 12 203mm 2S7 SP guns). Some only MRL.
Some 7 AB bde, (each 4 inf bn; arty, SAM, ATK; spt tps).
8 SF (*Spetsnaz*) bde.
24 SSM bde (20, incl 3 trg *Scud*, 4 SS-21).
18 ATK bde/regt.
15 SAM bde/regt
Avn: regt assigned at army and MD; some 40 attack regt with 24 Mi-8 and 40 Mi-24 attack hel.
Other Front and Army tps: engr, pontoon-bridge, pipe-line, signals, EW, CW def, tpt, supply bde/regt/bn.

EQUIPMENT:
MBT: about 29,000 incl: some 5,500 T-54/-55, 5,500 T-62, some 1,500 T-64A/-B, 11,000 T-72L/-M and 5,300 T-80/-M 9, plus some 21,000 in store east of Urals (incl Kazakhstan, Uzbekistan); types n.k.
LIGHT TANKS: 800 PT-76 (410).
RECCE: 6,000: incl some 2,000 BRDM-2.
AIFV: about 28,000 incl: BMP-1 (73mm gun/AT-3 ATGW), BMP-2 (30mm gun/AT-5 ATGW); some 2,400 BMD (AB), ε300 BMP-3.
APC: over 23,000 incl: BTR-50P/-60P/-70/-80/-152, 700 BTR-D; 6,000 MT-LB, plus 'look alikes'.
TOTAL ARTY: 22,000, plus some 21,000, mainly obsolete types, in store east of the Urals.
TOWED ARTY: about 12,500 incl 122mm: 4,500 D-30, 4,000 M-30; 152mm: 1,500 D-20, 1,500 *Giatsint-B* 2A36, 750 *MSTA-B* 2A65; 203mm: 24 B-4M.
SP ARTY: some 6,000 incl 122mm: 2,600 *Gvozdika* 2S1; 152mm: 2,000 *Acatsia* 2S3, 600 *Giatsint-S* 2S5, 130 *MSTA-S* 2S19; 203mm 240 *Pion* 2S7.
COMBINED GUN/MORTAR: about 700: 120mm: 650 *Nona-S* 2S9 SP, 40 *Nona-K* 2B16.
MRL: about 4,500 incl: 122mm: 3,000 BM-21, 30 9P138.
220mm: 1,250 9P140 *Uragan*.
300mm: 100 *Smerch* 9A52.
MORTARS: about 2,000 incl: 120mm: 1,500 2S12, 250 PM-38; 160mm: 50 M-160; 240mm: 100 M-240, 120 *Tulpan* 2S4 SP.
SSM: (nuclear-capable): 900 launchers, incl about 600 *FROG* (Luna)/SS-21 *Scarab* (Tochka), 300 *Scud* B/-C mod (R-17).
ATGW: AT-2 *Swatter*, AT-3 *Sagger*, AT-4 *Spigot*, AT-5 *Spandrel*, AT-6 *Spiral*, AT-7 *Saxhorn*, AT-9, AT-10.
ATK GUNS: 57mm: ASU-57 SP; 76mm; 85mm: D-44/SD-44, ASU-85 SP; 100mm: T-12/-12A/M-55 towed.
AD GUNS: 23mm: ZU-23, ZSU-23-4 SP; 30mm: 2S6 SP with 8 SA-19 SAM; 37mm; 57mm: S-60, ZSU-57-2 SP; 85mm: M-1939; 100mm: KS-19; 130mm: KS-30.

SAM: SA-4 A/B *Ganef* (twin): (Army/Front weapon).
SA-6 *Gainful* (triple): (div weapon).
SA-7 *Grail* (man-portable).
SA-8 *Gecko* (2 twin or 2 triple): (div weapon).
SA-9 *Gaskin* (2 twin): (regt weapon).
SA-11 *Gadfly* (quad): (replacing SA-4/-6).
SA-12A *Gladiator*: (replacing SA-4).
SA-X-12B *Giant*: under development (possible
    ATBM role).
SA-13 *Gopher* (2 twin): (replacing SA-9).
SA-14 *Gremlin*: (replacing SA-7).
SA-15: (replacing SA-6/SA-8).
SA-16: (replacing SA-7 and some SA-14).
SA-17: replacing SA-4/SA-11.
SA-18: replacing SA-7/SA-14.
SA-19 (2S6 SP): (8 SAM plus twin 35mm
    gun).
HELICOPTERS: some 3,200:
  ATTACK: 1,100 Mi-24.
  TRANSPORT: some 1,300 incl 270 Mi-6, 1,000
    Mi-8 (some armed), 35 Mi-26 (hy).
  EW/ECM: 200 Mi-8.
  GENERAL PURPOSE: 580: incl 500 Mi-2, 80 Mi-8
    (comms).

AIR FORCE: 300,000 (some 180,000 conscripts)
  incl 25,000 with Strategic Aviation.
10 Air army, 3 MD air forces.
  Some 3,700 cbt ac. Forces' strengths vary,
    mostly org with div of 3 regt of 3 sqn (total
    90–135 ac), indep regt (30–60 ac). Regt roles
    incl AD, interdiction, recce, tac air spt; div
    roles may be mixed.
FGA: some 1,800: incl 610 MiG-27, 330 Su-17/-22,
  480 Su-24, 340 Su-25.
FIGHTER: some 1,500: incl 310 MiG-21, 510
  MiG-23, 110 MiG-25, 430 MiG-29, 140 Su-27.
RECCE: some 365: incl 20 MiG-21, 85 MiG-25 , 100
  Su-17, 160 Su-24.
ECM: 40 Yak-28.
TRAINING: some 1,500 L-29, L-39 (not cbt ac).
HELICOPTERS: Some 320 Mi-24 (attack) (in trg units
  and in regt resubordinated from the army).
AAM: AA-2 *Atoll*, AA-7 *Apex*, AA-8 *Aphid*, AA-9
  Amos, AA-10 *Alamo*, AA-11 *Archer*.
ASM: AS-7 *Kerry*, AS-10 *Karen*, AS-11 *Kilter*,
  AS-12 *Kegler*, AS-13 *Kingbolt*, AS-14 *Kedge*,
  AS-16 *Kickback*.

MILITARY TRANSPORT AVIATION (VTA):

5 div, each 3 regt, each 30 ac; some indep regt.
EQUIPMENT: some 620 ac: 100 An-12, 435
  Il-76M/MD *Candid* B (replacing An-12), 55
  An-22, 29 An-124.
Additional ac (VTA augmentation force): Tpt ac in
  comd other than VTA: org in indep regt and sqn:
  1,200+: Tu-134, Tu-154, An-2, An-12, An-72, Il-18.
Civilian Aeroflot fleet: 1,700 med- and long-range
  passenger ac, incl some 220 An-12 and Il-76.

DEPLOYMENT:
GROUPS OF FORCES:
WESTERN GROUP OF FORCES (Germany)

(HQ Zossen-Wünsdorf): (177,000):
GROUND: 4 Army HQ: 6 TD, 3 MRD, plus 1 arty
  div; 1 indep MR, 4 SS-21, 1 *Scud*, 2 arty, 1 ATK,
  5 SAM bde, 6 attack hel regt, 2,600 MBT, 2,900
  AIFV, 900 APC, 2,000 arty/MRL/mors, 27 *Scud*,
  72 SS-21, 240 attack hel.
AIR: 1 air army; 2 FGA div, 6 regt, (215: MiG-23,
  MiG-27, Su-17, Su-25); 2 ftr div, 5 regt (170:
  MiG-23, MiG-29); 2 recce regt (65: MiG-25,
  Su-24 (some ECM)). 2 attack hel regt (84 Mi-24).

NORTHERN GROUP OF FORCES (Poland)

(HQ Legnica): (20,000):
GROUND: elm 1 TD, 1 MRD, 220 MBT, 600
  ACV, 120 arty/MRL/mor.
AIR: 1 air army (HQ Legnica): 1 bbr div (70:
  Su-24), 1 ftr div (60: Su-27), 1 recce regt (25
  Su-24, MiG-25), 1 attack hel regt (20 Mi-24).

NORTH-WESTERN GROUP OF FORCES

(HQ Kaliningrad):
RUSSIA: (Kaliningrad Oblast) (50,000).
GROUND: 1 army HQ, 2 TD, 2 MRD, plus 1 arty
  div (1 bde, 5 regt), 2 *Scud*, 1 AB, 1 SAM bde, 1
  MRL, 1 ATK, 1 attack hel regt, 750 MBT, 600
  AIFV, 300 APC, 600 arty/MRL/mors, 24 *Scud*,
  16 SS-21, 48 attack hel.
AIR DEFENCE:
FIGHTER: 1 regt (35 Su-27).
SAM: 250.
ESTONIA: (23,000)
GROUND: 1 MRD, 1 *Scud*, 1 *Spetsnaz* bde, 190
  MBT, 160 AIFV, 130 APC, 20 arty/MRL/mor,
  12 *Scud*, 4 *FROG*/SS-21.
AIR DEFENCE:
FIGHTERS: 3 regt (120 MiG-23).
SAM: 250.
LATVIA: (40,000).
GROUND: 1 TD (trg), 1 attack hel regt, 130 MBT,
  80 AIFV, 80 arty/MRL/mor, 24 attack hel.
AIR: 1 FGA regt (60: MiG-23, MiG-27), 1 recce
  regt (30: Su-17, Su-24), 1 tpt hel regt (20
  Mi-8).
AIR DEFENCE:
FIGHTER: 1 regt (40 Su-27).
SAM: 250.
LITHUANIA: (43,000)
GROUND: 1 MRD, 2 ABD (1 trg), plus 2 arty
  bde/regt, 180 MBT, 780 AIFV, 800 APC, 260
  arty/MRL/mor, 4 *FROG*/SS-21.
AIR: 1 FGA regt (50: MiG-27)
AIR DEFENCE
SAM: 125.

TERRITORY OF THE FORMER SOVIET UNION:
REPUBLIC AND RUSSIAN MILITARY DISTRICT BORDERS

NAVY
1 Coastal Defence div (270 MBT, 320 AIFV, 160 arty).

MILITARY DISTRICTS OF RUSSIA:

LENINGRAD MD (HQ St. Petersburg):
GROUND: 1 army HQ, 2 corps HQ; 6 MRD (1 trg), 1 ABD; plus 1 arty div, 3 arty bde/regt, 2 ATK, 5 *Scud* (2 trg), 1 AB, 1 *Spetsnaz*, 1 SAM bde, 1 attack hel regt, 1,350 MBT, 700 AIFV, 1,140 APC, 1,170 arty/MRL/mors, 50 attack hel.
AIR: 1 air army; 2 bbr regt (60: Su-24), 1 recce regt (35: MiG-25, Su-17).

MOSCOW MD (HQ Moscow):
GROUND: 1 Army HQ, 3 TD (1 trg), 1 MRD, 1 ABD, plus 1 arty trg div, 4 arty bde/regt, 2 ATK, 2 *Scud*, 1 indep MR, 1 *Spetsnaz*, 1 SAM bde, 2 attack hel regt, 1,500 MBT, 1,320 AIFV, 570 APC, 1,020 arty/MRL/mors, 24 *Scud*, 16 FROG/SS-21, 120 attack hel.
AIR: 1 ftr div, 2 regt (85: MiG-29, Su-17, Su-22, Su-24, Su-25, Su-27), 1 ftr regt (30: MiG-23), 4 trg div/centre (405: MiG-21*, MiG-23*, MiG-25*, MiG-29*, Su-17*, Su-24*, Su-25*, Su-27*; 320 L-29, L-39).

VOLGA MD (HQ Kuybyshev):
GROUND: 2 MRD (1 trg) plus 1 arty bde/regt, 1 trg *Scud*, 1 SAM bde, 1 ATK, 1 attack hel regt. 360 MBT, 300 AIFV, 500 APC, 170 arty/MRL/mor, 150 attack hel.
AIR: 1 trg regt (110 L-29), 2 attack hel trg regt (220 Mi-24).

URAL MD (HQ Sverdlovsk):
2 TD (1 trg), 2 MRD, 2 arty bde/regt, 1 ATK bde. 800 MBT, 1,000 AIFV, 600 APC, 1,000 arty/MRL/mor.

NORTH CAUCASUS MD (HQ Rostov):
GROUND: 1 Army, 2 corps HQ, 4 MRD (1 trg) plus 1 arty div, 1 arty bde/regt, 2 *Scud*, 2 SAM bde, 2 ATK regt, 550 MBT, 180 AIFV, 530 arty/MRL/mor, 24 *Scud*.
AIR: 5 trg div, 14 trg regt, (470: MiG-21*, MiG-23*, MiG-27*, Su-17*, Su-22*, Su-24*, Su-25*, 800: L-29, L-39).

SIBERIAN MD (HQ Novosibirsk):
GROUND: 8 MRD, 1 arty div, 3 arty bde/regt, 1 *Spetsnaz*, 1 ATK bde, 1,600 MBT, 1,950 arty/MRL/mor.

TRANSBAYKAL MD (HQ Chita):
GROUND: 3 army HQ, 4 TD (1 trg), 11 MRD (1 trg), plus 2 MG/arty div, 1 arty div, 5 arty bde/regt, 1 *Spetsnaz*, 1 ATK, 3 SAM bde, 2 attack hel regt, 3,700 MBT, 3,500 arty/MRL/mor, 100 attack hel.
AIR: 1 air army, 2 FGA div, 6 regt (160: MiG-27, Su-24), 1 ftr div, 2 regt (60: MiG-23), 1 recce regt (20: Su-24).

FAR EASTERN MD (HQ Khabarovsk):
GROUND: 4 army, 1 corps HQ, 3 TD (1 trg), 16 MRD (2 trg), plus 6 MG/arty div, 1 arty div, 11 arty bde/regt, 2 AB, 4 *Scud*, 1 *Spetsnaz*, 4 ATK bde, 6 attack hel regt, 4,400 MBT, 4,950 arty/MRL/mor, 50 *Scud*, 400 attack hel.
AIR: 3 air army, 3 FGA div, 8 regt (280 MiG-27, Su-24, Su-25) 1 ftr div, 3 regt (130: MiG-23, MiG-29, Su-27), 2 recce regt (60: MiG-21, MiG-25, Su-24).

FORCES IN CIS REPUBLICS:
MOLDOVA (14th Army): 1 army HQ, 2 MRD (Dnestr, Ukraine), 2 arty bde (Moldova), 2 *Scud* bde (Moldova), 1 attack hel regt (Ukraine) 230 MBT, 70 AIFV, 330 arty/MRL/mor, 24 *Scud*, 40 attack hel.

'TRANS-CAUCASUS MD':
ARMENIA
GROUND: (23,000): 1 Army HQ, 4 MRD, 2 arty regt, 250 MBT, 350 AIFV, 350 arty/MRL/mor, 7 attack hel.

AZERBAIJAN
GROUND (62,000): 1 Army HQ, 3 MRD, 1 ABD, 2 arty regt, 400 MBT, 720 AIFV, 470 arty/MRL/mors, 14 attack hel.
AIR: 1 bbr regt (30 Su-24), 1 FGA regt (30 Su-25), 1 recce regt (30 MiG-25, Su-24).

GEORGIA
GROUND (20,000): 1 MD HQ, 1 Corps HQ, 4 MRD (1 trg), 1 AB bde, 1 ATK regt, 1 attack hel regt, 850 MBT, 680 AIFV, 370 arty/MRL/mors, 48 attack hel.
AIR: 1 air army HQ, 1 bbr div HQ, 2 regt (60 Su-24), 1 ftr div, 2 regt (80 MiG-23, MiG-29), 1 recce regt (30 Su-17).

CENTRAL ASIA (former Turkestan MD)
KAZAKHSTAN
GROUND (63,000): 1 Army HQ, 1 TD, 5 MRD (1 trg), 1 AB bde, 2 arty bde, 1 ATK bde, 1 *Spetsnaz* bde, 1 attack hel regt, 1,200 MBT, 1,500 arty/MRL/mor, 25 attack hel.
AIR: 1 FGA div (140 MiG-27, Su-24), 1 ftr div: (100 MiG-23), 1 recce regt (70 MiG-25, Su-17, Su-24).

KYRGYZSTAN
GROUND (8,000): 1 MRD, 30 MBT, 75 arty/MRL/mor.
AIR: 1 trg centre (200+ MiG-21).

TAJIKISTAN
GROUND (6,000): 1 MRD, 260 MBT, 420 ACV, 360 arty/MRL/mors.

TURKMENISTAN
GROUND (34,000): 1 Corps HQ, 4 MRD (1 trg), 1 AB bde, 3 arty, 1 *Spetsnaz* bde, 750 MBT, 1,000+ ACV, 1,400 arty/MRL/mor.
AIR: 2 FGA regt (60 MiG-27, Su-17), 1 trg regt (30 MiG-29).

UZBEKISTAN
GROUND (15,000): 1 MRD, 1 ABD, 1 arty bde, 1 attack hel regt, 280 MBT, 780 arty/MRL/mors, 24 attack hel.

AIR: 2 FGA regt (100 Su-17, Su-24, Su-25), 2 ftr regt (100 MiG-29, Su-15, Su-17), 1 recce regt (35 Su-17, Su-24).

AIR DEFENCE TROOPS (VPVO): 356,000
(ε 230,000 conscripts). 5 Air Defence Armies: air regt and indep sqn; AD regt.

AIRCRAFT: (*Aviation of Air Defence* – APVO):

FIGHTER: some 2,200, plus some 300 in store: incl 130 MiG-21 (trg), 860 MiG-23 (6 AAM); 340 MiG-25 (4 AAM); 330 MiG-31 (4 AA-9); 300 Su-15 (2 AAM); 250 Su-27. (Incl some 500 trainer variants, in trg units plus each regt holds 4–5 trainer variants).

TRAINING: 350 L-39, 200 L-29 (not cbt ac)

AEW AND CONTROL: 15 Il-76

AAM: AA-2 *Atoll*, AA-3 *Anab*, AA-6 *Acrid*, AA-7 *Apex*, AA-8 *Aphid*, AA-9 *Amos*, AA-10 *Alamo*, AA-11 *Archer*.

DEPLOYMENT:
RUSSIA:
NORTH-WEST GROUP OF FORCES
> **Russia:** 1 regt: 35 Su-27.
> **Estonia:** 3 regt: 120 MiG-23
> **Latvia:** 1 regt: 40 Su-27

MOSCOW MD: 9 regt: 170 MiG-23, 30 MiG-25, 60 MiG-31, 30 Su-15, plus in store 100 Tu-128, 10 MiG-23, 20 Su-15, 1 trg centre: 60 MiG-23, MiG-25, MiG-31, Su-27 (half are trainer variants).

VOLGA AND URAL MDS: 3 regt: 80 MiG-23, 40 MiG-25, plus in store 25 MiG-23, 110 Su-15.

LENINGRAD MD: 9 regt: 40 MiG-23, 70 MiG-25, 90 MiG-31, 60 Su-15, 70 Su-27.

NORTH CAUCASUS MD: 3 regt, 30 MiG-23, 40 MiG-25, 40 Su-27, 2 trg centre: 280: MiG-21, MiG-23, Su-15 (half are trainer variants), 270 L-29/L-39.

FAR EAST REGION: 15 regt: 180 MiG-23, 100 MiG-25, 90 MiG-31, 90 Su-15.

GEORGIA: 2 regt: 40 Su-15, 30 Su-27.

AZERBAIJAN: 1 regt: 30 MiG-25.
> 2 trg regt: 150 L-29/L-39.

KAZAKHSTAN: 2 regt: 35 MiG-21, 45 MiG-31.

TURKMENISTAN: 2 regt: 55 MiG-23, 30 MiG-25.

UZBEKISTAN: 1 regt: 30 Su-27.

SAM: some 7,000 launchers in some 900 sites:
> SA-2 *Guideline*: 2,000 (being replaced by SA-10).
> SA-3 *Goa*: 800 (2 or 4 launcher rails, 200 sites.
> SA-5 *Gammon*: 1,800 launchers (110 complexes).
> SA-10 *Grumble*: some 2,400 quad.

DEPLOYMENT:

RUSSIA: 5,300.	**GEORGIA:** 175.
ARMENIA: 80.	**KAZAKHSTAN:** 150.
AZERBAIJAN: 135.	**KYRGYZSTAN:** 55.

MOLDOVA: 80.		**ESTONIA:** 250.
TAJIKISTAN: 40.		**LATVIA:** 450.
TURKMENISTAN: 75.		**LITHUANIA:** 125.
UZBEKISTAN: 100.		

At this time it is not possible to give SAM deployment by type.

FORCES ABROAD (other than in republics of former USSR or in Groups of Forces):

MONGOLIA: 3,000 (withdrawal to be completed by end 1992).

VIETNAM: (500); naval base; 1 Tu-142, 8 Tu-16 MR ac on det; AA, SAM, electronic monitoring station.

OTHER: Algeria 500; Angola 50; Cambodia 500; Congo 20; Cuba some 4,300 (1 bde (2,100), 2,100 SIGINT and 100 mil advisers); India 500; Libya 1,000; Mali 20; Mozambique 25; Peru 50; Syria 500; Yemen 300; Africa (remainder) 100.

UN AND PEACEKEEPING:
CAMBODIA (UNTAC): Naval unit and Observers (56).
CROATIA (UNPROFOR): 1 AB bn (900).
GEORGIA/SOUTH OSSETIA: 1 inf bn.
IRAQ/KUWAIT (UNIKOM): 20 Observers.
MIDDLE EAST (UNTSO): 35 Observers.
MOLDOVA/DNESTR: 6 AB bn.
WESTERN SAHARA: (MINURSO) 20 Observers.

PARAMILITARY: 520,000.

BORDER TROOPS Committee for the Protection of State Borders (previously KGB): 220,000.
EQUIPMENT:
> 30 T-80 MBT, 2,200 ACV (incl BMP, BTR).
> 90 arty (incl 2S1, 2S9, 2S12).

PATROL AND COASTAL COMBATANTS: About 212:
> **OFFSHORE PATROL:** About 25:
> > 7 *Krivak-III* with 1 × Ka-27 hel, 1 × 100mm gun.
> > 12 *Grisha-II*, 6 *Grisha-III*.
> **COASTAL PATROL:** About 32: 25 *Pauk*, 7 *Svetlyak*.
> **INSHORE PATROL:** About 155: 110 *Stenka*, 15 *Muravey*, 30 *Zhuk*.

RIVERINE MONITORS: About 135: 21 *Yaz*, 10 *Piyavka*, 8 *Vosh*, 96 *Shmel⟨*.

SUPPORT AND MISCELLANEOUS: About 26:
> 8 *Ivan Susanin* armed icebreakers, 18 *Sorum* armed ocean tugs.

MVD (*Ministerstvo Vnutrennikh Del*): internal security tps; 1 div, op regt (30,000); special police regt (40,000); guards and escorts (some 100,000) Eqpt incl 1,200 APC, 20 D-30. MVD troops mostly under national control.

OPPOSITION FORCES:
CHECHENIA-INGUSHETIA
National Guard: 62,000
Emergency Volunteer Corps: 300,000

The Middle East and North Africa

Political Developments

The Middle East Peace Conference got under way in Madrid in October 1991, with separate bilateral talks being held by Israel with Jordan/Palestinians, Lebanon and Syria. Although no substantive progress was made, at least the talks had started. By the time the Israeli elections were held on 23 June, four further rounds of talks had taken place in Washington and the parties' positions had been laid out. The multilateral regional talks were perhaps less successful as a number of countries boycotted different sessions. Syria did not attend the opening session in Moscow. Four separate talks were held in May on Refugees, Economics, Water, and on Arms Control; Israel was not present at the first two; Syria and Lebanon boycotted all four sessions. The new Prime Minister, Yitzhak Rabin, following the Likud party's defeat in the Israeli elections, has said he aims to complete negotiations on autonomy within a year.

The UN Security Council adopted Resolution 733 on 23 January 1992, which called on all parties to cease hostilities and imposed a 'general and complete embargo' on the delivery of arms and military equipment to Somalia. Following talks in New York with the Somali factions, the UN sent a technical team to Mogadishu at the end of March, tasked with preparing a plan for monitoring the ceasefire and for ensuring the delivery of humanitarian assistance. The Security Council, by its Resolution 751, decided to establish a peacekeeping operation in Somalia (UNOSOM). UNOSOM consists of 50 observers and an infantry battalion mainly for the protection of relief supplies convoys which had not deployed to Somalia by 1 August 1992.

Iraq and the United Nations

UN economic sanctions imposed on Iraq by Resolution 661 adopted in August 1990 were still in force two years later, and there had been no agreement by Iraq to the proposal made by the UN to allow it to sell oil in order to purchase relief supplies of food and medicine. Although the air and sea blockades remain in place, trade is undoubtedly taking place across Iraq's land borders.

The UN Special Commission set up to supervise the destruction of Iraq's stocks of weapons of mass destruction and their means of manufacture has made a considerable number of visits to Iraq with varying measures of success. All declared that ballistic missiles have been destroyed, as have a number of installations for their manufacture and modification. Whether there are still hidden stocks of missiles remains a matter of speculation, although the Commission has verified that Iraq had destroyed acknowledged ballistic missiles and production equipment. The Commission has still not yet received the full disclosure of Iraq's weapons programme and so cannot categorically state that Iraq has no production capability for ballistic missiles.

The International Atomic Energy Agency (IAEA), which is carrying out the destruction of Iraq's nuclear weapon capability on behalf of the UN, has made several visits to Iraq, and its work has been much aided by the discovery and removal of much of the weapons programme's archives at its headquarters in Baghdad. In April, the IAEA supervised the demolition of buildings at the main nuclear production facility at Al Atheer, while at nearby Al Hateen a high-explosive test firing bunker which could not be blown up was filled in with concrete, and other buildings were demolished.

In the CBW field all declared stocks of unfilled and unsafe ammunition have been destroyed. By summer 1992 the task of safely destroying agent stocks was about to begin at Al Muthanna, where a destruction plant has been assembled. The Executive Chairman of the Special Commission is quoted as saying 'Iraq had a very advanced military offensive programme in biological research, so it is peculiar that we have not found a real BW production plant yet'. The Special Commission continues to conduct short-notice inspections of undeclared but suspect sites.

Military Developments

Although the manpower of a number of armies has increased considerably, we have not yet noted a similar increase in weapons inventories. A number of states, notably Iran and Syria, are known to have ambitious weapon procurement plans.

The **Algerian** Army has increased its manpower strength by 13,000. The army is being reorganized on a divisional basis: there are to be four divisions, two armoured and two mechanized. Weapon deliveries include 60 M-1943 160mm mortars, three *El Yadekh* patrol craft and four more Su-24 FGA aircraft. Paramilitary forces have been greatly strengthened by the formation of National Security Forces of some 16,000 men with small arms only, and a 1,200-strong Republican Guard Brigade equipped with light tanks and other armoured vehicles, while Gendarmerie strength has increased by 12,000. Six Coast Guard patrol craft have been purchased.

The **Egyptian** Army holding of M-109A2 155 SP guns has increased by 50, and it now has 175 122mm Yugoslav-made M-88 MRL. There have been reports of test firings of the *Sakr* SSM, which is believed to have a range of 80km with a 200-kg payload.

While it is reported that **Iran** is seeking to buy large numbers of aircraft, tanks and SAM from Russia, and patrol boats and possibly SSM from China, we can only report the delivery of ten Su-24 FGA and ten MiG-29 fighters from Russia, and 12 F-7 fighters from China. Artillery holdings have been reassessed; there are around 300 more towed guns than previously thought. Iran is rumoured to be acquiring a submarine force. It is probable that a consignment of North Korean upgraded *Scud* PIP en route for Syria were landed in Iran after it was clear that passage through the Suez Canal would be barred.

Fresh information has allowed a reassessment of **Iraqi** divisions. While it is clear that 42 divisions were deployed into Kuwait and southern Iraq before *Operation Desert Storm* was launched, it is estimated that there were some 16 divisions which were not deployed to the theatre of operations, which were likely to be under-strength and manned by low-grade soldiers. A number of new divisions were formed during the war; a number of these and the uncommitted divisions were broken up. The best estimate of Iraq's current strength is that there are 29 divisions, of which 21 can be traced to divisions deployed in the Kuwait Theatre of Operations; three which had not been deployed, and three which are newly created formations. Of these 29, seven are Republican Guard armoured and mechanized divisions. A new force, the 'Presidential Guard and Special Security Force' has been formed at about divisional strength. Its role is to protect the government and it is probably manned by troops from the Republican Guard. Although rather more Iraqi naval vessels survived the war than was originally thought, the Navy is likely to have only a minimal capability for several years. The Iraqi Air Force fixed-wing aircraft are still grounded and will take some time to become operational once flying is allowed. There have been rumours of Iraqi Air Force training in Yemen, to which some aircraft may have been evacuated before the war.

The **Israeli** Army has disposed of a number of its older tanks, mainly M-48 and T-54/-55, but has increased its holding of *Merkava* MBT by 140. It is now assessed that the Israeli artillery can field some 100 MRL of varying types; the army would like to buy MLRS. The air force has taken delivery of 15 more F-15 and 40 more F-16 aircraft and added three more Israeli-built 1124 *Seascan* to its maritime reconnaissance force. Israel now has four *Patriot* batteries. The Israeli Defence Forces are under great economic pressure, and savings can only come from reducing 'career' manpower (although conscript strength can be increased as new immigrants from the former Soviet Union become eligible for army service). Procurement priority will be given to tanks, helicopters and combat aircraft; no money is available for AIFV.

Kuwaiti armed forces' strength has increased by 3,500. The army has taken delivery of the full order of 200 M-84 MBT (Yugoslav-produced T-72), 18 GCT 155mm SP guns and six M-30 107mm SP mortars. The air force has received eight F/A-18 FGA aircraft, 12 *Hawk* 64 and 16 *Tucano* trainers (both COIN capable aircraft) and four more SA-342 helicopters armed with HOT ATGW. In **Lebanon** the armed forces are some 20,000 stronger than previously thought. The only new equipment identified is an additional 12 M-102 105mm guns. Tank holdings have been reassessed; the overall total is unchanged, but there are 90 not 175 M-48, and 150 not 70 T-54/-55. **Libyan** holdings of Su-24 FGA have increased by five aircraft.

Oman has formed a second special forces unit, directly subordinate to the Royal Household. Two *Vosper* 83-m corvettes have been ordered for the Navy. **Qatar** has taken delivery of 12 G5 155mm towed howitzers and four *ASTROS* II MRL, and has ordered four *Vita* fast missile boats armed with *Exocet* SSM for its navy. **Saudi Arabian** manpower has increased considerably: the army by 28,000 and the National Guard by 20,000 men. New weaponry includes: ten more *ASTROS* MRL, ten S-70A-1 and 15 Bell 406CS helicopters for the army; the first *Al Jawf* (UK *Sandown*-class) mine countermeasures ship and 12 AS-332 *Super Puma* helicopters (six armed with *Exocet* SSM) for the navy; and 17 *Tornado* IDS FGA aircraft and 18 F-15C fighters for the air force. A large number of orders for military equipment are expected to be placed, but so far only equipment for 16 more *Patriot* batteries at a cost of $3.3bn has been ordered.

The **Sudanese** Army has received an additional 50 Chinese Type-59 MBT. Artillery holdings have been reassessed and show considerably higher numbers than previously thought. **Syria** has received some 200 T-72 tanks from Czechoslovakia despite some problems over shipping them. Syria is widely believed to have ordered M-9 SSM from China, with a range of 600km, and upgraded *Scud* PIP with a range of 500km from North Korea. There is no confirmation of delivery of M-9 missiles and a consignment of *Scuds* thought to be destined for Syria have been offloaded in Iran. The **UAE** has increased its manpower by 10,000 men; 40 G-6 155mm SP guns have been delivered. The navy has taken delivery of two *Mubaraz* (German 50-m Lürssen) missile craft with *Exocet* SSM, and the air force five more *Hawk* aircraft (three FGA, two trainers).

ALGERIA

GDP	1990ε:	D 428.30bn ($47.81bn)	
	1991ε:	D 735.00bn ($39.79bn)	
Growth	1990:	−1.0%	1991ε: 2.3%
Inflation	1990:	16.6%	1991ε: 30.0%
Debt	1990:	$26.00bn	1991: $23.80bn
Def bdgt[a]	1990:	D 8.100bn ($904m)	
	1991:	D 10.349bn ($660m) ~	
Def exp	1990ε:	D 17.02bn ($1.90bn)	
$1 = D	1989:	7.608	1990: 8.958
	1991:	18.473	1992: 22.600
D = dinar			

[a] Excl eqpt and internal security costs.

Population: 27,073,400

	13–17	18–22	23–32
Men	1,625,000	1,405,000	2,167,300
Women	1,534,400	1,327,800	2,049,200

TOTAL ARMED FORCES:
ACTIVE: 139,000 (84,000 conscripts).
Terms of service: Army only 18 months (6 months basic, 1 year civil projects).
RESERVES: Army: some 150,000, to age 50.

ARMY: 120,000 (84,000 conscripts).
6 Military Regions. Reorganizing into div structure. Numbers of indep bde, regt unclear.
2 armd div (each 3 tk, 1 mech regt).
2 mech div (each 3 mech, 1 tk regt).
9 mot inf bde (3 inf, 1 tk, 1 arty, 1 engr bn).
1 AB/SF bde.
31 indep inf, 4 para bn.
7 indep arty, 5 AD bn.
4 engr bn.
12 coy desert troops.

EQUIPMENT:
MBT: some 960: 330 T-54/-55, 330 T-62, 300 T-72.
RECCE: 120 BRDM-2.
AIFV: 915: 690 BMP-1, 225 BMP-2.
APC: 460 BTR-50/-60.
TOWED ARTY: 425: 122mm: 25 D-74, 100 M-1931/37, 40 M-30, 190 D-30; 130mm: 10 M-46; 152mm: 60 M-1938.
SP ARTY: 200: 122mm: 150 2S1; 152mm: 25 ISU-152, 25 2S3.
MRL: 128: 122mm: 48 BM-21; 140mm: 50 BM-14-16; 240mm: 30 BM-24.
MORTARS: 120mm: 120 M-1943, 150 M-1937; 160mm: 60 M-1943.
ATGW: 40 AT-3 *Sagger* (some SP/BRDM-2), *Milan*.
RCL: 178: 82mm: 120 B-10; 107mm: 58 B-11.
ATK GUNS: 296: 57mm: 156 ZIS-2; 85mm: 80 D-44; 100mm: 10 T-12, 50 SU-100 SP.
AD GUNS: 880: 14.5mm: 65 ZPU-2/-4; 20mm: 100; 23mm: 100 ZU-23 towed, 210 ZSU-23-4 SP; 37mm: 150 M-1939; 57mm: 75 S-60; 85mm: 20 KS-12; 100mm: 150 KS-19; 130mm: 10 KS-30.
SAM: SA-7/-8/-9.

NAVY: ε7,000.

BASES: Mers el Kebir, Algiers, Annaba, Jijel.
SUBMARINES: 2:
2 Sov *Kilo* with 533mm TT.
FRIGATES: 3 *Mourad Reis* (Sov *Koni*) with 2 × 12 ASW RL.
PATROL AND COASTAL COMBATANTS: 23:
CORVETTES: 3 *Rais Hamidou* (Sov *Nanuchka II*) with 4 × SS-N-2C *Styx* SSM.
MISSILE CRAFT: 11 *Osa* with 4 × SS-N-2 SSM.
PATROL: 9.
  COASTAL: 3 local-built *Djebel Chinoise.*
  INSHORE: about 6 *El Yadekh* PCI.
MINE WARFARE: 1 Sov T-43 MSC.
AMPHIBIOUS: 3:
2 *Kalaat beni Hammad* LST: capacity 240 tps, 10 tk, hel deck.
1 *Polnocny* LSM: capacity 100 tps, 5 tk.
SUPPORT AND MISCELLANEOUS: 3
1 *El Idrissi* AGHS, 1 div spt, 1 *Poluchat* torpedo recovery vehicle.

COAST GUARD (under naval control): 580;
6 Ch *Chui-E* PCC, about 6 *El Yadekh* PCI, 16 PCI⟨, 1 spt.

AIR FORCE: 12,000; 242 cbt ac, 58 armed hel.
FGA: 3 sqn:
  1 with 30 MiG-17;   1 with 10 Su-24.
  1 with 17 MiG-23BN/MF;
  FIGHTER: 10 sqn:
  6 with 95 MiG-21MF/bis;
  1 with 14 MiG-25;
  3 with 40 MiG-23B/E.
RECCE: 1 sqn with 3 MiG-25R.
MR: 1 sqn with 2 *Super King Air* B-200T.
TRANSPORT: 2 sqn with 6 An-12, 10 C-130H, 6 C-130H-30, 1 *Aero Commander* 680 (survey);
  VIP: 1 Il-18, 2 *Falcon* 900, 3 *Gulfstream* III, 2 *Super King Air* 200, 4 Il-76, 3 F-27.
HELICOPTERS: 7 sqn:
  ATTACK: 4 sqn with 38 Mi-24, 1 sqn with 20 Mi-8/-17.
  TRANSPORT: (hy): 1 sqn with 1 Mi-4, 1 Mi-6, 8 Mi-8/-17; (med): 1 sqn with 4 Mi-6, 1 Mi-8/-17.
TRAINING: 3 MiG-15, 25* MiG-17, 3* MiG-21U, 5* MiG-23U, 3* MiG-25U, 6 T-34C, 30 L-39, plus 30 ZLIN-142.
AAM: AA-2.
AD: GUNS: 3 bde+: 85mm, 100mm, 130mm.
  SAM: 3 regt: 1 with 30 SA-2, 21 SA-3, 2 with SA-6.

FORCES ABROAD:
UN AND PEACEKEEPING:
ANGOLA (UNAVEM II): 15 Observers.
CAMBODIA: (UNTAC): 19 Observers.

PARAMILITARY:
GENDARMERIE: (Ministry of Interior): 35,000;
44 Panhard AML-60/M-3 APC, 28 Mi-2 hel.
NATIONAL SECURITY FORCES: (Ministry of Interior): 16,000; small arms.
REPUBLICAN GUARD BDE: 1,200; AMX-13 lt tks, AML-60, M3 recce.

FOREIGN FORCES:
RUSSIA: 500 military advisers.

BAHRAIN

GDP	1990:	D 1.51bn ($4.01bn)	
	1991:	D 1.54bn ($4.09bn)	
Growth	1990:	2.9%	1991: −3.0%
Inflation	1990:	0.9%	1991: 0.8%
Debt	1989:	$339m	
Def bdg*a*	1991:	D 83.00m ($220.80m)	
	1992:	D 89.00m ($236.77m)	
$1	=	D 1989–92: 0.3759	

D = dinar
a Excl a subsidy from the Gulf Cooperation Council (GCC) of $1.8bn (1984–94) shared between Bahrain and Oman.

Population: 511,200

	13–17	18–22	23–32
Men	23,000	20,700	45,300
Women	23,000	19,800	36,600

TOTAL ARMED FORCES:
ACTIVE: 6,150.

ARMY: 5,000.
1 bde: 2 inf, 1 tk, 1 SF bn, 1 armd car sqn, 2 arty, 2 mor bty.
EQUIPMENT:
MBT: 81 M-60A3.
RECCE: 22 AML-90, 8 *Saladin*, 8 *Ferret*, 10 *Shorland*.
APC: some 10 AT-105 *Saxon*, 110 Panhard M-3.
TOWED ARTY: 105mm: 8 lt; 155mm: 14 M-198.
MORTARS: 81mm: 9; 120mm: 9.
ATGW: 15 BGM-71A *TOW*.
RCL: 106mm: 30 M-40A1; 120mm: 6 MOBAT.
SAM: 40+ RBS-70, 20+ *Stinger*, Crotale.

NAVY: ε500.
BASE: Mina Sulman.
PATROL AND COASTAL COMBATANTS: 10:
CORVETTES: 2 *Al Manama* (Ge Lürssen 62-m) with 2 × 2 MM-40 *Exocet* SSM, 1 × *Dauphin* II hel (AS-15 ASM).

MISSILE CRAFT: 4 *Ahmad el Fateh* (Ge Lürssen 45-m) with 2 × 2 MM-40 *Exocet*.
PATROL: 4: 2 *Al Riffa* (Ge Lürssen 38-m PFI). 2 PFI⟨.
SUPPORT AND MISCELLANEOUS: 1: 1 LCU design spt ship.

AIR FORCE: 650; 24 cbt ac, 12 armed hel.
FGA: 1 sqn with 8 F-5E, 4 F-5F.
FIGHTER: 1 sqn with 8 F-16C, 4 -D.
TRANSPORT: 2 *Gulfstream* (1 -II, 1 -III; VIP).
HELICOPTERS: 1 sqn with 12 AB-212 (8 armed), 4 Bo-105 (armed).
MISSILES:
 ASM: AS-11, AS-12.
 AAM: AIM-9P *Sidewinder*.

PARAMILITARY: (Ministry of Interior):
COAST GUARD ε400; 1 PCI, 7 PCI⟨ some 10 motor dhows, plus boats; 2 landing craft, 1 hovercraft.
POLICE 9,000; 2 Hughes 500, 2 Bell 412, 1 Bell 205 hel.

DJIBOUTI

GDP	1989ε:	frD 73.04bn ($410.9m)	
	1990:	frD 72.00bn ($405.1m)	
Growth:	1989ε: 1%		
Inflation:	1988: 6.4%	1989: 3.7%	
Debt	1990: $194.6m		
Def bdgt[a]	1989:	frD 4.71bn ($26m)	
	1990ε:	frD 5.50bn ($31m)	
Def exp	1987:	frD 6.10bn ($34m)	
	1988:	frD 6.35bn ($36m)	
FMA[b]	1992: $5.18m (US)		
$1 = frD	1988–92: 177.72		

frD = Djibouti francs

[a] Following the Gulf War, Djibouti has received substantial amounts of economic aid from Saudi Arabia ($38m). In December 1991, arms worth $10–12m were purchased from China.
[b] Approximately half of Djibouti's economy is subsidized by France, directly or indirectly, through military or development aid.

Population: 426,800

	13–17	*18–22*	*23–32*
Men	23,800	19,600	30,200
Women	23,300	19,400	29,500

TOTAL ARMED FORCES:
ACTIVE: some 3,800, incl 600 Gendarmerie.

ARMY: ε3,000.
 3 Comd (North, Central, South).
 1 inf bn, incl mor, ATK pl.
 1 armd sqn.   1 AB coy.
 1 spt bn.   1 arty bty.
 1 border cdo bn.
EQUIPMENT:
RECCE: 15 M-11 VBL, 4 AML-60, 20 AML-90, 20 AML-245.
APC: 10 BTR-60.
TOWED ARTY: 105mm: M-56 pack how; 122mm: D-30.
MORTARS: 81mm: 25; 120mm: 20.
RL: 73mm; 89mm: LRAC; 120mm: Brandt.
RCL: 106mm: M-40A1.
AD GUNS: 20mm: 5 M-693 SP; 23mm: 5 ZU-23; 40mm: L/70.

NAVY: 100.
BASE: Djibouti.
PATROL CRAFT, INSHORE: Some 9⟨; plus boats.

AIR FORCE: 100; no cbt ac or armed hel.
TRANSPORT: 2 C-212, 2 N-2501, lt: 1 Cessna U206G, 1 Socata 235GT.
HELICOPTERS: 3 AS-355, 2 SE-3130.
(defected from Ethiopia: some 18 ac and hel incl MiG-23, An-12 ac, Mi-8, Mi-24 hel).

PARAMILITARY:
GENDARMERIE: (Ministry of Defence): 600: 1 bn, 1 patrol boat.
NATIONAL SECURITY FORCE: (Ministry of Interior): 1,200.

OPPOSITION:
FRONT FOR THE RESTORATION OF UNITY AND DEMOCRACY: ε4,500.

FOREIGN FORCES:
FRANCE: 4,000, incl 1 inf, 1 Foreign Legion regt, 1 sqn: 10 *Mirage* F-1C, 1 C-160, 3 *Alouette*.

EGYPT

GDP	1990:	£E 78.91bn ($39.45bn)	
	1991:	£E 98.66bn ($29.63bn)	
Growth	1990: 2.6%	1991: 2.3%	
Inflation	1990: 16.8%	1991: 19.8%	
Debt	1990: $39.89bn	1991: $39.70bn	
Def exp	1989:	£E 4.70bn ($4.27bn)	
Def bdgt	1991:	£E 7.42bn ($2.23bn)	
	1992:	£E 8.24bn ($2.47bn)	
FMA[a]	1992: $2,116.8m (US)		
$1 = £E	1989: 1.100	1990: 2.000	
	1991: 3.330	1992: 3.340	

[a] Incl $815m as Economic Support

Population: 57,263,600

	13–17	18–22	23–32
Men	3,158,000	2,693,700	4,610,200
Women	2,999,200	2,536,500	4,301,700

TOTAL ARMED FORCES:
ACTIVE: 410,000 (some 252,000 conscripts).
Terms of service: 3 years (selective).
RESERVES: 604,000. Army 500,000; Navy 14,000; Air Force 20,000; AD 70,000.

ARMY: 290,000 (perhaps 180,000 conscripts).
4 Military Districts, 2 Army HQ:
  4 armd div (each with 2 armd, 1 mech bde).
  8 mech/mot inf div (type: 2 mech, 1 armd bde).
1 Republican Guard armd bde.

2 indep armd bde.	2 airmobile bde.
3 indep inf bde.	1 para bde.
4 indep mech bde.	7 cdo gp.
15 indep arty bde.	2 hy mor bde.

2 SSM bde (1 with *FROG*-7, 1 with *Scud* B).
EQUIPMENT:[b]
MBT: 3,090: 1,040 T-54/-55 (260 being mod), 600 T-62, 1,450 M-60 (700A1, 750A3).
RECCE: 300 BRDM-2.
AIFV: 470: 220 BMP-1, some 250 BMR-600P.
APC: 2,890: 650 *Walid*, 165 *Fahd*, 1,075 BTR-50/OT-62, 1,000 M-113A2.
TOWED ARTY: 1,108: 122mm: 48 M-31/37, 400 M-1938, 220 D-30M; 130mm: 440 M-46.
SP ARTY: 155mm: 200 M-109A2.
MRL: 122mm: 75 BM-11, 60 BM-21/as-Saqr-18/-30, 175 M-88.
MORTARS: 82mm (some 50 SP); 107mm: some 100 M-30 SP; 120mm: 900 M-43; 160mm: 35 M-160.
SSM (launchers): 12 *FROG*-7, *Sakr*-80 (trials), 9 *Scud* B.
ATGW: 1,400 AT-3 *Sagger* (incl BRDM-2); 220 *Milan*; 200 *Swingfire*; 520 *TOW* (incl 52 on M-901 (M-113) SP).
RCL: 82mm: B-10. 107mm: B-11.
AD GUNS: 14.5mm: ZPU-2/-4; 23mm: 460 ZU-23-2, 117 ZSU-23-4 SP, 45 *Sinai*; 37mm: 150 M-1939; 57mm: 300 S-60, 40 ZSU-57-2 SP.
SAM: 1,300 SA-7/'*Ayn as-Saqr*, 26 M-54 SP *Chaparral*.

NAVY: 20,000 (ε12,000 conscripts).
BASES: Alexandria (HQ, Mediterranean), Port Said, Mersa Matruh, Safaqa, Port Tewfig; Hurghada (HQ, Red Sea).
SUBMARINES: 4:
  4 Sov *Romeo*† with 533mm TT, (plus 4 Ch Type-033 awaiting refit).

PRINCIPAL SURFACE COMBATANTS: 5:
DESTROYER: 1: *El Fateh* (UK 'Z') (trg) with 4 × 114mm guns, 5 × 533mm TT.
FRIGATES: 4:
  2 *El Suez* (Sp *Descubierta*) with 2 × 3 ASTT, 1 × 2 ASW RL; plus 2 × 4 *Harpoon* SSM.
  2 *Al Zaffir* (Ch *Jianghu*) with 2 × ASW RL; plus 2 × CSS-N-2 (HY-2) SSM.
PATROL AND COASTAL COMBATANTS: 39:
MISSILE CRAFT: 21:
  6 *Ramadan* with 4 *Otomat* SSM.
  4 Sov *Osa-I* with 4 × SS-N-2A *Styx* SSM.
  6 *October*⟨ with 2 *Otomat* SSM (ε3 non-op).
  5 Ch *Hegu* (*Komar*-type)⟨ with 2 HY-2 SSM.
PATROL: 18:
  8 Ch *Hainan* PFC with 4 × ASW RL.
  6 Sov *Shershen* PFI, 2 with 4 × 533mm TT and BM-21 (8-tube) 122mm MRL; 4 with SA-N-5 and 1 BM-24 (12-tube) 240mm MRL.
  4 Ch *Shanghai* II PFI.
MINE WARFARE: 8:
MINE COUNTERMEASURES: 8:
  4 *Aswan* (Sov *Yurka*) MSC.
  4 *Assiout* (Sov 43 class) MSC.
AMPHIBIOUS: 3 Sov *Polnocny* LSM, capacity 100 tps, 5 tk, plus 11 LCU (some in reserve).
SUPPORT AND MISCELLANEOUS: 19:
  6 AOT (small), 5 trg, 6 tugs, 1 diving spt, 1 misc.

NAVAL AVIATION: 17 armed hel.
HELICOPTERS: 5 *Sea King* Mk 47 (ASW, anti-ship); 12 SA-342 (anti-ship).

COASTAL DEFENCE: (Army tps, Navy control):
GUNS: 130mm: SM-4-1.
SSM: 30 *Otomat* and *Samlet*.

AIR FORCE: 30,000 (10,000 conscripts); (incl AD comd).[b]
492 cbt ac, 74 armed hel.
FGA: 8 sqn:

1 with 14 *Alpha Jet*.	4 with 50 Ch J-6.
2 with 33 F-4E.	1 with 16 *Mirage* 5E2.

FIGHTER: 16 sqn:

2 with 33 F-16A.	5 with 100 MiG-21.
2 with 40 F-16C.	3 with 54 *Mirage* 5E.
3 with 52 Ch J-7.	1 with 16 *Mirage* 2000C.

RECCE: 2 sqn with 6 *Mirage* 5SDR, 14 MiG-21.
EW: 2 C-130H (ELINT), 4 Beech 1900 (ELINT) ac; 4 *Commando* 2E hel (ECM).
AEW: 5 E-2C.
MR: 2 Beech 1900C surveillance ac.
TRANSPORT: 3 sqn with 19 C-130H, 5 DHC-5D, 1 *Super King Air*.
HELICOPTERS: 15 sqn:
  ATTACK: 4 sqn with 74 SA-342K/-L (44 with *HOT*, 30 with 20mm gun).

TACTICAL TRANSPORT: hy: 14 CH-47C; **med:** 40
Mi-8, 25 *Commando* (5 -1 tpt, 17 -2 tpt, 3 -2B
VIP), 2 S-70 (VIP); **lt:** 12 Mi-4, 17 UH-12E
(trg), 10 *Chetak* (trg).
TRAINING: incl 28* *Alpha Jet*, 4 DHC-5, 54
EMB-312, 6* F-16B, 6* F-16D, 36 *Gumhuria*,
16* JJ-6, 40 L-29, 10 L-39, MiG-21U, 5* *Mirage*
5SDD, 3* *Mirage* 2000B, 10 PZL-104, Z-526.
MISSILES:
  ASM: AGM-65 *Maverick*, *Exocet* AM-39, AS-5
  Kelt, AS-12, AS-30, AS 30L *HOT*.
  ARM: *Armat*.
  AAM: AA-2 *Atoll*, AIM-7F *Sparrow*, AIM-9F/L/P
  Sidewinder, R-530, R-550 *Magic*.
RPV: 48 R4E-50 *Skyeye*.
29 Teledyne-Ryan 324.

AIR DEFENCE COMMAND: 70,000

(50,000 conscripts).
5 div: regional bde.   100 AD arty bn.
40 SA-2, 58 SA-3, 14 SA-6 bn.
12 bty *Improved HAWK*
10 bty *Chaparral*.   12 bty *Crotale*
EQUIPMENT:
AD GUNS: some 2,000: 20mm, 23mm, 37mm,
57mm, 85mm, 100mm.
SAM: 756+: some 360 SA-2, 240 SA-3, 60 SA-6, 72
Improved HAWK, 24 *Crotale*.
AD SYSTEMS: some 18 *Amoun* (*Skyguard*/RIM-7F
Sparrow, some 36 twin 35mm guns, some 36
quad SAM). *Sinai-23* short-range AD (Dassault
6SD-20S radar, 23mm guns, *'Ayn as-Saqr* SAM).

FORCES ABROAD: Advisers in Oman, Saudi
Arabia, Somalia, Sudan, Zaire.
UN AND PEACEKEEPING:
ANGOLA (UNAVEM II): 15 Observers.
WESTERN SAHARA (MINURSO): 9 Observers.
CROATIA (UNPROFOR): 3 Observers.

PARAMILITARY:
COAST GUARD: ε2,000.
  PATROL, INSHORE: 30:
    12 *Timsah* PCI, 9 *Swiftships*, 3 *Nisr*†,
    6 *Crestitalia* PFI⟨, plus some 60 boats.
CENTRAL SECURITY FORCES: 300,000.
NATIONAL GUARD: 60,000: *Walid* APC.
FRONTIER GUARD FORCES: 12,000; 13 Frontier Regt.

FOREIGN FORCES:
PEACEKEEPING (MFO): some 2,600. Contingents
from Canada, Colombia, Fiji, France, Italy,
Netherlands, New Zealand, Norway, Uruguay
and US.

---

[b] Most Soviet eqpt now in store, incl MBT and some cbt ac.

IRAN

GDP	1990:	r 34,590.0bn ($59.49bn)		
	1991ε:	r 41,508.0bn ($60.49bn)		
Growth	1990:	10%	1991ε:	8%
Inflation	1990:	21%	1991:	28%
Debt	1990:	$9.01bn		
Def bdgt[a]	1990ε:	r 895.0bn ($3.18bn)		
	1991ε:	r 1,273.0bn ($4.27bn)		
$1 = r[b]	1989:	530.00	1990:	581.45
	1991:	686.20	1992:	705.76

r = rial

[a] The defence budget in dollar terms represents the
estimated value of defence expenditure in PPP terms and
may not include arms purchases which are primarily
funded by all exports or by foreign exchange at the
official rate of exchange ($1 = r 69.7). Opposition sources
claim that Iran spent $19bn on defence in 1991 and has
put aside $14.5bn for military spending in 1992,
including purchase of arms.
[b] Official exchange rate 1991 $1= r 69.70.
Floating exchange rate 1990 $1= r 1,350–1,430.

Population: 55,483,800

	13–17	18–22	23–32
Men	3,165,600	2,732,700	4,311,900
Women	2,965,700	2,588,700	4,169,200

TOTAL ARMED FORCES:
ACTIVE: 528,000.
Terms of service: 24 months.
RESERVES: Army: 350,000, ex-service
volunteers.

ARMY: 305,000 (perhaps 250,000
conscripts).
ε3 Army HQ.
4 armd div (2 of 3, 2 of 4 bde).
7 inf div.
1 AB bde.
1 SF div (4 bde).
Some indep armd, inf bde (incl 'coastal
force').
5 arty gps.
RESERVES: *'Qods'* bn (ex-service).
EQUIPMENT:†
MBT: 700+ incl: T-54/-55, Ch T-59, T-62, some
T-72, *Chieftain* Mk 3/5, M-47/-48, M-60A1.
LIGHT TANKS: 40 *Scorpion*.
RECCE: 130 EE-9 *Cascavel*.
AIFV: 50+ BMP-1.
APC: 700: BTR-50/-60, M-113.
ARTY: 1,300+.
  TOWED: 105mm: M-101A1; 122mm: D-30, Ch
  Type-54/Type-60; 130mm: 200 M-46/Type-59;
  155mm: 50 M-71, 18 FH-77B, ε130 GHN-45,
  ε50 G-5; 203mm: some 30 M-115.

SP: 122mm: 15+ 2S1; 155mm: some 95 M-109;
175mm: 30 M-107; 203mm: 10 M-110.
MRL: 107mm: 40 Ch Type-63; 122mm: 65 BM-21,
Ch Type-81, BM-11; 230mm: *Oghab*; 333mm:
Shahin 2; 355mm: *Nazeat*; *Iran*-130 reported.
MORTARS: 1,200 incl: 81mm; 107mm: M-30
4.2-in.; 120mm.
SSM: *Scud*; local manufacture msl reported under
development.
ATGW: *ENTAC*, SS-11/-12, *Dragon, TOW*, AT-3
Sagger (some SP).
RCL: 57mm: M-18.
AD GUNS: 1,500: 23mm: ZU-23 towed, ZSU-23-4
SP; 35mm: 92; 37mm; 57mm: ZSU-57-2 SP.
SAM: SA-7, some HN-5.
AIRCRAFT: incl 40+ Cessna (185, 310, O-2A), 2 F-27,
2 *Falcon* 20, 15 PC-6, 5 *Shrike Commander*.
HELICOPTERS: 100 AH-1J (attack); 31 CH-47C (hy
tpt); 100 Bell 214A; 20 AB-205A; 50 AB-206.

REVOLUTIONARY GUARD CORPS

(*Pasdaran Inqilab*): Some 170,000.
GROUND FORCES: some 150,000; 11 Regional
Commands: loosely org in bn of no fixed size,
grouped into perhaps 24 inf, 4 armd div and
many indep bde, incl inf, armd, para, SF, arty
(incl SSM), engr, AD and border defence units,
serve indep or with Army; small arms, spt
weapons from Army; controls *Basij* (see
Paramilitary) when mob.
NAVAL FORCES: some 20,000; five island bases
(Al Farsiyah, Halul (oil platform), Sirri, Abu
Musa, Larak); some 40 Swedish Boghammar
Marin boats armed with ATGW, RCL, machine
guns. Italian SSM reported. Controls coast
defence elm incl arty and CSS-N-2 (HY-2)
Silkworm SSM in at least 3 sites, each 3–6 msl.
Now under joint command with Navy.
MARINES: 3 bde reported.

NAVY: 18,000, incl naval air and marines†.
BASES: Bandar Abbas (HQ), Bushehr, Kharg,
Bandar-e-Anzelli, Bandar-e-Khomeini, Chah
Bahar.
PRINCIPAL SURFACE COMBATANTS: 8:
SUBMARINES:
Iran is expected to take delivery of 1 Sov *Kilo* SS
during 1992.
DESTROYERS: 3:
1 *Damavand* (UK *Battle*) with 4 × 2 SM-1
(boxed) SSM, 2 × 2 114mm guns; plus 1 × 3
AS mor.
2 *Babr* (US *Sumner*) with 4 × 2 SM-1 SSM
(boxed), 2 × 2 127mm guns; plus 2 × 3 ASTT.
FRIGATES: 5:
3 *Alvand* (UK Vosper Mk 5) with 1 × 5 *Sea Killer*
SSM, 1 × 3 AS mor, 1 × 114mm gun.
2 *Bayandor* (US PF-103).

PATROL AND COASTAL COMBATANTS: 33:
MISSILE CRAFT: 10 *Kaman* (Fr *Combattante* II)
PFM some fitted for *Harpoon* or Ch C801 SSM.
PATROL INSHORE: 23:
3 *Kaivan*, 3 *Parvin* PCI, 3 N. Korean *Chaho*
PFI⟨, plus some 14 hovercraft⟨ (about 7 in
Refit/Reserve).
MINE WARFARE: 3:
2 *Shahrokh* MSC (1 in Caspian Sea trg), 1 *Riazi*
(US *Cape*) MSI.
(2 *Iran Ajr* LST used for minelaying).
AMPHIBIOUS: 10:
4 *Hengam* LST, capacity 9 tk, 225 tps, 1 hel.
3 *Iran Hormuz 24* (S. Korean) LST, capacity
8 tk, 140 tps.
2 *Iran Ajr* LST.
1 *Foque* LHA, capacity 120t.
Plus craft: 3 LCT.
SUPPORT AND MISCELLANEOUS: 14:
1 *Kharg* AOR, 2 *Bandar Abbas* AOR, 1 repair, 2
water tankers, 7 *Delva* spt vessels, 1 AT.

MARINES: 3 bn.

NAVAL AIR: 9 armed hel.
ASW: 1 hel sqn with ε3 SH-3D, 6 AB-212 ASW.
MCM: 1 hel sqn with 2 RH-53D.
TRANSPORT: 1 sqn with 4 *Commander*, 4 F-27, 1
Falcon 20 ac; AB-205, AB-206 hel.

AIR FORCE: 35,000. Some 262 cbt ac (less than
50% of US ac types serviceable); no armed hel.†
(112 cbt ac flew from Iraq to Iran during the
Gulf War. They consisted of Su-24, MiG-25, F-1,
Su-22, Su-25 and MiG-23. Probably non-op and
not incl in these totals.)
FGA: 9 sqn:
4 with some 60 F-4D/E.   1 with ε10 Su-24.
4 with some 60 F-5E/F.
FIGHTER: 7 sqn:
4 with 60 F-14.   1 with ε12 F-7.
2 with 30 MiG-29.
MR: 5 P-3F, 1 RC-130.
RECCE: 1 sqn (det) with some 5 RF-5, 3 RF-4E.
TANKER/TRANSPORT: 1 sqn with 4 Boeing 707.
TRANSPORT: 5 sqn: 9 Boeing 747F, 11 Boeing 707,
1 Boeing 727, 2 Boeing-747, 20 C-130E/H, 3
Commander 690, 9 F-27, 2 *Falcon* 20.
HELICOPTERS: 2 AB-206A, 39 Bell 214C, 5 CH-47.
TRAINING: incl 26 Beech F-33A/C, 40 EMB-312, 45
PC-7, 7 T-33, 5* MiG-29B, 5* FT-7, 20*
F-5B.
MISSILES:
ASM: AGM-65A *Maverick*.
AAM: AIM-7 *Sparrow*, AIM-9 *Sidewinder*,
AIM-54 *Phoenix*.

SAM: 12 bn with 30 *Improved HAWK*, 5 sqn with 30 *Rapier*, 25 *Tigercat*, 35 HQ-2J (Ch version of SA-2). Probable SA-5.

FORCES ABROAD:
LEBANON: Revolutionary Guard 1,500.
SUDAN: Military Advisers.

PARAMILITARY:
BASIJ 'Popular Mobilization Army' volunteers, mostly youths: strength has been as high as 1 million during periods of offensive operations. Org in up to 500 300–350-man 'bn' of 3 coy, each 4 pl and spt; small arms only. Not currently embodied for mil ops.
GENDARMERIE: (45,000 incl border guard elm); Cessna 185/310 lt ac, AB-205/-206 hel, patrol boats, 96 coastal, 40 harbour craft.†
KURDS: Kurdish Democratic Party armed wing *Pesh Merga*, ε12,000.

OPPOSITION:
KURDISH COMMUNIST PARTY OF IRAN (KOMALA): strength unknown.
DEMOCRATIC PARTY OF IRANIAN KURDISTAN (DPIK): perhaps 10,500.
NATIONAL LIBERATION ARMY (NLA): ε4,500. Org in bde, armed with captured eqpt. Perhaps 100+ tanks. Iraq-based.

IRAQ

There is insufficient data on Iraq's economy to produce figures for 1991. The UN embargo on oil exports is believed to have had a serious effect on the economy with industrial production down by 50% but the Iraqi leadership is still in control.

GDP	1989: D 18.200bn ($58.53bn)	
	1990ε: D 19.66bn ($40.78bn)	
Growth	1989: 3.5%	1990ε: −30% to −40%
Inflation	1989: 20.0%	1990ε: 40.0%
Debt	1989: $80.00bn	1990[a]: $109.67bn
Def bdgt	1990: D 4.150bn ($8.61bn)	
$1 = D	1989: 0.3109	1990: 0.3109
	1991: 0.3109	

(official exchange rate)
D = dinar
[a] Does not incl any est of war reparations.

Population: 18,400,000[b]
[b] Population estimates tentative due to unknown casualties in Iran–Iraq and Gulf War.

TOTAL ARMED FORCES:
ACTIVE: perhaps 382,500.
Terms of service: 18–24 months.
RESERVES: 650,000.

ARMY: ε350,000 (incl perhaps ε100,000 recalled reserves).
6 corps HQ.
22 armd/mech/inf div.
7 Republican Guard Force div (4 armd/mech, 3 inf div).
15 SF/cdo bde (for COIN ops).
(Presidential Guard/Special Security Force.
EQUIPMENT:
It is not possible to give numbers of individual weapons types. Weapons destroyed or captured during the war in 1991 incl: 3,000 tanks, 1,860 armoured vehicles and 2,140 artillery pieces.
MBT: perhaps 2,300 incl T-54/-55/M-77, Ch T-59/-69, T-62, T-72, *Chieftain* Mk 3/5, M-60, M-47.
RECCE: perhaps 1,500 incl BRDM-2, AML-60/-90, EE-9 *Cascavel*, EE-3 *Jararaca*.
AIFV: perhaps 900 BMP-1/-2.
APC: perhaps 2,000 incl BTR-50/-60/-152, OT-62/-64, MTLB, YW-531, M-113A1/A2, Panhard M-3, EE-11 *Urutu*.
TOWED ARTY: perhaps 1,200 incl 105mm: incl M-56 pack; 122mm: D-74, D-30, M-1938; 130mm: incl M-46, Type 59-1; 155mm: some G-5, GHN-45, M-114.
SP ARTY: incl 122mm: 2S1; 152mm: 2S3; 155mm: M-109A1/A2, AUF-1 (GCT).
MRL: perhaps 250 incl 107mm; 122mm: BM-21; 127mm: *ASTROS* II; 132mm: BM-13/-16.
MORTARS: 81mm; 120mm; 160mm: M-1943; 240mm.
ATGW: AT-3 *Sagger* (incl BRDM-2), AT-4 *Spigot* reported, SS-11, *Milan*, *HOT* (incl 100 VC-TH).
RCL: 73mm: SPG-9; 82mm: B-10; 107mm.
ATK GUNS: 85mm; 100mm towed.
HELICOPTERS: ε500 (120 armed) incl.
  ATTACK: ε120 Bo-105 with AS-11/*HOT*, Mi-24, SA-316 with AS-12, SA-321 (some with *Exocet*), SA-342.
  TRANSPORT: ε350 hy: Mi-6; med: AS-61, Bell 214 ST, Mi-4, Mi-8/-17, SA-330; lt: AB-212, BK-117 (SAR), Hughes 300C, -500D, -530F.
AD GUNS: ε5,500: 23mm: ZSU-23-4 SP; 37mm: M-1939 and twin; 57mm: incl ZSU-57-2 SP; 85mm; 100mm; 130mm.
SAM: SA-2/-3/-6/-7/-8/-9/-13/-14/-16, *Roland*.

NAVY: ε1,000.
BASES: Basra (limited facilities), Az Zubayr, Umm Qasr, (currently closed).
FRIGATES: 1: *Ibn Marjid* (ex-*Khaldoum*) (trg)† with 2 × ASTT.
PATROL AND COASTAL COMBATANTS: Some 10: 1 PFI, 6 PFI⟨, 3 PCI⟨, plus boats.

MINE WARFARE: 4
> 2 Sov *Yevgenya*
> 2 Yug *Nestan* MSI⟨.

SUPPORT AND MISCELLANEOUS: 2:
> 1 *Agnadeen* (It *Stromboli*) AOR (laid-up in Alexandria).
> 1 Yacht.

AIR FORCE: 30,000 incl 15,000 AD personnel; Total Iraqi air losses cannot be est. 35 ac were lost in air-to-air cbt, over 100 destroyed on ground, 112 cbt ac flown to Iran; these ac are not included in the totals.

BOMBERS: ε6 incl: H-6D, Tu-16, Tu-22.
FGA: ε130 incl J-6, MiG-23BN, MiG-27, *Mirage* F1EQ5/-200, Su-7, Su-20, Su-25.
FIGHTER: ε180 incl: Ch J-7, MiG-21, MiG-25, *Mirage* F-1EQ, MiG-29.
RECCE: incl: MiG-25.
AEW: incl: Il-76 *Adnan*.
TKR: incl: 2 Il-76.
TRANSPORT: incl: An-2, An-12, An-24, An-26, Il-76.
TRAINING: incl: AS-202, EMB-312, some 40 L-29, some 40 L-39, MB-233, *Mirage* F-1BQ, 25 PC-7, 30 PC-9.
MISSILES:
ASM: AM-39, AS-4, AS-5, AS-11, AS-12, AS-30L, C-601.
AAM: AA-2/-6/-7/-8, R-530, R-550.

PARAMILITARY:
FRONTIER GUARDS: ε20,000
SECURITY TROOPS: 4,800.

OPPOSITION:
KURDISH DEMOCRATIC PARTY (KDP): 25,000 (30,000 more in militia); small arms, some Iranian lt arty, MRL, mor, SAM-7.
KURDISH WORKERS' PARTY: ε20,000; breakaway from KDP, anti-Iran, Syria-based.
PATRIOTIC UNION OF KURDISTAN (PUK): ε12,000 cbt (plus 6,000 spt). Some T-54/-55 MBT; 450 mor (60mm, 82mm, 120mm); 106mm RCL; some 200 12.5mm AA guns; SA-7 SAM.
SOCIALIST PARTY OF KURDISTAN: ε500.
SUPREME ASSEMBLY OF THE ISLAMIC REVOLUTION (SAIRI): ε1 'bde'; Iran-based; Iraqi dissidents, ex-prisoners of war.

FOREIGN FORCES:
UN (UNIKOM): some 300 observers from 33 countries.

ISRAEL

GDP	1990:	NS 103.27bn ($51.22bn)	
	1991:	NS 133.16bn ($58.43bn)	
Growth	1990:	5.1%	1991: 4.9%
Inflation	1990:	17.3%	1991: 18.9%
Debt	1990:	$24.33bn	1991: $23.70bn
Def bdgt	1991:	NS 13.21bn ($5.79bn)	
	1992:	NS 17.58bn ($6.76bn)	
$1 = NS	1989:	1.9164	1990: 2.0162
	1991:	2.2790	1992: 2,5000
FMA[a]	1992:	$3,000m (US)	

NS = new sheqalim
[a] Incl $1,200m as Economic Support

Population: 5,090,000[b]

	13–17	18–22	23–32
Men	246,300	251,800	417,600
Women	234,500	239,300	391,600

[b] 4,175,000 Jews, 7,000 Muslims, 130,000 Christians, 85,000 Druze.

TOTAL ARMED FORCES:
ACTIVE: 175,000 (139,500 conscripts).
> *Terms of service:* officers 48 months, men 36 months, women 24 months (Jews and Druze only; Christians, Circassians and Muslims may volunteer). Annual trg as cbt reservists to age 45 thereafter to age 54 for men, 24 (or marriage) for women.

RESERVES: 430,000: Army 365,000; Navy 10,000; Air Force 55,000. Male commitment until 54 in reserve op units may be followed by voluntary service in the Civil Guard or Civil Defence.

STRATEGIC:
It is widely believed that Israel has a nuclear capability with up to 100 warheads. Delivery means could include ac, *Jericho* 1 SSM (range up to 500km), *Jericho* 2 (tested 1987–9, range ε1,500km) and *Lance*.

ARMY: 134,000 (114,700 conscripts, male and female); some 598,000 on mob.
> 3 territorial, 1 home front comd.
> 3 corps HQ
> 3 armd div (2 armd, 1 arty bde, plus 1 armd, 1 mech inf bde on mob).
> 2 div HQ (op control of anti-*intifida* units).
> 3 regional inf div HQ (border def).
> 4 mech inf bde (incl 1 para trained).
> 1 *Lance* SSM bn.
> 3 arty bn with 203mm M-110 SP.

RESERVES:
> 9 armd div (2 or 3 armd, 1 affiliated mech inf, 1 arty bde).
> 1 airmobile/mech inf div (3 bde manned by para trained reservists).
> 10 regional inf bde (each with own border sector).
> 4 arty bde.

EQUIPMENT:
MBT: 3,890 incl 1,080 *Centurion*, 400 M-48A5, 750 M-60/A1, 650 M-60A3, 100 T-54/-55, 110 T-62, 800 *Merkava* I/II/III.
RECCE: about 400 incl *Ramta* RBY, M-2/-3, BRDM-2, ε8 *Fuchs*.
APC: ε5,000 M-113A1/A2, ε80 *Nagmashot*, BTR-50P, ε3,000 M-2/-3 half track.
TOWED ARTY: ε400: 105mm: M-101; 122mm: D-30; 130mm: M-46; 155mm: Soltam M-68/-71, M-839P/-845P.
SP ARTY: 1,020: 105mm: 34 M-7; 155mm: L-33, 200 M-50, 530 M-109A1/A2; 175mm: M-107; 203mm: 220 M-110.
MRL: 100: 122mm: BM-21; 160mm: LAR-160; 240mm: BM-24; 290mm: MAR-290.
MORTARS: 5,500 incl: 81mm; 120mm: ε 250; 160mm (some SP).
SSM: 12 *Lance* some *Jericho* 1/2.
ATGW: *TOW* (incl *Ramta* (M-113) SP), *Dragon*, AT-3 *Sagger*, *Mapats*.
RL: 82mm: B-300.
RCL: 84mm: *Carl Gustav*; 106mm: 250 M-40A1.
AD GUNS: 20mm: 850: incl TCM-20, M-167 *Vulcan*, 30 M-163 *Vulcan*/M-48 *Chaparral* gun/msl systems; 23mm: ZU-23 and 60 ZSU-23-4 SP; 37mm: M-39; 40mm: L-70.
SAM: *Stinger*, *Redeye*.

NAVY: 10,000 (3,000 conscripts), 10,000 on mob.
BASES: Haifa, Ashdod, Eilat.
SUBMARINES: 3 *Gal* (UK Vickers) SSC with Mk 37 HWT, *Harpoon* USGW.
PATROL AND COASTAL COMBATANTS: 61:
MISSILE CRAFT: 19 PFM:
    2 *Aliya* with 4 *Harpoon*, 4 *Gabriel* SSM, 1 SA-366G *Dauphin* hel (OTHT).
    3 *Romat* with 8 *Harpoon*, 8 *Gabriel*.
    8 *Reshef* with 2–4 *Harpoon*, 4–6 *Gabriel*,
    6 *Mivtach*/*Sa'ar* with 2–4 *Harpoon*, 3–5 *Gabriel*.
PATROL, INSHORE: 40:
    Some 40 *Super Dvora*/*Dvora*/*Dabur* PFI⟨.
AMPHIBIOUS: Craft only; 3 LCT, 1 LCVP.
SUPPORT AND MISCELLANEOUS: 1: 1 tpt.

MARINES: Naval cdo: 300.

AIR FORCE: 32,000 (21,800 conscripts, mainly in AD), 37,000 on mob; 662 cbt ac (plus perhaps 102 stored), 93 armed hel.
FGA/FIGHTER: 16 sqn:
    4 with 112 F-4E (plus 13 in store); (converting 50 to *Phantom* 2000, some 30 now converted).
    2 with 63 F-15 (36 -A, 2 -B, 18 -C, 7 -D);
    6 with 209 F-16 (57 -A, 7 -B, 89 -C, 56 -D).
    4 with 95 *Kfir* C2/C7 (plus 75 in store);
FGA: 4 sqn with 121 A-4H/N, plus 14 in store.
RECCE: 14 RF-4E.

AEW: 4 E-2C.
EW: 6 Boeing 707 (ELINT/ECM), 1 C-130H, 2 EV-1E (ECM), 4 IAI-201 (ELINT), 4 RC-12D, 6 RC-21D (ELINT), 3 RU-21A.
MR: 3 IAI-1124 *Seascan*.
TANKER: 5 Boeing-707, 4 KC-130H.
TRANSPORT: 1 wing: incl 3 Boeing 707, 19 C-47, 24 C-130H, 10 IAI-201, 3 IAI-1124.
LIAISON: 4 *Islander*, 41 Cessna U-206, 2 -172, 2 -180, 6 Do-27, 9 -28D, 12 *Queen Air* 80.
TRAINING: 6 Cessna 152, 80 CM-170 *Tzukit*, 16* F-4E, 5* *Kfir* TC2/7, 35 *Super Cub*, 20* TA-4H, 7* TA-4J.
HELICOPTERS:
ATTACK: 40 AH-1G/S, 35 Hughes 500MD, 18 AH-64A;
SAR: 2 HH-65A;
TRANSPORT: **hy:** 32 CH-53 (2 -A, 30 -D); **med:** 12 UH-1D; **lt:** 54 Bell 212, 40 Bell 206A.
MISSILES:
ASM: AGM-45 *Shrike*, AGM-62A *Walleye*, AGM-65 *Maverick*, AGM-78D *Standard*, *Luz*, *Gabriel* III (mod).
AAM: AIM-7 *Sparrow*, AIM-9 *Sidewinder*, R-530, *Shafrir*, *Python* III.
SAM: 17 bty with MIM-23 *Improved HAWK*, 4 bty *Patriot*.

PARAMILITARY:
BORDER POLICE: 6,000; 600 *Walid* 1, BTR-152 APC.
COAST GUARD: ε50; 1 US PBR, 3 other patrol craft.

JORDAN

GDP	1990:	D 2.57bn ($3.87bn)		
	1991ε:	D 2.80bn ($4.11bn)		
Growth	1990:	−5.7%	1991:	1.0%
Inflation	1990:	16.1%	1991:	8.2%
Debt	1990:	$7.69bn	1991:	$7.20bn
Def bdgt	1991:	D 393.5m ($577.83m)		
	1992ε:	D 357.0m ($508.55m)		
FMA*a*	1992:	$57.0m (US)		
$1 = D	1989:	0.570	1990:	0.664
	1991:	0.681	1992:	0.702

D = dinar
a Incl $30m as Economic Support.

Population: 4,410,400

	13–17	18–22	23–32
Men	289,400	254,800	386,500
Women	255,100	222,600	331,000

TOTAL ARMED FORCES:
ACTIVE: 99,400.
    Terms of service: selective conscription, 2 years authorized.

RESERVES: 35,000 (all services): Army 30,000 (obligation to age 40).

ARMY: 85,000.
2 armd div (each 2 tk, 1 mech inf, 1 arty, 1 AD bde).
2 mech inf div (each 2 mech inf, 1 tk, 1 arty, 1 AD bde).
1 indep Royal Guards bde.
1 SF bde (3 AB bn).1 fd arty bde (4 bn).

EQUIPMENT:
MBT: some 1,131: 260 M-47/-48A5 (in store), 218 M-60A1/A3, 360 *Khalid/Chieftain*, 293 *Tariq (Centurion)*.
LIGHT TANKS: 19 *Scorpion*.
RECCE: 150 *Ferret*.
AIFV: some 30 BMP-2.
APC: 1,100 M-113, *Saracen*, some 25 EE-11 *Urutu*.
TOWED ARTY: 118: 105mm: 50 M-102; 155mm: 15 M-1 (*Long Tom*), 38 M-114 towed, 11 M-59; 203mm: 4 M-115 towed (in store).
SP ARTY: 350 incl: 105mm: M-52; 155mm: M-44, 220 M-109A1/A2; 203mm: 100 M-110.
MORTARS: 81mm: 350; 120mm: 300.
ATGW: 330 *TOW* (incl 50 SP), 310 *Dragon*.
RL: 94mm: LAW-80; 112mm: *APILAS*.
RCL: 106mm: 330 M-40A1.
AD GUNS: 360: 20mm: 100 M-163 *Vulcan* SP; 23mm: 44 ZSU-23-4 SP; 40mm: 216 M-42 SP.
SAM: SA-7B2, 50 SA-8, 50 SA-13, 250 SA-14, 240 SA-16, 250 *Redeye*.

NAVY 400.
BASE: Aqaba.
PATROL: 3:
3 *Al Hussein* (Vosper 30-m) PFI, plus boats.

AIR FORCE: 14,000; 113 cbt ac, 24 armed hel.
FGA: 4 sqn with 62 F-5 (55 -E, 7 -F).
FIGHTER: 2 sqn with 32 *Mirage* F-1 (14 -CJ, 16 -EJ, 2 -BJ).
TRANSPORT: 1 sqn with 6 C-130 (2 -B, 4 -H), 3 C-212A.
VIP: 1 sqn with 2 Boeing 727, 2 *Gulfstream* III (VIP) ac; 4 S-76 hel, 1 L-1011.
HELICOPTERS: 5 sqn:
  ATTACK: 2 sqn with 24 AH-1S (with *TOW* ASM).
  TRANSPORT: 1 sqn with 10 S-76, 3 S-70; 1 sqn with 12 AS-332M; 1 sqn with 8 Hughes 500D.
TRAINING: 16 *Bulldog*, 15 C-101, 12 PA-28-161, 6 PA-34-200, *19 F-5 (15 -A, 4 -B).
AD: 2 bde: 14 bty with 126 *Improved HAWK*.
MISSILES:
  ASM: AGM-65 *Maverick*, *TOW*.
  AAM: AIM-9 *Sidewinder*, R-530, R-550 *Magic*.

FORCES ABROAD:
UN AND PEACEKEEPING:
ANGOLA (UNAVEM II): 15 Observers.
CROATIA (UNPROFOR): 860.

PARAMILITARY:
PUBLIC SECURITY DEPARTMENT: (Ministry of Interior) 6,000; some APC.
CIVIL MILITIA 'PEOPLE'S ARMY': 225,000; men 16–65, women 16–45.
PALESTINE LIBERATION ARMY (PLA): 3,000; 1 bde (Palestinians supervised by Jordanian Army).

KUWAIT

GDP	1989:	D 6.779bn ($24.30bn)		
	1990:	D 7.950bn ($25.86bn)		
Growth[a]	1989:	6.8%	1991ε:	40%
Inflation[a]	1989:	3.4%		
Debt	1991ε:	$13.0bn		
Def exp[b]	1991:	D 4.76bn ($16.76bn)		
Def bdgt	1990:	D 450m ($1.53bn)		
	1991:	D 2.64bn ($9.30bn)		
$1 = D	1989:	0.293	1990:	0.300
	1991:	0.284	1992:	0.294

D = dinar
[a] There is insufficient data for Kuwait's 1990 macroeconomic figures. At the moment, most of Kuwait's efforts are aimed at defence and the rebuilding of infrastructure. The budget deficit for 1991–92 will reach 86% of total spending ($18.67bn).
[b] Incl $7.46bn in off-budget payments for *Operation Desert Storm*. Total war-related expenses are estimated to reach $10.3bn in addition to the $9.3bn defence budget in fiscal 1991–92.

Population: 400,000[c] (mid-1991)
[c] Nationals: 205,000. Non-nationals: 195,000. The pre-invasion population of Kuwait numbered 2,100,000, of which 580,000 were Kuwaiti nationals. The Kuwaiti government has made it clear it intends to restrict the numbers of non-nationals. By the end of 1992 the population is estimated to reach approximately half its pre-war level.

TOTAL ARMED FORCES:
ACTIVE: 11,700.
  Terms of service: voluntary.
RESERVES: 19,000: Obligation for 14 years following regular service. 1 month annual trg.

ARMY: 8,000.
2 mech bde (-).
2 armd bde (-).
1 reserve bde (-)
1 arty bde (-).
EQUIPMENT:
MBT: 200 M-84.
AIFV: 39 BMP-2.
APC: 37 M-113, 44 *Fahd*.

TOWED ARTY: 105mm: 8 M-101.
SP ARTY: 155mm: 3 M-109A2, 18 GCT.
MORTARS: 81mm; 107mm: 6 M-30 SP.
ATGW: *TOW/Improved TOW* (incl 7 M-901 SP).
RCL: 84mm: 200 *Carl Gustav.*

NAVY: 1,200.
BASE: Ras al Qalaya.
PATROL AND COASTAL COMBATANTS: 2:
MISSILE CRAFT: 2:
  1 *Istiqlal* (Ge Lürssen FPB-57) PFM with 2 ×
  MM-40 *Exocet* SSM.
  1 *Al Sanbouk* (Ge Lürssen TNC-45) with 2 ×
  MM-40 *Exocet.*
SUPPORT AND MISCELLANEOUS: 1 log spt.

AIR FORCE: 2,500
  73 cbt ac, 20 armed hel.
FGA: 22 A-4/TA KU, 8 F/A18.
FIGHTER: 15 *Mirage* F1CK/BK.
COIN/TRAINING: 1 sqn with 12 *Hawk* 64, 16
  Shorts *Tucano.*
TRANSPORT: 2 L-100-30, 1 DC-9.
HELICOPTERS: 3 sqn:
  TRANSPORT: 4 AS-332 (tpt/SAR/attack), 9
  SA-330.
  TRAINING/ATTACK: 16 SA-342 (with *HOT*).

PARAMILITARY:
NATIONAL GUARD: 5,000.
COAST GUARD: 500; boats only.

FOREIGN FORCES:
UN (UNIKOM): some 400, incl 300 Observers from
  33 countries.
US: *Patriot* trg bty.

LEBANON

GDP	1990ε:	LP 2,340.0bn ($3.37bn)		
	1991ε:	LP 3,744.0bn ($4.03bn)		
Growth	1990ε:	−8.0%	1991ε:	35%
Inflation	1990ε:	53%	1991ε:	35%
Debt	1990:	$1.93bn	1991:	$2.2bn
Def bdgt[a]	1991:	LP 139.98bn ($151.0m)		
	1992:	LP 241.69bn ($173.0m)		
FMA[b]	1992:	$2.4m (US)		
$1 = LP	1989:	469.69	1990:	695.09
	1991:	928.2	1992:	1,400.0

LP = Lebanese Pound
[a] Def budget does not include aid packages from the west
aimed at providing spares and maintenance for existing
eqpt worth more than $100m.
[b] Incl $2m as Economic Support.

Population: 2,697,800[c]

	13–17	18–22	23–32
Men	154,300	153,600	215,500
Women	150,200	152,300	246,300

[c] Population figures should be treated with caution as
available data is scarce and unreliable.

NATIONAL ARMED FORCES:
ACTIVE: ε36,800.

ARMY: some 35,700.
  11 bde (-) incl Presidential Guard, SF.
EQUIPMENT:
MBT: some 90 M-48A1/A5, 150 T-54/-55.
LIGHT TANKS: 32 AMX-13 (with 75mm or 105mm guns).
RECCE: 50 *Saladin*, 10 *Ferret.*
APC: 200 M-113, *Saracen*, 20 VAB-VTT, AMX-VCI.
TOWED ARTY: 105mm: 15 M-101A1;
  122mm: 30 M-102, M-1938/D-30; 130mm: 5
  M-46; 155mm: 40 incl: Model 50, M-114A1, M-198.
MORTARS: 81mm: 150; 120mm: 30.
ATGW: *ENTAC, Milan*, 20 BGM-71A TOW.
RL: 85mm: RPG-7; 89mm: M-65.
RCL: 106mm: M-40A1.
AD GUNS: 20mm; 23mm: ZU-23; 30mm: towed;
  40mm: 63 M-42 SP.

NAVY: ε400†
  Base: Juniye.
PATROL CRAFT: Inshore: about 7 PCI⟨ of
  doubtful operational status.
AMPHIBIOUS: Craft only; 2 *Sour* (Fr *Edic*) LCT†.

AIR FORCE: Some 800.
EQUIPMENT: (Numerous ac destroyed 1989–90;
  operational status of remainder is doubtful):
FIGHTERS: 3 *Hunter* (2 F-70, 1 T-66).
HELICOPTERS:
  ATTACK: 2 SA-342 with AS-11/-12 ASM;
  TRANSPORT: (med): 4 AB-212, 6 SA-330;
   (lt): 2 SA-313, 3 SA-319.
TRAINING: 3 *Bulldog*, 3 CM-170.
TRANSPORT: 1 *Dove*, 1 *Turbo-Commander* 690A.

PARAMILITARY:
INTERNAL SECURITY FORCE (Ministry of
  Interior): ε7,000 (being reorganized); 30
  Chaimite APC.
CUSTOMS: 2 *Tracker*, inshore patrol craft⟨.

MILITIAS: Most militias are being disbanded
  and heavy weapons handed over to the National
  Army. Reports suggest that large quantities have
  been placed in hidden stockpiles.
CHRISTIAN:
LEBANESE FORCES MILITIA: ε3,000 (incl The
  Phalange).

EQUIPMENT:
MBT: some 12 T-55, M-48.
LIGHT TANKS: some 5 AMX-13.
ARTY: some.
MORTARS: some.
RL: RPG-7.
AD: 12.7mm, 14.5mm, 23mm guns.

MUSLIM:
AMAL (Shi'i, pro-Syria): ε2,000 active; some 15,000 all told. Most eqpt has been handed over to Syria and the National Army.
HIZBOLLAH ('The Party of God'; Shi'i, fundamentalist, pro-Iranian): ε3,000 active; some 15,000 all told.
EQUIPMENT incl: APC, arty, RL, RCL, ATGW, (AT-3 *Sagger*) AA guns.

DRUZE:
PROGRESSIVE SOCIALIST PARTY (PSP): 4,000 active; perhaps 15,000 all told. Eqpt handed over to the Syrian Army.

SOUTH LEBANESE ARMY (SLA): ε2,500
active, (mainly Christian, some Shi'i and Druze, trained, equipped and supported by Israel, occupies the 'Security Zone' between Israeli border and area controlled by UNIFIL)
EQUIPMENT:
MBT: 40 M-4, 30 T-54/-55.
APC: M-113.
TOWED ARTY: 122mm: M-1938; 130mm: M-46; 155mm: M-198.

FOREIGN FORCES:
UNITED NATIONS (UNIFIL): some 5,900; Contingents from Fiji, Finland, France, Ghana, Ireland, Italy, Nepal, Norway and Sweden.

SYRIA: 30,000.
BEIRUT: elm 1 armd bde, elm 7 SF regt.
METN: elm 1 mech bde.
BEKAA: corps HQ, 1 inf, possibly elm 1 mech inf bde.
TRIPOLI: 2 SF regt, elm PLA.

IRAN: Revolutionary Guards: some 1,500 including locally recruited Shi'i Lebanese; may be withdrawn.

PALESTINE LIBERATION
ORGANIZATION (PLO):c
All significant factions of the PLO and other Palestinian military groups are listed here irrespective of the country in which they are based. The faction leader is given after the full title. Strengths are estimates of the number of active 'fighters', these could be trebled perhaps to give an all-told figure. PLO in Lebanon have agreed to hand over their heavy and medium weapons.

FATAH: 4,500.
PLF (Palestine Liberation Front, Al-Abas): ε300.
FATAH (dissidents, Abu Musa): 1,000.
PFLP (Popular Front for Liberation of Palestine, Habash): 900.
PFLP (GC) (Popular Front for Liberation of Palestine, (General Command), Jibril): 500.
SAIQA (al-Khadi): 600.
PSF (Popular Struggle Front, Ghisha): ε500.
DFLP (Democratic Front for Liberation of Palestine, Hawatmah): ε1,000.
FRC (Fatah Revolutionary Council, Abu Nidal): ε500.

Only the main Militia groups have been listed.
c The Palestine Liberation Army is not part of the PLO but is the name for Palestinian units either forming part of, or closely monitored by, host nation armed forces, 3–4 bde.

LIBYA

GDP	1990:	D 7.82bn ($28.96bn)	
	1991:	D 8.60bn ($32.09bn)	
Growth	1990ε: 1.5%		1991ε: 9%
Inflation	1989ε: 15.0%		1990ε: 11.0%
Debt	1989: $5.38bn		
Def bdgt	1989ε: D 440m ($1.51bn)		
$1 = D	1989: 0.292		1990: 0.270
	1991: 0.268		1992: 0.294
D = dinar			

Population: 4,956,000

	13–17	18–22	23–32
Men	281,000	234,000	176,000
Women	271,500	223,000	159,300

TOTAL ARMED FORCES:
ACTIVE: 85,000.
Terms of service: selective conscription, 2–4 years.
RESERVES: People's Militia, some 40,000.

ARMY: 55,000.
4 Military Districts.
28 bde (11 armd, 11 mech, 5 inf, 1 National Guard).

42 tk bn.	53 arty bn.
48 mech inf bn.	14 AD arty bn.
19 para/cdo bn.	

7 SSM bde.
EQUIPMENT:
MBT: 2,150 (incl 1,200 in store): 1,500 T-54/-55, 350 T-62, 300 T-72.
RECCE: 250 BRDM-2, 380 EE-9 *Cascavel*.
AIFV: 1,000 BMP-1.
APC: 850 BTR-50/-60, 100 OT-62/-64, 40 M-113, 100 EE-11 *Urutu*.

TOWED ARTY: some 720: 105mm: some 60 M-101;
122mm: 270 D-30, 60 D-74; 130mm: 330 M-46.
SP ARTY: some 350: 122mm: 130 2S1; 152mm: 40
2S3, *DANA*; 155mm: 160 *Palmaria*, 20 M-109.
MRL: some 650: 107mm: Type 63; 122mm:
BM-21/RM-70, BM-11.
MORTARS: 82mm; 120mm; 160mm: M-43; 240mm.
SSM launchers: 40 *FROG*-7, 80 *Scud* B.
ATGW: 3,000: *Vigilant, Milan,* AT-3 *Sagger* (incl
BRDM SP), AT-4 *Spigot.*
RCL: 106mm: 220 M-40A1.
AD GUNS: 600: 23mm: ZU-23, ZSU-23-4 SP; 30mm:
M-53/59 SP; 40mm: L/70; 57mm: 92 S-60.
SAM: SA-7/-9/-13, 24 quad *Crotale.*
HELICOPTERS:
  TRANSPORT: 18 CH-47.
  LIAISON: 5 AB-206, 11 SA-316.
DEPLOYMENT:
Aouzou Strip: ε2,000.

NAVY: 8,000 incl Coast Guard.
BASES: Tripoli, Benghazi, Derna, Tobruk, Sidi
Bilal, Al Khums.
SUBMARINES: 6 *Al Badr* (Sov *Foxtrot*) with
533mm and 406mm TT.
FRIGATES: 3:
  1 *Dat Assawari*† (UK Vosper Mk 7) with 2 × 3
  ASTT; plus 4 *Otomat* SSM, 1 × 114mm gun.
  2 *Al Hani* (Sov *Koni*) with 4 × ASTT, 2 × ASW
  RL; plus 4 SS-N-2C SSM.
PATROL AND COASTAL COMBATANTS: 45:
CORVETTES: 7:
  4 *Assad al Bihar*† (It *Assad*) with 4 *Otomat* SSM;
  plus 2 × 3 ASTT (A244S LWT).
  3 *Ean al Gazala* (Sov *Nanuchka*) with 2 × 2
  SS-N-2C *Styx* SSM.
MISSILE CRAFT: 24
  9 *Sharara* (Fr *Combattante* II) with 4 *Otomat* SSM;
  12 *Al Katum* (Sov *Osa* II) with 4 SS-N-2C SSM;
  3 *Susa*⟨ with 8 SS-12M SSM.
PATROL CRAFT: 14:
  INSHORE: 14: 4 *Garian*, 3 *Benina*, 7⟨.
MINE WARFARE: 8 *Ras al Gelais* (Sov *Natya* MSO).
  (tpt *El Temsah* has mine-laying capability)
AMPHIBIOUS: 5:
  2 *Ibn Ouf* LST, capacity 240 tps, 6 tk, 1 hel.
  3 Sov *Polnocny* LSM, capacity 180 tps, 6 tk.
  Plus craft: 3 LCT.
SUPPORT AND MISCELLANEOUS: 4:
  1 log spt/dock, 1 salvage, 1 diving spt, 1 tpt.

NAVAL AVIATION: 31 armed hel.
HELICOPTERS: 2 sqn:
  1 with 25 Mi-14 (ASW);
  1 with 12 SA-321 (6 ASW, 6 SAR).

AIR FORCE: 22,000 (incl Air Defence); (some
Syrian pilots, Russian, N. Korean and Pakistani

instructors); 409 cbt ac, 45 armed hel (many ac
in store, number n.k.)
BOMBERS: 1 sqn with 5 Tu-22.
FGA: 7 sqn:
  20 MiG-23BN, 8 MiG-23U, 22 *Mirage* 5D/DE,
  10 *Mirage* 5DD, 8 *Mirage* F-1AD, 15 Su-24,
  45 Su-20/-22.
FIGHTER: 9 sqn:
  50 MiG-21, 100 MiG-23, 12 -23U, 55 MiG-25,
  3 -25U, 12 *Mirage* F-1ED, 6 -BD.
COIN: 1 sqn with 30 J-1 *Jastreb.*
RECCE: 1 sqn with 6 *Mirage* 5DR, 7 MiG-25R.
TRANSPORT: 2 sqn:
  11 An-26, 12 Lockheed (7 C-130H, 2 L-100-20,
  3 L-100-30), 20 G-222, 16 Il-76, 15 L-410.
HELICOPTERS:
  ATTACK: 35 Mi-24, 10 Mi-35.
  TRANSPORT: hy: 18 CH-47C; **med:** 7 Mi-8,
  50 Mi-4; **lt:** 10 Mi-2, 4 SA-316.
TRAINING:
  89 *Galeb* G-2 ac; 20 Mi-2 hel; other ac incl
  2 Tu-22, 70 L-39ZO, 77 SF-260WL.
MISSILES:
  ASM: AT-2 *Swatter* ATGW (hel-borne).
  AAM: AA-2 *Atoll,* AA-6 *Acrid,* AA-7 *Apex,* AA-8
  Aphid, R-530, R-550 *Magic.*

AIR DEFENCE COMMAND:
  'Senezh' AD comd and control system.
  3 bde with SA-5A: each 2 bn of 6 launchers,
  some 4 AD arty gun bn; radar coy.
  3 Regions: 2 bde each 18 SA-2; 2–3 bde each 12
  twin SA-3; ε3 bde each 20–24 SA-6/-8.
  Some 2,000 Russian personnel reportedly support
  the Air Defence system. Expatriates form a
  large proportion of the technical support staff.

PARAMILITARY:
LIWA HARIS AL-JAMAHIRIYA (Revolution Guard
Corps): some 3,000: T-54/-55/-62/-72, armd cars,
APC, MRL, ZSU-23-4, SA-8 (Army inventory).
ISLAMIC PAN-AFRICAN LEGION, some 2,500:
reports of 1 armd, 1 inf, 1 para/cdo bde. Some
T-54/-55, EE-9 AIFV, BTR-50/-60.

PEOPLE'S CAVALRY FORCE: parade unit.

CUSTOMS/COAST GUARD (Naval control):
14 PCI; (counted in naval totals).

FOREIGN FORCES:
RUSSIA: 1,000 advisers.

MAURITANIA

| GDP | 1989ε: OM 82.53bn ($994m) |
| | 1990ε: OM 84.00bn ($1.04bn) |

Growth	1989ε: 1%		
Inflation	1990: 6.5%	1991ε: 8.0%	
Debt	1989: $2.08bn	1990: $2.3bn	
Def exp	1990: OM 3.24bn ($40.20m)		
	1991: OM 3.24bn ($39.55m)		
FMA	1988: $10.13m (US, Fr)		
$1 = OM	1989: 83.051	1990: 80.609	
	1991: 81.946	1992: 82.000	

OM = ouguiyas

Population: 2,042,000

	13–17	18–22	23–32
Men	113,500	98,000	141,000
Women	109,500	95,000	146,000

TOTAL ARMED FORCES:
ACTIVE: 9,600.

Terms of service: conscription (2 years) authorized.

ARMY: 9,000.
6 Military Regions.
7 mot inf bn.   1 arty bn.
1 para/cdo bn.   4 AD arty bty.
2 Camel Corps bn.
1 armd recce sqn
1 engr coy.
EQUIPMENT:
RECCE: 39 AML-60, 20 -90, 40 *Saladin*.
TOWED ARTY: 105mm: 10 M-101A1/HM-2; 122mm: 20 D-74, 10 D-30.
MORTARS: 81mm: 70; 120mm: 15 AR-51/-EC1A-L/SL.
ATGW: 4 *Milan*.
RCL: 75mm: M-20; 106mm: M-40A1.
AD GUNS: 23mm: 20 ZU-23-2; 37mm: 12 M-1939; 100mm: 12 KS-19.
SAM: SA-7.

NAVY: 400.
BASES: Nouadhibou.
PATROL CRAFT, INSHORE: 5:
3 *El Vaiz* (Sp *Barcelo*) PFI†.
1 *El Nasr* (Fr *PATRA*) PCI.
1 *Z'Bar* (Ge *Neustadt*) PFI.

AIR FORCE: 200.
7 cbt ac, no armed hel.
COIN: 5 BN-2 *Defender*, 2 FTB-337 *Milirole*.
MR: 2 *Cheyenne* II.
TRANSPORT: 2 Cessna F-337, 1 DHC-5D, 1 *Gulfstream* II, 1 *Skyvan* 3M.

PARAMILITARY:
GENDARMERIE 1,800; 6 regional coy (Ministry of Interior).

NATIONAL GUARD: (Ministry of Interior) 2,800 plus 1,000 auxiliaries.
BORDER GUARD: 100.

MOROCCO

GDP	1990: D 207.96bn ($25.23bn)		
	1991: D 230.84bn ($26.51bn)		
Growth	1990: 2.6%	1991ε: 4.2%	
Inflation	1990: 6.9%	1991: 8.0%	
Debt	1990: $23.52bn	1991: $21.47bn	
Def exp[a]	1990ε: D 11.10bn ($1.35bn)		
Def bdgt	1991: D 8.56bn ($983m)		
	1992: D 10.00bn ($1.13bn)		
FMA[b]	1992: $53.15m (US)		
$1 = D	1989: 8.488	1990: 8.242	
	1991: 8.707	1992: 8.850	

D = dirham
[a] Incl border and internal security costs.
[b] Incl $12m as Economic Support.

Population: 26,077,800

	13–17	18–22	23–32
Men	1,459,500	1,375,000	2,183,000
Women	1,406,000	1,325,500	1,637,000

TOTAL ARMED FORCES:
ACTIVE: 195,500.

Terms of service: conscription 18 months authorized; most enlisted personnel are volunteers.

RESERVES: 100,000: obligation to age 50.

ARMY: 175,000.
3 Comd (South, Northwest Atlas, Border).
3 mech inf bde HQ. 1 lt sy bde.
2 para bde.   11 mech inf regt.
Independent units:
  10 arty bn.   3 mot (camel corps) bn.
  1 AD gp.   3 cav bn.
  9 armd bn.   1 mtn bn.
  37 inf bn.   4 engr bn.
ROYAL GUARD: 1,500: 1 bn, 1 cav sqn.
EQUIPMENT:
MBT: 224 M-48A5, 60 M-60A1.
LIGHT TANKS: 5 AMX-13, 100 SK-105 *Kuerassier*.
RECCE: 16 EBR-75, 80 AMX-10RC, 190 AML-90, 38 AML-60-7.
AIFV: 30 *Ratel* 20, some 30 -90, 45 VAB-VCI.
APC: 420 M-113, 320 VAB-VTT, some 45 OT-62/-64 may be operational.
TOWED ARTY: 105mm: 30 lt (L-118), 20 M-101, 36 HM2 (Fr M-101A1); 130mm: 18 M-46; 155mm: 20 M-114.
SP ARTY: 105mm: 5 Mk 61; 155mm: 98 F-3, 44 M-109, 20 M-44.

MRL: 122mm: 40 BM-21.
MORTARS: 81mm: 1,100; 120mm: 600 (incl 20 VAB SP).
ATGW: 440 *Dragon*, 80 *Milan*, 150 *TOW* (incl 42 SP), *HOT*.
RL: 66mm: *LAW*; 88mm: M-20 3.5-in.
RCL: 106mm: 350 M-40A1.
ATK GUNS: 90mm: 28 M-56; 100mm: 8 SU-100 SP.
AD GUNS: 14.5mm: 180 ZPU-2, 20 ZPU-4; 20mm: 40 towed, 60 M-163 *Vulcan* SP; 23mm: 90 ZU-23-2; 37mm: 25 M-38/-39; 100mm: 12 KS-19 towed.
SAM: 37 M-54 SP *Chaparral*, 70 SA-7.

NAVY: 7,000 incl 1,500 marines.
BASES: Casablanca, Agadir, Al Hoceima, Dakhla.
FRIGATE: 1 *Lt Col. Errhamani* (Sp *Descubierta*) with 2 × 3 ASTT (Mk 46 LWT), 1 × 2 375mm AS mor; plus 4 × MM-40 *Exocet* SSM.
PATROL AND COASTAL COMBATANTS: 27:
MISSILE CRAFT: 4 *Cdt El Khattabi* (Sp *Lazaga* 58-m) PFM with 4 × MM-38 *Exocet* SSM.
PATROL: 23:
  COASTAL: 13:
    2 *Okba* (Fr PR-72) PFC.
    6 *LV Rabhi* (Sp 58-m B-200D) PCC.
    5 *El Hahiq* (Dk *Osprey* 55) PCC. (incl 2 with customs).
  INSHORE: 10 *El Wacil* (Fr P-32) PFI⟨. (incl 4 with customs).
AMPHIBIOUS: 3 *Ben Aicha* (Fr *Champlain BATRAL*) LSM, capacity 140 tps, 7 tk. Plus craft; 1 LCU.
SUPPORT: 3: 2 log spt, 1 tpt.

MARINES: (1,500). 1 naval inf bn.

AIR FORCE: 13,500; 90 cbt ac, 24 armed hel.
FGA: 2 sqn.
  1 with 15 F-5E, 3 F-5F.
  1 with 14 *Mirage* F-1EH.
FIGHTER: 1 sqn with 15 *Mirage* F-1CH.
COIN: 2 sqn:
  1 with 23 *Alpha Jet*; 1 with 23 CM-170.
RECCE: 1 sqn with 4 OV-10, 2 C-130H (with side-looking radar).
EW: 1 C-130 (ELINT), 1 *Falcon* 20 (ELINT).
TANKER: 1 Boeing 707; 3 KC-130H (tpt/tanker).
TRANSPORT: 11 C-130H, 7 CN-235, 3 Do-28, 1 *Falcon* 20, 1 *Falcon* 50 (VIP), 1 *Gulfstream* II (VIP), 5 *King Air* 100, 3 *King Air* 200.
HELICOPTERS:
  ATTACK: 24 SA-342 (12 with *HOT*, 12 with cannon).
  TRANSPORT: hy: 7 CH-47; **med:** 27 SA-330, 27 AB-205A; **lt:** 20 AB-206, 3 AB-212.
TRAINING: 10 AS-202, 2 CAP-10, 4 CAP-230, 12 T-34C.
LIAISON: 2 *King Air* 200.
AAM: AIM-9B/D/J *Sidewinder*, R-530, R-550 *Magic*.
ASM: AGM-65B *Maverick* (for F-5E), *HOT*.

DEPLOYMENT:
ARMY:
  Northwest Atlas: 1 Royal Guard, 1 mtn bn; 1 armd bn, 1 mech bn, 2 cav bn, 1 arty bn.
  South (incl West Sahara): 3 mech inf bde, 1 lt sy bde; 9 mech inf regt; 25 inf, 2 para, 2 Camel Corps bn; 4 armd bn, 1 mech bn; 4 mech bn (UR-416 APC); 7 arty bn.
  Border: 2 mech inf regt; 3 inf, 1 Camel Corps bn; 2 armd bn, 1 arty bn.

FORCES ABROAD:
EQUATORIAL GUINEA: 360: 1 bn.
UAE: some 5,000.
UN AND PEACEKEEPING:
ANGOLA (UNAVEM II): 14 Observers.

PARAMILITARY: 40,000.
GENDARMERIE ROYALE: 10,000;
  1 bde, 2 mobile gp, air sqn, coast guard unit; 18 boats, 2 *Rallye* ac; 3 SA-315, 3 SA-316, 2 SA-318, 6 *Gazelle*, 6 SA-330, 2 SA-360 hel.
FORCE AUXILIAIRE: 30,000 incl Mobile Intervention Corps (5,000).
CUSTOMS/COAST GUARD: 2 PCC, 4 PFI⟨ (included in Navy nos) plus boats.

OPPOSITION:
POLISARIO: Military Wing: Sahrawi People's Liberation Army: 10,000 (perhaps 4,000 active) org in bn.
EQUIPMENT: T-55, T-62 tk; BMP-1, 20–30 EE-9 *Cascavel* MICV; M-1931/37 122mm how; BM-21 122mm MRL; 120mm, 160mm mor; AT-4 *Spigot* ATGW; ZSU-23-2 23mm SP AA guns; SA-6/-7/-9 SAM.
(Captured Moroccan eqpt incl AML-90, *Eland* armd recce, *Ratel* 20, Panhard APC, Steyr SK-105 *Kuerassier* lt tks.)

FOREIGN FORCES:
UN (MINURSO): some 370 in Western Sahara from 24 countries.

OMAN

GDP	1990: R 4.09bn ($10.62bn)	
	1991ε: R 4.66bn ($12.13bn)	
Growth	1990: 9.1%	1991ε: 7.0%
Inflation	1990: 10.8%	1991: 7.2%
Debt	1990: $3.00bn	1991: $2.90bn
Def bdgt[a]	1991: R 572m ($1.49bn)	
	1992: R 665m ($1.73bn)	
Def exp	1990: R 742m ($1.93bn)	
FMA[b]	1992: $20.10m (US)	

$1 = R   1989–92   0.3845
R = rial
a Excl $1.8bn military subsidy from GCC between 1984
and 1994, shared with Bahrain.
b Incl $15m as Economic Support.

Population: ε1,589,000

	13–17	*18–22*	*23–32*
Men	87,800	72,700	128,400
Women	85,400	67,700	104,300

TOTAL ARMED FORCES:
ACTIVE: 35,700 (incl Royal Household tps, and
some 3,700 foreign personnel).

ARMY: 20,000. (Regt are of bn size.)
1 div HQ.
2 bde HQ.
2 armd regt (3 tk sqn).
1 armd recce regt (3 armd car sqn).
4 arty (2 fd, 1 med (2 bty), 1 AD (2 bty)) regt.
8 inf regt (incl 3 Baluch).
1 inf recce regt (3 recce coy), 2 indep recce coy.
1 fd engr regt (3 sqn).
1 AB regt.
Musandam Security Force (indep rifle coy).
EQUIPMENT:
MBT: 6 M-60A1, 43 M-60A3, 29 *Qayid al-Ardh*
(*Chieftain*).
LIGHT TANKS: 37 *Scorpion*, 6 VBC-90.
AIFV: 2 VAB PC.
APC: 6 VAB VCI.
TOWED ARTY: 66: 105mm: 42 ROF lt; 130mm: 12
M-46, 12 Type 59-1.
MORTARS: 81mm; 107mm: 12 M-30 4.2-in.;
120mm: 12 Brandt.
ATGW: 18 *TOW*, 32 *Milan* (incl 2 VCAC).
AD GUNS: 20mm (incl 2 VAB VD); 23mm: 4
ZU-23-2; 40mm: 12 *Bofors* L/60.
SAM: *Blowpipe*, 28 *Javelin*, SA-7.

NAVY: 3,000.
BASES: Seeb (HQ), Wudam (main base), Ray Sut,
Ghanam Island, Alwi.
PATROL AND COASTAL COMBATANTS: 12:
MISSILE CRAFT: 4 *Dhofar*, 1 with 2 × 3 MM-40, 3
with 2 × 4 MM-40 *Exocet* SSM.
PATROL: 8:
4 *Al Wafi* (UK 37-m) PCC, 4 *Seeb* (UK 25-m) PCI‹.
AMPHIBIOUS: 2:
1 *Nasr el Bahr* LST, capacity 240 tps, 7 tk, hel
deck.
1 *Al Munassir* LST, capacity 200 tps, 8 tk, hel
deck (non-op, harbour trg).
Plus craft; 3 LCM, 2 LCU.
SUPPORT: 2: 1 spt, 1 trg with hel deck.

AIR FORCE: 3,500; 52 cbt ac (plus 10 in store),
no armed hel.
FGA: 2 sqn with 15 *Jaguar* S(O) Mk 1, 1 GR1, 4
T-2 (plus 10 in store).
FGA/RECCE: 1 sqn with 10 *Hunter* FGA-73, 3 T-67.
COIN/TRAINING: 1 sqn with 12 BAC-167 Mk 82, 7
BN-2 *Defender*.
TRANSPORT: 3 sqn:
1 with 3 BAC-111; 2 with 15 *Skyvan* 3M
(7 radar-equipped, for MR), 3 C-130H.
HELICOPTERS: 2 med tpt sqn with 20 AB-205, 3
AB-206, 3 AB-212, 10 AB-214.
TRAINING: 2 AS-202-18.
AD: 2 sqn with 28 *Rapier* SAM, *Martello* radar.
MISSILES:
ASM: *Exocet* AM-39.
AAM: AIM-9P *Sidewinder*.

ROYAL HOUSEHOLD: 6,000.
Royal Guard bde: (4,500).
2 SF regt: (700).
Royal Yacht Squadron (based Muscat): (150);
1 Royal Yacht, 3,800t with hel deck.
1 *Fulk Al Salamah* tps and veh tpt with
2 AS-332C *Puma* hel.
Royal Flight: (250); 2 AS-202-18, 2 Boeing-747 SP,
2 *Gulfstream*, 1 *Falcon* 20 ac; 2 AS-332, 4
SA-330 hel.

PARAMILITARY:
TRIBAL HOME GUARD (*Firqat*): 3,500.
POLICE COAST GUARD: 400: 15 AT-105 APC, 18
inshore patrol craft.
POLICE AIR WING: 1 Boeing 727, 3 DHC-5D, 2
Do-228, 2 *Learjet* (1 -25B, 1 -35A), 2 *Merlin* IVA
ac; 6 Bell 214, 1 Hughes 369 hel.

QATAR

GDP	1990: R 26.87bn ($7.38bn)	
	1991ε: R 27.90bn ($7.66bn)	
Growth	1990ε: 9.0%	1991ε: 2.0%
Inflation	1990: 3.0%	1991ε: 3.0%
Debt	1990: $1.08bn	1991: $1.15bn
Def bdgt	1991ε: R 3.4bn ($934.07m)	
$1 =R	1989–92: 3.640	
R = rial		

Population: 454,800

	13–17	*18–22*	*23–32*
Men	18,300	17,900	44,900
Women	16,500	13,400	24,000

TOTAL ARMED FORCES:
ACTIVE: 7,500.

ARMY: 6,000.
1 Royal Guard regt.
1 tk bn.
3 mech inf bn.
1 SF 'bn' (coy).
1 fd arty regt.
1 SAM bty with *Rapier*.
EQUIPMENT:
MBT: 24 AMX-30.
AIFV: 30 AMX-10P.
APC: 160 VAB.
TOWED ARTY: 155mm: 12 G5.
SP ARTY: 155mm: 6 AMX Mk F-3.
MRL: 4 *ASTROS* II.
MORTARS: 81mm (some SP).
ATGW: 100 *Milan*, *HOT* (incl 24 VAB SP).
RCL: 84mm: *Carl Gustav*.
SAM: *Blowpipe*, 12 *Stinger*.

NAVY: 700 incl Marine Police.
BASE: Doha.
PATROL AND COASTAL COMBATANTS: 9:
MISSILE CRAFT: 3 *Damsah* (Fr *Combattante* III)
   with 2 × 4 MM-40 *Exocet* SSM.
PATROL, INSHORE: 6:
   6 *Barzan* (UK 33-m) PCI.
   plus some 44 small craft operated by marine police.
AMPHIBIOUS: Craft only, 1 LCT.
COAST DEFENCE: 3 × 4 MM-40 *Exocet*.

AIR FORCE: 800; 18 cbt ac, 20 armed hel.
FGA: Tac spt unit with 6 *Alpha Jet*.
FIGHTER: 1 AD sqn with 12 *Mirage* F1 (11 -E, 1 -D).
TRANSPORT: 1 sqn with 2 Boeing 707, 1 -727.
HELICOPTERS:
   ATTACK: 12 SA-342L (with *HOT*), 8 *Commando*
   Mk 3 (*Exocet*).
   TRANSPORT: 4 *Commando* (3 Mk 2A tpt, 1 Mk
   2C VIP).
   LIAISON: 2 SA-341G.
MISSILES:
   ASM: *Exocet* AM-39, *HOT*.
   SAM: 6 *Roland*, *Rapier*.

SAUDI ARABIA

GDP	1990ε: R 371.65bn ($99.24bn)		
	1991ε: R 393.95bn ($105.19bn)		
Growth	1990: 18.2%	1991:	6.6%
Inflation	1990: 2.2%	1991:	4.4%
Debt	1990: $22.50bn	1991:	$29.0bn
Def exp[a]	1990ε: R 86.75bn ($23.16bn)		
	1991ε: R 132.98bn ($35.51bn)		

Def bdgt[b]	1991: R 51.90bn ($13.86bn)	
	1992: R 54.30bn ($14.50bn)	
$1 = R	1989–92: 3.745	
R = rial		

[a] Def exp 1990, 1991 include costs of contributions to Allies for the Gulf War and costs of arms purchases made during the war.
[b] No budget was announced for 1991, projection for 1991 has been carried over from previous year. The estimated defence expenditure for 1992 may be as high as $35bn if arms purchases and defence construction projects are included.

Population: 10,600,000[c]

	13–17	18–22	23–32
Men	585,800	473,500	841,400
Women	403,600	440,200	652,500

[c] Incl approximately 3m expatriates.

TOTAL ARMED FORCES:
ACTIVE: 102,000 (plus 55,000 active National Guard).

ARMY: 73,000.
2 armd bde.
5 mech bde.
1 AB bde (2 AB bn, 3 SF coy).
1 Royal Guard regt (3 bn).
5 arty bn.
EQUIPMENT:
MBT: 700: 300 AMX-30, 400 M-60A3.
RECCE: 235 AML-60/-90.
AIFV: 500+ AMX-10P, 200 M-2 *Bradley*.
APC: 1,700 M-113 (incl variants), 30 EE-11 *Urutu*,
   150 Panhard M-3.
TOWED ARTY: 105mm: 100 M-101/-102 (in store);
   155mm: 40 FH-70 (in store), 90 M-198, M-114.
SP ARTY: 160: 155mm: 100 M-109A1B/A2, 60 GCT.
MRL: 70 *ASTROS* II.
MORTARS: 400 incl: 107mm: M-30 4.2-in.;
   120mm: Brandt.
SSM: Some 30 Ch CSS-2 (50 msl).
ATGW: BGM-71A *TOW* (incl 200 VCC-1 SP), M-47
   Dragon, *HOT* (incl 90 AMX-10P SP).
RCL: 75mm: M-20; 84mm: 450 *Carl Gustav*; 90mm:
   M-67; 106mm: M-40A1.
AVIATION:
HELICOPTERS: 11 S-70A-1, 6 UH-60 (tpt), 6
   SA-365N (medevac), 15 Bell 406CS.
SAM: *Crotale*, *Stinger*, 500 *Redeye*.

NAVY: 11,000 (incl 1,500 marines);
BASES: Riyadh (HQ Naval Forces). Western Fleet:
   Jiddah (HQ), Yanbu. Eastern Fleet: Al-Jubayl
   (HQ), Ad-Dammam, Ras al Mishab, Ras al Ghar.
FRIGATES: 8:
   4 *Madina* (Fr F.2000) with 4 × 533mm, 2 ×
   406mm ASTT, 1 × AS-365N hel (AS 15 ASM);
   plus 8 *Otomat-2* SSM, 1 × 100mm gun.

4 *Badr* (US Tacoma) (ASUW) with 2 × 4
Harpoon SSM, 2 × 3 ASTT (Mk 46 LWT).

PATROL AND COASTAL COMBATANTS: 12:
MISSILE CRAFT: 9 *As Siddiq* (US 58-m) PFM with 2
× 2 *Harpoon*.
TORPEDO CRAFT: 3 *Dammam* (Ge *Jaguar*) with 4 ×
533mm TT.
MINE WARFARE: 5:
1 *Al Jawf* (UK *Sandown* MCC).
4 *Addriyah* (US MSC-322) MCC.
AMPHIBIOUS: Craft only; 4 LCU, 8 LCM.
SUPPORT AND MISCELLANEOUS: 7:
2 *Boraida* (mod Fr *Durance*) AOR, 3 ocean
tugs, 1 salvage tug, 1 Royal Yacht.

NAVAL AVIATION: 20 armed hel.
HELICOPTERS: 24 AS-365N, (4 SAR, 20 with
AS-15TT ASM), 12 AS 332B/F (6 tpt, 6 with
AM-39 *Exocet*).

MARINES: (1,500): 1 inf regt (2 bn), with 140
BMR-600P.

AIR FORCE: 18,000+; 293 cbt ac, no armed hel.
FGA: 6 sqn:
3 with 52 F-5E;
3 with 45 *Tornado* IDS.
FIGHTER: 3 sqn with 78 F-15C.
2 with 24 *Tornado* ADV.
RECCE: 1 sqn with 10 RF-5E.
AEW: 1 sqn with 5 E-3A.
TANKER: 8 KE-3A, 7 KC-130H.
OCU: 2 with 14* F-5B, 21* F-5F, 20* F-15D.
TRANSPORT: 3 sqn:
41 C-130 (7 -E, 34 -H), 5 L-100-30HS (hospital
ac), 35 C-212.
HELICOPTERS: 2 sqn: 8 AB-205, 13 AB-206B, 27
AB-212, 7 KV-107 (SAR, tpt).
TRAINING: 32 BAC-167, 30* *Hawk* Mk 60, 30 PC-9,
1 *Jetstream* 31.
ROYAL FLIGHT:
ac: 4 BAe 125, 2 C-140, 4 CN-235, 2 *Gulfstream*
III, 2 *Learjet* 35, 6 VC-130H, 1 Cessna 310.
hel: 3 AS-61, AB-212, 1 Boeing-747 SP, 2
Boeing 707-320.
MISSILES:
ASM: AGM-65 *Maverick*, AS-15.
ARM: AGM-45 *Shrike*, ALARM.
AAM: AIM-9J/L/P *Sidewinder*, AIM-7F *Sparrow*,
ALARM.

AIR DEFENCE FORCES: 4,000:
33 SAM bty:
16 with 128 *Improved HAWK*;
17 with 68 *Shahine* fire units and AMX-30SA
30mm SP AA guns.
73 *Shahine/Crotale* fire units as static defence.

EQUIPMENT:
AD GUNS: 20mm: 92 M-163 *Vulcan*; 30mm: 50
AMX-30SA; 35mm: 128; 40mm: 150 L/70 (in
store).
SAM: 141 *Shahine*, 128 MIM-23B *Improved HAWK*.

NATIONAL GUARD: (Directly under Royal
command) 75,000 (55,000 active; 20,000 tribal
levies):
2 mech inf bde each 4 all arms bn.
4 inf bde.
1 ceremonial cav sqn.
EQUIPMENT:
APC: 1,100 V-150 *Commando*.
TOWED ARTY: 105mm: 30 M-102; 155mm: 4 M-198.
RCL: 106mm: M-40A1.
ATGW: *TOW*.

PARAMILITARY:
FRONTIER FORCE: 10,500.
COAST GUARD: (4,500) 4 PFI, about 30 PCI⟨, 16
hovercraft, 1 Royal Yacht (5,000t), about 350 boats.
**GENERAL CIVIL DEFENCE ADMINISTRATION
UNITS:** 10 KV-107 hel.
SPECIAL SECURITY FORCE: 500: UR-416 APC.

FOREIGN FORCES:
PENINSULAR SHIELD FORCE: ε5,000; 1 inf
bde (elm from all GCC states).
US: Air Force units on rotational det, numbers vary
(incl: F-4G, F-15, F-16, F-117, C-130, KC-135,
U-2, JSTARS) 1 *Patriot* bn.

SOMALI REPUBLIC

GDP	1988ε:	S sh 113.56bn ($666m)	
	1989ε:	S sh 295.76bn ($601.8m)	
Growth	1988:	−2%	1989: −5%
Inflation	1988:	81.9%	1989ε: 140%
Debt	1989:	$2.14bn	1990: $2.35bn
Def exp	1986ε:	S sh 6.0bn ($83m)	
Def bdgt	1988ε:	S sh 7.92bn ($46m)	
	1989ε:	S sh 8.86bn ($18.05m)*a*	
FMA	1988:	$4.65m (US)	
$1 = S sh	(1989): 490.68	(1990):1,800	
	(1991): 3,800		

S sh = Somali shillings
a Incl military and internal sy bdgt.

Population: 6,654,000

	13–17	18–22	23–32
Men	366,800	295,700	449,500
Women	364,500	299,100	466,900

Following the 1991 revolution, no National Armed
Forces have yet been formed. The Somali National

Movement has declared Northern Somalia as the independent Republic of Somaliland, whilst in the south competing insurgent groups lay claim to Mogadishu. Military equipment is in a poor state of repair or inoperable; no attempt has been made to itemize and quantify equipment.

SUDAN

GDP	1990:	£S 206.96bn ($9.95bn)	
	1991ε:	£S 356.41bn ($8.16bn)	
Growth	1989:	−2.3%	1990ε: −6.0%
Inflation	1990:	110%	1991ε: 126%
Debt	1989:	$12.70bn	1990: $13.00bn
Def exp	1989:	£S 2.88bn ($460m)	
Def bdgt	1989:	£S 3.6bn ($570m)	
	1990ε:	£S 4.3bn ($320m)[a]	
$1 = £S[b]	1989:	8.336	1990: 20.800
	1991:	43.680	1992ε: 90.000

[a] Incl bdgt for internal sy.

[b] Adjusted exchange rates. The Sudanese Pound was floated on 2 February 1992 abandoning the official rate of $1 = £S 15.2.

Population: 26,886,000

	13–17	18–22	23–32
Men	1,551,000	1,296,000	1,959,000
Women	1,474,000	1,226,000	1,888,500

TOTAL ARMED FORCES:
ACTIVE: 82,500.

Terms of service: conscription, (males 18–30), 3 years.

ARMY: ε75,000.
1 Military District.	3 mech inf bde.
6 inf div.	20 inf bde.
1 armd div.	3 arty regt.
1 engr div.	6 AD arty bde.
1 AB div (incl 1 SF bn).	

EQUIPMENT:†
MBT: 250 T-54/-55, 20 M-60A3, 50 Ch Type-59.
LIGHT TANKS: 70 Ch Type-62.
RECCE: 6 AML-90, 15 *Saladin*, 50 *Ferret*, 60 BRDM-1/-2.
APC: 286: 40 BTR-50/-152, 30 OT-62/-64, 36 M-113, 80 V-100/-150, 100 *Walid*.
TOWED ARTY: 231: 105mm: 18 M-101 pack, 6 Model 56 pack; 122mm: 4 D-74, 24 M-1938, 80 Type-54/D-30; 130mm: 27 M-46/Ch Type 59-1; 152mm: 60 D-20; 155mm: 12 M-114A1.
SP ARTY: 155mm: 6 AMX Mk F-3.
MRL: 122mm: 50 BM-21.
MORTARS: 81mm: 138; 120mm: 12 M-43, 24 AM-49.
ATGW: 4 *Swingfire*.

RCL: 106mm: M-40A1.
ATK GUNS: 76mm: 18 M-1942; 100mm: 20 M-1944.
AD GUNS: 20mm: M-167 towed, M-163 SP; 23mm: ZU-23-2; 37mm: 120 M-1939/Type-63; 40mm: 60 L/60; 85mm: KS-12; 100mm: KS-19 towed.
SAM: SA-7, *Redeye*.

NAVY: ε1,500.
BASES: Flamingo Bay, Khartoum, Port Sudan HQ.
PATROL CRAFT: 2:
2 *Kadir* PCI⟨, 4 riverine boats, about 10 other armed boats.
AMPHIBIOUS: Craft only; 2 *Sobat* (Yug DTM-221) LCT.

AIR FORCE: 6,000 (incl Air Defence).
†51 cbt ac, 2 armed hel.
FGA: 9 F-5 (7 -E, 2 -F), 10 Ch J-5, 9 Ch J-6.
FIGHTER: 8 MiG-21, 3 MiG-23, 6 Ch J-6.
COIN: 1 sqn with 3 BAC-167 Mk 90, 3 *Jet Provost* Mk 55.
MR: 2 C-212.
TRANSPORT: 5 An-24, 5 C-130H, 4 C-212, 2 DHC-5D, 6 EMB-110P, 1 F-27, 2 *Falcon* 20/50.
HELICOPTERS: 1 sqn with 11 AB-412, 15 IAR/SA-330, 4 Mi-4, 14 Mi-8, 2 Mi-24 (armed).
TRAINING: incl 4 MiG-15UTI, 4 MiG-21U, 2 JJ-5, 2 JJ-6.
AD: 5 bty SA-2 SAM (18 launchers).
AAM: AA-2 *Atoll*.

PARAMILITARY:
POPULAR DEFENCE FORCE: ε15–20,000: mil wing of National Islamic Front.

OPPOSITION:
SUDANESE PEOPLE'S LIBERATION ARMY
(SPLA): ε55,000: two factions, each org in bn; mainly small arms plus 60mm mor, 14.5mm AA, SA-7 SAM; arty reported; operating mainly in southern Sudan.

SYRIA

GDP[a]	1990ε:	£S 278.63bn ($14.36bn)	
	1991ε:	£S 390.09bn ($13.89bn)	
Growth	1990ε:	9.5%	1991ε: 6.0%
Inflation	1990ε:	50.0%	1991ε: 70.0%
Debt[b]	1989:	$16.88bn	1990: $16.45bn
Def bdgt[c]	1990ε:	£S 37.10bn ($1.48bn)	
	1991ε:	£S 50.8bn ($1.13bn)	
$1 = £S[d]	1989:	18.520	1990: 25.004
	1991:	45.007	

[a] Syria's GDP in £S is unrealistically low, due to that country's large black economy. The dollar figures, however, represent the estimated real value of the economy through the use of exchange rates adjusted for real inflation. Official inflation figures are also far lower at around 8% for 1991.

b Most of Syria's foreign debt is military debt to the former USSR in concessional form.

c Syria's official defence budget is £S 30bn for 1991/92 but may not include arms purchasing.

d Exchange rates adjusted for inflation.

Population: 13,186,600

	13–17	*18–22*	*23–32*
Men	789,400	651,800	1,015,500
Women	784,500	633,000	959,900

TOTAL ARMED FORCES:
ACTIVE: 408,000.

Terms of service: conscription, 30 months.

RESERVES (to age 45): 400,000. Army 300,000 active; Navy 8,000.

ARMY: 300,000 (130,000 conscripts, 50,000 reservists).
2 corps HQ:
6 armd div (each 3 armd, 1 mech bde, 1 arty regt).
3 mech div (-) (each 2 armd, 2 mech bde, 1 arty regt).
1 Republican Guard div (-) (2 armd, 1 mech bde).
1 SF div (3 SF regt).
(1 bde in each div at cadre strength).
3 indep mech inf bde.
2 indep arty bde.
8 indep SF regt.
3 SSM bde:
2 (each 3 bn) with *FROG, Scud*; 1 (3 bn) with SS-21.
1 coastal def SSM bde with SS-C-1B *Sepal* and SS-C-3.
1 Border Guard bde.
2 indep ATK regt.
RESERVES: 9 mech and inf bde.
EQUIPMENT:
MBT: 4,600: 2,100 T-54/-55, 1,000 T-62M/K, 1,500 T-72/-72M. (Total incl some 900 in static positions and in store.)
RECCE: 500 BRDM-2.
AIFV: 2,250 BMP-1.
APC: 1,500 BTR-40/-50/-60/-152, OT-64.
TOWED ARTY: some 2,000 incl; 122mm: 100 M-1931/-37 (in store), 150 M-1938, 500 D-30; 130mm: 650 M-46; 152mm: 50 M-1937; 180mm: 10 S23.
SP ARTY: 122mm: 250 2S1, 36 T-34/D-30; 152mm: 50 2S3.
MRL: 122mm: 280 BM-21.
MORTARS: 82mm; 120mm: 400 M-1943; 160mm: 100 M-1943; 240mm: ε8 M-240.
SSM launchers: 18 *FROG*-7, some 18 SS-21, 20 *Scud* B/-C; SS-C-1B *Sepal*, SS-C-3 coastal.
ATGW: 4,700 AT-3 *Sagger* (incl 4,000 SP), 200 AT-4 *Spigot* and 200 *Milan*.

AD GUNS: some 1,985: 23mm: 600 ZU-23-2 towed, 400 ZSU-23-4 SP; 37mm: 300 M-1939; 57mm: 675 S-60, 10 ZSU-57-2 SP; 100mm: some KS-19.
SAM: SA-7/-9, 20 SA-13.

NAVY: 8,000.
BASES: Latakia, Tartus, Minet el-Baida.
SUBMARINES: 3 Sov *Romeo*† with 533mm TT.
FRIGATES: 2 Sov *Petya* II with 4 × ASW RL, 5 × 533mm TT.
PATROL AND COASTAL COMBATANTS: 30:
MISSILE CRAFT: 19: 14 Sov *Osa* I and II PFM with 4 SS-N-2 *Styx* SSM, 5 Sov *Komar* with 2 SS-N-2 *Styx* SSM.
PATROL: 11:
8 Sov *Zhuk* PFI⟨.
1 Sov *Natya* (ex-MSO).
2 *Hamelin* PFI⟨.
MINE COUNTERMEASURES: 9:
1 Sov T-43, 1 *Sonya* MSC.
2 Sov *Vanya*, 5 *Yevgenya* MSI.
AMPHIBIOUS: 3 *Polnocny* LSM, capacity 100 tps, 5 tk.
SUPPORT AND MISCELLANEOUS: 2: 1 spt, 1 trg.

NAVAL AVIATION: 17 armed hel.
ASW: 12 Mi-14, 5 Ka-25 (Ka-28 to replace) hel.

AIR FORCE: 40,000; 639 cbt ac; 100 armed hel.*e*
FGA: 10 sqn:
4 with 70 Su-22.   1 with 20 Su-20;
4 with 60 MiG-23 BN.   1 with 20 Su-24.
FIGHTERS: 18 sqn:
8 with 172 MiG-21, 2 with 30 MiG-25, 5 with 80 MiG-23, 3 with 20 MiG-29.
RECCE: 6 MiG-25R.
EW: 10 Mi-8 *Hip* J/K hel.
TRANSPORT: 6 An-12, 4 An-24, civil-registered ac incl: 5 An-26, 2 *Falcon* 20, 4 Il-76, 7 Yak-40.
HELICOPTERS:
ATTACK: 50 Mi-25, 50 SA-342L.
TRANSPORT: 10 Mi-2, 10 Mi-6, 130 Mi-8, 40 Mi-17.
ASW (Navy-assigned): 4 Ka-25, 20 Mi-14.
TRAINING: incl 10 L-29, 90* L-39, 20 MBB-223, 50* MiG-21U, 16* MiG-23UM, 5* MiG-25U.
MISSILES:
ASM: AT-2 *Swatter*, AS-7 *Kerry*, AS-12, *HOT*.
AAM: AA-2 *Atoll*, AA-6 *Acrid*, AA-7 *Apex*, AA-8 *Aphid*, AA-10 *Alamo*.

AIR DEFENCE COMMAND: ε60,000;
22 AD bde (some 95 SAM bty):
11 (some 60 bty) with some 450 SA-2/-3;
11 (27 bty) with some 200 SA-6 and AD arty.
2 SAM regt (each 2 bn of 2 bty) with some 48 SA-5, 60 SA-8.

FORCES ABROAD:
LEBANON: 30,000: 1 corps HQ, elm 1 armd, elm 2 mech, 1 indep inf, elm 2 arty bde, elm 8 SF regt.

PARAMILITARY:
PALESTINE LIBERATION ARMY: 4,500; 3 bde (in Syria/Lebanon, some Syrian officers); 60 T-54/-55 MBT; some arty; MRL; AT-3 *Sagger* ATGW; SA-7 SAM.
GENDARMERIE (Ministry of Interior): 8,000.
BA'TH PARTY: Workers' Militia (People's Army).

FOREIGN FORCES:
UNITED NATIONS (UNDOF): some 1,300, contingents from Austria, Canada, Finland and Poland.
RUSSIA: ε500 advisers, mainly in Air Defence.

e Some ac may be in store.

TUNISIA

GDP	1990:	D 10.99bn ($12.51bn)			
	1991:	D 12.12bn ($13.11bn)			
Growth	1990:	7.6%		1991:	3.5%
Inflation	1990:	6.8%		1991:	8.2%
Debt	1990:	$7.53bn		1991:	$6.92bn
Def bdgt	1991:	D 403.0m ($435.86m)			
	1992:	D 468.0m ($508.70m)			
FMA*a*	1992:	$14.25m			
$1 = D	1989:	0.9493		1990:	0.8783
	1991:	0.9246		1992:	0.9200

D = dinar
a Incl $3m as Economic Support.

Population: 8,375,400

	13–17	18–22	23–32
Men	474,700	439,900	739,300
Women	446,700	410,200	711,600

TOTAL ARMED FORCES:
ACTIVE: 35,000 (26,400 conscripts).
Terms of service: 12 months selective.

ARMY: 27,000 (25,000 conscripts) (being reorg).
2 mech bde (each with 1 armd, 2 mech inf bn).
(1 more mech bde forming).
1 Sahara bde.
1 SF bde.
1 ATK regt.
3 fd arty regt.
1 armd recce regt.
1 AD bde (2 AD regt).
1 engr regt.

EQUIPMENT:
MBT: 84: 54 M-60A3, 30 M-60A1.
LIGHT TANKS: 55 SK-105 *Kuerassier*.
RECCE: 24 *Saladin*, 35 AML-90.
APC: 268: 140 M-113A1/-A2, 18 EE-11 *Urutu*, 110 Fiat F-6614.
TOWED ARTY: 117: 105mm: 48 M-101A1/A2; 155mm: 12 M-114A1, 57 M-198.
SP ARTY: 28: 105mm: 10 M-108; 155mm: 18 M-109.
MORTARS: 81mm: 95; 107mm: 40 4.2-in; 120mm: 18.
ATGW: 65 *TOW* (incl some SP), 500 *Milan*.
RL: 89mm: 300 LRAC-89, 300 M-20 3.5-in.
RCL: 57mm: 140 M-18; 106mm: 70 M-40A1.
AD GUNS: 20mm: 100 M-55; 37mm: 10 M-1939/Type-55.
SAM: 48 RBS-70, 25 M-54 *Chaparral*.

NAVY: 4,500 (ε700 conscripts).
BASES: Bizerte, Sfax, Kelibia.
FRIGATE: 1 *Inkhad* (US *Savage*) with 2 × 3 ASTT (under repair).
PATROL AND COASTAL COMBATANTS: 20:
MISSILE CRAFT: 6:
    3 *La Galite* (Fr *Combattante* III) PFM with 8 MM-40 *Exocet* SSM;
    3 *Bizerte* (Fr P-48) with 8 × SS-12 SSM.
PATROL: 14:
    INSHORE: 14: 2 *Gafsah* (Ch *Shanghai*) PFI, 2 *Tazarka* (UK Vosper 31-m) PCI, 10⟨.

AIR FORCE: 3,500 (700 conscripts);
38 cbt aircraft, 18 armed hel.
FGA: 15 F-5E/F.
COIN: 1 sqn with 7 MB-326K, 4 MB-326L.
TRANSPORT: 2 C-130H.
LIAISON: 2 S-208M.
TRAINING: 21 SF-260 (9 -C, *12 -W), 8 MB-326B.
HELICOPTERS:
    ARMED: 5 SA-341 (attack), 5 AB 205A-1 (aslt), 8 AB-205 (aslt).
    TRANSPORT: 1 wing with 13 AB-205, 6 AS-350B, 1 AS-365, 6 SA-313, 5 SA-316, 4 UH-1H, 2 UH-1N.
AAM: AIM-9J *Sidewinder*.

FORCES ABROAD:
UN AND PEACEKEEPING:
CAMBODIA (UNTAC): 426.
WESTERN SAHARA (MINURSO): 9 Observers.

PARAMILITARY:
PUBLIC ORDER BRIGADE: 3,500: (Ministry of Interior); army trained; 3 bn; EBR-75 AFV; V-150 Commando APC.
NATIONAL GUARD: 10,000; incl Coastal Patrol with some 10 craft⟨.

UNITED ARAB EMIRATES (UAE)

GDP	1990:	Dh 124.0bn ($33.78bn)	
	1991:	Dh 123.6bn ($33.67bn)	
Growth	1990:	11.0%	1991: −2.0%
Inflation	1990:	8.0%	1991: 2.0%
Debt	1990:	$9.9bn	1991: $10.7bn
Def exp[a]	1990:	Dh 9.508bn ($2.59bn)	
	1991:	Dh 17.99bn ($4.90bn)	
Def bdgt	1990:	Dh 5.70bn ($1.55bn)	
	1991ε:	Dh 5.85bn ($1.59bn)	
$1 = Dh	1989–92:	3.671	
Dh = dirham			

Population: 1,757,000

	13–17	18–22	23–32
Men	74,000	58,800	150,000
Women	69,500	49,000	77,400

[a] Def exp 1990 est and incl $1bn in contributions to UK and US for military exp. Def exp 1991 est and incl $3.3bn in contributions and pledges to US and UK.

TOTAL ARMED FORCES:[b]
ACTIVE: 54,500 (perhaps 30% expatriates).

ARMY: 50,000 (incl Dubai: 6,000).
MoD (Dubai); GHQ (Abu Dhabi).
INTEGRATED:
1 Royal Guard 'bde'.   1 armd bde.
1 mech inf bde.   2 inf bde.
1 arty bde.
NOT INTEGRATED:
1 inf bde (Dubai)
EQUIPMENT:
MBT: 131: 95 AMX-30, 36 OF-40 Mk 2 (*Lion*).
LIGHT TANKS: 76 *Scorpion*.
RECCE: 90 AML-90, 70 *Saladin* (in store), 30 *Ferret* (in store).
AIFV: 15 AMX-10P.
APC: 390: 50 VCR (incl variants), 240 Panhard M-3, 100 EE-11 *Urutu*.
TOWED ARTY: 97: 105mm: 59 ROF lt, 18 M-56 pack; 130mm: 20.
SP ARTY: 155mm: 20 Mk F-3, 40+ G-6.
MRL: 122mm: 25 *FIROS*-25.
MORTARS: 81mm: 80; 120mm: 21.
ATGW: 230 *Milan*, *Vigilant*, 25 *TOW*, *HOT* (incl 20 SP).
RCL: 84mm: *Carl Gustav*; 106mm: 30.
AD GUNS: 20mm: 48 M-3VDA SP; 30mm: 20 GCF-BM2.
SAM: 20+ *Blowpipe*, 10 SA-16.

NAVY: ε2,000.
BASES: Abu Dhabi: Dalma, Mina Zayed; **Ajman; Dubai:** Mina Rashid, Mina Jabal 'Ali; **Fujairah; Ras al Khaimah:** Mina Sakr; **Sharjah:** Taweela (main base), Mina Khalid, Khor Fakkan.

PATROL AND COASTAL COMBATANTS: 19:
CORVETTES: 2 *Muray Jip* (Ge Lürssen 62-m) with 2 × 2 MM-40 *Exocet* SSM, plus 1 SA-316 hel.
MISSILE CRAFT: 8: 6 *Ban Yas* (Ge Lürssen TNC-45) PFM with 2 × 2 MM-40 *Exocet* SSM.
2 *Mubarraz* (Ge Lürssen 50-m) with 2 × 2 MM-40 *Exocet* SSM, plus 1 × 6 *Sadral* SAM.
PATROL, INSHORE: 9: 6 *Ardhana* (UK Vosper 33-m) PFI, 3⟨.
AMPHIBIOUS: Craft only, 2 *Jananah* LCT, 1 LCM.
SUPPORT AND MISCELLANEOUS: 4: 1 div spt, 2 log spt, 1 tug.

AIR FORCE: (incl Police Air Wing): 2,500 (incl Dubai: 700); 105 cbt ac, 19 armed hel.
FGA: 2 sqn:
1 with 14 *Mirage* IIIEAD;
1 with 18 *Hawk* Mk 63 (FGA/trg).
FIGHTER: 1 sqn with 12 *Mirage* 5 AD, 22 *Mirage* 2000 EA.
COIN: 1 sqn with 6 MB-326 (4 -KD, 2 -LD), 5 MB-339A.
OCU: *9 *Hawk* Mk 61, *2 MB-339A, *6 *Mirage* 2000 DAD.
RECCE: 8 *Mirage* 2000 RAD, 3 *Mirage* 5-R.
EW: 4 C-212.
TRANSPORT: incl 1 BN-2, 4 C-130H, 2 L-100-30, 1 G-222.
HELICOPTERS:
ATTACK: 2 AS-332F (anti-ship, with *Exocet* AM-39), 10 SA-342K (with *HOT*), 7 SA-316/-319 (with AS-11/-12).
TRANSPORT: 8 AS-332 (2 VIP), 1 AS-350, 12 Bell (2 -205, 5 -206A, 1 -206L, 4 -214), 11 SA-330.
SAR: 3 Bo-105.
TRAINING: 24 PC-7, 6 SF-260 (5 -TP, 1 -W).
MISSILES:
ASM: *HOT*, AS-11/-12, AS-15TT, *Exocet* AM-39.
AAM: R-550 *Magic*, AIM 9L.
AD:
1 AD bde (3 bn).
5 bty *Improved HAWK* (still forming).
12 *Rapier*, 8 *Crotale*, 13 RBS-70 SAM.

PARAMILITARY:
COAST GUARD: (Ministry of Interior): some 40 PCI⟨, plus boats.

FOREIGN FORCES:
MOROCCO: some 5,000; army, gendarmerie and police.

[b] The Union Defence Force and the armed forces of the UAE (Abu Dhabi, Dubai, Ras Al Khaimah and Sharjah) were formally merged in 1976; Abu Dhabi and Dubai still maintain a degree of independence.

REPUBLIC OF YEMEN

The Yemen Arab Republic and The People's Democratic Republic of Yemen joined to form the Republic of Yemen on 22 May 1990. A major reorganization of the armed forces continues. The unified Air Forces and Air Defences is now under one command. The Navy has concentrated at Aden.

GDP	1990:	R 77.10bn ($7.90bn)	
	1991:	R 97.10bn ($8.11bn)	
Growth	1989:	6%	1990ε: −4%
Inflation	1989:	15.2%	1990: 34.2%
Debt	1990:	$6.80bn	1991: $7.80bn
Def bdgt	1991:	R 12.73bn ($1.06bn)	
	1992:	R 11.20bn ($935m)	
FMA	1990:	$1.6m (US)	
$1 = R^a	1990:	12.003	1991: 11.980
	1992:	12.000	
R = rial			

Population:^{b} 11,500,000

	13–17	18–22	23–32
Men	538,200	473,600	725,400
Women	532,400	469,900	732,000

^{a} Official exchange rate.
^{b} Since the end of the Gulf War, an estimated 700,000 Yemenis have returned to the Republic of Yemen swelling the unemployment figures to 30%.

TOTAL ARMED FORCES:
ACTIVE: 63,500 (perhaps 45,000+ conscripts).
Terms of service: conscription, 2 years.
RESERVES: Army: perhaps 40,000.

ARMY: 60,000 (perhaps 45,000 conscripts).
9 armd bde (-).
19 inf bde.
5 mech bde.
2 AB/cdo bde.
5 militia bde.
7 arty bde.
2 SSM bde.
EQUIPMENT:
MBT: 1,275: 250 T-34, 725 T-54/-55, 250 T-62, 50 M-60A1.
RECCE: 125 AML-90, 60 AML-245, 150 BRDM-2.
AIFV: 300 BMP-1/-2.
APC: 670: 70 M-113, 600 BTR-40/-60/-152.
TOWED ARTY: 547: 85mm: 100 D-44; 105mm: 35 M-101A1; 122mm: 30 M-1931/37, 150 D-30, 90 M-1938; 130mm: 90 M-46; 152mm: 10 D-20; 155mm: 12 M-114.
ASSAULT GUNS: 85mm: 20 SU-85; 100mm: 70 SU-100.
MRL: 122mm: 290 BM-21; 132mm: 50 BM-13; 140mm: 30 BM-14; 240mm: 35 BM-24.

MORTARS: 81mm: 250; 82mm; 120mm: 110; 160mm: 100.
SSM: 6 *Scud* B, 17 SS-21, 12 *FROG*-7.
ATGW: 200 *TOW*, 500 *Dragon*.
RCL: 82mm: M-43.
ATK GUNS: 100mm: 42 M-1944 (BS-3).
AD GUNS: 20mm: 52 M-167, 20 *Vulcan* SP; 23mm: 200 ZU-23, ZSU-23-4; 37mm: 200 M-1939; 57mm: 120 S-60; 85mm: 40 KS-12; 130mm: 225 KS-30.
SAM: SA-7, SA-9.

NAVY: ε1,500.
MAIN BASES: Aden, Hodeida
FACILITIES: Al Muka, Perim Island, Al Mukalla, Socotra.
PATROL AND COASTAL COMBATANTS: 16:
CORVETTES: 2 *Tarantul* I with 1 × 2 SA-N-4, 2 × 12 ASW RL; plus 2 × 2 76mm gun.
MISSILE CRAFT: 6 Sov *Osa* II with 4 × SSN-2B *Styx* SSM.
PATROL CRAFT, INSHORE: 8:
3 *Sana'a* (US *Broadsword* 32-m) PFI, 5 Sov *Zhuk*⟨.
MINE COUNTERMEASURES: 9:
2 Sov *Natya* MSO.
1 Sov *Sonya* MSC.
6 Sov *Yevgenya* MSI.
AMPHIBIOUS: 5:
1 Sov *Ropucha* LST, capacity 200 tps, 9 tk.
2 Sov *Polnocny* LSM, capacity 100 tps, 5 tk.
2 Sov *Ondatra* LCU, plus 4 LCVP.
SUPPORT AND MISCELLANEOUS: 3: 1 AR, 2
small tankers (1,300 tons).

AIR FORCE: 2,000;
101 cbt ac, 20 armed hel.
FGA: 4 sqn:
1 with 11 F-5E;
3 with 37 Su-20/-22.
FIGHTER: 4 sqn with 47 MiG-21.
TRANSPORT: 3 An-12, 1 An-24, 10 An-26, 2 C-130H, 4 C-47, 3 *Twin Otter*, 2 F-27, 2 *Skyvan* 3M.
HELICOPTERS: 5 AB-212, 2 AB-214, 40 Mi-8, 20 Mi-24/-35 (attack).
TRAINING: *3 F-5B, 3* MiG-21U.
AD: 12 SAM bty: 4 with SA-2; 3 with SA-3; 5 with SA-6.
ASM: AS-7, AS-9, AT-2, AT-6.
AAM: AA-2 *Atoll*, AIM-9 *Sidewinder*.

PARAMILITARY:
CENTRAL SECURITY ORGANISATION: 20,000.
TRIBAL LEVIES: at least 20,000.
Customs service some 6 PFI⟨.

FOREIGN FORCES:
RUSSIA: 300 advisers.

Central and Southern Asia

Following the break-up of the Soviet Union, *The Military Balance* has reorganized the Asian chapter into two separate sections. This section contains the five Central Asian republics of the former Soviet Union (Kazakhstan, Kyrgyzstan, Tajikistan, Turkmenistan and Uzbekistan), Afghanistan, Nepal, the three countries of the Indian subcontinent, Sri Lanka and Myanmar (Burma). Given its long border with China and Thailand, Myanmar could arguably be placed in the East Asia section, but on balance and considering its history, we have opted for this section. Although Iran borders on three Central Asian states: Turkmenistan, Afghanistan and Pakistan, the IISS believes that its strategic position lies more with the Middle East.

Nuclear Developments

The continent of Asia now contains: two nuclear states in which nuclear weapons are deployed – China and Kazakhstan; two states which have the capability to assemble nuclear weapons if they have not done so already – India and Pakistan; and a state suspected of having a nuclear weapons development programme – North Korea.

Kazakhstan signed a Protocol in Lisbon on 23 May 1992 in which it, with the other nuclear-armed republics of the former USSR, assumed the obligations of the former USSR under the START Treaty. It further declared that it would adhere to the Treaty on Non-Proliferation of Nuclear Weapons (NPT) as a non-nuclear state 'in the shortest possible time' (START allows seven years for its conditions to be fully implemented). At the time of the signing of START, Kazakhstan had 104 SS-18 ICBM and 40 Tu-95 *Bear* bombers deployed on its territory.

In accordance with the agreement reached in December 1990, **India** and **Pakistan** exchanged information regarding their nuclear installations which they had agreed would not be attacked. Both sides have accused each other of not declaring all their nuclear installations, in both cases a gas centrifuge enrichment plant. For the second year, President Bush was unable to certify to the US Congress that Pakistan did not have unsafeguarded, military-capable nuclear facilities. In February 1992 Pakistan's Foreign Minister acknowledged that it had 'elements which, if put together would become a device'. Pakistan has proposed that both it and India should sign the NPT. India has rejected the idea, as it considers the NPT 'unequal and discriminatory' and will not join as long as China possesses nuclear weapons.

The Central Asian Republics of the Former Soviet Union

The eventual status of units of the former Soviet armed forces in the Central Asian republics is not yet clear. Kazakhstan, Kyrgyzstan and Tajikistan have signed the majority of the agreements on the future of armed forces reached at the four CIS summits held since December 1991. Turkmenistan and Uzbekistan have signed about two-thirds of the agreements. A full list of the relevant agreements with the signatories of each is shown at p. 245.

Kazakhstan, while originally firmly supporting the formation of Joint General Purpose Forces, has more recently issued two decrees regarding its own armed forces. First, on 20 April 1992 the Kazakhstan President claimed command of the 14th Army, although the army remained within the CIS combined armed forces. Second, on 8 May 1992 the Kazakh Armed Forces were created and all property of CIS forces transferred to Kazakh jurisdiction. This second decree also forbade the redeployment of units and military equipment beyond the borders of Kazakhstan; however, it also stated 'at the same time the conditions of all agreements on the CIS unified armed forces must be strictly obeyed'. The exact status of forces in Kazakhstan is somewhat ambiguous.

Kyrgyzstan also supported the formation of Joint General Purpose Forces; it has agreed that its conscripts may serve in the territories of other republics. On 29 June, however, the Chairman of the State Defence Committee told parliament that the concept of national armed forces implied the creation of a regular army of 5,000 to 7,000 men and a reserve. On mobilization the army would number some 18,000. Armed forces now stationed in Kyrgyzstan would be reduced by between 30 and 40%. It has also been reported that the 8th Motorized Infantry Division had been transferred to Kyrgyzstan and would become the basis for the national army.

Recognizing that it too cannot afford its own armed forces, **Tajikistan** supports the formation of Joint General Purpose Forces.

In May 1992 the President of **Turkmenistan** proposed that the armed forces there should be under joint control with Russia. Turkmenistan would fund local administration, while Russia would provide for equipment and maintenance. Air defence would be a Russian responsibility. Only those conscripts who can speak Russian would serve outside Turkmenistan, and all conscripts destined for construction units would serve only in Turkmenistan.

Uzbekistan has not yet formally declared itself in support of Joint General Purpose Forces and did not sign the Kiev agreement on their status. However, it has taken no steps towards assuming jurisdiction over forces on Uzbek territory. At the autumn 1991 call-up it was decided that conscripts would not serve in the Trans-Caucasus, Ukraine or the Baltic region and those called to construction units would serve only in Uzbekistan. By May 1992, and the spring call-up, it had been decided that only those conscripts who volunteered would serve outside Uzbekistan.

In the entries for the Central Asian republics we have listed the forces of the former Soviet Union under the heading 'Forces under Joint Control' and then listed the details of any newly formed republican forces.

Military Developments

Following the collapse of the Najibullah regime in **Afghanistan**, it is unclear how much of the army is now loyal to the new regime and which of the *Mujaheddin* forces are considered armed forces of the state. Many conscripts will have deserted and strengths must be treated with particular caution. The listings for the army and air force reflect the organization and equipment holding at the time of the fall of Najibullah.

The **Indian** Army has brought into service some 400 additional locally-made T-72/-M1 MBT; a reassessment of air defence units shows that many more SAM are held by the army than previously thought. We have also reassessed the manpower strengths of the many paramilitary forces; overall, their strength is over 200,000 more than previously listed. In addition, we have listed the Home Guard, a reserve force of some 438,000, which is receiving more training and could replace active paramilitary forces in their garrison duties. It is not suggested that any, bar a few specialist groups, of the paramilitary forces would add to India's conventional military capability, but the regular armed forces could concentrate on operations without being concerned with rear-area security, civil unrest, or problems on borders away from the scene of any conflict. There have been only two additions to Indian naval strength in the last 12 months; a third *Shishumar*-class (German T-209) submarine, the first built in India, and a second *Vibhuti*-class missile corvette armed with four *Styx* SSM have commissioned. In addition, a further *Shishumar*-class submarine has been launched and will come into service during 1993–94. The air force has added 44 MiG-27 fighters to its inventory. The **Pakistani** Army has added some 15,000 men to its strength and formed two more independent infantry brigades. Aircraft strength has been reassessed and there are fewer J-6/JJ-6 fighters (100 not 110) and more J-7 FGA aircraft (75 not 40) than previously thought. The **Sri Lankan** Army, which continues its long campaign to defeat the Tamil Tigers guerrilla movement, has increased its manpower strength by some 17,000. It has taken delivery of its first MBT: some 25 T-54/-55. The navy has commissioned three Chinese *Shanghai II*-class fast patrol boats and two fast passenger/cargo craft, each with a capacity of 120 men; they are not equipped with ramps and so cannot take part in beach landings. In **Myanmar** the army now has 30 T-6911 Chinese MBT. Last year these were incorrectly reported as Type-63 light tanks, of which the army has only 30. The navy has acquired three Danish *Osprey*-class coastal patrol craft, and the air force brought into service its first armed helicopters, ten Mi-2, as well as 12 PZL W-3 *Sokol* Polish helicopters.

AFGHANISTAN

GDP	1987:	Afs 198.31bn ($3.92bn)
	1988:	Afs 187.22bn ($3.70bn)
Growth	1988:	2.3%	1989: 0%
Inflation	1990:	42%	1991: 57%
Debt	1986ε:	+$30bn
Def bdgt	1985:	Afs 14.50bn ($286.56m)
FMAε:	1990:	$3.5–$4.5bn
$1 = Afs	1987–92: 50.60
Afs = afghanis

Population: ε21,320,000

	13–17	18–22	23–32
Men	1,240,300	1,049,000	1,625,000
Women	1,193,400	1,005,900	1,552,000

TOTAL ARMED FORCES:
ACTIVE: 45,000.
Terms of service: Males 15–40: conscription 2 years followed by a break of 3 years, then another 2 years.
RESERVES: No formal force identified; call-up from ex-servicemen, Youth League and tribesmen from age 20 to age 40.

ARMY: 40,000 (mostly conscripts).[a]
5 corps HQ.
16 inf div.
3 armd bde.
5 Special Guard bde.
1 mech inf div/bde.
5 cdo bde.
1 arty, 1 SSM (*Scud*) bde.
(Following the change of government in April 1992, no new structure for the armed forces has yet been established.)
EQUIPMENT:
MBT: 1,200: T-54/-55, T-62.
LIGHT TANKS: 60 PT-76.
RECCE: 250 BRDM-1/-2.
AIFV: 550 BMP-1/-2.
APC: 1,100 BTR-40/-60/-70/-80/-152.
TOWED ARTY: 2,000+: 76mm: M-1938, M-1942; 85mm: D-48; 100mm: M-1944; 122mm: M-30, D-30; 130mm: M-46; 152mm: D-1, D-20, M-1937 (ML-20).
MRL: 122mm: BM-21; 140mm: BM-14; 220mm: BM-22.
MORTARS: 1,000+: 82mm: M-37; 107mm; 120mm: 100 M-43.
SSM: 10 *Scud*, 12 *FROG*-7 launchers.
ATGW: AT-1 *Snapper*, AT-3 *Sagger*.
RCL: 73mm: SPG-9; 82mm: B-10.
AD GUNS: 600+ 14.5mm; 23mm: ZU-23, 20 ZSU-23-4 SP; 37mm: M-1939; 57mm: S-60; 85mm: KS-12; 100mm: KS-19.

SAM: SA-7.

AIR FORCE:[b] ε5,000 (incl AD comd);
233 cbt ac, 80 armed hel.†
FGA: 9 sqn:
2 with 30 MiG-23;
7 with 80 Su-7/-17/-22.
FIGHTER:
7 sqn with 80 MiG-21F.
ATTACK HELICOPTERS: 8 sqn with 25 Mi-8, 35 Mi-17, 20 Mi-25.
RECCE: 1 An-30.
TRANSPORT:
AIRCRAFT:
1 VIP sqn with 2 Il-18D;
2 sqn with 10 An-2, 10 An-12, 15 An-26, some An-32.
HELICOPTERS: 12 Mi-4.
TRAINING: 25* L-39, 18* MiG-21.
MISSILES:
AAM: AA-2.
AD: 1 div:
2 SAM bde (each 3 bn) with 115 SA-2, 110 SA-3;
1 AD arty bde (2 bn) with 37mm, 85mm, 100mm guns;
1 radar bde (3 bn).

PARAMILITARY:
BORDER GUARD (under Army): ε3,000; 10 'bde'.
TRIBAL MILITIAS: ε60,000+.
SARANDOY (Ministry of Interior): ε12,000.

OPPOSITION:
Afghan insurgency is a broad national movement. The extent of integration of insurgent forces within the new government is unknown. Some groups will probably remain as armed opposition to central authority.

The military elements, *mujaheddin* fighters, make up numerous groups affiliated to either one of the seven parties of the Peshawar-based Resistance Alliance or one of the predominantly Shi'i groups based in Iran, plus a few indep groups. It is not possible to give accurate strengths; of the Peshawar groups, however, some 40,000 are reported to be active, supported by a further 120,000.
Peshawar groups; leaders' names follow strengths.

TRADITIONALIST MODERATE:
NATIONAL LIBERATION FRONT (*Jabhāt-Nijāt-Millī*): ε15,000. Sibghatullah Modjaddi.
NATIONAL ISLAMIC FRONT (*Mahaz-Millin Islāmī*): ε15,000. Sayyed Amhad Gailani.
ISLAMIC REVOLUTIONARY MOVEMENT (*Harakāt-Inqilāb-Islāmī*): ε25,000. Mohammed Nabi Mohammed.

ISLAMIC FUNDAMENTALIST:
ISLAMIC PARTY (*Hizbi-Islāmi-Khālis*): ε40,000.
Yūnis Khālis.
ISLAMIC PARTY (*Hizbi-Islāmi-Gulbaddin*):
ε50,000. Gulbaddin Hekmatyar.
ISLAMIC UNION (*Ittihād-Islāmi*): ε18,000. Abdul
Rasul Sayyaf.
ISLAMIC SOCIETY (*Jamiāt Islāmi*): ε60,000.
Burhanuddin Rabāni.

IRAN-BASED:
SAZMAN-E-NASR (some 50,000).
HARAKAT-E-ISLAMI (20,000).
PASDARAN-E-JEHAD (8,000).
HEZBOLLAH (4,000).
NEHZAT (4,000).
SHOORA-E-ITTEFAQ (some 30,000+).
EQUIPMENT: (predominantly captured): T-34, T-55
MBT; BMP MICV, BTR-40/-60 APC; 76mm
guns; 122mm D-30 how; 107mm, 122mm MRL;
82mm M-41, 120mm mor; *Milan* ATGW; RPG-7
RL; 12.7mm, 14.5mm, 20mm AA guns;
Blowpipe, Stinger, SA-7 SAM.

---

a Actual strength suspect. Divisions reported to average
2,500 (about quarter strength). Desertion is common.
b Air Force org uncertain after the defeat of the
government by the *Mujaheddin*. Org and inventory
represents the situation prior to the defeat of the
Najibullah regime.

BANGLADESH

GDP	1990:	Tk 750.41bn ($21.71bn)	
	1991ε:	Tk 846.62bn ($23.13bn)	
Growth	1990:	4.5%	1991ε: 4%
Inflation	1990:	8.1%	1991: 7.2%
Debt	1990:	$10.8bn	1991: $11.4bn
Def bdgt	1990:	Tk 11.12bn ($321.68m)	
	1991:	Tk 11.10bn ($303.31m)	
Def exp	1990:	Tk 11.30bn ($326.90m)	
$1 = Tk	1989:	32.270	1990: 34.569
	1991:	36.596	1992: 38.950
Tk = Taka			

Population: 118,426,600

	13–17	18–22	23–32
Men	7,219,600	6,593,700	9,450,400
Women	6,976,400	6,219,000	8,880,300

TOTAL ARMED FORCES:
ACTIVE: 107,000.

ARMY: 93,000.
6 inf div HQ.
14 inf bde (some 26 bn).
1 armd bde (2 armd regt).
6 arty regt.
6 engr bn.

EQUIPMENT:†
MBT: 20 Ch Type-59, 30 T-54/-55.
LIGHT TANKS: some 40 Ch Type-62.
TOWED ARTY: 105mm: 30 Model 56 pack,
50 M-101; 122mm: 20 Ch Type-54.
MORTARS: 81mm; 82mm: Ch Type-53; 120mm: 50
Ch Type-53.
RCL: 106mm: 30 M-40A1.
ATK GUNS: 57mm: 18 6-pdr; 76mm: 50 Ch Type-54.
AD GUNS: 37mm: 16; 57mm.

NAVY:† ε7,500.
BASES: Chittagong (HQ), Dhaka, Khulna, Kaptai.
FRIGATES: 4:
1 *Osman* (Ch *Jianghu II*) with 2 × 5 ASW mor,
plus 2 × 2 CSS-N-2 *Hai Ying*-2 (HY-2) SSM, 2
× 2 100mm guns.
1 *Umar Farooq* (UK *Salisbury*) with 1 × 3 *Squid*
ASW mor, 1 × 2 114mm guns.
2 *Abu Bakr* (UK *Leopard*) with 2 × 2 114mm guns.
PATROL AND COASTAL COMBATANTS: 35:
MISSILE CRAFT: 8:
4 *Durdarsha* (Ch *Huangfeng*) with 4 × HY-2
SSM.
4 *Durbar* (Ch *Hegu*) PFM⟨ with 2 ×
HY-2 SSM.
TORPEDO CRAFT: 4 Ch *Huchuan* PFT⟨ with 2 ×
533mm TT.
PATROL, COASTAL: 5:
2 *Durjoy* (Ch *Hainan*) with 4 × 5 ASW RL.
2 *Meghna* fishery protection.
1 *Shahjalal*.
PATROL, INSHORE: 13:
8 *Shahead Daulat* (Ch *Shanghai II*) PFI.
2 *Karnaphuli*, 2 *Padma*, 1 *Bishkali* PCI.
RIVERINE: 5 *Pabna*⟨.
AMPHIBIOUS: 1 *Shahamanat* LCU; plus craft: 4
LCT, 3 LCVP.
SUPPORT AND MISCELLANEOUS: 3:
1 coastal tanker, 1 repair, 1 ocean tug.

AIR FORCE:† 6,500;
85 cbt ac, no armed hel.
FGA: 3 sqn with 18 J-6/JJ-6, 16 Q-5, 12 Su-7BM
(ex-Iraqi ac).
FIGHTER: 2 sqn with 17 J-7M, 16 MiG-21MF,
2 MiG-21U.
TRANSPORT: 1 sqn with 1 An-24, 4 An-26, 1 DHC-3.
HELICOPTERS: 3 sqn with 2 Bell 206L, 10 -212,
6 Mi-8, 3 UH-1N.
TRAINING: 20 Ch CJ-6, 8 CM-170, 4* JJ-7, 4
MiG-15UTI, 3 Su-7U.

FORCES ABROAD:
UN AND PEACEKEEPING:
CAMBODIA (UNTAC): 907: 1 inf bn.
CROATIA (UNPROFOR): 4 Observers.
IRAQ/KUWAIT (UNIKOM): 7 Observers.
WESTERN SAHARA (MINURSO): 1 Observer.

PARAMILITARY:
BANGLADESH RIFLES: 30,000 (border guard); 37 bn.
ARMED POLICE: 5,000.
ANSARS (Security Guards): 20,000.

OPPOSITION:
SHANTI BAHINI (Peace Force), Chakma tribe Chittagong Hills, ε5,000.

INDIA

GDP	1990ε:	Rs 4,959.0bn ($283.31bn)	
	1991ε:	Rs 5,715.1bn ($251.30bn)	
Growth	1990:	4.5%	1991ε: 3%
Inflation	1990:	9.0%	1991: 13.9%
Debt	1990:	$70.12bn	1991: $77.2bn
Def exp	1990:	Rs 176.84bn ($10.1bn)	
	1991ε:	Rs 183.55bn ($8.07bn)	
Def bdgt	1991:	Rs 168.5bn ($7.41bn)	
	1992:	Rs 175.0bn ($6.75bn)	
$1 = Rs*a*	1989:	16.226	1990: 17.504
	1991:	22.742	1992: 25.914

Rs = rupees
a 20% devaluation in mid-1991.

Population: 873,673,400

	13–17	*18–22*	*23–32*
Men	49,263,700	44,677,900	72,983,900
Women	46,671,700	41,212,400	66,510,400

TOTAL ARMED FORCES:
ACTIVE: 1,265,000.
RESERVES: (obligation to age 60) Army 300,000 (first-line reserves within 5 years of full-time service, a further 600,000 have a commitment until the age of 60); Territorial Army (volunteers) 160,000; Air Force 140,000; Navy 55,000.

ARMY: 1,100,000.
HQ: 5 Regional Comd (= Fd Army), 10 Corps (1 more forming).
  2 armd div (each 2/3 armd, 1 SP arty (2 SP fd, 1 med regt) bde).
  1 mech div (each 3 mech (4/6 mech bn), 3 armd regt, 1 arty bde).
  22 inf div (each 2–5 inf, 1 arty bde; some have armd regt).

10 mtn div (each 3–4 bde, 1 or more arty regt).
14 indep bde: 5 armd, 7 inf, 1 mtn, 1 AB/cdo.
3 indep arty bde.
6 AD bde.
4 engr bde.
These formations comprise:
  53 tk regt (bn).
  25 mech, 332 inf bn.
  9 AB/cdo bn.
  164 arty regt (bn): incl 1 hy, 5 MRL, 50 med (11 SP), 69 fd (3 SP), 39 mtn.
  29 AD arty regt; perhaps 10 SAM gp (3–5 bty each).
Army Aviation:
  7 sqn Air Observation,
  6 ATK/tpt, 4 liaison hel sqn.
EQUIPMENT:
MBT: 3,800: some 800 T-55, 1,300 T-72/-M1, 1,700 *Vijayanta*.
LIGHT TANKS: 100 PT-76.
RECCE: BRDM-2.
AIFV: 800 BMP-1/-2 (*Sarath*).
APC: 400 OT-62/-64, 50 BTR-60.
TOWED ARTY: ε3,000 incl: 75mm: 900 75/24 mtn, 215 Yug M-48; 100mm: 185 M-1944; 105mm: some 800 (incl M-56 pack), some 100 IFG Mk II; 130mm: 550 M-46; 155mm: 410 FH-77B.
SP ARTY: 105mm: 80 *Abbot*; 130mm: 100 mod M-46.
MRL: 122mm: 80 BM-21.
MORTARS: 81mm: L16A1; 120mm: 1,000 M-43; 160mm: 200 M-43.
ATGW: *Milan*, AT-3 *Sagger*, AT-4 *Spigot*, AT-5 *Spandrel*.
RCL: 57mm: M-18; 84mm: *Carl Gustav*; 106mm: 1,000+ M-40A1.
AD GUNS 2,750: 23mm: 140 ZU 23-2, 75 ZSU-23-4 SP; 40mm: 1,245 L40/60, 790 L40/70.
SAM: 100 SA-6, 620 SA-7, 48 SA-8A/-B, 200 SA-9, 50 SA-11, 45 SA-13, 90 SA-16.
HELICOPTERS: 9 sqn with 50 *Chetak*, 40 *Cheetah*, 30 *Krishnar* Mk II.
RESERVES: Territorial Army: 30 inf bn.
DEPLOYMENT:
North – 1 Corps with 3 inf, (1 indep) div; 1 mtn, 1 indep inf, 1 indep arty bde. 1 Corps with 4 inf, 1 mtn div; 2 indep armd, 2 indep inf, 2 indep arty bde.
West – 1 Corps with 1 armd, 1 mech, 2 inf div; 2 Corps each with 2 inf div.
Central – 1 Corps with 1 armd, 2 inf div, plus 3 indep inf div.
East – 3 Corps each with 3 mtn div.
South – 1 Corps with 4 inf div.

NAVY: 55,000, incl 5,000 Naval Air Force and 1,000 Marines.
PRINCIPAL COMMANDS: Western, Eastern, Southern.
Sub-Commands: Submarine, Naval Air.
BASES: Bombay (HQ Western Cmd), Goa (HQ Naval Air), Lakshadweep (Laccadive Is), Karwar (building); Cochin (HQ Southern Cmd), Visakhapatnam (HQ Eastern and Submarines),

Calcutta, Madras, Port Blair (Andaman Is), Arakkonam (new NAS building).

FLEETS: Western (based Bombay), Eastern (based Visakhapatnam).

SUBMARINES: 15:
SS: 15:
 8 *Sindhughosh* (Sov *Kilo*) with 533mm TT.
 3 *Shishumar* (Ge T-209/1500) with 533mm TT.
 4 *Kursura* (Sov *Foxtrot*) with 533mm TT. (plus 3 non-op).

PRINCIPAL SURFACE COMBATANTS: 28:
CARRIERS: 2:
 1 *Viraat* (UK *Hermes*) (29,000t) CVV.
 1 *Vikrant* (UK *Glory*) (19,800t) CVV.
 Air group typically:
  ac: 8 *Sea Harrier* fighter/attack.
  hel: 6 *Sea King* ASW/ASUW (*Sea Eagle* ASM).
DESTROYERS: 5:
 5 *Rajput* (Sov *Kashin*) DDG with 2 × 2 SA-N-1 *Goa* SAM; plus 4 SS-N-2C *Styx* SSM, 5 × 533mm TT, 2 × ASW RL, 1 Ka-25 or 27 hel (ASW).
FRIGATES: 21:
 3 *Godavari* FFH with 2 × *Sea King* hel, 2 × 3 ASTT; plus 4 × SS-N-2C *Styx* SSM.
 2 *Talwar* (UK *Whitby*) FFH with 3 × SS-N-2A *Styx*, 1 *Chetak* hel.
 6 *Nilgiri* (UK *Leander*) with 2 × 3 ASTT, 4 with 1 × 3 *Limbo* ASW mor, 1 *Chetak* hel, 2 with 1 *Sea King*, 1 × 2 ASW RL; plus 2 × 114mm guns.
 5 *Kamorta* (Sov *Petya*) with 4 ASW RL, 3 × 533mm TT.
 4 *Khukri* (ASUW) with 4 *Styx*, hel deck.
 1 *Betwa* (UK *Leopard*) (trg).
PATROL AND COASTAL COMBATANTS: 39:
CORVETTES: 14:
 3 *Vijay Durg* (Sov *Nanuchka* II) with 4 × SS-N-2B *Styx* SSM.
 5 *Veer* (Sov *Tarantul*) with 4 × *Styx* SSM.
 2 *Vibhuti* (similar to *Tarantul*) with 4 × *Styx* SSM.
 4 *Abhay* (Sov *Pauk*) (ASW) with 4 × ASTT, 2 × ASW mor.
MISSILE CRAFT: 8 *Vidyut* (Sov *Osa* II) with 4 × *Styx*.
PATROL, OFFSHORE: 5 *Sukanya* PCO.
PATROL, INSHORE: 12:
 12 SDB Mk 2/3.
MINE WARFARE: 20:
MINELAYERS: None, but *Kamorta* FF and *Pondicherry* MSO have minelaying capability.
MINE COUNTERMEASURES: 20:
 12 *Pondicherry* (Sov *Natya*) MSO.
 2 *Bulsar* (UK 'Ham') MSI.
 6 *Mahé* (Sov *Yevgenya*) MSI⟨.
AMPHIBIOUS: 9:
 1 *Magar* LST, capacity 200 tps, 12 tk, 1 hel.
 8 *Ghorpad* (Sov *Polnocny* C) LSM, capacity 140 tps, 6 tk.
 Plus craft; 7 *Vasco da Gama* LCU.

SUPPORT AND MISCELLANEOUS: 20:
 2 *Deepak* AO, 1 *Amba* (Sov *Ugra*) sub spt, 1 div spt, 2 ocean tugs, 4 AO sm, 5 *Sandhayak* and 4 *Makar* AGHS, 1 *Tir* trg.

NAVAL AIR FORCE: (5,000);
 46 cbt ac, 75 armed hel.
ATTACK: 1 sqn with 21 *Sea Harrier* FRS Mk-51, 3 T-60 trg.
ASW: 6 hel sqn with 26 *Chetak*, 7 Ka-25, 10 Ka-28, 32 *Sea King* Mk 42A/B.
MR: 2 sqn: 9 BN-2, 5 Il-38, 8 Tu-142M *Bear* F.
COMMUNICATIONS: 1 sqn with 5 BN-2 *Islander*, Do-228 ac; 3 *Chetak* hel.
SAR: 1 hel sqn with 6 *Sea King* Mk 42C.
TRAINING: 2 sqn: 6 HJT-16, 8 HPT-32 ac; 2 *Chetak*, 4 Hughes 300 hel.

MARINES: (ε1,000);
 1 regt (2nd forming).

AIR FORCE: 110,000;
 674 cbt ac, 36 armed hel. 5 Air Comd.
BOMBERS: 1 lt bbr sqn with 9 *Canberra*.
FGA: 28 sqn:
 5 with 80 *Jaguar* IS.
 14 with 112 MiG-21 MF/PFMA.
 3 with 54 MiG-23 BN/UM.
 6 with 100 MiG-27.
FIGHTER: 17 sqn:
 4 with 74 MiG-21 FL/U.
 6 with 108 MiG-21 bis/U.
 2 with 26 MiG-23 MF/UM.
 3 with 54 MiG-29/UB.
 2 with 36 *Mirage* 2000H/TH.
MARITIME ATTACK: 8 *Jaguar* with *Sea Eagle*.
ATTACK HELICOPTERS: 2 sqn:
 1 with 18 Mi-25;
 1 with 18 Mi-35.
RECCE: 3 sqn:
 1 with 8 *Canberra* PR-57;
 1 with 6 MiG-25R, 2 MiG-25U;
 1 with 4 HS-748.
MR/SURVEY: 2 *Gulfstream* IV SRA, 2 *Learjet* 29.
TRANSPORT:
 AIRCRAFT: 12 sqn:
  1 with 15 An-12B (being withdrawn);
  6 with 105 An-32 *Sutlej*;
  1 with 16 BAe-748;
  2 with 30 Do-228;
  2 with 24 Il-76 *Gajraj*;
 HELICOPTERS: 11 sqn with 80 Mi-8, 50 Mi-17, 10 Mi-26 (hy tpt).
VIP: 1 HQ sqn with 2 Boeing 707-337C, 4 Boeing 737, 7 BAe-748.
LIAISON: flt and det: 16 BAe-748.
TRAINING: 24 BAe-748, 7 *Canberra* T-4/-13/-67, 120 HJT-16, 56 *Kiran* II, 20 HPT-32, 60 HT-2, 20

Hunter T-66, 5* *Jaguar* IB, 5 MiG-29UB, 44
TS-11 ac; 20 *Chetak*, 2 Mi-24, 2 Mi-35 hel.
MISSILES:
  ASM: *Akash*, AM-39 *Exocet*, AS-7 *Kerry*, AS-11B
    (ATGW), AS-30, *Sea Eagle*.
  AAM: AA-2 *Atoll*, AA-7 *Apex*, AA-8 *Aphid*, AA-10
    Alamo, AA-11 *Archer*, R-550 *Magic*, Super 530D.
SAM: 30 bn: 280 *Divina* V75SM/VK (SA-2), SA-3, SA-5.

FORCES ABROAD:
UN AND PEACEKEEPING:
ANGOLA (UNAVEM II): 15 Observers.
CAMBODIA (UNTAC): 470: 1 inf bn.
CROATIA (UNPROFOR): 1 Observer.
EL SALVADOR (ONUSAL): 7 Observers.
IRAQ/KUWAIT (UNIKOM): 7 Observers.

PARAMILITARY:
NATIONAL SECURITY GUARDS: 7,500:
  anti-terrorism contingency deployment force.
  Comprises elm of the Armed Forces, CRPF,
  Border Guard.
CENTRAL RESERVE POLICE FORCE (CRPF):
  (Ministry of Home Affairs) 125,000; 70 bn,
  internal security duties.
BORDER SECURITY FORCE: (Ministry of Home
  Affairs) 171,000; some 147 bn, small arms, some
  lt arty, tpt/liaison air spt.
ASSAM RIFLES: (Ministry of Home Affairs)
  35,000; 31 bn, security within north-eastern states.
LADAKH SCOUTS: 5,000.
INDO-TIBETAN BORDER POLICE: (Ministry of
  Home Affairs) 29,000; 28 bn.
SPECIAL FRONTIER FORCE: 10,000.
CENTRAL INDUSTRIAL SECURITY FORCE:
  (Ministry of Home Affairs) 74,000.
DEFENCE SECURITY CORPS: 31,000.
RAILWAY PROTECTION FORCES: 70,000.
PROVINCIAL ARMED CONSTABULARY: 400,000.
NATIONAL RIFLES: (being formed, to be 10,000).
HOME GUARD: 438,000

COAST GUARD: ε3,000;
PATROL CRAFT: 37:
  9 *Vikram* PCO, 8 *Tara Bai* PCI, 5 *Rajhans* PFI,
  7 *Jija Bai* PCI, 8⟨.
AVIATION: 3 air sqn with 9 Do-228, 2 Fokker F-27,
  5 BN-2 *Islander* ac, 4 *Chetak* hel.

KAZAKHSTAN

GDP	1991:	r 91.95bn ($54.09bn)
Growth[a]	1991:	−10%
Inflation[b]	1991:	82.9%
Debt	1991:	$3.1bn
$1 = r	1991:	1.70

r = rouble
[a] NMP growth
[b] Year average

Population: 16,691,000 (38% Russian)

13–17	18–22	23–32
1,614,300	1,418,800	2,069,700

STRATEGIC NUCLEAR FORCES: (CIS
  controlled forces on Kazakhstan territory).
ICBM: 104
  SS-18 *Satan* (RS-20), 104 at 2 sites.
BOMBERS: 40
  40 Tu-95H (ALCM-equipped).

FORCES UNDER JOINT CONTROL:
ARMY (63,000)
  1 Army HQ.
  1 TD
  5 MRD (1 trg).
  1 AB bde.
  2 arty bde
  1 ATK bde.
  1 *Spetsnaz* bde.
  1 attack hel regt.
EQUIPMENT
  Some 1,200 MBT, 1,500 arty/MRL/mor, 40
    FROG/SS-21, 25 attack hel, plus over 1,000
    MBT in store.

AIR FORCE:
FGA: 1 div: 140 MiG-27, Su-24.
FIGHTER: 1 div with 4 regt: 100 MiG-23.
RECCE: 1 regt: 70 MiG-25, Su-17, Su-24.

AIR DEFENCE:
FIGHTER: 2 regt: 60 MiG-25, MiG-31.
SAM: 150.

NATIONAL FORCES
To form National Guard (3–5,000).

KYRGYZSTAN

GDP	1991:	r 15.2bn ($8.94bn)
Growth[a]	1991:	−5%
Inflation[b]	1991:	88.2%
Debt	1991:	$700m
Def bdgt	1992:	r 730m
$1 = r	1991:	1.70

[a] NMP growth
[b] Year average
r = roubles

Population: 4,367,000 (21.5% Russian)

13–17	18–22	23–32
466,600	393,000	506,600

Terms of service: 18 months.

FORCES UNDER JOINT CONTROL:
ARMY: (8,000).
1 MRD.
EQUIPMENT: 30 MBT, 170 ACV, 75 arty/MRL/mor.

AIR:
1 trg centre: 200+ MiG-21, L-29, L-39.

AIR DEFENCE:
SAM: 55

NATIONAL FORCES:
To be formed 5–7,000 active, 11,000 reserve.

MYANMAR (BURMA)

GDP	1989:	K 110.92bn ($16.54bn)	
	1990ε:	K 138.1bn ($21.92bn)	
Growth	1990:	5.1%	1991ε: 4.2%
Inflation	1990:	17.6%	1991: 32.3%
Debt	1990:	$4.50bn	1991ε: $5bn
Def bdgt	1990:	K 6.72bn ($1,060.2m)	
	1992ε:	K 7.9bn ($1,257.16m)	
$1 = Kᵃ	1989:	6.705	1990: 6.339
	1991:	6.284	1992: 6.30

K = kyats
ᵃ Official rate. Black market rate may be as high as
$1 = K10.

Population: 42,267,600

	13–17	18–22	23–32
Men	2,272.200	2,137,400	3,563,400
Women	2,229,100	2,105,200	3,530,200

TOTAL ARMED FORCES:
ACTIVE: ε286,000.

ARMY: 265,000.
10 lt inf div (each 3 tac op comd (TOC)).
10 Regional Comd (8 with 3 TOC, 2 with 4 TOC).
32 TOC with 145 garrison inf bn.
Summary of cbt units:
223 inf bn.
3 armd bn.
7 arty bn.
1 AA arty bn.

EQUIPMENT:†
MBT: 26 *Comet*, 30 Ch T-69II.
LIGHT TANKS: 30 Type-63.
RECCE: 45 *Ferret*, 40 *Humber*, 30 *Mazda* (local manufacture).
APC: 20 *Hino* (local manufacture).
TOWED ARTY: 76mm: 100 M-1948; 88mm: 50 25-pdr; 105mm: 96 M-101; 140mm: 5.5-in.
MRL: 122mm: Type-63 reported.
MORTARS: 81mm; 82mm; 120mm: 80 Soltam.
RCL: 84mm: 500 *Carl Gustav*; 106mm: M40A1.
ATK GUNS: 60: 57mm: 6-pdr; 76.2mm: 17-pdr.
AD GUNS: 37mm: 24 Type-74; 40mm: 10 M-1; 57mm: 12 Type-80.

NAVY:† 12,000–15,000 (incl 800 Naval Infantry).
BASES: Bassein, Mergui, Moulmein, Seikky, Rangoon (Monkey Point), Sittwe.
PATROL AND COASTAL COMBATANTS: 60:
CORVETTES: 2:
    1 *Yan Taing Aung* (US PCE-827)
    1 *Yan Gyi Aung* (US *Admirable* MSF).
PATROL: 58:
    COASTAL: 11: 2 *Nawarat*, 3 *Indaw* (Dk *Osprey*) (fishery protection), 6 *Yan Sit Aung* (Ch *Hainan*).
    INSHORE: 18: 10 US PGM-401/412, 2 imp Yug Y-301 PCI, 3 Yug PFI⟨, 3 US *Swift* PGM (fishery protection).
    RIVERINE: 29: 10 Yug Y-301, 19⟨ and some 25 boats.
AMPHIBIOUS: 5
    5 *Aiyar Lulin* LCT plus craft: 10 LCM.
SUPPORT: 4: 1 coastal tpt, 2 AGHS, 1 PC spt.
NAVAL INFANTRY: 800: 1 bn.

AIR FORCE: 9,000;
37 cbt ac, 10 armed hel.
FIGHTERS: 1 sqn: 10 F-7, 2 FT-7.
COIN: 2 sqn: 15 PC-7, 4 PC-9, 6 *Super Galeb*.
TRANSPORT: 1 F-27, 4 FH-227, 5 PC-6A/-B.
LIAISON: 6 Cessna 180, 1 -550.
HELICOPTERS: 4 sqn: 12 Bell 205, 6 -206, 9 SA-316, 10 Mi-2 (armed), 12 PZL W-3 *Sokol*.

PARAMILITARY:
PEOPLE'S POLICE FORCE: 50,000.
PEOPLE'S MILITIA: 35,000.
FISHERY DEPT: ε250: 6 patrol boats plus some 6 armed boats (incl in Navy totals).

OPPOSITION:
Numerous rebel groups with loose and varying alliances. Only main groups listed.
NATIONAL DEMOCRATIC FRONT (NDF):
Some 20,000: coalition of numerous ethnic gp, mainly in border areas incl Kachin (8,000), Shan and Karen (5,000) groups.

ROHINGYA SOLIDARITY ORGANISATION:
ε6,000.
ARAKAN ROHINGYA ISLAMIC FRONT: ε500.
PRIVATE ARMIES (mainly narcotics linked)
Mong Tai Army (formerly Shan United Army)
  Chang Shee Fu 'Khun Sa' (narcotics warlord):
  2,100. Kan Chit: 450. United Revolutionary
  Army: ε1,000; Kuomintang-linked. Loi Maw
  Rebels/Army: ε3,000.

NEPAL

GDP	1990:	NR 88.71bn ($3.02bn)	
	1991ε:	NR 100.60bn ($2.70bn)	
Growth	1990:	3.6%	1991ε: 4.1%
Inflation	1990:	8.3%	1991ε: 16.0%
Debt	1989:	$1.36bn	1990: $1.62bn
Def bdgt	1990:	NR 1.15bn ($37.93m)	
	1991:	NR 1.24bn ($33.19m)	
$1 = NR	1989:	27.189	1990: 29.369
	1991:	37.255	1992: 42.700

NR = Nepalese rupees

Population: 19,895,400

	13–17	18–22	23–32
Men	1,129,200	967,800	1,487,200
Women	1,066,800	928,300	1,435,100

TOTAL ARMED FORCES:
ACTIVE 35,000 (to be 40,000).
RESERVES none.

ARMY: 34,800
1 Royal Guard bde: incl 1 cav sqn, 1 garrison
  bn.
5 inf bde.
1 spt bde: incl AB bn, arty regt, engr bn, armd
  recce sqn.
1 log bde.
EQUIPMENT:
RECCE: 25 *Ferret*.
TOWED ARTY: 75mm: 6 pack; 94mm: 5 3.7-in mtn;
  105mm: 6 pack.
MORTARS: 81mm; 120mm: 18.
AD GUNS: 14.5mm: 30 Ch; 40mm: 2 L/60.

AIR FORCE: 200
No cbt ac, or armed hel.
TRANSPORT:
AIRCRAFT: 1 BAe-748, 2 *Skyvan*, 1 *Twin Otter*.
HELICOPTERS: 2 AS-332 (Royal Flight), 1 Bell
  206L, 2 *Chetak*, 2 SA-330.

FORCES ABROAD:
UN AND PEACEKEEPING:
CROATIA (UNPROFOR): 21 Observers.
LEBANON (UNIFIL): 1 inf bn (849).

PARAMILITARY:
POLICE FORCE: 28,000.

PAKISTAN

GDP	1990:	Rs 862.45bn ($39.73bn)	
	1991:	Rs 1,016.73bn ($42.72bn)	
Growth	1990:	5.3%	1991: 6.5%
Inflation	1990:	9.0%	1991: 6.6%
Debt	1989:	$18.31bn	1990: $20.68bn
Def exp	1990:	Rs 63.20bn ($2.91bn)	
	1991:	Rs 76.96bn ($3.23bn)	
Def bdgt	1991:	Rs 70.95bn ($2.98bn)	
	1992:	Rs 82.15bn ($3.29bn)	
$1 = Rs	1989:	20.541	1990: 21.707
	1991:	23.801	1992: 25.000

Rs = rupees

Population: 118,355,800 (excl Afghan refugees)

	13–17	18–22	23–32
Men	7,017,700	6,092,800	9,593,000
Women	6,283,000	5,442,800	8,659,500

TOTAL ARMED FORCES:
ACTIVE: 580,000.
RESERVES: 513,000; Army 500,000: obligation to
  ages 45 (men) or 50 (officers); active liability for
  8 years after service. Navy 5,000. Air 8,000.

ARMY: 515,000.
9 Corps HQ, 1 area comd.
2 armd div.
19 inf div.
6 indep armd bde.
8 indep inf bde.
7 corps arty bde (2 more forming).
7 AD arty bde.
7 engr bde.
3 armd recce regt.
1 SF gp (3 bn).
Avn: 1 ac, 6 hel sqn; indep observation flt.
EQUIPMENT:
MBT: 1,980+: 150 M-47, 280 M-48A5, 50 T-54/-55,
  1,300 Ch Type-59, 200 Ch Type-69, T-85 reported.
APC: 800 M-113.
TOWED ARTY: 1,405: 85mm: 200 Ch Type-56;
  88mm: 200 25-pdr; 105mm: 300 M-101, 50 M-56
  pack; 122mm: 200 Ch Type-60, Ch Type-54;
  130mm: 200 Ch Type-59-1; 140mm: 45 5.5in;

155mm: 30 M-59, 60 M-114, 100 M-198;
203mm: 20 M-115.
SP ARTY: 240: 105mm: 50 M-7; 155mm: 150
M-109A2; 203mm: 40 M-110A2.
MRL: 122mm: 45 BM-11.
MORTARS: 81mm: 500; 120mm: 225 AM-50,
M-61.
SSM: 18 *Hatf*-1, *Hatf*-2.
ATGW: 800: *Cobra*, *TOW* (incl 24 on M-901 SP), Ch
Red Arrow.
RL: 89mm: M-20 3.5-in.
RCL: 75mm: Type-52; 106mm: M-40A1.
AD GUNS: 2,000+ incl: 14.5mm; 35mm: 200
GDF-002; 37mm: Ch Type-55/-65; 40mm: M1,
100 L/60; 57mm: Ch Type-59.
SAM: 350 *Stinger*, *Redeye*, RBS-70, 500 *Anza*.

AVIATION:
AIRCRAFT:
  SURVEY: 1 *Commander* 840.
  LIAISON: 1 Cessna 421, 2 *Commander* 690,
    80 *Mashshaq*.
  OBSERVATION: 40 O-1E, 50 *Mashshaq*.
HELICOPTERS:
  ATTACK: 20 AH-1F (*TOW*).
  TRANSPORT: 7 Bell 205, 10 -206B, 16 Mi-8, 6
    IAR/SA-315B, 23 IAR/SA-316, 35 SA-330,
    5 UH-1H.

NAVY: ε20,000 (incl Naval Air and maritime
security agency).
BASE: Karachi (Fleet HQ).
SUBMARINES: 6:
  2 *Hashmat* (Fr *Agosta*) with 533mm TT (F-17
  HWT), *Harpoon* USGW.
  4 *Hangor* (Fr *Daphné*) with 533mm TT (L-5
  HWT), *Harpoon* USGW.
  Plus 3 SX-756 SSI SF insertion craft.
PRINCIPAL SURFACE COMBATANTS: 13.
DESTROYERS: 3:
  1 *Babur* (UK *Devonshire*) DDH with 1 × *Sea
  King* Mk-45 hel (ASW/ASUW), plus 2 × 2
  114mm guns.
  2 *Alamgir* (US *Gearing*) (ASW) (trg) with 1 × 8
  ASROC; plus 2 × 3 ASTT, 2 × 2 127mm guns,
  3 × 2 *Harpoon* SSM.
(Plus 2 *Alamgir* in store.)
FRIGATES: 10:
FFG: 4 *Badr* (US *Brooke*) with 1 × SM-1 MR SAM,
  1 × 8 *ASROC*, 2 × 3 ASTT, 1 × 127mm gun and
  equipped for SA-316B hel (on 5-yr lease).
FF: 6:
  2 *Shamsher* (UK *Leander*) with SA-316 hel, 1 × 3
  ASW mor, plus 2 × 114mm guns.
  4 *Saif* (US *Garcia*) with 1 × 8 *ASROC*, 2 × 3
  ASTT, plus 2 × 127mm guns equipped for
  SA-316 hel (on 5-yr lease).
PATROL AND COASTAL COMBATANTS: 25:

MISSILE CRAFT: 8:
  4 Ch *Huangfeng* with 4 × *Hai Ying 2* SSM.
  4 Ch *Hegu*⟨ with 2 × *Hai Ying 2*.
TORPEDO CRAFT: 4 Ch *Huchuan* PHT with 2 ×
533mm TT (in reserve).
PATROL: 13:
  COASTAL: 4 *Baluchistan* (Ch *Hainan*) PFC with 4
    × ASW RL.
  INSHORE: 9:
    8 *Quetta* (Ch *Shanghai*) PFI (some in reserve),
    1 *Rajshahi* PCI.
MINE WARFARE: 2 *Mahmood* (US-MSC 268) MSC.
SUPPORT AND MISCELLANEOUS: 5:
  1 *Nasr* (Ch *Fuqing*) AO, 1 *Dacca* AO, 1 AGOR, 1
  ocean tug, 1 repair.

NAVAL AIR:
4 cbt ac, 9 armed hel.
ASW/MR: 1 sqn with 4 *Atlantic* (operated by Air Force).
ASW/SAR: 2 hel sqn: 1 with 4 SA-316B (ASW), 5
Sea King Mk 45 (ASW).
COMMUNICATIONS: 2 Fokker F-27 ac (Air Force).
ASM: *Exocet* AM-39.

AIR FORCE: 45,000; 352 cbt ac, (plus 48
Mirage IIIO in store), no armed hel.
FGA: 8 sqn:
  1 with 18 *Mirage* (15 IIIEP (some with AM-39
    ASM), 3 IIIDP (trg));
  3 (1 OCU) with 58 *Mirage* 5 (54 -5PA/PA2, 4
    -5DPA/DPA2);
  4 with 50 Q-5.
FIGHTER: 9 sqn:
  4 with 100 J-6/JJ-6;
  3 (1 OCU) with 39 F-16 (27 -A, 12 -B);
  2 (1 OCU) with 75 J-7.
RECCE: 1 sqn with 12 *Mirage* IIIRP.
TRANSPORT: 12 C-130 (5 -B, 7 -E), 1 L-100;
  3 Boeing 707, 3 *Falcon* 20, 2 F-27-200
  (1 with Navy), 2 Beech (1 *Travel Air*, 1 *Baron*).
SAR: 1 hel sqn with 6 SA-319.
TRANSPORT HELICOPTERS: 1 sqn with 12 SA-316,
  4 SA-321.
TRAINING: 12 CJ-6, 30 JJ-5, *24 *Mashshaq*, 6
  MiG-15UTI, 10 T-33A, 53 T-37B/C.
AD: 7 SAM bty:
  6 each with 24 *Crotale*;
  1 with 6 CSA-1 (SA-2).
MISSILES:
  ASM: AM-39 *Exocet*.
  AAM: AIM-7 *Sparrow*, AIM-9 *Sidewinder*, R-530,
    R-550 *Magic*.

FORCES ABROAD:
SAUDI ARABIA: some 500 military/technical advisors.
UN AND PEACEKEEPING:
CAMBODIA (UNTAC): 1,055: 1 inf bn.
IRAQ/KUWAIT (UNIKOM): 9 Observers.

WESTERN SAHARA (MINURSO): 1 Observer.

PARAMILITARY:
NATIONAL GUARD: 180,000; incl Janbaz Force; National Cadet Corps; Women Guards.
FRONTIER CORPS: (Ministry of Interior) 65,000, 45 UR-416 APC.
PAKISTAN RANGERS: (Ministry of Interior) 23,000.
MARITIME SECURITY AGENCY: (ε2,000)
1 *Alamgir* (US *Gearing* DD) (no *ASROC* or TT), 4 *Barakat* PCC.
COASTGUARD: Some 23 PFI, plus boats.

SRI LANKA

GDP	1990:	Rs 321.06bn ($8.01bn)	
	1991ε:	Rs 384.00bn ($9.28bn)	
Growth	1990:	6.2%	1991ε: 4.8%
Inflation	1990:	21.5%	1991: 12.2%
Debt	1990:	$5.3bn	1991: $5.7bn
Def bdgt	1990:	Rs 17.60bn ($439.31m)	
	1991ε:	Rs 18.62bn ($450.06m)	
$1 = Rs	1989:	36.047	1990: 40.063
	1991:	41.372	1992: 43.000
Rs = rupees			

Population: 17,829,200			
	13–17	*18–22*	*23–32*
Men	893,200	864,100	1,571,300
Women	868,700	855,000	1,601,900

TOTAL ARMED FORCES: some 105,900
incl recalled reservists.
ACTIVE: 22,000.
RESERVES: some 12,000; Army 2,500; Navy 1,000; Air 8,500. Obligation: 7 years post-Regular service.

ARMY: 89,000, incl recalled reservists (being re-org).
3 div, 4 Task Force HQ.
9 inf bde HQ.
11 op bde gp.
1 indep SF bde (1 cdo, 1 SF regt).
1 armd regt (bn).
2 recce regt (bn) (1 reserve).
4 fd arty (incl 1 reserve), 4 fd engr regt.
EQUIPMENT:
MBT: 25 T-54/-55.
RECCE: 31 *Saladin*, 33 *Ferret*, 12 Daimler *Dingo*.
APC: 19 Ch Type-85, 10 BTR-152, 37 *Buffel*, 73 *Unicorn*, 8 Shorland, 9 *Hotspur*, 41 *Saracen*.
TOWED ARTY: 76mm: 14 Yug M-48; 85mm: 12 Ch Type-56; 88mm: 24 25-pdr; 130mm: 12 Ch Type-59-1.
MORTARS: 81mm: 176; 82mm: 36; 120mm: 36 M-43.

RCL: 105mm: 20 M-65; 106mm: 40 M-40.
AD GUNS: 40mm: 7 L-40; 94mm: 3 3.7-in.

NAVY: 8,900.
BASES: Colombo (HQ), Trincomalee (main base): Karainagar, Tangalle, Kalpitiya, Galle, Kochchikade, Welisara.
PATROL AND COASTAL COMBATANTS: 44:
PATROL, COASTAL: 2 *Jayesagara* PCC.
PATROL, INSHORE: 42:
5 *Sooraya*, 3 *Rana* (Ch *Shanghai* II) PFI.
12 Is *Dvora* PFI⟨.
3 S. Korean PFI⟨.
19 PCI⟨, plus some 30 boats.
AMPHIBIOUS: craft only; 4 LCM, 2 fast personnel carrier.
SUPPORT AND MISCELLANEOUS: 3:
3 *Abheetha* spt/cmd.

AIR FORCE: 8,000 (incl 2,000 reservists);
30 cbt ac, 12 armed hel.
FGA: 4 F-7M.
COIN: 11 SF-260TP.
ATTACK HELICOPTERS: 13 Bell 212, 4 -412.
MR: 1 sqn with 6 Cessna 337 ac; 2 SA-365 hel.
TRANSPORT: 1 sqn with 5 BAe 748, 1 Cessna 421C, 1 *Super King Air*, 2 Ch Y-8, 9 Y-12.
HELICOPTERS: 7 Bell 206.
TRAINING: incl 6 Cessna 150, 4 DHC-1, 2* FT-5, 1* FT-7, 12* SF-260 MB, 5 *Chipmunk*.
RESERVES: Air Force Regt, 3 sqn; Airfield Construction Regt, 1 sqn.

PARAMILITARY:
POLICE FORCE: (Ministry of Defence) 30,000 active, incl 1,000 women, (22,000 reserves, increase to 28,000 planned) incl Special Task Force: 3,000-man anti-guerrilla unit.
NATIONAL AUXILIARY VOLUNTEER FORCE: 12,000 reported.
HOME GUARD: 15,200.

OPPOSITION:
LIBERATION TIGERS OF TAMIL EELAM (LTTE):
Leader: Veluppillai Prabaharan: ε2,000.

TAJIKISTAN

GDP	1991:	r 13.0bn ($7.65bn)
Growth[a]	1991:	−8.7%
Inflation[b]	1991:	103%
Debt	1991:	$700m
Def bdgt[c]	1992:	r 1.5bn
$1 = r	1991:	1.70
r = rouble		

[a] NMP growth.
[b] Year average.
[c] Contribution to CIS defence budget.

Population: 5,248,000 (10.4% Russian)

13–17	18–22	23–32
621,500	498,600	556,300

FORCES UNDER JOINT CONTROL:
ARMY: (6,000)
  1 MRD
EQUIPMENT: 260 MBT, 420 ACV, 360 arty/MRL/
  mors, 4 *FROG*/SS-21.

AIR DEFENCE:
SAM: 40.

NATIONAL FORCES:
  Nil

TURKMENISTAN

GDP	1991:	r 18.60bn ($10.94bn)
Growth[a]	1991:	−0.6%
Inflation[b]	1991:	90.4%
Debt	1991:	$600m
$1 = r	1991:	1.70

r = rouble
[a] NMP growth
[b] Year average

Population: 3,622,000 (12.6% Russian)

13–22	18–22	23–32
424,300	362,200	405,700

FORCES UNDER JOINT CONTROL:
ARMY: (34,000)
  1 Corps HQ.
  4 MRD (1 trg).
  1 AB bde.
  3 arty bde.
  1 *Spetsnaz* bde.
EQUIPMENT:
  750 MBT, 1,000+ ACV, 1,400 arty/MRL/mor,
  24 SSM.

AIR FORCE:
  2 FGA regt: with 60 MiG-27, Su-17.
  1 trg regt: 30 MiG-29.

AIR DEFENCE:
FIGHTER: 2 regt: 85 MiG-23, 30 MiG-25.
SAM: 75.

UZBEKISTAN

GDP	1991:	r 56.30bn ($33.12bn)
Growth	1991:	−0.5%
Inflation[a]	1991:	82.2%
Debt	1991:	$2.70bn
$1 = r	1991:	1.70

[a] Year average
r = rouble

Population: 20,322,000 (10.8% Russian)

13–17	18–22	23–32
2,348,600	1,930,600	2,235,400

FORCES UNDER JOINT CONTROL:
ARMY: (15,000)
  1 MRD.
  1 ABD.
  1 arty bde.
  1 attack hel regt.
EQUIPMENT:
  280 MBT, 700 ACV, 780 arty/MRL/mors,
  8 SSM, 24 attack hel, plus up to 5,000
  MBT in store.

AIR FORCE:
  2 FGA regt: 100 Su-17, Su-24, Su-25.
  2 ftr regt: 100 MiG-29, Su-15, Su-27.
  1 recce regt: 35 Su-17, Su-24.

AIR DEFENCE:
FIGHTER: 1 regt, 30 Su-27.
SAM: 100.

NATIONAL FORCES:
PARAMILITARY:
National Guard: 1 bde 700.
National Security Service.

East Asia and Australasia

Political Developments

Both **North** and **South Korea** gained admission to the United Nations on 17 September 1991. A peace agreement intended to end the 12-year civil war in **Cambodia** was signed in Paris on 23 October 1991. The agreement allowed for the establishment of the United Nations Transitional Authority in Cambodia (UNTAC) to play a major role in the government of Cambodia until UN-supervised elections take place in 1993. The peacekeeping force of UNTAC has begun to deploy and is disarming and demobilizing some 70% of the forces of both the government and opposition parties. After a protracted campaign of opposition in the *Diet*, **Japan** passed a bill allowing the Japanese Self-Defense Forces to take part in UN peacekeeping operations. Without further specific legislation, participation is limited to a maximum of 2,000 men in non-combat roles only. Japan is expected to contribute troops to UNTAC and a government mission has visited Cambodia to examine what role Japan could take on. The US has not renewed its lease on the Subic Bay naval base in the Philippines; arrangements for the use of facilities in all five ASEAN countries have been concluded. A small US team is already established in Singapore. There is growing concern about the dispute over the ownership of the Spratly Islands and the Paracels in the South China Sea. China, Taiwan, Vietnam, Malaysia, Brunei and the Philippines all have overlapping claims to parts of the archipelagoes where it is believed there are extensive oil deposits. The most recent development was the landing of Chinese troops and construction materials to erect a marker on Da Lac on 8 July. Vietnam immediately protested.

Nuclear Developments

China formally acceded to the Nuclear Non-Proliferation Treaty (NPT) on 12 March 1992, when it deposited its instrument of accession with the US and UK. It has informed the International Atomic Energy Agency (IAEA) that it will start providing the Agency with information on its relevant exports. It has not yet signed a safeguards agreement. Shortly after joining the NPT, China carried out a large-yield nuclear test at Lop Nor; several monitoring organizations have reported that the yield of the underground explosion could have been as high as one megaton. It is also reported that China is developing a new generation of ballistic missiles which could come into service in the late 1990s. There are no reports of any further development of ballistic missile submarines. China has only ever completed one *Xia* SSBN which has proved unsatisfactory and does not patrol far from its home port, where it spends most of the time. China has also given assurances that it will abide by the guidelines laid down by the Missile Technology Control Regime, but it is also understood that this would not halt deliveries of missiles for which contracts already exist. It is suspected that both Iran and Syria have ordered missiles from China.

There has been intense interest in **North Korea's** suspected nuclear weapons programme. As a signatory of the NPT, the country came under increasing pressure to reach agreement with the IAEA on a safeguards inspection regime, which it did on 30 January 1992. A team led by the Director-General of the IAEA visited North Korea in May 1992 and saw nuclear facilities at Yongbyon. While the IAEA consider the authorities in Pyongyang to have been cooperative, they are concerned that a radio-chemical laboratory at Yongbyon could be a plutonium extraction plant. Officials have admitted that North Korea had produced a small quantity of plutonium. The IAEA plans further inspections and hopes to conclude a subsidiary agreement specifying inspection procedures shortly.

Conventional Military Developments

The **Australian** Navy commissioned the fifth *Adelaide*-class frigate; the final ship in this class is expected to commission in late 1993. The first of a new class, the *Anzac*, has been laid down but will not commission until 1995/96. One *Oberon*-class submarine has been retired. A new class of submarine, the *Collins*, is under construction with three of six laid down and the first expected to commission in 1995.

A reassessment of forces in **Cambodia** shows the strength of the army to be some 80,000 men, 25,000 more than previously thought. The strength of the Khmer People's National Liberation Armed Forces (KPNLAF) is also greater than previously assessed: 20,000 as opposed to 12,000. Even these much higher figures may be too low; the UN estimates there are some 200,000 men backed by 250,000 militia split between the government forces and the three opposition factions. Manpower strengths should be viewed with caution, however, as the various parties are suspected of inflating their own figures in order to obtain a larger share of the new Cambodian Army, which will number some 60,000 men representing all four parties.

The **Chinese** Navy has commissioned four new warships; a fifth *Han*-class nuclear-powered submarine, two more improved *Ming*-class diesel submarines and the first of a new class of frigate – the *Jiangwei* – with two more in the final stages of construction. At least six *Jiangwei* are to be built. It is estimated that nearly 50 of the navy's 84 Soviet *Romeo*-class submarines are non-operational. The navy has an ambitious programme of expansion. In addition to the *Jiangwei* frigate, a new class of destroyer, the *Luhu* (the first commissioning possibly in 1993), and a new missile craft, the *Houang* (of which one is already operational with several more still undergoing operational training), are being introduced. The *Anshan*-class destroyers have been retired, as have ten *Huangteng/Hola* missile craft which the *Houang*-class is replacing. Two new types of amphibious ship are being built. There is no confirmation that China is bidding to buy the still uncompleted aircraft carrier under construction at Nikolayev in Ukraine.

A reassessment of the Chinese Army reveals that for some years *The Military Balance* has overestimated the size of airborne forces; there are only three brigades (one with a training role), and not the four divisions previously listed. It is understood that the army has developed 'rapid deployment forces'; two armies (said to be the 38th and 39th) provide the heavy-armoured and mechanized elements and other more lightly armed divisions also have a deployment role.

Fiji has now formed a separate air wing. The navy has retired two US *Reading*-class and taken delivery of four Israeli *Dabur*-class patrol craft. The **Indonesian** Navy has commissioned two more German Lürssen 57-metre fast patrol craft and two more US LST-512 amphibious ships. The army has taken delivery of 25 more *Rapier* SAM fire units.

The **Japanese** Maritime Self-Defense Force has retired two *Yamagumo*-class frigates and two *Juichi-go*-class torpedo craft. The first of a new class of destroyer, the *Yukikaze* (equipped with the *Aegis* command-and-control system) is expected to commission in 1993; two more have been laid down. The third *Harushio*-class submarine commissioned in 1992; four more are under construction. The Air Self-Defense Force has added ten more F-15J/DJ fighters to its inventory.

The Military Balance has reassessed the organization of the **North Korean** Army. There are 15 not 17 corps: one armoured, four mechanized, eight infantry, one artillery and a new corps called 'The Capital Defence Corps'.

The **South Korean** Army has increased its holdings of Type 88 tanks by 200, and KIFV by about 500. We now assess the total number of SP guns available as 500, but cannot break this down between the three types (M-107, M-109 and M-110) in service. The army has 37 more attack helicopters: 17 AH-1F/-J and 20 *Hughes* 500 MD; and also over 80 more utility helicopters, including its first 30 UH-23. The navy has commissioned a fourth *Tolgorae*-class submarine and not a German T-209/1400 as reported by *The Military Balance*; three T-209/1400 are under construction, one in Germany and two in Korea. Three more *Po Hang*-class frigates have commissioned. Twelve *Lynx* ASW helicopters have been delivered.

The **Malaysian** Army has formed a tenth infantry brigade. Malaysia has placed orders for two frigates to be built in the UK, and for ten *Hawk* trainers and 18 *Hawk* 200 multirole aircraft for delivery from October 1993 to March 1995. The **Singaporean** Army has taken delivery of 22 AMX-10 PAC 90 armoured reconnaissance vehicles and 22 AMX-10P APCs; and 28 more 155mm FH-88 towed gun howitzers.

The **Taiwanese** Army has formed a sixth armoured brigade but has not, as yet, increased its tank holding. The navy will commission two US *Knox*-class frigates later in 1992. Eight French *Lafayette*-class frigates have been ordered. Only unarmed hulls are to be delivered. The revised number of US *Adjutant*-class *Yung Chou* coastal minesweeper is 13 not eight.

In **Thailand** the army has taken delivery of 50 plus M-60 tanks. The navy has commissioned two more frigates, one Chinese *Jianghu*-III-class and one *Jianghu*-IV-class; this last can operate a helicopter. Two more *Kramronsin*-class corvettes have become operational. There have been unconfirmed reports that Thailand may order an aircraft carrier from Spain.

AUSTRALIA

GDP	1990:	$A 376.81bn ($US 294.61bn)
	1991:	$A 376.30bn ($US 293.18bn)

Growth	1990:	1.6%	1991:	−2.2%
Inflation	1990:	7.3%	1991:	3.3%
Debt	1990:	$US120.76bn		
	1991:	$US125.00bn		
Def bdgt	1991:	$A 9.07bn ($US7.06bn)		
	1992:	$A 9.44bn ($US7.27bn)		
Def exp	1990:	$A 9.31bn ($US7.27bn)		
$US 1 = $A	1989:	1.262	1990:	1.279
	1991:	1.284	1992:	1.299

$A = Australian dollars

Population: 17,067,000

	13–17	18–22	23–32
Men	660,500	693,600	1,457,900
Women	631,500	658,600	1,353,200

TOTAL ARMED FORCES:
ACTIVE: 67,900 (incl 8,500 women).
RESERVES: 29,200. Army: 26,000; Navy: 1,600; Air: 1,600.

ARMY: 30,300 (incl 3,100 women).
LAND COMD: 6 military districts, 1 northern comd.
Comd tps:
   1 AD regt +
   1 engr regt (construction)
   1 avn regt.
1 SF regt (3 sqn)
1 inf div
   1 mech bde (1 armd, 1 mech, 1 para inf bn)
   2 inf bde (each 2 inf bn)
   1 recce regt +
   1 APC regt
   3 arty regt (1 med, 2 fd)
   1 engr regt +
   1 avn regt (3 hel, 1 ac sqn).
   (2 reserve inf bde see below)

RESERVES:
   1 div HQ, 7 bde HQ, 2 recce regt, 1 APC regt plus 2 APC sqn, 15 inf bn, 1 cdo, 5 arty (1 med, 4 fd) regt, 1 fd arty bty, 4 engr (2 fd, 2 construction) regt, 3 regional surveillance units.

EQUIPMENT:
MBT: 103 *Leopard* 1A3.
AIFV: 53 M-113 with 76mm gun.
APC: 725 M-113 (incl variants, 205 in store), 15 LAV.
TOWED ARTY: 105mm: 142 M2A2/L5, 63 *Hamel*; 155mm: 34 M-198.
MORTARS: 81mm: 294.
ATGW: 10 *Milan*.
RCL: 84mm: 597 *Carl Gustav*; 106mm: 68 M-40A1.
SAM: 20 *Rapier*, 19 RBS-70.
AIRCRAFT: 13 GAF N-22B *Missionmaster*, 14 PC-6.
HELICOPTERS: 34 S-70 (Army/Air Force crews), 44 OH-58 *Kalkadoon*, 6 UH-1H (armed).
MARINE: 16 LCM, 85 LARC-5 amph craft.

NAVY: 15,300 (incl 900 Fleet Air Arm, 1,800 women).
Maritime Command, Support Command, 6 Naval Area cmd.
BASES: Sydney, NSW. (Maritime Command HQ). Base for: 4 SS, 3 DDG, 6 FF, 1 patrol, 1 LST, 1 AOR, 1 AGT, 2 LCT. Cockburn Sound, WA. Base for: 2 SS, 3 FF, 3 patrol, 1 survey, 1 AOR. Cairns, Qld: 5 patrol. 1 survey, 2 LCT Darwin, NT: 6 patrol, 1 LCT.
SUBMARINES: 5 *Oxley* (mod UK *Oberon*) (3 in refit) with Mk 48 HWT and *Harpoon* SSM.
PRINCIPAL SURFACE COMBATANTS: 11: incl 2 at 14 days notice for ops.
DESTROYERS: 3 *Perth* (US *Adams*) DDG with 1 SM-1 MR SAM/*Harpoon* SSM launcher; plus 2 × 3 ASTT (Mk 46 LWT), 2 × 127mm guns.
FRIGATES: 8:
   5 *Adelaide* (US *Perry*) FFG, with S-70B-2 *Sea Hawk*, 2 × 3 ASTT; plus 1 × SM-1 MR SAM/*Harpoon* SSM launcher.
   2 *Swan*, 1 *Paramatta* FF with 2 × 3 ASTT; plus 2 × 114mm guns.
PATROL AND COASTAL COMBATANTS: 19:
INSHORE: 19:
   15 *Fremantle* PFI, 2 *Attack* PCI (Reserve trg).
   2 *Banks* PCC (Reserve trg).

MINE WARFARE: 5:
   2 *Rushcutter* MHI.
   2 *Bandicoot* and 1 *Brolga* auxiliary MSI.
AMPHIBIOUS: 1:
   1 *Tobruk* LST, capacity 14 tk, 350 tps, hel deck.
   Plus craft; 6 LCT, capacity 3 tk (1 more in store).
SUPPORT AND MISCELLANEOUS: 12:
   1 *Success* (mod Fr *Durance*) AOR, 1 *Westralia*
   AO, 1 *Protector* sub trials and safety, 1 trg/log spt
   (ex-ferry), 2 AGHS, 4 small AGHS, (2 AGOR in
   store), 2 tugs.

FLEET AIR ARM: (900);
   no cbt ac, 15 armed hel.
ASW: 1 hel sqn with 7 *Sea King* Mk 50/50A (ASW),
   1 hel sqn with 16 S-70B-2 (ASW/trg).
UTILITY/SAR: 1 sqn with 6 AS-350B, 3 Bell 206B; 1
   with 2 BAe-748 (EW trg), 1 F-27 (survey).

AIR FORCE: 22,300 (incl 3,500 women);
   157 cbt ac, no armed hel.
FGA/RECCE: 2 sqn with 18 F-111C,
   4 RF-111C.
FIGHTER/FGA: 3 sqn with 52 F-18 (50 -A, 2 -B).
TRAINING: 2 sqn with 46* MB-326H.
MR: 2 sqn with 19 P-3C.
OCU: 1 with 18* F-18B.
FAC: 1 flt with 4 CA-25 *Winjeel*.
TANKER: 4 Boeing 707-32OC.
TRANSPORT: 7 sqn:
   2 with 24 C-130 (12 -E, 12 -H);
   1 with 6 Boeing 707 (4 fitted for air-to-air refuelling);
   2 with 21 DHC-4;
   1 VIP with 5 *Falcon*-900.
   1 with 10 HS-748 (8 for navigation trg, 2 for VIP tpt).
TRAINING: 64 PC-9, 45 CT-4/4A.
SUPPORT: 4 *Dakota*, 2 *Nomad*, 2 DHC-4.
MISSILES:
   ASM: AGM-84A.
   AAM: AIM-7 *Sparrow*, AIM-9L/M *Sidewinder*.
AD: *Jindalee* OTH radar: 1 experimental, 3 planned.
   3 control and reporting units (1 mobile).

FORCES ABROAD:
MALAYSIA: Army: 1 inf coy (on 3-month
   rotational tours). Air Force: det with P-3C ac.
PAPUA NEW GUINEA: 100; trg unit, 1 engr unit,
   85 advisers.
Advisers in Indonesia, Solomon Is., Vanuatu,
   Tonga, W. Samoa and Kiribati.
UN AND PEACEKEEPING
CAMBODIA (UNTAC): 423.
CROATIA (UNPROFOR): 1 Observer.
MIDDLE EAST (UNTSO): 13 Observers.
WESTERN SAHARA (MINURSO): 43.

PARAMILITARY:
BUREAU OF CUSTOMS: 10 GAF N-22B
   Searchmaster MR ac; 6 boats.

FOREIGN FORCES:
US: 700: Air Force: 300; Navy: 400, joint
   facilities at NW Cape (until October 1993),
   Pine Gap and Nurrungar.
NEW ZEALAND: Air Force: 6 A-4K/TA-4K
   (providing trg for Australian Navy).

BRUNEI

GDP	1989ε: $B 6.44bn ($US 3.29bn)	
	1990ε: $B 6.55bn ($US 3.49bn)	
Growth	1989ε: 2.5%	1990ε: 1.0%
Inflation	1989ε: 2.5%	1990ε: 1.5%
Def bdgt	1987ε: $B 410.00m ($US 193.21m)	
	1988: $B 499.53m ($US 233.1m)	
$US 1 = $B 1989: 1.960	1990: 1.867	
1991: 1.750	1992: 1.610	
$B = Brunei dollars		

Population: 283,000

	13–17	18–22	23–32
Men	12,700	11,600	26,700
Women	13,000	11,700	20,600

TOTAL ARMED FORCES: (all services form
   part of the Army): (Malays only eligible for service.)
ACTIVE: 4,450 incl 250 women.
RESERVES: Army: to be 900.

ARMY: 3,600.
   3 inf bn.
   1 armd recce sqn.
   1 SAM bty: 2 tps with *Rapier*.
   1 engr sqn.
EQUIPMENT:
LIGHT TANKS: 16 *Scorpion*.
APC: 24 Sankey AT-104, 26 VAB.
MORTARS: 81mm: 18.
SAM: 12 *Rapier* (with *Blindfire*).
RESERVES: 1 bn (forming).

NAVY: ε550.
BASE: Muara.
PATROL AND COASTAL COMBATANTS: 6†:
MISSILE CRAFT: 3 *Waspada* PFM with 2 × MM-38
   Exocet SSM.
PATROL: 3 *Perwira* PFI⟨.
RIVERINE: Boats only.
AMPHIBIOUS: Craft only; 2 LCM⟨.

AIR FORCE: 300;
4 cbt ac, 7 armed hel.
COIN: 1 sqn with 7 Bo-105 armed hel.
HELICOPTERS: 1 sqn with 10 Bell 212,
1 -214 (SAR).
VIP tpt: 2 S-70 hel, 2 Bell 214ST.
TRAINING: *4 SF-260W (COIN, trg) ac, 2 Bell 206B hel.

PARAMILITARY:
GURKHA RESERVE UNIT: 900+: 2 bn.
ROYAL BRUNEI POLICE: 1,750, 3 PCI⟨, boats.

FOREIGN FORCES:
UK: some 800. (Army) 1 Gurkha inf bn, 1 hel flt.
SINGAPORE: some 500: trg school incl hel det (5 UH-1).

CAMBODIA

NMP	1989ε:	$US 917.84m		
Growth	1989ε:	0%		
Inflation	1989ε:	13.5%	1990ε:	105%
Debt:	1989ε:	$1.0bn		
FMA*a*	1992:	$5m (US)		
$1 = riel	1989:	180.0	1990:	580.0
	1991:	1000.0*b*	1992:	846.6

a Security assistance to the Cambodian resistance as Economic Support.
b December 1991.

Population: 8,515,400			
	13–17	*18–22*	*23–32*
Men	305,600	370,400	796,200
Women	308,200	366,200	773,500

TOTAL ARMED FORCES:
ACTIVE: some 135,000 incl provincial forces.
Terms of service: conscription, 5 years; ages 18 to 35. Militia serve 3 to 6 months with Regulars.

ARMY: some 80,000.
5 Military Regions.
7 inf div.
3 indep inf bde.
14 indep inf regt.
3 armed regt.
Some indep recce, arty, AD bn.
EQUIPMENT:
MBT: 150 T-54/-55/-59.
LIGHT TANKS: 10 PT-76.
APC: 210 BTR-60/-152, M-113.
TOWED ARTY: some 490: 76mm: M-1942; 122mm: M-1938, D-30; 130mm: Type 59.

MRL: 107mm: Type-63; 122mm: 8 BM-21; 132mm: BM-13-16; 140mm: 20 BM-14-16.
MORTARS: 82mm: M-37; 120mm: M-43; 160mm: M-160.
RCL: 82mm: B-10; 107mm: B-11.
AD GUNS: 14.5mm: ZPU 1/-2/-4; 37mm: M-1939; 57mm: S-60.
SAM: SA-7.

NAVY: ε4,000.
PATROL AND COASTAL COMBATANTS: 12†:
2 Sov *Turya* PFI (no TT).
4 Sov *Stenka* PFI (no TT), about 6⟨.

AIR FORCE: ε1,000.
17 cbt ac; no armed hel.
FIGHTER: 17 MiG-21.
TRANSPORT: 3 An-24, Tu-134.
HELICOPTERS: 11 Mi-8/-17.

PROVINCIAL FORCES: some 50,000.
Reports of at least 1 inf regt per province: with varying number of inf bn with lt wpn.

PARAMILITARY:
MILITIA: Some 220,000 local forces, org at village level for local defence. ε10–20 per village. Not all armed.

OPPOSITION:
KHMER ROUGE (National Army of Democratic Kampuchea) some 27,000 org in 20 'bde': perhaps further 15,000 spt and log.
KHMER PEOPLE'S NATIONAL LIBERATION ARMED FORCES (KPNLAF): some 20,000 org in 5 div and 3 indep bde.
ARMÉE NATIONALE SIHANOUKISTE (ANS): perhaps 17,500 org in 5 div.

EQUIPMENT: T-54, Type-62 tk; 122mm: M-1938; 130mm arty; 60mm, 82mm mor; RPG-7 RL, RCL, SA-7 SAM reported.

FOREIGN FORCES:
RUSSIA: some 500 advisers.
UNITED NATIONS (UNTAC): some 10,200 from 29 countries incl inf bn from Bangladesh, France, India, Indonesia, Malaysia, Netherlands, Pakistan and Uruguay.

CHINA

GNP	1990:	Y 1,768.6bn ($369.77bn)
	1991ε:	Y 1,975.9bn ($371.20bn)

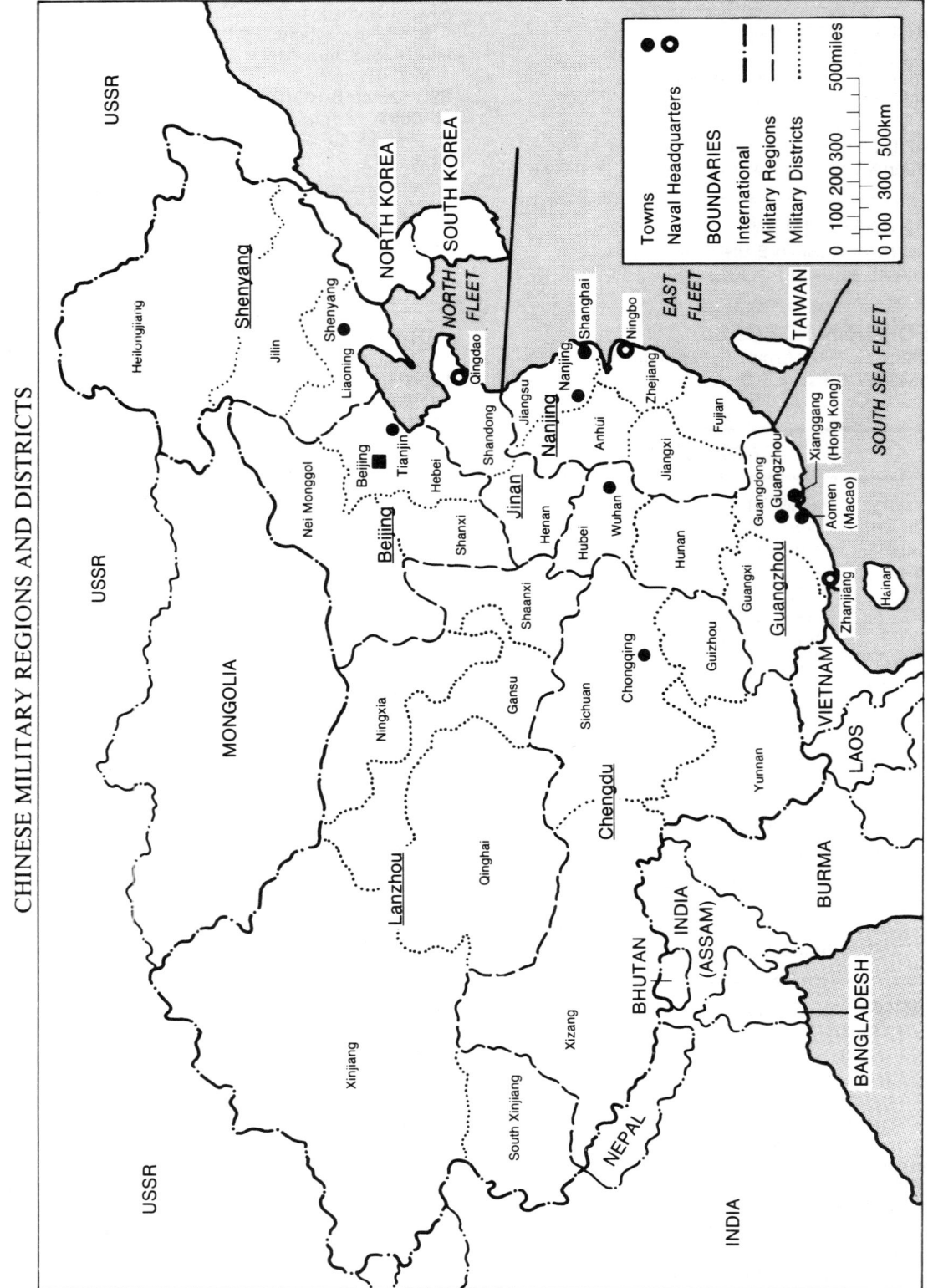

CHINESE MILITARY REGIONS AND DISTRICTS

Growth	1990: 4.9%	1991ε: 6.2%
Inflation	1990: 6.0%	1991ε: 3%
Debt	1990: $45.4bn	1991: $53bn
Def exp	1990: Y 54bn ($11.3bn)	
	1991: Y 63bn ($11.85bn)	
Def bdgt[a]	1991: Y 32.5bn ($6.11bn)	
	1992: Y 37bn ($6.76bn)	
$1 = yuan	1989: 3.765	1990: 4.783
	1991: 5.323	1992: 5.470

Y = yuan

[a] Official budget; the real level of defence spending in China is estimated at between $11bn and $23bn for 1990.

Population: 1,148,593,200

	13–17	18–22	23–32
Men	53,457,000	61,715,200	112,732,600
Women	49,630,100	57,594,200	105,496,800

TOTAL ARMED FORCES:

ACTIVE: some 3,030,000 (perhaps 1,350,000 conscripts, some 136,000 women), being reduced. *Terms of service:* selective conscription; Army, Marines 3 years; Navy, Air Force 4 years.

RESERVES: 1,200,000+ militia reserves being formed on a province-wide basis.

STRATEGIC MISSILE FORCES:

OFFENSIVE (Strategic Rocket Units): (90,000).
MISSILES: org in 6 bases (army level) with bde/regt incl 1 msl testing and trg regt; org varies by msl type.
ICBM: 8:
  2 CSS-4 (DF-5); mod tested with MIRV.
  6 CSS-3 (DF-4).
IRBM: 60 CSS-2 (DF-3), some updated.
SUBMARINES: 1:
SSBN: 1 *Xia* with 12 CSS-N-3 (J-1).
  (Note: Chinese SSBN programme is continuing, but extremely slowly. No further *Xia*-class are expected but a new design is believed to be close to construction.)

DEFENSIVE:
(a) Tracking stations: Xinjiang (covers Central Asia) and Shanxi (northern border).
(b) Phased-array radar complex. Ballistic missile early warning.

ARMY: 2,300,000 (perhaps 1,075,000 conscripts), (reductions continue).
  7 Military Regions (MR), 28 Military Districts, 3 Garrison Comd.
  24 Integrated Group Armies (GA, equivalent to Western corps) org varies, normally with 3 inf div, 1 tk, 1 arty, 1 AD bde or 3 inf, 1 tk div, 1 arty, 1 AD bde, cbt readiness category varies.
  Summary of Combat units:
    84 inf div (incl 1 mech 'all arms').
  10 armd div (normally 3 regt, 323 MBT).
  7 field, 4 AD arty div.
  14 indep armd, 21 indep fd arty, 28 indep AA bde.
  50 indep engr regt.
  6 Rapid Deployment Force bn.
  Avn: 3 group hel bn (2 more forming); 1 hel trg regt.
  AB (manned by Air Force):
    1 corps of 3 bde (2 para, 1 trg bde; each bde 3 para, 1 arty, 1 ATK, 1 AD bn).
  Spt tps.

EQUIPMENT:
MBT: some 7,500–8,000: T-54, 6,000 Type-59, 200 T-69 (mod Type-59), some Type-79, Type-80, Type-85 II reported.
LIGHT TANKS: 1,200 Type-63 amph, 800 Type-62.
AIFV: WZ-501, YW-307/-309.
APC: 2,800 Type-531 C/-D/-E, YW-534, Type-85 (YW-531H), Type-55 (BTR-40), -56 (BTR-152), -63, Type-77-1/-2 (Sov BTR-50PK amph); Type-523.
TOWED ARTY: 14,500:
  100mm: Type-59 (fd/ATK), Type-86; 122mm: Type-54, Type-60, Type-83, D-30; 130mm: Types-59/-59-1; 152mm: Type-54, Type-66, Type-83; 155mm: WAC-21.
SP ARTY: 122mm: Type-54-1 (Type-531 chassis), Type-85; 152mm: Type-83.
MRL: 3,800: 107mm: Types-63 towed /-81 SP (being replaced by 122mm); 122mm: Type-81, Type-83; 130mm: Type-63, Type-70 SP, Type-82, Type-85; 140mm: BM-14-16; 273mm: Type-83; 284mm: Type-74 minelayer; 320mm: WS-1; 425mm: Type-762 mine clearance.
MORTARS: 82mm: Type-53 (incl SP); 120mm: Type-55 (incl SP); 160mm: Type-56.
SSM: M-9 (range 500km); M-11 (range 120–150km).
ATGW: HJ-73 (*Sagger*-type), HJ-8 (*TOW/ Milan*-type).
RCL: 75mm: Type-52, Type-56; 82mm: Type-65.
RL: 90mm: Type-51.
ATK GUNS: 57mm: Type-55; 76mm: Type-54; 100mm: Type-73, Type-86.
AD: GUNS: 15,000: incl 23mm: (ZSU-23 type); 37mm: Types-55/-65/-74, -63 twin SP; 57mm: Types-59, -80 SP; 85mm: Type-56; 100mm: Type-59.
SAM: HN-5, HN-5A/-C (SA-7 type); HQ-61 twin SP.
HELICOPTERS: 30 Z-9, 8 SA-342 (with *HOT*), 24 S-70.

RESERVES: (undergoing major reorganization on a provincial basis) perhaps 600,000: ε54 inf div.

DEPLOYMENT:

North-East: Shenyang MR (Heilongjiang, Jilin, Liaoning MD): 5 GA, 3 armd, 15 inf, 1 arty div.
North: Beijing MR (Beijing, Tianjin Garrison Comds; Nei Monggol, Hebei, Shanxi MD): 6 GA, 2 armd, 20 inf, 1 AB (Air Force), 2 arty, 2 AD div.

West: Lanzhou MR (incl Ningxia, Shaanxi, Gansu, Qinghai, Xinjiang, South Xinjiang MD): 2 GA, 1 armd, 12 inf div.

South-West: Chengdu MR (incl Sichuan, Guizhou, Yunnan, Xizang MD): 2 GA, 7 inf, 1 arty div.

South: Guangzhou MR (Hubei, Hunan, Guangdong, Guangxi, Hainan): 2 GA, 6 inf, 1 arty, 1 AD div; 2 AB bde (Air Force).

Centre: Jinan MR (Shandong, Henan, MD): 4 GA, 2 armd, 13 inf, 1 arty div; 1 AB bde (Air Force).

East: Nanjing MR (Shanghai Garrison Comd; Jiangsu, Zhejiang, Fujian, Jiangxi, Anhui MD): 3 GA, 2 armd, 11 inf, 1 arty, 1 AD div.

NAVY: ε260,000 incl Coast Defence (27,000), Naval Air (2,500) and Marines (6,000) (some 35,000 conscripts);

SUBMARINES: 46:
STRATEGIC SUBMARINES: 1 SSBN.
TACTICAL SUBMARINES: 44:
SSN: 5 *Han* with 533mm TT.
SSG: 1 modified *Romeo* (Type ES5G), with 6 C-801 (YJ-6, *Exocet* derivative) SSM; plus 533mm TT.
SS: 38:
5 *Improved Ming* (Type ES5E) with 533mm TT.
33 *Romeo* (Type ES3B)† with 533mm TT.
(Note: probably additional 49 *Romeo*-class non-operational).
OTHER ROLES: 1 *Golf* (SLBM trials)
PRINCIPAL SURFACE COMBATANTS: 54:
DESTROYERS: 17:
2 modified *Luda* with 2 × 3 CSS-N-2 *Hai Ying-2* (HY-2 *Styx* derivative) SSM, 1 × 2 130mm guns, 2 Z-9A (Fr *Dauphin*) hel (OTHT), 2 × 3 ASTT.
15 *Luda* (Type-051) (ASUW) with 2 × 3 HY-2 SSM, 2 × 2 130mm guns; plus 2 × 12 ASW RL
FRIGATES: 37:
27 *Jianghu*; 4 variants:
About 13 Type I, with 4 × 5 ASW RL, plus 2 × 2 HY-2 SSM, 2 × 100mm guns.
About 9 Type II, with 2 × 5 ASW RL, plus 2 × 2 HY-2, 2 × 2 100mm guns.
About 3 Type III, with 8 × C-801 SSM, 2 × 2 100mm guns; plus 4 × 5 ASW RL.
About 2 Type IV, with 1 Z-9A hel, 2 × 3 ASTT, 2 × 5 ASW RL, 2 × 2 HY-2 SSM, 1 × 100mm gun.
1 *Jiangdong* with 2 × 5 ASW RL, 2 × 2 CSA-NX-2 SAM, 2 × 2 100mm guns.
5 *Jiangnan* with 2 × 5 ASW RL, 3 × 100mm guns.
4 *Chengdu* with 1 × 2 HY-2 SSM, 3 × 100mm guns.
PATROL AND COASTAL COMBATANTS: About 860:
MISSILE CRAFT: 207:
1 *Huang* with 6 × C-801 SSM.
1 *Houxin* with 4 × C-801 SSM.
Some 115 *Huangfeng/Hola* (Sov *Osa* I-type) with 6 or 8 × C-801 SSM; some with 4 × HY-2.
About 90 *Hegu/Hema*⟨ (*Komar*-Type) with 2 × HY-2 or 4 × C-801 SSM.

TORPEDO CRAFT: About 160:
100 *Huchuan*, some 20 P-4 and 40 P-6, all ⟨ with 2 × 533mm TT.
PATROL: About 490:
COASTAL: About 100:
4 *Haijui* with 3 × 5 ASW RL
About 80 *Hainan* with 4 × ASW RL.
12 Sov *Kronshtadt* with 2 × ASW RL.
INSHORE: About 350:
300 *Shanghai*, 3 *Huludao* PFI, about 50 *Shantou*⟨.
RIVERINE: About 45⟨.
(Note: some minor combatants have reportedly been assigned to paramilitary forces – People's Armed Police, border guards, the militia and to the Customs Service – or into store. Totals therefore may be high.)
MINE WARFARE: About 130:
MINELAYERS: 1 *Beleijan* reported. In addition *Luda, Anshan, Jiangnan* and *Chengdu* class DD/FF, *Hainan, Kronshtadt* and *Shanghai* PC and T-43 MSO have minelaying capability.
MCM: About 130:
35 Sov T-43 MSO.
2 *Wosao* Cl MSC.
About 80 *Lienyun* aux MSC.
10 *Fushun* MSI; plus about 60 drone MSI⟨.
AMPHIBIOUS: 61:
3 *Yukan* LST, capacity about 200 tps, 10 tk.
13 *Shan* (US LST-1) LST, capacity about 150 tps, 16 tk.
30 *Yuliang*, 1 *Yuling*, 4 *Yudao* LSM, capacity about 100 tps, 3 tk.
10 *Hua* (US LSM-1), capacity 50 tps, 4 tk.
Plus about 400 craft: 320 LCU, 40 LCP, 10 LCT and some hovercraft.
SUPPORT AND MISCELLANEOUS: About 150:
2 *Fuqing* AO, 33 AOT, 1 AF, 10 submarine spt, 1 sub rescue, 2 repair, 9 *Qiong Sha* tps tpt, 30 tpt, 33 survey/research/experimental, 4 icebreakers, 25 ocean tugs, 1 trg.

COASTAL REGIONAL DEFENCE FORCES: (27,000).
ε35 indep arty and SSM regt deployed in 25 coastal defence regions to protect naval bases, offshore islands and other vulnerable points.
GUNS: 85mm, 100mm, 130mm.
SSM: CSS-C-2 (*Hai Ying 2* variant, '*Silkworm*').

MARINES: (Naval Infantry): (some 6,000).
1 bde.
Special recce units.
RESERVES: On mob to total 8 div (24 inf, 8 tk, 8 arty regt), 2 indep tk regt.
(3 Army div also have an amph role.)

EQUIPMENT:
MBT: T-59.
LIGHT TANKS: T-60/-63, PT-76.
APC: Type-531, LVT; some Type-77.
ARTY: how: 122mm: Type-54 (incl -54-1 SP).
MRL: Type-63.

NAVAL AIR FORCE: (25,000);
880 shore-based cbt ac, 65 armed hel.
Org in 3 bbr, 6 ftr div, incl:
BOMBERS: some 30 H-6, some H-6D reported with
C-601 anti-ship ALCM.
About 130 H-5 torpedo-carrying lt bbr.
FGA: some 100 Q-5.
FIGHTER: some 600, incl J-5/-6/-7.
RECCE: H-5.
MR/ASW: 15 ex-Sov Be-6 *Madge*, 5 PS-5 (Y-8 mod).
HELICOPTERS: ASW: 15 SA-321, 40 Z-5, 10 Z-9.
MISCELLANEOUS: some 60 lt tpt ac; JJ-5/-6 trg ac.
ALCM: FL-1/C-601.
Naval fighters are integrated into the national
AD system.

DEPLOYMENT AND BASES:
NORTH SEA FLEET: Coastal defence from Korean
border (Yalu River) to south of Lianyungang
(approx 35°10′N); equates to Shenyang, Beijing
and Jinan Military Regions; and to seaward.
BASES: Qingdao (HQ), Dalian (Luda), Huludao,
Weihai, Chengshan.
9 coastal defence districts.
FORCES: 2 submarine, 3 escort, 1 mine warfare, 1
amph sqn; plus Bohai Gulf trg flotillas. About
325 patrol and coastal combatants.
EAST SEA FLEET: Coastal defence from south of
Lianyungang to Dongshan (35°10′N to 23°30′N
approx); equates to Nanjing Military Region, and
to seaward:
BASES: Shanghai (HQ), Wusong, Dinghai, Hangzhou.
7 coastal defence districts.
FORCES: 2 submarine, 2 escort, 1 mine warfare, 1
amph sqn. About 270 patrol and coastal combatants.
Marines: 1 cadre div.
Coastal Regional Defence Forces: Nanjing
Coastal District.
SOUTH SEA FLEET: Coastal defence from
Dongshan (approx 23°30′N) to Vietnam border;
equates to Guangzhou Military Region, and to
seaward (including Paracel and Spratly Islands).
BASES: Zhanjiang (HQ), Shantou, Guangzhou,
Haikou, Yulin, Beihai, Huangpu; plus outposts
on Paracel and Spratly Is.
9 coastal defence districts.
FORCES: 2 submarine, 2 escort, 1 mine warfare, 1
amph sqn. About 320 patrol and coastal combatants.
Marines: 1 bde.

AIR FORCE: 470,000, incl strategic forces and
220,000 AD personnel (160,000 conscripts);

some 4,970 cbt ac, few armed hel.
7 Military Air Regions, HQ Beijing.
Combat elm org in armies of varying numbers of
air div (each with 3 regt of 3 sqn of 3 flt of 4–5
ac, 1 maint unit, some tpt and trg ac).
Tpt ac in regt only.
BOMBERS:
MEDIUM: 120 H-6 (some may be nuclear-capable).
Some carry C-601 ASM.
LIGHT: Some 350 H-5 (some with C-801 ASM).
FGA: 500 Q-5.
FIGHTER: ε4,000, incl 400 J-5, some 60 regt with
about 3,000 J-6/B/D/E, 500 J-7, 100 J-8, 24
Su-27, 4 Su-27B.
RECCE: ε40 HZ-5, 150 JZ-5, 100 JZ-6 ac.
TRANSPORT: some 600, incl 18 BAe *Trident* 1E/2E,
30 Il-14, 10 Il-18, 50 Li-2, 300 Y-5, 25 Y-7, 25
Y-8, 15 Y-11, 2 Y-12.
HELICOPTERS: some 400: incl 6 AS-332, 4 Bell 214,
24 Mi-17, 20 S-70C-2, 30 Mi-8, 250 Z-5, 100
Z-6, 15 Z-8, 50 Z-9.
TRAINING: incl CJ-5/-6, HJ-5, J-2, JJ-2,
JJ-4/-5/-6.
MISSILES:
AAM: PL-2/-2A, PL-5B *Atoll*-type, PL-7.
ASM: HOT: C-601 subsonic ALCM (anti-ship,
perhaps HY-2 SSM derivative); C-801
surface skimmer.
AD ARTY:
16 div: 16,000 35mm, 57mm, 85mm and 100mm
guns;
28 indep AD regts (100 SAM units with
HQ-2/-2B, -2J (CSA-1), -61 SAM).

FORCES ABROAD:
UN AND PEACEKEEPING:
CAMBODIA (UNTAC): 426 incl observers and
engrs.
MIDDLE EAST (UNTSO): 5 Observers.
IRAQ/KUWAIT(UNIKOM): 20 Observers.
WESTERN SAHARA (MINURSO): 20 Observers.

PARAMILITARY: some 12,000,000,
Ministry of Public Security: People's Armed Police:
1.2 million: 60 div, duties incl border and
internal security.

FIJI

GDP	1990: $F 1.82bn ($US 1.23bn)	
	1991ε: $F 1.91bn ($US 1.29bn)	
Growth	1990: 5.3%	1991ε: 3.5%
Inflation	1990: 8.1%	1991: 6.5%
Debt	1989: $US 405.2m	1990: $US 339.1m
Def exp	1989: $F 37.3m ($US 25.15m)	
Def bdgt	1990: $F 38.0m ($US 25.66m)	
	1991: $F 39.4m ($US 26.58m)	

$US 1 = $F 1989: 1.483   1990: 1.481
             1991: 1.476   1992: 1.494
$F = Fiji dollar

Population: 763,400

	13–17	18–22	23–32
Men	41,400	38,400	66,500
Women	39,200	36,800	65,700

TOTAL ARMED FORCES:
ACTIVE: 5,000 (incl recalled reserves).
RESERVES: some 5,000 (to age 45).

ARMY: 4,700 (incl reserves).
   5 inf bn (incl 4 cadre).
   1 engr bn.
EQUIPMENT:
MORTARS: 81mm: 12.

NAVY: 300.
BASE: Suva.
PATROL AND COASTAL COMBATANTS: 6:
   4 *Vai* (Is *Dabur*) PCI⟨.
   2 *Lautoka* PCI⟨.
SUPPORT AND MISCELLANEOUS: 1 *Tovuto* AGHS.

AIR WING:
   1 AS-355, 1 SA-365.

FORCES ABROAD: 1,100.
UN AND PEACEKEEPING:
EGYPT (MFO): 400. 1 inf bn.
IRAQ/KUWAIT (UNIKOM): 12 Observers.
LEBANON (UNIFIL): 718; 1 inf bn.

INDONESIA

GDP	1990:	Rp 197,721bn ($107.29bn)
	1991ε:	Rp 227,463.0bn ($116.63bn)
Growth	1990:	7.4% 1991ε: 5.5%
Inflation	1990:	7.4% 1991: 9.2%
Debt	1989:	$53.11bn 1990: $57.56bn
Def exp	1990:	Rp 2,965.8bn ($1.61bn)
Def bdgt	1991:	Rp 3,015.00bn ($1.55bn)
	1992:	Rp 3,380.00bn ($1.65bn)
FMA[a]	1992:	$7.3m (US)
$1 = Rp	1989:	1,770.1 1990: 1,842.8
	1991:	1,950.3 1992: 2,050

Rp = rupiahs
[a] Incl $5m as Economic Support

Population: 185,647,600

	13–17	18–22	23–32
Men	10,703,400	9,812,600	15,217,700
Women	10,279,200	9,337,800	15,169,200

TOTAL ARMED FORCES:
ACTIVE: 283,000.
   Terms of service: 2 years selective conscription
   authorized.
RESERVES: 400,000: Army (planned): cadre
   units; numbers, strengths unknown, obligation to
   age 45 for officers.

ARMY: 215,000.
Strategic Reserve (KOSTRAD).
   2 inf div HQ.
   3 inf bde (9 bn).
   3 AB bde (9 bn).
   2 fd arty regt (6 bn).
   1 AD arty regt (2 bn).
   2 engr bn
10 Military Area Comd (KODAM)
(Provincial (KOREM) and District (KORIM) comd)
   65 inf bn (incl 4 AB).
   8 cav bn.
   8 fd arty, 8 AD bn.
   8 engr bn.
   1 composite avn sqn, 1 hel sqn.
SF (KOPASSUS): 2 SF gp (each 2 bn).
EQUIPMENT:
LIGHT TANKS: some 125 AMX-13, 30 PT-76†.
RECCE: 60 *Saladin*, 45 *Ferret*.
APC: 200 AMX-VCI, 45 *Saracen*, 200 V-150
   Commando, 20 *Commando Ranger*, 140 BTR-40,
   25 BTR-50.
TOWED ARTY: 76mm: M48; 105mm: 170 M-101.
MORTARS: 81mm: 800; 120mm: 75 Brandt.
RCL: 90mm: 90 M-67; 106mm: 45 M-40A1.
AD GUNS 20mm: 125; 40mm: 90 L/70; 57mm: 200 S-60.
SAM: 50 *Rapier*, 40 RBS-70.
AVIATION:
   AIRCRAFT: 1 BN-2 *Islander*, 2 C-47, 4 NC-212, 2
      Cessna 310, 2 *Commander* 680, 18 *Gelatik* (trg).
   HELICOPTERS: 10 Bell 205, 15 Bo-105, 4 NB-412,
      10 Hughes 300C (trg).
MARINE: LST: 1; **LCU:** 20 300t; 14 tpt.

NAVY: ε44,000, incl ε1,000 Naval Air and
   12,000 Marines.
PRINCIPAL COMMANDS:
WESTERN FLEET (HQ) Jakarta/Tanjung Priok:
BASES: Jakarta, Tanjungpinang (Riau Is.), Sabang,
   Belawan (Sumatra).
EASTERN FLEET (HQ Surabaya);
BASES: Surabaya, Manado (Celebes), Ambon
   (Moluccas), Usung Pandang.
MILITARY SEA TRANSPORT COMMAND:
   (KOLINLAMIL): Controls some amph and tpt
   ships used for inter-island comms.
SUBMARINES: 2 *Cakra* (Ge T-209/1300) with
   533mm TT (Ge HWT).

FRIGATES: 17

6 *Ahmad Yani* (Nl *Van Speijk*) with 1 *Wasp* hel (ASW) (Mk 44 LWT), 2 × 3 ASTT; plus 2 with 2 × 4 *Harpoon* SSM.

3 *Fatahillah* with 2 × 3 ASTT (not *Nala*), 1 × 2 ASW mor, 1 *Wasp* hel (*Nala* only); plus 2 × 2 MM-38 *Exocet*, 1 × 120mm gun.

3 *M.K. Tiyahahu* (UK *Ashanti*) with 1 *Wasp* hel, 1 × 3 *Limbo* ASW mor; plus 2 × 114mm guns.

4 *Samadikun* (US *Claud Jones*) with 2 × 3 ASTT, (probably 3 in store).

1 *Hajar Dewantara* (trg) with 2 × 533mm TT, 1 ASW mor; plus 2 × 2 MM-38 *Exocet*.

PATROL AND COASTAL COMBATANTS: 48:

MISSILE CRAFT: 4 *Mandau* PFM with 4 × MM-38 *Exocet* SSM.

TORPEDO CRAFT: 2 *Singa* (Ge Lürssen 57-m (NAV I)) with 2 × 533mm TT and 1 × 57mm gun.

PATROL: 42:

COASTAL: 8:

2 *Pandrong* (Ge Lürssen 57-m (NAV II)) PFC, with 1 × 57mm gun.

2 *Barakuda* (Sov *Kronshtadt*).

4 *Kakap* (Ge Lürssen 57-m (NAV III)) PFC, with 40mm gun and hel deck.

INSHORE: 34:

3 Yug *Kraljevica* (in reserve), 8 *Siliman* (Aus *Attack*) PCI,

5 *Bima Samudera* PHM, 18⟨.

MINE WARFARE: 2:

2 *Pulau Rengat* (mod Nl *Alkmaar*) MCC (mainly used for coastal patrol).

AMPHIBIOUS: 16:

6 *Teluk Semangka* LST, capacity about 200 tps, 17 tk, 4 with 3 hel (2 fitted as comd ships and 1 as hospital ship).

1 *Teluk Amboina* LST, capacity about 200 tps, 16 tk.

7 *Teluk Langsa* (US LST-512) and 2 *Teluk Banten* (mod US LST-512) LST, capacity: 200 tps, 16 tks).

(3 LST assigned to Mil Sea Tpt Comd.)

Plus about 50 craft: 5 LCU, some 45 LCM.

SUPPORT AND MISCELLANEOUS: 18:

1 *Sorong* AO, 1 cmd/spt, 1 repair, 8 tpt (Mil Sea Tpt Comd), 1 ocean tug, 6 survey/ research.

NAVAL AIR: (ε1,000); 18 cbt ac, 15 armed hel.

ASW: 9 *Wasp* HAS-1 hel.

MR: 12 N-22 *Searchmaster* B, 6 *Searchmaster* L, 6 CN-235-100 IPTN/CASA.

OTHER:

AIRCRAFT: incl 4 *Commander*, 4 NC-212; 2 *Bonanza* F33 (trg), 6 PA-38 (trg).

HELICOPTERS: 4 NAS-332F, *6 NBo-105, 2 SA-313.

MARINES: (12,000);

2 inf bde (6 bn);

1 SF bn(-).

1 cbt spt regt (arty, AD)

EQUIPMENT:

LIGHT TANKS: 80 PT-76†.

RECCE: 20 BRDM.

AIFV: 10 AMX-10 PAC-90.

APC: 100: 25 AMX-10P, 75 BTR-50P.

TOWED ARTY: 122mm: 40 M-38.

MRL: 140mm: BM-14.

AD GUNS: 40mm, 57mm.

AIR FORCE: 24,000;

81 cbt ac, no armed hel.

2 Air Operations Areas:

FGA: 2 sqn with 28 A-4 (26 -E, 2 TA-4H).

1 with 12 F-16 (8 -A, 4 -B).

FIGHTER: 1 sqn with 14 F-5 (10 -E, 4 -F).

COIN: 2 sqn:

1 with 15 *Hawk* Mk 53 (COIN/trg);

1 with 12 OV-10F.

MR: 1 sqn with 3 Boeing 737-200, 1 C-130H-MP.

TANKER: 2 KC-130B.

TRANSPORT:

19 C-130 (9 -B, 3 -H, 7 -H-30), 1-L100-30.

1 Boeing 707, 5 Cessna 401, 2 -402, 7 F-27-400M, 1 F-28-1000, 10 NC-212, 1 *Skyvan* (survey), 30 CN-235M.

HELICOPTERS: 3 sqn:

1 with 12 S-58T;

2 with 2 Bell 204B, 2 -206B, 10 Hughes 500, 12 NBo-105, 13 NSA-330, 3 SE-3160.

TRAINING: 4 sqn with 40 AS-202, 2 Cessna 172, 5 -207 (liaison), 23 T-34C, 10 T-41D.

AIRFIELD DEFENCE: 5 bn *Rapier*.

FORCES ABROAD:

UN AND PEACEKEEPING:

CAMBODIA (UNTAC): 1,180: 1 inf bn.

IRAQ/KUWAIT (UNIKOM): 6 Observers.

PARAMILITARY:

POLICE (POLRI): some 180,000: incl Police 'Mobile bde' (BRIMOB) org in coy: some 8,000 incl Police COIN unit (GEGANA); 3 *Commander*, 1 Beech 18, 7 lt ac; 10 Bo-105, 3 Bell 206 hel.

MARINE: About 10 PCC and 9 PCI and 6 PCI⟨ (all armed).

KAMRA (People's Security): 1.5m: some 300,000 a year get 3 weeks' basic trg. Part-time police auxiliary.

WANRA (People's Resistance): part-time local military auxiliary force under comd of Regional Military Commands (KOREM).

CUSTOMS: About 72 PFI⟨, armed.

MARITIME SECURITY AGENCY: 9 SAR PCI plus boats.

MILITARY SEA TRANSPORT COMMAND
(Transport Ministry):
8 tpt (also listed under Navy).
3 LST (also listed under Navy).
28 LST (for Army use).
Some LCU.

OPPOSITION:
FRETILIN (Revolutionary Front for an Independent
East Timor): some 100 incl spt; small arms.
FREE PAPUA MOVEMENT (OPM): perhaps
500–600 (100 armed).
FREE ACEH MOVEMENT (Gerakan Aceh
Merdeka): 750 armed reported.

JAPAN

GDP	1990:	¥ 425,735bn ($2,940.36bn)	
	1991:	¥ 452,976bn ($3,362.73bn)	
Growth^a	1990:	5.7%	1991ε: 4.2%
Inflation^b	1990:	3.1%	1991: 3.3%
Debt	1990:	$425bn	
Def bdgt^c	1991:	¥ 4,402.3bn ($32.68bn)	
	1992:	¥ 4,551.8bn ($34.30bn)	
$1 = ¥	1989:	137.96	1990: 144.79
	1991:	134.71	1992: 132.70

¥ = yen
^{a} GNP
^{b} Real inflation is higher, national accounting not
considering housing costs which are substantial.
^{c} ¥ 100bn were cut from the 1991 def bdgt to finance
contributions to various countries due to Gulf War.

Population: 124,593,000

	13–17	18–22	23–32
Men	4,562,900	4,798,800	8,671,100
Women	4,370,900	4,589,700	8,329,100

TOTAL ARMED FORCES:
ACTIVE: 246,000 incl Central Staffs (reducing).
RESERVES: Army 46,000; Navy 1,300; Air 1,100.

ARMY: (Ground Self-Defense Force): 156,000
(reducing).
5 Army HQ (Regional Commands).
1 armd div.
12 inf div (5 at 7,000, 7 at 9,000 men each).
2 composite bde.
1 AB bde.
1 arty bde; 2 arty gp.
2 AD bde; 3 AD gp.
4 trg bde; 2 trg regt.
1 hel bde: 24 hel sqn.
2 ATK hel pl, 1 more forming.

EQUIPMENT:
MBT: 1,210: some 307 Type-61 (retiring), some 873
Type-74, 30 Type-90.
RECCE: 67 Type-87.
AIFV: some 17 Type-89.
APC: 300 Type-60, 298 Type-73, some 170 Type-82.
TOWED ARTY: 557: 105mm: 290 M-101;
155mm: 227 FH-70; 203mm: 40 M-115.
SP ARTY: 302: 105mm: 20 Type-74; 155mm: 200
Type-75; 203mm: 82 M-110A2.
MRL: 130mm: some 120 Type-75 SP.
MORTARS: 1,900 incl 81mm: 820 (some SP);
107mm: 560 (some SP).
SSM: 50 Type-30, 16 Type-88 coastal.
ATGW: 220 Type-64, some 128 Type-79, some 72
Type-87.
RL: 89mm: 110 3.5-in M-20.
RCL: 3,130: 75mm; 84mm: *Carl Gustav*; 106mm
(incl Type 60 SP).
AD GUNS: 130: 35mm: 70 twin; 37mm SP; 40mm SP.
SAM: 180 *Stinger*, some 90 Type 81, 200
Improved HAWK.
AVIATION:
AIRCRAFT: 18: 16 LR-1, 2 TL-1 (trg).
HELICOPTERS:
ATTACK: 63 AH-1S;
TRANSPORT: 3 AS-332L (VIP), 23 CH-47J, 39
KV-107, 189 OH-6D/J, 141 UH-1B/H; 33
TH-55 (trg).

NAVY: (Maritime Self-Defense Force): 44,000
(including ε12,000 MSDF air).
BASES: Yokosuka, Kure, Sasebo, Maizuru, Ominato.
Fleet: Surface Units org into 4 escort flotillas, of
6–8 DD/FF each; based at Yokosuka (2), Sasebo
and Maizuru. Submarines org into 2 flotillas
based at Kure and Yokosuka. Remainder
assigned to 10 regional/district units.
SUBMARINES: 17:
TACTICAL SUBMARINES: 13:
2 *Harushio* with 533mm TT (Jap Type-89 HWT)
with *Harpoon* USGW.
10 *Yuushio* with 533mm TT (US Mk 37, GRX-2
HWT), 7 with *Harpoon* USGW.
1 *Uzushio* with 533mm TT (Mk 37 HWT).
OTHER ROLES: 4: 3 *Uzushio* (trg), 1 *Uzushio* (trials).
PRINCIPAL SURFACE COMBATANTS: 64:
DESTROYERS: 6 DDG:
2 *Hatakaze* with 1 × SM-1-MR *Standard* SAM;
plus 2 × 4 *Harpoon* SSM, 1 × 8 *ASROC*
SUGW (Mk 46 LWT) 2 × 3 ASTT, 2 ×
127mm guns.
3 *Tachikaze* with 1 × SM-1-MR; plus 1 × 8
ASROC, 2 × 3 ASTT, 8 × *Harpoon*, 2 ×
127mm guns.
1 *Amatsukaze* with 1 × SM-1-MR; plus 1 × 8
ASROC, 2 × 3 ASTT.
FRIGATES: 58: (incl 5 training):

FFH: 24:

2 *Shirane* with 3 × SH-60J *Sea Hawk* ASW hel, 1 × 8 *ASROC*, 2 × 3 ASTT; plus 2 × 127mm guns.

2 *Haruna* with 3 × *Sea King* hel, 1 × 8 *ASROC*, 2 × 3 ASTT; plus 2 × 127mm guns.

8 *Asagiri* with 1 *Sea King* hel, 1 × 8 *ASROC*, 2 × 3 ASTT; plus 2 × 4 *Harpoon* SSM.

12 *Hatsuyuki* with 1 *Sea King*, 1 × 8 *ASROC*, 2 × 3 ASTT; plus 2 × 4 *Harpoon* SSM.

FF: 34:

4 *Abukuma* with 1 × 8 *ASROC*, 2 × 3 ASTT; plus 2 × 4 *Harpoon* SSM.

4 *Takatsuki* with 1 × 8 *ASROC*, 2 × 3 ASTT, 1 × 4 ASW RL; plus 2 with 2 × 4 *Harpoon* SSM, 1 × 127mm gun; 2 with 2 × 127mm guns.

4 *Yamagumo* with 1 × 8 *ASROC*, 2 × 3 ASTT, 1 × 4 ASW RL.

3 *Minegumo* with 1 × 8 *ASROC*, 2 × 3 ASTT, 1 × 4 ASW RL.

2 *Yubari* with 2 × 3 ASTT, 1 × 4 ASW RL; plus 2 × 4 *Harpoon* SSM.

1 *Ishikari* with 2 × 3 ASTT, 1 × 4 ASW RL; plus 2 × 4 *Harpoon* SSM.

11 *Chikugo* with 1 × 8 *ASROC*, 2 × 3 ASTT.

4 *Isuzu* (trg) with 1 × 4 ASW RL; plus 4 × 2 76mm gun.

1 *Katori* (trg) with 2 × 3 ASTT, 1 × ASW RL.

PATROL AND COASTAL COMBATANTS: 11:

TORPEDO CRAFT: 2 *Juichi-go* PFT with 4 × 533mm TT.

PATROL: 9 *Jukyu-go* PCI⟨.

MINE WARFARE: 43:

MINELAYERS: 1:

1 *Souya* (460 mines) plus hel deck, 2 × 3 ASTT, also MCM spt/comd.

MINE COUNTERMEASURES: 42:

1 *Hayase* MCM cmd with hel deck, 2 × 3 ASTT, plus minelaying capacity (116 mines).

25 *Hatsushima*, 5 *Takami* MCC.

4 *Nana-go* MSI⟨.

6 *Takami* coastal diver spt ships (ex MSC).

1 *Utone* coastal MCM spt.

AMPHIBIOUS: 6:

3 *Miura* LST, capacity 200 tps, 10 tk.

3 *Atsumi* LST, capacity 130 tps, 5 tk.

Plus craft; 4 LCT, 15 LCM, 21 LCVP.

SUPPORT AND MISCELLANEOUS: 18:

3 *Towada*, 1 *Sagami* AOE, 2 sub rescue, 2 *Akizuki* trg, 2 trg spt, 7 survey/experimental, 1 icebreaker.

MSDF AIR ARM: (12,000);

99 cbt ac (plus 15 in store), 72 armed hel.

7 Air Groups.

MR: 8 sqn:

7 (1 trg) with 66 P-3C (plus 15 in store);

1 with 10 P-2J.

ASW: 6 hel sqn (1 trg) with 81 HSS-2A/B, plus 24 in store.

MCM: 3 hel sqn with 5 KV-107A, 12 S-80.

EW: 1 sqn with 2 EP-2J, 2 EP-3C.

TRANSPORT: 1 sqn with 4 YS-11M.

TEST: 1 sqn with 3 P-3C, 3 UP-2J, 4 U-36A ac; 2 HSS-2B, 2 SH-60J hel.

SAR: 1 sqn (7 flt) with 8 US-1/1A.

3 rescue sqn with 10 S-61 hel.

TRAINING: 9 sqn with 30 KM-2, 10* P-3C, 22 *Queen Air* 65, 8 T-5, 23 TC-90/UC-90, 10 YS-11T ac; 10 HSS-2A/B, 12 OH-6D/J hel.

AIR FORCE: (Air Self-Defense Force): 46,000;

440 cbt ac (plus 54 in store), no armed hel.

7 cbt air wings; 1 cbt air unit; 1 recce gp; 1 AEW unit.

FGA: 3 sqn with 73 F-1.

1 with 21 F-4EJ (anti-ship).

FIGHTER: 10 sqn:

7 with 158 F-15J/DJ.

3 with 72 F-4EJ (being upgraded); 50 more in store.

RECCE: 1 sqn with 10 RF-4EJ. 4 more in store.

AEW: 1 sqn with 12 E-2C.

EW: 1 flt with 1 C-1, 4 YS-11.

AGGRESSOR TRAINING: 1 sqn with 20 T-2, 2 T-33.

TRANSPORT: 5 sqn:

3 with 30 C-1, 15 C-130H, 10 YS-11;

2 heavy-lift hel sqn with 10 CH-47J.

2 747-400 (VIP).

SAR: 1 wing (10 det) with 30 MU-2 ac; 22 KV-107, 6 CH-47J hel. (UH-60J hel being delivered.)

CALIBRATION: 1 wing with 2 MU-2J, 1 YS-11.

TRAINING: 5 wings: 10 sqn: 40* T-1A/B, 64* T-2, 40 T-3, 60 T-4, 10 T-33A (to be replaced by T-4).

LIAISON: 11 *Queen Air* 65, 126 T-33.

TEST: 1 wing with C-1, 3 F-4EJ, F-15J.

MISSILES:

ASM: ASM-1.

AAM: AAM-1, AIM-7 *Sparrow*, AIM-9 *Sidewinder*.

AIR DEFENCE:

Ac control and warning: 4 wings; 30 radar sites.

SAM: 6 AD msl gp (18 sqn) with 180 *Nike*-J (*Patriot* replacing).

Air Base Defense Gp with 20mm *Vulcan* AA guns, Type 81 *Tan*, *Stinger* SAM.

PARAMILITARY:

MARITIME SAFETY AGENCY: (Coast Guard) 12,000:

PATROL VESSELS: Some 335:

OFFSHORE: (over 1,000 tons): 48, incl 1 *Shikishima* with 2 *Super Puma* hel, 2 *Mizuho* with 2 Bell 212, 8 *Soya* with 1 Bell 212 hel and 2 *Izu* and 28 *Shiretoko*.

COASTAL: 11 (under 1,000 tons): 36.

INSHORE: about 244: 3 PFI, 15 PCI, some 225⟨.

MISCELLANEOUS: 90 service, 81 tender/trg vessels;

AIRCRAFT: 5 NAMC YS-11A, 2 Short *Skyvan*, 16 *King Air*, 1 Cessna U-206G.

HELICOPTERS: 32 Bell 212, 4 Bell 206, 2 Hughes 369.

FOREIGN FORCES:

US: 39,300: Army (2,200): 1 Corps HQ; Navy (5,500) bases at Yokosuka (HQ 7th Fleet) and Sasebo; Marines (21,300): 1 MEF in Okinawa; Air (10,300): 1 Air HQ, 96 cbt ac.

KOREA: DEMOCRATIC PEOPLE'S REPUBLIC (NORTH)

GNP*a*	1990ε:	won 47.8bn ($22.76bn)	
	1991ε:	won 45.0bn ($20.45bn)	
Growth	1991ε:	−5%	
Inflation	1990ε: 2%		1991ε: 2%
Debt	1990:	$6.78bn	1991: $8.30bn
Def exp	1991ε:	won 12.0bn ($5.45bn)	
Def bdgt	1991ε:	won 5.20bn ($2.36bn)	
	1992ε:	won 6.00bn ($2.75bn)	
$1 = won*b*	1988:	0.956	1989: 0.977
	1990:	0.995	1991: 1.000

---

a Dollar figures reflect the real value of the economy and mark a departure from the use of official exchange rates to a more realistic commercial rate.
b Official exchange rate; commercial rate $1 = 2.20 Won (1991)

Population: 23,760,000

	13–17	*18–22*	*23–32*
Men	1,309,000	1,195,000	1,993,000
Women	1,252,000	1,158,000	2,028,000

TOTAL ARMED FORCES:

ACTIVE: 1,132,000.

Terms of service: Army 5–8 years; Navy 5–10 years; Air Force 3–4 years, followed by compulsory part-time service in the Pacification Corps to age 40. Thereafter service in the Worker/Peasant Red Guard to age 60.

RESERVES: Army 500,000, Navy 40,000. Mob claimed in 12 hours; up to 5,000,000 have some Reserve/Militia commitment. See Paramilitary.

ARMY: 1,000,000.

15 Corps (1 armd, 4 mech, 8 inf, 1 arty, 1 capital defence)
30 inf/mot inf div.
15 armd bde.
20 mot/mech inf bde.
4 indep inf bde.
1 Special Purpose Corps: 60,000: 22 bde incl 3 cdo, 4 recce, 1 river crossing regt, 3 amph, 3 AB bn, 22 lt inf bn. 'Bureau of Reconnaissance SF' (8 bn).

Arty:
Army tps: 8 hy arty bde (incl MRL).
Corps tps: 14 bde incl 122mm, 152mm SP, MRL.

RESERVE: Pacification Corps: some 1.2m. 22–26 inf div, 18 inf bde.

EQUIPMENT:

MBT: some 3,000: 300 T-34, 900 T-54/-55, 1,800 T-62, Type-59.
LIGHT TANKS: 500 Type-63, 50 Type-62, M-1985.
RECCE: 140 BA-64.
AIFV: 200 BMP-1/BMP-2.
APC: 4,000 BTR-40/-50/-60/-152, Ch Type-531, N. Korean Type M-1973.
TOWED ARTY: 2,300: 76mm: M-1942; 85mm: D-44/SD-44; 100mm: M-1944; 122mm: M-1931/-37, D-74, Type-54, Type-60, D-30; 130mm: M-46, Ch Type-59; 152mm: M-1937 M-1938, M-1943, Ch Type-66.
SP ARTY: Some 4,500: 122mm: M-1981, M-1985; 130mm: M-1975; 152mm: M-1974, M-1977; 180mm: M-1978.
MRL: 2,400: 107mm: Type-63; 122mm: BM-21, 240mm: BM-24.
MORTARS: 9,000: 82mm: M-37; 120mm: M-43.
SSM: 54 *FROG*-3/-5/-7; some 15 *Scud* B/-C.
ATGW: AT-1 *Snapper*, AT-3 *Sagger*.
RCL: 107mm: 1,000 B-11.
AD GUNS: 8,800: 14.5mm: ZPU-2/-4 SP; 23mm: ZU-23, ZSU-23-4 SP; 37mm: Ch Type-55, M-1939; 57mm: ZSU-57-2 SP, S-60, Ch Type-59; 85mm: KS-12; 100mm: KS-19. N. Korean SP AA, type unknown.
SAM: 5,000+ HN-5A (SA-7 type).

NAVY: ε40,000.

BASES: East Coast: Toejo (HQ), Changjon, Munchon, Songjon-pardo, Mugye-po, Mayang-do, Chehollodongjagu, Puan-Dong, Najin.
West Coast: Nampo (HQ), Pipaqo, Sagwon-ri, Chodo-ri, Koampo, Tasali.
2 Fleet HQ.

SUBMARINES: 26:
22 Ch Type-031/Sov *Romeo* with 533mm TT
4 *Sov Whiskey* with 533mm and 406mm TT.
(plus some 48 midget submarines mainly used for SF ops, but some with 2 × TT).

FRIGATES: 3:
1 *Soho* with 4 × ASW RL, plus 4 × SS-N-2 *Styx* SSM, 1 × 100mm gun.
2 *Najin* with 2 × 5 ASW RL, 1 with 3 × 533mm TT; plus 2 × 100mm guns. 2 SS-N-2 *Styx* SSM.

PATROL AND COASTAL COMBATANTS: 379:

CORVETTES: 3 *Sariwon* with 1 × 100mm gun.
MISSILE CRAFT: 39:
11 *Soju*, 8 Sov *Osa*, 4 Ch *Huangfeng* PFM with 4 × SS-N-2 *Styx*
6 *Sohung*, 10 Sov *Komar* PFM⟨ with 2 × SS-N-2.

TORPEDO CRAFT: 173:
3 Sov *Shershen* with 4 × 533mm TT.
Some 170⟨ with 2 × 533mm TT.
PATROL: 164:
COASTAL: 16: 6 *Hainan* PFC with 4 × ASW RL,
10 *Taechong*.
INSHORE: some 148:
13 SO-1, 12 *Shanghai* II, 3 *Chodo*, some
120⟨.
MINE WARFARE: About 23 MSI⟨.
AMPHIBIOUS: craft only; 24 LCM, 7 LCU, about
100 LCVP⟨ plus about 60 hovercraft.
SUPPORT AND MISCELLANEOUS: 7: 2 ocean
tugs, 1 AS, 4 survey.
COAST DEFENCE: SSM: 2 regt: *Samlet* in 6 sites;
GUNS: 122mm: M-1931/-37; 130mm: SM-4-1;
152mm: M-1937.

AIR FORCE: 92,000;
732 cbt ac, 50 armed hel.
BOMBERS: 3 lt regt with 80 H-5.
FGA: 10 regt:
5 with 150 J-5;
3 with 100 J-6;
1 with 40 Q-5;
1 with 20 Su-7, 36 Su-25.
FIGHTER: 12 regt:
2 with 80 J-5;
2 with 60 J-6;
1 with 40 J-7;
4 with 120 MiG-21;
2 with 46 MiG-23;
1 with 30 MiG-29.
ATTACK HELICOPTERS: 50 Mi-24.
TRANSPORT:
AIRCRAFT: 10 An-24, 5 Il-14, 5 Il-18, 4 Il-62M, 2
Tu-134, 4 Tu-154, 250 Y-5.
HELICOPTERS: 1 Hughes 300C, 80 -500D, 6
-500E, 100 Mi-2, 60 Mi-8/17, 30 Z-5.
TRAINING: incl 120 CJ-5, 30 CJ-6, *H-5, 50
MiG-15UTI, *MiG-19U, 10* MiG-21U,
Yak-11.
AAM: AA-2 *Atoll*, AA-7 *Apex*.
SAM: 4 bde (12 bn, 40 bty) with 72 SA-2 in 45 sites,
2 regt with ε32 SA-3, 2 regt with ε72 SA-5.

FORCES ABROAD: Advisers in some 12
African countries.

PARAMILITARY:
SECURITY TROOPS (Ministry of Public Security):
115,000 incl Border guards.
WORKER/PEASANT RED GUARD: some 3.8m.
Org on a provincial/town/village basis. Comd
structure is bde – bn – coy – pl. Small arms with
some mor and AD guns (but many units
unarmed).

KOREA: REPUBLIC OF (SOUTH)

GDP	1990: won 172,724bn ($244.04bn)	
	1991: won 207,517bn ($282.97bn)	
Growth	1990: 9.2%	1991: 8.4%
Inflation	1990: 8.6%	1991: 9.7%
Debt	1990: $34.00bn	1991: $38.20bn
Def bdgt	1991: won 7,900.0bn ($10.77bn)	
	1992: won 9,470bn ($12.35bn)	
$1 = won	1989: 671.46	1990: 707.76
	1991: 733.35	1992: 766.5

Population: 44,908,400

	13–17	*18–22*	*23–32*
Men	2,127,100	2,204,000	4,509,800
Women	2,032,400	2,078,000	4,231,400

TOTAL ARMED FORCES:
ACTIVE: 633,000.
Terms of service: conscription, Army 26 months,
Navy and Air Force 30 months, then First
Combat Forces (Mobilization Reserve Forces)
or Regional Combat Forces (Homeland
Defence Forces) to age 33.
RESERVES: 4,500,000; being reorganized.

ARMY: 520,000.
HQ: 3 Army, 9 Corps.
3 mech inf div (each 3 bde: 3 mech inf,
3 tk, 1 recce, 1 engr bn; 1 fd arty bde).
19 inf div (each 3 inf regt, 1 recce, 1 tk,
1 engr bn; 1 arty regt (4 bn)).
2 indep inf bde.
7 SF bde.
3 counter-infiltration bde.
3 SSM bn with NHK-I/-II (*Honest John*).
3 AD arty bde.
3 *HAWK* bn (24 sites), 2 *Nike Hercules* bn (10
sites).
1 avn comd.
RESERVES: 1 Army HQ, 23 inf div.
EQUIPMENT:
MBT: 1,800: 450 Type 88, 400 M-47, 950 M-48.
AIFV: some 1,000 (KIFV).
APC: some 1,550 incl 300 M-113, 275 Fiat
6614/KM-900/-901.
TOWED ARTY: some 4,000: 105mm: M-101, KH-178;
155mm: M-53, M-114, KH-179; 203mm: M-115.
SP ARTY: 500: 155mm: M-109A2; 175mm: M-107;
203mm: M-110
MRL: 130mm: 140 *Kooryong* (36-tube).
MORTARS: 5,300: 81mm: KM-29; 107mm: M-30.
SSM: 12 NHK-I/-II.
ATGW: *TOW*.
RCL: 57mm, 75mm, 90mm: M67; 106mm: M40A2.
ATK GUNS: 76mm: 8 M-18; 90mm: 50 M-36 SP.

AD GUNS: 600: 20mm: incl 60 M-167 *Vulcan*; 35mm: 20 GDF-003; 40mm: 80 L60/70, M-1.

SAM: 350 *Javelin*, 60 *Redeye*, 130 *Stinger*, 110 *HAWK*, 200 *Nike Hercules*.

AVIATION:

AIRCRAFT: 10 O-1A.

HELICOPTERS:

ATTACK: 65 AH-1F/-J, 70 Hughes 500 MD.

TRANSPORT: 15 CH-47D.

UTILITY: 175 Hughes 500, 125 UH-1H, 5 UH-60, 30 UH-23.

NAVY: 60,000 (ε19,000 conscripts) incl 25,000 marines.

BASES: Chinhae (HQ), Cheju, Inchon, Mokpo, Mukho, Pukpyong, Pohang, Pusan.
3 Fleet Commands.

SUBMARINES: 4: 3 KSS-1 *Tolgorae* SSI (175t) with 2 × 406mm TT.
1 Ge T-209/1400 with 8 × 533 TT.

PRINCIPAL SURFACE COMBATANTS: 38:

DESTROYERS: 9:

7 *Chung Buk* (US *Gearing*) with 2 or 3 × 2 127mm guns; plus 2 × 3 ASTT; 5 with 2 × 4 *Harpoon* SSM, 1 *Alouette* III hel (OTHT), 2 with 1 × 8 *ASROC*.

2 *Dae Gu* (US *Sumner*) with 3 × 2 127mm guns; plus 2 × 3 ASTT, 1 *Alouette III* hel.

FRIGATES: 29:

7 *Ulsan* with 2 × 3 ASTT (Mk 46 LWT); plus 2 × 4 *Harpoon* SSM.

22 *Po Hang* with 2 × 3 ASTT; some with 2 × 1 MM-38 *Exocet*.

PATROL AND COASTAL COMBATANTS: 81:

CORVETTES: 4 *Dong Hae* (ASW) with 2 × 3 ASTT.

MISSILE CRAFT: 11:

8 *Pae Ku*-52, 3 with 4 *Standard* (boxed) SSM, 5 with 2 × 2 *Harpoon* SSM.

1 *Pae Ku*-51 (US *Asheville*), with 2 × *Standard* SSM.

2 *Kilurki-71* (*Wildcat*) with 2 × MM-38 *Exocet* SSM.

PATROL, INSHORE: 66:

32 *Kilurki-11* ('*Sea Dolphin*') 33-m PFI.

34 *Chebi-51* ('*Sea Hawk*') 26-m PFI⟨ (some with 2 × MM-38 *Exocet* SSM).

MINE WARFARE: 10:

3 '*Kang Kyong*' (mod It *Lerici*) MHC.

7 *Kun San* (US MSC-268/289) MSC.

AMPHIBIOUS: 14:

7 *Un Bong* (US LST-511) LST, capacity 200 tps, 16 tk.

7 *Ko Mun* (US LSM-1) LSM, capacity 50 tps, 4 tk.

Plus about 36 craft; 6 LCT, 10 LCM, about 20 LCVP.

SUPPORT AND MISCELLANEOUS: 11:

3 spt tankers, 2 ocean tugs, 2 salv/div spt, about 4 survey (civil manned, Ministry of Transport funded).

NAVAL AIR: 15 cbt ac; 47 armed hel.

ASW: 2 sqn:

1 ac with 15 S-2E;

1 hel with 25 Hughes 500MD (maritime patrol);

10 flt with 10 SA-316 hel (maritime patrol), 2 Bell 206 (liaison), 12 *Lynx* (ASW).

Lynx being delivered; to replace SA-316.

MARINES: (25,000).

2 div, 1 bde.

Spt units.

EQUIPMENT:

MBT: 40 M-47.

APC: 60 LVTP-7.

TOWED ARTY: 105mm, 155mm.

SSM: *Harpoon* (truck-mounted).

AIR FORCE: 53,000;

403 cbt ac plus 52 in store, no armed hel. 7 cbt, 2 tpt wings.

FGA: 8 sqn:

2 with 48 F-16 (36 -C, 12 -D),

6 with 142 F-5 (42-A, 100 -E) plus 16 in store.

FIGHTER: 4 sqn with 96 F-4D/E. Plus 36 in store.

COIN: 1 sqn with 23 A-37B, 6 T-28D.

FAC: 20 O-1, 10 O-2A, 25 OA-37B.

RECCE: 1 sqn with 18 RF-4C, 10 RF-5A.

SAR: 1 hel sqn with 15 Bell UH-1B, 2 UH-1N.

TRANSPORT: 2 wings, 5 sqn:

AIRCRAFT: 2 BAe 748 (VIP), 1 Boeing 737-300 (VIP), 9 C-54, 1 C-118, 10 C-123J/K, 10 C-130H, 3 *Commander*.

HELICOPTERS: 7 Bell 212, 3 -412, 5 UH-1D, 5 -H.

TRAINING: 25* F-5B, 35* -F, 25 T-33A, 14 T-37, 20 T-41D.

MISSILES:

ASM: AGM-65A *Maverick*.

AAM: AIM-7 *Sparrow*, AIM-9 *Sidewinder*.

PARAMILITARY:

CIVILIAN DEFENCE CORPS (to age 50): 3,500,000.

COAST GUARD: (ε3,500)

PATROL CRAFT: 75:

PATROL CRAFT, OFFSHORE: 13:

1 *Mazinger* (HDP-1000) (CG flagship).

6 *Han Kang* (HDC-1150)

6 *Sea Dragon/Whale* (HDP-600)

COASTAL: 24:

22 *Sea Wolf/Shark*

2 *Bukhansan*

INSHORE: 38: 18 *Seagull*; about 20⟨, plus numerous boats.

HELICOPTERS: 9 Hughes 500D.

FOREIGN FORCES:
US: 35,500. Army (26,500): 1 army HQ, 1 inf div. Air Force (9,000): 1 Air Force HQ: 2 wings: 84 cbt ac.

LAOS

GDP	1989	kip 291.60bn ($526.19m)	
	1990ε:	kip 379.08bn ($521.83m)	
Growth	1990:	9.1%	
Inflation	1990:	18.6%	1991ε: 15%
Debt	1989:	$949.00m	1990: $1.06bn
Def bdgt	1989ε:	kip 10.5bn ($18.94m)	
$1 = kip	1989:	554.17	1990: 726.44
	1991:	714.00	1992: 710.0

Population: 4,305,800

	13–17	*18–22*	*23–32*
Men	252,300	234,700	296,200
Women	247,400	235,500	302,000

TOTAL ARMED FORCES:
ACTIVE: 37,000.
Terms of service: conscription, 18 months minimum.

ARMY: 33,000.
4 Military Regions	5 arty, 9 AD arty bn.
5 inf div	65 indep inf coy.
7 indep inf regt	1 lt ac liaison flt.
3 engr (2 construction) regt.	

EQUIPMENT:
MBT: 30 T-54/-55, T-34/85.
LIGHT TANKS: 25 PT-76.
APC: 70 BTR-40/-60/-152.
TOWED ARTY: 75mm: M-116 pack; 105mm: 25 M-101; 122mm: 40 M-1938 and D-30; 130mm: 10 M-46; 155mm: M-114.
MORTARS: 81mm; 82mm; 107mm: M-2A1, M-1938; 120mm: M-43.
RCL: 57mm: M-18/A1; 75mm: M-20; 106mm: M-40; 107mm: B-11.
AD GUNS: 14.5mm: ZPU-1/-4; 23mm: ZU-23, ZSU-23-4 SP; 37mm: M-1939; 57mm: S-60.
SAM: SA-3, SA-7.

NAVY: ε500.
PATROL CRAFT, river: some 8 PCI‹, 4 LCM and about 50 patrol boats‹.

AIR FORCE: 3,500;
31† cbt ac; no armed hel.
FGA: 1 regt with some 29 MiG-21.
TRANSPORT: 1 sqn with 5 An-24, 2 An-26, 2 Yak-40.

HELICOPTERS: 1 sqn with 2 Mi-6, 10 Mi-8.
TRAINING: *2 MiG-21U.
AAM: AA-2 *Atoll.*

PARAMILITARY:
MILITIA SELF-DEFENCE FORCES: 100,000+: village 'homeguard' org for local defence.

OPPOSITION:
Numerous factions/groups. Total armed strength ε2,000. Largest group United Lao National Liberation Front (ULNLF).

MALAYSIA

GDP	1989:	$M 101.54bn ($US 37.48bn)	
	1990:	$M 114.616bn ($US 42.37bn)	
Growth	1990:	9.8%	1991ε: 8.5%
Inflation	1990:	3.1%	1991: 4.5%
Debt	1989:	$US 19.17bn	1990: $US 19.50bn
Def bdgt	1991:	$M 4.73bn ($US 1.72bn)	
	1992:	$M 5.0bn ($US 1.94bn)	
Def exp	1990:	$M 4.68bn ($1.7bn)	
FMA	1992:	$1.1m (US)	
$US1 = $M	1989:	2.709	1990: 2.705
	1991:	2.750	1992: 2.580
$M = ringgit			

Population: 18,076,400

	13–17	*18–22*	*23–32*
Men	966,500	880,200	1,617,100
Women	925,300	846,000	1,568,200

TOTAL ARMED FORCES:
ACTIVE: 127,500.
RESERVES: 44,300: Army 41,000; Navy 2,700; Air 600.

ARMY: 105,000 (reducing to 85,000).
2 Military Regions, 1 corps, 4 div HQ.
10 inf bde, consisting of 36 inf bn (1 APC, 2 AB), 4 armd, 5 fd arty, 1 AD arty, 5 engr regt. 1 SF regt (3 bn).
RESERVES: 1 div HQ; 1 bde HQ; 12 inf regt; 4 highway sy bn.
EQUIPMENT:
LIGHT TANKS: 26 *Scorpion* (90mm).
RECCE: 156 SIBMAS, 140 AML-60/-90, 92 *Ferret* (60 mod).
APC: 184 V-100/-150 *Commando*, 25 *Stormer*, 460 *Condor*, 32 M-3 *Panhard*.
TOWED ARTY: 105mm: 150 Model 56 pack, 40 M-102A1 († in store); 155mm: 9 FH-70.

MORTARS: 81mm: 300.
ATGW: SS-11.
RL: 89mm: M-20.
RCL: 84mm: *Carl Gustav*; 106mm: 150 M-40;
    120mm: 5 *Wombat*.
AD GUNS: 35mm: 8 Oerlikon; 40mm: 36 L40/70.
SAM: 48 *Javelin*, 12 *Rapier*.
ASSAULT CRAFT: 165 Damen.

NAVY: 10,500.
Two Regional Commands: plus Fleet.
    Area 1: Malayan Peninsula (west of 109°E).
    Area 2: Borneo Area (east of 109°E).
BASES: Area 1: Lumut (HQ), Tanjong Gelang,
    Kuantan; Woodlands (Singapore), trg base.
Area 2: Labuan (HQ), Sungei Antu (Sarawak).
FRIGATES: 4:
    2 *Kasturi* (FS-1500) with 2 × 2 ASW mor, deck
        for *Wasp* hel; plus 2 × 2 MM-38 *Exocet* SSM,
        1 × 100mm gun.
    1 *Hang Tuah* (UK *Mermaid*) with 1 × 3 *Limbo*
        ASW mor, hel deck for *Wasp*; plus 1 × 2
        102mm gun.
    1 *Rahmat* with 1 × 3 ASW mor, 1 × 114mm gun
        hel deck.
PATROL AND COASTAL COMBATANTS: 37:
MISSILE CRAFT: 8
    4 *Handalan* (Sw *Spica*) with 4 MM-38 *Exocet* SSM.
    4 *Perdana* (Fr *Combattante* II) with 2 *Exocet* SSM.
PATROL: 29:
    OFFSHORE: 2 *Musytari* with 1 × 100mm gun,
        hel deck.
    INSHORE: 27: 6 *Jerong* PFI, 3 *Kedah*, 4 *Sabah*, 14
        Kris PCI.
MINE WARFARE: 5:
    4 *Mahamiru* (mod It *Lerici*) MCO.
    1 diving tender (inshore).
AMPHIBIOUS: 2:
    2 *Sri Banggi* (US LST-511) LST, capacity 200
        tps, 16 tk (but usually employed as tenders to
        patrol craft).
    Plus 33 craft: 5 LCM, 13 LCU, 15 LCP.
SUPPORT AND MISCELLANEOUS: 3:
    2 logistic/fuel spt, 1 survey.

NAVAL AIR:
    No cbt ac, 6 armed hel.
HELICOPTERS: 6 *Wasp* HAS-1.

AIR FORCE: 12,000;
    69 cbt ac, no armed hel; 4 Comd.
FGA: 2 sqn: with 33 A-4 (27 A-4PTM, 6 TA-4);
FIGHTER: 1 sqn with 13 F-5E, 4 -F.
RECCE: 1 recce/OCU sqn with 2 RF-5E, 2 F-5F.
MR: 1 sqn with 3 C-130HMP.
TRANSPORT:
    AIRCRAFT: 4 sqn:

1 with 5 C-130H;
2 with 14 DHC-4;
1 with 2 BAe-125 (VIP), 1 *Falcon*-900 (VIP), 2
    HU-16 (1 tpt, 1 VIP), 12 Cessna 402B ac; 1
    NAS-332 hel.
HELICOPTERS: 4 sqn with 30 S-61A, 20
    SA-316A/B (liaison), 3 AS-322.
TRAINING: 4 trg units:
    AIRCRAFT: 11* MB-339, 40 PC-7 (4* wpn trg);
    HELICOPTERS: 8 SE-3160, 5 Bell 47, 4 S-61.
AAM: AIM-9 *Sidewinder*.
AIRFIELD DEFENCE TROOPS: 1 sqn.

FORCES ABROAD:
UN AND PEACEKEEPING:
ANGOLA (UNAVEM II): 15 Observers.
CAMBODIA (UNTAC): 887: 1 inf bn.
IRAQ/KUWAIT (UNIKOM): 7 Observers.
WESTERN SAHARA (MINURSO): 1 Observer.

PARAMILITARY:
POLICE FIELD FORCE: 18,000; 4 bde HQ: 21 bn
    (incl 2 Aboriginal); *Shorland* armd cars, 140
    AT-105 *Saxon*, SB-301 APC.
MARINE POLICE: 48 Inshore Patrol Craft:
    15 *Lang Hitam* (38-m) PFI
    6 *Sangitan* (29-m) PFI
    27 PCI⟨ plus boats.
POLICE AIR WING: 4 Cessna 206, 7 PC-6 ac, 1
    Bell 206L3, 2 AS-355F2.
AUXILIARY POLICE FIELD FORCE: (Area Security
    Units), 3,500 men in 89 units.
BORDER SCOUTS (in Sabah, Sarawak): 1,200.
PEOPLE'S VOLUNTEER CORPS (RELA):
    200,000.
CUSTOMS SERVICE: 56 patrol craft: 6 *Perak*
    (Vosper 32-m) armed PFI, about 50 craft⟨.

FOREIGN FORCES:
AUSTRALIA: Army: 1 inf coy. Air Force: det with
    P-3C ac.

MONGOLIA

GDP	1987ε: t 7.71bn ($2.30bn)	
	1988ε: t 8.10bn ($2.41bn)	
Growth	1990ε: 0%	1991ε: −13%
Inflation	1990ε: 90.0%	
Debt	1990ε: $2.00bn	1991: $2.5bn
Def exp	1987: t 837.0m ($249.44m)	
Def bdgt	1992: t 914.2m ($130.0m)	
$1 = t[a]	1986–91: 3.355	

t = tugrik
[a] Several devaluations in 1991 brought official rate
down to $1 = t5.6 at beginning of 1991. Black
market rates as high as $1 = t120.

Population: 2,265,200

	13–17	18–22	23–32
Men	127,300	113,500	180,100
Women	124,000	112,200	180,400

TOTAL ARMED FORCES:
ACTIVE: 15,500 (perhaps 11,000 conscripts).
Terms of service: Conscription: males 18–28 years; 2 years.
RESERVES: Army 200,000.

ARMY: 14,000 (perhaps 11,000 conscripts).
4 MRD (understrength).
EQUIPMENT:
MBT: 650 T-54/-55/-62.
RECCE: 135 BRDM-2.
AIFV: 420 BMP-1.
APC: 300 BTR-40/-60/-152.
TOWED ARTY: 300: 122mm: M-1938/D-30; 130mm: M-46; 152mm: M-1937.
MRL: 122mm: 135+ BM-21.
MORTARS: 140: 82mm, 120mm, 160mm.
ATK GUNS: 100mm: T-12.
AD GUNS: 100: 14.5mm: ZPU-4; 37mm: M-1939; 57mm: S-60.
SAM: 300 SA-7.

AIR FORCE: 1,500; 15 cbt ac; 10 armed hel.
FIGHTER: 1 sqn with 12 MiG-21.
ATTACK HELICOPTERS: 10 Mi-24.
TRANSPORT: at least 2 sqn:
15 An-2, 18 An-24, 3 An-26, 1 An-32, 1 Tu-154.
HELICOPTERS: 1 sqn with 10 Mi-4, 4 Mi-8.
TRAINING: 2 MiG-15U, 3* MiG-21U, 3 PZL-104, 6 Yak-11, Yak-18.

PARAMILITARY:
MILITIA (Ministry of Public Security):
10,000: internal security troops, frontier guards; BTR-60/-152 APC.

FOREIGN FORCES:
RUSSIA: 3,000 (withdrawal complete by end 1992).

NEW ZEALAND

GDP	1990:	$NZ 73.75bn ($US 44.03bn)
	1991:	$NZ 73.09bn ($US 42.32bn)
Growth	1990: 0.2%	1991: −2.1%
Inflation	1990: 6.1%	1991: 2.6%
Debt	1989: $US 28.80bn	1990: $US 29.50bn
Def exp	1989: $NZ 1.37bn ($US 818.17m)	
	1990: $NZ 1.38bn ($US 826.27m)	

Def bdgt	1991:	$NZ 1.36bn ($US 785.76m)
	1992:	$NZ 1.22bn ($US 663.40m)
$US 1 = $NZ	1989: 1.671	1990: 1.675
	1991: 1.727	1992: 1.839

$NZ = New Zealand dollars

Population: 3,396,800

	13–17	18–22	23–32
Men	136,300	144,900	296,500
Women	130,700	138,000	281,200

TOTAL ARMED FORCES:
ACTIVE: 10,900 incl 1,300 women.
RESERVES: 8,500. *Regular* 2,900: Army 1,650, Navy 1,050, Air 200. *Territorial* 5,650: Army 4,600, Navy 600, Air 400.

ARMY: 4,800 (incl 400 women).
2 inf bn.
1 lt armd sqn.
1 fd arty bty.
2 SF sqn (1 reserve).
RESERVES: Territorial Army: 6 inf bn, 6 fd, 1 med arty bty, 2 armd sqn (1 APC, 1 lt recce).
EQUIPMENT:
LIGHT TANKS: 26 *Scorpion.*
APC: 76 M-113 (incl variants).
TOWED ARTY: 105mm: 20 M-101A1 (8 in store), 24 *Hamel.*
MORTARS: 81mm: 72.
RL: *LAW.*
RCL: 84mm: 61 *Carl Gustav.*

NAVY: 2,400 (incl 300 women).
BASE: Auckland (Fleet HQ).
FRIGATES: 4 *Waikato* (UK *Leander*) with 1 *Wasp* hel, 3 with 2 × 3 ASTT and 2 × 114mm guns, 1 with *Ikara* SUGW (incl 1 in refit).
PATROL AND COASTAL COMBATANTS: 4:
4 *Moa* PCI (reserve trg).
SUPPORT AND MISCELLANEOUS: 4:
1 *Endeavour* AO, 1 AGHS, 1 AGOR, 1 diving spt.
IN STORE: 4 *Pukaki* PCI (to be sold).

NAVAL AIR:
No cbt ac, 7 armed hel.
HELICOPTERS: 7 *Wasp* (see Air Force).

AIR FORCE: 3,700 (incl 600 women);
41 cbt ac, no armed hel.
OPERATIONAL GROUP:
FGA: 2 sqn with 16 A-4K, 5 TA-4K.
MR: 1 sqn with 6 P-3K *Orion.*
LIGHT ATTACK/TRG: 1 sqn for ab initio and ftr lead-in trg with 18 MB-339C.

ASW: 7 *Wasp* HAS-1 (Navy-assigned) (plus 2 in store).
TRANSPORT: 3 sqn:
  AIRCRAFT: 2 sqn:
    1 with 5 C-130H, 2 Boeing 727;
    1 with 9 *Andover*.
  HELICOPTERS: 1 with 14 UH-1H.
COMMUNICATIONS: 1 flight with 3 Cessna 421C.
SUPPORT GROUP:
  TRAINING: 1 wing with 4 *Airtourer*, 18 CT-4, 3 F-27 ac; 4 Bell 47 hel.
MISSILES:
  ASM: AGM-65 *Maverick*.
  AAM: AIM-9H *Sidewinder*.

FORCES ABROAD:
SINGAPORE: 20: spt unit.
UN AND PEACEKEEPING:
ANGOLA (UNAVEM II): 13 Observers.
CAMBODIA (UNTAC): 65.
CROATIA (UNPROFOR): 4 Observers.
EGYPT (MFO): 25.
MIDDLE EAST (UNTSO): 5 Observers.

PAPUA NEW GUINEA

GDP	1990:	K 3.059bn ($3.20bn)	
	1991ε:	K 3.4bn ($3.57bn)	
Growth	1990:	−3.7%	1991:	8%
Inflation	1990:	6.9%	1991:	6.9%
Debt	1989:	$2.45bn	1990:	$2.61bn
Def exp	1989:	K 39.0m ($45.57m)	
	1990:	K 47.6m ($49.82m)	
Def bdgt	1990:	K 44.0m ($46.03m)	
$1 = K	1989:	0.855	1990:	0.955
	1991:	0.952	1992:	0.959

K = kina

Population: 4,127,000

	13–17	18–22	23–32
Men	236,900	217,400	347,400
Women	220,600	198,600	301,600

TOTAL ARMED FORCES:
ACTIVE: about 3,800.

ARMY: 3,200.
  2 inf bn.
  1 engr bn.

NAVY: 500.
BASES: Port Moresby (HQ), Lombrum (Manaus Is.).

PATROL AND COASTAL COMBATANTS: 5:
  4 *Tarangau* (Aus Pacific Forum 32-m) PCI
  1 *Madang* (Aus *Attack*) PCI.
AMPHIBIOUS: craft only: 2 *Salamaua* (Aus *Balikpapan*) LCT plus 6 other landing craft. (4 civilian manned and operated by Dept of Transport).

AIR FORCE: 100. 3 cbt ac, no armed hel.
MR: 3 N-22B *Searchmaster* B.
TRANSPORT: 5 C-47, 1 N-22B *Missionmaster*.
  HELICOPTERS: 3† *Arava*, 4† UH-1H.

OPPOSITION FORCES:
Bougainville Revolutionary Army: 2,000.

FOREIGN FORCES:
AUSTRALIA: 100; 1 engr unit, 82 advisers.

PHILIPPINES

GDP	1990:	P 1,074.3bn ($44.19bn)	
	1991:	P 1,238.7bn ($45.08bn)	
Growth	1990:	2.4%	1991:	−1.0%
Inflation	1990:	14.2%	1991:	18.7%
Debt	1989:	$28.47bn	1990:	$30.46bn
Def exp	1990ε:	P 22.56bn ($927.97m)	
Def bdgt	1991:	P 27.12bn ($986.76m)	
	1992ε:	P 26.70bn ($1,026.92m)	
FMA	1992:	$322.8mª (US)	
$1 = P	1989:	21.737	1990:	24.311
	1991:	27.479	1992:	26.000

P = pesos
ª Incl $120m as Economic Support

Population: 64,250,800

	13–17	18–22	23–32
Men:	3,691,100	3,243,800	5,391,900
Women:	3,578,900	3,150,600	5,223,600

TOTAL ARMED FORCES:
ACTIVE: 106,500.
RESERVES: 131,000. Army 100,000 (some 75,000 more have commitments); Navy 15,000; Air 16,000 (to age 49).

ARMY: 68,000.
  6 Area Unified Comd (joint service).
  8 inf div (each with 3 inf bde).
  1 lt armd bde ('regt').
  3 engr bde; 1 construction bn.
  8 arty bn.

1 SF bde.
1 Presidential Security Group.
EQUIPMENT:
LIGHT TANKS: 41 *Scorpion.*
AIFV: 85 YPR-765 PRI.
APC: 100 M-113, 20 *Chaimite,* 165 V-150.
TOWED ARTY: 105mm: 230 M-101, M-102, M-26
and M-56; 155mm: 12 M-114 and M-68.
MORTARS: 81mm: M-29; 107mm: 40 M-30.
RCL: 75mm: M-20; 90mm: M-67; 106mm: M-40 A1.

NAVY:† 23,000 (incl 8,500 Marines, 2,000 Coast
Guard to be a separate service from August
1992). 6 Naval Districts .
BASES: Sangley Point/Cavite, Zamboanga, Cebu.
FRIGATES: 1:
1 *Datu Siratuna* (US *Cannon*) with ASW mor.
PATROL AND COASTAL COMBATANTS: 42:
PATROL OFFSHORE: 8:
2 *Rizal* (US *Auk*)
5 *Miguel Malvar* (US PCE-827) (plus 2
reserve/refit).
1 *Magat Salamat* (US-MSF).
INSHORE: 34:
1 *Negros Oriental* (US PC-461) PCC.
1 *Aguinaldo,* 3 *Kagitingan,* 4 *Basilan* (US
PGM-39/42) and about 25⟨ PCI.
AMPHIBIOUS: 7:
some 7 *Agusan del Sur* (US LST-511) LST,
capacity: either 16tk or 10tk plus 200 tps.
Plus about 39 craft; 30 LCM, 3 LCU, some 6 LCVP.
SUPPORT AND MISCELLANEOUS: 12:
1 AOT (small), 2 repair ships, 4 survey/research,
2 spt, 2 water tankers, 1 yacht.

NAVAL AVIATION: 5 cbt ac, no armed hel.
MR/SAR: 5 BN-2A *Defender,* 1 *Islander;* 14 Bo-105
(SAR) hel.

MARINES: (8,500):
4 bde (10 bn).
EQUIPMENT:
APC: 30 LVTP-5, 55 LVTP-7.
ARTY: towed: 105mm: 150 M-101.
MORTARS: 4.2-in. (107mm): M-30.

COAST GUARD: (2,000).
EQUIPMENT: Some 65 patrol craft incl 1 ex-USCG
tender, 2 lt ac.

AIR FORCE: 15,500;
49 cbt ac, some 94 armed hel.
FIGHTER: 1 sqn with 9 F-5 (7 -A, 2 -B).
COIN:
AIRCRAFT: 1 sqn with 16 T-28D (to be retired this
year), 24 OV-10 *Broncos.*

HELICOPTERS: 3 sqn with 55 Bell UH-1H/M, 11
AUH-76 (S-76 gunship conversion), 28 Hughes
500/520MD.
MR: 2 F-27M.
RECCE: 3 RT-33A.
SAR: 4 HU-16 ac, 10 Bo-105C hel.
PRESIDENTIAL AIRCRAFT WING:
AIRCRAFT: 1 F-27, 1 F-28.
HELICOPTERS: 1 Bell 212, 1 S-70A, 2 SA-330.
TRANSPORT: 7 sqn:
AIRCRAFT:
1 with 3 C-130H, 3 L-100-20;
2 with 3 C-47, 7 F-27;
2 with 10 BN-2 *Islander,* 9 N-22B *Missionmaster.*
HELICOPTERS: 2 sqn with 55 Bell 205, 17 UH-1H.
LIAISON: 6 Cessna 180, 2 -210, 1 -310, 5 DHC-2,
15 U-17A/B.
TRAINING: 4 sqn:
1 with 5 T-33, 3 RT-33.
1 with 20 T-41D;
1 with 14 SF-260MP, 9* -WP.
1 with 15* S-211.
AAM: AIM-9B *Sidewinder.*

FORCES ABROAD:
UN AND PEACEKEEPING:
CAMBODIA (UNTAC): 92.

PARAMILITARY:

PHILIPPINE NATIONAL POLICE (Department of
Interior and Local Government): ε90,000; 14
Regional Comd, 234 provincial coy.

**CITIZEN ARMED FORCE GEOGRAPHICAL UNITS
(CAFGU):** Militia: 45,000, 56 bn. Part-time units
which can be called up for extended periods.

OPPOSITION:

NEW PEOPLE'S ARMY (NPA; Communist): 15,000.
BANGSA MORO ARMY (armed wing of Moro
National Liberation Front (MNLF), Muslim):
ε15,000.
MORO ISLAMIC LIBERATION FRONT (breakaway
from MNLF; Muslim): 2,900.
MORO ISLAMIC REFORMIST GROUP (breakaway
from MNLF): 900.

FOREIGN FORCES:
US: Navy: 1,500, base at Subic Bay ε1,000.
Marines: 500 (to close by end 1992).

SINGAPORE

| GDP | 1990: | S 62.71bn ($34.60bn) |
| | 1991ε: | S 68.61bn ($39.70bn) |

Growth	1990:	8.3%	1991ε: 6.5%
Inflation	1990:	3.5%	1991: 3.4%
Def bdgt	1990:	S 3.08bn ($1.70bn)	
	1991:	S 3.68bn ($2.13bn)	
$1 = S	1989:	1.950	1990: 1.813
	1991:	1.728	1992: 1.650
S = $ Singapore			

Population: 2,744,400

	13–17	18–22	23–32
Men	103,900	109,300	259,800
Women	97,600	102,900	247,000

TOTAL ARMED FORCES:
ACTIVE: 55,500 (34,800 conscripts).
Terms of service: conscription 2 years.
RESERVES: Army 250,000; annual trg to age 40 for men, 50 for officers. Navy ε4,500. Air Force ε7,500. People's Defence Force: ε30,000.

ARMY: 45,000 (30,000 conscripts).
1 combined arms div:
  2 inf bde (each 3 inf bn).
  1 mech bde.
  1 recce, 2 arty, 1 AD, 1 engr bn.
1 cdo bn.
1 arty, 1 SP mor bn.
1 engr bn.
RESERVES:
2 div, 1 mech, 6 inf bde HQ; 18 inf, 1 cdo, 10 arty, 2 AD arty, 3 engr bn.
People's Defence Force: some 30,000; org in 2 comd, 7 bde gp, ε21 bn.
EQUIPMENT:
LIGHT TANKS: ε350 AMX-13SM1.
RECCE: 22 AMX-10 PAC 90.
APC: 720 M-113, 30 V-100, 250 V-150/-200 *Commando*, 22 AMX-10P.
TOWED ARTY: 155mm: 38 Soltam M-71, 16 M-114A1 (may be in store), M-68 (may be in store), 52 FH88.
MORTARS: 81mm (some SP); 120mm: 50 (some SP in M-113); 160mm: 12 Tampella.
ATGW: 30 *Milan*.
RL: *Armbrust*; 89mm: M-20 3.5-in.
RCL: 84mm: *Carl Gustav*; 106mm: 90 M-40A1 (in store).
AD GUNS: 20mm: 30 GAI-CO1 (some SP).
SAM: RBS-70 (some SP in V-200).

NAVY: 4,500 (1,800 conscripts).
BASE: Pulau Brani (Singapore).
PATROL AND COASTAL COMBATANTS: 30:
CORVETTES: 6 *Victory* (Ge Lürssen 62-m) with 8 × *Harpoon* SSM, 2 × 3 ASTT.
MISSILE CRAFT: 6 *Sea Wolf* (Ge Lürssen 45-m) PFM with 2 × 2 *Harpoon*, 2 × *Gabriel* SSM.

PATROL, INSHORE: 18:
  6 *Independence/Sovereignty* (33-m).
  12 *Swift*⟨ plus boats.
MINE WARFARE: 1 *Mercury* (US *Bluebird* MSC plus *Jupiter* has mine-hunting capability.
AMPHIBIOUS: 5.
  5 *Endurance* (US LST-511) LST, capacity 200 tps, 16 tk.
  Plus craft; 8 LCM and some 400 boats.
SUPPORT AND MISCELLANEOUS: 1 *Jupiter* div spt and salvage.

AIR FORCE: 6,000 (3,000 conscripts);
192 cbt ac, 6 armed hel.
FGA: 5 sqn:
  3 with 62 A-4S/SI, 13 TA-4S/SI.
  1 with 20 *Hunter* F-74, 4 T-75.
  1 with 8 F-16 (4 -A, 4 -B).
FIGHTER: 2 sqn with 29 F-5E, 9 F-5F.
RECCE: 8 RF-5E.
AEW: 1 sqn with 4 E-2C.
MR: 3 Fokker, 50 *Enforcer* 2.
ARMED HELICOPTERS: 6 AS-350.
TRANSPORT:
  AIRCRAFT: 2 sqn:
    1 with 4 C-130B (tkr/tpt), 4 C-130B, 6 C-130H.
    1 with 6 *Skyvan* 3M (tpt/SAR).
  HELICOPTERS: 3 sqn:
    1 with 18 UH-1B;
    1 with 4 AB-205, 5 Bell 205;
    1 with 22 AS-332M (incl 3 SAR).
TRAINING: 3 sqn:
  2 with 30* SIAI S-211;
  1 with 26 SF-260 (14 -MS, 12* -WS).
AD: 3 bn: 2 SAM, 1 arty:
  1 with 10 *Rapier* (with *Blindfire*);
  1 with 12 *Improved HAWK*.
  1 with 35mm Oerlikon (towed) guns.
AIRFIELD DEFENCE: 1 field defence sqn (reservists).
AAM: AIM-9 J/P *Sidewinder*.

FORCES ABROAD:
BRUNEI: (500); trg school, incl hel det (with 5 UH-1).
TAIWAN: trg camp.
UN AND PEACEKEEPING:
ANGOLA (UNAVEM II): 8 Observers.
IRAQ/KUWAIT (UNIKOM): 9 Observers.

PARAMILITARY:
POLICE/MARINE POLICE: 11,600; incl some 750 Gurkhas, about 80 boats.
CIVIL DEFENCE FORCE: ε100,000 (incl regulars, conscripts, ε34,000 former army reservists). 1 construction bde (2,500 conscripts).

FOREIGN FORCES:
NEW ZEALAND: 20: spt unit.
UNITED STATES: 150: Navy (120); Air Force (30).

TAIWAN

GNP	1990:	$NT 4,316.5bn ($US 160.70bn)	
	1991:	$NT 4,670.0bn ($US 173.22bn)	
Growth	1990:	5.2%	1991ε: 6%
Inflation	1990:	4.1%	1991ε: 4%
Debt	1990:	$US 950m	1991: $US 1,146m
Def bdgt	1991:	$NT 250.5bn ($US 9.29bn)	
	1992ε:	$NT 264.0bn ($US 9.71bn)	
$1 = $NT	1989:	26.01	1990: 26.86
	1991:	26.96	1992: 27.20

$NT = New Taiwan dollars

Population: 21,265,000

	13–17	18–22	23–32
Men	989,600	950,000	1,938,000
Women	934,500	899,800	1,861,900

TOTAL ARMED FORCES:
ACTIVE: 360,000.
Terms of service: 2 years.
RESERVES: 1,657,500. Army: 1,500,000 have
some Reserve obligation to age 30. Navy 32,500,
Marines 35,000, Air 90,000.

ARMY: 260,000.
3 Army, 1 SF HQ.
20 inf div.
2 mech inf div.
1 AB bde.
6 indep armd bde.
1 SF gp.
22 fd arty bn.
5 SAM bn: 2 with *Nike Hercules*, 3 with *HAWK*.
6 avn sqn.
RESERVES: 7 inf div.
EQUIPMENT:
MBT: 309 M-48A5, 150 M-48H.
LIGHT TANKS: 230 M-24 (90mm gun), 675
M-41/Type 64.
RECCE: M-8.
AIFV: 225 M-113 with 20/30mm cannon.
APC: 40 M-2 half-track, 650 M-113, 300 V-150
Commando.
TOWED ARTY: 105mm: 650 M-101 (T-64);
155mm: M-44, 90 M-59, 250 M-114 (T-65);
203mm: 70 M-115.
SP ARTY: 105mm: 100 M-108; 155mm: 45 T-69,
110 M-109A2; 203mm: 60 M-110.
MRL: 117mm: KF VI; 126mm: KF III/IV towed and SP.
MORTARS: 81mm: M-29 (some SP); 107mm.

SSM: *Hsiung Feng* (*Gabriel*-type) coastal defence.
ATGW: 1,000: *Kun Wu* (*TOW*-type), *TOW* (some SP).
RCL: 90mm: M-67; 106mm: 500 M-40A1/Type 51.
ATK GUNS: 76mm: 150 M-18 SP.
AD GUNS: 35mm; 40mm: 400 (incl M-42 SP, Bofors).
SAM: 40 *Nike Hercules*, 100 *HAWK*, some
Chaparral; *Tien Kung* (*Sky Bow*)-1/-2.
AVIATION:
  AIRCRAFT: 20 O-1.
  HELICOPTERS: 100 UH-1H, 12 KH-4.
DEPLOYMENT:
QUEMOY: 55,000,
MATSU: 18,000.

NAVY: 30,000.
3 Naval Districts.
BASES: Tsoying (HQ), Makung (Pescadores),
Keelung.
SUBMARINES: 4:
  2 *Hai Lung* (Nl mod *Zwaardvis*) with 533mm TT.
  2 *Hai Shih* (US *Guppy* II) with 533mm TT.
PRINCIPAL SURFACE COMBATANTS: 33:
DESTROYERS: 24:
  DDG: 8 *Chien Yang* (US *Gearing*), (*Wu Chin* III
    conversion) with 10 × SM-1 MR SAM (boxed)
    plus 1 × 8 *ASROC*, 2 × 3 ASTT plus 1 *Hughes*
    MD-500 hel.
  DD: 16.
  6 *Fu Yang* (US *Gearing*) (ASW); 13 with 1
    Hughes MD-500 hel, 4 with 1 × 8 *ASROC*, all
    with 2 × 3 ASTT; plus 1 or 2 × 2 127mm guns,
    5 or 3 *Hsiung Feng-II* (HF-2) (Is *Gabriel*) SSM.
  6 *Po Yang* (US *Sumner*) with 1 or 2 × 2 127mm
    guns; plus 2 × 3 ASTT; 5 or 6 HF-2 SSM, 2
    with 1 *Hughes* MD-500 hel.
  4 *Kun Yang* (US *Fletcher*) with 2 or 3 × 127mm
    guns; 1 × 76mm gun; plus 2 × 3 ASTT with 5
    HF-2 SSM.
FRIGATES: 10:
  9 *Tien Shan* (US *Lawrence/Crosley*), 8 with 2 × 3
    ASTT; plus 2 × 127mm guns.
  1 *Tai Yuan* (US *Rudderow*) with 2 × 3 ASTT;
    plus 2 × 127mm guns.
  (Plus 2 ex-US *Knox* with 1 × 8 *ASROC*, 1 ×
    SH-2F hel, 4 × ASTT; plus *Harpoon* (from
    ASROC launchers), 1 × 127mm gun by
    September 1992).
PATROL AND COASTAL COMBATANTS: 93:
MISSILE CRAFT: 52:
  2 *Lung Chiang* PFM with 2 × HF-2 SSM
  50 *Hai Ou* (mod Is *Dvora*)⟨ with 2 × HF-2 SSM
PATROL, OFFSHORE: 3 *Ping Jin* (US *Auk* MSF) with
  1 × 3 ASTT plus 2 × 76mm guns.
INSHORE: 38: 22 Vosper-type 32-m PFI.
  About 16 PCI⟨.
MINE WARFARE: 13:
MINELAYERS: Nil but *Tai Yuan* and 1 *Ping Jin*
  have capability.

MINE COUNTERMEASURES: 13
    13 *Yung Chou* (US *Adjutant*) MSC.
AMPHIBIOUS: 26
    1 *Kao Hsiung* (US LST 511) amph comd.
    20 *Chung Hai* (US LST 511) LST, capacity 16 tk, 200 tps.
    4 *Mei Lo* (US LSM-1) LSM, capacity about 4 tk.
    1 *Cheng Hai* (US *Cabildo*) LSD, capacity 3 LCU or 18 LCM.
    Plus about 400 craft; 22 LCU, some 260 LCM, 120 LCVP.
SUPPORT AND MISCELLANEOUS: 28:
    4 spt tankers, 2 repair/salvage, 1 *Wu Yi* combat spt with hel deck, 6 *Yuen Feng* ATK tpt, 2 tpt, 3 survey/research, 7 ocean tugs, 3 tugs.

NAVAL AIR: 32 cbt ac; 12 armed hel.
MR: 1 sqn with 32 S-2 (25 -E, 7 -G).
HELICOPTERS: 1 sqn with 12 Hughes 500MD ASW *Defender*.

MARINES: 30,000.
    2 div, spt elm.
EQUIPMENT:
APC: LVT-4/-5.
TOWED ARTY: 105mm, 155mm.
RCL: 106mm.

AIR FORCE: 70,000;
    486 cbt ac, no armed hel. 5 cbt wings.
FGA/FIGHTER: 14 sqn with 8 F-5B, 215 -E, 55 -F, 8 F-104D/DJ, 82 -G, 20 -J, 32 TF-104G.
RECCE: 1 sqn with 6 RF-104G.
SAR: 1 sqn with 8 HU-16B ac, 12 S-70, 12 UH-1H hel.
TRANSPORT: 8 sqn:
   AIRCRAFT: 2 with 8 C-47, 2 C-54, 1 C-118B, 1 DC-6B;
     3 with 30 C-119G, 10 C-123B/K;
     1 with 12 C-130H.
     1 with 12 Beech 1900.
     1 VIP with 1 Boeing 707-720B, 4 -727-100.
   HELICOPTERS: 5 CH-34, 3 CH-47C, 1 S-62A (VIP), 14 S-70.
TRAINING: incl 60* AT-3, T-28A, 30 T-33A, 42 T-34C, 30 T-CH-1 ac; 12 Bell 47G/OH-13, 6 Hughes 500 hel.
MISSILES:
   ASM: AGM-65A *Maverick*.
   AAM: AIM-4D *Falcon*, AIM-9J/P *Sidewinder*, *Shafrir*.

PARAMILITARY:
SECURITY GROUPS (Ministry of Defence): 25,000: incl National Police Administration. Bureau of Investigation. Military Police HQ.

CUSTOMS SERVICE (Ministry of Finance):
    4 PCO, 2 PCC, 6 PCI; most armed.

FOREIGN FORCES:
SINGAPORE: trg camp.

THAILAND

GDP	1990:	b 2,051.2bn ($80.17bn)	
	1991ε:	b 2,383.3bn ($93.40bn)	
Growth	1990:	10.0%	1991: 7.9%
Inflation	1990:	6.0%	1991ε: 5.7%
Debt	1990:	$25.30bn	1991: $26.90bn
Def bdgt	1991:	b 60.58bn ($2.40bn)	
	1992:	b 68.81bn ($2.69bn)	
FMA	1992:	$5m*a* (US)	
$1 = b	1989:	25.702	1990: 25.585
	1991:	25.571	1992: 25.60

b = baht
a Incl $2.5m as Economic Support

Population: 58,438,800

	13–17	*18–22*	*23–32*
Men	3,116,100	3,132,100	5,494,500
Women	2,995,500	3,009,100	5,330,700

TOTAL ARMED FORCES:
ACTIVE: 283,000.
    Terms of service: conscription 2 years.
RESERVES: 500,000.

ARMY: 190,000 (80,000 conscripts).
    4 Regional Army HQ, 2 Corps HQ.
    1 armd div.
    1 cav (lt armd) div (2 cav, 1 arty regt).
    2 mech inf div.
    6 inf div (incl Royal Guard, 5 with 1 tk bn) (1 to be mech, 1 to be lt).
    2 SF div.
    1 arty div, 1 AD arty div (6 AD arty bn).
    19 engr bn.
    1 indep cav regt.
    8 indep inf bn.
    4 recce coy.
    Armd air cav regt with 3 air-mobile coy.
    Some hel flt.
RESERVES: 4 inf div HQ.
EQUIPMENT:
MBT: 50+ Ch Type-69 (in store), 100 M-48A5, 53 M-60.
LIGHT TANKS: 154 *Scorpion*, 250 M-41, 106 *Stingray*.
RECCE: 32 *Shorland* Mk 3.
APC: 340 M-113, 150 V-150 *Commando*, 450 Ch Type-85 (YW-531H).
TOWED ARTY: 105mm: 200 M-101/-101 mod, 12 M-102, 32 M-618A2 (local manufacture);

130mm: 15 Ch Type-59; 155mm: 56 M-114, 62
M-198, 32 M-71.
MORTARS: 81mm, 107mm.
ATGW: *TOW*, 300 *Dragon*.
RL: M-72 *LAW*.
RCL: 75mm: M-20; 106mm: 150 M-40.
AD GUNS: 20mm: 24 M-163 *Vulcan*, 24 M-167
Vulcan; 37mm: 122 Type-74; 40mm: 80
M-1/M-42 SP, 28 L/70; 57mm: 24.
SAM: *Redeye*, some *Aspide*.
AVIATION:
TRANSPORT: 1 Beech 99, 4 C-47, 10 Cessna 208,
1 Short 330, 1 *Beech King Air*.
LIAISON: 63 O-1A, 17 -E, 5 T-41A, 13 U-17A.
TRAINING: 16 T-41D.
HELICOPTERS:
ATTACK: 4 AH-1F.
TRANSPORT: 10 Bell 206, 9 -212, 6 -214, 70
UH-1H.
TRAINING: 36 Hughes 300C, 3 OH-13, 7 TH-55.

NAVY: 50,000 (some conscripts) incl naval air
and marines.
BASES: Bangkok, Sattahip (Fleet HQ), Songkhla,
Phang Nga, Nakhon Phanom (HQ Mekong River
Operating Unit), Trat.
FRIGATES: 8:
FFG: 3:
2 *Chao Phraya* (Ch *Jianghu*-III) with 8 × C-801
SSM, 2 × 2 100mm guns; plus 2 × 5 ASW RL.
1 *Kraburil* (Ch *Jianghu*-IV type) with 8 × C-801
SSM, 1 × 2 100mm guns; plus 2 × 5 ASW RL
and hel deck.
FF: 5.
1 *Makut Rajakumarn* with 2 × 3 ASTT (*Sting
Ray* LWT); plus 2 × 114mm guns.
2 *Tapi* (US PF-103) with 2 × 3 ASTT (Mk 46 LWT).
2 *Tachin* (US *Tacoma*) (trg) with 2 × 3 ASTT.
PATROL AND COASTAL COMBATANTS: 65:
CORVETTES: 5:
2 *Rattanakosin* with 2 × 3 ASTT (*Sting Ray*
LWT); plus 2 × 4 *Harpoon* SSM.
3 *Khamronsin* with 2 × 3 ASTT; plus 1 × 76mm gun.
MISSILE CRAFT: 6:
3 *Ratcharit* (It Breda 50-m) with 4 × MM-38
Exocet SSM.
3 *Prabparapak* (Ge Lürssen 45-m) with 5 *Gabriel* SSM.
PATROL: 54:
COASTAL: 14:
3 *Chon Buri* PFC, 6 *Sattahip*, 5 *Sarasin* (US
PC-461) PCC.
INSHORE: 40: 10 T-11 (US PGM-71), about 30 PCI⟨.
MINE WARFARE: 7:
2 *Bang Rachan* (Ge Lürssen T-48) MCC.
4 *Ladya* (US 'Bluebird' MSC) MSC.
1 *Thalang* MCM spt with minesweeping capability.
plus some 5 MSB.
AMPHIBIOUS: 8:

2 *Sichang* (Fr PS-700) LST, capacity 14 tk, 300
tps with hel deck.
4 *Angthong* (US LST-511) LST, capacity 16 tk,
200 tps (1 trg).
2 *Kut* (US LSM-1) LSM, capacity about 4 tk.
Plus 40 craft; 10 LCU, about 30 LCM.
SUPPORT AND MISCELLANEOUS: 7:
1 small tanker, 3 survey, 3 trg.

NAVAL AIR: (900); 26 cbt ac; 8 armed hel.
MR/ASW: 1 sqn with 3 Do-228, 3 F-27MPA, 5
N-24A *Searchmaster* L.
ASW HELICOPTERS: 8 Bell 212 ASW.
MR/SAR: 1 sqn with 2 CL-215.
MR/ATTACK: 10 Cessna T-337.
SAR: 1 hel sqn with 8 Bell 212, 2 -214, 4 UH-1H.
ASM: AGM-84 *Harpoon* (for F-27MPA).

MARINES:
1 div HQ, 6 inf regt, 1 arty regt (3 fd, 1 AA bn);
1 amph aslt bn; recce bn.
EQUIPMENT:
APC: 33 LVTP-7.
TOWED ARTY: 155mm: 18 GC-45.
ATGW: *TOW*, *Dragon*.

AIR FORCE: 43,000;
166 cbt ac, no armed hel.
FGA: 1 sqn with 8 F-5A, 4 -B.
14 F-16A, 4 -B.
FIGHTER: 2 sqn with 38 F-5E, 6 -F.
COIN: 7 sqn:
1 with 15 A-37B;
1 with 7 AC-47;
3 with 24 AU-23A;
2 with 30 OV-10C.
ELINT: 1 sqn with 3 IAI-201.
RECCE: 3 RF-5A, 3RT-33A.
SURVEY: 1 *Commander* 690, 3 *Learjet* 35A, 2
Merlin IVA, 2 *Queen Air*.
TRANSPORT: 4 sqn:
1 with 3 C-130H, 3 C-130H-30, 3 DC-8-62F.
1 with 10 C-123B/-K, 6 BAe-748.
1 with 10 C-47.
1 with 20 N-22B *Missionmaster*.
VIP: Royal flight: 2 Boeing 737-200, 1 *King Air*
200, 3 *Merlin* IV ac; 2 Bell 412 hel.
TRAINING: 24 CT-4, 16 *Fantrainer* V-600, 16
SF-260, 10 T-33A, 20 PC-9, 13 T-37B, 6 -C, 11
T-41, 4 D-1A *Bird Dog*.
LIAISON: 3 *Commander*, 2 *King Air* E90, 30 O-1.
HELICOPTERS: 2 sqn:
1 with 18 S-58T.
1 with 21 UH-1H.
AAM: AIM-9B/J *Sidewinder*.
AD: *Blowpipe* and *Aspide* SAM. 1 AA arty bty: 4
Skyguard, 1 *Flycatcher* radars, each with 4 fire
units of 2 × 30mm Mauser guns.

FORCES ABROAD:
UN AND PEACEKEEPING:
CAMBODIA (UNTAC): 710: 1 engr bn.
CROATIA (UNPROFOR): 4 Observers.
IRAQ/KUWAIT (UNIKOM): 7 Observers.

PARAMILITARY:
THAHAN PHRAN ('Hunter Soldiers'): 18,500
   volunteer irregular force; 27 regt of some 200 coy.
NATIONAL SECURITY VOLUNTEER CORPS:
   43,000.
MARINE POLICE: ε1,700; 2 PFC, 3 PFI, some 57 PCI⟨.
POLICE AVIATION: 500; 1 *Airtourer*, 3 AU-23, 1
   C-47, 2 Cessna 310, 1 CT-4, 3 DHC-4, 1 Do-28,
   4 PC-6, 1 Short 330 ac; 27 Bell 205A, 14 -206, 3
   -212, 6 UH-12, 5 KH-4, 1 S-62 hel.
BORDER PATROL POLICE: 28,000.
PROVINCIAL POLICE: ε50,000 incl Special Action
   Force (ε500).

VIETNAM

NMP[a]			
	1989ε:	d 235.0bn ($14.52bn)	
	1990ε:	d 240.6bn ($14.9bn)	
Growth	1990:	2.4%	1991ε: 3.8%
Inflation	1990:	90%	1991ε: 70%
Debt	1990:	$14.60bn	1991: $15.30bn
Def bdgt	1988ε:	$2.54bn	1989ε: $2.32bn
$1 = d	1989:	4,540.2	1990: 8,700.0
	1991:	11,000.0	1992: 11,145.1

d = dong

[a] NMP in dong is expressed in constant rather than
current terms. $ figures are est as conversion through the
official rate of exchange is meaningless.

Population: 73,778,600

	13–17	18–22	23–32
Men	4,073,000	3,687,400	6,534,700
Women	3,982,400	3,577,300	6,367,700

TOTAL ARMED FORCES:
ACTIVE: 857,000 (referred to as 'Main Force').
   Terms of service: 2 years, specialists 3 years, some
   ethnic minorities 2 years.
RESERVES 'Strategic Rear Force' some 3–4m
   manpower potential, see also Paramilitary.

ARMY: 700,000.
8 Military Regions, 2 Special areas.
14 Corps HQ.
62 inf div.[b]
3 mech div.
10 armd bde.

15 indep inf regt.
SF incl AB bde, demolition engr regt.
some 10 fd arty bde.
8 engr div.
10–16 economic construction div; 20 indep engr bde.[c]
EQUIPMENT:†
MBT: 1,300: T-34/-54/-55, T-62, Ch Type-59, M-48A3.
LIGHT TANKS: 600 PT-76, Ch Type-62/63.
RECCE: 80 BRDM-1/-2.
AIFV: 300 BMP.
APC: 1,100 BTR-40/-50/-60/-152, YW-531, M-113.
TOWED ARTY: 2,300: 100mm: M-1944, T-12;
   105mm: M-101/-102; 122mm: Type-54, Type-60,
   M-1938, D-30, D-74; 130mm: M-46; 152mm:
   D-20; 155mm: M-114.
SP ARTY: 152mm: 30 2S3; 175mm: M-107.
ASSAULT GUNS: 100mm: SU-100; 122mm: ISU-122.
MRL: 107mm: 320 Type 63; 122mm: 350 BM-21;
   140mm: BM-14-16.
MORTARS: 82mm, 120mm: M-43; 160mm: M-43.
ATGW: AT-3 *Sagger*.
RCL: 75mm: Ch Type-56; 82mm: Ch Type-65, B-10;
   88mm: Ch Type-51.
AD GUNS: 12,000: 14.5mm; 23mm: incl ZSU-23-4
   SP; 30mm; 37mm; 57mm; 85mm; 100mm.
SAM: SA-6/-7/-9.

NAVY:† ε42,000 (incl 30,000 Naval Infantry).
   Five Naval Regions.
BASES: Hanoi (HQ): Cam Ranh Bay, Da Nang,
   Haiphong, Ha Tou, Ho Chi Minh City, Can Tho
   plus several smaller bases.
FRIGATES: 7:
   1 *Phan Ngu Lao* (US *Barnegat*) (ASUW), with 2
   × SS-N-2 *Styx* SSM, 1 × 127mm gun.
   5 Sov *Petya* II with 4 × ASW RL, 3
   × 533mm TT.
   1 *Dai Ky* (US *Savage*) with 2 × 3 ASTT.
PATROL AND COASTAL COMBATANTS: 55:
MISSILE CRAFT: 8 Sov *Osa* II with 4 × SS-N-2 SSM.
TORPEDO CRAFT: 19:
   3 Sov *Turya* PHT with 4 × 533mm TT.
   16 Sov *Shershen* PFT with 4 × 533mm TT.
PATROL: 28:
   INSHORE: 28:
   8 Sov SO-1, 3 US PGM-59/71, 11 *Zhuk*⟨, 4⟨.
   2 Sov *Turya* (no TT).
MINE WARFARE: 11:
   2 *Yurka* MSC, 4 *Sonya* MSC, 2 Ch *Lienyun*
   MSC, 1 *Vanya* MSI, 2 *Yevgenya* MSI⟨, plus
   5 K-8 boats.
AMPHIBIOUS: 7:
   3 US LST-510-511 LST, capacity 200 tps, 16 tk.
   3 Sov *Polnocny* LSM, capacity 180 tps, 6 tk.
   1 US LSM-1 LSM, capacity about 50 tps, 4 tk.
   Plus about 30 craft; 12 LCM, 18 LCU.
SUPPORT AND MISCELLANEOUS: 19:
   1 survey, 4 small tankers, about 12 small tpt, 2
   ex-Sov Floating Docks.

NAVAL INFANTRY: (30,000) (amph, cdo).

AIR FORCE: 15,000; 185 cbt ac, 20 armed hel
(plus many in store).† 4 Air Div.
FGA: 2 regt:
    1 with 20 Su-17;
    1 with 40 Su-22.
FIGHTER: 5 regt with 125 MiG-21bis/PF.
ATTACK HELICOPTERS: 20 Mi-24.
MR: 4 Be-12.
ASW HEL: 8 Ka-25.
SURVEY: 2 An-30.
TRANSPORT: 3 regt: incl 12 An-2, 4 An-24, 30
    An-26, 8 Tu-134, 14 Yak-40.
HELICOPTERS: 1 div (3 regt) with 200 hel incl 5
    Mi-6, 30 Mi-8.
TRAINING: 3 regt with 53 ac incl L-39, *MiG-21U.
AAM: AA-2 *Atoll*.

AIR DEFENCE FORCE: 100,000.
14 AD div:
    SAM: some 66 sites with SA-2/-3/-6;

4 AD arty bde: 37mm, 57mm, 85mm, 100mm,
    130mm; plus People's Regional Force: ε1,000
    units.
6 radar bde: 100 sites.

PARAMILITARY:
LOCAL FORCES: Some 4–5m. Incl People's Self
Defence Force (urban units), People's Militia
(rural units). Comprise: static and mobile cbt
units, log spt and village protection pl. Some
arty, mor and AD guns. Acts as reserve.

OPPOSITION:
**UNITED FRONT FOR THE LIBERATION OF THE
OPPRESSED RACES** (FULRO) ε2,500;
montagnards; Cambodian border.
NATIONAL SALVATION MOVEMENT.
ARMY OF THE REPUBLIC OF VIETNAM
(remnants; *Hoa Hao*).

b Inf div strengths vary from 5,000 to 12,500.
c Men beyond normal mil age; unit strength about 4,000
each, fully armed, with mil and economic role.

Caribbean and Latin America

Political Developments

On 13 December 1991 Argentina and Brazil signed agreements with the IAEA for the application of safeguards, although neither have signed the NPT. On 14 February 1992, the 25th anniversary of the signing of the Treaty of Tlatelolco (Latin American and Caribbean nuclear-free zone), the Presidents of Argentina and Brazil issued a joint statement of their intention to submit, at the earliest opportunity, some technical amendments to the Treaty. Argentina, Brazil and Chile also signed a declaration on 5 September 1991 banning the production and use of chemical and biological weapons.

The United Nations Observer Group in Central America (ONUCA), which had been established in 1989 to monitor the implementation of the Esquipulas II agreement and to take delivery of the arms of the demobilized Nicaraguan Resistance, completed its task in January 1992, and its resources were transferred to the United Nations Observer Mission in El Salvador (ONUSAL). ONUSAL became operational in July 1991 and is monitoring the cease-fire and any human-rights violations and is helping to establish a police force in the democratic tradition. A programme of demobilization of both FMLN and the army has been published and is due to be completed by December 1992.

Military Developments

A major reorganization of the **Argentinian** Army is in progress. Divisions are being formed, the make-up of which is not yet clear; nor is it known whether Corps HQ will be retained. The navy's aircraft carrier has been retired but kept in preservation. The **Brazilian** Army has added to its inventory an additional 100 EE-9 *Cascavel* and 190 EE-3 *Jararaca* armoured reconnaissance vehicles and 50 more EE-11 *Urutu* APC. A second *Inhauma*-class frigate which mounts *Exocet* and a *Lynx* helicopter has commissioned. The **Chilean** Army has retired its M-4A3 tanks and taken delivery of 50 more EE-11 *Urutu* APC. The navy has retired the 55-year-old *O'Higgins* (US *Brooklyn*-class cruiser) and commissioned a fourth UK *Leander*-class frigate. Four AS-365 and four AS-532SC ASW helicopters have been delivered.

Cuban Army tank holdings have been reassessed; there are 1,200 T-54/-55 and 400 T-62. The army has received a further 100 BMP-1. In **Ecuador** the air force has taken delivery of six more A-37B COIN aircraft. In **El Salvador** the paramilitary National Guard and Treasury Police have been placed under army command. The *Ouragan* fighter squadron, whose aircrafts' operational capability has been suspect for some time, has been disbanded. The **Guatemalan** Air Force has taken delivery of six Israeli-built IAI-201 liaison aircraft and six more Bell 212/412 attack helicopters.

There has been a reorganization of **Honduran** Army units. The **Mexican** Army has taken delivery of 40 Mex-1 reconnaissance vehicles. The two US-511-class LST which *The Military Balance* last listed in 1987–88 are still in service. Demobilization of the **Nicaraguan** Army continues. Manpower strength has been reduced to about 13,000 and there is now only one brigade. A number of inshore patrol craft have been retired. The **Peruvian** Navy has retired its US *Guppy*-class submarine which is to be used for alongside training. The navy has taken delivery of two more *Super King Air* B 200T ASW/MR aircraft. The **Uruguay** Army has been reorganized and has formed six more brigades: three infantry and three cavalry. The air force has taken delivery of four more A-37B COIN aircraft. In **Venezuela** the navy has taken delivery of two more AB-212 ASW helicopter, and the air force 14 more OV-10E COIN aircraft and four more armed UH-1H helicopters.

ARGENTINA

GDP*a*	1990:	P 4.01bn ($66.82bn)	
	1991ε:	P 4.20bn ($69.36bn)	
Growth	1990:	0.5%	1991: 3.8%
Inflation	1990:	2,312%	1991: 81%
Debt	1990:	$61.14bn	1991ε: $58.0bn
Def exp*b*	1991:	P 1,408m ($1.41bn)	
Def bdgt	1992:	P 1,739m ($1.75bn)	
FMA	1992:	$1.2m (US)	
$1 = A	1989:	423.34	1990: 4,876.0
$1 = P	1991:	0.9536	1992: 0.9906

A = Australes
P = Pesos

a On 1 Jan 1992, the Peso Argentino, equal to 10,000 Australes, was introduced. All GDP figures are in 1985 prices and exchange rates and have been converted into Pesos.
b Def bdgt and exp are in current prices and exchange rates.

Population: 33,479,000

	13–17	*18–22*	*23–32*
Men	1,565,000	1,373,000	2,391,000
Women	1,529,000	1,344,000	2,350,000

TOTAL ARMED FORCES:
ACTIVE: 65,000 (12,800 conscripts).
Terms of service: all services up to 14 months; conscripts may actually serve less than 7 months.
RESERVES: 377,000: Army 250,000 (National Guard 200,000; Territorial Guard 50,000); Navy 77,000; Air 50,000.

ARMY: 35,000 (8,000 conscripts).
(Many units cadre status only.)
3 corps HQ (reorganizing on div basis).
6 regional div with:-
  2 armd cav bde (each 3 tk regt, 1 SP arty bn, 1 armd recce sqn, 1 engr coy).
  2 mech inf bde (each 2 inf regt of 1 bn, 1 tk regt, 1 arty bn, 1 armd recce sqn, 1 engr coy).
  2 mtn inf bde (each 3 inf, 1 arty bn, 1 SF, 1 engr coy).
  2 inf bde (1 with 3 inf regt each 1 bn, 1 arty bn, 1 armd recce sqn, 1 engr coy, 1 with 1 inf, 1 jungle, 1 mtn regt, 1 arty bn, 1 armd recce sqn, 1 engr coy).
  1 jungle bde (4 lt inf, 2 arty (how) bn, 1 armd recce sqn, 2 engr coy).
  1 AB bde (3 AB regt of 1 bn, 1 arty bn, 1 engr coy).
Army Tps:
  Army HQ Escort Regt: 1 mot inf regt of 1 bn (ceremonial).
  Presidential Escort: 1 mot cav regt (ceremonial).
  1 indep mech inf bde (3 inf regt of 1 bn, 1 arty bn, 1 armd recce sqn, 1 engr coy).
  1 AD arty, 2 engr, 1 avn bn.
  1 SF coy.
Corps Tps;
  each corps 1 armd cav regt (recce), 1 arty, 1 AD arty, 1 engr bn.
EQUIPMENT:
MBT: 266: 96 M-4 *Sherman*, 170 TAM.
LIGHT TANKS: 60 AMX-13, 106 SK-105 *Kuerassier*.
RECCE: 50 AML-90.
AIFV: 30 AMX-VCI, some 160 *TAM* VCTP.
APC: ε75 M-3 half-track, 240 M-113, 80 MOWAG *Grenadier* (mod *Roland*).
TOWED ARTY: 250: 105mm: 150 M-56; 155mm: 100 CITEFA Models 77/-81.
SP ARTY: 125: 155mm: Mk F3, L33.
MRL: 105mm: SLAM *Pampero*; 127mm: SLAM SAPBA-1.
MORTARS: 81mm: 1,000; 120mm: 130 (some SP in VCTM AIFV).
ATGW: 600 SS-11/-12, *Cobra (Mamba)*, 2,100 *Mathogo*.
RCL: 75mm: 75; 90mm: 100; 105mm: 150.
AD GUNS: 20mm: 130; 30mm: 40; 35mm: 15 GDF-001; 40mm: 80 L/60, 15 L/70; 90mm: 20.
SAM: *Tigercat, Blowpipe, Roland,* SAM-7.
AVIATION:
  AIRCRAFT: 5 Cessna 207, 5 *Commander* 690, 2 DHC-6, 3 G-222, 1 *Merlin* IIIA, 4 -IV, 3 *Queen Air*, 1 *Sabreliner*, 5 T-41.
  HELICOPTERS: 6 A-109, 3 AS-332B, 5 Bell 205, 4 FH-1100, 4 SA-315, 3 SA-330, 10 UH-1H, 8 UH-12.

NAVY: 20,000 incl naval air force and marines (incl 2,500 conscripts).
3 Naval Areas: Centre: from River Plate to 42°45' S; South: from 42°45' S to Cape Horn; and Antarctica.
BASES: Buenos Aires, Puerto Belgrano (HQ Centre), Mar del Plata (submarine base), Ushuaia (HQ South), Puerto Deseado.
SUBMARINES: 4:
  2 *Santa Cruz* (Ge TR-1700) with 533mm TT (SST-4 HWT).
  2 *Salta* (Ge T-209/1200) with 533mm TT (SST-4 HWT) (both in major refit).
PRINCIPAL SURFACE COMBATANTS: 13:
DESTROYERS: 6:
  2 *Hercules* (UK Type 42) with 1 × 2 *Sea Dart* SAM; plus 1 SA-319 hel (ASW), 2 × 3 ASTT, 4 × MM-38 *Exocet* SSM, 1 × 114mm gun.
  4 *Almirante Brown* (Ge *MEKO-360*) ASW with 2 × SA-316 hel, 2 × 3 ASTT; plus 8 × MM-40 *Exocet* SSM, 1 × 127mm gun.
FRIGATES: 7:

4 *Espora* (Ge *MEKO-140*) with 2 × 3 ASTT, hel deck; plus 8 × MM-40 *Exocet*.

3 *Drummond* (Fr A-69) with 2 × 3 ASTT; plus 4 × MM-38 *Exocet*, 1 × 100mm gun.

ADDITIONAL IN STORE: 1 carrier: 1 *Veinticinco de Mayo* CVS (UK *Colossus*).

PATROL AND COASTAL COMBATANTS: 13:

TORPEDO CRAFT: 2 *Intrepida* (Ge Lürssen 45-m) PFT with 2 × 533mm TT (SST-4 HWT)

PATROL CRAFT: 11:

OFFSHORE: 7:

1 *Teniente Olivieri* (ex-US oilfield tug).

2 *Irigoyen* (US *Cherokee* AT).

2 *King* (trg) with 3 × 105mm guns.

2 *Somellera* (US *Sotoyomo* AT).

INSHORE; 4 *Baradero* PCI⟨.

MINE WARFARE: 6:

4 *Neuquen* (UK 'Ton') MSC.

2 *Chaco* (UK 'Ton') MHC.

AMPHIBIOUS: 1 *Cabo San Antonio* LST (hel deck), capacity 600 tps, 18 tk.

Plus 20 craft; 4 LCM, 16 LCVP.

SUPPORT AND MISCELLANEOUS: 9:

1 AGOR, 3 tpt, 1 ocean tug, 1 icebreaker, 2 trg, 1 research.

NAVAL AVIATION: (2,000);

42 cbt ac, 10 armed hel.

ATTACK: 1 sqn with 12 *Super Etendard*.

MR/ASW: 1 sqn with 3 L-188, 6 S-2E.

EW: 1 L-188E.

HELICOPTERS: 2 sqn: 1 ASW/tpt with 4 ASH-3H (ASW) and 4 AS-61D (tpt); 1 spt with 6 SA-316/-319 (with SS-11).

TRANSPORT: 1 sqn with 1 BAe-125, 3 F-28-3000, 3 L-188, 4 *Queen Air* 80, 9 *Super King Air*, 4 US-2A.

SURVEY: 3 PC-6B (Antarctic flt).

TRAINING: 2 sqn:

7* EMB-326, 9* MB-326, 5* MB-339A, 10 T-34C.

MISSILES:

ASM: AGM-12 *Bullpup*, AM-39 *Exocet*, AS-12, Martín *Pescador*.

AAM: AIM-9 *Sidewinder*, R-550 *Magic*.

MARINES: (3,000).

Fleet Forces: 2: each 2 bn, 1 amph recce coy, 1 fd arty bn, 1 ATK, 1 engr coy.

Amph spt force: 1 marine inf bn.

1 AD arty regt (bn).

2 indep inf bn.

EQUIPMENT:

RECCE: 12 ERC-90 *Lynx*.

APC: 19 LVTP-7, 15 LARC-5, 6 MOWAG *Grenadier*, 24 Panhard.

TOWED ARTY: 105mm: 15 M-101/M-56; 155mm: 6 M-114.

MORTARS: 81mm: 20.

RL: 89mm: 60 3.5-in M-20.

ATGW: 50 *Bantam*, *Cobra* (*Mamba*).

RCL: 105mm: 30 M-1968.

AD GUNS: 30mm: 10 HS-816.

SAM: *Tigercat*.

AIR FORCE: 10,000 (2,300 conscripts);

174 cbt ac, 14 armed hel, 9 air bde, 10 AD arty bty, SF (AB) coy.

AIR OPERATIONS COMMAND (9 bde):

BOMBERS: 1 sqn with 4 *Canberra* B-62, 2 T-64.

FGA/FIGHTER: 4 sqn:

2 (1 OCU) with 20 *Mirage* IIIC (17 -CJ, 1 -BE, 2 -BJ), 15 *Mirage* IIIEA; 2 with 8 *Mirage* 5P, 23 *Dagger* (*Nesher* ; 20 -A, 3 -B).

FGA: 2 sqn with 16 A-4P.

COIN: 3 sqn:

2 with 36 IA-58A, 16 IA-63, 24 MS-760;

1 armed hel with 11 Hughes MD500, 3 UH-1H.

MR: 1 Boeing 707.

SURVEY: 3 *Learjet* 35A, 4 1A-50.

TANKER: 2 Boeing 707, 2 KC-130H.

SAR: 4 SA-315 hel.

TRANSPORT: 5 sqn with:

AIRCRAFT: 3 Boeing 707, 6 C-47, 2 C-130E, 5 -H, 1 L-100-30, 6 DHC-6, 12 F-27, 6 F-28, 15 IA-50, 2 *Merlin* IVA. Antarctic spt unit with 1 DHC-6, 1 LC-47.

HELICOPTERS: 7 Bell 212, 2 CH-47C, 1 S-61R.

CALIBRATION: 1 sqn with 2 Boeing 707, 3 IA-50, 2 *Learjet* 35, 1 PA-31.

LIAISON: 1 sqn with 20 Cessna 182, 1 -320, 7 *Commander*, 1 *Sabreliner*.

AIR TRAINING COMMAND:

28 EMB-312, 10* MS-760, 30 T-34B ac.

4 Hughes 500D hel.

MISSILES:

ASM: ASM-2 *Martín Pescador*.

AAM: AIM-9B *Sidewinder*, R-530, R-550, *Shafrir*.

FORCES ABROAD:

UN AND PEACEKEEPING:

ANGOLA (UNAVEM II): 15 Observers.

CAMBODIA (UNTAC): 2.

CROATIA (UNPROFOR): 884: 1 inf bn.

IRAQ/KUWAIT (UNIKOM): 7 Observers.

MIDDLE EAST (UNTSO): 6 Observers.

WESTERN SAHARA (MINURSO): 7 Observers.

PARAMILITARY:

GENDARMERIE (Ministry of Defence): 17,000; 5 Regional Comd.

EQUIPMENT: *Shorland* recce, 40 UR-416; 81mm mor; ac: 3 Piper, 5 PC-6; hel: 5 SA-315.

PREFECTURA NAVAL (Coast Guard): (13,000); 7 comd.

EQUIPMENT: 5 *Mantilla*, 1 *Delfin* PCO, 4 PCI, 19⟨; 5 C-212, 4 Short *Skyvan* ac; 3 SA-330, 6 MD-500 hel.

THE BAHAMAS

| GDP | 1990ε: $B 2.62bn ($US 2.62bn) |
| | 1991ε: $B 2.82bn ($US 2.82bn) |

Growth	1990: 3.0%	1991: −1.0%
Inflation	1990: 4.5%	1991: 8.0%
Debt	1990: $US 207.0m	1991ε: $US 212.0m
Sy bdgt*a*	1991: $B 63.66m ($US 63.66m)	
	1992ε: $B 66.96m ($US 66.96m)	

$US1 = $B 1987–92: 1.0
$B = Bahamian dollars
a Incl Police allocation.

Population: 268,200

	13–17	18–22	23–32
Men	14,700	15,000	22,500
Women	14,500	15,000	23,700

TOTAL SECURITY FORCES:
ACTIVE: 2,400: Police (1,700); Defence Force (700).

NAVY: (850).
(ROYAL BAHAMIAN DEFENCE FORCE)
BASE: Coral Harbour, New Providence Island.
PATROL AND COASTAL COMBATANTS: 15:
  INSHORE: 3 *Yellow Elder* PFI, 1 *Marlin*, 6 *Fenrick Sturrup* (ex-USCG *Cape Higgon* Cl) PCI, 5 PCI⟨, plus some ex-fishing vessels boats.
MISCELLANEOUS: 1 converted LCM (ex USN), 1 small auxiliary.
AIRCRAFT: 1 *Cessna* 404, 1 *Cessna* 421.

BELIZE

| GDP | 1990: $BZ 733.2m ($US 366.6m) |
| | 1991ε: $BZ 791.2m ($US 395.6m) |

Growth	1990: 6.5%	1991: 5.0%
Inflation	1990: 3.1%	1991: 5.6%
Debt	1990: $US 158.0m	
Def bdgt	1989ε: $BZ 19.88m ($US 9.94m)	
	1990ε: $BZ 19.36m ($US 9.68m)	

$US1 = $BZ 1987–92: 2.0
$BZ = $ Belize

Population: 204,600

	13–17	18–22	23–32
Men	13,200	11,800	16,000
Women	13,200	11,900	16,000

TOTAL ARMED FORCES:
ACTIVE: 660.
RESERVES (militia): 500.

ARMY: 600.
1 inf bn (3 inf, 1 spt, 1 trg, 3 Reserve coy).
EQUIPMENT:
MORTARS: 81mm: 6.
RCL: 84mm: 8 *Carl Gustav*.

MARITIME WING: 50.
PATROL: 2 PCI⟨, plus some 6 armed boats.

AIR WING: 15: 2 cbt ac, no armed hel.
MR/TRANSPORT: 2 BN-2B *Defender*.

FOREIGN FORCES:
UNITED KINGDOM: 1,500. Army: some 1,200; 1 inf bn + spt elm (incl *Rapier*). RAF: 300; 1 *Harrier* (FGA) flt, *Puma* hel flt.

BOLIVIA

| GDP | 1990: B 17.54bn ($5.53bn) |
| | 1991: B 21.69bn ($6.06bn) |

Growth	1990: 2.6%	1991: 4.1%
Inflation	1990: 17.1%	1991: 21.5%
Debt	1990: $4.30bn	1991: $3.47bn
Def bdgt	1991: B 440m ($122.88m)	
	1992: B 456m ($119.69m)	
FMA	1992: $65.9m*a* (US)	
$1 = B	1989: 2.691	1990: 3.173
	1991: 3.581	1992: 3.810

B = Bolivianos
a Incl $25m as Economic Support

Population: 7,622,000

	13–17	18–22	23–32
Men	434,300	365,700	556,500
Women	429,900	368,200	577,000

TOTAL ARMED FORCES:
ACTIVE: 31,500 (some 19,000 conscripts).
Terms of service: 12 months, selective.

ARMY: 23,000 (some 15,000 conscripts).
  HQ: 6 Military Regions.
  Army HQ direct control:
    2 armd bn.
    1 mech cav regt.

1 Presidential Guard inf regt.
10 'div'; org, composition varies; comprise:
8 cav gp (5 horsed, 2 mot, 1 aslt); 1 mot inf regt with 2 bn. 22 inf bn (incl 5 inf aslt bn); 1 armd bn; 1 arty 'regt' (bn); 5 arty gp (coy); 1 AB 'regt' (bn); 6 engr bn.

EQUIPMENT:
LIGHT TANKS: 36 SK-105 *Kuerassier*.
RECCE: 24 EE-9 *Cascavel*.
APC: 98: 40 M-113, 10 V-100 *Commando*, 24 MOWAG *Roland*, 24 EE-11 *Urutu*.
TOWED ARTY: 75mm: 70 incl M-116 pack, ε10 Bofors M-1935; 105mm: 30 incl M-101, FH-18.
MORTARS: 81mm: 250; 107mm: M-30.
RCL: 90mm: 30.
AVIATION: 4 Cessna 206, 1 *King Air* B90, 1 *Super King Air* 200 (VIP).

NAVY: 4,500 (incl 2,000 marines) (some conscripts).
6 Naval Districts; covering Lake Titicaca and the rivers; each 1 Flotilla.
BASES: Riberalta (HQ), Tiquina (HQ), Puerto Busch, Puerto Guayaramerín (HQ), Puerto Villaroel, Trinidad (HQ), Puerto Suárez (HQ) Cobija (HQ).
RIVER PATROL CRAFT: some 10⟨; plus some 8 US *Boston* whalers.
SUPPORT: 1 *Libertador Bolivar* ocean tpt (uses Arg/Uruguay ports).
Some 20 riverine craft/boats.

NAVAL AVIATION:
AIRCRAFT: 1 Cessna 206, 1 402.
MARINES: 6 bn (1 in each District).

AIR FORCE: 4,000 (perhaps 2,000 conscripts); 50 cbt ac, 10 armed hel.
FIGHTER: 1 sqn with 12 AT-33N, 4 F-86F (ftr/trg).
COIN: 2 AT-6G, 12 PC-7.
SPECIAL OPS: 1 sqn with 10 Hughes 500M hel.
SAR: 1 hel sqn with 4 HB-315B, 2 SA-315B, 1 UH-1.
SURVEY: 1 sqn with 5 Cessna 206, 1 210, 1 402, 3 *Learjet* 25, 1 PA-31.
TRANSPORT: 3 sqn:
1 VIP tpt with 1 L-188, 1 *Sabreliner*, 2 *Super King Air*.
2 tpt with 9 C-130, 4 F-27-400, 1 IAI-201, 2 *King Air*, 5 C-47.
LIAISON:
AIRCRAFT: 9 Cessna 152, 2 -185, 13 -206, 2 -402, 1 *Commander* 500.
HELICOPTERS: 2 Bell 212, 25 UH-1H.
TRAINING: 1 Cessna 152, 2 172, 11* PC-7, 6 SF-260CB, 15 T-23, 9* T-33A, 3 T-41D.
1 air-base defence regt (Oerlikon twin 20mm, some truck-mounted guns).

PARAMILITARY:
NATIONAL POLICE: some 15,000.
NARCOTICS POLICE: some 1,200.

BRAZIL

GDP[a]	1990:	Cr 1,527.0bn ($246.59bn)	
	1991ε:	Cr 1,545.3bn ($249.55bn)	
Growth	1990:	−4.0%	1991: 1.2%
Inflation	1990:	2,900%	1991: 440%
Debt	1990:	$116.17bn	1991: $117.0bn
Def bdgt	1991ε:	Cr 935.20bn ($2.30bn)	
	1992:	Cr 7,423.0bn ($2.12bn)	
$1 = Cr	1989:	2.83	1990: 68.30
	1991:	406.61	1992ε 3,500.0

Cr = Cruzeiro
[a] All GDP figures are in 1985 prices and exchange rates.

Population: 155,954,000

	13–17	18–22	23–32
Men	8,067,000	7,339,000	13,267,000
Women	8,004,000	7,326,000	13,275,000

TOTAL ARMED FORCES:
ACTIVE: 296,700 (128,500 conscripts).
Terms of service: 12 months (can be extended by 6 months).
RESERVES: Trained first-line 1,115,000; 400,000 subject to immediate recall. Second-line 225,000.

ARMY: 196,000; (126,500 conscripts).
HQ: 7 Military Comd, 12 Military Regions;
8 div (3 with Region HQ).
1 armd cav bde (2 mech, 1 armd, 1 arty bn).
3 armd inf bde (each 2 inf, 1 armd, 1 arty bn).
4 mech cav bde (each 3 inf, 1 arty bn).
12 motor inf bde (26 bn).
1 mtn bde.
2 'jungle' bde (7 bn).
1 frontier bde (6 bn).
1 AB bde (3 AB, 1 SF bn).
2 coast and AD arty bde.
3 cav guard regt.
28 arty gp (4 SP, 6 med, 18 fd).
2 engr gp each 4 bn; 10 bn (incl 2 railway) (to be increased to 34 bn).
Avn: hel bde forming, to comprise 46 hel.
EQUIPMENT:
LIGHT TANKS: some 520, some 150 M-3, some 80 X-1A, 40 X-1A2 (M-3 mod); 250 M-41C.
RECCE: 300 EE-9 *Cascavel*, 250 EE-3 *Jararaca*, 30 M-8.
APC: 845: 225 EE-11 *Urutu*, 20 M-59, 600 M-113.
TOWED ARTY: 570: 105mm: 420 M-101/-102, Model 56 pack; 155mm: 150 M-114.

SP ARTY: 105mm: 120 M-7/-108.
COAST ARTY: some 240 57mm, 75mm, 120mm, 150mm, 152mm, 305mm.
MRL: 108mm: SS-06; 180mm: SS-40; 300mm: SS-60 incl SP; 4 *ASTROS* II.
MORTARS: 81mm; 107mm: M-30; 120mm.
ATGW: 300 *Cobra*.
RCL: 57mm: 240 M-18A1; 75mm: 20; 105mm; 106mm: M-40A1.
AD GUNS: 20mm; 35mm: 38 GDF-001; 40mm: 60 L-60/-70.
SAM: 4 *Roland* II, BOFI AD system (40mm L/70 gun with RBS-70 SAM).
HELICOPTERS: 36 SA-365 and 10 HB-350 to be delivered.

NAVY: 50,000 (2,000 conscripts) incl 700 naval air and 15,000 marines.
  5 Oceanic Naval Districts plus 1 Riverine; 1 Comd.
BASES: OCEAN: Rio de Janeiro (HQ I Naval District), Salvador (HQ II District), Natal (HQ III District), Belém (HQ IV District), Rio Grande do Sul (HQ V District).
RIVERINE: Ladario (HQ VI District), Manaus.
SUBMARINES: 5:
  1 *Tupi* (Ge T-209/1400) with 533mm TT (UK *Tigerfish* HWT).
  3 *Humaita* (UK *Oberon*) with 533mm TT (*Tigerfish* HWT).
  1 *Goias/Bahia* (US *Guppy* III/II)† with 533mm TT (trg only).
PRINCIPAL SURFACE COMBATANTS: 19:
CARRIER: 1 *Minas Gerais* (UK *Colossus*) CVS (ASW), capacity 20 ac: typically 7–8 S-2E ASW ac, 8 ASH-3H hel.
DESTROYERS: 6:
  2 *Marcilio Dias* (US *Gearing*) ASW with 1 *Wasp* hel (Mk 46 LWT), 1 × 8 *ASROC*, 2 × 3 ASTT; plus 2 × 2 127mm guns.
  4 *Mato Grosso* (US *Sumner*) ASW, 4 with 1 *Wasp* hel, all with 2 × 3 ASTT; plus 3 × 2 127mm guns.
FRIGATES: 12:
  4 *Para* (US *Garcia*) with 1 × 8 *ASROC*, 2 × 3 ASTT, 1 × *Lynx* hel; plus 2 × 127mm guns.
  4 *Niteroi* ASW with 1 *Lynx* hel, 2 × 3 ASTT, *Ikara* SUGW, 1 × 2 ASW mor; plus 2 × MM-40 *Exocet* SSM, 1 × 114mm gun.
  2 *Niteroi* GP; weapons as ASW, except 4 × MM-40 *Exocet*, 2 × 114mm guns, no *Ikara*.
  2 *Inhauma*, with 1 *Lynx* hel, 2 × 3 ASTT, plus 4 × MM-40 *Exocet*, 1 × 114mm gun.
PATROL AND COASTAL COMBATANTS: 30:
  9 *Imperial Marinheiro* PCO.
  2 *Grauna* PCC.
  6 *Piratini* (US PGM) PCI, 3 *Aspirante Nascimento* PCI (trg).
  4 *Tracker* PCI⟨.
  6 Riverine patrol: 3 *Roraima* and 2 *Pedro Teixeira*, 1 *Parnaiba*.

MINE WARFARE: 6: 6 *Aratü* (Ge *Schütze*) MSI.
AMPHIBIOUS: 3:
  2 *Ceara* (US *Thomaston*) LSD capacity 350 tps, 38 tk.
  1 *Duque de Caxais* (US *de Soto County* LST), capacity 600 tps, 18 tk.
Plus some 39 craft; 3 LCU, 6 LCM, 30 LCVP.
SUPPORT AND MISCELLANEOUS 19:
  1 AOR, 1 repair ship, 1 submarine rescue, 4 tpt, 6 survey/oceanography, 1 mod *Niteroi* FF (trg), 5 ocean tugs.

NAVAL AVIATION: (700); 13 armed hel.
ASW: 1 hel sqn with 7 ASH-3A.
ATTACK: 1 with 6 *Lynx* HAS-21.
UTILITY: 2 sqn with 5 AS-332, 8 AS-350B, 9 AS-355.
TRAINING: 1 hel sqn with 15 TH-57.
ASM: AS-11, AS-12, *Sea Skua*.

MARINES: (15,000).
Fleet Force:
  1 amph div (1 comd, 3 inf bn, 1 arty gp).
Reinforcement Comd:
  5 bn incl 1 engr, 1 special ops.
Internal Security Force:
  6 regional gp.
EQUIPMENT:
RECCE: 6 EE-9 Mk IV *Cascavel*.
AAV: 12 LVTP-7A1
APC: 30 M-113.
TOWED ARTY: 105mm: 12 M-101; 155mm: 6 M-114.
RL: 89mm: 3.5-in. M-20.
RCL: 106mm: M-40A1.
AD GUNS: 40mm: 6 L/70 with BOFI.

AIR FORCE: 50,700; 307 cbt ac, 8 armed hel.
AD COMMAND: 1 Gp:
FIGHTER: 2 sqn with 14 F-103E (*Mirage* IIIEBR), 4 F-103D (*Mirage* IIIDBR).
TACTICAL COMMAND: 10 Gp:
FGA: 3 sqn with 49 F-5E, 4 -B, 4 -F, 15 AMX.
COIN: 3 sqn with 48 AT-26.
COIN/TRG: 30 T-27.
RECCE: 2 sqn with 8 RC-95, 12 RT-26, 3 *Learjet* 35.
LIAISON/OBSERVATION: 7 sqn: 1 ac with 8 T-27; 1 hel with 8 UH-1H (armed), 5 ac/hel with 31 U-7 ac and 30 UH-1H hel.
MARITIME COMMAND: 4 Gp.
ASW (afloat): 1 sqn with 11 S-2E.
MR/SAR: 3 sqn with 11 EMB-110B, 10 EMB-111.
TRANSPORT COMMAND: 6 Gp (6 sqn), 7 regional indep sqn:
  HEAVY 2 sqn:
    1 with 9 C-130E, 5 -H;
    1 with 2 KC-130H, 4 KC-137 tkr/tpt.
  MED/LT: 2 sqn:
    1 with 12 C-91;

1 with 23 C-95A/B/C.
TACTICAL: 1 sqn with 12 C-115.
VIP: 1 sqn with 1 VC-91, 10 VC/VU-93, 2 VC-96, 5 VC-97, 5 VU-9, ac; 3 VH-4 hel.
REGIONAL: 7 sqn with 7 C-115, 82 C-95A/B/C, 6 EC-9 (VU-9).
HELICOPTERS: 9 AS-332, 13 AS-355, 2 Bell 206, 6 SA-330, 30 SA-350, 6 SH-1H.
LIAISON: 50 C-42, 3 Cessna 208, 30 U-42.
TRAINING COMMAND:
AIRCRAFT: 50* AT-26, 70 EMB-110, 25 T-23, 98 T-25, 78* T-27.
HELICOPTERS: 4 OH-6A, 25 OH-13.
CALIBRATION: 1 unit with 2 C-95, 1 EC-93, 4 EC-95, 1 U-93.
AAM: AIM-9 *Sidewinder*, R-530.

FORCES ABROAD:
UN AND PEACEKEEPING:
ANGOLA (UNAVEM II): 15 Observers, 14 medical.
EL SALVADOR (ONUSAL): 47 Observers, 8 medical.

PARAMILITARY:
PUBLIC SECURITY FORCES (R): some 243,000 in state military police org (State Militias) under Army control and considered an Army Reserve.

CHILE

GDP	1990:	pCh 8,477.9bn ($27.79bn)	
	1991:	pCh 10,939.2bn ($31.31bn)	
Growth	1990:	2.2%	1991: 6.0%
Inflation	1990:	26.1%	1991: 21.9%
Debt	1990:	$19.11bn	1991: $17.91bn
Def bdgt	1990:	pCh 282.79bn ($927m)	
	1991:	pCh 349.37bn ($1,000m)	
FMA	1992:	$1.15m (US)	
$1 = pCh	1989:	267.16	1990: 305.06
	1991:	349.37	1992: 347.00

pCh = pesos Chilenos

Population: 13,290,000

	13–17	18–22	23–32
Men	616,800	591,000	1,165,700
Women	601,600	576,800	1,148,600

TOTAL ARMED FORCES:
ACTIVE: 91,800 (30,800 conscripts).
Terms of service: 2 years all services.
RESERVES: Army 45,000.

ARMY: 54,000 (27,000 conscripts).
6 Military Regions, 2 Corps HQ.

6 div:
  1 with 3 mot inf, 1 armd cav, 1 arty, 1 engr regt, 1 ATK bn;
  1 with 2 mot inf, 5 mtn, 1 armd cav, 1 arty, 1 engr regt;
  1 with 2 inf, 3 mtn, 2 armd cav, 1 arty, 1 engr regt;
  1 with 1 inf, 2 mtn, 2 armd cav, 1 arty, 1 engr regt;
  1 with 2 inf, 2 armd cav, 1 arty, 1 engr regt, 1 cdo bn;
  1 with 2 inf, 1 mtn, 2 armd cav, 1 arty, 1 engr regt.
1 bde with 1 mtn, 1 inf, 1 arty regt, 1 recce sqn.
Army tps: 1 avn, 1 engr regt.
EQUIPMENT:
MBT: 171: 150 M-51, 21 AMX-30.
LIGHT TANKS: 157: 60 M-24, 50 M-41, 47 AMX-13 (in store).
RECCE: 200 EE-9 *Cascavel*.
AIFV: 20 MOWAG *Piranha* with 90mm gun.
APC: 50 M-113, 180 Cardoen/MOWAG *Piranha*, 300 EE-11 *Urutu*.
TOWED ARTY: 150: 105mm: 120 incl M-101, Model 56; 155mm: 30 M-68.
SP ARTY: 155mm: 10 Mk F3.
MORTARS: 81mm: 300 M-29; 107mm: 15; 120mm: 110 ECIA (incl 50 SP).
ATGW: *Milan/Mamba*.
RL: 89mm: 3.5-in. M-20.
RCL: 150 incl: 57mm: M-18; 75mm; 106mm: M-40A1.
AD GUNS: 20mm: some SP (Cardoen/MOWAG).
SAM: *Blowpipe, Javelin*.
AIRCRAFT:
  TRANSPORT: 6 C-212, 1 *Citation* (VIP), 3 CN-235, 4 DHC-6, 3 PA-31, 8 PA-28 Piper *Dakota*.
  TRAINING: 16 Cessna R-172.
HELICOPTERS: 2 AB-206, 3 AS-332, 15 Enstrom 280 FX, 5 Hughes 530F (armed trg), 10 SA-315, 9 SA-330.

NAVY: ε25,000 (3,000 conscripts), incl naval air, marines and Coast Guard.
DEPLOYMENT AND BASES:
3 main commands: Fleet (includes CC, DD and FF), Submarine Flotilla, Transport. Remaining forces allocated to 4 Naval Zones:
  1st Naval Zone (26°S – 36°S approx).
    Valparaiso (HQ).
  2nd Naval Zone (36°S – 43°S approx).
    Talcahuano, (HQ), Puerto Montt.
  3rd Naval Zone (43°S to Cape Horn), Punta Arenas, (HQ), Puerto Williams.
  4th Naval Zone (north of 26°S approx) Iquique (HQ).
SUBMARINES: 4:
  2 *O'Brien* (UK *Oberon*) with 533mm TT (Ge HWT).
  2 *Thompson* (Ge T-209/1300) with 533mm TT (HWT).
PRINCIPAL SURFACE COMBATANTS: 10:
DESTROYERS: 6:

2 *Capitan Prat* (UK *Norfolk*) DDG with 1 × 2
Seaslug-2 SAM, 4 × MM-38 *Exocet* SSM, 1 × 2
114mm guns, 1 hel.

2 *Blanco Encalada* (UK *Norfolk*) DDH with 4 ×
MM-38, 1 × 2 114 mm guns, 2 NAS-332 hel.
(*Cochrane* in refit).

2 *Almirante Riveros* (ASUW) with 4 × MM-38
Exocet SSM, 4 × 102mm guns; plus 2 × 3
ASTT (Mk 44 LWT), 2 × 3 ASW mor.

FRIGATES: 4 *Condell* (mod UK *Leander*) with 2 × 3
ASTT, 1 hel; plus 4 × MM-38 *Exocet*, 1 × 2
114mm guns.

PATROL AND COASTAL COMBATANTS: 10:
MISSILE CRAFT: 4:
2 *Casma* (Is *Reshef*) PFM with 4 *Gabriel* SSM.
2 *Iquique* (Is *Sa'ar*) PFM with 6 *Gabriel* SSM.
TORPEDO CRAFT: 4 *Guacolda* (Ge Lürssen 36-m)
with 4 × 533mm TT.
PATROL: 2:
1 PCO (ex-US tug).
1 *Papudo* PCC (ex-US PC-1638).
AMPHIBIOUS: 3:
3 *Maipo* (Fr *BATRAL*) LSM, capacity 140 tps, 7 tk.
Plus craft; 2 LCT.
SUPPORT AND MISCELLANEOUS: 9:
1 *Almirante Jorge Montt* (UK 'Tide') AO, 1
Araucano AO, 1 submarine spt, 1 tpt, 1 survey,
1 *Uribe* trg. 1 Antarctic patrol, 2 tugs/spt.

NAVAL AVIATION: (500);
6 cbt ac, 12 armed hel. 4 sqn.
MR: 1 sqn with 6 EMB-111N, 2 *Falcon* 20.
ASW HEL: 4 AS-332F, 4 AS-365, 4 AS-532SC.
LIAISON: 1 sqn with 3 C-212A, 3 EMB-110N, 2
IAI-1124, 1 PA-31.
HELICOPTERS: 1 sqn with 3 AB-206, 3 SH-57.
TRAINING: 1 sqn with 10 PC-7.

MARINES: (ε4,000).
4 gp: each 1 inf bn (+), 1 cdo coy, 1 fd arty, 1
AD arty bty. 1 amph bn.
EQUIPMENT:
APC: 40 MOWAG *Roland*, 30 LVTP-5.
TOWED ARTY: 105mm: 16 M-101; 155mm: 36 M-114†.
COAST GUNS: 155mm: 16 GPFM-3.
MORTARS: 60mm: 50; 81mm: 50.
SAM: *Blowpipe*.

COAST GUARD: (1,600)
PATROL CRAFT: 17:
2 PCC (Buoy Tenders), 1 *Castor* PCI, 2 *Alacalufe*
PCI, 12 PCI⟨, plus about 12 boats.
HELICOPTER: 1 Bell 206B.

AIR FORCE: 12,800 (800 conscripts);
106 cbt ac, no armed hel. 5 Air Bde: 4 wings.

FGA: 2 sqn:
1 with 32 *Hunter* (17 F-71, 8 FGA-9, 4 FR-71, 3
T-72);
1 with 16 F-5 (13 -E, 3 -F).
COIN: 2 sqn with 24 A-37B, 20 A-36.
FIGHTER/RECCE: 1 sqn with 15 *Mirage* 50 (8 -FCH,
6 -CH, 1 -DCH).
RECCE: 2 photo units with 2 *Canberra* PR-9, 1 *King
Air* A-100, 2 *Learjet* 35A.
TRANSPORT: 1 sqn with:
AIRCRAFT: 4 Boeing 707, 2 C-130H, 2 C-130B, 3
Beech 99 (ELINT, tpt, trg), 14 DHC-6 (5 -100,
9 -300).
HELICOPTERS: 5 SA-315B.
LIAISON HELICOPTERS: 6 Bo-105CB, 4 UH-1H.
TRAINING: 1 wing, 3 flying schools:
AIRCRAFT: 16 PA-28, 60 T-35A/B, 20 T-36, 26
T-37B/C, 8 T-41D.
HELICOPTERS: 6 UH-1H.
MISSILES:
ASM: AS-11/-12.
AAM: AIM-9B *Sidewinder*, *Shafrir*.
AD: 1 regt (5 gp) with: 20mm: S-639/-665, GAI-CO1
twin; 35mm: 36, K-63 twin; *Blowpipe*, 12
Cactus (Crotale).

===

FORCES ABROAD:
UN AND PEACEKEEPING:
CAMBODIA (UNTAC): 19 Observers.
INDIA/PAKISTAN (UNMOGIP): 3 Observers.
IRAQ/KUWAIT (UNIKOM): 48: incl air unit of 6
UH-1H hel.
MIDDLE EAST (UNTSO): 4 Observers.

===

PARAMILITARY:
CARABINEROS: 27,000.
EQUIPMENT:
APC: MOWAG *Roland*.
MORTARS: 60mm, 81mm.
AIRCRAFT: 1 *Metro*.
HELICOPTERS: 2 Bell 206, 12 Bo-105.

===

OPPOSITION:
**FRENTE PATRIOTICO MANUEL RODRIGUEZ/
DISSIDENT (FPMR/D):** ε1,000; leftist.
**MOVEMENT OF THE REVOLUTIONARY LEFT
(MIR):** some 500.

COLOMBIA

GDP	1990:	pC 20,234.1bn ($40.29bn)		
	1991:	pC 26,708.9bn ($42.19bn)		
Growth	1990:	4.1%	1991:	1.5%
Inflation	1990:	29.1%	1991:	30.4%
Debt	1990:	$17.24bn	1991:	$17.75bn

Def bdgt 1990: pC 454.07bn ($904.06m)
1991: pC 749.30bn ($1.18bn)
FMA[a] 1992: $60.3m (US)
$1 = pC 1989: 382.57 1990: 502.26
1991 633.05 1992: 750.00
pC = pesos Colombianos
[a] Redirected to the Police Forces from the Military.

Population: 32,314,000

	13–17	18–22	23–32
Men	1,715,000	1,636,000	2,958,000
Women	1,671,000	1,605,000	2,950,000

TOTAL ARMED FORCES:
ACTIVE: 139,000 (some 40,400 conscripts).
Terms of service: 1–2 years, varies (all services).
RESERVES: 116,900: Army 100,000; Navy 15,000; Air 1,900.

ARMY: 120,000 (38,000 conscripts).
4 div HQ.
12 inf bde (Regional):
8 with 3 inf, 1 arty bn, 1 engr gp, 1 mech or horsed cav gp;
4 with 2 inf bn only.
Army Tps:
2 COIN bde (9 bn).
1 trg bde.
1 Presidential Guard bn (mech).
1 mech gp.
1 AB, 1 cdo, 1 ranger, 1 AD arty bn.
EQUIPMENT:
LIGHT TANKS: 12 M-3A1.
RECCE: 4 M-8, 120 EE-9 *Cascavel*.
APC: 80 M-113, 76 EE-11 *Urutu*.
TOWED ARTY: 105mm: 130 M-101;
MORTARS: 81mm: 125 M-1; 107mm: 148 M-2; 120mm: 120 Brandt.
ATGW: *TOW*.
RCL: 75mm: M-20; 106mm: M-40A1.
AD GUNS: 40mm: 30 Bofors.

NAVY: 12,000 (incl 6,000 marines) (some 500 conscripts).
BASES: OCEAN: Cartagena (main), Buenaventura, Malala (Pacific).
RIVER: Puerto Leguízamo, Puerto Orocué, Puerto Carreño, Leticia.
SUBMARINES: 2:
2 *Pijao* (Ge T-209/1200) with 533mm TT (Ge HWT).
Plus 2 *Intrepido* (It SX-506) SSI (SF delivery).
FRIGATES: 5: 4 *Almirante Padilla* with 1 × Bo-105 hel (ASW), 2 × 3 ASTT; plus 8 × MM-40 *Exocet* SSM.
1 *Boyaca* (US *Courtney*) with 2 × 3 324mm TT, 2 × 76mm gun; plus hel deck (used HQ ship).

PATROL AND COASTAL COMBATANTS: 26:
PATROL:
OFFSHORE: 3 *Pedro de Heredia* (ex-US tugs).
INSHORE: 9: 2 *Quito Sueno* (US *Asheville*) PFI.
1 *Castillo Y Rada* (Swiftships 32-m) PCI.
6 PCI⟨.
RIVERINE: 14: 3 *Arauca*, 11⟨.
SUPPORT AND MISCELLANEOUS: 4:
1 tpt, 2 research, 1 trg.

MARINES: (6,000); 5 bn, 2 bn naval police.
No hy eqpt (to get EE-9 *Cascavel* recce, EE-11 *Urutu* APC).

NAVAL AVIATION: 500
AIRCRAFT: 3 *Commander*, 3 PA-28, 2 PA-31.
HELICOPTERS: 2 Bo-105.

AIR FORCE: 7,000 (some 1,900 conscripts); 68 cbt ac, 51 armed hel.
AIR COMBAT COMMAND:
FGA: 2 sqn:
1 with 15 *Mirage 5* (11 -COA, 2 -COD trg, 2 -COR recce);
1 with 13 *Kfir* (11 -C2, 2 -TC2).
COIN: 1 AC-47, 10 AT-33A, 3 IA-58, 8 A-37B, 17 OA-37B, 18 OV-10, 4 OA-37B ac; 6 UH-1B, 23 -H armed hel.
TACTICAL AIR SUPPORT COMMAND:
COIN: 1 sqn hel with 12 OH-6/Hughes 500D, 18 Hughes 500MG/530MG hel.
RECCE: 1 sqn with:
AIRCRAFT: 3 RT-33A;
HELICOPTERS: 5 Hughes 300C, 4 -500D, 2E.
MILITARY AIR TRANSPORT COMMAND:
AIRCRAFT: 1 sqn with 1 BAe 748, 1 Boeing 707, 8 C-47, 4 C-54, 2 C-130B, 1 -E, 2 -H-30, 2 Cessna 310, 1 -340, 4 -404, 1 *Commander* 560A, 4 DC-6, 10 DHC-2, 2 F-28, 2 IAI-201, 2 PA-31, 1 PA-32, 1 PA-34, 1 PA-44, 5 PC-6B, 4 *Queen Air*.
HELICOPTERS: 10 Bell 205, 3 212, 2 412, 8 UH-60.
AIR TRAINING COMMAND:
AIRCRAFT: 20 T-34A/B, 30 T-41D.
HELICOPTERS: 2 Hughes 500C, 8 OH-13, 6 TH-55.
AAM: AIM-7 *Sparrow*, R-530.

FORCES ABROAD:
UN AND PEACEKEEPING:
CROATIA (UNPROFOR): 4 Observers.
EGYPT (MFO): 500.
EL SALVADOR (ONUSAL): 8 Observers.

PARAMILITARY:
NATIONAL POLICE FORCE: 85,000; 35 ac, 25 hel.
COAST GUARD: 1,500
PATROL CRAFT: 2 PCI.

OPPOSITION:

COORDINADORA NACIONAL GUERRILLERA SIMON BOLIVAR (CNGSB): loose coalition of guerrilla gp incl: Revolutionary Armed Forces of Colombia (FARC): some 5,000 active, pro-Soviet; Ejército de Liberación Nacional (ELN): ε2,000, pro-Cuban; Ejército Poplar de Liberación (EPL-D).

COSTA RICA

GDP	1990:	C 522.21bn ($5.70bn)		
	1991:	C 672.95bn ($5.50bn)		
Growth	1990:	3.6%	1991:	1.3%
Inflation	1990:	19.0%	1991:	28.7%
Debt	1990:	$3.77bn		
Sy bdgt[a]	1991:	C 6.77bn ($55.31m)		
	1992ε:	C 8.19bn ($60.70m)		
FMA[b]	1992:	$22.59m (US)		
$1 = C	1989:	81.504	1990:	91.580
	1991:	122.430	1992:	135.000

C = colones

[a] No armed forces. Figures are for sy and Police.

[b] Incl $20m as Economic Support.

Population: 3,032,000

	13–17	18–22	23–32
Men	156,900	144,500	276,100
Women	151,100	138,700	268,100

TOTAL SECURITY FORCES:
ACTIVE (Paramilitary): 7,500.

CIVIL GUARD: 4,300.
6 Border Sy Comd (4 North, 2 South)
Presidential Guard: 1 bn, 7 coy.
MARINE: (150)
PATROL, INSHORE: 6:
   1 *Isla del Coco* (US *Swift* 32-m), 1 *Astronauta Franklin Chang* (US *Cape Higgon*) PFI, 4 PFI⟨ plus about 10 boats.
AIRCRAFT: 4 Cessna 206, 1 *Commander* 680, 3 O-2 (surveillance), 2 PA-23, 3 PA-28, 1 PA-31, 1 PA-34.
HELICOPTERS: 2 Hughes 500E, 1 Hiller FH-1100.

RURAL GUARD: (Ministry of Government and Police): 3,200; small arms only.

CUBA

GSP[a]	1990ε:	pC 27.2bn ($33.84bn)
	1991ε:	pC 23.1bn ($25.98bn)

Growth	1990ε: −4.0%	1991ε: −25%	
Inflation	1989ε: 4.0%	1990ε: 3.5%	
Debt[b]	1989: $6.80bn	1990ε: $6.40bn	
Def bdgt	1990ε: pC 1.36bn ($1.69bn)		
	1991ε: pC 1.16bn ($1.16bn)		
$1 = pC	1989: 0.762	1990: 0.804	
	1991ε: 0.890	1992ε: 1.000	

pC = pesos Cubanos

[a] Gross Social Product: excl the so-called 'non-productive' service sectors of the economy, such as education and housing which are included in GDP. GSP figures in dollars are exaggerated by the official exchange rate. The actual size of the economy is estimated to be up to 30% smaller in real dollar terms.

[b] Excl debt to socialist countries. Cumulative debt to CMEA ε $35–40bn.

Population: 10,824,000

	13–17	18–22	23–32
Men	447,000	532,000	1,062,000
Women	427,000	509,000	1,010,000

TOTAL ARMED FORCES:
ACTIVE: 175,000 incl ε15,000 Ready Reserves, (79,500 conscripts).
Terms of service: 2 years.
RESERVES: Army: 135,000 Ready Reserves (serve 45 days per year) to fill out Active and Reserve units; See also Paramilitary.

ARMY: 145,000 (incl ε15,000 Ready Reservists). (ε60,000 conscripts)
HQ: 4 Regional Command; 3 Army, 1 Isle of Youth.
   1 armd div (Cat A).
   13 mech inf div, (3 mech inf, 1 armd, 1 arty, 1 AD arty regt) (Cat B).
   9 inf div (3 inf, 1 arty, 1 AD arty regt) (Cat B/C).
   1 indep armd bde.
   AD: AD arty regt and SAM bde (Cat varies: SAM εCat A, AD arty B or C).
   1 AB bde (Cat A).
   Forces combat readiness system: Cat A div fully manned by active tps; Cat B: partial manning augmented by reservists on mob; Cat C: Active cadre, full manning by reservists on mob.
EQUIPMENT:
MBT: 1,700: 100 T-34 (in store), 1,200 T-54/-55, 400 T-62.
LIGHT TANKS: 70 PT-76.
RECCE: 200 BRDM-1/-2.
AIFV: 400 BMP-1.
APC: 1,100 BTR-40/-50/-60/-152.
TOWED ARTY: 76mm: M-1942; 122mm: M-1931/37, D-74; 130mm: M-46; 152mm: M-1937, D-20, D-1.
SP ARTY: 122mm: 2S1; 152mm: 2S3.
MRL: 122mm: BM-21; 140mm: BM-14; 240mm: BM-24.
MORTARS: 82mm: M-41/-43; 120mm: M-38/-43.

STATIC DEFENCE ARTY: some 15 JS-2 (122mm) hy tk, T-34 (85mm), SU-100 (100mm) SP guns.
ATGW: AT-1 *Snapper*, AT-3 *Sagger*.
ATK GUNS: 85mm: D-44; 100mm: SU-100 SP.
AD GUNS: 1,600 incl 23mm: ZU-23, ZSU-23-4 SP; 30mm: M-53 (twin)/BTR-60P SP; 37mm: M-1939; 57mm: S-60 towed, ZSU-57-2 SP; 85mm: KS-12; 100mm: KS-19.
SAM: 12 SA-6, SA-7/-8/-9/-13/-14.

NAVY: 13,500 (8,500 conscripts).
3 Naval Districts, 4 Operational Flotillas.
BASES: Cienfuegos, Cabanas, Havana, Mariel, Punta Movida, Nicaro.
SUBMARINES: 3 Sov *Foxtrot* with 533mm and 406mm TT (incl 1 in refit).
FRIGATES: 3 Sov *Koni* with 2 × ASW RL.
PATROL AND COASTAL COMBATANTS: 28:
MISSILE CRAFT: 18:
  18 Sov *Osa-I/-II* with 4 × SS-N-2 *Styx* SSM.
PATROL: 10:
  COASTAL: 1:
    1 Sov *Pauk* II PFC with 2 × ASW RL, 4 × ASTT.
  INSHORE: 9:
    9 Sov *Turya* PHI.
MINE WARFARE: 16:
  4 Sov *Sonya* MSC
  12 Sov *Yevgenya* MSI.
AMPHIBIOUS: 2 Sov *Polnocny* LSM, capacity 6 tk, 200 tps.
SUPPORT AND MISCELLANEOUS 5:
  1 AO, 1 AGI, 1 survey, 1 ocean tug, 1 trg.

NAVAL INFANTRY: (550+).
1 amph aslt bn.

COASTAL DEFENCE:
ARTY: 122mm: M-1931/37; 130mm: M-46; 152mm: M-1937.
SSM: 2 SS-C-3 systems.

AIR FORCE: ε17,000+, incl AD (11,000 conscripts); 162 cbt ac, 85 armed hel.
FGA: 2 sqn:
  2 with 20 MiG-23BN.
FIGHTER: 4 sqn:
  2 with 30 MiG-21F;
  1 with 50 MiG-21bis;
  1 with 40 MiG-23MF.
  6 MiG-29.
ATTACK HELICOPTERS: 10 Mi-8, 40 Mi-17, 30 Mi-25.
ASW: 5 Mi-14 hel.
TRANSPORT: 4 sqn: 8 An-2, 3 An-24, 21 An-26, 2 An-3, 4 Yak-40, 2 Il-76 (Air Force ac in civilian markings).

HELICOPTERS: 60 Mi-8/-17.
TRAINING: 25 L-39, 15 MiG-15, 15 MiG-15UTI, 8* MiG-21U, 4* MiG-23U, 2* MiG-29UB, 20 Z-326.
MISSILES:
  ASM: AT-2, AT-3.
  AAM: AA-2, AA-8.
AD: 200+ SAM launchers: SA-2, SA-3, SA-6, SA-9, SA-13.
Civil Airline: 10 Il-62, 7 Tu-154, 12 Yak-42 used as troop tpt.

PARAMILITARY:
YOUTH LABOUR ARMY: 100,000:
CIVIL DEFENCE FORCE: 50,000:
TERRITORIAL MILITIA (R): 1,300,000.
STATE SECURITY (Ministry of Interior): 15,000.
BORDER GUARDS (Ministry of Interior): 4,000.
  About 30 Sov *Zhuk* and 3 Sov *Stenka* PFI⟨, plus boats.

FOREIGN FORCES:
US: 2,300: Navy: 1,900; Marine: 400: 1 reinforced coy at Guantánamo Bay.
RUSSIA: 4,300: 1 motor rifle bde (2,100); SIGINT personnel (2,100); mil advisers (ε100).

DOMINICAN REPUBLIC

GDP[a]	1990:	$RD 60.56bn ($US 4.95bn)
	1991:	$RD 91.41bn ($US 4.93bn)
Growth	1990: −5.4%	1991: −0.5%
Inflation	1990: 59.5%	1991: 53.9%
Debt	1990: $US 4.40bn	1991: $US 4.80bn
Def bdgt	1990ε: $RD 423.9m ($US 49.72m)
	1991: $RD 441.5m ($US 34.79m)
FMA[b]	1992: $7.9m (US)
$US 1 =	$RD 1989: 6.340	1990: 8.290
	1991: 12.692	1992: 12.950

$RD = pesos República Dominicana
[a] GDP in $US is calculated in 1985 prices and exchange rates.
[b] Incl $US 5m as Economic Support.

Population: 7,479,000

	13–17	18–22	23–32
Men	414,000	388,000	669,000
Women	401,000	375,000	640,000

TOTAL ARMED FORCES:
ACTIVE: 22,200.

ARMY: 15,000.
5 Defence Zones.

4 inf bde (with 17 bn).
1 armd, 1 Presidential Guard, 1 arty, 1 engr bn.

EQUIPMENT:
LIGHT TANKS: 2 AMX-13 (75mm), 12 M-41A1 (76mm).
RECCE: 8 V-150 *Commando*.
APC: 20 M-2/M-3 half-track.
TOWED ARTY: 105mm: 22 M-101.
MORTARS: 81mm: M-1; 120mm: 24 ECIA.
RCL: 106mm: M-40A1.
AD GUNS: 40mm: 20 L/60.

NAVY: ε3,000.
BASES: Santo Domingo (HQ), Las Calderas.
PATROL AND COASTAL COMBATANTS: 18:
OFFSHORE: 9:
1 *Mella* (Cdn *River*) (comd/trg)
3 *Cambiaso* (US *Cohoes*).
3 armed ocean tugs.
2 *Prestol Botello* (US *Admirable*).
INSHORE: 9: 1 *Betelgeuse* (US PGM-71), 8⟨.
AMPHIBIOUS: craft only;
1 LCU.
SUPPORT AND MISCELLANEOUS: 1:
1 AOT (small harbour).

AIR FORCE: 4,200; 10 cbt ac, no armed hel.
COIN: 1 sqn with 8 A-37B.
TRANSPORT: 1 sqn with 3 C-47, 1 *Commander* 680,
1 MU-2.
LIAISON: 1 Cessna 210, 5 O-2A, 2 PA-31, 3 *Queen Air*, 80 1 *King Air*.
HELICOPTERS: 8 Bell 205, 1 OH-6A, 2 SA-318C, 1 SA-365 (VIP), 1 SA-360.
TRAINING: 2* AT-6, 6 T-34B, 3 T-41D.
AB: 1 AB sqn.
AD: 1 bn with 4 20mm guns.

PARAMILITARY:
NATIONAL POLICE: 15,000 incl 'special ops unit': 1,000.

ECUADOR

GDP	1990: ES 8,349.7bn ($10.88bn)	
	1991: ES 12,691.5bn ($12.13bn)	
Growth	1990: 2.4%	1991: 1.2%
Inflation	1990: 48.5%	1991: 48.7%
Debt	1990: $12.11bn	1991: $12.25bn
Def bdgt	1990: ES 193.0bn ($251.38m)	
	1991ε: ES 273.0bn ($260.92m)	
FMA	1992: $5.8m (US)	
$1 = ES	1989: 526.35	1990: 767.75
	1991: 1,046.30	1992: 1,400.0

ES = Ecuadorean sucres

Population: 11,319,000

	13–17	18–22	23–32
Men	643,000	570,000	919,000
Women	627,000	557,000	904,000

TOTAL ARMED FORCES:
ACTIVE: 57,500.
Terms of service: conscription 1 year, selective.
RESERVES: 100,000; ages 18–55.

ARMY: 50,000.
4 Defence zones.
1 inf div.
1 armd bde.
4 inf bde.
3 jungle bde.
Army tps:
1 SF (AB) bde (2 gp).
1 AD arty gp.
1 avn gp.
3 engr bn

EQUIPMENT:
LIGHT TANKS: 45 M-3, 108 AMX-13.
RECCE: 35 AML-60/-90, 10 EE-9 *Cascavel*.
APC: 20 M-113, 60 AMX-VCI, 20 EE-11 *Urutu*.
TOWED ARTY: 105mm: 50 M2A2; 155mm: 10 M-198.
SP ARTY: 155mm: 10 Mk F3.
MORTARS: 300: 81mm: M-29; 107mm: 4.2-in M-30; 160mm: 12 Soltam.
RCL: 400: 90mm: M-67; 106mm: M-40A1.
AD GUNS: 20mm: 20 M-1935; 35mm: 30 GDF-002 twin; 40mm: 30 L/70.
SAM: 75 *Blowpipe*.
AVIATION:
AIRCRAFT:
SURVEY: 1 Cessna 206, 1 *Learjet* 24D.
TRANSPORT: 1 CN-235, 1 DHC-5, 3 IAI-201, 1 *King Air* 200, 3 PC-6.
LIAISON/TRG/OBS: 1 Cessna 172, 1 -182.
HELICOPTERS:
SURVEY: 3 SA-315B.
TRANSPORT/LIAISON: 10 AS-332, 4 AS-350B, 1 Bell 214B, 3 SA-315B, 3 SA-330, 30 SA-342.

NAVY: 4,500, incl some 1,500 Marines.
BASES: Guayaquil (main base), Jaramijo, Galápagos Islands.
SUBMARINES: 2 *Shyri* (Ge T-209/1300) with 533mm TT (Ge SUT HWT).
PRINCIPAL SURFACE COMBATANTS: 2:
FRIGATES: 2 *Presidente Eloy Alfaro* (ex-UK *Leader Batch II*) with hel, 2 × 3 ASTT; plus 4 × MM-38 *Exocet* SSM.
PATROL AND COASTAL COMBATANTS: 12:
CORVETTES: 6 *Esmeraldas* with 2 × 3 ASTT, hel deck; plus 6 × MM-40 *Exocet* SSM.
MISSILE CRAFT: 6:

3 *Quito* (Ge Lürssen 45-m) with 4 × MM-38 *Exocet*.

3 *Manta* (Ge Lürssen 36-m) with 4 × *Gabriel* II SSM.

AMPHIBIOUS: 1:

1 *Hualcopo* (US LST-511) LST, capacity 200 tps, 16 tk.

SUPPORT AND MISCELLANEOUS: 6:

1 survey, 1 AOT (small), 1 water carrier, 2 tugs, 1 trg.

NAVAL AVIATION:
AIRCRAFT:
  LIAISON: 1 *Citation* I, 1 *Super King Air*, 1 CN-235.
  TRAINING: 2 Cessna 172, 3 -337, 3 T-34C.
HELICOPTERS: 5 Bell 206.

MARINES: (1,500): 3 bn: 2 on garrison duties, 1 cdo (no hy weapons/veh).

AIR FORCE: 3,500; 85 cbt ac, no armed hel.
OPERATIONS COMMAND: 1 wing, 5 sqn:
FGA: 2 sqn:
  1 with 8 *Jaguar* S, 1 -B;
  1 with 9 *Kfir* C-2, 1 TC-2.
FIGHTER: 1 sqn with 13 *Mirage* F-1JE, 1 F-1JB.
COIN: 1 sqn with 20 A-37B.
COIN/TRAINING: 1 sqn with 9 *Strikemaster* Mk 89.
MILITARY AIR TRANSPORT GROUP:
  2 civil/military airlines:
TAME: 4 Boeing 727, 2 BAe-748, 2 C-130H, 3 DHC-6, 1 F-28, 1 L-100-30.
ECUATORIANA: 3 Boeing 707-720, 4 -707, 1 DC-10-30.
LIAISON: 1 *King Air* E90, 1 *Sabreliner*.
LIAISON/SAR hel flt: 2 AS-332, 1 Bell 212, 6 Bell-206B, 6 SA-316B, 1 SA-330, 2 UH-1B, 24 UH-1H.
TRAINING: incl 23* AT-33, 20 Cessna 150, 5 -172, 19 T-34C, 4 T-41.
AAM: R-550 *Magic*, *Super* 530, *Shafrir*.
1 AB sqn.

FORCES ABROAD:
UN AND PEACEKEEPING:
EL SALVADOR (ONUSAL): 42 Observers.

PARAMILITARY:
COAST GUARD 200:
PATROL INSHORE: 7:
  2 25 *de Julio*, 2 5 *de Agosta*, 3 PCI⟨, plus some 15 boats.

EL SALVADOR

| GDP | 1990: C 41.06bn ($5.11bn) |
| | 1991: C 47.79bn ($5.91bn) |

Growth	1990: 3.4%	1991: 3.5%
Inflation	1990: 23.9%	1991: 14.4%
Debt	1989: $2.07bn	1990: $2.13bn
Def bdgt[a]	1991: C 1.15bn ($141.87m)	
	1992ε: C 1.18bn ($145.0m)	
FMA[b]	1992: $206.4m (US)	
$1 = C	1989: 5.00	1990: 8.03
	1991: 8.08	1992: 8.16

C = colones
[a] Incl sy bdgt.
[b] Incl $1.20m as Economic Support.

Population: 5,467,000

	13–17	18–22	23–32
Men	352,000	302,000	382,000
Women	342,000	295,000	411,000

TOTAL ARMED FORCES:
ACTIVE: 43,700 (excl paramilitary and civil defence force).
  Terms of service: selective conscription, 2 years: all services.
RESERVES: ex-soldiers registered.

ARMY: 40,000 (some conscripts).
  6 Military Zones (14 Departments).
  6 inf bde (20 inf bn).
  1 border guard εbde (former National Guard).
  8 inf det (20 inf bn).
  1 internal affairs unit (ε4 inf bn of former Treasury Police).
  1 engr det (1 engr, 2 inf bn).
  1 arty bde (4 fd, 1 AD).
  1 mech cav regt (2 bn).
  Air Force comd:
    1 AB, 1 AD arty, 2 base sy bn.
    1 special ops gp.
EQUIPMENT:
LIGHT TANKS: 5 M-3A1 (in store).
RECCE: 10 AML-90.
APC: 54 M-37B1 (mod), 14 M-113, 8 UR-416.
TOWED ARTY: 105mm: 36 M-101/102, 14 M-56.
MORTARS: 81mm: incl 300 M-29;
  120mm: 60 UB-M52, M-74.
RL: *LAW*.
RCL: 90mm: 400 M-67; 106mm: 20+ M-40A1 (some SP).
AD GUNS: 20mm: 24 Yug M-55, 4 SP.
SAM: some captured SA-7 may be in service.

NAVY: 1,300 (some 600 marines).
BASES: La Unión, La Libertad, Acajutla and El Triunfo.
PATROL AND COASTAL COMBATANTS: 5:
PATROL INSHORE: 3 Camcraft 30-m, 2 PCI⟨ plus boats.
AMPHIBIOUS: Craft only, 3 LCM, plus boats.

MARINES: (600); 2 bn.

AIR FORCE: 2,400 (incl AD);
30 cbt ac, 25 armed hel.
COIN:
  AIRCRAFT: 1 sqn with 10 A-37B, 3 AC-47, 11 O-2A.
  HELICOPTERS: 1 sqn with 10 Hughes (armed: 3 MD 500D, 7 -E), 15 UH-1M (armed), 35 UH-1H (tpt).
TRANSPORT: 1 gp:
  4 C-47, 2 C-47 Turbo-67, 2 C-123K, 1 *Commander*, 1 DC-6B, 3 IAI-201, 1 *Merlin* IIIB, 9 *Rallye*.
LIAISON: 6 Cessna 180, 1 Cessna 182, 1 Cessna 185 ac.
TRAINING: 6* CM-170 (COIN/trg;†), 4 T-41A/D.

PARAMILITARY:
NATIONAL POLICE: 6,000: 6 comds with 4 police, 38 police coy.
DEFENSA CIVIL (territorial civil defence force): 24,000 armed.

OPPOSITION:
FARABUNDO MARTI NATIONAL LIBERATION FRONT (FMLN): 6–7,000 combatants, coalition of 5 groups: People's Revolutionary Army (ERP); Popular Liberation Forces (FPL); Armed Forces of National Resistance (FARN or RN); Revolutionary Party of Central American Workers (PRTC); and Armed Forces of Liberation (FAL).

FOREIGN FORCES:
UNITED NATIONS (ONUSAL): 291 mil observers from 10 countries, plus 600 police and 100+ civilians.

GUATEMALA

GDP	1990:	q 34.29bn ($7.64bn)	
	1991:	q 46.99bn ($9.34bn)	
Growth	1990:	3.1%	1991: 3.3%
Inflation	1990:	41.2%	1991: 33.2%
Debt	1990:	$2.78bn	1991: $2.90bn
Def bdgt	1992:	q 565.0m ($112.80m)	
FMA[a]	1992:	$32.4m	
$1 = q	1989:	2.816	1990: 4.486
	1991:	5.029	1992: 5.010

q = quetzales
[a] Incl $30m as Economic Support.

Population: 9,566,000

	13–17	*18–22*	*23–32*
Men	584,000	486,000	718,000
Women	568,000	471,000	701,000

TOTAL ARMED FORCES: (National Armed Forces are combined; the Army provides log spt for Navy and Air Force).
ACTIVE: 44,600.
Terms of service: Conscription; selective, 30 months.
RESERVES: Army 4,500 (trained), Navy (some), Air 200.

ARMY: 42,000.
19 Military Zones (some 23 inf bn).
3 Strategic Reserve bde (each 2–3 inf bn).
4 Tactical Security Group (each 2 inf bn).
1 SF gp (2 bn).
1 AB bn.
some indep arty bty.
1 engr bn.
(Summary of cbt units: 40 inf bn).
EQUIPMENT:
LIGHT TANKS: 10 M-41A3.
RECCE:† 10 M-8, 10 RBY-1.
APC: 9 M-113, 7 V-150 *Commando*, 25 *Armadillo*.
TOWED ARTY: 75mm: 10 M-116; 105mm: 4 M-101, 8 M-102, 56 M-56.
MORTARS: 81mm: 55 M-1; 107mm: 12 M-30; 120mm: 18 ECIA.
RL: 89mm: 3.5-in. M-20.
RCL: 106mm: M-65.
AD GUNS: 20mm: 20 incl 4 M-55, 12 Oerlikon;

NAVY: 1,200 incl 700 marines.
BASES: Santo Tomás de Castillas (Atlantic), Puerto Quetzal, (Pacific).
PATROL CRAFT, INSHORE 8:
  1 *Kukulkan* (US '*Broadsword*' 32-m) PFI, 7 PCI⟨,
  plus boats.
AMPHIBIOUS: craft only.

MARINES: (700); 1 bn.

AIR FORCE: 1,400; 22 cbt ac, 12 armed hel.
Serviceability of ac is less than 50%.
COIN: 1 sqn with 8 Cessna A-37B, 8 PC-7, 6 IAI-201.
ATTACK HELICOPTERS: 6 Bell 212, 6 Bell 412.
TRANSPORT: 1 sqn with 6 C-47, 3 F-27, 1 *Super King Air* (VIP).
LIAISON: 1 sqn with 3 Cessna 206, 1 -310.
  HELICOPTERS: 1 sqn with 9 Bell 206, 5 UH-1D/-H, 3 S-76.
TRAINING: 6 T-41.

PARAMILITARY:
NATIONAL POLICE: 12,000: 3 bn, 28 coy, 21 sub-units, 14 mobile teams.

TREASURY POLICE: 2,100.
TERRITORIAL MILITIA (R) (CVDC): ε500,000.

OPPOSITION:
**UNIDAD REVOLUCIONARIA NACIONAL
   GUATEMALTECA** (URNG): some 1,500;
   coalition of 4 groups: Ejército Guerrillero de los
   Pobres (EGP): 700. Partido Guatemalteco del
   Trabajo (PGT). Fuerzas Armadas Rebeldes
   (FAR): 300. Organización del Pueblo en Armas
   (ORPA): 400.

GUYANA

GDP[a]   1989: $G 6.96bn ($US 425.35m)
           1990: $G 10.13bn ($US 398.83m)
Growth   1989: −4.8%   1990: −6.2%
Inflation 1989ε: 60%   1990ε: 100%
Debt   1989: $1.86bn   1990: $1.96bn
Def bdgt   1986: $G 277.71m ($US 65.00m)
           1988: $G 138.1m ($US 14.4m)
FMA   1992: $2m (US Economic Support)
$US 1 = $G 1989: 27.159 1990: 39.533
           1991: 111.800 1992: 123.000
$G = $ Guyanese
[a] $US figures are in 1985 prices and exchange
rates.

Population: 848,600
	13–17	18–22	23–32
Men	47,000	43,500	79,000
Women	45,500	42,000	76,800

TOTAL ARMED FORCES: (Combined
Guyana Defence Force):
ACTIVE: 2,000.
RESERVES: some 2,000 People's Militia.
(see Paramilitary).

ARMY: 1,700.
1 inf, 1 guard, 1 SF, 1 spt wpn, 1 engr bn.
EQUIPMENT:
RECCE: 3 *Shorland*†.
TOWED ARTY: 130mm: 6 M-46.
MORTARS: 81mm: 12 L16A1; 82mm: 18 M-43;
   120mm: 18 M-43.
SAM: SA-7.

NAVY:† 100;
BASES: Georgetown, New Amsterdam.
   About 4 boats.

AIR FORCE: 200; No cbt ac, no armed hel.

TRANSPORT:
   AIRCRAFT: 4 BN-2A, 1 *Super King Air* B-200
   (VIP).
   HELICOPTERS: 1 Bell 206, 1 -212, 1 -412, 2 Mi-8.

PARAMILITARY:
GUYANA PEOPLE'S MILITIA (GPM): some 2,000.
GUYANA NATIONAL SERVICE (GNS): 1,500.

HAITI

GDP   1990: G 12.51bn ($2.50bn)
           1991: G 12.86bn ($2.57bn)
Growth   1990: −0.7%   1991: −0.8%
Inflation 1990: 21.5%   1991: 15.4%
Debt   1989: $802.0m   1990: $874.0m
Def bdgt   1990: G 85.0m ($17.0m)
           1991: G 147.0m ($29.40m)
FMA[a]   1992: $26.87m
$1 = G   1987–92: 5.0
G = gourdes
[a] Incl $24m as Economic Support

Population: 6,767,600
	13–17	18–22	23–32
Men	377,000	344,500	538,000
Women	373,000	345,000	558,000

TOTAL ARMED FORCES:
ACTIVE: 7,400.

ARMY: 7,000 (has police/gendarmerie,
fire-fighting, immigration, etc, roles).
   1 defence unit (3 inf, 1 hy wpn coy).
   9 military departments (27 coy).
EQUIPMENT:†
APC: 5 M-2, 6 V-150 *Commando*.
TOWED ARTY: 75mm: 5 M-116; 105mm: 4 M-101;
MORTARS: 60mm: 36 M-2; 81mm: M-1.
ATK GUNS: 37mm: 10 M-3A1; 57mm: 10 M-1.
RCL: 57mm: M-18; 106mm: M-40A1.
AD GUNS: 20mm: 6 TCM-20, 4 other; 40mm: 6 M-1.

NAVY: ε250 (Coast guard).
BASE: Port au Prince
PATROL CRAFT: 1 PCO (ex-US *Sotoyomo*-class
   tug), boats.

AIR FORCE: 150; 2 cbt ac, no armed hel.
TRANSPORT: 1 *Baron*, 1 DHC-6, 2* Cessna 337.
TRAINING: 3 Cessna 150, 1 -172, 5 SF-260TP, 1
Twin Bonanza.

HONDURAS

GDP[a]	1990:	L 12.54bn ($4.25bn)	
	1991:	L 16.41bn ($4.34bn)	
Growth	1990:	0.1%	1991: 2.2%
Inflation	1990:	23.3%	1991: 34%
Debt	1989:	$3.33bn	1990: $3.48bn
Def exp	1990:	L 276.0m ($138.0m)	
Def bdgt	1990:	L 247.0m ($123.5m)	
FMA[b]	1992:	$70.2m	
$1 = L	1989–90:	2.00	
	1991–1992:	5.40	

L = lempiras
[a] $US figures are in 1985 prices and exchange rates.
[b] Incl $50m as Economic Support.

Population: 5,485,000

	13–17	18–22	23–32
Men	329,000	283,000	417,000
Women	315,000	279,000	420,000

TOTAL ARMED FORCES:
ACTIVE: 16,800 (reducing); (11,200 conscripts).
Terms of service: conscription, 24 months.
RESERVES: 60,000 ex-servicemen registered.

ARMY: 14,000 (10,000 conscripts).
10 Military Zones:
    2 inf bde (2 with 3 inf, 1 arty bn).
    1 inf bde (incl special tac gp) with 2 inf bn, 1 ranger gp, 1 arty, 1 engr bn, 2 trg units.
    1 territorial force (2 inf, 1 SF, 1 AB bn).
    1 armd cav regt (2 bn).
    1 arty, 1 engr bn.
RESERVES:
    3 inf bde.
EQUIPMENT:
LIGHT TANKS: 15 *Scorpion*.
RECCE: 3 *Scimitar*, 1 *Sultan*, 72 *Saladin*, 12 RBY Mk 1.
TOWED ARTY: 105mm: 24 M-102; 155mm: 4 M-198.
MORTARS: 400 60mm; 81mm; 120mm: 60 Brandt; 160mm: 30 *Soltam*.
RL: 84mm: 120 *Carl Gustav*.
RCL: 106mm: 80 M-40A1.
AD GUNS: 80: 20mm: incl M-55.

NAVY: 1,000 incl 400 marines (500 conscripts).
BASES: Puerto Cortés, Puerto Castilla (Atlantic), Amapala (Pacific).
PATROL CRAFT: 11:
INSHORE: 11:
    3 *Guaymuras* (US Swiftships 31-m) PFI, 2 *Copan* (US Lantana 32-m) PFI⟨, 6 other PCI⟨, plus boats.
AMPHIBIOUS: craft only; 1 *Punta Caxinas* LCT; plus some 3 ex-US LCM.

MARINES: (400); 1 bn.

AIR FORCE: some 1,800 (700 conscripts);
46 cbt ac, no armed hel.
FGA: 2 sqn:
    1 with 13 A-37B;
    1 with 10 F-5E, 2 -F.
FIGHTER: 1 sqn with 8 *Super Mystère* B2 (non operational).
TRANSPORT: 9 C-47, 1 C-123, 4 C-130A, 2 DHC-5, 1 L-188, 2 IAI-201, 1 IAI-1123, 1 -1124.
LIAISON: 1 sqn with 1 *Baron*, 3 Cessna 172, 2 -180, 2 -185, 4 *Commander*, 1 PA-31, 1 PA-34.
HELICOPTERS: 9 Bell 412, 4 Hughes 500, 7 TH-55, 8 UH-1B, 11 UH-1H, 1 S-76.
TRAINING: 4* C-101BB, 6 U-17A, 11* EMB-312, 5 T-41A.

PARAMILITARY:
PUBLIC SECURITY FORCES (Ministry of Public Security and Defence) 5,500: 11 regional comd.

FOREIGN FORCES:
US: Army: 800.

JAMAICA

GDP	1990:	$J 28.20bn ($US 3.93bn)	
	1991ε:	$J 43.00bn ($US 3.55bn)	
Growth	1990:	3.8%	1991: 2.4%
Inflation	1990:	21.9%	1991: 51.1%
Debt	1990:	$US 4.60bn	1991: $US 4.00bn
Def bdgt	1989:	$J 159.0m ($US 27.68m)	
	1990:	$J 233.6m ($US 32.52m)	
FMA[a]	1992:	$US18.5m	
$US 1 = $J	1989:	5.745	1990: 7.184
	1991:	12.116	1992: 23.000

$J = $ Jamaican
[a] Incl $US 15m in Economic Support

Population: 2,431,000

	13–17	18–22	23–32
Men	133,900	134,000	243,000
Women	128,800	130,000	242,000

TOTAL ARMED FORCES (all services
form combined Jamaica Defence Force):
ACTIVE: some 3,350.
RESERVES: some 870: Army 800; Coast guard: 50; Air wing: 20.

ARMY: 3,000. 2 inf bn, 1 spt bn.
APC: 15 V-150 *Commando*.
MORTARS: 81mm: 12 L16A1.
RESERVES: 800: 1 inf bn.

COAST GUARD: ε150.
BASE: Port Royal
PATROL CRAFT: 5 inshore:
1 *Fort Charles* PFI (US 34-m), 4 PFI⟨.

AIR WING: 170; no cbt ac, no armed hel.
AIRCRAFT: 2 BN-2, 1 Cessna 210, 1 *King Air*, 1 Cessna 337.
HELICOPTERS: 4 Bell 206, 2 -212, 4 UH-1H.

MEXICO

GDP[a]	1990:	pM 642,271.5bn ($193.84bn)
	1991ε:	pM 802,838.7bn ($201.59bn)
Growth	1990: 3.8%	1991: 3.6%
Inflation	1990: 26.7%	1991: 22.7%
Debt	1990: $96.81bn	1991: $85.0bn
Def bdgt	1992: pM 4,713.0bn ($1.52bn)	
$1 = pM	1989: 2,461.5	1990: 2,812.6
	1991: 3,030.0	1992: 3,100.0

pM = pesos Mexicanos
[a] $US figures are in 1985 prices and exchange rates.

Population: 93,120,000

	13–17	18–22	23–32
Men	5,525,000	5,031,000	7,838,000
Women	5,362,000	4,896,000	7,728,000

TOTAL ARMED FORCES:
ACTIVE: 175,000 (60,000 conscripts).
Terms of service: 1 year conscription by lottery.
RESERVES: 300,000.

ARMY: 130,000 regular (incl ε60,000 conscripts).
36 Zonal Garrisons: incl 1 armd, 19 mot cav, 1 mech inf, 3 arty regt, 80 inf bn.
1 armd bde (3 armd, 1 mech inf regt).
1 Presidential Guard bde (4 inf, 1 arty bn).
3 inf bde (each 3 inf bn, 1 arty bn).
1 AB bde (3 bn).
AD, engr and spt units.
EQUIPMENT:
RECCE: 50 M-8, 120 ERC-90F *Lynx*, 40 M-11 VBL, 70 DN-3/-5 *Caballo*, 30 MOWAG, 40 Mex-1.
APC: 40 HWK-11, 30 M-3 halftrack, 40 VCR/TT.
TOWED ARTY: 75mm: 18 M-116 pack; 105mm: 100 M-2A1/M-3, M-101, M-56.
SP ARTY: 75mm: 5 M-8.

MORTARS: 1,500 incl 81mm.
ATGW: *Milan* (incl 8 M-11 VBL).
ATK GUNS: 37mm: 30 M-3.
AD GUNS: 12.7mm: 40 M-55.

NAVY: 37,000, incl 500 naval air force and 8,000 marines.
6 Navy regions covering 2 Areas:
Gulf: 6 Naval Zones.
Pacific: 11 Naval Zones.
BASES: Gulf: Vera Cruz (HQ), Tampico, Chetumal, Ciudad del Carmen, Yukalpetén.
Pacific: Acapulco (HQ), Ensenada, La Paz, San Blas, Guaymas, Mazatlán, Manzanillo, Salina Cruz, Puerto Madero, Lázaro Cárdenas, Puerto Vallarta.
DESTROYERS: 3:
2 *Quetzalcoatl* (US *Gearing*) ASW with 1 × 8 ASROC, 2 × 3 ASTT; plus 2 × 2 127mm guns, hel deck.
1 *Cuitlahuac* (US *Fletcher*) with 5 × 533mm TT, 5 × 127mm guns.
PATROL AND COASTAL COMBATANTS: 94:
PATROL, OFFSHORE: 43:
2 *S.J. Holzinger* (ex *Uxmal*) (imp *Uribe*) with Bo-105 hel.
6 *Cadete Virgilio Uribe* (Sp 'Halcon') with Bo-105 hel.
1 *Comodoro Manuel Azueta* (US *Edsall*) (trg).
3 *Zacatecas* (US *Lawrence/Crosley*) with 1 × 127mm gun.
1 *Durango* (trg) with 1 × 102mm gun.
17 *Leandro Valle* (US *Auk* MSF).
1 *Guanajuato* with 1 × 102mm gun.
12 D-01 (US *Admirable* MSF).
PATROL, INSHORE: 33:
31 *Quintana Roo* (UK *Azteca*) PCI.
2 ex-US *Cape Higgon* PCI.
PATROL, RIVER: 18⟨.
AMPHIBIOUS:
2 *Panuco* (US-511) LST.
SUPPORT AND MISCELLANEOUS: 16:
1 *V. Guerrero* PCI spt, 4 log spt, 6 ocean tugs, 3 survey, 2 tpt.

NAVAL AVIATION: (500);
9 cbt ac, no armed hel.
MR: 1 sqn with 9 C-212, 6 HU-16 (SAR).
MR HEL: 12 Bo-105 (8 afloat).
TRANSPORT: 1 C-212, 2 Cessna 180, 3 -310, 1 DHC-5, 4 FH-227, 1 *King Air* 90, 1 *Learjet* 24.
LIAISON: 3 Cessna 150, 2 -337, 2 -402.
HELICOPTERS: 3 Bell 47, 4 SA-315.

MARINES: (8,000).
3 bn (incl 1 Presidential Guard).
15 gp.

EQUIPMENT:
AMPH VEH: 25 VAP-3550.
TOWED ARTY: 105mm: 8 M-56.
MORTARS: 100 incl 60mm, 81mm.
RCL: 106mm: M-40A1.

AIR FORCE: 8,000 (incl 1,500 AB bde);
113 cbt ac, 25 armed hel.
FIGHTER: 1 sqn with 9 F-5E, 2 -F.
COIN: 9 sqn:
  6 with 70 PC-7;
  1 with 12 AT-33;
  1 with 10 IAI-201;
  1 hel with 5 Bell 205, 5 -206, 15 -212.
RECCE: 1 photo sqn with 10 *Commander* 500S.
TRANSPORT: 5 sqn with 2 BN-2, 12 C-47, 4 C-54,
  8 C-117, 2 C-118, 9 C-130A, 1 *Citation*, 5
  Commander 500, 1 -680, 3 *Skyvan*.
PRESIDENTIAL TRANSPORT:
  AIRCRAFT: 7 Boeing 727, 2 Boeing 737, 1 L-188,
    3 FH-227, 1 *Jetstar*, 1 *Merlin*, 5 T-39.
  HELICOPTERS: 1 A-109, 1 AS-332, 4 Bell 206, 1
    -212, 2 SA-330.
LIAISON: 3 *Baron*, 1 Cessna 310, 1 *King Air*, 1
  Queen Air 80.
TRAINING:
  AIRCRAFT: 41 *Bonanza*, 20 CAP-10, 20
    Musketeer, 10 PC-7.
  HELICOPTERS: 4 MD 500E.

PARAMILITARY:
RURAL DEFENCE MILITIA (R): 14,000.

NICARAGUA

GDP[a]	1990:	$C 1,164.0 tr ($US 2.49bn)	
	1991:	$C 33,144.0 tr ($US 2.46bn)	
Growth	1990:	−3.8%	1991: −0.7%
Inflation	1990:	7,500%	1991: 675%
Debt	1990:	$ 10.50bn	1991: $ 10.80bn
Def bdgt	1991ε:	$US 225.0m	
	1992ε:	$US 214.50m	
FMA[b]	1992:	$US 150m	
$US 1 = $C	1989:	15,655 1990: 705,000.0	
	1991:	21,354,000.0	
	1992:	25,000,000.0	

$C = córdobas
[a] $US figures in 1985 prices and exchange rates.
[b] All Economic Support.

Population: 4,038,000

	13–17	*18–22*	*23–32*
Men	243,800	207,200	314,000
Women	236,400	202,600	312,300

TOTAL ARMED FORCES:
ACTIVE: 14,700.
Terms of service: voluntary, 18–36 months.
RESERVES: numbers/details not yet known.

ARMY: ε13,000.
Reorganization in progress.
6 Regional Commands; 2 Military Department.
1 mot inf bde.
4 inf, 1 SF bn.
10 inf coy.
EQUIPMENT:
MBT: some 130 T-54/-55.
LIGHT TANKS: 27 PT-76.
RECCE: 80 BRDM-2.
APC: 19 BTR-60, 100 BTR-152.
TOWED ARTY: 122mm: 36 D-30; 152mm: 60
  D-20.
MRL: 107mm: 30 Type-63; 122mm: 30 BM-21.
MORTARS: 82mm: 500; 120mm: 20 M-43.
ATGW: AT-3 *Sagger* (12 on BRDM-2).
ATK GUNS: 57mm: 325 ZIS-2; 76mm: 84 Z1S-3;
  100mm: 24 M-1944 (BS-3).
SAM: 500+ SA-7/-14/-16.

NAVY: ε500.
PATROL AND COASTAL COMBATANTS: 23:
PATROL, INSHORE: 17:
  2 Sov *Zhuk* PFI⟨, 9 North Korea *Sin Hung*
    PFI⟨, 6 PCI⟨.
MINE COUNTERMEASURES: 5:
  2 Sov *Yevgenya*, 3 K-8 MSI⟨.

AIR FORCE: 1,200;
16† cbt ac, 9 armed hel.
COIN: 1 sqn with 6 Cessna 337†, 6 L-39ZO†, 4
SF-260 WL†.
ATTACK HELICOPTERS: 9 Mi-25.
TRANSPORT: 1 sqn with 5 An-26.
  HELICOPTERS: 1 sqn with 31 Mi-8/-17.
LIAISON: ac: 8 An-2, 4 *Commander* ; plus 1 Cessna
  172, 2 -185†
  hel: 5 Mi-2.
TRAINING: 4 PA-18.
ASM: AT-2 *Swatter* ATGW.
AD GUNS: 800: 14.5mm: ZPU-1/-2/-4; 23mm: ZU-23;
  37mm: M-1939; 57mm: S-60; 100mm: KS-19.

PANAMA

GDP	1990:	B 4.95bn ($4.95bn)	
	1991:	B 5.40bn ($5.40bn)	
Growth	1990:	4.6%	1991: 9.3%
Inflation	1990:	1.0%	1991: 1.0%
Debt	1989:	$6.27bn	1990: $6.68bn

Def bdgt   1991: B 75.0m ($75.0m)
FMA*a*   1992: $10m (US)
$1 = B   1987–92:   1.00
B = balboas
a All Economic Support

Population: 2,480,000
	13–17	*18–22*	*23–32*
Men	136,100	128,800	220,800
Women	131,700	124,500	210,200

TOTAL PUBLIC FORCES:
ACTIVE: 11,700.

NATIONAL POLICE FORCE: 11,000.
No hy mil eqpt, small arms only.

NATIONAL MARITIME SERVICE: ε350.
BASES: Balboa (HQ), Colón.
PATROL CRAFT:
INSHORE: 3:
   1 *Panquiaco* (UK Vosper 31.5-m), 1 ex-USCG
   Cape Higgon, 1⟨.
AMPHIBIOUS: craft only; 2 LCM.

NATIONAL AIR SERVICE: 350.
TRANSPORT: 1 CN-235-2A, 1 BN-2B, 2 PA-34, 3
   CASA C-221.
TRAINING: 10 T-35D.†
HELICOPTERS: 2 Bell 205, 3† -212, 1† UH-1B, 1†
   -H, 1-N.†

FOREIGN FORCES:
US: 10,500. Army: 7,700; 1 inf bde and spt elm.
Navy: 500. Marines: 200. Air Force; 2,100; 1
air div.

PARAGUAY

GDP*a*	1990: Pg 6,474.4bn ($5.50bn)	
	1991: Pg 7,545.3bn ($5.64bn)	
Growth	1990: 3.1%	1991: 2.5%
Inflation	1990: 38.2%	1991: 24.3%
Debt	1990: $2.39bn	1991: $2.13bn
Def bdgt	1988ε: Pg 46.37bn ($84.32m)	
	1989ε: Pg 64.0bn ($60.59m)	
$1 = Pg	1989: 1,056.2	1990: 1,229.8
	1991: 1,325.2	1992: 1,430.0

Pg = guaraníes
a $US figures are in 1985 prices and exchange
rates.

Population: 4,514,000
	13–17	*18–22*	*23–32*
Men	247,800	220,500	378,000
Women	238,600	212,000	363,500

TOTAL ARMED FORCES:
ACTIVE: 16,500 (11,000 conscripts).
Terms of service: 18 months; Navy 2
   years.
RESERVES: some 45,000.

ARMY: 12,500 (8,600 conscripts).
   3 corps HQ.
   9 div HQ (6 inf, 3 cav).
   6 inf regt (bn).   4 cav regt (horse).
   6 frontier bn.   2 arty bn.
   1 armd cav regt.   5 engr bn.
   1 mech cav regt.
EQUIPMENT:
MBT: 5 M-4A3.
LIGHT TANKS: 18 M-3A1.
RECCE: 5 M-3, 30 EE-9 *Cascavel*.
APC: 10 EE-11 *Urutu*.
TOWED ARTY: 75mm: 20 Model 1927/1934;
   105mm: 15 M-101; 152mm: 6 Mk V 6-in (anti-ship).
MORTARS: 81mm: 75.
RCL: 75mm: M-20.
AD GUNS: 20mm: 20 Bofors; 40mm: 10 M-1A1.

NAVY: 3,000 (ε1,500 conscripts) (incl Marines,
   Harbour and River Guard).
BASES: Asunción (Puerto Sajonia), Bahía Negra,
   Ciudad Del Este.
PATROL AND RIVERINE COMBATANTS: 7:
   COASTAL: 6
      2 *Paraguay* with 4 × 120mm guns.
      3 *Nanawa* (Arg *Bouchard* MSO)
      1 *Itaipu* (riverine).
   RIVERINE: 1 *Capitan Cabral* (built 1908).
SUPPORT AND MISCELLANEOUS: 4:
   1 tpt, 1 *Boqueron* spt (ex-US LSM with hel
   deck), 1 trg/tpt, 1 survey⟨.

MARINES: 500 (200 conscripts)).
   1 marine bn.
   1 cdo bn.

NAVAL AVIATION: (50). 2 cbt ac, no armed hel.
COIN: 2 AT-6G.
TRANSPORT: 1 C-47.
LIAISON: 3 Cessna 150, 3 -206, 1 -210.
HELICOPTERS: 2 HB-350, 1 OH-13, 2 UH-12E.

AIR FORCE: 1,000 (700 conscripts);
   17 cbt ac, no armed hel.

COMPOSITE SQN: .
COIN: 5 AT-26, 7 EMB-326.
LIAISON: 1 Cessna 185, 2 -206, 1 -337, 1 -402, 2 T-41.
HELICOPTER: 3 HB-350, 1 UH-1B, 4 UH-12.
TRANSPORT: 1 sqn with 5 C-47, 4 C-212, 3 DC-6B, 1 DHC-6 (VIP).
TRAINING: 5* EMB-312, 6 T-6, 10 T-23, 5 T-25, 6 T-27, 1 T-41, 15 T-25.

PARAMILITARY:
SPECIAL POLICE SERVICE: 8,000.

PERU

GDP[a]	1990:	NS 6.80bn ($15.63bn)	
	1991:	NS 38.10bn ($16.08bn)	
Growth	1990:	−4.7%	1991: 2.8%
Inflation	1990:	7,460%	1991: 410%
Debt	1990:	$21.11bn	1991: $22.64bn
Def bdgt	1990:	NS 120.61m ($641.94m)	
	1992:	NS 787.20m ($656.80m)	
Def exp	1991:	NS 541.52m ($750.03m)	
FMA	1992:	$40m (US)	
$1 = I/.	1989:	2,666.2	
$1 = NS	1990:	0.187	1991: 0.723
	1992:	1.250	

I/. = New inti
NS[b] = New Sol
[a] $US figures are in 1985 prices and exchange rates.
[b] On 1 July 1991 the new Sol equal to one million Intis, was introduced.

Population: 21,616,000

	13–17	18–22	23–32
Men	1,186,000	1,141,000	1,830,000
Women	1,165,500	1,116,000	1,866,000

TOTAL ARMED FORCES:
ACTIVE: 112,000 (69,000 conscripts).
Terms of service: 2 years, selective.
RESERVES: 188,000 (Army only).

ARMY: 75,000 (52,000 conscripts).
5 Military Regions:
Army Troops:
 1 AB 'div' (bde: 3 cdo, 1 para bn, 1 arty gp).
 1 Presidential Escort regt.
 1 AD arty gp.
Regional Troops:
 2 armd div (bde, each 2 tk, 1 armd inf bn, 1 arty gp, 1 engr bn).
 1 armd gp (3 indep armd cav, 1 fd arty, 1 AD arty, 1 engr bn).
 1 cav div (3 mech regt, 1 arty gp).
 8 inf div (bde, each 3 inf bn, 1 arty gp).
 1 jungle div.
 2 med arty gp; 2 fd arty gp.
 1 indep inf bn.
 1 indep engr bn.
 3 hel sqn.

EQUIPMENT:
MBT: 300 T-54/-55† (ε100 serviceable).
LIGHT TANKS: 110 AMX-13.
RECCE: 60 M-8/-20, 20 Fiat 6616, 15 BRDM-2.
APC: 300 M-113, 225 UR-416.
TOWED ARTY: 105mm: 50 Model 56 pack, 130 M-101; 122mm: 30 D-30; 130mm: 30 M-46; 155mm: 36 M-114.
SP ARTY: 155mm: 12 M-109A2, 12 Mk F3.
MRL: 122mm: 14 BM-21.
MORTARS: 81mm: incl some SP; 107mm: incl some SP; 120mm: 300 Brandt, ECIA.
RCL: 106mm: M40A1.
AD GUNS: 23mm: 35 ZSU-23-4 SP; 40mm: 40 L60/70.
SAM: SA-7.
AVIATION:
 AIRCRAFT: 1 Cessna 182, 2 -U206, 1 -337, 1 *Queen Air* 65, 3 U-10, 3 U-17.
 HELICOPTERS: 2 Bell 47G, 2 Mi-6, 28 Mi-8, 14 Mi-17, 6 SA-315, 5 SA-316, 3 SA-318, 2 *Agusta* A-109.

NAVY: 22,000 (10,000 conscripts) incl naval air, marines.
3 Naval Force Areas: Pacific, Lake Titicaca, Amazon River.
BASES: ocean: Callao, San Lorenzo Island, Paita, Talara. **lake:** Puno. **river:** Iquitos, Puerto Maldonado.
SUBMARINES: 9:
 6 *Casma* (Ge T-209/1200) with 533mm TT (It A184 HWT).
 3 *Abtao* (US *Mackerel*)† with 533mm TT.
 (Plus 1 *Pedrera* (US *Guppy* I) with 533mm TT (Mk 37 HWT) alongside trg only).
PRINCIPAL SURFACE COMBATANTS: 12:
CRUISERS: 2:
 1 *Almirante Grau* (Nl *De Ruyter*) with 4 × 2 152mm guns, 8 *Otomat* SSM.
 1 *Aguirre* (Nl *De 7 Provincien*) with 4 × SH-3D *Sea King* hel (ASW/ASUW) (Mk 46 LWT/AM-39 *Exocet*), 2 × 2 152mm guns.
DESTROYERS: 6:
 2 *Palacios* (UK *Daring*) with 4 × 2 MM-38 *Exocet*, 3 × 2 114mm guns, hel deck.
 4 *Bolognesi* (Nl *Friesland*) with 4 × 120mm guns, 2 × 4 ASW RL.
FRIGATES: 4 *Carvajal* (mod It *Lupo*) with 1 AB-212 hel (ASW/OTHT), 2 × 3 ASTT; plus 8 *Otomat* SSM, 2 × 20 105mm MRL, 1 × 127mm gun.

PATROL AND COASTAL COMBATANTS: 7:
MISSILE CRAFT: 6 *Velarde* PFM (Fr PR-72 64-m)
with 4 × MM-38 *Exocet*.
PATROL: 1 *Unanue* (ex-US *Sotoyomo*) PCC
(Antarctic ops).
AMPHIBIOUS: 4 *Paita* (US *Terrebonne Parish*)
LST, capacity 300 tps, 16 tk.
SUPPORT AND MISCELLANEOUS: 9
2 AO, 3 AOT, 1 tpt, 2 survey, 1 ocean tug.
RIVER AND LAKE FLOTILLAS: 10:
4 gunboats, 6 patrol⟨.

NAVAL AVIATION: 8 cbt ac, 12 armed hel.
ASW/MR: 4 sqn with:
AIRCRAFT: 4 S-2E, 4 -G, 5 *Super King Air* B
200T.
HELICOPTERS: 6 AB-212 ASW, 6 SH-3D.
TRANSPORT: 2 C-47.
LIAISON: 4 Bell 206B, 6 UH-1D hel, 2 SA-319.
TRAINING: 1 Cessna 150, 5 T-34C.
ASM: *Exocet* AM-39 (on SH-3 hel).

MARINES: (3,000).
1 Marine bde (5 bn, 1 recce, 1 cdo coy).
EQUIPMENT:
RECCE: V-100.
APC: 15 V-200 *Chaimite*, 20 BMR-600.
RCL: 106mm.
RL: 84mm.
MORTARS: ε18 120mm.
AD GUNS: twin 20mm SP.

COAST DEFENCE: 3 bty with 18 155mm how.

AIR FORCE: 15,000 (7,000 conscripts);
107 cbt ac, 10 armed hel.
BOMBERS:
1 Gp (2 sqn) with 13 *Canberra*.
FGA: 2 Gp: 6 sqn:
3 with 41 Su-22 (incl 4* Su-22U);
3 with 25 Cessna A-37B.
FIGHTER: 3 sqn:
1 with 10 *Mirage* 2000P, 2 -DP;
2 with 14 *Mirage* 5P, 2 -DP.
ATTACK HELICOPTERS: 1 hel sqn with 10 Mi-25
RECCE: 1 photo-survey unit with 2 *Learjet* 25B, 2 -36A.
TANKER: 1 Boeing KC 707-323C.
TRANSPORT: 3 Gp (7 sqn):
AIRCRAFT: 14 An-32, 4 C-130A, 6 -D, 5
L-100-20, 2 DC-8-62F, 12 DHC-5, 8 DHC-6,
1 FH-227, 9 PC-6, 6 Y-12.
PRESIDENTIAL FLT: 1 F-28, 1 *Falcon* 20F.
HELICOPTERS: 3 sqn with 8 Bell 206, 15 -212, 5
-214, 1 -412, 10 Bo-105C, 5 Mi-6, 5 Mi-8, 5
SA-316.
LIAISON: 2 Beech 99, 3 Cessna 185, 1 -320, 15
Queen Air 80, 3 *King Air* 90, 1 PA-31T.

LIAISON HELICOPTERS: 8 UH-1D.
TRAINING: 2 Cessna 150, 29 EMB-312, 13
MB-339A, 20 T-37B/C, 35 T-41A/-D.
TRAINING HELICOPTERS: 12 Bell 47G.
MISSILES:
ASM: AS-30.
AAM: AA-2 '*Atoll*', R-550 *Magic*.
AD: 3 SA-2, 6 SA-3 bn with 18 SA-2, 24 SA-3 launchers.

FORCES ABROAD:
UN AND PEACEKEEPING:
WESTERN SAHARA (MINURSO): 12.

PARAMILITARY:
NATIONAL POLICE: 84,000 (amalgamation of
Guardia Civil, Republican Guard and Policia
Investigacionara Peruana); MOWAG *Roland*
APC.
COAST GUARD: 600; 5 PCC, 3 PCI, some 7 riverine⟨.
RONDAS CAMPESINAS (peasant self-defence
force): perhaps 2,000 *rondas* 'groups', up to pl
strength, some with small arms. Deployed
mainly in emergency zone.

OPPOSITION:
SENDERO LUMINOSO (Shining Path): some
ε5–8,000; maoist.
**MOVIMIENTO REVOLUCIONARIO TUPAC
AMARU** (MRTA): 500; mainly urban gp.

FOREIGN FORCES:
RUSSIA: 50.

SURINAME

GDP	1989:	gld 2.51bn ($1.40bn)	
	1990ε:	gld 2.89bn ($1.62bn)	
Growth	1989:	1.5%	1990: 0.4%
Inflation	1989:	15%	1990: 14%
Debt	1989:	$123m	1990: $123m
Def exp	1990:	gld 162.0m ($90.76m)	
Def bdgt	1989:	gld 69.62m ($39.00m)	
	1990:	gld 119.0m ($67m)	
$1 = gld	1987–92:	1.785	
gld = guilders			

Population: 459,200

	13–17	*18–22*	*23–32*
Men	23,200	23,200	42,400
Women	22,700	23,100	43,300

TOTAL ARMED FORCES:
(all services form part of the Army):
ACTIVE: 1,800.

ARMY: 1,400.
1 inf bn (4 inf coy).
1 mech cav sqn.
1 Military Police 'bde' (bn).
EQUIPMENT:
RECCE: 6 EE-9 *Cascavel*.
APC: 9 YP-408, 15 EE-11 *Urutu*.
MORTARS: 81mm: 6.
RCL: 106mm: M-40A1.

NAVY: 250.
BASE: Paramaribo.
PATROL CRAFT: 5 inshore:
3 S-401 (Nl 32-m), 2⟨.

AIR FORCE: ε150; 5 cbt ac, no armed
hel.
COIN: 3 BN-2 *Defender*, 2 PC-7.
LIAISON: 1 Cessna U206.
HELICOPTERS: 2 SA-316.

TRINIDAD & TOBAGO

GDP 1990: $TT 20.79bn ($US 4.89bn)
1991ε: $TT 21.83bn ($US 5.14bn)
Growth 1990: 0.7% 1991: 2.0%
Inflation 1990: 11.0% 1991: 3.8%
Debt 1990: $US 2.31bn 1991: $US 2.40bn
Def bdgt 1989: $TT 250.75m ($59.0m)
1992ε: $TT 314.50m ($74.0m)
$US 1 = $TT 1989–92 4.25
$TT = $ Trinidad & Tobago

Population: 1,326,200

	13–17	18–22	23–32
Men	63,800	61,600	120,600
Women	62,100	59,100	123,000

TOTAL ARMED FORCES:
(all services are part of the Army):
ACTIVE: 2,650.

ARMY: 2,000.
1 inf bn.
1 reserve bn (3 coy).
1 spt bn.
EQUIPMENT:
MORTARS: 60mm: ε40;
81mm: 6 L16A1.
RL: 82mm: 13 B-300.

COAST GUARD: 600.
BASE: Staubles Bay (HQ) Hart's Cut, Fort Fortin,
Tobago.
PATROL CRAFT: Inshore: 10:
2 *Barracuda* PFI (Sw *Karlskrona* 40-m).
1 *Buccoo Reef* PCI (UK Vosper 31.5-m), 7⟨,
plus boats and 8 ex-marine police spt vessels.

AIR WING: 50.
AIRCRAFT: 1 Cessna 310, 1 -402, 1 Cessna 172.

PARAMILITARY:
POLICE: 4,800.

URUGUAY

GDP 1990: pU 9,623.7bn ($8.22bn)
1991ε: pU 19,300.0bn ($8.85bn)
Growth 1990: 0.9% 1991: 1.9%
Inflation 1990: 112.6% 1991: 102%
Debt 1989: $3.76bn 1990: $3.71bn
Def exp 1990: pU 210.78bn ($180.0m)
1991: pU 524.88bn ($240.8m)
FMA 1992: $ 1.3m (US)
$1 = pU 1989: 605.62 1990: 1,171.0
1991: 2,180.0 1992: 3,100.00
pU = pesos Uruguayos

Population: 3,168,000

	13–17	18–22	23–32
Men	135,000	129,000	239,000
Women	131,000	125,000	233,000

TOTAL ARMED FORCES:
ACTIVE: 24,700.

ARMY: 17,200.
4 Military Regions/div HQ.
5 inf bde (4 of 3 inf bn, 1 of 1 mech, 1 mot, 1
para bn).
1 engr bde (3 bn).
3 cav bde (10 cav bn (4 horsed, 3 mech, 2 mot,
1 armd)).
1 arty bde (2 arty, 1 AD arty bn).
3 arty, 4 cbt engr bn.
EQUIPMENT:
LIGHT TANKS, 17 M-24, 28 M-3A1, 22 M-41A1.
RECCE: 20 FN-4-RM-62, 25 EE-3 *Jararaca*,
10 EE-9 *Cascavel*.
APC: 15 M-113, 50 *Condor*.
TOWED ARTY: 75mm: 12 Bofors M-1902; 105mm:
50 M-101A/M-102; 155mm: 5 M-114A1.
MORTARS: 81mm: 50 M-1; 107mm: 8 M-30.
ATGW: 5 *Milan*.
RCL: 57mm: 30 M-18; 106mm: 20 M-40A1.

AD GUNS: 20mm: 6 M-167 *Vulcan*; 40mm: 11 L/60.

NAVY: 4,500 incl 300 naval air, 500 naval
infantry, 2,000 Prefectura Naval (coast guard).
BASES: Montevideo (HQ), La Paloma Y Fray Bentos.
FRIGATES: 3:
3 *General Artigas* (Fr *Cdt. Rivière*) with 2 × 3
ASTT, 1 × 2 ASW mor, 2 × 100mm guns.
PATROL AND COASTAL COMBATANTS: 8:
OFFSHORE: 1:
1 *Campbell* (US *Auk* MSF) PCO (Antarctic
patrols).
INSHORE: 7:
2 *Colonia* PCI (US *Cape*).
3 *15 de Noviembre* PFI (Fr *Vigilante* 42-m).
1 *Salto* PCI, 1 *Paysandu* PCI⟨.
MINE WARFARE:
4 *Temerario* MSC (Ge *Kondor*).
AMPHIBIOUS: craft only; 2 LCM, 2 LCVP.
SUPPORT AND MISCELLANEOUS: 5:
1 tanker (VLCC, civilian charter), 1 trg, 2 salvage.
1 ocean tug.

NAVAL AVIATION: (300); 6 cbt ac, no armed hel.
ASW: 1 flt with 3 S-2A, 3 -G.
MR: 1 *Super King Air* 200T.
TRAINING/LIAISON: 1 *Super Cub*, 2 T-28, 2 T-34B, 2
T-34C, 1 PA-34-200T, 1 C-182 *Skylane*, 1 CH-34C.
HELICOPTERS: 1 CH-34C, 2 Wessex 60, 1 Bell 47G.

NAVAL INFANTRY: (500); 1 bn.

AIR FORCE: 3,000; 37 cbt ac, no armed hel.
COIN: 2 sqn:
1 with 12 A-37B, 6 AT-33.
1 with 6 IA-58B, 6 T-33A.
SURVEY: 1 EMB-110B1.
SAR: 1 sqn with: 2 Bell 212, 2 UH-1B, 3 UH-1H
hel.
TRANSPORT: 3 sqn with 3 C-212 (tpt/SAR), 3
EMB-110C, 1 F-27, 1 FH-227.
LIAISON: 2 Cessna 182, 1 *Queen Air* 80, 4 U-17,
1 U-206.
TRAINING: *7 AT-6A, 7 T-33, 30 T-34A/B, 6 T-41D.

FORCES ABROAD:
UN AND PEACEKEEPING:
CAMBODIA (UNTAC): 79.
EGYPT (MFO): 64.
INDIA/PAKISTAN (UNMOGIP): 1 adviser.
IRAQ/KUWAIT (UNIKOM): 8 Observers.

PARAMILITARY:
METROPOLITAN GUARD: 700.
REPUBLICAN GUARD: 500.
COAST GUARD: The Prefectura Naval (PNN) is
part of the Navy.

VENEZUELA

GDP	1990:	Bs 2,264.0bn ($48.27bn)	
	1991:	Bs 2,995.4bn ($52.72bn)	
Growth	1990:	5.7%	1991: 9.2%
Inflation	1990:	40.8%	1991: 34.2%
Debt	1990:	$33.31bn	1991: $33.0bn
Def exp	1990:	Bs 26.99bn ($573.56m)	
	1991:	Bs 107.95bn ($1.89bn)	
Def bdgt	1990:	Bs 24.35bn ($519.19m)	
	1991:	Bs 97.40bn ($1.62bn)	
$1 = Bs	1989:	34.684	1990: 46.900
	1991:	56.816	1992: 65.500
Bs = bolívares			

Population: 20,498,000

	13–17	18–22	23–32
Men	1,128,000	1,014,000	1,745,500
Women	1,094,000	983,000	1,695,000

TOTAL ARMED FORCES:
ACTIVE: 75,000 incl National Guard (ε18,000
conscripts).
Terms of service: 2 years (Navy 2¹/₂ years)
selective, varies by region for all services.

ARMY: 34,000 (incl conscripts).
6 inf div.
1 armd bde.
1 cav bde.
7 inf bde (18 inf, 1 mech inf, 4 fd arty bn).
1 AB bde.
1 Ranger bde (6 Ranger bn).
1 avn regt.
EQUIPMENT:
MBT: 70 AMX-30.
LIGHT TANKS: 75 M-18, 36 AMX-13, ε50 *Scorpion*.
RECCE: 10 AML-245, 25 M-8.
APC: 25 AMX-VCI, 100 V-100, 30 V-150, 100
Dragoon (some with 90mm gun), 35 EE-11 *Urutu*.
TOWED ARTY: 105mm: 40 Model 56, 40 M-101;
155mm: 12 M-114;
SP ARTY: 155mm: 5 M-109, 10 Mk F3.
MRL: 160mm: 20 LAR SP.
MORTARS: 81mm: 165; 120mm: 65 Brandt.
ATGW: AT-4, AS-11.
RCL: 106mm: M-40A1.
AVIATION:
AIRCRAFT: 3 IAI-202, 2 Cessna 172, 2 -206, 2 -207.
HELICOPTERS:
ATTACK: 6 A-109 (ATK);
TRANSPORT: 4 AS-61A, 3 Bell 205, 6 UH-1H.
LIAISON: 2 Bell 206.

NAVY: 11,000 incl naval air, marines and coast
guard (ε4,000 conscripts).

5 Commands: Fleet, Marines, Naval Avn, Coast guard, Fluvial (River Forces).

5 Fleet sqn: submarine, frigate, patrol, amph, service.

BASES: Caracas (HQ), Puerto Cabello (submarine, frigate, amph and service sqn), Punto Fijo (patrol sqn). Minor bases: Puerto de Hierro, Puerto La Cruz, El Amparo (HQ Arauca River), Maracaibo, La Guaira, Ciudad Bolívar (HQ Fluvial Forces).

SUBMARINES: 2:
2 *Sabalo* (Ge T-209/1300) with 533mm TT. (SST-4 HWT) (1 refitting in Germany).

FRIGATES: 6 *Mariscal Sucre* (It *Lupo*) with 1 AB-212 hel (ASW/OTHT), 2 × 3 ASTT (A-244S LWT); plus 8 × *Otomat* SSM, 1 × 127mm gun, 2 × 20 105mm MLR.

PATROL AND COASTAL COMBATANTS: 6:

MISSILE CRAFT: 6: 3 *Constitución* PFM (UK Vosper 37-m), with 2 × *Otomat*.
3 *Constitución* PFI with 4 × *Harpoon* SSM.

AMPHIBIOUS: 5:
4 *Capana* LST, capacity 200 tps, 12 tk.
1 *Amazonas* (US-1152) LST, capacity 200 tps, 16 tk.
Plus craft; 2 LCU (river comd), 11 LCVP.

SUPPORT AND MISCELLANEOUS: 3:
1 log spt, 1 trg, 1 *Punta Brava* AGHS.

NAVAL AVIATION: (2,000);
4 cbt ac, 8 armed hel.

ASW: 1 hel sqn (afloat) with 8 AB-212.

MR: 1 sqn with 4 C-212.

TRANSPORT: 2 C-212, 1 DHC-7, 1 *Rockwell Commander* 680.

LIAISON: 1 Cessna 310, 1 -402, 1 *King Air* 90.

HELICOPTERS: 2 Bell 47J.

MARINES: (6,000).
4 inf bn.
1 arty bn (3 fd, 1 AD bty).
1 amph veh bn.
1 river patrol, 1 engr, 2 para/cdo unit.

EQUIPMENT:

AAV: 11 LVTP-7 (to be mod to -7A1).

APC: 25 EE-11 *Urutu*, 10 *Fuchs/Transportpanzer* 1.

TOWED ARTY: 105mm: 18 Model 56.

AD GUNS: 40mm: 6 M-42 twin SP.

COAST GUARD: (ε750).

BASE: La Guaira; operates under Naval Command and Control, but organizationally separate.

PATROL, OFFSHORE: 3:
2 *Almirante Clemente* (It FF type),
1 *Larrazabal* (ex-US ocean tug).

PATROL INSHORE: 5: 4 *Manaure* (riverine) PCI⟨, 1 PCI⟨ plus about 15 boats.

AIR FORCE: 7,000 (some conscripts);
120 cbt ac, 30 armed hel.

FIGHTER/FGA: 3 Air Gp: 1 with 10 F-5A, 10 -B, 19 T-2D; 1 with 4 *Mirage* IIIEV, 2 -5V, 2 -5DV, 5 *Mirage* 50EV; 1 with 18 F-16A, 6 -B.

COIN: 1 Air Gp with 12 EMB-312, 25 OV-10E.

ATTACK HELICOPTERS: 1 Air Gp with 10 SA-316, 12 UH-1D, 8 UH-1H.

TRANSPORT: 7 C-123, 6 C-130H, 8 G-222, 2 HS-748, 2 B-707 (tkr).

TRANSPORT HELICOPTERS: 3 Bell 214, 4 -412, 5 AS-332B, 2 UH-1N.

PRESIDENTIAL FLT: 1 Boeing 737, 3 *Falcon* 20, 1 *Gulfstream* II, 1 -III, 1 *Learjet* 24D.

LIAISON: 9 *Cessna* -182, 1 *Citation* I, 1 -II, 2 *Queen Air* 65, 5 *Queen Air* 80, 5 *Super King Air* 200, 12 SA-316B *Alouette III*.

TRAINING: 1 Air Gp: 28 EMB-312, *7 F-5 (1 CF-5D, 6 NF-5B), 20 T-34.

AAM: R-530 *Magic*, AIM-9P *Sidewinder*.

AD GUNS: 110: 20mm: some Panhard M-3 SP; 35mm; 40mm: Bofors L/70 towed, Breda towed.

SAM: 10 *Roland*.

NATIONAL GUARD: *Fuerzas Armadas de Cooperación:* 23,000 (internal sy, customs).

EQUIPMENT: 25 UR-416 AIFV, 204 Fiat-6614 APC, 100 60mm mor, 10 81mm mor.

AC: 1 *Baron*, 1 BN-2A, 2 Cessna 185, 5 -U206, 1 -337, 1 -402C, 4 IAI-201, 1 *King Air* 90, 1 *King Air* 200C, 2 *Queen Air* 80, 2 F-28C.

HEL: 4 A-109, 15 Bell 206.

PATROL CRAFT: inshore: 22⟨; some 60 boats.

FORCES ABROAD:

UN AND PEACEKEEPING:

CROATIA (UNPROFOR): 3 Observers.

EL SALVADOR (ONUSAL): 38 Observers.

IRAQ/KUWAIT (UNIKOM): 7 Observers.

WESTERN SAHARA (MINURSO): 15 Observers.

Sub-Saharan Africa

The encouraging developments of late 1991 and early 1992 have not led to much progress in settling the many internal disputes in Africa. Most agreements reached earlier have been maintained, but without achieving the aim of true peace.

In **Ethiopia** the OROMO Liberation Front (OLF) is breaking away from the government formed by the Ethiopian People's Revolutionary Democratic Front, and a new civil war may break out. In **Angola** the planned merger of government forces with those of UNITA has not taken place, nor has any real progress been made in settling the internal problems of **Mozambique**. Some small progress has been made in **Liberia**, and the peacekeeping force established by the Economic Community of West African States (ECOWAS) has extended the area under its control. When rioting broke out in Kinshasa, Belgian and French troops were temporarily deployed to **Zaire** in September 1991 to protect their nationals. In early September 1991, **Libya** and **Chad** signed a security agreement; since then fighting in Chad has broken out intermittently between government forces and the supporters of the deposed President, Hissène Habré.

African states are now playing a much larger role in UN peacekeeping operations: eight countries contribute to six UN operations, a total of 19 separate contributions. (In 1989 six countries contributed to four operations in nine separate contributions.)

Military Developments

There is little information available on military developments in this region, so once again there are few significant changes to its armed forces. What information is available to *The Military Balance* shows there to have been an increase in army manpower strength, with little or no concomitant increase in military hardware; if anything, a number of older equipments have been retired without replacement.

In **Angola**, where about 60% of government troops and 75% of UNITA's have collected in containment camps, demobilization and integration is well behind schedule. Government forces' manpower has been reassessed at some 127,000, some 30,000 more than previous assessments. Weapons holdings are generally lower than before. Army strength in **Chad** is some 7,000 higher than previously thought; *Stinger* SAM have been obtained. In **Ghana** army strength is some 4,500 men fewer. This could be partly accounted for by the formation of a Presidential Guard Battalion, although the provision of three battalions for peacekeeping (ECOMOG in Liberia, UNTAC in Cambodia, UNIFIL in Lebanon) argues for an increase in manpower. Two of the navy's four ships are in refit in France. The reorganization of the **Nigerian** armed forces has reduced the army's strength by 18,000 men. The two mechanized and one armoured divisions have each lost one brigade which have been disbanded; initial deliveries of a further 80 Vickers Mk 3 tank are now being made and 70 MOWAG *Piranha* APCs have been procured. The navy's two frigates, corvette and three missile craft are still in refit. In **Zaire** there are 4,000 more men in the army, and the Presidential Guard has been raised to divisional status (previously two brigades). In **Botswana**, some 1,500 more men have been added to the army which is now organized into two brigades; one infantry battalion has converted to a 'commando' role. Six more 105mm light guns have been delivered. The **South African** Army now fields some 40 G-6 155mm SP guns, 30 more than previously assessed.

The **Zimbabwean** Air Force has only 12 Chinese J-7 fighters and not the 48 reported last year; whether the total of 48 are eventually to be procured or not, is not known. **Zambian** Army strength has been reassessed and shows an increase of 4,000 men. **Ugandan** Army manpower has probably been underestimated in the past and could be as high as 100,000 men, but there are plans to reduce the size of the army to some 60,000 men. The **Kenyan** Army is 1,500 men stronger; a third armoured battalion has been formed, but armoured holdings are only up by four Vickers MBT and 12 AML-90 armoured reconnaissance vehicles. The artillery battalions have been concentrated in an artillery brigade and 18 more 105mm light guns have been brought into service. The air force has taken delivery of 12 *Tucano* COIN aircraft.

ANGOLA

GDP	1989ε:	K 230.00bn ($7.56bn)	
	1990ε:	K 475.00bn ($7.90bn)	
Growth	1987ε:	13.9%	1988: 9.2%
Inflation	1991ε:	180.0%	
Debt	1989:	$6.95bn	1990: $7.71bn
Def exp	1989:	K 81.75bn ($2.69bn)	
$1 = K	1990:	29.9	1991: 60.0
	1992:	537.581	

K = kwanza

All dollar figures are highly misleading due to the difference between the official ($1 = 60K) and the parallel market exchange rate ($1 = 800 to 1,200K).

Population: 10,632,000

	13–17	18–22	23–32
Men	593,500	499,500	753,000
Women	592,900	503,100	769,000

Following the end of a 15-year civil war the Angolan government and its opponent UNITA have agreed to merge their armed forces to form a new 50,000-strong National Army. Details outlined below reflect the general situation and estimated status as of early 1992. Demobilization and integration is well behind schedule. About 60% of government tps and 75% of UNITA are in containment camps. Numbers and org fluctuate.

TOTAL ARMED FORCES:
ACTIVE: ε127,500.
Terms of service: conscription, authorized.

ARMY: ε120,000.
15 Military Zones (some may be fd HQ).
73+ bde (each with inf, tk, APC, arty and AA units as required. Bde = ε1,000 men).
EQUIPMENT:†
MBT: 100 T-34†, 130 T-54/-55, some T-62.
LIGHT TANKS: some 10 PT-76.
AIFV: 70+ BMP.
RECCE: some 40+ BRDM-2.
APC: 300 BTR-60/-152.
TOWED ARTY: 500: incl 76mm: M-1942 (ZIS-3); 85mm: D-44; 122mm: D-30; 130mm: M-46.
ASSAULT GUNS: SU-100.
MRL: 122mm: 50 BM-21, some BM-24.
MORTARS: 82mm: 250; 120mm: 40+ M-43.
ATGW: AT-3 *Sagger.*
RCL: 500: 82mm: B-10; 107mm: B-11.
AD GUNS: 200+: 14.5mm: ZPU-4; 23mm: ZU-23-2, 20 ZSU-23-4 SP; 37mm: M-1939; 57mm: S-60 towed, 40 ZSU-57-2 SP.
SAM: SA-7/-14.

NAVY:† ε1,500.
BASES: Luanda (HQ), Lobito, Namibe.
PATROL AND COASTAL COMBATANTS: 17:
MISSILE CRAFT: 6 Sov *Osa*-II with 4 × SS-N-2 *Styx* SSM.
TORPEDO CRAFT: 4 *Shershen*† with 4 × 533mm HWT.
PATROL, INSHORE 7: 4 Port *Argos*†, 2 Sov *Poluchat*, 1 Sov *Zhuk*⟨.
MINE WARFARE: 2 Sov *Yevgenya* MHI.
AMPHIBIOUS: 3 Sov *Polnocny* LSM, capacity 100 tps. 6 tk.
Plus craft; 1 LCT, about 8 LCM.
COASTAL DEFENCE: SS-C-l *Sepal* at Luanda.

AIR FORCE/AIR DEFENCE: ε6,000;
146 cbt ac, 40 armed hel.†
FGA: 25 MiG-17, 25 MiG-23, 30 Su-22, 10 Su-25.
FIGHTER: 35 MiG-21 MF/bis.
COIN/RECCE: 16 PC-7.
MR: 2 EMB-111, 1 F-27MPA.
ATTACK HELICOPTERS: 28 Mi-25/35, 6 SA-365M (guns), 6 SA-342 (*HOT*).
TRANSPORT: 2 sqn with 12 An-12, 20 An-26, 6 BN-2, 3 C-47, 6 C-212, 2 L-100-20, 4 PC-6B.
HELICOPTERS: 2 sqn with 30 IAR-316, 10 SA-316, 25 Mi-8, 13 Mi-17, 1 SA-315, 10 SA-365.
LIAISON: 10 An-2, 5 Do-27.
TRAINING: 3 Cessna 172, 3 MiG-15UTI, 6 MiG-21U, 5* Su-22, 6 Yak-11.
AD: 5 SAM bn. 10 bty; with 40 SA-2, 12 SA-3, 25 SA-6, 15 SA-8, 20 SA-9, 10 SA-13.
MISSILES:
ASM: *HOT.*
AAM: AA-2 *Atoll.*

PARAMILITARY:
BORDER GUARD (TGFA): 7,000.

OPPOSITION:
UNITA (*Union for the Total Independence of Angola*): some 28,000 'regulars' (1–2 years service), 37,000 'militia' (spt and log); to merge with government forces.
EQUIPMENT: captured T-34/-85, 70 T-55 MBT reported, misc APC (not in service); BM-21 122mm MRL; 75mm, 76mm, 122mm fd guns; 81mm, 82mm, 120mm mor; 85mm RPG-7 RL; 75mm RCL; 12.7mm hy machine guns; 14.5mm, 20mm and ZU-23-2 23mm AA guns; *Stinger,* SAM-7.
FNLA (*National Front for the Liberation of Angola*): (Bakongo tribesmen) claims up to 5,000, actual strength ε250; small arms only.
FLEC (*Front for the Liberation of the Cabinda Enclave*): (claims 5,000, actual strength ε600); small arms only.

FOREIGN FORCES:
RUSSIA: ε50 advisers and technicians.
UNITED NATIONS (UNAVEM II): 366 military observers and 90 police observers from 24 countries.

BENIN

GDP	1989:	fr 562.07bn ($1.76bn)	
	1990ε:	fr 548bn ($2.01bn)	
Growth	1990:	0.9%	1991: 3%
Debt	1989:	$1.18bn	1990: $1.43bn
Def bdgt	1991ε:	fr 5.77bn ($20.47m)	
	1992ε:	fr 7.20bn ($25.71m)	
$1 = fr	1990:	272.26	1991: 282.11
	1992:	280.0	

fr = francs CFA (Communauté financière africaine)
Benin's economy is to a large extent subsidized by the French government which is covering part of the country's bdgt deficit through economic aid.

Population: 5,083,600

	13–17	18–22	23–32
Men	281,240	230,000	331,160
Women	294,160	246,320	376,200

TOTAL ARMED FORCES: (all services form part of the Army):
ACTIVE: 4,350.
Terms of service: conscription (selective), 18 months.

ARMY 3,800.
3 inf, 1 AB/cdo, 1 engr bn, 1 armd sqn, 1 arty bty.
EQUIPMENT:
LIGHT TANKS: 20 PT-76.
RECCE: 9 M-8, 14 BRDM-2, 10 VBL M-11.
TOWED ARTY: 105mm: 4 M-101.
MORTARS: 81mm.
RL: 89mm: LRAC.

NAVY:† ε150.
BASE: Cotonou.
PATROL AND COASTAL COMBATANTS: 1:
PATROL, INSHORE: 1 *Patriote* PFI (Fr 38-m)⟨.
SUPPORT AND MISCELLANEOUS: 1: 1 tug.
In store: 4 Sov *Zhuk*⟨ PFI.

AIR FORCE:† 350; no cbt ac, 1 armed hel.
AIRCRAFT: 3 An-2, 2 An-26, 2 C-47, 1 *Commander* 500B, 2 Do-128.
HELICOPTERS:
 ATTACK: 1 SA-355M.
 TRANSPORT: 2 AS-350B, 1 Ka-26, 1 SE-3130.

PARAMILITARY:
GENDARMERIE: 2,000; 4 mobile coy.
PUBLIC SECURITY FORCE.
PEOPLE'S MILITIA: 1,500–2,000.

BOTSWANA

GDP	1990:	P 6.047bn ($3.25bn)	
	1991:	P 6.58bn ($3.02bn)	
Growth	1990:	5.1%	1991: 8.3%
Inflation	1990:	11.4%	1991: 11.7%
Debt	1990:	$515.60m	
Def bdgt	1989ε:	P 221.40m ($110.01m)	
	1990ε:	P 243.54m ($130.94m)	
FMA	1991:	$1.4m	
$1 = P	1990:	1.860	1991: 2.175
	1992:	2.128	

P = pula

Population: 1,347,400

	13–17	18–22	23–32
Men	79,800	65,600	89,800
Women	81,100	67,200	101,100

TOTAL ARMED FORCES: (both services form part of the Army):
ACTIVE: 6,100+.

ARMY: 6,000+
2 bde:
4 inf bn; 2 fd arty, 2 AD arty, 1 engr regt, 1 cdo unit.
EQUIPMENT:
RECCE: 10 *Shorland*, 12 V-150 *Commando* (11 with 90mm gun).
APC: 30 BTR-60†.
TOWED ARTY: 105mm: 12 lt, 4 Model 56 pack.
MORTARS: 81mm; 120mm.
ATGW: *TOW* reported.
RCL: 84mm: *Carl Gustav.*
AD GUNS: 20mm: M-167.
SAM: 12 SA-7.

AIR FORCE: 100+. 13 cbt ac, no armed hel.
COIN: 1 sqn with 8 BAC-167 Mk 83, 5 BN-2 *Defender.*
TRANSPORT: 1 sqn with 2 *Defender*, 2 CN-235, 2 *Skyvan* 3M, 1 BAe 125-800 (VIP).
LIAISON/TRAINING: 1 sqn with 1 Cessna 152, 7 PC-7.
HELICOPTERS: 2 AS-350L, 5 Bell 412.

PARAMILITARY:
POLICE MOBILE UNIT: 1,000.

BURKINA FASO

GDP   1989:   fr 698.74bn ($2.19bn)
            1990:   fr 733.68bn ($2.69bn)
Growth   1989:   9.9%   1990:   4.5%
Inflation   1990:   −0.5%   1991ε: 3.1%
Debt   1989: $717m   1990: $834m
Def bdgt   1990ε: fr 20,800.0m ($76.40m)
            1991ε: fr 28,160.0m ($108.10m)
FMA   fr (Fr) 5.7m (France)
$1 = fr   1990:   272.26   1991:   282.11
            1992:   280.0
fr = francs CFA (Communauté financière africaine)

Population: 9,623,600

	13–17	18–22	23–32
Men	512,960	428,120	689,000
Women	531,520	463,000	700,480

TOTAL ARMED FORCES: (all services incl
Gendarmerie form part of the Army):
ACTIVE: 8,700.

ARMY: 7,000.
6 Military Regions.
   5 inf 'regt': HQ, 3 'bn' (each 1 coy of 5 pl).
   1 AB 'regt': HQ, 1 'bn', 2 coy.
   1 tk 'bn': 2 pl.
   1 arty 'bn': 2 tps.
   1 engr 'bn'.
EQUIPMENT:
RECCE: 83: 15 AML-60/-90, 24 EE-9 *Cascavel*,
   10 M-8, 4 M-20, 30 *Ferret*.
APC: 13 M-3.
TOWED ARTY: 105mm: 8 M-101.
MRL: 107mm: Ch Type-63.
MORTARS: 81mm.
RL: 89mm: LRAC, M-20.
RCL: 75mm: Ch Type-52.
AD GUNS: 14.5mm: 30 ZPU.
SAM: SA-7.

AIR FORCE: 200; 18 cbt ac, no armed hel.
FIGHTER: 1 sqn with 8 MiG-21.
COIN: 4 SF-260W, 6 SF-260WP.
TRANSPORT: 2 C-47, 1 *Commander* 500B, 2
   HS-748, 2 N-262.
LIAISON: 3 MH-1521M, 2 SA-316, 2 SA-365.
HELICOPTERS: 2 SA-316B, 2 SA-365N.

PARAMILITARY: 1,750:
GENDARMERIE: 1,500; 6 coy (2 mobile).
SECURITY COMPANY (CRG): 250.
PEOPLE'S MILITIA(R): 45,000 trained; 2 years
   part-time; men and women 20–35 (military and
   civil duties).

BURUNDI

GDP   1989:   fr 174.50bn ($1.10bn)
            1990:   fr 189.142bn ($1.10bn)
Growth   1989:   1.4%   1990:   3.4%
Inflation   1990:   7.1%   1991:   9.0%
Debt   1990: $906m
Def bdgt   1987:   fr 3,910.0m ($31.64m)
            1988:   fr 4,500.0m ($32.05m)
$1 = fr   1990:   171.36   1991:   181.51
            1992:   210.00
fr = Burundi francs

Population: 5,786,600

	13–17	18–22	23–32
Men	304,640	259,280	444,840
Women	306,520	258,840	451,640

TOTAL ARMED FORCES:
(all services incl Gendarmerie form part of the
Army):
ACTIVE: ε7,200 (incl Gendarmerie).

ARMY: 5,500.
   2 inf, 1 AB, 1 cdo bn.
   1 armd car coy.
EQUIPMENT:
RECCE: 6 AML-60, 12 -90, 7 *Shorland*.
APC: 29: 9 M-3, 20 BTR-40 and *Walid*.
MORTARS: 82mm: 18 M-43.
RL: 83mm: *Blindicide*.
RCL: 75mm: 15 Ch Type-52.
AD GUNS: 14.5mm: 15 ZPU-4.

NAVY: ε50.
BASE: Bujumbura.
PATROL BOATS: river: ε3⟨.

AIR: 150.
   3 cbt ac, no armed hel.
COIN: 3 SF-260W.
TRANSPORT: 1 C-47.
HELICOPTERS: 3 SA-316B,
   4 SA-342L.
LIAISON: 3 Reims-Cessna 150,
   1 Do-27Q.
TRAINING: 7 SF-260 (3 -C, 4 -TP).

PARAMILITARY:
GENDARMERIE: ε1,500.

CAMEROON

GDP	1989ε:	fr 3,506.0bn ($10.99bn)
	1990ε:	fr 3,130.9bn ($11.50bn)
Growth	1989ε:	−7.0% 1990ε: 1.0%
Inflation	1989:	0% 1990ε: −0.5%
Debt	1989:	$4.786bn 1990: $6.02bn
Def bdgt	1989:	fr 45.520bn ($142.7m)
	1990:	fr 51.977bn ($190.9m)
FMA	1988:	$8.28m (Fr, US)
$1 = fr	1989:	319.101 1990: 272.26
	1991:	282.11 1992: 280

fr = francs CFA (Coopération financière en Afrique centrale)

Population: 13,003,600

	13–17	18–22	23–32
Men	717,280	553,600	827,560
Women	717,080	556,960	843,520

TOTAL ARMED FORCES:
ACTIVE: 11,700 (incl Gendarmerie).

ARMY: 6,600.
3 Military Regions; 7 Military Sectors: coy gp under cmd.
Presidential Guard: 1 guard, 1 armd recce bn, 3 inf coy.
1 AB/cdo bn.
5 inf bn (1 trg).
1 engr bn.
1 arty bn (5 bty).
1 AA bn (6 bty).
EQUIPMENT:
RECCE: 8 M-8, *Ferret*, 8 V-150 *Commando* (20mm gun), 5 VBL M-11.
AIFV: 12 V-150 *Commando* (90mm gun).
APC: 29 V-150 *Commando*, 12 M-3 half-track.
TOWED ARTY: 22: 75mm: 6 M-116 pack; 105mm: 16 M-101.
MORTARS: 81mm (some SP); 120mm: 16 Brandt.
ATGW: *Milan*.
RL: 89mm: LRAC.
RCL: 57mm: 13 Ch Type-52; 106mm: 40 M-40A2.
AD GUNS: 14.5mm: 18 Ch Type-58; 35mm: 18 GDF-002; 37mm: 18 Ch Type-63.

NAVY: ε800.
BASES: Douala (HQ), Limbe, Kribi.
PATROL AND COASTAL COMBATANTS: 2:
MISSILE CRAFT: 1 *Bakassi* (Fr P.48) PFM with 2 × 4 MM-40 *Exocet* SSM.
PATROL, INSHORE: 1:
1 *L'Audacieux* (Fr P.48) PFI.
RIVERINE: Boats only, some 30 US Swiftsure-38, 4 SM-36 type.

AMPHIBIOUS: craft only: 2 LCM, 5 LCVP.

AIR FORCE: 300; 16 cbt ac, 4 armed hel.
1 composite sqn.
1 Presidential flt.
FGA/COIN: 5 *Alpha Jet*, 11 CM-170.
MR: 2 Do-128D-6.
ATTACK HELICOPTERS: 4 SA-342L (with *HOT*).
TRANSPORT: 3 C-130H/-H-30, 1 DHC-4, 4 DHC-5D, 1 IAI-201, 2 PA-23.
HELICOPTERS: 3 Bell 206, 3 SE-3130, 1 SA-318, 4 SA-319.

PARAMILITARY:
GENDARMERIE: 4,000: 10 regional groups.
PATROL BOATS: about 10 US Swiftsure-38 (included in Navy entry).

CAPE VERDE

GDP	1987:	CV E 17.984bn ($248.0m)
	1988:	CV E 20.64bn ($286.0m)
Growth	1987:	9.3% 1988: 7.7%
Inflation	1987:	3.8% 1988: 8.2%
Debt	1989:	$135.3m 1990: $152.0m
$1 = CV E	1988:	72.068 1989: 77.978
	1990:	70.031 1991: 71.408

CV E = Cape Verde escudos

Population: 389,400

	13–17	18–22	23–32
Men	23,120	21,200	28,960
Women	22,960	21,800	36,480

TOTAL ARMED FORCES:
ACTIVE: 1,300.
Terms of service: conscription (selective).

ARMY: 1,000 (Popular Militia).
2 bn.
EQUIPMENT:
RECCE: 3 BRDM-2.
TOWED ARTY: 75mm: 6; 76mm: 12.
MORTARS: 82mm: 6. 120mm: 6 M-1943.
RL: 89mm: 3.5-in.
AD GUNS: 23mm: 12 ZU-23.

NAVY: 200.
BASE: Praia, Porto Grande.
PATROL AND COASTAL COMBATANTS: 5:
2 Sov *Shershen* PFI (no TT), 3 Sov *Zhuk*⟨.
SUPPORT AND MISCELLANEOUS:
1 survey.†

AIR FORCE: under 100; no cbt ac.
TRANSPORT: 2 An-26.

CENTRAL AFRICAN REPUBLIC

GDP	1989:	fr 350.90bn ($1.10bn)
	1990:	fr 363.7bn ($1.34bn)
Growth	1989: 3.7%	1990: 1.86%
Inflation[a]	1990: −0.1%	1991ε: −2.6%
Debt	1989: $716.00m	1990: $901m
Def bdgt	1987:	fr 5,610.0m ($18.67m)
	1988ε:	fr 6,546.6m ($21.98m)
$1 = fr	1989: 319.101	1990: 272.260
	1991: 282.11	1992: 280.0

fr = francs CFA (Coopération financière en Afrique
  centrale)

[a] Inflation figures represent the consumer price index for
African households. CPI for European households shows
an inflation rate of 6.2% for 1989.

Population: 3,154,400

	13–17	18–22	23–32
Men	172,000	156,840	215,760
Women	172,800	151,280	221,640

TOTAL ARMED FORCES:
ACTIVE: 6,500 incl Gendarmerie.
  Terms of service: conscription (selective),
    2 years; Reserve obligation thereafter, term
    unknown.

ARMY: 3,500.
  1 Republican Guard regt (2 bn).
  1 territorial defence regt (bn).
  1 combined arms regt (1 mech, 1 inf bn).
  1 spt/HQ regt.
  1 Presidential Guard bn.
EQUIPMENT:†
MBT: 4 T-55.
RECCE: 10 *Ferret*.
APC: 4 BTR-152, some 10 VAB, 25+ ACMAT.
MORTARS: 81mm; 120mm: 12 M-1943.
RL: 89mm: LRAC.
RCL: 106mm: 14 M-40.
RIVER PATROL CRAFT: 9⟨.

AIR FORCE: 300; No cbt ac, no armed hel.
TRANSPORT: 2 C-47, 2 Cessna 337, 1 DC-4.
LIAISON: 8 AL-60, 6 MH-1521.
HELICOPTERS: 1 AS-350, 1 SE-3130.

PARAMILITARY:
GENDARMERIE: 2,700;

3 Regional Legions, 8 'bde'.

FOREIGN FORCES:
FRANCE: 1,200. 1 inf bn gp, 1 armd cav sqn, 1
  arty bty. 5 *Jaguar*, 3 C-160.

CHAD

GDP	1989ε: fr 330.70bn ($1.04bn)
	1990ε: fr 334.40bn ($1.23bn)
Growth	1988: 1.7%	1989: −2.0%
Inflation	1989: −4.9%	1990: 0.6%
Debt	1989: $368.4m	1990: $491.5m
Def bdgt	1988: fr 23,200m ($77.89m)
	1989: fr 18,500m ($57.99m)
FMA	1991: $2.4m (US); fr (CFA) 5bn
	(France)
$1 = fr	1989: 319.01	1990: 272.26
	1991: 282.11	1992: 280.0

fr = francs CFA (Coopération financière en
  Afrique centrale).

Population: 5,981,800

	13–17	18–22	23–32
Men:	310,920	266,680	430,200
Women:	311,080	268,760	436,400

TOTAL ARMED FORCES:
ACTIVE: some 25,200.
  Terms of service: conscription, 3 years.

ARMY: ε25,000.
  7 Military Regions.
EQUIPMENT:
AFV: some 63: 4 Panhard ERC-90, some 50
  AML-60/-90, 9 V-150 with 90mm.
TOWED ARTY: 105mm: 5 M-101.
MORTARS: 81mm; 120mm: AM-50.
ATGW: *Milan*.
RL: 89mm: LRAC.
RCL: 106mm: M-40A1; 112mm: *APILAS*.
AD GUNS: 20mm, 30mm.

AIR FORCE: 200; 4 cbt ac, no armed hel.
COIN: 2 PC-7, 2 SF-260W.
TRANSPORT: 3 C-47, 1 C-130A, 2 -B, 1 -H, 1 C-212,
  2 DC-4.
HELICOPTERS: 4 SA-330, 1 SA-341.
LIAISON: 2 PC-6B, 5 Reims-Cessna FTB 337.

PARAMILITARY:
GENDARMERIE: 4,500.

OPPOSITION:
WESTERN ARMED FORCES: strength unknown.
MOVEMENT FOR DEVELOPMENT AND DEMOCRACY: strength unknown.

FOREIGN FORCES:
FRANCE: 750. 2 inf coy, AD arty units; 3 C-160.

CONGO

GDP	1989:	fr 647.00bn ($2.03bn)	
	1990:	fr 535.60bn ($1.97bn)	
Growth	1988:	−2.8%	1989: −5.2%
Inflation	1989:	4.1%	1990: 2.1%
Debt	1989:	$4.33bn	1990: $5.12bn
Def bdgt	1987:	fr 30,208.0m ($100.51m)	
$1 = fr	1989:	319.101	1990: 272.260
	1991:	282.11	1992: 280.0

fr = francs CFA (Coopération financière en Afrique centrale)

Population: 2,419,600
	13–17	18–22	23–32
Men:	130,400	113,160	170,720
Women:	129,400	112,520	172,480

TOTAL ARMED FORCES:
ACTIVE: 10,850.

ARMY: 10,000.
    2 armd bn.
    2 inf bn gp (each with lt tk tp, 76mm gun bty).
    1 inf bn.   1 engr bn.
    1 arty gp (how, MRL)   1 AB/cdo bn.
EQUIPMENT:†
MBT: 25 T-54/-55, 15 Ch Type-59. (Some T-34 in store.)
LIGHT TANKS: 10 Ch Type-62, 3 PT-76.
RECCE: 25 BRDM-1/-2.
APC: M-3, 80 BTR (30 -50, 30 -60, 20 -152).
TOWED ARTY: 76mm; 100mm: 10 M-1944; 122mm: 10 D-30; 130mm: 5 M-46; 152mm: some D-20.
MRL: 122mm: 8 BM-21; 140mm: BM-14-16.
MORTARS: 82mm; 120mm: 10 M-43.
RCL: 57mm: M-18.
ATK GUNS: 57mm: 5 M-1943.
AD GUNS: 14.5mm: ZPU-2/-4; 23mm: ZSU-23-4 SP; 37mm: 28 M-1939; 57mm: S-60; 100mm: KS-19.

NAVY:† ε350.
BASE: Point Noire.
PATROL AND COASTAL COMBATANTS: 6:
PATROL, INSHORE: 6:
    3 *Marien N'gouabi* PFI (Sp *Barcelo* 33-m).

3 Sov *Zhuk* PFI⟨.
RIVERINE: Boats only.

AIR FORCE:† 500. 22 cbt ac, no armed hel.
FGA: 10 MiG-17, 12 MiG-21.
TRANSPORT: 5 An-24, 1 An-26, 1 Boeing 727, 1 N-2501.
TRAINING: 4 L-39, 1 MiG-15UTI.
HELICOPTERS: 2 SA-316, 2 SA-318, 1 SA-365.

FORCES ABROAD:
UN AND PEACEKEEPING:
ANGOLA (UNAVEM II): 15 Observers.

PARAMILITARY: 6,100:
GENDARMERIE: 1,400; 20 coy.
PEOPLE'S MILITIA: 4,700.

FOREIGN FORCES:
RUSSIA: 20 military advisers.

CÔTE D'IVOIRE

GDP	1990:	fr 2,647.6bn ($9.72bn)	
	1991ε:	fr 2,660.8bn ($9.43bn)	
Growth	1990:	−3%	1991: 0.5%
Inflation	1990:	−0.4%	1991ε: 1.53%
Debt	1989:	$15.61bn	1990: $17.96bn
Def bdgt	1989ε:	fr 59,272.2m ($185.0m)	
FMA	$4.0m (Economic Support, US)		
$1 = fr	1989:	319.01	1990: 272.26
	1991:	282.11	1992: 280.0

fr = francs CFA (Communauté financière africaine)

Population: 12,849,800
	13–17	18–22	23–32
Men	714,880	613,400	927,960
Women	704,720	584,040	833,320

TOTAL ARMED FORCES:
ACTIVE: 7,100.
    Terms of service: conscription (selective), 6 months.
RESERVES: 12,000.

ARMY: 5,500.
    4 Military Regions:
        1 armd, 3 inf bn, 1 arty gp.
        1 AB, 1 AA, 1 engr coy.
EQUIPMENT:
LIGHT TANKS: 5 AMX-13.
RECCE: 7 ERC-90 *Sagaie*, ε16 AML-60/-90.
APC: 16 M-3, 13 VAB.

TOWED ARTY: 105mm: 4 M-1950.
MORTARS: 81mm; 120mm: 16 AM-50.
RL: 89mm: LRAC.
RCL: 106mm: M-40A1.
AD GUNS: 20mm: 16 incl 6 M-3 VDA SP;
40mm: 5 L/60.

NAVY: 700.
BASE: Locodjo (Abidjan).
PATROL AND COASTAL COMBATANTS: 4:
MISSILE CRAFT: 2:
2 *L'Ardent* (Fr *Auroux* 40-m) with 4 × SS-12 SSM.
PATROL: 2 *Le Vigilant* (Fr SFCN 47-m) PCI.
AMPHIBIOUS: 1 *L'Eléphant* (Fr *BATRAL*) LSM,
capacity 140 tps, 7 tk, hel deck.

AIR FORCE: 900; 6 cbt ac, no armed hel.
FGA: 1 sqn with 6 *Alpha Jet*.
TRANSPORT: 1 hel sqn with 1 SA-318, 1 SA-319, 1
SA-330, 4 SA-365C.
PRESIDENTIAL FLIGHT:
  AIRCRAFT: 1 F-28, 1 *Gulfstream* IV, 1 Fokker 100.
  HELICOPTERS: 1 SA-330.
TRAINING: 6 Beech F-33C, 2 Reims Cessna 150H.
LIAISON: 1 Cessna 421, 2 *Super King Air* 200.

PARAMILITARY: 7,800:
PRESIDENTIAL GUARD: 1,100.
GENDARMERIE: 4,400; VAB APC, 4 patrol boats.
MILITIA: 1,500.
MILITARY FIRE SERVICE: 800.

FOREIGN FORCES:
FRANCE: 500: 1 marine inf regt; 1 AS-350 hel.

EQUATORIAL GUINEA

GDP	1989:	fr 46.27bn ($145m)	
Growth	1989:	−1.5%	1990: 0.3%
Inflation	1989:	5.5%	1990: 0%
Debt	1989:	$226.9m	1990: $237.4m
$1 = fr	1989:	319.101	1990: 272.26
	1991:	282.11	1992: 280.00

fr = francs CFA (Coopération financière en Afrique centrale)

Population: 440,200

	13–17	18–22	23–32
Men:	21,520	19,200	31,800
Women:	22,360	19,840	32,920

TOTAL ARMED FORCES:
ACTIVE: 1,300.

ARMY: 1,100.
3 inf bn.
EQUIPMENT:
RECCE: 6 BRDM-2.
APC: 10 BTR-152.

NAVY†: 120.
BASES: Malabo (Santa Isabel), Bata.
PATROL COMBATANTS: 3 PFI, 1 PCI, all⟨.

AIR FORCE: 100;
no cbt ac or armed hel.
TRANSPORT: 1 Yak-40.

PARAMILITARY: some 2,000.
GUARDIA CIVIL: 2 coy.

FOREIGN FORCES:
MOROCCO: 360: 1 bn.

ETHIOPIA

GDP	1990:	EB 12.533bn ($6.11bn)	
	1991:	EB 12.722bn ($6.06bn)	
Growth	1989:	0.9%	1990: −2.0%
Inflation	1990:	5.1%	1991: 35.8%
Debt	1989:	$3.024bn	1990: $3.250bn
Def bdgt	1989ε:	EB 1,110.15m ($536.30m)	
	1990:	EB 2,691.00m ($1.31bn)	
$1 = EB*a*	1989:	2.070	1990: 2.051
	1991:	2.100	1992: 2.034

EB = birr
a Official rate fixed at $1 = EB 2.07

Population: 52,154,400

	13–17	18–22	23–32
Men	2,939,160	2,540,520	3,894,040
Women	2,859,320	2,461,600	3,809,480

Following the defeat and dissolution of the former government of Ethiopia by forces of the Ethiopian People's Revolutionary Democratic Front (EPRDF) and Eritrean People's Liberation Front (EPLF), no national armed forces have yet been formed. Strengths of the two groups are assessed as:
EPRDF – an est 110,000, of whom the majority are members of the Tigray People's Liberation Front (TPLF). Some 15–20,000 belong to the Oromo Liberation Front and other smaller groups.
EPLF – about 85,000.
Eqpt previously held by the government of Ethiopia is now largely in EPRDF and EPLF hands.

Estimated numbers in service must be treated with some caution.

GROUND FORCES:†
MBT: ε350 T-54/-55, T-62.
RECCE/AIFV/APC: ε200 incl: BRDM, BMP, BTR-60/-152.
TOWED ARTY: 76mm: ZIS-3; 85mm: D-44; 122mm: D-30/M-30; 130mm: M-46.
MRL: BM-21.
MORTARS: 82mm: M-1937; 120mm: M-1938.
ATGW: AT-3 *Sagger*.
RCL: 82mm: B-10; 107mm: B-11.
AD GUNS: 23mm: ZU-23, ZSU-23-4 SP; 37mm: M-1939; 57mm: S-60.
SAM: 20 SA-2, 30 SA-3, 300 SA-7, SA-9.

NAVY: †3,500 in 1990.
No organization exists. Prior to the final EPLF/EPRDF offensives of spring 1991, the Ethiopian Navy numbered some 27 vessels as shown below. With the fall of the Eritrean ports, the op portion of the navy dispersed. Many vessels remain in Yemen, Saudi Arabia and Djibouti. Non-op ships and craft were sunk or scuttled in port.

The EPLF naval forces number about 300 and are reported as operating about 10–12 Ethiopian naval vessels plus some 25 armed boats and about 50 armed dhows.

BASES: Massawa, Assab.
FRIGATES: 2 *Zerai Deres* (Sov *Petya* II) with 2 × ASW RL, 10 × 406mm TT.
PATROL AND COASTAL COMBATANTS: 14:
MISSILE CRAFT: 4 Sov *Osa* with 4 × SS-N-2 *Styx* SSM.
TORPEDO CRAFT: 4: 2 Sov *Turya* PHT, 2 *Mol* PFT all with 4 × 533mm TT.
PATROL INSHORE: 6 PFI: 3 US Swiftships 32-m, 3 Sov *Zhuk*⟨.
AMPHIBIOUS: 2 Sov *Polnocny* LSM, capacity 100 tps, 6 tk.
Plus craft; 3 LCT (2 *Chamo*, 1 Fr EDIC), 4 LCM.
SUPPORT AND MISCELLANEOUS: 2:
1 AOT (small), 1 trg.

AIR FORCE:† 58 cbt ac, 18 armed hel.
No recognizable org remains. There is a residue of former maintenance technicians under contract remaining to man and service a future air force, however the availability of pilots remains limited. The op status before the spring offensive of 1991 was less than 50% for all types. Types and numbers of remaining ac are assessed as follows.
FGA: 40 MiG-21MF; 18 MiG-23BN
TRANSPORT: 6 An-12, 2 DH-6, 2 L-100-30 (liaison), 1 Yak-40 (VIP).
TRAINING: 14 L-39.

HELICOPTERS:
ATTACK: 18 Mi-24.
TRANSPORT: 1 IAR-330, 30 Mi-8, 3 UH-1, 2 Mi-14.

GABON

GDP	1990:	fr 1,084.60bn ($3.98bn)	
	1991ε:	fr 1,232.10bn ($4.37bn)	
Growth	1988:	−2.0%	1989ε: 4.0%
Inflation	1989:	6.9%	1990: 8.7%
Debt	1989:	$3.18bn	1990: $3.65bn
Def bdgt	1988ε:	fr 45,800.0m ($153.77m)	
	1989ε:	fr 46,510.0m ($145.79m)	
$1 = fr	1989:	319.01	1990: 272.260
	1991:	282.11	1992: 280.0

fr = francs CFA (Communauté financière africaine)

Population: 1,206,200

	13–17	18–22	23–32
Men	56,200	49,760	84,200
Women	57,720	51,400	86,720

TOTAL ARMED FORCES:
ACTIVE: 4,750.

ARMY: 3,250.
Presidential Guard bn gp (1 recce/armd, 3 inf coy, arty, AA bty) (under direct Presidential control).
8 inf, 1 AB/cdo, 1 engr coy.
EQUIPMENT:
RECCE: 16 EE-9 *Cascavel*, 24 AML-90, 6 ERC-90 *Sagaie*, 12 EE-3 *Jararaca*, 14 VBL M-11.
AIFV: 12 EE-11 *Urutu* with 20mm gun.
APC: 9 V-150 *Commando*, Panhard M-3, 12 VXB-170.
TOWED ARTY: 105mm: 4 M-101.
MRL: 140mm: 8 *Teruel*.
MORTARS: 81mm: 35; 120mm: 4 Brandt.
ATGW: 4 *Milan*.
RL: 89mm: LRAC.
RCL: 106mm: M40A1.
AD GUNS: 20mm: 4 ERC-20 SP; 23mm: 24 ZU-23-2; 37mm: 10 M-1939; 40mm: 2 Bofors.

NAVY: ε500.
BASE: Port Gentil (HQ).
PATROL AND COASTAL COMBATANTS: 3:
MISSILE CRAFT: 1 *General Nazaire Boulingu* PFM (Fr 42-m) with 4 SS-12 SSM.
PATROL COASTAL: 2 *General Ba'Oumar* (Fr P.400 55-m).
AMPHIBIOUS: 1 *President Omar Bongo* (Fr *BATRAL*) LSM, capacity 140 tps, 7 tk.
Plus craft; 1 LCM.

AIR FORCE: 1,000. 20 cbt ac, 7 armed hel.

FGA: 9 *Mirage* 5 (2 -G, 4 -GII, 3 -DG).
MR: 1 EMB-111P1.
TRANSPORT: 1 C-130H, 1 L-100-20, 2 L-100-30, 3 EMB-110, 1 *Falcon* 50, 1 *Gulfstream* III, 2 YS-11A.
HELICOPTERS:
   ATTACK: 2 AS-350, 5 SA-342.
   TRANSPORT: 3 SA-330C/-H.
   LIAISON: 3 SA-316/-319.
PRESIDENTIAL GUARD:
   COIN: 6 CM-170, 4 T-34.
   TRANSPORT: 1 ATR-42F, 1 EMB-110.

PARAMILITARY:
COAST GUARD: ε2,800; boats only.
GENDARMERIE: 2,000; 3 'bdes', 11 coy, 2 armd sqn, air unit.

FOREIGN FORCES:
FRANCE: 500: 1 marine inf regt; 1 AS-35 hel, 1 C-160 (tpt).

THE GAMBIA

GDP	1990:	D 2,345m ($297.50m)		
	1991:	D 2,689.4m ($305.51m)		
Growth	1990:	2.0%	1991ε:	3.0%
Inflation	1990:	12.2%	1991:	8.6%
Debt	1989:	$340.5m	1990:	$352.2m
Def bdgt	1988:	D 20.10m ($3.00m)		
$1 = D	1989:	7.585	1990:	7.883
	1991:	8.803	1992:	8.900
D = dalasi				

Population: 928,200

	13–17	*18–22*	*23–32*
Men	49,080	40,440	65,640
Women	48,360	40,640	68,120

TOTAL ARMED FORCES:
ACTIVE: 800.

GAMBIAN NATIONAL ARMY (GNA):
   1 inf bn (4 coy), engr sqn.
MARINE UNIT: About 70.
BASE: Banjul.
PATROL, INSHORE: 3:
   2 *Gonjur* (Ch *Shanghai-II*) PFI, 1 PFI⟨, boats.

FORCES ABROAD:
LIBERIA: about 100, forming part of ECOWAS force.

FOREIGN FORCES:
NIGERIA: 50+ trg team.

GHANA

GDP	1990:	C 2,031.7bn ($6.23bn)	
	1991ε:	C 2,438.0bn ($6.62bn)	
Growth	1990:	3.3%	1991ε: 4%
Inflation	1990:	37.0%	1991: 18.0%
Debt	1990:	$3.5bn	1991: $3.1bn
Def bdgt	1989ε:	C 11,200m ($41.48m)	
	1990:	C 14,811m ($45.39m)	
$1 = C	1989:	270.00	1990: 326.33
	1991:	367.83	1992: 395.00
C = cedi			

Population: 15,929,400

	13–17	*18–22*	*23–32*
Men	913,640	753,680	1,120,800
Women	911,440	756,000	1,141,240

TOTAL ARMED FORCES:
ACTIVE: 7,200.

ARMY: 5,000.
   2 Command HQ:
      2 bde (comprising 6 inf bn (incl 1 trg, 1 UNIFIL, 1 ECOMOG), spt units).
      1 recce regt (2 sqn).
      1 AB force (incl 1 para coy).
      1 arty 'regt' (mor bn).
      1 fd engr regt (bn).
EQUIPMENT:
RECCE: 3 *Saladin*, 3 EE-9 *Cascavel*.
AIFV: 50 MOWAG *Piranha*.
MORTARS: 81mm: 50; 120mm: 28 Tampella.
RCL: 84mm: 50 *Carl Gustav*.

NAVY: ε1,000 Commands: Western and Eastern.
BASES: Sekondi (HQ, West), Tema (HQ, East).
PATROL AND COASTAL COMBATANTS: 4:
COASTAL: 2 *Achimota* (Ge Lürssen 57-m) PFC (incl 1 in refit).
INSHORE: 2 *Dzata* (Ge Lürssen 45-m) PCI (incl 1 in refit).

AIR FORCE: 1,200. 18 cbt ac, no armed hel.
COIN: 1 sqn with 4 MB-326K†, 2 MB-339.
TRANSPORT: 3 sqn:
   1 VIP with 3 Fokker (2 F-27, 1 F-28);
   1 with 3 F-27, 1 C-212.
   1 with 6 *Skyvan*.
HELICOPTERS: 2 Bell 212 (VIP), 2 Mi-2, 4 SA-318.
TRAINING: 1 sqn with 10 *Bulldog* 122†, 12* L-29.

FORCES ABROAD:
LIBERIA: about 1,000 forming part of ECOWAS force.
UN AND PEACEKEEPING:
CAMBODIA: (UNTAC): 719.
CROATIA (UNPROFOR): 3 Observers.
IRAQ/KUWAIT (UNIKOM): 14 Observers.
LEBANON (UNIFIL): 1 inf bn (890).
WESTERN SAHARA (MINURSO): 1 Observer.

PARAMILITARY:
PEOPLE'S MILITIA: 5,000: part-time force with
    police duties.
PRESIDENTIAL GUARD: 1 inf bn.

GUINEA

GDP	1990: G fr 1,930.0bn ($2.92bn)		
	1991ε: G fr 2,411.0bn ($3.04bn)		
Growth	1991ε: 4.0%		
Inflation	1988: 33%	1989:	28%
Debt	1989: $2.18bn	1990:	$2.50bn
Def exp	1989ε: $27m		
$1 = G fr	1989: 302.3	1990:	660.3
	1991: 792.6	1992:	812.6

G fr = Guinean franc

Population: 7,297,000

	13–17	18–22	23–32
Men	366,320	311,840	511,200
Women	380,280	327,360	538,960

TOTAL ARMED FORCES:
ACTIVE: 9,700 (perhaps 7,500 conscripts).
    Terms of service: conscription, 2 years.

ARMY: 8,500.

1 armd bn.	1 cdo bn.
5 inf bn.	1 SF bn.
1 arty bn.	1 engr bn.
1 AD bn.	

EQUIPMENT:†
MBT: 30 T-34, 8 T-54.
LIGHT TANKS: 20 PT-76.
RECCE: 25 BRDM-1/-2, 2 AML-90.
APC: 40 BTR (16 -40, 10 -50, 8 -60, 6 -152).
TOWED ARTY: 76mm: 8 M-1942; 85mm: 6 D-44;
    122mm: 12 M-1931/37.
MORTARS: 82mm: M-43; 120mm: 20 M-1938/43.
RCL: 82mm: B-10.
ATK GUNS: 57mm: M-1943.
AD GUNS: 30mm: twin M-53; 37mm: 8 M-1939;
    57mm: 12 S-60, Ch Type-59; 100mm: 4 KS-19.
SAM: SA-7.

NAVY: 400.
BASES: Conakry, Kakanda.
PATROL AND COASTAL COMBATANTS: 9:
PATROL: 9
    1 *Kaba* Sov T-58C PCO†
    Some 3 Sov 39-m (*Osa* hull & machinery) PFI
    2 Sov *Zhuk*, 1 US Swiftships-77, 2 other PCI, all‹.

AIR FORCE:† 800; 12 cbt ac, no armed hel.
FGA: 4 MiG-17F, 8 MiG-21.
TRANSPORT: 2 An-12, 4 An-14.
TRAINING: 3 L-29, 2 MiG-15UTI, 6 Yak-18.
HELICOPTERS: 1 IAR-330, 4 Mi-4, 1 SA-316B, 1
    SA-330, 1 SA-342K.

FORCES ABROAD:
LIBERIA: some 400, forming part of ECOWAS force.
UN AND PEACEKEEPING:
WESTERN SAHARA (MINURSO): 2 Observers.

PARAMILITARY:.
PEOPLE'S MILITIA: 7,000.
GENDARMERIE: 1,000.
REPUBLIC GUARD: 1,600.

GUINEA-BISSAU

GNP	1990ε: pG 403.63bn ($181m)		
Growth	1988ε: 4.1%	1989ε:	5.0%
Inflation	1989ε: 40%	1990ε:	25%
Debt	1989: $498.4m	1990:	$592.8m
Def bdgt	1989: pG 8,027.0m ($4.43m)		
$1 = pG	1989: 1,811.4	1990:	2,230.0
	1991: 650.0	1992:	5,000.0

pG = Guinea pesos

Population: 1,027,400

	13–17	18–22	23–32
Men	60,040	52,040	73,200
Women	55,520	48,360	76,680

TOTAL ARMED FORCES: (all services incl
    Gendarmerie are part of the Army):
ACTIVE: 9,200.
    Terms of service: conscription (selective).

ARMY: 6,800.
    1 armd 'bn' (sqn).
    5 inf, 1 arty bn, 1 recce, 1 engr coy.
EQUIPMENT:
MBT: 10 T-34.
LIGHT TANKS: 20 PT-76.

RECCE: 10 BRDM-2.
APC: 35 BTR-40/-60/-152, 20 Ch Type-56.
TOWED ARTY: 85mm: 8 D-44; 122mm: 18 M-1938/D-30.
MORTARS: 82mm: M-43; 120mm: 8 M-1943.
RL: 89mm: M-20.
RCL: 75mm: Ch Type-52; 82mm: B-10.
AD GUNS: 23mm: 18 ZU-23; 37mm: 6 M-1939; 57mm: 10 S-60.
SAM: SA-7.

NAVY: 300.
BASE: Bissau.
PATROL AND COASTAL COMBATANTS: 8:
PATROL INSHORE: 8:
  3 Sov 39-m (*Osa* hull & machinery), 2 Ch *Shantou* PFI, 3 PCI⟨.

AIR FORCE: 100. 3 cbt ac, no armed hel.
FIGHTER: 3 MiG-17.
HELICOPTERS: 1 SA-318, 2 SA-319.

FORCES ABROAD:
UN AND PEACEKEEPING:
ANGOLA (UNAVEM II): 15 Observers.

PARAMILITARY:
GENDARMERIE: 2,000.

KENYA

GDP	1990:	sh 200.65bn ($8.76bn)	
	1991ε:	sh 234.76bn ($8.53bn)	
Growth	1990:	3.5%	1991: 2.2%
Inflation	1990:	11.8%	1991: 14.8%
Debt	1989:	$5.8bn	1990: $6.84bn
Def bdgt	1992ε:	sh 5.30bn ($151.43m)	
Def expε	1988:	sh 4,886.0m ($275.42m)	
	1989:	sh 6,048.2m ($294m)	
FMA	1991:	$5.1m (US)	
$1 = sh	1989:	20.572	1990: 22.915
	1991:	27.508	1992: 35.000
sh = Kenyan shillings			

Population: 27,101,400

	13–17	18–22	23–32
Men:	1,635,800	1,290,240	1,800,800
Women:	1,638,080	1,298,560	1,822,480

TOTAL ARMED FORCES:
ACTIVE: 24,200.

ARMY: 20,500.
  1 armd bde (3 armd bn).
  2 inf bde (1 with 2, 1 with 3 inf bn); 1 indep inf bn.
  1 arty bde (3 bn).
  1 engr bde.
  1 AD arty bn.
2 engr bn.
1 indep air cav bn.
EQUIPMENT:
MBT: 80 Vickers Mk 3.
RECCE: 52 AML-60/-90, 12 *Ferret*, 8 *Shorland*.
APC: 52 UR-416, 10 Panhard M-3.
TOWED ARTY: 105mm; 58 lt, 8 pack.
MORTARS: 81mm: 50; 120mm: 12 Brandt.
ATGW: 40 *Milan*, 14 *Swingfire*.
RCL: 84mm: 80 *Carl Gustav*; 120mm: 20 *Wombat*.
AD GUNS: 20mm: 50 TCM-20, 12 *Oerlikon*; 40mm: 13 Bofors.

NAVY: 1,200.
BASE: Mombasa.
PATROL AND COASTAL COMBATANTS: 10:
MISSILE CRAFT 6:
  2 *Nyayo* (UK Vosper 56-m) PFM, with 4 *Otomat* II SSM.
  1 *Mamba*, 3 *Madaraka* (UK Brooke Marine 37-m/32-m) PFM with 4 × *Gabriel* II SSM.
PATROL, INSHORE: 4: 3 *Simba* (UK Vosper 31-m) PCI, 1 PCI⟨.

AIR FORCE: 2,500: 40 cbt ac, 38 armed hel.
FGA: 11 F-5 (9 -E, 2 -F).
COIN: 5 *Strikemaster* Mk 87, 12 *Hawk* Mk 52, 12 *Tucano*.
TRANSPORT: 7 DHC-5D, 7 Do-28D, 1 PA-32.
TRAINING: 8 *Bulldog* 103/127.
HELICOPTERS:
  ATTACK: 15 Hughes 500MD (with TOW), 8 500ME, 15 500M.
  TRANSPORT: 9 IAR-330, 3 SA-330, 1 SA-342.
  TRAINING: 2 Hughes 500D.
MISSILES:
  ASM: AGM-65 *Maverick*, TOW.
  AAM: AIM-9 *Sidewinder*.

FORCES ABROAD:
UN AND PEACEKEEPING:
CROATIA (UNPROFOR): 33 Observers.
IRAQ/KUWAIT (UNIKOM): 13 Observers.
WESTERN SAHARA (MINURSO): 10 Observers.

PARAMILITARY:
POLICE GENERAL SERVICE UNIT: 5,000.
POLICE AIR WING: 7 Cessna lt ac, 3 Bell hel (1 206L, 2 47G).
POLICE NAVAL SQN: about 5 PCI⟨ (2 Lake Victoria), some 12 boats.

LESOTHO

GDP	1989:	M 1,287.3m ($492.09m)	
	1990:	M 1,504.7m ($581.86m)	
Growth	1989ε:	6%	1990ε: 4%
Inflation	1990:	11.6%	1991: 17.69%
Debt	1989:	$324.7bn	1990: $389.7bn
Def exp	1989:	M 83.3m ($31.84m)	
$1 = M	1989:	2.616	1990: 2.586
	1991:	2.756	1992: 2.900

M = maloti

Population: 1,868,600

	13–17	18–22	23–32
Men	99,240	82,760	126,080
Women	101,000	85,560	135,400

TOTAL ARMED FORCES:
ACTIVE: 2,000.

ARMY:
7 inf coy.
1 spt coy (incl recce/AB, 81mm mor).
1 air sqn.
EQUIPMENT:
RECCE: 10 Is RAMTA, 8 *Shorland*.
ARTY: 105mm: 2.
MORTARS: 81mm: some.
AIRCRAFT: 2 C-212 *Aviocar* 300.
HELICOPTERS: 2 Bo-105, 3 Bell 412.

LIBERIA

GDP	1986:	$L 1,034.80m ($US 1,034.80m)	
	1987ε:	$L 990m ($US 990m)	
Growth	1987:	−1.1%	1988: −1.5%
Inflation	1988:	9.7%	1989: 5.84%
Debt	1990:	$US 3.5bn	
Def bdgt	1988ε:	$L 28.07m ($US 28.07m)	
	1989ε:	$L 37.62m ($US 37.62m)	
$1 = $L*a*	1986–92:	1.00	

a $1 = $L fluctuates on parallel market; unofficial
estimate $1 = $L8–10

Population: 2,784,200

	13–17	18–22	23–32
Men	149,440	121,760	186,040
Women	151,880	123,840	190,760

As a result of civil war the Armed Forces of Liberia
(AFL) with a cbt strength of ε5,000 are now
confined to the capital city Monrovia. Eqpt held by
the AFL has been destroyed or is unserviceable.
They are opposed by the National Patriotic Forces
of Liberia (NPFL) who control most of the country
with a cbt strength of ε15,000. A six-nation
peacekeeping force (ECOMOG) provided by the
Economic Community of West African States
(ECOWAS) is deployed within the country and is
composed of forces from:
The Gambia – ε100; Ghana – ε1,000; Guinea –
ε400; Nigeria – ε4,000; Senegal – ε1,200; Sierra
Leone – ε400.

MADAGASCAR

GDP	1989:	fr 3,117.67bn ($1.94bn)	
	1990ε:	fr 3,610.26bn ($2.42bn)	
Growth	1989:	3.5%	1990: 4%
Inflation	1990:	11.8%	1991: 12.8%
Debt	1990:	$3.94bn	1991: $4.5bn
Def bdgt	1990:	fr 52,300.0m ($35.00m)	
	1991:	fr 58,600.0m ($36.63m)	
FMA	1988:	$2.88m (Fr, US)	
$1 = fr	1989:	1,603.40	1990: 1,494.10
	1991:	1,835.4	1992: 2,020.0

fr = Malagasy francs

Population: 12,807,200

	13–17	18–22	23–32
Men	734,320	607,080	921,840
Women	724,360	596,240	895,120

TOTAL ARMED FORCES:
ACTIVE: 21,000.
Terms of service: conscription (incl for civil
purposes), 18 months.

ARMY: some 20,000.
2 bn gp.	1 service regt.
1 engr regt.	7 construction regt.
1 sigs regt.	

EQUIPMENT:
LIGHT TANKS: 12 PT-76.
RECCE: 8 M-8, ε20 M-3A1, 10 *Ferret*, ε35 BRDM-2.
APC: ε30 M-3A1 half-track.
TOWED ARTY: 76mm: 12 ZIS-3; 105mm: some
M-101; 122mm: 12 D-30.
MORTARS: 82mm: M-37; 120mm: 8 M-43.
RL: 89mm: LRAC.
RCL: 106mm: M-40A1.
AD GUNS: 14.5mm: 50 ZPU-4; 37mm: 20 Type 55.

NAVY: 500 (incl some 100 marines).
BASES: Diégo-Suarez, Tamatave, Fort Dauphin,
Tuléar, Majunga.
PATROL CRAFT: 1 *Malaika* (Fr PR48-m) PCI.

AMPHIBIOUS: 1 *Toky* (Fr *BATRAM*) LSM, with 8 × SS-12 SSM, capacity 30 tps, 4 tk.
Plus craft; 1 LCT (Fr EDIC), 1 LCA, 3 LCVP.
SUPPORT AND MISCELLANEOUS: 1 tpt/trg.

AIR FORCE: 500; 12 cbt ac, no armed hel.
FGA: 1 sqn with 4 MiG-17F, 8 MiG-21FL.
TRANSPORT: 4 An-26, 3 BN-2, 2 C-212, 2 Yak-40 (VIP).
HELICOPTERS: 1 sqn with 6 Mi-8.
LIAISON: 1 Cessna 310, 2 -337, 1 PA-23.
TRAINING: 4 Cessna 172.

PARAMILITARY:
GENDARMERIE: 7,500, incl maritime police with some 5 PCI⟨.

MALAWI

GDP	1990:	K 5.07bn ($1.86bn)	
	1991:	K 6.10bn ($2.18bn)	
Growth	1990:	4.8%	1991: 4.8%
Inflation	1990:	11.7%	1991: 12.7%
Debt	1989:	$1.39bn	1990: $1.54bn
Def bdgt	1988:	K 53.10m ($20.73m)	
	1989ε:	K 60.76m ($22.02m)	
FMA	1991:	$1.25m (US)	
$1 = K	1989:	2.7595	1990: 2.7289
	1991:	2.8033	1992: 2.9000

K = kwacha

Population: 8,844,600

	13–17	18–22	23–32
Men:	500,240	409,920	595,680
Women:	501,360	417,000	635,120

TOTAL ARMED FORCES: (all services form part of the Army):
ACTIVE: 10,750.
RESERVES: Army: some 1,000; ex-soldiers have a 5-year obligation.

ARMY: 10,500. 3 inf bn; 1 spt bn (incl 1 recce sqn).
EQUIPMENT:
RECCE: 20 *Fox*, 10 *Ferret*, 13 *Eland*.
TOWED ARTY: 9 105mm lt.
MORTARS: 81mm: L16.
RL: 89mm: M-20.
RCL: 57mm: M-18.
AD GUNS: 14.5mm: 50 ZPU-4.
SAM: 15 *Blowpipe*.

MARINE: 100.
BASE: Monkey Bay. (Lake Nyasa).

PATROL CRAFT: 1 PCI⟨, 2 LCVP, some boats.

AIR: 150; No cbt ac, 4 armed hel.
TRANSPORT: 1 sqn with 4 Do-228, 2 C-47, 1 HS-125-800 (VIP), 1 *King Air* C90
HELICOPTERS:
ATTACK: 4 AS-350.
TRANSPORT: 3 SA-330, 1 SA-365.

FORCES ABROAD:
MOZAMBIQUE: 1,500.

PARAMILITARY:
POLICE: 6,000: 3 BN-2T *Defender* (border patrol), 1 *Skyvan* 3M ac; 2 AS-350 hel. Some boats.
Mobile Force (1,000).

MALI

GDP	1990:	fr 683.30bn ($2.51bn)	
	1991ε:	fr 693.54bn ($2.46bn)	
Growth	1990:	2.4%	1991: −0.2%
Inflation	1990:	0.5%	1991ε: 1.56%
Debt	1989:	$2.16bn	1990: $2.43bn
Def bdgt	1987ε:	fr 18,310m ($60.92m)	
	1988ε:	fr 19,010m ($63.82m)	
$1 = fr	1989:	319.01	1990: 272.26
	1991:	282.11	1992: 280.0

fr = francs CFA (Communauté financière africaine)

Population: 9,011,600

	13–17	18–22	23–32
Men	516,240	444,000	595,200
Women	516,160	443,760	620,560

TOTAL ARMED FORCES: (all services form part of the Army):
ACTIVE: 7,350.
Terms of service: conscription (incl for civil purposes), 2 years (selective).

ARMY: 6,900.
2 tk, 4 inf, 1 AB, 2 arty, 1 engr, 1 SF bn, 2 AD, 1 SAM bty.
EQUIPMENT:†
MBT: 21 T-34.
LIGHT TANKS: 18 Type 62.
RECCE: 20 BRDM-2.
APC: 30 BTR-40, 10 BTR-152, 10 BTR-60.
TOWED ARTY: 85mm: 6 D-44; 100mm: 6 M-1944; 122mm: 8 D-30.
MRL: 122mm: 2 BM-21.
MORTARS: 82mm: M-43; 120mm: 30 M-43.

AD GUNS: 37mm: 6 M-1939; 57mm: 6 S-60.
SAM: 12 SA-3.

NAVY:† About 50.
BASES: Bamako, Mopti, Segou, Timbuktu.
RIVER PATROL CRAFT: 3⟨.

AIR FORCE: 400; 16 cbt ac, no armed hel.†
FGA: 5 MiG-17F.
FIGHTER: 11 MiG-21.
TRANSPORT: 2 An-2, 2 An-24, 2 An-26.
TRAINING: 6 L-29, 1 MiG-15UTI, 4 Yak-11, 2 Yak-18.
HELICOPTERS: 2 Mi-4, 1 Mi-8.

PARAMILITARY:
GENDARMERIE: 1,800; 8 coy.
REPUBLICAN GUARD: 2,000.
MILITIA: 3,000.
NATIONAL POLICE: 1,000.

FOREIGN FORCES:
RUSSIA: 20 military advisers.

MOZAMBIQUE

GDP	1989ε:	M 825.24bn ($1.19bn)	
	1990ε:	M 990.29bn ($1.06bn)	
Growth	1990:	1.5%	1991: 0.9%
Inflation	1990:	47%	1991ε: 30–35%
Debt	1989:	$4.50bn	1990: $4.72bn
Def bdgt[a]	1990ε:	M 105,200m ($113.09m)	
	1991ε:	M 206,000m ($114.44m)	
$1 = M	1989:	691.23	1990: 930.25
	1991:	1,356.0	1992: 2,356.0

(Official exchange rate $1 = M 1,800)
M = meticais
[a] Incl sy. Demob programme est $50m.

Population: 16,896,000

	13–17	18–22	23–32
Men	916,280	778,320	1,205,320
Women	949,200	812,960	1,226,480

TOTAL ARMED FORCES:
ACTIVE: 50,200.
> *Terms of service:* conscription (selective, blacks only), 2 years (incl women), extended during emergency.

ARMY: ε45,000 (perhaps 85% conscripts; all units well under strength.)
10 Provincial Commands.

1 tk bde.
7 inf bde.
1 lt inf bde.
Many indep cbt and cbt spt bn and sy units.
6 AA arty bn.
EQUIPMENT:†
MBT: some 100 T-54/-55 (300+ T-34, T-54/-55 non-op).
RECCE: 30 BRDM-1/-2.
AIFV: 40 BMP-1.
APC: 150+ BTR-60, 100 BTR-152.
TOWED ARTY: 250+: 76mm: M-1942; 85mm: 150+: D-44, D-48, Type-56; 100mm: 24 M-1944; 105mm: M-101; 122mm: M-1938, D-30; 130mm: 24 M-46; 152mm: 20 D-1.
MRL: 122mm: 30 BM-21.
MORTARS: 82mm: M-43; 120mm: M-43.
RCL: 75mm: M-20; 82mm: B-10; 107mm: B-11.
AD GUNS: 400: 20mm: M-55; 23mm: 90 ZU-23-2; 37mm: 100 M-1939; 57mm: 90: S-60 towed, ZSU-57-2 SP.
SAM: SA-7.

NAVY†: 1,200.
BASES: Maputo (HQ), Beira, Nacala, Pemba, Inhambane, Quelimane (ocean); Metangula (Lake Nyasa) where 3 PCI⟨† are based.
PATROL AND COASTAL COMBATANTS: 12:
INSHORE: 12†:
 2 Sov SO-1, 3 *Zhuk* PFI⟨.
 7 PCI⟨.
MINE WARFARE: 2 Sov *Yevgenya* MSI.
AMPHIBIOUS: craft only; 2 LCU†.

AIR FORCE: 4,000 (incl AD units);
43 cbt ac†, 6 armed hel.†
FGA: 5 sqn with 43 MiG-21.
TRANSPORT: 1 sqn with 5 An-26, 2 C-212, 2 Cessna 152, 1 -172.
HELICOPTERS:
 ATTACK: 6 Mi-24.
 TRANSPORT: 5 Mi-8.
TRAINING: 4 Cessna 182, 4 PA-32.
AD SAM:† SA-2, 10 SA-3.

PARAMILITARY:
BORDER GUARD: 5,000; 1 bde.
PROVINCIAL MILITIA: 9 bn; 1 bn (less Nyasa) per province.

OPPOSITION:
MOZAMBIQUE NATIONAL RESISTANCE: (MNR or RENAMO): 20,000, ε10,000+ trained.
8 bn (active).
EQUIPMENT: RCL: 82mm B-10, RPG-7.
 MORTARS: 60mm, 82mm, 120mm M-1943.
 AD GUNS: 12.7mm and 14.5mm.

FOREIGN FORCES:
ZIMBABWE: Some 3,000–5,000 (varies).
MALAWI: 1,500 (varies).
MILITARY ADVISERS: Russia 25, North Korea 40(-).

NAMIBIA

GDP	1990ε: R 4.98bn ($1.92bn)			
	1991ε: R 5.60bn ($2.17bn)			
Growth	1990ε: 2.9%		1991ε: 1%	
Inflation	1990ε: 14.2%		1991: 18.1%	
Debt	1988: $758.00bn	1989: $663.00bn		
Def bdgt	1989: R 220.00m ($84.10m)			
	1990: R 122.68m ($47.44m)			
FMA*a*	1991: $5.18m (US)			
$ 1 = R	1989: 2.616	1990: 2.586		
	1991: 2.583	1992: 2.8058		

R = rand

a Incl $5m as Economic Support.

Population: 1,397,200

	13–17	18–22	23–32
Men	76,840	63,960	98,840
Women	77,320	64,840	100,560

TOTAL ARMED FORCES:
ACTIVE: 7,500.

ARMY: 7,400.
1 Presidential Guard bn.
4 mot inf bn.
1 arty bn.
1 AD arty bn.
1 ATK bn.
EQUIPMENT:
APC: some *Casspir*.
MRL: BM-21.
MORTARS: 81mm.

NAVY: ε100.
PATROL: Boats only.

NIGER

GDP	1989: fr 676.9bn ($2.12bn)		
	1990ε: fr 628.1bn ($2.31bn)		
Growth	1987: –2.0%	1988: –4.6%	
Inflation	1990: –0.8%	1991: –7.81%	
Debt	1989: $1.58bn	1990: $1.83bn	
Def bdgt	1988: fr 5,490.0m ($17.6m)		
	1989 fr 6,700m ($21.0m)		
FMA	1991: $0.8m (US)		

$1 = fr	1989: 319.01	1990: 272.26	
	1991: 282.11	1992: 280.0	

fr = francs CFA (Communauté financière africaine)

Population: 7,957,000

	13–17	18–22	23–32
Men:	435,800	356,200	546,100
Women:	440,900	363,400	561,500

TOTAL ARMED FORCES:
ACTIVE: 3,300.
Terms of service: selective conscription (2 years).

ARMY: 3,200.
3 Military Districts.
2 armd recce sqn.
6 inf, 1 AB, 1 engr coy.
EQUIPMENT:
RECCE: 50+: 10 M-8, 18 AML-90,
18 AML-60-7, some AML-60-20.
APC: 14 M-3.
MORTARS: 81mm: 30 Brandt; 120mm: 15 Brandt.
RL: 89mm: LRAC.
RCL: 57mm: 8 M-18; 75mm: 6 M-20.
AD GUNS: 20mm: 10 M-3 VDA SP.

AIR FORCE: 100+; no cbt ac or armed hel.
TRANSPORT: 1 C-54, 2 C-130H, 2 Do-228, 3
N-2501. 1 Boeing 737-200 (VIP).
LIAISON: 2 Cessna 337D, 2 Do-28D.

PARAMILITARY:
GENDARMERIE: 900; 7 groups.
PRESIDENTIAL GUARD: 200.
REPUBLICAN GUARD: 1,900.
NATIONAL POLICE: 1,500.

NIGERIA

GDP	1990: N 260.64bn ($32.43bn)	
	1991: N 315.53bn ($31.84bn)	
Growth	1990: 5.1%	1991: 4.3%
Inflation	1990: 7.5%	1991: 13.01%
Debt	1990: $36bn	
Def exp	1990: N 2,285m ($284.27m)	
Def bdgt*a*	1991: N 2,415.0m ($243.72m)	
	1992: N 3,060.0m ($255.0m)	
$1 = N	1989: 7.365	1990: 8.038
	1991: 9.909	1992: 12.0

N = naira

a Excl Police and Police Affairs Dept, and Internal
Affairs Ministry.

Population:*b* 90,491,000

	13–17	*18–22*	*23–32*
Men	5,006,000	4,095,000	6,046,000
Women	4,993,000	4,110,000	6,152,000

[b] In March 1992, the National Population Commission announced the provisional results of the 1991 census showing a huge discrepancy with UN and other agencies' projection.

TOTAL ARMED FORCES:
ACTIVE: 76,000.
RESERVES: planned; none organized.

ARMY: 62,000.
1 armd div (2 armd bde).
1 composite div (incl 1 mot,
    1 amph bde, 1 AB bn).
2 mech div (each 1 mech, 1 mot bde).
1 AD bde.
Div tps: each div 1 arty, 1 engr bde, 1 recce bn.
EQUIPMENT:
MBT: 157: 60 T-55†, 97 Vickers Mk 3.
LIGHT TANKS: 100 *Scorpion*.
RECCE: 20 *Saladin*, ε120 AML-60, 60 AML-90, 55 *Fox*.
APC: 10 *Saracen*, 300 4K-7FA, 70 MOWAG *Piranha*.
TOWED ARTY: 105mm: 200 M-56; 122mm: 200 D-30/-74; 155mm: 24 FH-77B.
SP ARTY: 155mm: 25 *Palmaria*.
MORTARS: 81mm: 200.
RCL: 84mm: *Carl Gustav*; 106mm: M-40A1.
AD GUNS: 20mm: some 60; 23mm: ZU-23, 30 ZSU-23-4 SP; 40mm: L/60.
SAM: 48 *Blowpipe*, 16 *Roland*.

NAVY: 4,500.
BASES: Apapa (Lagos; HQ Western Command), Calabar (HQ Eastern Command), Warri, Port Harcourt.
FRIGATES: 2:
    1 *Aradu* (Ge *Meko*-360) with 1 *Lynx* hel, 2 × 3 ASTT; plus 8 × *Otomat* SSM, 1 × 127mm gun (in refit).
    1 *Obuma* with hel deck; plus 1 × 2 102mm guns (in refit and conversion to trg role).
PATROL AND COASTAL COMBATANTS: 54:
CORVETTES: 3:
    2† *Erinomi* (UK Vosper Mk 9) with 1 × 2 ASW mor.
    1 *Otobo* (UK Vosper Mk 3) (in Italy, refitting to PCO).
MISSILE CRAFT: 6:
    3 *Ekpe* (Ge Lürssen 57-m) PFM with 4 × *Otomat* SSM.
    3 *Siri* (Fr *Combattante*) with 2 × 2 MM-38 *Exocet* SSM (in France refitting).
PATROL, INSHORE: 45:
    4 *Makurdi* (UK Brooke Marine 33-m), some 41 PCI⟨.

MINE WARFARE: 2 *Ohue* (mod It *Lerici*) MCC.
AMPHIBIOUS: 2 *Ambe* (Ge) LST, capacity 220 tps, 5 tk.
SUPPORT AND MISCELLANEOUS: 6: 1 survey, 4 tugs, 1 nav trg.
NAVAL AVIATION:
HELICOPTERS: 2 *Lynx* Mk 89 MR/SAR.

AIR FORCE: 9,500;
95 cbt ac†,
15 armed hel†.
FGA/FIGHTER: 3 sqn:
    1 with 21 *Alpha Jet* (FGA/trg);
    1 with †6 MiG-21MF, †4 MiG-21U, †12 MiG-21B/FR.
    1 with †15 *Jaguar* (12 -SN, 3 -BN).
COIN/TRAINING: 23 L-39MS, 12 MB-339AN.
ATTACK HELICOPTERS: †15 Bo-105D.
MR/SAR: 1 sqn with:
    AIRCRAFT: †2 F-27MR (armed);
    HELICOPTERS: 4 Bo-105D.
TRANSPORT: 2 sqn with 6 C-130H, 3 -H-30, 3 Do-228 (VIP), 5 G-222.
    PRESIDENTIAL FLT: 1 Boeing 727, 1 *Falcon*, 1 BAe 125-700, 2 *Gulfstream*, 1 BAe 125-100.
    LIGHT TPT: 3 sqn with 18 Do-28D, 18 Do-128-6.
    HELICOPTERS: incl 4 AS-322, 3 Bo-105CB, 2 SA-330.
TRAINING:
    AIRCRAFT:† 25 *Bulldog*;
    HELICOPTERS: 14 Hughes 300.
MISSILES:
    AAM: AA-2 *Atoll*.

FORCES ABROAD:
LIBERIA: some 4,000; contingent forms major part of ECOWAS force.
THE GAMBIA: 50+ trg team.
SIERRA LEONE: 800.
UN AND PEACEKEEPING:
ANGOLA (UNAVEM II): 15 Observers.
CROATIA (UNPROFOR): 18 Observers.
IRAQ/KUWAIT (UNIKOM): 8 Observers.
WESTERN SAHARA (MINURSO): 1 Observer.

PARAMILITARY:
COAST GUARD: 1 PCI⟨, some 60 boats.
PORT SECURITY POLICE: 12,000.
SECURITY AND CIVIL DEFENCE CORPS
    (Ministry of Internal Affairs): Police: UR-416, 70 AT-105 *Saxon*† APC; 1 Cessna 500, 3 Piper (2 *Navajo*, 1 *Chieftain*) ac, 4 Bell (2 -212, 2 -222) hel; 68 small craft, 7 hovercraft (5 AV *Tiger*).

RWANDA

GDP	1990:	fr 176.5bn ($2.14bn)		
	1991:	fr 193.8bn ($1.55bn)		
Growth	1990:	−7.0%	1991ε:	−9%
Inflation	1990:	4.2%	1991:	19.62%
Debt	1989:	$648.2m	1990:	$740.7m
Def bdgt	1988:	fr 2.80bn ($36.63m)		
Def exp	1989ε:	fr 2.96bn ($37m)		
$1 = fr	1989:	79.98	1990:	82.60
	1991:	125.14	1992:	120.0

fr = Rwanda francs

Population: 7,741,400

	13–17	18–22	23–32
Men	419,200	338,000	564,000
Women	423,100	342,200	566,000

TOTAL ARMED FORCES: (all services
form part of the Army):
ACTIVE: 5,200.

ARMY: 5,000.
1 cdo bn.
1 recce, 8 inf, 1 engr coy.
EQUIPMENT:
RECCE: 12 AML-60,
16 VBL M-11.
APC: 16 M-3.
MORTARS: 81mm: 8.
RL: 83mm: *Blindicide.*
ATK GUNS: 57mm: 6.
AVIATION:
TRANSPORT: 2 C-47,
1 Do-27Q-4.
HELICOPTERS: 2 SE-3160.

AIR: 200;
2 cbt ac, no armed hel.
COIN: 2 R-235 *Guerrier.*
TRANSPORT: 2 BN-2, 1 N-2501, 1 *Falcon* 50 (VIP).
LIAISON: 5 SA-316, 6 SA-342L hel.

PARAMILITARY:
GENDARMERIE: 1,200.

OPPOSITION:
RWANDA PATRIOTIC FRONT

FOREIGN FORCES:
FRANCE: 200; 1 para coy.

SENEGAL

GDP	1989ε:	fr 1,478.20bn ($4.63bn)		
	1990:	fr 1,591.98bn ($5.84bn)		
Growth	1989:	1.0%	1990ε:	4.5%
Inflation	1990:	0.3%	1991:	−1.8%
Debt	1989:	$3.30bn	1990:	$3.80bn
Def bdgt	1990:	fr 30,453m ($111.85m)		
	1991[a]:	fr 43,584m ($154.49m)		
FMA[b]	1991:	$4.53m (US)		
$1 = fr	1989:	319.01	1990:	272.26
	1991:	282.11	1992:	280.0

fr = francs CFA (Communauté financière africaine)
[a] Exceptional budget to cover 18 months from July 1991 to January 1993 (government is bringing fiscal year into line with civil year); the annualized budget is approximately fr 30.0bn ($106.3m).
[b] Incl Economic Support of $3.0m.

Population: 8,137,000

	13–17	18–22	23–32
Men	464,600	384,100	574,500
Women	462,800	387,800	581,000

TOTAL ARMED FORCES:
ACTIVE: 9,700.
Terms of service: conscription, 2 years selective.
RESERVE: exists, no details known.

ARMY: 8,500 (mostly conscripts).
4 Military Zone HQ.

1 armd bn.	1 cdo bn.
6 inf bn.	1 arty bn.
1 AB bn.	1 engr bn.

1 Presidential Guard (horsed). 3 construction coy.
EQUIPMENT:
RECCE: 10 M-8, 4 M-20, 30 AML-60, 27 -90.
APC: some 16 Panhard M-3, 12 M-3 half-track.
TOWED ARTY: 18: 75mm: 6 M-116 pack; 105mm: 6 M-101/HM-2; 155mm: ε6 Fr Model-50.
MORTARS: 81mm: 8 Brandt; 120mm: 8 Brandt.
ATGW: *Milan.*
RL: 89mm: LRAC.
AD GUNS: 20mm: 21 M-693; 40mm: 12 L/60.

NAVY: 700.
BASES: Dakar, Casamance.
PATROL AND COASTAL COMBATANTS: 10:
PATROL COASTAL: 2:
1 *Fouta* (Dk *Osprey*) PCC.
1 *Njambuur* (Fr SFCN 59-m) PFC.
INSHORE: 8:
3 *Senegal* II PFI⟨.
2 *Challenge* (UK *Tracker*) PFI⟨.
3 *Saint Louis* (Fr 48-m) PCI.
AMPHIBIOUS: craft only; 2 LCT, 2 LCM.

AIR FORCE: 500;

9 cbt ac, no armed hel.
COIN: 1 sqn with 5 CM-170, 4 R-235 *Guerrier*.
MR/SAR: 1 EMB-111.
TRANSPORT: 1 sqn with 6 F-27-400M, 2 MH-1521.
1 PA-23 (liaison).
HELICOPTERS: 2 SA-318C, 2 SA-330, 1 SA-341H.
TRAINING: 2 *Rallye* 160, 2 -235A.

FORCES ABROAD:

LIBERIA: ε1,200 forms part of ECOWAS force.
UN AND PEACEKEEPING:
ANGOLA (UNAVEM II): 15 Observers.
CAMBODIA (UNTAC): 2 Observers.
IRAQ/KUWAIT (UNIKOM): 7 Observers.

PARAMILITARY:

GENDARMERIE: 12 VXB-170 APC.
CUSTOMS: 2 PCI⟨, boats.

FOREIGN FORCES:

FRANCE: 1,200: 1 marine inf regt, MR and tpt
ac/hel.

SEYCHELLES

GDP	1988:	SR 1,523.9m ($283.06m)		
	1989:	SR 1,702.8m ($301.61m)		
Growth	1988:	6.0%	1989:	7.0%
Inflation	1990:	3.9%	1991:	1.9%
Debt	1989:	$168.40m	1990:	$197.3m
Def bdgt	1989ε:	SR 70.0m ($12.40m)		
	1991:	SR 84.20m ($15.92m)		
FMAᵃ	$3.40m (US)			
$1 = SR	1989:	5.65	1990:	5.34
	1991:	5.29	1992:	5.35

SR = Seychelles rupees
ᵃ Incl Economic Support of $3.30m.

Population: 69,600

	13–17	*18–22*	*23–32*
Men	4,000	4,000	7,000
Women	4,000	3,760	6,300

TOTAL ARMED FORCES: (all services

form part of the Army):
ACTIVE: 1,300.

ARMY: 1,000.

1 inf bn (3 coy).
2 arty tps.
Spt coy.

EQUIPMENT:

RECCE: 6 BRDM-2, ε8 *Shorland*.
APC: 4 BTR-152.
TOWED ARTY: 122mm: 3 D-30.
MRL: 122mm: 2 BM-21.
MORTARS: 82mm: 6 M-43.
RL: RPG-7.
SAM: 10 SA-7.

MARINE: 200.

BASE: Port Victoria.
PATROL AND COASTAL COMBATANTS: 6:
COASTAL: 1 *Topaz* (Fr *Sirius*).
INSHORE: 5:
1 *Andromache* (It Pichiotti 42-m) PFI
1 *Zoroaster* (Sov *Turya*, no foils or TT) PFI.
2 *Zhuk* PFI⟨, 1 PCI⟨.
AMPHIBIOUS: craft only; 1 LCT.

AIR: 100. 1 cbt ac, no armed hel.

MR: 1 BN-2 *Defender*.
LIAISON: 1 *Citation* 5, 1 R-235E.
HELICOPTERS: 2 *Chetak*.
TRAINING: 1 Cessna 152, 1 *Rallye* 235E.

PARAMILITARY:

PEOPLE'S MILITIA: 800.

SIERRA LEONE

GDPᵃ	1989:	Le 43,946.8m ($840.76m)		
	1990:	Le 70,133.5m ($699.85m)		
Growth	1989:	2.2%	1990:	4.1%
Inflation	1990:	111.0%	1991:	102.66%
Debt	1989:	$1,082m	1990:	$1,189m
Def exp	1989ε:	Le 308.0m ($5.15m)		
$1 = Le	1989:	59.81	1990:	151.45
	1991:	295.34	1992:	500.00

Le = leones
ᵃ Dollar values have been adjusted for inflation and
rapid devaluation of the leone.

Population: 4,369,600

	13–17	*18–22*	*23–32*
Men	235,100	199,000	309,100
Women	232,600	197,800	311,500

TOTAL ARMED FORCES:

ACTIVE: 6,150.

ARMY: ε6,000.

2 inf bn.   1 engr sqn.
2 arty bty.

EQUIPMENT:
APC: 10 MOWAG *Piranha*, 4 *Saracen*.
MORTARS: 81mm.
RCL: 84mm: *Carl Gustav*.
SAM: SA-7.
AVIATION:
  HELICOPTERS: 2 AS-355, 1 Bo-105.

NAVY: ε150.
BASE: Freetown.
PATROL AND COASTAL COMBATANTS: 3:
  2 Ch *Shanghai-II* PFI.
  1 Swiftships 32-m PFI.
  Plus some 3 modern boats.

FORCES ABROAD:
LIBERIA: ε400; contingent forms part of
  ECOWAS force.

PARAMILITARY:
1 SF bn (State Security Division).

FOREIGN FORCES:
NIGERIA: 800.

SOUTH AFRICA

GDP	1990: R 263.82bn ($102.02bn)	
	1991: R 296.67bn ($107.64bn)	
Growth	1990: −0.5%	1991: −0.6%
Inflation	1990: 14.4%	1991: 15.3%
Debt	1991: $19.4bn	
Def exp[a]	1989: R 9.411bn ($3.60bn)	
	1990: R 11.164bn ($4.32bn)	
Def bdgt[b]	1991: R 10.62bn ($3.85bn)	
	1992: R 9.7bn ($3.32bn)	
$1 = R	1989: 2.616	1990: 2.586
	1991: 2.756	1992: 2.924

R = rand
[a] Incl additional estimates and supplements
[b] Excl Intelligence and Police (internal sy) bdgt, which in 1988/9 amounted to R 1.8bn, and Namibian expenditure.

Population: 26,288,400

	13–17	18–22	23–32
Men:	1,429,200	1,254,500	2,035,100
Women:	1,420,600	1,245,000	2,030,600

TOTAL ARMED FORCES:
ACTIVE: 72,400 (of the total 8,000 are Medical
  Services not listed below); (36,400 white
  conscripts; 3,700 women).
  Terms of service: 12 months National Service for
  whites, followed by 12 years part-time service

in Citizen Force (CF) (in any 2-year period of
call-up, duty not to exceed 60 days trg).
Thereafter continued voluntary service in CF
(to age 55) or 5 years with no commitment in
Active Citizen Force Reserve. Then may be
allocated to Commandos to age 55 with annual
commitment of 12 days. Races other than
whites volunteer for Full Time Force, National
Service and Commandos but are not
conscripted.
RESERVES:
  Citizen Force 360,000; Active Citizen Force
  Reserve 135,000; Commandos ε140,000.

ARMY: ε49,900. Full Time Force: 18,900 (12,000
  White; 5,400 Black and Coloured; ε1,500
  women). National Service: ε 31,000.
FULL TIME FORCE (FT):
13 army (area) comd.
  1 AB bde (1 FT, 1 trg, 2 CF AB bn, 1 CF arty bn
    with 120mm mor).
  1 mech bde.
  SF: 5 recce coy (4 FT, 1 CF)
9 inf bn (2 coloured, 7 black)
Training Units (all with cbt capability)
  2 armd bn
  9 inf bn (8 white (2 mech, 6 mot), 1 black (mot))
  2 arty regt
  1 AD arty regt
  1 engr regt.
RESERVES:
CITIZEN FORCE (CF):
  1 Corps HQ (FT administered)
    2 mech div (each 1 armd, 2 mech bde) (being
      reorganized into 3 mech div).
  Indep units (being reorganized):
    2 armd recce regt   2 AD regt
    16 inf bn   3 engr regt
    2 arty regt
COMMANDOS:
  Some 250 inf coy home defence units.
EQUIPMENT:
MBT: some 250 *Centurion/Olifant* 2B.
RECCE: 1,600 *Eland*-60/-90, *Ferret* Mk 2, some *Rooikat*.
AIFV: 1,500 *Ratel*-20/-60/-90.
APC: 1,500 *Buffel*, *Casspir*, *Wolf*.
TOWED ARTY: 350 incl: 25-pdr (88mm): 30; 5.5-in
  (140mm): 75 G-2; 155mm: ε250 G-5.
SP ARTY: 155mm: ε40 G-6.
MRL: 150 incl: 127mm: 120 *Bateleur* (40 tube),
  Valkiri 22 SP (24 tube); some *Valkiri* 5 towed.
MORTARS: 81mm: 4,000 (incl some SP); 120mm: +120.
ATGW: ZT-3 *Swift* (some SP).
RL: 100mm: FT-5.
RCL: 106mm: M-40A1.
AD GUNS: 600: 20mm: GAI, *Ystervark* SP; 23mm:
  ZU-23-2; 35mm: 150 GDF-002 twin.
SAM: SA-7/-14.

NAVY: ε4,500, (ε900 conscripts; ε300 women).
Naval HQ; Pretoria.
Three Flotillas: Submarine, Strike, Mine Warfare.
BASES: Simonstown, Durban, Walvis Bay (log spt only).
SUBMARINES: 3 *Maria Van Riebeek* (Mod Fr *Daphné*) with 550mm TT.
PATROL AND COASTAL COMBATANTS: 9:
MISSILE CRAFT: 9:
9 *Jan Smuts* (Is *Reshef*) with 6 *Skerpioen* (Is *Gabriel*) SSM (3 in reserve).
MINE WARFARE: 8:
1 *Kimberley* (UK 'Ton') MSC.
3 *Walvisbaai* (UK 'Ton') MSC.
4 *Umzimkulu* MHC.
SUPPORT AND MISCELLANEOUS: 8:
2 AOR, each with 2 hel and extempore amph capability (perhaps 200 tps), 1 AGHS, 1 Diving spt, 1 Antarctic tpt with 2 hel (operated by Dept of Economic Affairs), 3 tugs.

AIR FORCE: 10,000 (3,000 conscripts; ε400 women); 259 cbt ac, 14+ armed hel.
2 Territorial Area Comds, Air Defence, Tac Spt, Log, Trg Comd.
FGA: 4 sqn.
2 with 75 *Impala* II;
1 with 29 *Mirage* F-1AZ;
1 with 12 *Cheetah* E;
FTR: 1 sqn:
1 with 14 *Mirage* F-1 CZ;
EW: 1 sqn with 4 Boeing 707-320 (ELINT/tkr).
MR: 1 sqn with 8 C-47;
TRANSPORT: 3 sqn:
1 with 7 C-130B, 9 C-160Z;
1 (VIP) with 4 HS-125 -400B (civil registration), 2 *Super King Air* 200, 1 *Citation*.
1 with 1 *Viscount* 781 (civil registration), 19 C-47 (being modified to C-4 TP), 4 DC-4.
HELICOPTERS: 6 sqn with 63 SA-316/-319 (some armed), 63 SA-330.
LIAISON/FAC: 1 sqn with 34 AM-3C.
TRAINING COMMAND (incl OCU): 7 schools:
AIRCRAFT: 12 C-47, *14 *Cheetah* D, 130 T-6G *Harvard* IIA/III (80 to be updated), *115 *Impala* I.
HELICOPTERS: 30 SE-3130, 7 SA-316.
MISSILES:
ASM: AS-11/-20/-30.
AAM: R-530, R-550 *Magic*, AIM-9 *Sidewinder*, V-3C *Darter*, V-3A/B *Kukri*.
SAM: 20 *Cactus* (*Crotale*), 32 *Tigercat*, SA-8/-9/-13.

MEDICAL SERVICE: 8,000 (1,500 conscripts; 1,500 women). A separate service within SADF, organized territorially to support all three services.

PARAMILITARY:
SOUTH AFRICAN POLICE: 100,000; Police Reserves: 37,000.
Coast guard to form; 7 MR ac planned.

OPPOSITION:
AFRICAN NATIONAL CONGRESS (ANC): combat wing *Umkhonto we Sizwe:* (MK) perhaps 10,000 trained.
PAN AFRICANIST CONGRESS (PAC): Azanian People's Liberation Army: perhaps 350.

HOMELANDS

Each homeland has its own armed forces, not included in South African data. Currency in all cases is the South African Rand.

BOPHUTHATSWANA
Def bdgt 1990: R 97.89m, 1991: R 132.45m
Population: 2,352,000.
ARMED FORCES: ε3,100
2 inf bn.
1 AB/SF unit (coy-).
2 indep inf coy gp.
Air Wing: 1 recce, 1 lt tpt, 1 hel flt.
EQUIPMENT:
APC: *Buffalo*.
MORTARS: 81mm.
AIRCRAFT: 2 C-212, 3 PC-7, 1 PC-6B, 1 CN-235.
HELICOPTERS: 2 BK-117, 2 SA-316, 1 SA-365.

CISKEI
Def bdgt 1989: R 91.2m (incl police)
Population: 1,025,000.
ARMED FORCES: ε1,000:
1 inf bn.
1 AB coy
EQUIPMENT:
APC: *Buffalo*.
MORTARS: 81mm.
AIRCRAFT: 2 BN-2, 1 IAI-1124 (VIP), 2 *Skyvan*, 3 Cessna 152.
HELICOPTERS: 3 BK-117, 1 Bo-105.

TRANSKEI
Def bdgt 1989: R 109.2m. 1990: R 120.4m (incl police)
Population: 4,367,000.
ARMED FORCES: ε2,000:
1 inf bn.
1 SF regt: 1 SF coy, AB coy, mounted sqn, marine gp.
Air wing.
EQUIPMENT:
MORTARS: 81mm.
AIRCRAFT: 2 C-212.

HELICOPTERS: 2 BK-117.

VENDA
Def bdgt 1988: R 45.9m (incl police)
Population: 665,000.
ARMED FORCES: ε900:
2 inf bn.
Engr tp.
Air wing.
EQUIPMENT:
APC: *Buffalo*.
MORTARS: 81mm.
AIRCRAFT: 1 C-212-200.
HELICOPTERS: 2 BK-117, 1 SA-316B.

TANZANIA

GDP	1989:	sh 406.54bn ($2.84bn)	
	1990:	sh 495.86bn ($2.54bn)	
Growth	1990:	3.6%	1991: 3.4%
Inflation	1990:	24.4%	1991: 15.72%
Debt	1989:	$5.07bn	1990: $5.87bn
Def bdgt	1987ε:	sh 7.66bn ($119.20m)	
	1989ε:	sh 15.80bn ($110.20m)	
$1 = sh	1989:	143.377	1990: 195.060
	1991:	219.16	1992: 270.00
sh = Tanzanian shilling			

Population: 28,560,000

	13–17	18–22	23–32
Men	1,582,400	1,306,700	1,881,800
Women	1,608,600	1,342,400	1,949,900

TOTAL ARMED FORCES:
ACTIVE: 46,800 (perhaps 20,000 conscripts).
Terms of service: national service incl civil duties, 2 years.
RESERVE: 10,000: armed elm of Citizen's Militia.

ARMY: 45,000 (some 20,000 conscripts).
3 div HQ.
8 inf bde.
1 tk bde.
2 fd arty bn, 2 AA arty bn (6 bty).
2 mor, 2 ATK bn.
1 engr regt (bn).
1 SAM bn with SA-3, SA-6.
EQUIPMENT:†
MBT: 30 Ch Type-59, 32 T-54/-55.
LIGHT TANKS: 30 Ch Type-62, 40 *Scorpion*.
RECCE: 40 BRDM-2.
APC: 45 BTR-40/-152, 30 Ch Type-56.
TOWED ARTY: 76mm: 45 ZIS-3; 85mm: 80 Ch Type-56; 122mm: 20 D-30, 100 M-30; 130mm: 40 M-46.

MRL: 122mm: 58 BM-21.
MORTARS: 82mm: 300 M-43; 120mm: 50 M-43.
RCL: 75mm: 540 Ch Type-52.
AD GUNS: 14.5mm: 280 ZPU-2/-4; 23mm: 40 ZU-23; 37mm: 120 Ch Type-55.
SAM: 9 SA-3, 12 SA-6, SA-7.

NAVY:† 800.
BASES: Dar es Salaam, Zanzibar, Mwanza (Lake Victoria – 4 boats).
PATROL AND COASTAL COMBATANTS: 20:
TORPEDO CRAFT: 4 Ch *Huchuan* PHT⟨ with 2 × 533mm TT.
PATROL, INSHORE: 16:
6 Ch *Shanghai* II PFI, some 10 PCI⟨, (4 in Zanzibar).
(Note: Spares are short; many vessels are not operational.)

AIR FORCE: 1,000; 24 cbt ac, no armed hel†.
FIGHTER: 3 sqn with 3 Ch J-4, 10 J-6, 11 J-7.
TRANSPORT: 1 sqn with 5 DHC-5D, 1 Ch Y-5, 3 HS-748, 2 F-28.
HELICOPTERS: 4 AB-205.
LIAISON: 7 Cessna 310, 2 -404, 5 PA-28, 1 -32 ac; 2 Bell 206B hel.
TRAINING: 2 MiG-15UTI, 5 PA-28.

PARAMILITARY:
POLICE FIELD FORCE: 1,400.
POLICE AIR WING: 1 Cessna U206 ac; 2 AB-206A, 2 -B, 2 Bell 206L hel, 2 Bell 47G.
POLICE MARINE UNIT: (100).
CITIZENS' MILITIA: 100,000.

TOGO

GDP	1989:	fr 413.93bn ($1.30bn)	
	1990:	fr 426.34bn ($1.57bn)	
Growth	1989:	3.6%	1990: 2.6%
Inflation	1990:	1.0%	1991ε: 0.2%
Debt	1989:	$1.19bn	1990: $1.30bn
Def bdgt	1987ε:	fr 13,047m ($43.42m)	
$1 = fr	1989:	319.01	1990: 272.26
	1991:	282.11	1992: 280.00
fr = francs CFA (Communauté financière africaine)			

Population: 3,821,200

	13–17	18–22	23–32
Men:	208,500	171,800	244,200
Women:	220,900	184,000	281,400

TOTAL ARMED FORCES:
ACTIVE: some 5,250.

Terms of service: conscription, 2 years
(selective).

ARMY: 4,800.
2 inf regt:
  1 with 1 mech bn, 1 mot bn;
  1 with 2 armd sqn, 3 inf coy; spt units (trg).
1 Presidential Guard regt: 2 bn (1 cdo), 2 coy.
1 para cdo regt: 3 coy.
1 spt regt: 1 fd arty bty; 2 AD arty bty; 1
  log/tpt/engr bn.
EQUIPMENT:
MBT: 2 T-54/-55.
LIGHT TANKS: 9 *Scorpion.*
RECCE: 6 M-8, 3 M-20, 3 AML-60, 7 -90, 36 EE-9
  Cascavel, 2 VBL M-11.
APC: 4 M-3A1 half-track, 30 UR-416.
TOWED ARTY: 105mm: 4 HM-2.
MORTARS: 82mm: 20 M-43.
RCL: 57mm: 5 ZIS-2; 75mm: 12 Ch Type-52/-56;
  82mm: 10 Ch Type-65.
AD GUNS: 14.5mm: 38 ZPU-4; 37mm: 5 M-39.

NAVY: 200 incl marine inf unit.
BASE: Lomé.
PATROL AND COASTAL COMBATANTS: 2
INSHORE: 2 *Kara* (Fr Esterel) PFI⟨.

AIR FORCE: 250; 16 cbt ac, no armed hel.
COIN/TRAINING: 5 *Alpha Jet,* 4 CM-170, 4
  EMB-326G, 3 TB-30.
TRANSPORT: 2 *Baron,* 2 DHC-5D, 1 Do-27, 1
  F-28-1000 (VIP), 1 *Falcon* 10 (VIP), 2
  Reims-Cessna 337.
HELICOPTERS: 2 SA-313, 2 SA-315, 1 SA-330.

PARAMILITARY:
GENDARMERIE (Ministry of Interior): 750; 1 trg
  school, 2 regional sections, 1 mobile sqn.

UGANDA

GDP	1989:	N sh 1,128.41bn ($5.06bn)		
	1990:	N sh 1,537.10bn ($3.58bn)		
Growth	1989:	7.4%	1990:	4.3%
Inflation	1990ε:	45%	1991ε:	60%
Debt	1990:	$2.73bn	1991:	$2.6bn
Def bdgt	1990ε:	N sh 31,790m ($74.13m)		
	1991ε:	N sh 53,800m ($73.29m)		
FMA	1988:	$11.15m (US, Fr)		
$1 = N sh	1989:	223.09	1990:	428.85
	1991:	734.00	1992:	1,050.00

N sh = Ugandan shillings

Population: 18,395,000

	13–17	*18–22*	*23–32*
Men	1,062,800	873,800	1,275,000
Women	1,062,200	878,700	1,304,900

TOTAL ARMED FORCES:
ACTIVE: ε70,000–100,000.

NATIONAL RESISTANCE ARMY (NRA):
7 'div' (closer to weak bde).
EQUIPMENT:†
MBT: some T-54/-55.
APC: some BTR-60, 4 OT-64 SKOT.
TOWED ARTY: 76mm: 60 M-1942; 122mm: 20 M-1938.
MORTARS: 82mm; 120mm: Soltam.
ATGW: 40 AT-3 *Sagger.*
AD GUNS: 14.5mm: ZPU-1/-2/-4; 23mm: ZU-23;
  37mm: M-1939.
SAM: SA-7.
AVIATION: 10 cbt ac†, 5 armed hel.
  FGA: 4 MiG-17F.
  TRAINING: 3 L-39, 4* S-211, 4 SF-260, 2* -260W.
  HELICOPTERS:
    ATTACK: 5 AB-412.
    TRANSPORT: 3 Bell 205, 4 Bell 206, 2 Bell
      412, 1 Bell 212, 4 Mi-17.
TRANSPORT/LIAISON: 2 AS-202B, 1-L100, 1
  Gulfstream II.
POLICE AIR WING:
  AIRCRAFT: 1 DHC-2, 1 DHC-4, 1 DHC-6.
  HELICOPTERS: 2 Bell 206, 4 Bell 212.

OPPOSITION:
HOLY SPIRIT MOVEMENT: ε500, small arms only.

ZAIRE

GDP*a*	1989:	Z 3,441bn ($7.66bn)	
	1990:	Z 6,239bn ($7.46bn)	
Growth	1989:	-1.29%	1990: -2.6%
Inflation	1990ε:	265%	1991: 2,154.6%
Debt	1989:	$9.18bn	1990: $10.12bn
Def bdgt	1987:	Z 5,200m ($46.26m)	
	1988:	Z 12,500m ($66.82m)	
FMA	1991:	$3.3m (US)	
$1 = Z*b*	1989:	381.445	1990: 718.60
	1991:	15,587	1992: 150,000

Z = zaires

a Dollar figures in 1985 prices and exchange rates.
b Estimate of the value of the Zaire is difficult due to
extremely rapid devaluation since 1990.

Population: 37,886,400

	13–17	*18–22*	*23–32*
Men:	2,125,900	1,774,600	2,695,700
Women:	2,127,200	1,775,600	2,689,800

TOTAL ARMED FORCES:
ACTIVE: 54,100 (incl Gendarmerie).

ARMY: 26,000.
8 Military Regions.
1 inf div (3 inf bde).
1 Presidential Guard div.
1 para bde (3 para, 1 spt bn) (2nd forming).
1 SF (cdo/COIN) bde.
1 indep armd bde.
2 indep inf bde (each 3 inf bn, 1 spt bn).

EQUIPMENT:
MBT: some 60 Ch Type-62, 20 Ch Type-59.
RECCE:† 250 AML-60, 60 -90.
APC: 12 M-113, 12 YW-531, 60 M-3.
TOWED ARTY: 75mm: 30 M-116 pack; 85mm: 20 Type 56; 122mm: 20 M-1938/D-30, 15 Type 60, 130mm: 8 Type 59.
MRL: 107mm: 20 Type 63; 122mm: 10 BM-21.
MORTARS: 81mm; 107mm: M-30; 120mm: 50 Brandt.
RCL: 57mm: M-18; 75mm: M-20; 106mm: M-40A1.
AD GUNS: 14.5mm: ZPU-4; 37mm: 40 M-1939/Type 63; 40mm: L/60.
SAM: SA-7.

NAVY: 1,300 incl marines.
BASES: Banana (coast), Boma, Matadi, Kinshasa (all river), Kalémié (Lake Tanganyika – 4 boats).
PATROL AND COASTAL COMBATANTS: 4:
INSHORE: Some 4 Ch *Shanghai* II PFI.
RIVERINE: About 20 armed boats.

MARINES: 600.

AIR FORCE: 1,800; 28 cbt ac, no armed hel.
FGA/FIGHTER: 1 sqn with 7 *Mirage* 5M, 1 -5DM.
COIN: 1 sqn with 8 MB-326 GB, 6 -K, 6 AT-6G.
TRANSPORT: 1 wing with 1 Boeing 707-320, 1 BN-2, 8 C-47, 5 C-130H, 3 DHC-5.
HELICOPTERS: 1 sqn with 1 AS-332, 7 SA-319, 9 SA-330.
LIAISON: 6 Cessna 310R, 2 Mu-2J (VIP).
TRAINING: incl 12 Cessna 150, 3 -310, 9 SF-260C ac; 6 Bell 47 hel.

PARAMILITARY:
GENDARMERIE: 25,000 (to be 27,000); 40 bn.
CIVIL GUARD: 10,000; some *Fahd* APC reported.

ZAMBIA

GDP	1990ε: K 107.5bn ($3.71bn)		
	1991ε: K 219.7bn ($3.56bn)		
Growth	1990: −2.0%	1991ε: −1.8%	
Inflation	1990: 111.0%	1991: 92.6%	
Debt	1990: $7.22bn	1991ε: $7.90bn	
Def exp	1989ε: K 1,529.7m ($186.01m)		
	1990ε: K 2,753.4m ($213.39m)		
$1 = K	1989: 12.903	1990: 28.985	
	1991: 61.728	1992: 155.000	

K = kwacha

Population: 8,593,800

	13–17	18–22	23–32
Men	499,800	410,000	597,000
Women	493,000	404,300	610,300

TOTAL ARMED FORCES:
ACTIVE: 24,000.

ARMY: 20,000.
3 bde HQ.
1 armd regt (incl 1 armd recce bn).
9 inf bn (3 reserve).
1 arty regt.
1 engr bn.

EQUIPMENT:
MBT: 10 T-54/-55, 20 Ch Type-59.
LIGHT TANKS: 30 PT-76.
RECCE: 88 BRDM-1/-2.
APC: 13 BTR-60.
TOWED ARTY: 76mm: 35 M-1942; 105mm: 18 Model 56 pack; 122mm: 25 D-30; 130mm: 18 M-46.
MRL: 122mm: 50 BM-21.
MORTARS: 81mm: 55; 82mm: 24; 120mm: 14.
ATGW: AT-3 *Sagger*.
RCL: 57mm: 12 M-18; 75mm: M-20; 84mm: *Carl Gustav*.
AD GUNS: 20mm: 50 M-55 triple; 37mm: 40 M-1939; 57mm: 55 S-60; 85mm: 16 KS-12.
SAM: SA-7.

AIR FORCE: 4,000; 67 cbt ac, some armed hel.
FGA: 1 sqn with 12 Ch J-6†;
FIGHTER: 1 sqn with 19 MiG-21 MF†.
COIN/TRAINING: 12 *Galeb* G-2, 16 MB-326GB, 8 SF-260MZ.
TRANSPORT: 1 sqn with 4 An-26, 4 C-47, 2 DC-6B, 3 DHC-4, 4 DHC-5D;
VIP: 1 flt with 1 HS-748, 3 Yak-40.
LIAISON: 7 Do-28.
TRAINING: 2-F5T, 2 MiG-21U†.

HELICOPTERS: 1 sqn with 4 AB-205A, 5 AB-212, 12 Mi-8.
LIAISON HELICOPTERS: 12 AB-47G.
MISSILES:
  ASM: AT-3 *Sagger*.
  SAM: 1 bn; 3 bty: SA-3 *Goa*.

PARAMILITARY:
POLICE MOBILE UNIT (PMU): 700; 1 bn of 4 coy.
POLICE PARAMILITARY UNIT (PPMU): 700; 1 bn of 3 coy.

ZIMBABWE

GDP	1989:	$Z 11.27bn ($US 5.33bn)	
	1990:	$Z 13.03bn ($US 5.32bn)	
Growth	1989: 4.5%	1990:	1.9%
Inflation	1990: 17.4%	1991:	24.3%
Debt	1990: $US 3.0bn	1991:	$US 3.2bn
Def bdgt	1990: $Z 884.8m ($US 361.45m)		
	1991: $Z 1,145m ($US 334.01m)		
$1 = $Z	1989: 2.1132	1990:	2.4480
	1991: 3.4280	1992:	4,8000

Population: 10,593,000

	13–17	*18–22*	*23–32*
Men	602,600	519,400	797,800
Women	601,600	510,000	805,000

TOTAL ARMED FORCES:
ACTIVE: 48,500.
  Terms of service: conscription, 12 months reported.

ARMY: 46,000.
  7 bde HQ (incl 1 Presidential Guard).
  1 armd regt.
  26 inf bn (incl 3 Guard, 2 mech, 1 cdo, 2 para, 1 mounted).

1 fd arty regt (incl 2 AD bty).
  1 engr spt regt.
EQUIPMENT:
MBT: 30 Ch T-59, 10 Ch T-69.
RECCE: 90 EE-9 *Cascavel* (90mm gun), 20 AML-90 *Eland*.
APC: 8 YW-531, ε40 UR-416, 75 *Crocodile*.
TOWED ARTY: 122mm: 18 Ch Type-60, 12 Ch Type-54.
MRL: 107mm: 18 Ch Type-63.
MORTARS: 81mm: L16; 120mm: 4.
RCL: 106mm: 12 M-40A1.
AD GUNS: 14.5mm: ZPU-1/-2/-4; 23mm: ZU-23; 37mm: M-1939.
SAM: SA-7.

AIR FORCE: 2,500; 36† cbt ac, no armed hel.
FGA/COIN: 2 sqn:
  1 with 10 *Hunter* FGA-90, 1 T-81;
  1 with 6 *Hawk* Mk 60.
FIGHTER: 1 sqn with 12 Ch J-7.
COIN/RECCE: 1 sqn with 8 Reims-Cessna 337 *Lynx*.
TRAINING/RECCE/LIAISON: 1 sqn with 13 SF-260C/W *Genet*, 5 SF-260TP.
TRANSPORT: 1 sqn with 6 BN-2, 11 C-212-200 (1 VIP), 10 C-47.
HELICOPTERS: 2 sqn:
  1 with 2 AB-205, 7 SA-316;
  1 with 10 AB-412 (VIP).

FORCES ABROAD:
MOZAMBIQUE: some 3,000–5,000 (varies).
UN AND PEACEKEEPING:
ANGOLA (UNAVEM II): 15 Observers.

PARAMILITARY:
ZIMBABWE REPUBLIC POLICE FORCE, incl Air Wing: 15,000.
POLICE SUPPORT UNIT: 2,000.
NATIONAL MILITIA: 4,000.

2

_____

TABLES AND ANALYSES

Defence Expenditure: NATO, Japan, Sweden

These charts are expressed in local currency, based on 1985 prices and using a 1985 deflator. Where possible, the NATO definition of defence expenditure is used and is shaded on the chart. Unshaded columns for NATO countries represent IISS estimates, and for Japan and Sweden they represent

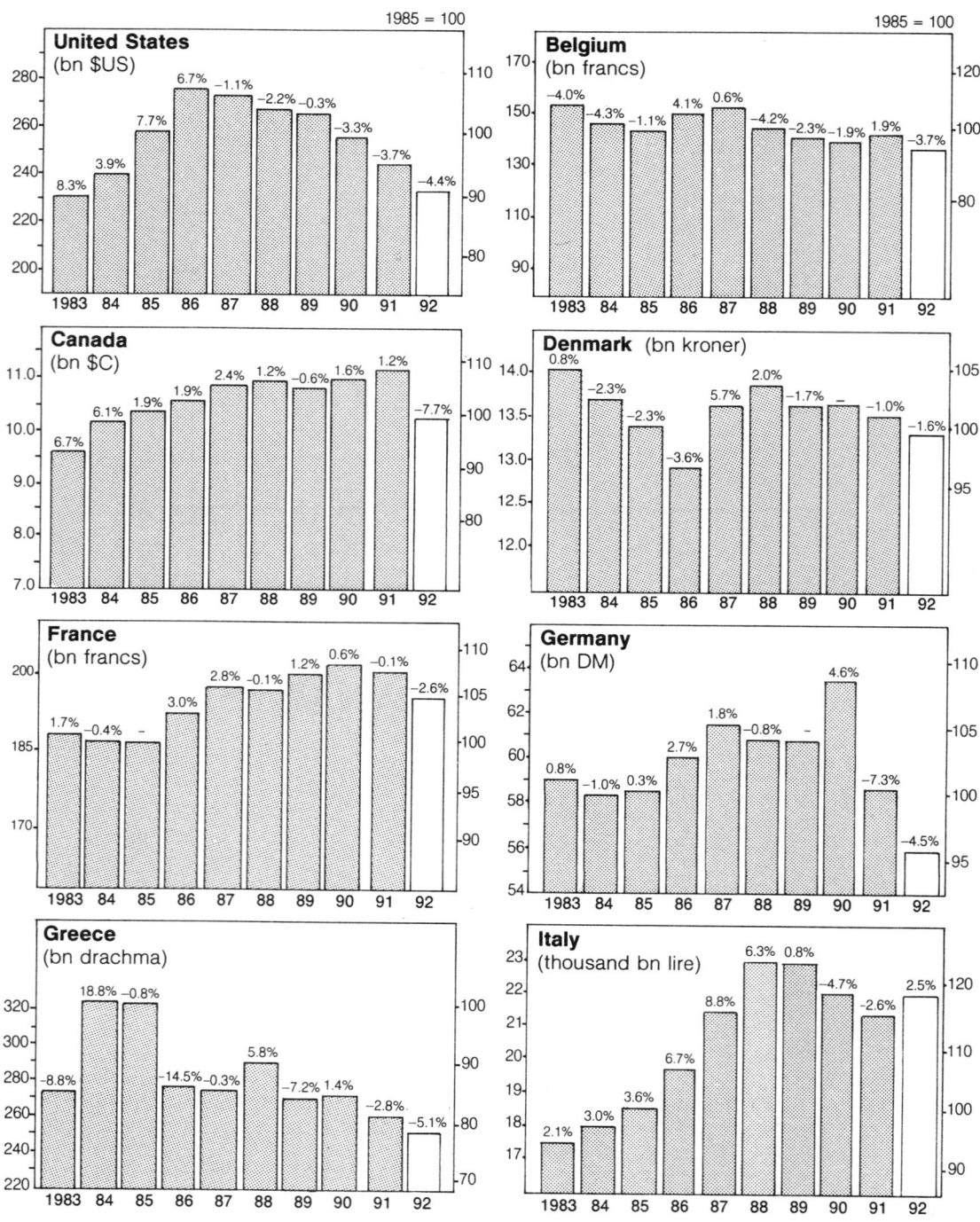

national definitions. The figure above each column shows the percentage increase, or decrease, from the previous year. The right-hand index shows changes measured against a base of 100 in 1985 (the scale of this index varies for each country).

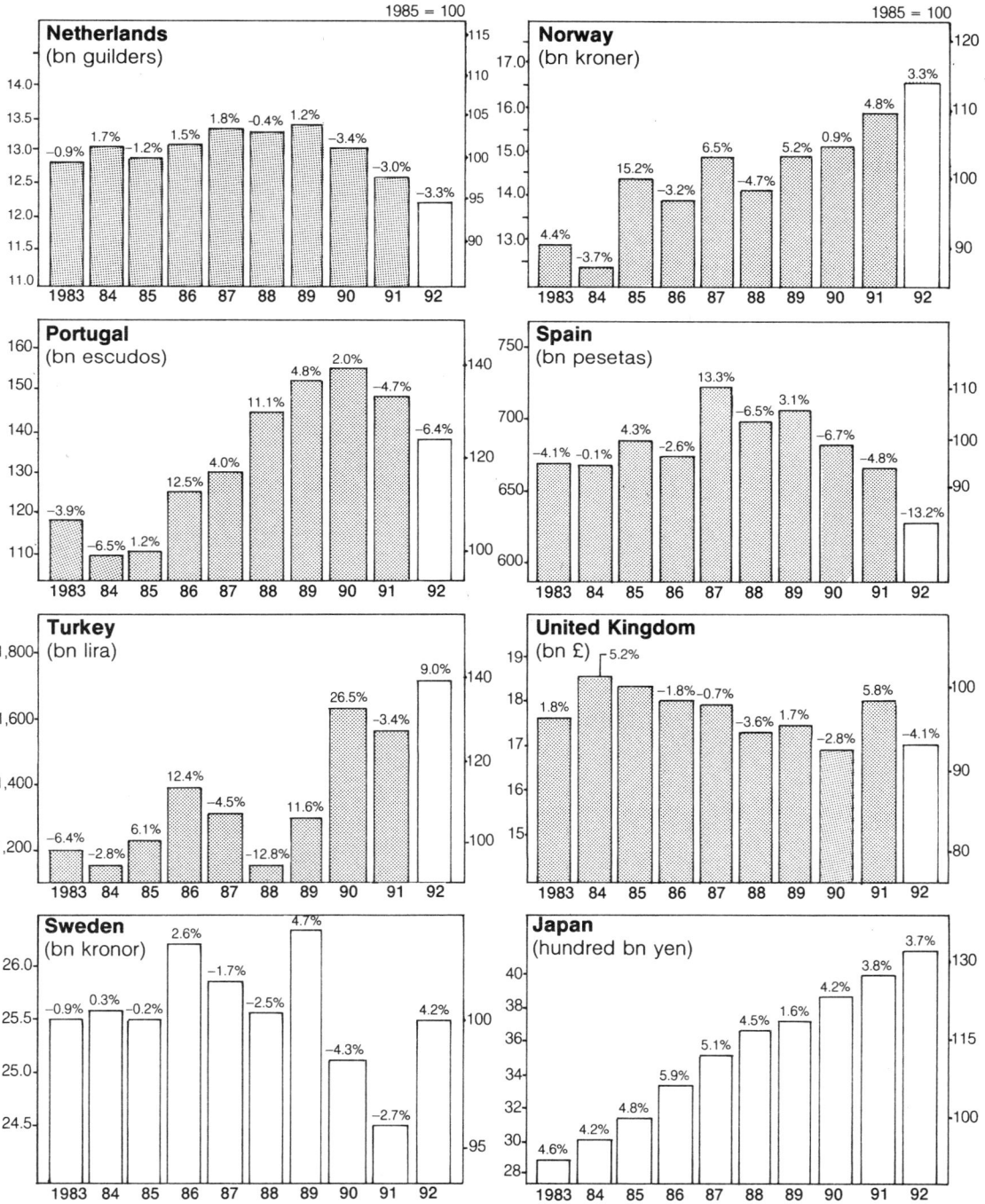

COMPARISONS OF DEFENCE EXPENDITURE AND MILITARY MANPOWER 1985–1991[a]

| Country | Defence Expenditure | | | | | | | | | Numbers in armed forces (000) | | Est. reservists[d] (000) | Para-military[e] (000) |
| | $ million[b] (1985 prices & exchange rates) | | | $ per capita[b] (1985 prices & exchange rates) | | | % of GDP/GNP[c] | | | | | | |
	1985	1990	1991	1985	1990	1991	1985	1990	1991	1985	1991	1991	1991
NATO													
Belgium	2,428	1,558	1,505	246	158	153	3.0	1.6	1.5	91.6	80.7	228.8	16.8
Denmark	1,259	1,253	1,272	246	247	251	2.2	2.0	2.0	29.6	29.2	72.4	0.0
France	20,780	18,113	18,044	377	320	317	4.0	2.9	2.8	464.3	453.1	419.0	91.8
Germany[f]	19,922	16,940	16,450	262	221	214	3.2	2.2	1.9	478.0	447.0	904.7	24.9
Greece	2,331	2,023	1,977	235	199	194	7.0	5.9	5.9	201.5	158.5	406.0	26.5
Italy	9,733	9,320	9,146	170	163	159	2.3	1.8	1.7	385.1	361.4	584.0	244.8
Luxembourg	38	52	54	104	142	148	0.9	1.1	1.2	0.7	0.8	n.k.	0.5
Netherlands	3,884	4,134	3,947	268	280	266	3.1	2.8	2.7	105.5	93.0	144.3	3.9
Norway	1,797	1,880	1,864	433	447	442	3.1	3.3	3.2	37.0	32.7	285.0	0.0
Portugal	654	707	638	64	67	60	3.1	2.4	2.4	73.0	55.3	190.0	43.5
Spain	3,969	3,742	3,484	103	94	86	2.4	1.7	1.6	320.0	217.0	498.0	64.6
Turkey	1,649	1,751	2,014	33	31	35	4.5	2.8	3.1	630.0	579.2	1,107.0	71.1
United Kingdom	23,791	21,669	22,420	421	382	395	5.2	4.1	4.2	327.1	293.5	353.0	0.0
NATO Europe													
Total	92,235	83,187	82,914	238	209	206	n.k.	n.k.	n.k.	3,143.4	2,801.4	5,192.2	588.4
Canada	7,566	7,064	7,358	298	265	272	2.2	1.8	1.9	83.0	84.0	29.7	n.k.
US	258,165	238,678	227,055	1,079	957	902	6.5	5.3	5.1	2,151.6	1,913.8	1,784.1	68.0
Total NATO	357,966	328,929	317,327	548	487	466	–	–	–	5,378.0	4,799.2	7,006.0	656.4
Soviet Union[g]	241,500	127,638	91,631	871	446	318	16.1	14.2	11.1	5,300.0	3,988.0	5,602.0	530.0
Other Europe													
Albania	189	160	103	64	48	30	4.1	4.9	n.k.	40.4	40.0	155.0	16.0
Austria	892	752	813	118	100	108	1.4	1.0	1.0	54.7	52.0	200.0	
Bulgaria[h]	1,656	2,010	1,790	185	222	197	3.9	6.4	6.9	148.5	107.0	472.5	16.0
Cyprus	87	211	174	131	302	246	3.6	5.9	4.9	10.0	8.0	88.0	3.7
Czechoslovakia[h]	4,849	4,320	2,800	313	275	177	4.7	3.9	2.9	203.3	145.8	495.0	15.5
Finland	807	938	1,084	164	187	215	1.5	1.4	1.7	36.5	32.8	700.0	4.4
Hungary[h]	2,402	1,450	1,230	226	137	117	3.6	2.4	2.3	106.0	80.8	192.0	23.5
Ireland	320	265	278	90	71	74	1.8	1.1	1.2	13.7	13.0	16.1	n.k.
Malta	14	16	15	39	45	41	1.4	1.0	0.9	0.8	1.7	n.k.	n.k.
Poland[h]	5,760	2,490	2,200	155	66	58	3.0	2.3	2.4	319.0	296.5	435.2	38.0
Romania[h]	1,395	1,330	1,150	61	58	51	1.4	3.0	3.1	189.5	200.0	593.0	50.0
Sweden	3,192	2,916	2,788	382	350	334	3.3	2.5	2.5	65.7	60.5	709.0	35.0
Switzerland	1,930	2,047	1,853	299	315	285	2.1	1.8	1.7	35.0	35.0	625.0	480.0
Yugoslavia	1,692	2,039	3,490	73	152	317	3.8	3.8	18.6	241.0	135.0	n.k.	n.k.

	C1	C2	C3	C4	C5	C6	C7	C8	C9	C10	C11	C12	C13
Middle East													
Algeria	953	988	971	44	38	36	1.7	1.9	1.4	170.0	139.0	150.0	52.2
Bahrain	151	205	222	362	416	434	3.5	5.0	5.4	2.8	6.2	n.k.	9.0
Djibouti	32	25	n.k.	85	61	n.k.	9.2	7.6	n.k.	3.0	3.8	n.k.	1.8
Egypt	4,143	3,433	3,582	319	62	63	8.5	7.5	7.5	445.0	410.0	604.0	372.0
Iran[h]	14,223	3,810	4,270	809	71	77	8.6	5.3	7.1	305.0	528.0	350.0	57.0
Iraq	12,868	7,490	n.k.	1,193	381	n.k.	25.9	21.1	n.k.	520.0	382.5	650.0	24.8
Israel	5,052	3,623	3,239	149	737	636	21.2	12.0	9.9	142.0	175.0	430.0	6.0
Jordan	523	619	594	1,050	146	135	12.8	14.6	14.1	70.3	98.3	35.0	9.0
Kuwait[i]	1,796	1,357	7,959	n.k.	688	3,907	9.1	5.7	33.0	12.0	11.7	19.0	9.0
Lebanon	n.k.	21	20	359	8	7	n.k.	4.2	3.7	17.4	36.8	n.k.	7.0
Libya	1,350	1,177	n.k.	n.k.	249	n.k.	n.k.	6.3	n.k.	73.0	85.0	40.0	5.5
Mauritania	641	30	27	29	15	13	5.4	3.9	n.k.	8.5	9.6	n.k.	4.7
Morocco	2,157	675	730	1,737	27	28	20.8	4.1	4.3	149.0	195.5	100.0	40.0
Oman	n.k.	n.k.	1,182	n.k.	1,081	744	n.k.	18.1	12.3	2.5	35.7	n.k.	3.5
Qatar	n.k.	n.k.	781	1,533	n.k.	1,718	19.6	n.k.	12.2	6.0	7.5	n.k.	n.k.
Saudi Arabia[i]	17,693	24,143	35,438	n.k.	2,238	3,343	4.6	23.3	33.8	62.5	102.0	75.0	11.0
Somali Republic	46	n.k.	n.k.	9	9	n.k.	3.4	n.k.	n.k.	62.7	64.5	n.k.	29.5
Sudan	207	222	222	9	n.k.	235	16.4	2.1	n.k.	56.6	82.5	n.k.	15.0
Syria	3,483	2,434	3,095	332	192	39	5.0	13.3	13.0	402.5	408.0	400.0	12.5
Tunisia	417	305	323	58	38	n.k.	7.6	3.2	3.3	35.1	35.0	n.k.	13.5
UAE[i]	2,043	2,291	4,249	1,487	1,363	2,418	8.9	7.7	14.6	43.0	54.5	n.k.	13.5
Yemen[j]	792	1,016	910	79	91	79	n.k.	12.5	13.1	64.1	63.5	40.0	40.0
Africa[k]													
Angola[l]	1,147	2,732	n.k.	131	280	n.k.	28.4	35.5	n.k.	49.5	100.0	50.0	7.0
Benin	21	n.k.	13	5	n.k.	3	1.8	n.k.	n.k.	4.5	4.4	n.k.	3.5
Botswana[l]	22	80	79	21	66	63	2.5	4.1	4.0	3.0	4.5	n.k.	1.0
Burkina Faso	34	47	62	4	5	6	3.3	2.8	3.6	4.0	8.7	n.k.	1.8
Burundi	35	n.k.	n.k.	7	n.k.	n.k.	3.0	n.k.	n.k.	5.2	7.2	n.k.	1.8
Cameroon[l]	159	82	94	16	7	8	1.9	1.3	1.7	7.3	11.7	n.k.	4.0
Cape Verde[l]	n.k.	n.k.	n.k.	n.k.	n.k.	n.k.	n.k.	n.k.	7.7	1.3	n.k.	n.k.	n.k.
Central African Republic[l]										2.3	6.5	n.k.	2.7
Chad[l]	37	46	n.k.	7	8	n.k.	5.9	5.6	n.k.	12.2	17.0	n.k.	5.7
Congo[l]	56	n.k.	n.k.	30	n.k.	n.k.	2.6	n.k.	n.k.	8.7	8.8	n.k.	6.1
Côte d'Ivoire[l]	76	114	n.k.	8	10	n.k.	1.1	2.0	n.k.	13.2	7.1	12.0	7.8
Equatorial Guinea[l]	n.k.	n.k.	n.k.	n.k.	n.k.	n.k.	n.k.	n.k.	21.5	2.2	1.3	n.k.	2.0
Ethiopia[l]	447	528	1,217	11	11	25	9.4	9.0	n.k.	217.0	320.0	n.k.	9.0
Gabon[l]	79	102	n.k.	79	92	n.k.	2.2	4.8	n.k.	2.4	4.8	n.k.	4.8
The Gambia[l]	2	n.k.	n.k.	n.k.	n.k.	n.k.	1.2	n.k.	0.7	0.5	0.9	n.k.	0.6
Ghana[l]	63	72	69	3	5	5	1.0	0.8	n.k.	15.1	12.2	0.0	5.0
Guinea[l]	n.k.	69	n.k.	5	4	n.k.	n.k.	1.1	n.k.	9.9	9.7	n.k.	9.6
Guinea Bissau[l]	11	n.k.	n.k.	4	13	n.k.	1.1	3.1	n.k.	8.6	9.2	n.k.	2.0
Kenya[l]	256	283	n.k.	13	12	n.k.	3.1	3.5	n.k.	13.7	23.6	n.k.	4.0
Lesotho[l]	n.k.	23	n.k.	13	13	n.k.	4.3	6.5	n.k.	2.0	2.0	n.k.	n.k.
Liberia[l]	28	30	n.k.	n.k.	12	n.k.	2.6	n.k.	n.k.	6.8	7.8	50.0	2.0
Madagascar	54	39	39	5	3	3	2.3	1.4	1.4	21.1	21.0	n.k.	7.5

| Country | Defence Expenditure | | | | | | | | | Numbers in armed forces (000) | | Est. reservists[d] (000) | Para-military[e] (000) |
| | $ million[b] (1985 prices & exchange rates) | | | $ per capita[b] (1985 prices & exchange rates) | | | % of GDP/GNP[c] | | | | | | |
	1985	1990	1991	1985	1990	1991	1985	1990	1991	1985	1991	1991	1991
Malawi[l]	21	16	n.k.	3	2	n.k.	1.9	1.4	n.k.	5.3	7.3	1.0	0.5
Mali[l]	30	n.k.	n.k.	4	n.k.	n.k.	2.7	n.k.	n.k.	4.9	7.3	n.k.	7.8
Mozambique	239	232	230	17	14	14	9.4	10.6	15.6	15.8	50.2	n.k.	5.0
Namibia[l]	n.k.	67	33	n.k.	52	25	n.k.	5.1	2.5	–	9.0	n.k.	n.k.
Niger[l]	12	17	n.k.	2	2	n.k.	0.8	1.0	n.k.	2.2	3.3	n.k.	4.5
Nigeria	1,251	849	814	16	10	9	1.3	0.9	0.8	94.0	76.0	n.k.	12.0
Rwanda[l]	n.k.	n.k.	n.k.	n.k.	n.k.	n.k.	n.k.	n.k.	n.k.	5.2	5.2	n.k.	1.2
Senegal	63	67	68	10	9	8	2.4	1.9	1.9	10.1	9.7	n.k.	n.k.
Seychelles	8	9	10	123	135	150	5.0	3.9	4.3	1.2	1.3	n.k.	0.8
Sierra Leone[l]	5	6	n.k.	1	1	n.k.	0.4	0.7	n.k.	3.1	6.2	n.k.	0.8
South Africa	1,951	2,309	2,063	83	90	78	3.6	3.9	3.6	106.4	72.4	650.0	100.0
Tanzania[l]	280	313	n.k.	13	12	n.k.	4.4	3.9	n.k.	40.4	46.8	10.0	1.4
Togo[l]	19	n.k.	70	6	n.k.	4	2.6	n.k.	n.k.	3.6	5.9	n.k.	1.6
Uganda	53	67	n.k.	4	4	n.k.	2.7	2.1	2.2	20.0	70.0	n.k.	n.k.
Zaire[l]	81	n.k.	n.k.	3	n.k.	n.k.	2.7	n.k.	n.k.	48.0	51.0	n.k.	50.0
Zambia[l]	295	71	61	44	9	8	4.1	3.8	2.6	16.2	16.2	n.k.	1.2
Zimbabwe	284	300	312	34	30	29	6.0	6.8	7.0	41.0	48.5	n.k.	21.0
Asia and Australia													
Afghanistan	287	n.k.	n.k.	16	n.k.	n.k.	8.7	n.k.	n.k.	47.0	45.0	n.k.	97.0
Australia	4,668	4,306	4,210	296	256	247	3.0	2.4	2.4	70.4	67.9	29.2	n.k.
Bangladesh	169	251	234	2	2	2	1.2	1.5	1.3	91.3	107.0	n.k.	55.0
Brunei[l]	205	n.k.	n.k.	915	n.k.	n.k.	6.0	n.k.	n.k.	4.1	4.2	0.9	2.7
Cambodia	n.k.	n.k.	n.k.	n.k.	n.k.	n.k.	n.k.	n.k.	n.k.	35.0	111.8	n.k.	50.0
China	10,615	10,617	12,025	10	9	10	3.6	3.1	3.2	3,900.0	3,030.0	1,200.0	12,000.0
Fiji	14	24	23	20	32	30	1.2	2.1	2.1	2.7	5.0	5.0	n.k.
India	6,263	8,506	7,990	8	10	9	3.0	3.2	2.9	1,260.0	1,265.0	655.0	1,280.5
Indonesia	2,341	1,776	1,739	14	10	9	2.8	1.4	1.3	278.1	283.0	400.0	480.0
Japan	13,151	16,059	16,464	109	130	132	1.0	1.0	1.0	243.0	246.0	48.4	n.k.
North Korea	4,156	5,434	5,328	204	235	224	23	25.2	26.7	838.0	1,132.0	540.0	200.0
South Korea	4,399	6,637	6,359	107	150	142	5.1	4.4	3.8	598.0	633.0	4,500.0	3.5
Laos[l]	n.k.	138	n.k.	n.k.	35	n.k.	n.k.	3.6	n.k.	53.7	55.1	n.k.	n.k.
Malaysia	1,764	1,557	1,670	113	89	92	5.6	3.7	3.7	110.0	127.5	44.3	22.7
Mongolia[l]	233	262	268	123	120	118	11.0	10.9	11.1	33.0	15.5	200.0	10.0
Myanmar (Burma)	228	335	298	6	8	7	3.3	4.9	4.2	186.0	286.0	n.k.	85.3
Nepal	36	37	35	2	2	2	1.5	1.3	1.2	25.0	35.0	n.k.	28.0
New Zealand	454	450	423	140	134	124	2.0	1.9	1.9	12.4	10.9	8.5	n.k.
Pakistan	2,076	2,803	3,014	22	25	25	6.9	7.2	7.0	482.8	580.0	513.0	270.0
Papua New Guinea[l]	34	32	37	10	8	9	1.5	1.3	1.6	3.2	3.5	n.k.	n.k.
Philippines	474	878	843	9	14	13	1.4	2.2	2.2	114.8	106.5	131.0	90.0

Singapore	1,188	1,313	1,518	464	485	553	6.7	4.9	5.4	55.0	55.5	292.0	111.6
Sri Lanka	228	361	340	14	21	19	3.8	5.5	4.8	21.6	105.9	12.0	57.2
Taiwan	4,136	5,304	5,474	213	254	257	6.6	5.4	5.4	444.0	360.0	1,657.5	25.0
Thailand	1,517	1,601	1,761	29	28	30	4.1	2.6	2.5	235.3	283.0	500.0	139.5
Vietnam[l]	n.k.	2,311	n.k.	n.k.	34	n.k.	n.k.	16.0	n.k.	1,027.0	1,041.0	1,000.0	2,600.0
Latin America													
Argentina	1,889	987	1,161	62	32	35	2.9	1.5	1.7	108.0	65.0	377.0	17.0
The Bahamas	n.k.	51	46	n.k.	196	173	n.k.	2.5	2.3	n.k.	0.8	0.5	n.k.
Belize[l]	4	9	9	24	49	45	1.8	3.0	2.6	0.6	0.8	n.k.	n.k.
Bolivia	127	116	122	20	16	16	2.0	1.9	2.0	27.6	31.5	n.k.	16.2
Brazil	1,731	1,059	1,081	13	7	7	0.8	0.9	0.8	276.0	296.7	1,515.0	243.0
Chile	1,242	750	735	103	57	55	7.8	3.5	3.2	101.0	91.8	45.0	27.0
Colombia	274	1,046	1,403	10	33	43	0.8	2.2	3.0	66.2	139.0	116.9	85.0
Costa Rica	29	52	48	11	18	16	0.7	1.1	1.0	n.k.	n.k.	n.k.	7.5
Cuba	1,597	1,491	1,272	158	140	117	9.6	5.0	5.0	161.5	175.0	1,435.0	169.0
Dominican Republic	51	32	22	8	4	3	1.1	0.7	0.5	22.2	22.2	n.k.	15.0
Ecuador	284	422	401	30	39	35	1.8	2.3	2.2	42.5	57.5	100.0	n.k.
El Salvador	252	155	201	53	29	37	4.4	2.7	2.4	41.7	43.7	n.k.	30.0
Guatemala	197	120	158	25	13	17	1.8	0.9	1.2	31.7	44.6	5.0	14.1
Guyana[l]	45	n.k.	n.k.	57	n.k.	n.k.	9.7	n.k.	n.k.	6.6	2.0	2.0	3.5
Haiti	31	14	21	5	2	3	1.5	0.7	1.1	6.9	7.4	n.k.	n.k.
Honduras[l]	72	61	82	16	12	16	2.1	1.5	2.0	16.6	17.5	60.0	5.0
Jamaica[l]	18	19	23	8	8	10	0.9	0.7	0.8	2.1	3.4	0.9	n.k.
Mexico[m]	1,241	n.k.	917	16	n.k.	10	0.7	n.k.	0.5	129.1	175.0	300.0	14.0
Nicaragua	637	n.k.	225	199	n.k.	56	14.2	n.k.	9.1	62.9	14.7	n.k.	n.k.
Panama	97	84	73	44	n.k.	29	2.0	n.k.	1.4	12.0	11.7	n.k.	n.k.
Paraguay[l]	60	n.k.	n.k.	16	16	n.k.	1.3	1.4	n.k.	14.4	16.0	45.0	8.0
Peru	641	540	605	34	20	28	4.5	4.1	3.8	128.0	112.0	188.0	84.0
Suriname[l]	23	13	16	59	26	35	2.4	2.8	4.1	2.0	3.0	n.k.	n.k.
Trinidad & Tobago*	73	71	n.k.	62	29	n.k.	1.0	1.4	2.8	2.1	2.7	n.k.	4.0
Uruguay	128	116	143	42	56	45	2.5	2.2	1.4	31.9	24.7	n.k.	1.2
Venezuela	824	n.k.	1,525	48	37	74	1.3	n.k.	2.2	49.0	75.0	23.0	3.6

Notes:

a In this edition total defence expenditures and per capita defence expenditures represent national definitions and are given in 1985 prices and in 1985 dollars. Where possible, exchange rates have been taken from the IMF, otherwise published average annual exchange rates have been calculated. The consumer price indices have been taken from the IMF where possible, or, where necessary, constructed from known inflation rates.

b Some military expenditures include internal security expenditures; in other cases these and research costs are born by other ministries' budgets.

c Based on local currency. See individual country entries. For most countries, GDP figures are used. For some countries, GNP figures are derived from NMP.

d Normally, only men within 5 years of their active service period are included, unless a country entry specifies a different parameter. Home Guard manpower has not been included.

e Part-time and reserve paramilitary forces are not included.

f Data is for former FRG only. Excl aid to West Berlin.

g Defence expenditure estimates are based on a re-evaluation of costs by function. Soviet published data has been used. Data for 1985 calculated using different criteria. See *The Military Balance 1989–1990* and *1991–1992*.

h The difficulty in calculating suitable exchange rates makes conversion to dollars and international comparison imprecise and unreliable. It is important to refer to individual country entries and to the *local-currency* figures for defence expenditures and the size of the economy.

i 1990 and 1991 data includes estimates of Gulf War costs and contributions.

j Republic of Yemen – all figures consolidated.

k A number of African countries for which there is insufficient data have been omitted.

l No economic data for 1991 available. Data for 1989 is shown in the 1990 column, for 1990 in the 1991 column.

m No economic data for 1990–91 available. Estimate for 1992 shown in the 1991 column.

Nuclear Developments

Over the last 12 months there has been a series of developments which affects not just the strategic nuclear balance but the future of nuclear weapons in general.

The last days of the US–Soviet dialogue

President Bush on 27 September and President Gorbachev on 5 October 1991, announced a number of disarmament measures in respect of sub-strategic nuclear weapons which each would implement unilaterally. Both presidents also proposed a number of other measures which they would be prepared to carry out if these were agreed to on a bilateral basis.

The US and the Soviet Union said they would withdraw and destroy all warheads for nuclear artillery and short-range surface-to-surface missiles. Negotiations on short-range nuclear forces (SNF) would have been the most likely topic for the next set of arms-control negotiations, and so the moves pre-empt some months of painstaking negotiation aimed at achieving the same result. Without a formal treaty, however, there is unlikely to be any provision for verification to ensure that destruction has been carried out. The relevance of ground-based SNF, which NATO planned to use against Warsaw Pact forces should they be massing for a breakthrough after several days of conventional fighting, has always been dubious. Now that the forces of the Soviet Union and NATO were to be separated by 1,000 kilometres, these weapons ceased to have a role in Europe. The number of warheads to be destroyed is just over 7,000: 2,150 US and about 5,000 Soviet. As with previous nuclear force cuts, there will be practical problems in dismantling such large numbers of weapons, and, of course, although the warheads will cease to exist, the core of nuclear explosive material is impossible to destroy and so must either be reprocessed or stored safely and securely.

The US and the USSR both said they would withdraw nuclear weapons (other than SLBM) from naval service, and that this would include bombs delivered by both carrier-borne and land-based naval aircraft. This would complete a process begun by the US some three years ago with the withdrawal from service of its two anti-submarine nuclear weapons – *ASROC* and *SUBROC*. In the age of smart weapons and highly lethal conventional missiles, such as *Exocet*, the use of nuclear weapons is an unnecessarily heavy-handed way to sink a ship; although perhaps only a nuclear weapon could be guaranteed to sink a US aircraft carrier. The US decision includes nuclear-armed *Tomahawk* SLCM. This unilateral move allows the continued deployment of conventionally-armed SLCM, which were so successful in the Gulf War. Conversely, under the INF Treaty all ground-launched cruise missiles, whether nuclear, conventional or unarmed, were eliminated. The development should make port visits around the world easier to arrange, even if the policy of 'neither confirming nor denying' the presence of nuclear weapons continues to be invoked. Some 6,000 naval warheads were to be withdrawn into storage – 3,400 Soviet and 2,500 US – but neither side has committed itself yet to destroying all such warheads.

The Soviet Union would also destroy its remaining atomic demolition mines (ADM), withdraw from service all its anti-aircraft nuclear warheads and destroy some. The US destroyed its ADM in 1987 and withdrew *Nike Hercules* SAM warheads in 1989. The Soviet Union was thought to have some 2,700 SAM warheads, but no firm estimate has ever been made for ADM numbers.

The Soviet Union also proposed that nuclear-armed weapons be withdrawn from non-strategic aircraft and placed in stores. NATO's Nuclear Planning Group met in Sicily on 17 October 1991; it approved the US cuts and further agreed that about 50% of air-delivered nuclear weapons (all free-fall bombs) would be withdrawn from Europe. It was estimated then that there were some 1,400 tactical nuclear bombs in Europe.

The UK followed America's lead in September 1991 and declared that all its naval nuclear weapons, in effect only air-delivered depth-bombs, would be withdrawn from ships and from shore-based maritime stations. The UK would also withdraw a proportion of its free-fall bombs located in Germany.

Presidents Bush and Gorbachev also made a number of decisions on the future of strategic weapons. Both sides stood their strategic bombers down from alert, as well as the ICBM scheduled for elimination under the START Treaty. For the US this involved 450 *Minuteman* II ICBM, and the Soviets stood down a total of 503 ICBM, including 154 SS-18. President Gorbachev also announced that three SSBN (most probably the sole *Yankee-II* and two *Yankee-I*) had been removed from service, to be followed by three more (presumably *Yankee-I*). The US has withdrawn from patrol its ten *Poseidon*-armed SSBN, each with 16 SLBM. President Bush terminated the development of the rail-mobile version of the MX *Peacekeeper*, the mobile elements of the small ICBM (*Midgetman*) programme and cancelled the new short-range attack missile (SRAM II). In response, Gorbachev abandoned Soviet programmes to develop a small mobile ICBM and a new rail-mobile ICBM; rail-mobile SS-24 ICBM would, in future, remain in their garrisons. Both the US and the Soviet Union placed their strategic nuclear assets under one central authority: in the US this is to be Strategic Command, and in the former Soviet Union the Strategic Deterrent Forces.

President Bush called for negotiations to agree the elimination of all ICBM with multiple warheads, while President Gorbachev proposed resuming the START talks with the aim of agreeing a further 50% reduction in strategic weapons after the full implementation of START-agreed cuts. The USSR also announced that it would suspend nuclear tests for the following year, an initiative subsequently endorsed by Russia. No doubt this move was designed to put pressure on the US to follow suit, given that the US resisted earlier moves to stop nuclear testing when the Soviet Union halted its testing between August 1985 and February 1987. In any event, the Soviet Union had some problems over test sites, as Kazakhstan has insisted that the Semipalatinsk site be shut down, and environmentalists were attempting to close the only other site at Novaya Zemlya in the Murmansk region of the Russian Republic. On 8 April 1992 France announced its intention to hold no more tests during 1992.

President Bush called on President Gorbachev to join the US (in the context of a world in which 15 nations have ballistic missiles) 'in taking concrete steps to permit the limited deployment of non-nuclear defences to protect against limited ballistic missile strikes – whatever their source – without undermining the credibility of existing deterrrent forces'. President Gorbachev's reply was 'we are ready to discuss US proposals on non-nuclear anti-aircraft systems, we propose to study the possibility of creating joint systems to avert nuclear missile attack with ground- and space-based systems'. The US could therefore be encouraged that its strategic defence programme, known as Global Protection Against Limited Strikes (GPALS), which if deployed might violate the Anti-Ballistic Missile (ABM) Treaty, might not have been automatically opposed by Moscow, which had said it would withdraw from START should the ABM Treaty be breached.

The creation of the CIS

On 8 December 1991 a 'commonwealth' was formed by Russia, Ukraine and Byelarus, following Ukraine's referendum vote in favour of independence. By 18 December Gorbachev had acknowledged the end of the Soviet Union, and on 21 December the republics of the former Soviet Union, with the exception of Georgia, agreed to form the 'Commonwealth of Independent States' (CIS). The control of nuclear weapons in the CIS was under the direction of Marshal Shaposhnikov, who was appointed Supreme Commander. The decision to use nuclear weapons would be taken by the President of Russia only with the agreement of the Presidents of Byelarus, Kazakhstan and Ukraine, and in consultation with the other CIS heads of state. Byelarus and Ukraine undertook to sign the Treaty on the Non-Proliferation of Nuclear Weapons (NPT) as non-nuclear states. All republics agreed to the withdrawal of tactical nuclear weapons to central storage in Russia for dismantling under joint supervision. Withdrawal of tactical nuclear weapons from Kazakhstan was quickly achieved, but problems arose with Ukraine, which complained that dismantling was not taking place; the withdrawal was halted on 12 March 1992 and resumed in April. The withdrawal from Byelarus was completed by 28 April 1992, and from Ukraine by 5 May 1992. In the preceding months several thousand tactical nuclear weapons had been transported to Russia from these and other republics (although most, if not all, warheads had been withdrawn from the Baltic and Trans-Caucasus republics earlier) – a considerable achievement in view of the circumstances.

In his State of the Union address on 28 January 1992, President Bush announced a number of unilateral measures that the US would take to reduce its strategic nuclear forces, and proposed further measures which would be taken if Russia agreed to eliminate its multiple-warhead ICBM. A day later, President Yeltsin broadcast his own list of proposals. Although welcome, these did not represent a response to the Bush proposals as they did not address the offer of downloading ICBM.

The main component of President Bush's proposal was that if it was agreed that all land-based multiple-warhead ballistic missiles were eliminated, then the US would: eliminate its 50 MX

Peacekeeper ICBM; reduce to one the number of warheads on *Minuteman* III ICBM; and reduce the number of warheads on SLBM by about one-third. A substantial portion of the strategic bomber force would be converted to conventional use, although under START they will still be countable as nuclear bombers. It was later clarified that the SLBM offer was based on the post-START warhead numbers and not the current level. It should be pointed out that, because START only permits the downloading of ICBMs by no more than four warheads, Russia would have to scrap all SS-18 and SS-24 ICBM which both have ten warheads, and the SS-19 with six. However, to gain Russian acceptance of the single warhead ICBM principle, it might be necessary to amend some START conditions. President Bush also committed the US to procuring only 20 B-2 bombers, cancelling the small ICBM (*Midgetman*) programme, ceasing production of the MX *Peacekeeper* missiles and the W-88 warhead (which is understood to have a yield of 300–475KT compared to the 100KT of the W-76 warhead it would replace); and stopping production of advanced cruise missiles (ACM) after 640 of the amended order for 1,000 missiles had been completed.

President Yeltsin in his statement on 29 January 1992 included a number of items that had already been announced by Gorbachev. The first point that Yeltsin made was that he would submit the START Treaty for ratification by the Russian Supreme Soviet. He stated that about 600 land- and sea-based missiles had been removed from operational readiness, that 130 ICBM silos had been, or were about to be destroyed, and six SSBN were decommissioning. (President Gorbachev had already said 503 ICBM had been taken off alert and three SSBN had decommissioned.) It had also been announced by a spokesman as far back as November 1990 that 40 ICBM silos had been destroyed. Yeltsin announced the end of production of Tu-95 *Bear* and Tu-160 *Blackjack* bombers, long-range ALCM, long-range SLCM and the end of development of new SLCM. He also offered, on a reciprocal basis, to end development of new long-range ALCM and to eliminate all long-range SLCM. He stated that the number of SSBN on patrol had been reduced by half and would be further reduced. Russia planned to implement the strategic weapons reductions required by START in three years rather than the seven allowed by the Treaty.

Regarding tactical nuclear weapons, President Yeltsin announced that production of warheads for SSM, artillery and mines would cease, and he confirmed that stocks of these warheads would be destroyed. One-third of sea-based tactical nuclear weapons and one half of anti-aircraft and air-launched nuclear weapons would also be eliminated. Finally, he proposed that negotiations should begin to achieve further reductions in strategic weapons down to 2,000–2,500 each for the US and Russia, in the hope that the other nuclear powers would join in the process of disarmament.

On 23 May 1992, Byelarus, Kazakhstan, Russia, Ukraine and the US signed a protocol to the START Treaty. It was agreed that these four republics of the former Soviet Union, as successor states, would assume the obligations of the former USSR under the Treaty. Byelarus, Kazakhstan and Ukraine further committed themselves to adhere to the NPT Treaty as non-nuclear weapon states in the shortest possible time, although START allows seven years for full implementation. The START protocol will enter into force on the date of the final exchange of instruments of ratification.

Beyond START

On 16 June 1992, Presidents Bush and Yeltsin met in Washington and signed a Joint Understanding on further substantial reductions in strategic offensive weapons; these would be effected in two stages. In the first stage, to be completed within seven years of START entering into force, strategic forces would be reduced to no more than: an overall total between 3,800 and 4,250 warheads; 1,200 MIRV ICBM warheads, 650 heavy (SS-18) ICBM warheads and 2,160 SLBM warheads. The second stage, to be completed by the year 2003 (or by the end of 2000 if the US contributes to the Russian elimination process), would reduce each side's overall warhead total to between 3,000 and 3,500. All MIRV ICBM would be eliminated, and no more than 1,750 SLBM warheads would be deployed by each side. A significant change to the START counting rules for bombers has been agreed. Instead of attributing a number of weapons (ten for US ALCM-equipped bombers and one for non-ALCM bombers) to aircraft which can be equipped to carry more, the new rule is that bombers will be counted as carrying the number of weapons they are equipped to carry. No specific attribution numbers have been published. It is not yet certain whether any other START articles or protocols will be altered. A short treaty-type document is to be rapidly drafted and submitted for ratification. The START rule for reducing the number of warheads on missiles –

'downloading' – which only allows missiles to be downloaded by no more than four warheads, means that Russia would have to destroy all its multiple-warhead ICBM as they have more than five warheads each, whereas the US can download its *Minuteman* III (but not MX). US fears of 'breakout' (the replacement of warheads into downloaded missiles) will lead it to argue that the downloading rule in START must remain unaltered.

In the analysis that follows it is assumed that the articles, statements, protocols and declarations of the START Treaty (other than bomber counting rules) will be adhered to.

The US Secretary of Defense's Annual Report to the President and the Congress announced US nuclear force posture both after the implementation of START and if the President's proposal to ban multiple-warhead ICBM was accepted.

US	Post-START		Post-Bush Proposal		16 June Agreement
	Delivery Weapons	Countable Warheads	Delivery Weapons	Countable Warheads	Actual Warheads
ICBM					
Minuteman II	200	600 ⎫	500	500[a]	500
Minuteman III	300	300[a] ⎬			
MX *Peacekeeper*	50	500	0	0	0
SLBM					
Trident I/C-4 (8)	192	1,536	192 ⎫	2,304[b]	1,728
Trident II/D-5(10)	240	1,920	240 ⎬		
Bombers					
B-52H (ALCM)	95	950	95	950	
B-1B	95	95	95	95	1,272
B-2	20	20	20	20	
Totals	**1,192**	**5,921**	**1,142**	**3,869**	**3,500**

Notes:
[a] Downloaded from three to one warhead.   [b] Warheads reduced by about one-third.

To bring the SLBM warhead total down to the new limit of 1,750 will require a further 554 warheads to be eliminated. This can be achieved by: reducing the number of submarines (only five *Trident* II boats have commissioned so far); reducing the number of missiles on submarines; and further downloading SLBM warheads. If the maximum START downloading of four warheads is applied to all SLBM, then the warhead total becomes 1,728. While it is clear that the US will deploy 500 ICBM and no more than 1,750 SLBM warheads, the situation on bombers is less straightforward. The Joint Understanding of 16 June 1992 clearly states that 'the number of warheads counted for heavy bombers will be the number they are actually equipped to carry'. There should be no problem over ALCM-capable bombers, as the internal common strategic rotary launchers (which can be loaded with eight ALCM, SRAM or free-fall bombs) or the external pylons can be removed. It is of course possible that the number of bombers will be reduced; the US already deploys a force of B-52 bombers in the conventional role, these could be increased to the maximum of 100 as laid down in the Joint Understanding. However, only bombers never equipped with long-range ALCM can be converted to the conventional role. It has been suggested that the B-1B force will be converted to the conventional role and that B-2 bombers will be equipped to carry 16 weapons. The remaining warheads (up to the maximum of 3,500) could be carried by B-52H bombers, which, if no external pylons were fitted, would count as eight weapons each, 20 if the current 12 pylons remain fitted. Until further information is released, *The Military Balance* has listed the bomber force as suggested above.

The ex-Soviet signatories of the START protocol have not yet stated how they will implement START, although it is possible to speculate about how most of the cuts will be taken – older weapons first and those not deployed in Russia (Byelarus, Kazakhstan and Ukraine have committed themselves to the removal of all nuclear weapons). The new agreement makes the task of estimating the final Russian force posture somewhat simpler. All SS-18, SS-19 and SS-24, which cannot be downloaded under START rules, would have to be eliminated. Older missiles – SS-11, SS-13, SS-17 – are already being retired, and this process is likely to be completed. This will leave Russia with only its road-mobile SS-25, of which there are currently some 340, including 80 in Byelarus (Byelarus expects these to be destroyed). Production has not yet been ended and so a somewhat larger force might be deployed. *Yankee-II* submarines are also decommissioning, and the remaining boats of this class are also likely to go. Further cuts to SLBM warheads will have to be made either by retiring older submarines (the most cost-effective option), or by downloading multiple-warhead SLBM. A future Russian nuclear force posture is set out below, but it is only one of a number of options open.

USSR/Russia		Delivery Weapons	Warheads	Totals
ICBM	SS-25[a]	500	500	500
SLBM[b]	SS-N-18[c] (14)	224	224	
	SS-N-23[d] (7)	112	224	1,648
	SS-N-20 (6)	120	1,200	
Bombers[e]	*Bear* ALCM	60	480	
	Bear	90	180	820
	Blackjack	20	160	
Totals		**1,126**	**2,968**	**2,968**

Notes:
[a] Assumes continued production to match *Minuteman* numbers.
[b] Assumes retirement of *Yankee-I* and *Delta-I* (with SS-N-8) submarines.
[c] Downloaded from three to one warhead.
[d] Downloaded from four to two warheads.
[e] Assumes eight weapons for ALCM bombers, two for others.

The postulated Russian force posture is similar to that of the US in numbers of warheads carried by each of the three arms of the triad: ICBM, SLBM and bombers. ICBM would comprise 15% of both sides' armoury; for SLBM it is 60% for Russia, compared with 52% for the US; for bombers it is 25% compared with 33%, respectively. Compared with pre-START strategic nuclear postures, both very large numbers of warheads, around 70%, will be eliminated as the Table shows, and the ratio between the three arms of the triad would be significantly altered, although, of course, Russia could adopt a quite different posture with possibly many more SS-25 ICBM based in silos vacated by MIRV ICBM. However, this would be much more expensive than the option outlined in the Table below.

	USSR/Russia		US	
	Pre-START	Post-16 June	Pre-START	Post-16 June
ICBM	6,612	500	2,450	500
SLBM	2,804	1,648	5,760	1,728
Bombers	855	820	2,665	1,272
Totals	**10,271**	**2,968**	**10,875**	**3,500**

Politically, this is a most encouraging development. Implementation is scheduled to take ten years, however, and it will be unrealistic to expect further force reductions, down to the undefined level of minimum deterrence, until the elimination process is well under way.

CIS Strategic Nuclear Forces: 1 September 1990, 1 June 1992 and Russian Strategic Nuclear Forces: 2003

Delivery vehicle type		With START counting rules for warheads						Actual warhead count		
		START data: 1 September 1990			Current situation: 1 June 1992			Post-16 June Agreement: 2003[a]		
		Launchers deployed	Warheads/ launchers	Total warheads	Launchers deployed	Warheads/ launchers	Total warheads	Launchers deployed	Warheads/ Launchers	Total Warheads
Heavy ICBM	SS-18	308	10	3,080	308	10	3,080	–	–	–
Mobile ICBM	SS-24	33	10	330	36	10	360	–	–	–
	SS-25	288	1	288	340	1	340	500	–	500
Sub-total Mobile ICBM		321	–	618	376	–	700	500	–	500
Other ICBM	SS-11	326	1	326	280	1	280	–	–	–
	SS-13	40	1	40	40	1	40	–	–	–
	SS-17	47	4	188	40	4	160	–	–	–
	SS-19	300	6	1,800	300	6	1,800	–	–	–
	SS-24	56	10	560	56	10	560	–	–	–
Sub-total ICBM		1,398	–	6,612	1,400	–	6,620	500[b]	–	500
SLBM	SS-N-6	192	1	192	96	1	96	–	–	–
	SS-N-8	280	1	280	280	1	280	–	–	–
	SS-N-17	12	1	12	–	–	–	–	–	–
	SS-N-18	224	3	672	224	3	672	224	1	224
	SS-N-20	120	10	1,200	120	10	1,200	120	10	1,200
	SS-N-23	112	4	448	112	4	448	112	2	224
Sub-total SLBM		940	–	2,804	832	–	2,696	456[c]	–	1,648
Total Ballistic Missiles		2,338	–	9,416	2,232	–	9,316	956	–	2,148
Bombers										
ALCM-equipped	Tu-95H-6/H-16	84	8	672	61	8	488	60[d]	8	480
	Tu-160	15	8	120	20	8	160	20[d]	8	160
Non-ALCM	Tu-95B/G	63	1	63	89	1	89	90[e]	2	180
Total Bombers		162	–	855	170	–	737	170	–	820
GRAND TOTAL		2,500	–	10,271	2,402	–	10,053	1,126	–	2,968

Notes:

[a] This column represents only a possible force posture.
[b] Assumes Russia will eliminate all ICBM other than SS-25.
[c] Assumes Russia will retire SS-N-6 and SS-N-8-armed SSBN, and that SS-N-23 will be downloaded from four to two warheads, and SS-N-18 from three to one warhead.
[d] Assumes Tu-95 and Tu-160 will be equipped to carry only eight ALCM.
[e] Assumes Tu-95 will only carry two nuclear bombs.

US Strategic Nuclear Forces: 1 September 1990, 1 June 1992, and 2003

Delivery vehicle type	With START counting rules for warheads						Actual warhead count		
	START data: 1 September 1990			Current situation: 1 June 1992			Post-16 June Agreement: 2003		
	Launchers deployed	Warheads/ launchers	Total warheads	Launchers deployed	Warheads/ launchers	Total warheads	Launchers deployed	Warheads/ Launchers	Total Warheads
ICBM									
Minuteman II	450	1	450	450	1	450	–	–	–
Minuteman III	500	3	1,500	500	3	1,500	500	1	500
MX	50	10	500	50	10	500	–	–	–
Sub-total ICBM	*1,000*	–	*2,450*	*1,000*	–	*2,450*	*500*	–	*500*
SLBM									
Poseidon C-3	192	10	1,920	192[a]	10	1,920	–	–	–
Trident C-4	384	8	3,072	384[b]	8	3,072	192[c]	4	768
Trident D-5	96	8	768	120	8	960	240[c]	4	960
Sub-total SLBM	*672*	–	*5,760*	*696*	–	*5,952*	*432*	–	*1,728*
Total Ballistic Missiles	*1,672*	–	*8,210*	*1,696*	–	*8,402*	*932*	–	*2,228*
Bombers									
ALCM-equipped									
B-52	150	10	1,500	150	10	1,500	95	[d]	952
B-52[e]	39	20	780	28	20	540	–	–	–
Non-ALCM									
B-52	290	1	290	278	1	278	–	–	–
B-1B	95	1	95	95	1	95	–	–	–
B-2	–	–	–	–	–	–	20	16	320
Total bombers	*574*	–	*2,665*	*551*	–	*2,413*	*115*	–	*1,272*
GRAND TOTAL	**2,246**	–	**10,875**	**2,247**	–	**10,815**	**1,047**	–	**3,500**

Notes:

[a] *Poseidon*-armed SSBN were withdrawn from patrol during 1992.
[b] Two *Trident* C-4-armed SSBN are to be retired by end FY1992.
[c] Assumes downloading of all *Trident* SLBM from 8 to 4 warheads.
[d] Assumes some B-52H will carry 8 weapons, others more.
[e] START rules allow only first 150 US ALCM-capable bombers to count 10 warheads, bombers in excess of 150 count as 20.

Nuclear-Capable Delivery Vehicles: NATO, Russia, CIS and China

Many delivery systems are dual-capable; we show the total number in service, even though a high proportion may not be assigned a nuclear role. Maximum aircraft loadings are given, though often fewer weapons may be carried. Some loadings differ from those under SALT/START counting rules. All ground-launched nuclear weapons (SSM and artillery) have been withdrawn to store in Russia and the US. We no longer list delivery systems of other states. All sea-launched weapons, other than SLBM, incl SLCM have been withdrawn from ships and from shore-based maritime air stations of the US, Russia and NATO. All CIS tactical nuclear weapons have been moved to Russia.

Category and type	Year deployed	Range (km)a	Throw-weightb	CEP (m)c	Launcher total	Munition/ warhead	Yield per warheadd	Remarks
UNITED STATES								
LAND-BASED								
Strategic								
ICBM								
LGM-30F *Minuteman II*	1966	11,300	8	370	450	Mk 11C; W-56	1.2MT	10 with Emergency Rocket Communications System
LGM-30G *Minuteman III*	1970	14,800	11.5	220	200	3 × Mk 12 MIRV; W-62	170KT	
	1980	12,900	11.5	220	300	3 × Mk 12A MIRV; W-78	335KT	
LGM-118 *Peacekeeper* (MX)	1986	11,000	39.5	100	50	10×Mk 21 MIRV; W-87	300 or 400KT	In mod *Minuteman* silos
Tactical:e All warheads for ground-launched weapons to be destroyed.								
SRBM								
MGM-52C *Lance*	1972	110	–	150–400	20	W-70 mods 0, 1, 2 / W-70 mod 3	3 values: 1–10KT / 1KT(–) or 1KT(+)	
*Artillery*f								
M-110A1/A2 203mm	1977/9	21.3	–	170	1,364	M-422 shell; W-33 / M-753 rocket-assisted projectile; W-79	0.5 or 10KT / 0.5, 1 or 2.5KT	Some 800 warheads / Some 300 warheads. Some enhanced radiation (ER) warheads stored in US
SP	1981	29	–	200–500				
M-109 155mm SP (3 mod)	1963	18/24/30	–	n.k.	2,573	M-454 shell; W-48	0.1KT	Some 900 warheads
M-198 155mm towed	1979	14	–	n.k.	1,193		under 2KT	
M-114 155mm towed	1940	19.3	–	n.k.	550			
SEA-BASED								
Strategic								
SLBM								
UGM-73A *Poseidon* C-3	1971	4,600	20	450	160	10 × Mk 3 MIRV; W-68	40KT	Installed in 10 SSBN (elimination in process)
UGM-93A *Trident* C-4	1980	7,400	15	450	384	8 × Mk 4 MIRV; W-76	100KT	Installed in 20 SSBN
UGM-133A *Trident* D-5	1989	12,000	28	120	120	8 × Mk 5 MIRV; W-88	300–475KT	Installed in 5 SSBN (W-88 production halted)
Tacticale								
SLCM								
BGM-109A *Tomahawk*g	1983	2,500	n.k.	280	–	TLAM-N; W-80	200KT	84 submarines, 49 surface combatants have launchers

For notes, see p. 236.

		Radius of action (km)[a]	Max speed (mach)	Weapon load (000 kg)	Missile total	Max ordnance load[i]	
AIR							
Strategic							
Long-range bombers[e]							
B-52C/D/E/F	—	—	—	—	—	—	218 awaiting conversion/elimination
B-52G	1959	4,600	0.95	29.5	40	Internal: 12 bombs (B-43/-53/-61/-83) or 8 SRAM. External: 12 ALCM	Plus 44 ac awaiting conversion/elimination. In conventional role but could re-role. Plus 19 ac awaiting conversion/elimination
					41	Internal: 12 bombs (B-43/-53/-61/-83) or 8 *Harpoon*	
B-52H	1962	6,140	0.95	29.5	94	Internal: 11 bombs (B-43/-53/-61/-83) or 8 SRAM or 8 ALCM. External: 12 ALCM	Plus 4 test ac
B-1B	1986	4,580	1.25	61	95	Internal: 8 ALCM plus 8 SRAM; or 24 SRAM; or 24 B-61 bombs	Plus 2 test ac. Not yet equipped for ALCM.
B-2	—	—	—	—	—	—	4 test aircraft
Tactical[e]							
Land-based							
F-111D/E/F/G	1967	1,750	2.2/2.5	13.1	275	3 bombs (B-43/-57/-61)	Plus 56 in store
F-4D/E	1969	840	2.4	5.9	34	3 bombs (B-28RE/-43/-57/-61)	Plus some 600 in store
F-16	1979	550/930	2+	5.4	1,440	1 bomb (B-43/-61)	Some in store
A-4M	1970	1,230	0.9	4.5	24	1 bomb (B-28/-43/-57/-61)	USMCR
Carrier-borne							
A-6E	1963	1,250	0.9	8.1	319	3 bombs (B-28/-43/-57/-61)	Incl 20 USMC
F/A-18	1982	850	2.2	7.7	864	2 bombs (B-57/-61)	Incl 201 USMC, some in store
S-3A (ASW)	1974	575	0.6	n.k.	99	1 B-57 depth charge	2 hrs endurance at radius of action. Total endurance 5 hrs
Maritime							
P-3 (ASW)	1961	1,140	0.66	19	310	2 B-57 depth charges	8 hrs endurance at radius of action; total endurance 18 hrs. Some in store.

		Range (km)[a]	Max speed (mach)	Weapon load (000 kg)	Missile total	Munition/ warhead	Yield per warhead[d]	
ALCM								
AGM-86B[e]	1982	2,400	0.66	—	1,660	W-80	170–200KT	
AGM-129 ACM	1991	3,000	n.k.	—	200	W-80	170–200KT	Production limited to 640
ASM								
AGM-69A (SRAM)	1972	56 (low) 220 (high altitude)	3.5	—	1,100	W-69	170KT	

BOMBS[h]

Type	Yield per warhead[d]	Wpn stockpile	Remarks
B-57	5–20KT	1,550	
B-61 (Strategic)	100–500KT(s)	900	Depth-charge capability In-flight yield selection and fusing, hard target penetration
B-61 (tactical)	1–345KT	1,925	Replacing B-28, B-53
B-83	1–2MT	650	

NATO (excluding US)[j]

Category and type	Year deployed	Range (km)[a]	CEP (m)[c]	Launcher total	Munition/warhead	Yield per warhead[d]	Remarks
LAND-BASED							
Intermediate-range							
IRBM							
SSBS S-3D	1980	3,500	n.k.	18	TN-61	1MT	Fr
Short-range							
Pluton	1974	120	150–300	24	AN-51	15 or 25KT	Fr
SEA-BASED							
Strategic							
SLBM							
Polaris A-3 TK	1967	4,600	900	48	3 × MRV; W-58 (*Chevaline*)	200KT	UK. In 3 SSBN, incl 1 in extended refit
M-4	1985	5,000	n.k.	64	6 × MIRV; TN-70/-71	150KT	Fr. In 4 SSBN plus 1 SSBN in conversion.

Category and type	Year deployed	Radius of action (km)[a]	Max speed (mach)	Weapon load (000 kg)	Munition/warhead (Max ordnance load)	Remarks
AIR[e]						
Tactical						
Land-based						
F-104G/S	1958	830	2.2	1.8	242 — 1 B-28/-57/-61 bombs	Gr (40), It (18), Tu (129)
F-4E/F	1967/73	840	2.4	5.9	321 — 1 B-61 bomb	Ge (152), Gr (54), Tu (135)
F-16	1982	930	2+	5.4	371 — 1 B-61 bomb	Be (72), Dk[k] (63), Gr (40), Nl (168), No[k] (61), Tu (92)
Mirage IVP	1986	930	2.2	9.3	15 — 1 *ASMP*	Fr. Plus 13 in store
Mirage 2000N	1988	690	2.2	6.3	45 — 1 *ASMP*	Fr

For notes, see p. 236.

Category and type	Year deployed	Radius of action (km)[a]	Max speed (mach)	Weapon load (000 kg)	Launcher total	Max ordnance load	Remarks
Jaguar A	1974	850	1.1	4.75	204	1 or 2 AN-52 bombs	Fr (89) (no longer in nuclear role) UK (115)
Tornado IDS	1981	1,390	0.92	6.8	430	n.k.	Ge (236), It (80), UK (114), plus 83 in store.
Carrier-borne							
Super Etendard	1980	650	0.98	2.1	38	ASMP	Fr. Plus 19 in store.
Sea Harrier	1980	460/750	0.98	2.3	40	1 (or 2) WE-177 bombs	UK
Maritime							
Buccaneer	1963	1,410	0.85	7.3	23		UK. Plus 38 in store.

Category and type	Year deployed	Range (km)[a]	Max speed (mach)	Weapon load (000 kg)	Launcher total	Munition/warhead	Yield per warhead[d]	Remarks
ASM								
ASMP	1986	100–300	2	n.a.	n.a.		45KT	Fr
Bombs								
AN-22		–	–	–	–		15, 300KT	Fr
WE-177		–	–	–	–		10, 200, 400KT	UK

COMMONWEALTH OF INDEPENDENT STATES (STRATEGIC) AND RUSSIA (TACTICAL)

LAND-BASED

Strategic

ICBM

Category and type		Year deployed	Range (km)[a]	Throw-weight[b]	CEP (m)[c]	Munition/warhead	Yield per warhead[d]	Remarks
SS-11 *Sego*	mod 2	1973	13,000	}12	1,100	single RV	1MT	Russia
	mod 3	1975	10,600			3 × MRV	100–300KT	Russia
SS-13 (RS-12) *Savage*	mod 2	1968	9,400	6	1,800	single RV	600KT	Russia
SS-17 (RS-16) *Spanker*	mod 3	1982	10,000	25.5	400	4 × MIRV	500KT	Russia

	Year deployed	Range (km)[a]	Throw-weight[b]	CEP (m)[c]	Launcher total	Munition/warhead[e]	Yield per warhead[d]	Remarks
SS-18 (RS-20) mod 4	1982	11,000	88	250	308	10 × MIRV	500KT	104 Kazakhstan, 204 Russia
Satan mod 5	–	ε9,000	88	n.k.		10 × MIRV	750KT	
SS-19 (RS-18) mod 3 *Stiletto*	1982	10,000	43.5	300	300	6 × MIRV	550KT	170 Russia, 130 Ukraine.
SS-24 (RS-22) *Scalpel*	1987/8	10,000	40.5	ε 200	92	10 × MIRV	100KT	36 rail-based, Russia, 56 silo-based: 10 Russia, 46 Ukraine
SS-25 (RS-12M) *Sickle*	1985/6	10,500	10	ε 200	340+	single RV	750KT	Road-mobile. 260+ Russia, 80 Byelarus
Short-range[e]								
SSM								
FROG-7 (Luna)	1965	70	–	400	600	–	200KT	
SS-21 *(Tochka) Scarab*	1978	120	–	30		–	100KT	
SS-1c (R-17) *Scud* D[e]	1965	300	–	450	300	–	KT range	–
GLCM								
SS-C-1b *Sepal*	1962	450	–	n.k.	40	–	350KT	Coastal defence. Nuclear role doubtful
Artillery[ef]								
2A36 152mm towed	1978	27	–	n.k.	1,500	–	2–5KT	
2S5 152mm SP	1980	27	–	n.k.	600	–	2–5KT	
D-20 152mm towed	1955	17.4	–	n.k.	1,650	–	2KT	
2S3 152mm SP	1972	27	–	n.k.	2,000	–	under 5KT	
2S7 203mm SP	1975	18 +	–	n.k.	240	–	2–5KT	
2S4 240mm SP mor	1975	12.7	–	n.k.	120	–	n.k.	
SAM								
SH-01 *Galosh*	1964	320	–	–		–	3MT	Deployed Moscow only.
SH-11 mod *Galosh*	1983/4	320	–	–	100	–	n.k.	
SH-08 *Gazelle*	1984	80	–	–		–	10KT	
SA-10 *Grumble*[e]	1981	100	–	–	2,400	–	n.k.	
SA-5 *Gammon*[e]	1967	300	–	–	1,800	–	n.k.	

For notes, see p. 236.

SEA-BASED

Strategic

SLBM

Category and type		Year deployed	Range (km)[a]	Throw-weight[b]	CEP (m)[c]	Launcher total	Munition/warhead	Yield	Remarks
SS-N-6 Serb	mod 1	1968	2,400	6.5	1,300	96	single RV	500KT–1MT	In 6 SSBN
	mod 3	1974	3,000	6.5	1,300		2 MRV	ε500KT	
SS-N-8 Sawfly	mod 1	1972	7,800	11	1,500	280	single RV	800KT	In 22 SSBN
	mod 2	1973	9,100	11	900		2 MRV	800KT	
SS-N-18	mod 1	1977	6,500	16.5	1,400	224	3 MIRV	20KT	In 14 SSBN
Stingray	mod 2	1977	8,000	16.5	900		single RV	450KT	7 warheads originally attributed in START, now 'downloaded' to 3.
	mod 3	1978	6,500	16.5	900		7 MIRV	100KT	
SS-N-20 Sturgeon		1981	8,300	25.5	500	120	10 MIRV	100KT	In 6 SSBN
SS-N-23 Skiff		1985	8,300	28	<900	112	4 MIRV	ε100KT	In 7 SSBN

Tactical

SLCM

Category and type	Year deployed	Range (km)[a]	Throw-weight[b]	CEP (m)[c]	Launcher total	Munition/warhead	Yield	Remarks
SS-N-3a/b Shaddock[e]	1962	450	–	n.a.	60	–	350KT	In some 6 SSGN/SSG[l], 1 CG, 3 DDG
SS-N-7 Starbright[e]	1968	n.a.	–	n.a.	56	–	200KT	In 7 SSGN
SS-N-9 Sirene[e]	1968/9	100	–	n.a.	256	–	200KT	In 5 SSGN, 36 corvettes
SS-N-12 Sandbox[e]	1973	550	–	n.a.	164	–	350KT	In some 13 SSGN[l], 3 CVV, 3 CG
SS-N-19 Shipwreck[e]	1980	550	–	n.a.	288	–	500KT	In 9 SSGN, 3 CGN, 1 CVV
SS-N-21 Sampson	1987	3,000	–	150	ε104	–	200KT	In 3 SSGN, 11 SSN (ε4 per SSN)
SS-N-22 Sunburn[e]	1981	400	–	n.k.	200	–	200KT	In 15 DDG, 20 corvettes
SS-NX-24	–	–	–	n.k.	ε12	–	n.k.	In trials SSGN

ASW

Category and type	Year deployed	Range (km)[a]	Throw-weight[b]	CEP (m)[c]	Launcher total	Munition/warhead	Yield	Remarks
SS-N-14 Silex[e]	1974	55	–	n.a.	306	*ASROC* type	1 to 5KT	In 1 CGN, 25 CG, 32 frigates
SS-N-15 Starfish	1982	45	–	n.k.	n.k.	*SUBROC* type	about 5KT	In 33 SSN
SUW-N-1 (FRAS-1)	1975	30	–	n.k.	8	*ASROC* type	5KT	In 2 CVV, 2 CGH
Type 53-68 HWT	1970	14	–	–	n.k.	torpedo	20KT	Usable from all 533mm TT
Type 65 HWT	1981	50	–	–	n.k.	torpedo	20KT	Usable from all 650mm TT

Mines

Category and type	Year deployed	Range (km)[a]	Throw-weight[b]	CEP (m)[c]	Launcher total	Munition/warhead	Yield	Remarks
Mines	n.k.	–	–	n.k.	–	–	5–20KT	

AIR	Year	Radius of action (km)[a]	Max speed (mach)	Weapon load (000 kg)	Weapon total	Max ordnance load	
Strategic							
Long-range bombers							
Tu-95 *Bear B/G* / *Bear H*	1956	5,690	0.9	11.3	45} / 84}	{4 bombs/2 AS-3/-4 ALCM / up to 10 AS-15 ALCM	Russia. Plus 8 test ac / 40 Kazakhstan, 22 Ukraine, 22 plus 20 trg Russia
Tu-160 *Blackjack*	1988	7,300	2.3	16.3	20	12 AS-15/24 AS-16	Ukraine
Medium-range bombers[e]							
Tu-16 *Badger*	1955	2,180	0.91	9	120	1–2 AS-5/-6 ALCM, 1 bomb	50 Strategic Aviation, 70 Navy, plus 45 in store
Tu-22 *Blinder*	1962	1,500	1.4	10	10	1 AS-4 ALCM, 1 bomb	10 Navy
Tu-26 (Tu-22M) *Backfire*	1974	4,430	1.92	12	273	1–2 AS-4 ALCM, 2 bombs	118 Strategic Aviation, 155 Navy
Tactical[e]							
Land-based							
MiG-27 *Flogger D/J*	1971	390/600	1.7	4.5	640	2 bombs	Incl 30 Navy
Su-17 *Fitter D/H/K*	1974	430/680	2.1	4	495	2 bombs	Incl 165 Navy
Su-24 *Fencer*	1974	320/1,130	2.3	8	580	2 bombs	Incl 100 Navy
Maritime ASW[e]							
Tu-142 *Bear F*	1972	1,510	0.83	10	58	2 bombs	8 hrs endurance at radius of action.
Il-38 *May*	1970	1,700	0.64	7	41	ε2 bombs	8 hrs endurance at radius of action. Total endurance 15 hrs
Be-12 *Mail*	1965	600	0.5	10	92	2 bombs	8 hrs endurance at radius of action. Total endurance 12 hrs

	Year	Range (km)[a]	Max speed (mach)	Weapon load (000 kg)	Weapon total	Yield[d]	
ALCM							
AS-4 *Kitchen*	1962	300	3.3	n.k.	n.k.	1MT	
AS-6 *Kingfish*	1977	300	3	n.k.	n.k.	350KT–1MT	
AS-15 *Kent*	1984	1,600	0.6	n.k.	n.k.	250KT	
AS-16 *Kickback*	1989	200	n.k.	n.k.	n.k.	350KT	
Bombs	n.k.	–	–	–	n.k.	Strategic: 5, 20, 50MT / Tactical: 250, 350KT	
Depth-charges	n.k.	–	–	–	n.k.	–	Known to exist; no details available

For notes, see p. 236.

CHINA	Year deployed	Range (km)[a]	CEP (m)[c]	Launcher total	Munition/warhead	Yield per warhead[d]	Remarks
LAND-BASED							
Strategic							
ICBM							
CSS-4 (DF-5)	1981	15,000	n.k.	2	single RV	5MT	
CSS-3 (DF-4)	1978/9	7,000	n.k.	6	single RV	3MT	
IRBM							
CSS-2 (DF-3)	1970	2,700	n.k.	60	single RV	2MT	
SEA-BASED							
Strategic							
SLBM							
CSS-N-3 (JL-1)	1983/4	2,200–3,000	n.k.	12	–	ε2MT	Installed in 1 SSBN

AIR		Radius of action (km)[a]	Max speed (mach)	Weapon load (000 kg)		Munition/warhead	Yield per warhead[d]
Strategic[g]						Maximum ordnance load	
Medium-range bombers							
H-6	1968/9	2,180	0.91	9	up to 120	ε2 bombs	n.k.

Chinese *tactical* nuclear weapons have been reported, but no details are available.

SOURCES: include Cochrane, Arkin and Hoenig, *Nuclear Weapons Databook*, vol. I (Cambridge MA: Ballinger, 1984); Cochrane, Arkin, Norris and Hoenig, *Nuclear Weapons Databook*, vol. II (Cambridge MA: Ballinger, 1987); Hansen, *US Nuclear Weapons, The Secret History* (New York: Orion, 1988); *Bulletin of the Atomic Scientists* (various issues); Treaty between the US and USSR on the Reduction and Limitation of Strategic Offensive Arms.

[a] Ranges and aircraft radii of action in km; for nautical miles, multiply by 0.54. A missile's range may be reduced by up to 25% if max payload is carried. Radii of action for ac are in normal configuration, at optimum altitude, with a standard warload, without in-flight refuelling. When two values are given, the first refers to a low-low-low mission profile and the second to a high-low-high profile.

[b] Throw-weight concerns the weight of post-boost vehicle (warhead(s), guidance systems, penetration aids and decoys). No definition of the term is given in the START Treaty document. Throw-weight is expressed in terms of kg (100s).

[c] CEP (circular error probable) = the radius of a circle around a target within which there is a 50% probability that a weapon aimed at that target will fall.

[d] Yields vary greatly; figures given are estimated maxima. KT range = under 1MT; MT range = over 1MT. Yield, shown as 1–10KT means the yield is between these limits. Yields shown as 1 or 10KT mean that either yield can be selected.

[e] Dual-capable.

[f] Numbers cited are totals of theoretically nuclear-capable pieces. Not all will be certified for nuclear use, and in practice relatively few are likely to be in a nuclear role at any one time. All artillery pieces listed are dual-capable.

[g] It is not possible to give launcher numbers as the vertical launch system (VLS) can mount a variety of missiles in any of its tubes.

[h] All bombs have five option fusing: freefall airburst or surface burst, parachute retarded airburst or surface burst, and retarded delayed surface burst (except B-57, which has no freefall/retarded surface burst, and B-53, which has no freefall surface burst).

[i] External loads are additional to internal loads.

[j] Except for French and UK national weapons, nuclear warheads held in US custody.

[k] No nuclear warheads held on Canadian, Danish, Norwegian, Spanish or Portuguese territory.

[l] Some SSGN/SSG can carry either SS-N-12 *Sandbox* or SS-N-3 *Shaddock*.

Conventional Forces in Europe

The Treaty on Conventional Armed Forces in Europe (CFE) was signed by the member states of NATO and the then Warsaw Pact on 19 November 1990. Since then much has happened. The Warsaw Pact has been dissolved, Germany has been unified, the Baltic states have regained their independence, and the Soviet Union has disintegrated into 12 independent republics.

With regard to the CFE Treaty, there have been three significant developments. First, the 12 republics of the former Soviet Union met in Tashkent on 15 May 1992 and issued a Joint Declaration in which as successor states of the USSR, they agreed that they would fulfil the obligations of the Treaty and they published the details of how the quota of treaty-limited equipments (TLE) allotted to the Soviet Union by the CFE Treaty would be apportioned beween them. Second, agreement was reached in Vienna at the CFE1a talks on the limitation of the personnel strength of conventional armed forces, and a Concluding Act was signed in Helsinki on 10 July 1992 by the members of NATO, Bulgaria, Czechoslovakia, Hungary, Poland, Romania, the seven republics of the former Soviet Union with forces located in the Atlantic to the Urals (ATTU) region (i.e., Armenia, Azerbaijan, Byelarus, Georgia, Moldova, Russia and Ukraine) and Kazakhstan, which has territory but no forces in the ATTU region. Third, at the CSCE Helsinki summit it was agreed that CFE would be provisionally applied from 17 July for 120 days or until the final party deposited its instrument of ratification. Only Byelarus and Armenia have yet to ratify CFE; they have affirmed their intention to do so and will implement CFE provisions where necessary before ratification.

CFE Implementation

After 17 July 1992 all TLE held above specified limits must be destroyed and not otherwise disposed of (by sale or movement out of the ATTU). By 16 August 1992 each party must have provided to all other parties the information concerning their forces and TLE holdings as laid down in the Treaty Annex on the exchange of information. The reductions required by CFE must be fully implemented by 17 January 1996 (25% of the reductions must have been effected within 16 months (November 1993) and 60% within 28 months (November 1994) of the Treaty coming into force).

Apportionment of TLE of the former Soviet Union

CFE laid down limits for TLE (tanks, armoured combat vehicles (ACV) artillery, combat aircraft and attack helicopters) for each side (NATO and Warsaw Pact). It also laid down the limit for TLE which any one state could retain, and geographical sub-limits for the zones into which the ATTU was divided. Each side then agreed the apportionment of TLE between the members of their alliance. This apportionment can be changed by mutual agreement of the two states concerned as long as no geographical sub-limits are violated. Aircraft and helicopter limits are set for the whole ATTU region only.

For ground forces TLE the ATTU has been divided into four zones, each of which has its own TLE limit. However, there are two complicating factors. First the zones do not 'stand alone' but are sequential; that is to say, as you move away from the former inter-alliance frontier, each zone also forms part of the zone beyond it. (For example, the innermost zone for the ex-Warsaw Pact, Zone 4, covers Czechoslovakia, the then GDR, Hungary and Poland. Zone 3 also includes this area, plus the four most westerly military districts (MD) of the Soviet Union). There are also specific limits for territory on the flanks, that is to say the territory not included in Zone 2. The second complicating factor is that the limits for some zones are for total numbers of TLE, and in others for those in active units. There is therefore considerable flexibility allowed to each side as to how they deploy their TLE.

For the territory of the former Soviet Union the Zones are as follows:

Zone 4: No part of the former Soviet Union lies in Zone 4, where limits apply to TLE in active units only.

Zone 3: Zone 4 plus four military districts: the Baltic (now redesignated the North-Western Group of Forces, which commands the forces in the Kaliningrad Oblast of Russia and Russian forces in the three Baltic republics until they are withdrawn), the Belorussian (now the Republic of Byelarus), and the Carpathian and Kiev (now forming part of Ukraine). Here the limit applies to TLE in active units only, however there is an additional sub-limit for all TLE in the Kiev MD.

Zone 2: Zone 3 plus the Moscow, Volga and Ural MDs of Russia. In this zone there are two limits: one for TLE in active units; and one for the total number. Stored TLE (with the exception of the Kiev MD), can be located anywhere in the zone (for example, all in Zone 4).

Zone 1: The whole ATTU. Again, there are two sets of limits, one for active units and one for the overall total. There are also a number of geographical sub-limits affecting the flanks. One limits the number of TLE in active units in the Leningrad, Odessa (now Ukraine), Trans-Caucasus (Armenia, Azerbaijan and Georgia) and North Caucasus MD, Bulgaria and Romania. Apart from some TLE in the Odessa MD and in the Leningrad MD of Russia, no additional TLE may be stored.

There was considerable discussion as to how TLE should be apportioned between the republics of the former Soviet Union, and naturally each held out for a larger share than the others were prepared to allow (and that which was finally agreed to). The Russians claimed that the apportionment should be calculated on the same basis as that used to decide the TLE limits of the USSR and its Warsaw Pact allies. That calculation was based on a combination of a state's land area, length of borders and size of population, and would have greatly favoured Russia, as can be seen by the following Table, which compares the proposals made by Byelarus, Russia and Ukraine.

TLE Category	Proposal by	For Russia	For Byelarus	For Ukraine	For Moldova	Combined Total for Armenia Azerbaijan Georgia
Tanks	Russia	8,800	1,125	2,800	65	360
	Byelarus	–	2,000	–	–	–
	Ukraine	5,888	2,000	4,800	–	462
ACV	Russia	13,400	1,560	4,440	90	510
	Byelarus	–	2,500	–	–	–
	Ukraine	12,050	2,500	5,000	–	450
Artillery	Russia	8,800	910	2,675	120	670
	Byelarus	–	1,700	–	–	–
	Ukraine	5,782	1,700	5,000	–	693
Combat Aircraft	Russia	4,046	260	730	0	114
	Byelarus	–	320	–	–	–
	Ukraine	3,020	515	1,100	–	515
Attack Helicopters	Russia	1,171	80	200	0	49
	Byelarus	–	130	–	–	–
	Ukraine	700	150	500	–	150

The quotas agreed for the smaller republics of Armenia, Azerbaijan, Georgia and Moldova are all expressed in TLE in active units (although some may be stored if wished). All four republics lie within the southern flanking area of Zone 1 and none are subject to any special restrictions.

	Armenia	Azerbaijan	Georgia	Moldova
Tanks	220	220	220	210
HACV	11	11	11	0
AIFV	135	135	135	130
Total ACV	220	220	220	210
Artillery	285	285	285	250
Combat Aircraft	100	100	100	50
Attack Helicopters	50	50	50	50

At present, these four republics have few TLE of their own, as these are mainly still held by units considered to be part of the Russian army. However, some items have been handed over to the newly forming national armies (or to the opposition in the case of Moldova, where it is suspected that weapons have been given to the forces of the Dnestr region) and others have been stolen in order to arm warring groups.

Byelarus is only constrained by the limit set for Zone 2. The Table shows the limit for both active units and stored TLE agreed for Byelarus, together with its current holding. It is not known whether any of the TLE still in Germany or Poland will be withdrawn to Byelarus.

| | TLE Limit | | | Current Holding |
	Active Units	Storage	Total	
Tanks	1,525	275	1,800	1,850
AIFV	–	–	1,590	2,460
HACV	–	–	130	10
Total ACV	2,175	425	2,600	3,340
Artillery	1,375	240	1,615	1,393
Combat Aircraft	–	–	260	617
Attack Helicopters	–	–	80	80

TLE in Ukraine are restricted by: the limits imposed on the Odessa MD (no more than 400 tanks and 500 artillery in storage); by the ceiling for Zone 2 which limits TLE in the Carpathian and Kiev MDs; and by the flanking areas sub-limit which restricts TLE in the Odessa MD. The agreed quota for Ukraine, shown in the Table below, is therefore divided between those in the Odessa MD and the remainder of Ukraine.

| | Odessa | | Carpathia/Kiev | | Total | |
TLE Category	Holding	TLE limit	Holding	TLE limit	Holding	TLE Limit
Tanks Active Units	–	280	–	2,850	–	3,130
Storage	–	400	–	550	–	950
Total	270	680	5,830	3,400	6,100	4,080
AIFV	373	–	3,307	–	3,680	3,095
HACV	3	–	177	–	180	253
All ACV Active Units	–	350	–	4,000	–	4,350
Storage	–	–	–	700	–	700
Total	1,320	350	5,840	4,700	6,160	5,050
Artillery Active Units	–	390	–	2,850	–	3,240
Storage	–	500	–	300	–	800
Total	518	890	2,558	3,150	3,076	4,040
Combat Aircraft	165	–	1,203	–	1,368	1,090
Attack Helicopters	0	–	240	–	240	330

The picture for Russia, while slightly more complicated, allows more flexibility, as the TLE limit for the flanks is an aggregate for both the Leningrad MD in the north, where there is a specific limit on stored TLE in the southern part of the MD, and the North Caucasus MD in the south.

TLE Category	Flanks: Leningrad and North Caucasus MD			Kaliningrad, Moscow, Volga and Ural MDs		Total	
	Holding Leningrad	N Caucasus	TLE Limit	Holding	TLE Limit	Holding	TLE Limit
Tanks Active Units	–	–	700	–	4,275	–	4,975
Storage	–	–	600	–	825	–	1,425
Total	1,350	550	1,300	3,200	5,100	5,100	6,400
AIFV	600	180	–	3,050	–	3,830	7,030
HACV	390	0	–	10	–	400	574
All ACV Active Units	–	–	580	–	9,945	–	10,525
Storage	–	–	800	–	155	–	955
Total	2,170	250	1,380	4,700	10,100	7,120	11,480
Artillery Active Units	–	–	1,280	–	3,825	–	5,105
Storage	–	–	400	–	910	–	1,310
Total	1,170	530	1,680	2,810	4,735	4,510	6,415
Combat Aircraft	350	880	–	1,050	–	2,280	3,450
Attack Helicopter	50	0	–	430	–	480	890

The Tashkent Declaration also took account of the various protocols to CFE concerning other forces:

a) Land-based naval aircraft are limited to no more than 400 for any one state. It is now agreed that Russia will have no more than 300 and Ukraine no more than 100.

b) The USSR was allowed, as a unique exception, to have no more than 100 Mi-24R and Mi-24K helicopters (all other Mi-24 types are attack helicopters) equipped for reconnaissance and CBW sampling. The 100 helicopters have been apportioned as follows:

Armenia	4	Georgia	4	Russia	50
Azerbaijan	4	Moldova	4	Ukraine	18
Byelarus	16				

c) The USSR was limited to holding no more than 462 armoured vehicle launched bridges (AVLB) in active units. There is no limit for AVLB in storage. AVLB have been apportioned as follows:

Armenia	8	Georgia	8	Russia	223
Azerbaijan	8	Moldova	7	Ukraine	144
Byelarus	64				

The Tashkent Declaration also took into account the legally binding statement made by the USSR regarding CFE TLE deployed with forces not covered by the Treaty: Strategic Rocket Forces (SRF), Coastal Defence Forces and Naval Infantry. The USSR had committed itself to limits of certain TLE in these forces and further committed itself to reducing the number of TLE held by forces covered by the Treaty by an identical number:

a) SRF: Soviet SRF could hold 1,701 APCs above the CFE limit. These are to be split between the nuclear-armed republics as follows: Byelarus – 585; Russia – 700; Ukraine – 416.

The quotas for Byelarus and Ukraine are to be transferred to Russia when SRF have been totally removed from their territories.

b) Coastal Defence Forces: The TLE allowed to Coastal Defence Forces have been split between Russia and Ukraine as follows:

	Russia	Ukraine
Tanks	542	271
ACV	407	470
Artillery	686	160

c) Naval Infantry: The TLE allowed to Naval Infantry has been split between Russia and Ukraine as follows:

	Russia	Ukraine
Tanks	120	nil
ACV	583	265
Artillery	186	48

The division of land-based maritime aircraft, Coastal Defence Forces and Naval Infantry has been agreed, with all elements of these forces in the Black Sea Fleet going to Ukraine, before any agreement on how the ships of the Fleet should be split has been reached.

The Tashkent Declaration failed to address two minor matters regarding exceptions to TLE limits:

a) Each state is permitted to have up to 1,000 AIFV (of which no more than 600 may be in the flanking area) held by organizations designed and structured to perform peacetime internal security functions. There has been no apportionment of this category of AIFV, and it is possible that newly independent states could argue that they are each entitled to 1,000 more AIFV (600 only in the case of Armenia, Azerbaijan, Georgia and Moldova).

b) Each state may retain no more than 550 trainer versions of combat aircraft (of which no more than 130 can be MiG-25U) so long as these have been totally disarmed according to a laid down procedure which includes the removal of sections of electric circuits. It could be argued that circuits could be replaced and aircraft rearmed far quicker and at much less cost than building new aircraft. There has been no apportionment of combat trainer aircraft.

Some consider CFE to have been overtaken by events and to have little purpose, given the changes that have taken place in eastern Europe. In the new circumstances many states will field far less TLE than allowed by CFE, certainly in active units. However, the cost of destroying large numbers of TLE may result in some states maintaining their full quota, albeit with many TLE in store.

TLE reduction is not the only purpose of CFE, however. Information exchange and inspection are two valuable confidence- and security-building measures (CSBM) in themselves, which, when coupled with CSCE CSBM (such as allowing observers at major exercises), and with 'Open Skies' observation flights, provide a very real degree of transparency. For those who still view Russia as a potential source of external conflict, inspection and CSBM will greatly aid intelligence collection. For intelligence on Soviet forces, NATO relied heavily on observation of the Western Group of Forces in Germany, particularly for information on new types of weapons, changes to unit organization, operating procedures and combat capability.

Personnel Strength of Conventional Armed Forces in Europe

The main significance of the Concluding Act signed at Helsinki is that it removed the situation of singularity imposed on Germany by the 'Two-plus-Four' Treaty, which laid down personnel strength limits for the German armed forces. All other signatories of the CFE Treaty have now declared personnel limits, agreed what types of forces are covered by those limits, and agreed to a number of measures concerning: information exchange, verification, intended unit strength increases and unit resubordination. States intending to revise their personnel limits upwards must notify all other participating states which can raise an objection and request an extraordinary conference to examine the intended revision.

The limit applies to all full-time military personnel serving in the ATTU with:

- Ground Forces (including air defence units).
- Air and Air Defence units.
- Central HQ, command and staff elements and centrally-controlled units and other organizations, including rear services but excluding naval personnel serving with these units.
- Land-based naval formations and units holding TLE or land-based naval aircraft.
- Other formations and units which hold TLE.

In addition, reserve personnel who have completed their initial training and are called up for a continuous period of more than 90 days are subject to the limit.

The following personnel, even if they fall into any of the categories listed above, are not included within the scope of the limitation:

– Internal security organizations.
– Transitees who remain in the ATTU for no more than seven days.
– Those serving under UN command.

The main military forces excluded from the personnel limit are therefore:

– Navies, although personnel in Coastal Defence, Naval Infantry (marines) and land-based aviation units are subject to the limit.
– Strategic Rocket Forces.

The personnel limits agreed are:

Armenia[a]		Germany	345,000	Poland	234,000
Azerbaijan[a]		Greece	158,621	Portugal	75,000
Belgium	70,000	Hungary	100,000	Romania	230,248
Bulgaria	104,000	Iceland	0	Russia	1,450,000
Byelarus	100,000	Italy	315,000	Spain	300,000
Canada	10,660	Kazakhstan	0	Turkey	530,000
Czechoslovakia	140,000	Luxembourg	900	Ukraine	450,000
Denmark	39,000	Moldova[a]		UK	260,000
France	325,000	Netherlands	80,000	US	250,000
Georgia[a]		Norway	32,000		

[a] These countries have not yet declared their personnel limit.

The provisions for information exchange on personnel strength are very comprehensive and will reveal more data than the information exchanges required by either CFE or the CSCE Vienna Document. Disclosure of manpower strengths will reveal the status (active, 50% strength, reserve etc.) of communications, support and logistic units and will help in forming assessments of readiness for war. Ground-based elements of air defence forces (SAM and anti-aircraft artillery separate from ground force formations) will be included for the first time, but only at the level above division or equivalent level (but no details of their armament or deployment will be given). Personnel strengths must also be exchanged on forces not covered by the Treaty limit: organizations designed and structured for peacetime internal security and those serving under command of the UN.

Three measures under the heading 'Stabilizing Measures' have been introduced. Increases in personnel strength of 1,000 or more planned for a brigade/regiment, or 500 for a wing/air regiment are to be notified at least 42 days before the increase takes place. Forty-eight days' notice of the call up of more than 35,000 reserve personnel by any state must be given, but in the case of emergency situations, notice need only be given on the day the 35,000 limit is exceeded. The notification must include: i) the total number to be called up and the number who will be recalled for more than 90 days; ii) a general description of the purpose of the call-up; iii) the planned start and end dates of the period; iv) the designation and location of any division or equivalent level formation to which more than 7,000 personnel will be called up, and of any army/army corps or equivalent level to which more than 9,000 will be called up. The resubordination of units whose personnel are subject to the manpower limit to organizations whose personnel are not subject to limitation must be notified before the resubordination takes place. There is also provision for verification of personnel numbers which will take place at the same time as normal CFE inspections of Objects of Verification (OOVs)

The Concluding Act is much less significant than the main CFE Treaty. The use of manpower is viewed quite differently by many states. Those with purely volunteer forces husband this expensive asset carefully and employ large numbers of civilians to carry out tasks often undertaken by conscripts in other armies. With the possible exception of Russia, it is unlikely that any state will maintain the number of men it is allowed.

Treaty on 'Open Skies'

The Treaty on 'Open Skies' which allows for observation flights to be made over the territory of other treaty signatories was signed in Helsinki on 24 March 1992. All members of NATO signed, as did the five former Warsaw Pact East European states. Byelarus, Georgia, Russia and Ukraine are the only republics of the former Soviet Union to have signed the Treaty so far. Belgium, the Netherlands and Luxembourg have opted (as allowed by the Treaty) to be considered as a single state party (Benelux), as have Russia and Byelarus. The Treaty is open to signature by the remaining republics of the former Soviet Union at any time before or after the Treaty enters into force. Other participating CSCE states may apply for accession during the first six months the Treaty is in force. After that accession is open to any state, subject to the approval of the Open Skies Consultative Commission.

The essence of the Treaty is that each state party is obliged to accept a number of observation flights over its territory in accordance with the quotas laid down in the Treaty (for example the US must accept 42 flights annually, France 12 and Portugal only two), and may make a similar number of flights over other state's territory. Each state may make the same number of flights over the territory of another state as that state can conduct over it (but it is not mandatory to have to do so). Each year a distribution of flights which can be made by each state is agreed to; the distribution for the nine months remaining of 1992 is shown as an Annex to the Treaty (for example: Romania may make one flight over Bulgaria, Greece, Hungary and Ukraine, while Poland must accept flights made by the Benelux countries, Canada, Norway and Ukraine).

Each state has nominated a number of 'Open Skies' airfields from which observation flights may start. The length of the flight allowed is laid down for each airfield and reflects the size of the overflown state's land mass (for example, flights of 4,900km may be made from Washington-Dulles, US, but only of 900km from Timisoara, Romania).

The sensors which may be used during observation flights are restricted to the following:

- Optical panoramic and framing cameras: only one panoramic camera, one vertically mounted and two obliquely-mounted frame cameras may be used. A ground resolution of no better than 30cm is allowed, using black and white film only.
- Video camera providing a ground resolution of no better than 30cm recording on magnetic tape. Real-time display in the observation aircraft is permitted.
- A single infra-red line scan device giving a ground resolution of no better than 50cm employing black and white film or magnetic tape.
- A single sideways-looking synthetic aperture radar capable of looking from either side of the aircraft, but not both simultaneously. A ground resolution of no better than 3m (calculated by the impulse response method) is permitted. Recording to be on magnetic tape.

All states have the right to request copies of the data collected by sensors during any observation flight.

At least 72 hours' warning of the intention to conduct an observation flight must be given. The observed party has the right to provide the observation aircraft if it wishes. If the observing party is providing the aircraft, then the observed party has the right to make a pre-flight inspection of the aircraft and its sensors.

The Treaty is a major confidence- and security-building measure. It is the first CSBM to have been agreed to which covers territory outside the CSCE zone (the Atlantic to the Urals) in that all Canadian, US and Russian territory is open to over-flight. It is the first treaty of its kind which will be open to states not participating in CSCE. It could act as a model for similar treaties in other areas of tension – the Middle East or India/Pakistan for instance.

Conventional Forces in Europe

Manpower and TLE: current holdings and CFE limits of the forces of the CFE signatories

Country	Manpower		Tanks[a]		ACV[a]		Arty[a]		Attack Hel		Combat Aircraft[b]	
	Holding	Limit	Holding	Limit	Holding	Limit	Holding	Limit	Holding	Limit	Holding	Limit
Armenia[c]	–		250	220	640	220	350	285	7	50	0	100
Azerbaijan[c]	–		400	220	1,260	220	470	285	14	50	120	100
Byelarus	125,000	100,000	1,850	1,800	3,870	2,600	1,393	1,615	80	80	617	260
Georgia[c]	–		850	220	1,160	220	370	285	48	50	240	100
Moldova[c]	–		230	210	300	210	330	250	0	50	30[d]	50
Russia[e]	1,536,000	1,450,000	11,000	6,400	18,300	11,480	9,200	6,415	710	890	3,950	3,450
Ukraine	230,000	450,000	6,300	4,080	6,170	5,050	3,080	4,040	240	330	1,380	1,090
Bulgaria	97,000	104,000	2,100	1,475	2,053	2,000	2,129	1,750	44	67	259	235
Czechoslovakia	145,000	140,000	3,208	1,435	4,286	2,050	3,414	1,150	56	75	402	345
Hungary	80,800	100,000	1,357	835	1,809	1,700	1,040	810	39	108	134	180
Poland	281,400	234,000	2,850	1,730	2,253	2,150	2,316	1,610	31	130	509	460
Romania	187,000	230,248	2,875	1,375	3,206	2,100	4,009	1,475	220	120	486	430
Belgium	71,300	70,000	359	334	2,009	1,099	376	320	0	46	196	232
Canada	5,100	10,660	77	77	277	277	38	38	12	13	45	90
Denmark	24,300	39,000	499	353	316	316	553	553	0	12	106	106
France	330,400	325,000	1,343	1,306	3,843	3,820	1,266	1,292	400	352	808	800
Germany	411,800	345,000	7,090	4,166	7,700	3,446	4,592	2,705	254	306	989	900
Greece	139,800	158,621	1,879	1,735	1,772	2,534	1,908	1,878	0	18	458	650
Italy	306,000	315,000	1,220	1,348	3,345	3,339	1,952	1,955	157	142	537	650
Netherlands	76,000	80,000	913	743	1,467	1,080	824	607	90	69	188	230
Norway	25,400	32,000	211	170	134	225	527	527	0	0	94	100
Portugal	45,500	75,000	129	300	317	430	306	450	0	26	83	160
Spain	173,200	300,000	794	794	1,182	1,588	1,355	1,310	28	71	207	310
Turkey[f]	512,000	530,000	2,800	2,795	1,650	3,120	3,250	3,523	0	43	400	750
UK	222,500	260,000	1,198	1,015	3,136	3,176	639	636	341	384	721	900
US	182,100	250,000	4,900	4,006	4,944	5,372	2,219	2,492	240	518	342	784

Notes:

a Incl TLE with land-based maritime forces (Marines, Naval Inf etc.).
b Does not incl land-based maritime aircraft for which a separate limit has been set.
c These countries have not yet declared their personnel limit, nor is it possible to assess accurately their full-time manpower. TLE holdings are still under Russian command; some may be handed over, some withdrawn.
d These aircraft are under Moldovan command.
e Incl TLE in Armenia, Azerbaijan, Georgia and Moldova.
f Manpower figure is for all Turkey, TLE is for that in ATTU zone only.

CIS Summit Meetings – Agreements and List of Signatories

Date	Place	Title	Armenia	Azerbaijan	Byelarus	Kazakhstan	Kyrgyzstan	Moldova	Russia	Tajikistan	Turkmenistan	Ukraine	Uzbekistan
1991													
21 Dec	Alma-Ata	Protocol on Commonwealth of Independent States	✓	✓	✓	✓	✓	✓	✓	✓	✓	✓	✓
21 Dec	Alma-Ata	Declaration Agreeing to Single Control of Nuclear Weapons	✓	✓	✓	✓	✓	✓	✓	✓	✓	✓	✓
22 Dec	Alma-Ata	Declaration on Nuclear Armaments	✓	✓	✓	✓	✓	✓	✓	✓	✓	✓	✓
30 Dec	Minsk	Agreement on Joint Research and Use of Space	✓	✓	✓	✓	✓	✓	✓	✓	✓	✓	✓
30 Dec	Minsk	Agreement on Armed Forces and Border Troops	✓	✓[a]	✓	✓	✓	✓	✓	✓	✓	✓	✓
30 Dec	Minsk	Agreement on Strategic Forces	✓	✓[b]	✓	✓	✓	✓	✓	✓	✓	✓	✓
30 Dec	Minsk	Agreement on Council of Heads of State and Government	✓	✓	✓	✓	✓	✓	✓	✓	✓	✓	✓
1992													
14 Feb	Minsk	Agreement on Status of Strategic Forces	✓	✓	✓	✓[c]	✓		✓	✓	✓	✓[d]	✓
14 Feb	Minsk	Agreement on General Purpose Forces for the Transitional Period	✓	✓	✓	✓	✓		✓	✓	✓		✓
14 Feb	Minsk	Agreement on Social and Legal Safeguards for Servicemen	✓	✓	✓	✓	✓	✓	✓	✓	✓		✓
14 Feb	Minsk	Agreement on Material Provision for Armed Forces	✓	✓	✓	✓	✓	✓	✓	✓	✓		✓
14 Feb	Minsk	Agreement on Single Defence Budget	✓	✓[e]	✓	✓	✓	✓	✓	✓	✓	✓[e]	✓
20 Mar	Kiev	Agreement on CIS Peacekeeping Force	✓	✓	✓	✓	✓	✓	✓	✓	✓	✓[f]	✓
20 Mar	Kiev	Agreement on Status of General Purpose Forces	✓	✓	✓	✓	✓		✓	✓	✓		✓
20 Mar	Kiev	Agreement on Maintaining Supplies to the CIS Armed Forces	✓	✓	✓	✓	✓	✓[g]	✓	✓	✓		✓
20 Mar	Kiev	Agreement on the Protection of State Frontiers	✓	✓	✓	✓	✓		✓	✓	✓	✓[h]	✓
20 Mar	Kiev	Declaration on the Non-Use of Force or Threat of its Use	✓	✓	✓	✓	✓	✓	✓	✓	✓	✓	✓
20 Mar	Kiev	Decision and Status on the Supreme Command of the Joint Armed Forces of the CIS	✓	✓	✓	✓	✓	✓	✓	✓	✓		✓
20 Mar	Kiev	Agreement on the Status of CIS Frontier Forces	✓		✓	✓	✓	✓	✓	✓	✓		✓
20 Mar	Kiev	Resolution and Provision on the Unified Frontier Forces Command	✓		✓	✓	✓	✓	✓	✓	✓		✓
15 May	Tashkent	Treaty on Collective Security	✓			✓	✓		✓	✓			✓
15 May	Tashkent	Agreement on Chemical Weapons	✓	✓		✓	✓		✓	✓	✓	✓	✓
15 May	Tashkent	Statement on Cutting Armed Forces	✓	✓		✓	✓		✓	✓	✓	✓	✓
15 May	Tashkent	Joint Declaration confirming adherence to CFE Treaty[i]	✓	✓		✓	✓		✓	✓	✓	✓	✓

[a] Azerbaijan qualified its agreement with 'the compulsory completion within a two month period of the handover of general purpose armed forces to the Azerbaijan Republic'.

[b] Azerbaijan qualified its agreement with 'the exception of financing'.

[c] Kazakhstan qualified its agreement with 'an agreement on proving [testing] grounds shall be concluded with the Republic of Kazakhstan'.

[d] Ukraine qualified its agreement by 'except for Article 2 item 2 (which refers to the security of financing)'.

[e] Azerbaijan and Ukraine are to assume the financing solely of the upkeep of strategic forces on their territory.

[f] Ukraine qualified its agreement by 'in each specific case the decision on participation of Ukraine is taken by the Supreme Soviet of Ukraine'.

[g] Moldova qualified its agreement by 'Moldova resolves the issues expounded in the present treaty only on a bilateral basis'.

[h] Ukraine signed separate versions of these articles: 'the state borders of CIS states are of identical status for the whole of their length'; 'collaboration by CIS border troops and member states' own border troops is implemented on the basis of separate agreements'.

[i] Georgia is not a member of the CIS but signed the Joint Declaration.

Extracts from Key Agreements reached at CIS Summit Meetings

Alma-Ata, 21 December 1991

Protocol to the Agreement on the Creation of the Commonwealth of Independent States and Alma Ata Declaration: 'Recognizes each other's territorial integrity and the inviolability of existing borders'; 'allied command of military-strategic forces and a single control over nuclear weapons will be preserved'; 'the Union of the Soviet Socialist Republics ceases to exist'.

Declaration on Nuclear Armaments: 'Confirm the obligation not to be the first to use nuclear weapons'; 'until nuclear weapons have been completely eliminated on the territory of Byelarus and Ukraine, decisions on the need to use them are taken, by agreement with heads of the member states of the Agreement, by the President of Russia'; 'Byelarus and Ukraine undertake to join the 1968 nuclear non-proliferation treaty as non-nuclear states'; 'Byelarus, Kazakhstan and Ukraine will ensure the withdrawal of tactical nuclear weapons to central factory premises for dismantling under joint supervision'.

Minsk, 30 December 1991

Agreement on Armed Forces and Border Troops: 'confirm member-states legitimate right to set up their own armed forces'; 'to examine and settle, jointly with the CinC of the armed forces, within two months, the issue of the procedure for controlling general-purpose forces'; 'instruct the CinC of Border Troops to work out, within two months, a mechanism for the activity of Border Troops'.

Agreement on Strategic Forces: 'the term "strategic forces" means groupings, formations, units, institutions and training institutes for the strategic missile forces, for the air force, for the navy and for the air defences; the directorates of the Space Command and of airborne troops and of strategic and operational intelligence'; 'recognise the need for joint command of strategic forces and for maintaining unified control of nuclear weapons and other types of weapons of mass destruction'.

Minsk, 14 February 1992

Agreement on the Status of Strategic Forces: 'Any member state of the CIS regardless of whether military formations and facilities are based on its territory may be party to the agreement'; 'Strategic Forces are designed to ensure the security of all state-parties to this agreement and shall be maintained through fixed contributions by the said states'; 'each agrees to the permanent or temporary stationing of military formations and facilities of strategic forces in basing areas as at the moment of signing'; 'the command of the Strategic Forces shall: work out plans of combat use, organise activities to ensure security of nuclear weapons in the regions of their deployment and on the routes of their movement, carry out measures to comply with the international treaties on nuclear arms and other weapons of mass destruction'.

Agreement on General Purpose Forces for the Transitional Period: 'the parties shall form joint General Purpose Forces (which means formations, units etc not belonging to the strategic forces of the CIS as well as the armed forces of the parties directly subordinated with their consent to the General Command of the Joint Armed Forces)'; 'each party shall have the right to withdraw from it after giving no less than six months notice'.

Kiev, 20 March 1992

Agreement on the Protection of State Frontiers: included definitions: 'state borders of member states of the CIS are the sections of state borders of CIS member states with states that are not in the Commonwealth'; 'own border troops are formations of border troops belonging to a CIS member state'; 'Commonwealth border troops are formations of border troops which are not own border troops'.

Tashkent, 15 May 1992

Treaty on Collective Security: 'confirm their commitment to refrain from the use or threat of force'; 'if one of the participating states is subjected to aggression by any state or group of states, this shall be perceived as aggression against all participating states'; 'all other participating states shall give the necessary assistance, including military assistance'.

Peacekeeping Operations

UNITED NATIONS

United Nations Truce Supervision Organization (UNTSO)

Mission: Established in June 1948 to assist the Mediator and the Truce Commission in supervising the observance of the truce in Palestine called for by the Security Council. At present, UNTSO assists and cooperates with UNDOF and UNIFIL in the performance of their tasks; Military Observers are stationed in Beirut, South Lebanon, Sinai, Jordan, Israel and Syria.

Strength: 300

Composition: Observers from Argentina, Australia, Austria, Belgium, Canada, Chile, China, Denmark, Finland, France, Ireland, Italy, Netherlands, New Zealand, Norway, Russia, Sweden, Switzerland, US.

United Nations Military Observer Group in India and Pakistan (UNMOGIP)

Mission: To supervise, in the State of Jammu and Kashmir, the cease-fire between India and Pakistan along the Line of Control.

Strength: 35

Composition: Observers from Belgium, Chile, Denmark, Finland, Italy, Norway, Sweden, Uruguay.

United Nations Peacekeeping Force in Cyprus (UNFICYP)

Mission: Established in 1964 to use its best efforts to prevent the recurrence of fighting and, as necessary, to contribute to the maintenance and restoration of law and order and a return to normal conditions. Since the hostilities of 1974, this has included supervising the cease-fire and maintaining a buffer zone between the lines of the Cyprus National Guard and of the Turkish and Turkish-Cypriot forces.

Strength: 2,200

Composition: Units from Austria (Infantry), Canada (Infantry), Denmark (Infantry), UK (Infantry, Helicopters, Logistics), Staff Officers from Finland, Ireland and Sweden. Civil Police detachments from Australia, Sweden.

United Nations Disengagement Observer Force (UNDOF)

Mission: To supervise the cease-fire between Israel and Syria, and to establish an area of separation and verify troop levels, as provided in the Agreement on Disengagement between Israeli and Syrian Forces of 31 May 1974.

Strength: 1,300

Composition: Units from Austria (Infantry), Canada (Logistics), Finland (Infantry), Poland (Logistics).

United Nations Interim Force in Lebanon (UNIFIL)

Mission: Established in 1978 to confirm the withdrawal of Israeli forces from southern Lebanon, to restore international peace and security and to assist the government of Lebanon in ensuring the return of its effective authority in the area.

Strength: 5,900

Composition: Units from Fiji (Infantry), Finland (Infantry), France (Logistics), Ghana (Infantry), Ireland (Infantry, Administration), Italy (Helicopters), Nepal (Infantry), Norway (Infantry, Maintenance), Poland (Medical), Sweden (Logistics).

United Nations Observer Group in Central America (ONUCA)

Mission: ONUCA was established in 1989 for the on-site verification of the security undertakings contained in the Guatemala Agreement (Esquipulas II) of 7 August 1987. These include the ending of aid to irregular forces and use of the territory of a state for attacking others. In March 1990 the mission was expanded to include taking delivery of and destroying arms and ammunition of the Nicaraguan

Resistance as they demobilized. ONUCA operates in El Salvador, Honduras and Nicaragua. Mission completed on 16 January 1992 and resources transferred to ONUSAL.

United Nations Observer Mission in El Salvador (ONUSAL)

Mission: ONUSAL became operational in July 1991 to monitor agreements concluded between the government and the FMLN. A peace agreement was signed between the government and the FMLN in January 1992 under which both sides would report their full strength of troops and weapons to ONUSAL, which would also dispose of FMLN weapons as they were handed over during demobilization. The UN disbanded ONUCA and transferred its manpower and equipment to ONUSAL. ONUSAL is to monitor the cease-fire (military observers), monitor human rights violations (civilian observers), and establish a police force on democratic lines.

Strength: 291

Composition: Observers from Brazil, Canada, Colombia, Ecuador, India, Ireland, Spain, Sweden and Venezuela.

United Nations Iraq/Kuwait Observer Mission (UNIKOM)

Mission: Established in April 1991 following the recapture of Kuwait from Iraq by Coalition Forces. Its mandate is to monitor the Khor Abdullah and a demilitarized zone (DMZ) extending 10km into Iraq and 5km into Kuwait from the agreed boundary between the two (Iraq/Kuwait Restoration of Friendly Relations, Recognition and Related Matters dated 4 October 1963). It is to deter violations of the boundary and to observe hostile or potentially hostile actions.

Composition: Units from Canada (Engineers), Chile (Air Wing), Denmark (Administrative Staff), Norway (Medical). Observers from Argentina, Austria, Bangladesh, Canada, China, Denmark, Fiji, Finland, France, Ghana, Greece, Hungary, India, Indonesia, Ireland, Italy, Kenya, Malaysia, Nigeria, Norway, Pakistan, Poland, Romania, Russia, Senegal, Singapore, Sweden, Thailand, Turkey, UK, Uruguay, US, Venezuela.

Security: Infantry companies from UNFICYP (Austria and Denmark) and UNIFIL (Fiji, Ghana, Nepal) provided security during the initial stages. All companies were withdrawn by the end of June 1991.

United Nations Mission for the Referendum in Western Sahara (MINURSO)

Established in April 1991 to supervise a referendum to choose between independence and integration into Morocco. A transitional period would begin with the coming into effect of a cease-fire and end when the referendum results were announced. Although a cease-fire came into effect on 6 September 1991, the transitional period did not begin as the UN had been unable to complete its registration of eligible voters. It is now apparent that, despite earlier agreements, substantial areas of difference between the two sides remain. MINURSO is therefore currently restricted to verifying the cease-fire.

Strength: 343

Composition: Units from Australia (signals), Canada (movement control), Switzerland (civilian medical). Observers from Argentina, Australia, Austria, Bangladesh, Canada, China, Egypt, France, Ghana, Greece, Guinea, Ireland, Italy, Kenya, Malaysia, Nigeria, Pakistan, Peru, Poland, Russia, Tunisia, UK, US, Venezuela.

United Nations Angola Verification Mission II (UNAVEM II)

Mission: Established June 1991. To verify the cease-fire as set out in the Peace Accords, agreed to by the government of Angola and UNITA, and to monitor the Angolan police as set out in the Protocol of Estoril.

Strength: 350 military and 90 police observers

Composition: Observers from Algeria, Argentina, Brazil, Canada, Congo, Czechoslovakia, Egypt, Guinea-Bissau, Hungary, India, Ireland, Jordan, Malaysia, Morocco, Netherlands, Nigeria, Norway, Senegal, Singapore, Spain, Sweden, Yugoslavia, Zimbabwe.

United Nations Transitional Authority in Cambodia (UNTAC)

Mission: A cease-fire in Cambodia entered into effect with the signing of an agreement on a comprehensive political settlement of the Cambodian conflict on 23 October 1991. Prior to the establishment of UNTAC, which became operational on 15 March 1992, the UN had established a small mission, the United Nations Advanced Mission in Cambodia (UNAMIC) to assist the parties in maintaining the cease-fire and provide training in mine clearance. UNTAC consists of seven distinct components: Human Rights (fostering an environment in which respect for human rights is ensured including a civic education programme); Electoral (to establish an electoral law, to carry out the registration of voters, and to supervise elections which are currently scheduled for April–May 1993); Civil Administration (UNTAC will have 'direct control' in the fields of foreign affairs, national defence, finance, public security and information. UNTAC will have a consultative role in areas such as education, communications and health); Police (supervision to ensure that law and order are maintained and human rights fully protected); Repatriation and Resettlement (organization of the return of an estimated 360,000 refugees within nine months including transportation, transit camp facilities, provision of agricultural land and assistance for one year.) Rehabilitation (coordination of international assistance, assistance with food, health, housing for all Cambodians, resettlement of internally displaced persons (ε170,000) and demobilized troops (ε150,000) and restoration of essential infrastructure). The seventh military component of UNTAC's mandate includes: Verification of the withdrawal and non-return of all foreign forces; Supervision of the cease-fire including the regroupment, disarmament and demobilization of up to 450,000 soldiers of the four factions; Weapons control; Assistance with mine clearance.

Strength: 14,300 (to rise to 15,900 during the demobilization phase)

Composition: Infantry Battalions from: Bangladesh, Bulgaria, France, Ghana, India, Indonesia, Malaysia, Netherlands, Pakistan, Tunisia and Uruguay. Military Observers from: Algeria, Argentina, Austria, Bangladesh, Belgium, Bulgaria, Cameroon, China, France, Ghana, India, Indonesia, Ireland, Malaysia, New Zealand, Pakistan, Poland, Russia, Senegal, Tunisia, UK and US. Logistic and Support Units: from Australia and New Zealand (Communications), China, France, Poland and Thailand (Engineers), France and Netherlands (Air), Canada, Chile, New Zealand, Philippines, Russia, UK and Uruguay (Naval), Germany and India (Medical), and Australia, Canada, Netherlands, Pakistan and Poland (Logistics).

United Nations Protection Force (UNPROFOR)

Mission: Established in March 1992. UNPROFOR, which includes military, police and civilian components, is deployed in three 'United Nations Protected Areas' (UNPAs) in Croatia to create the conditions of peace and security required to permit the negotiations of an overall political settlement of the Yugoslav crisis. UNPROFOR is responsible for ensuring that the UNPAs are demilitarized through the withdrawal or disbandment of all armed forces in them, and that all persons residing in them are protected from fear of armed attack. To this end, UNPROFOR is authorized to control access to the UNPAs, to ensure that they remain demilitarized, and to monitor the functioning of the local police there to help ensure non-discrimination and the protection of human rights. Outside the UNPAs, UNPROFOR Military Observers will verify the withdrawal of all Yugoslav National Army (JNA) and Serbian forces from Croatia, other than those disbanded and demobilized there. In Bosnia-Herzegovina, UNPROFOR will lend its good offices to help defuse inter-communal tension and conflict, and will attempt to secure the reopening of Sarajevo airport to facilitate the delivery of humanitarian supplies. The Canadian battalion deployed to Sarajevo from Croatia is to be replaced shortly by other units.

Strength: 9,700 (authorized 13,870 military and police, including 12 infantry battalions)

Composition: Units and observers from: Argentina (inf bn), Belgium (inf bn), Canada (inf bn and engr), Czechoslovakia (inf bn), Denmark (inf bn), Finland (construction bn), France (inf bn, log·bn), Jordan (inf bn), Kenya (inf bn), Luxembourg (inf pl), Netherlands (signals), Nepal (inf bn), Nigeria (inf bn), Norway (movement control), Poland (inf bn), Russia (inf (airborne) bn), Sweden (HQ/staff coy), UK (medical unit) and observers from Australia, Bangladesh, Colombia, Egypt, Ghana, India, Ireland, New Zealand, Portugal, Thailand, Venezuela.
Additional for Sarajevo airport: 1,500: inf bn from Egypt, France and Ukraine.

United Nations Operation in Somalia (UNOSOM)

Mission: The UN Security Council adopted Resolution 733 on 23 January 1992 which called on all parties to cease hostilities, and which imposed a general and complete embargo on the delivery of army and military equipment to Somalia. Following the visit of a UN team to Mogadishu, the Security Council, by its Resolution 751 on 21 April 1992, decided to establish an operation to monitor the cease-fire and to provide protection for relief supply convoys. ONOSOM would comprise 50 observers and an infantry battalion. Observers started to deploy on 5 July 1992, but the deployment of a battalion is not yet acceptable to the parties.

Composition: Observers from Bangladesh, Czechoslovakia, Egypt, Fiji, Finland, Indonesia, Jordan, Morocco, Pakistan, Zimbabwe. Inf bn on standby from Pakistan.

OTHERS

Multinational Force and Observers (MFO)

Mission: Established in August 1981 following the peace treaty between Israel and Egypt and the subsequent withdrawal of Israeli forces from Sinai. Its task is to verify the level of forces in the zones in which forces are limited by the treaty. Ensure freedom of navigation through the Strait of Tiran.

Strength: 2,600

Composition: Units from Colombia (Infantry), Fiji (Infantry), France (Fixed-Wing Aviation), Italy (Naval Coastal Patrol), Netherlands (Signals and Military Police), New Zealand (Training), Uruguay (Engineers and Transport), UK (Headquarters staff), US (Infantry and Logistics). Staff Officers from Canada and Norway.

Neutral Nations' Supervisory Commission for Korea (NNSC)

Mission: Established by the Armistice Agreement in July 1953 at the end of the Korean War. The Commission is to supervise, observe, inspect and investigate the armistice and to report on these activities to the Military Armistice Commission. Today its main role is to maintain and improve relations between both sides and thus keep open a channel of communications.

Composition: Diplomats and military officers from Czechoslovakia, Poland, Sweden and Switzerland.

Designations of Aircraft and Helicopters listed
in *The Military Balance*

The use of [square brackets] shows the type from which a variant was derived. 'Q-5 . . . [MiG-19]' indicates that the design of the Q-5 was based on that of the MiG-19.

(Parentheses) indicate an alternative name by which an aircraft is known – sometimes in another version. 'L-188 . . . *Electra* (P-3 *Orion*)' shows that in another version the

Lockheed Type 188 *Electra* is known as the P-3 *Orion*.

Names given in 'quotation marks' are NATO reporting names – e.g. 'Su-27 . . . *Flanker*' '.

When no information is listed under 'Origin' or 'Maker', take the primary reference given under 'Name/designation' and look it up under 'Type'.

Type	Name/designation	Origin	Maker
AIRCRAFT			
A-3	*Skywarrior*	US	Douglas
A-4	*Skyhawk*	US	MD
A-5	*Fantan*	China	Nanchang
A-6	*Intruder*	US	Grumman
A-7	*Corsair* II	US	LTV
A-10	*Thunderbolt*	US	Fairchild
A-36	*Halcón* (C-101)		
A-37	*Dragonfly*	US	Cessna
AC-130	(C-130)		
AC-47	(C-47)		
Airtourer		NZ	Victa
AJ-37	(J-37)		
Ajeet	(Folland *Gnat*)	India/UK	HAL
Alizé		France	Breguet
Alpha Jet		France/Ge	Dassault/Breguet/Dornier
AM-3	*Bosbok* (C-4M)	Italy	Aermacchi
An-2	'Colt'	Russia	Antonov
An-12	'Cub'	Russia	Antonov
An-14	'Clod'	Russia	Antonov
An-22	'Cock'	Russia	Antonov
An-24	'Coke'	Russia	Antonov
An-26	'Curl'	Russia	Antonov
An-30	'Clank'	Russia	Antonov
An-32	'Cline'	Russia	Antonov
An-124	'Condor' (*Ruslan*)	Russia	Antonov
Andover	[HS-748]		
Atlantic	(*Atlantique*)	France	Dassault/Breguet
AS-202	*Bravo*	Switz	FFA
AT-3		Taiwan	AIDC
AT-6	(T-6)		
AT-11		US	Beech
AT-26	EMB-326		
AT-33	(T-33)		
AU-23	*Peacemaker* [PC-6B]	US	Fairchild
AV-8	*Harrier* II	US/UK	MD/BAe
Aztec	PA-23	US	Piper
B-1		US	Rockwell
B-52	*Stratofortress*	US	Boeing
BAC-111		UK	BAe
BAC-167	*Strikemaster*	UK	BAe
BAe-146		UK	BAe
BAe-748	(HS-748)		
Baron	(T-42)		
Be-6	'Madge'	Russia	Beriev
Be-12	'Mail' (*Tchaika*)	Russia	Beriev
Beech 50	*Twin Bonanza*	US	Beech
Beech 95	*Travel Air*	US	Beech
BN-2	*Islander, Defender, Trislander*	UK	Britten-Norman
Boeing 707		US	Boeing
Boeing 727		US	Boeing
Boeing 737		US	Boeing
Boeing 747		US	Boeing
Bonanza		US	Beech
Bronco	(OV-10)		
Buccaneer		UK	BAe
Bulldog		UK	BAe
C-1		Japan	Kawasaki
C-2	*Greyhound*	US	Grumman
C-4M	*Kudu* (AM-3)	S. Africa	Atlas
C-5	*Galaxy*	US	Lockheed
C-7	DHC-7		
C-9	*Nightingale* (DC-9)		
C-12	*Super King Air* (*Huron*)	US	Beech
C-18	[Boeing 707]		
C-20	(*Gulfstream* III)		
C-21	(*Learjet*)		
C-22	(Boeing 727)		
C-23	(*Sherpa*)	UK	Short
C-42	(Neiva *Regente*)	Brazil	Embraer
C-45	*Expeditor*	US	Beech
C-46	*Commando*	US	Curtis
C-47	DC-3 (*Dakota*) (C-117 *Skytrain*)	US	Douglas
C-54	*Skymaster* (DC-4)	US	Douglas
C-91	HS-748		
C-93	HS-125		
C-95	EMB-110		
C-97	EMB-121		
C-101	*Aviojet*	Spain	CASA
C-115	DHC-5	Canada	De Havilland
C-117	(C-47)		
C-118	*Liftmaster* (DC-6)		
C-119	*Packet*	US	Fairchild
C-123	*Provider*	US	Fairchild
C-127	(Do-27)	Spain	CASA
C-130	*Hercules* (L-100)	US	Lockheed
C-131	Convair 440	US	Convair
C-135	[Boeing 707]		
C-137	[Boeing 707]		
C-140	(*Jetstar*)	US	Lockheed
C-141	*Starlifter*	US	Lockheed
C-160		Fr/Ge	Transall
C-212	*Aviocar*	Spain	CASA
C-235		Spain	CASA
CA-25	*Winjeel*	Aust	Commonwealth
Canberra	(B-57)	UK	BAe
CAP-10		France	Mudry
CAP-20		France	Mudry
CAP-230		France	Mudry
Caravelle	SE-210	France	Aérospatiale
CC-109	(Convair 440)	US	Convair
CC-115	DHC-5		

Type	Name/designation	Origin	Maker
CC-117	(*Falcon* 20)		
CC-132	(DHC-7)		
CC-137	(Boeing 707)		
CC-138	(DHC-6)		
CC-144	CL-600/-601	Canada	Canadair
CF-18	F/A-18		
CF-116	F-5		
Cheetah	[*Mirage* III]	S. Africa	Atlas
Cherokee	PA-28	US	Piper
Cheyenne	PA-31T [*Navajo*]	US	Piper
Chieftain	PA-31-350 [*Navajo*]	US	Piper
Chipmunk	DHC-1		
Citabria		US	Champion
Citation	(T-47)	US	Cessna
CJ-5	[Yak-18]	China	
CL-215		Canada	Canadair
CL-44		Canada	Canadair
CL-601	*Challenger*	Canada	Canadair
CM-170	*Magister* [*Tzukit*]	France	Aérospatiale
CM-175	*Zéphyr*	France	Aérospatiale
CN-235		Sp/Indon	CASA/IPTN
Cochise	T-42		
Comanche	PA-24	US	Piper
Commander	*Aero-/Turbo-Commander*	US	Rockwell
Commodore	MS-893	France	Aérospatiale
Corvette	SN-601	France	Aérospatiale
CP-3	P-3 *Orion*		
CP-121	S-2		
CP-140	*Aurora* (P-3 *Orion*)	US	Lockheed
CT-4	*Airtrainer*	NZ	Victa
CT-39	*Sabreliner*	US	Rockwell
CT-114	CL-41 *Tutor*	Canada	Canadair
CT-133	*Silver Star* [T-33]	Canada	Canadair
CT-134	*Musketeer*		
Dagger	(*Nesher*)		
Dakota		US	Piper
Dakota	(C-47)		
DC-3	(C-47)	US	Douglas
DC-4	(C-54)	US	Douglas
DC-6	(C-118)	US	Douglas
DC-7		US	Douglas
DC-8		US	Douglas
DC-9		US	MD
Deepak	(HT-32)		
Defender	BN-2		
DH-100	*Vampire*	UK	De Havilland
DHC-1	*Chipmunk*	Canada	DHC
DHC-2	*Beaver*	Canada	DHC
DHC-3	*Otter*	Canada	DHC
DHC-4	*Caribou*	Canada	DHC
DHC-5	*Buffalo*	Canada	DHC
DHC-6	*Twin Otter*	Canada	DHC
DHC-7	*Dash-7* (*Ranger*, CC-132)	Canada	DHC
DHC-8		Canada	DHC
Dimona	H-36	Ge	Hoffman
Do-27	(C-127)	Ge	Dornier
Do-28	*Skyservant*	Ge	Dornier
Do-128		Ge	Dornier
Do-228		Ge	Dornier
E-2	*Hawkeye*	US	Grumman
E-3	*Sentry*	US	Boeing
E-4	[Boeing 747]	US	Boeing
E-6	[Boeing 707]		
E-26	T-35A (*Tamiz*)	Chile	Enear
EA-3	[A-3]		
EA-6	*Prowler* [A-6]		
Electra	(L-188)		
EC-130	[C-130]		
EC-135	[Boeing 707]		
EMB-110	*Bandeirante*	Brazil	Embraer
EMB-111	*Maritime Bandeirante*	Brazil	Embraer
EMB-120	*Brasilia*	Brazil	Embraer
EMB-121	*Xingu*	Brazil	Embraer
EMB-312	*Tucano*	Brazil	Embraer
EMB-326	*Xavante* (MB-326)	Brazil	Embraer
EMB-810	[*Seneca*]	Brazil	Embraer
EP-3	(P-3 *Orion*)		
Etendard		France	Dassault
EV-1	(OV-1)		
F-1	[T-2]	Japan	Mitsubishi
F-4	*Phantom*	US	MD
F-5	-A/-B: *Freedom Fighter*, -E/-F: *Tiger* II	US	Northrop
F-5T	JJ-5	China	Shenyang
F-6	J-6		
F-7	J-7		
F-8	J-8		
F-8	*Crusader*	US	Republic
F-14	*Tomcat*	US	Grumman
F-15	*Eagle*	US	MD
F-16	*Fighting Falcon*	US	GD
F-18	[F/A-18]		
F-21	*Kfir*	Israel	IAI
F-27	*Friendship*	Nl	Fokker
F-28	*Fellowship*	Nl	Fokker
F-35	*Draken*	Sweden	SAAB
F-84	*Thunderstreak*	US	Lockheed
F-86	*Sabre*	US	N. American
F-100	*Super Sabre*	US	N. American
F-104	*Starfighter*	US	Lockheed
F-106	*Delta Dart*	US	Convair
F-111		US	GD
F-172	(Cessna 172)	France/US	Reims-Cessna
F/A-18	*Hornet*	US	MD
Falcon	*Mystère-Falcon*		
FB-111	(F-111)		
FH-227	(F-27)	US	Fairchild-Hiller
Flamingo	MBB-233	Ge	MBB
FT-5	JJ-5	China	CAC
FT-6	JJ-6		
FTB-337	[Cessna 337]		
G-91		Italy	Aeritalia
G-222		Italy	Aeritalia
Galaxy	C-5		
Galeb		Yug	SOKO
Gardian	(*Falcon* 20)		
Genet	SF-260W		
GU-25	(*Falcon* 20)		
Guerrier	R-235		
Gulfstream		US	Gulfstream Aviation
Gumhuria	(Bücker 181)	Egypt	Heliopolis Ac
H-5	[Il-28]	China	Harbin
H-6	[Tu-16]	China	Xian
H-36	*Dimona*		

LPD	landing platform(s), dock
LPH	landing platform(s), helicopter
LSD	landing ship(s), dock
LSM	landing ship(s), medium
LST	landing ship(s), tank
lt	light
LWT	light-weight torpedo(es)
m	million(s)
maint	maintenance
MBT	main battle tank(s)
MCC/I/O	mine countermeasures vessel(s), coastal/inshore/offshore
MCMV	mine countermeasures vessel(s)
MCR	Marine Corps Reserve (US)
MD	Military District(s)
mech	mechanized
med	medium
medevec	casualty transport/air ambulance
MEF/B/U	Marine Expeditionary Force(s)/Brigade(s)/Unit(s) (US)
MFO	Multinational Force and Observers
MG	machine gun
MHC/I/O	minehunter(s), coastal/inshore/offshore
MICV	mechanized infantry combat vehicle(s)
mil	military
MIRV	multiple independently-targetable re-entry vehicle(s)
misc	miscellaneous
Mk	mark (model number)
ML	minelayer
mob	mobilization
mod	modified/modification
mor	mortar(s)
mot	motorized
MPS	marine prepositioning squadron(s)
MR	maritime reconnaissance/motor rifle
MRBM	medium-range ballistic missile(s)
MRD	motor rifle division
MRL	multiple rocket launcher(s)
MRR	motor rifle regiment
MRV	multiple re-entry vehicle(s)
MSC/I/O	minesweeper(s), coastal/inshore/offshore
msl	missile(s)
MT	megaton(s)
mtn	mountain
n.a.	not applicable
NBC	nuclear, biological and chemical
NCO	non-commissioned officer
NGF	Northern Group of Forces (Rus)

n.k.	not known
Nl	Netherlands
NMP	net material product
NNSC	Neutral Nations' Supervisory Commission for Korea
No	Norway
NR	Naval Reserve (US)
NRF	Naval Reserve Surface
nuc	nuclear
NWGF	North-Western Group of Forces (Rus)
obs	observation
OCU	operational conversion unit(s)
off	official
OOA	Out of Area
OOV	Objects of Verification
op/ops	operational/operations
org	organized/organization
OTH	over-the-horizon
OTHR	over-the-horizon radar
OTHT	over-the-horizon targeting
para	parachute
pax	passenger(s)/passenger transport aircraft
PCC/I/O	patrol craft, coastal/inshore/offshore
pdr	pounder
PFC/I/O	fast patrol craft, coastal/inshore/offshore
PFM	fast patrol craft, SSM
PFT	fast patrol craft, torpedo
PHM/T	hydrofoil(s), SSM/torpedo
pl	platoon(s)
Pol	Poland
POMCUS	prepositioning of matériel configured to unit sets
Port	Portugal
RAS	replenishment at sea
RCL	recoilless launcher(s)
R&D	research and development
recce	reconnaissance
regt	regiment(s)
RL	rocket launcher(s)
Ro	Romania
ro-ro	roll-on, roll-off
RPV	remotely piloted vehicle(s)
Rus	Russia
RV	re-entry vehicle(s)
SAC	Strategic Air Command (US)
SALT	Strategic Arms Limitation Treaty
SAM	surface-to-air missile(s)
SAR	search and rescue
SDI	Strategic Defense Initiative
SES	surface-effect ship(s)
SF	Special Forces
SIGINT	signals intelligence
sigs	signals
SLBM	submarine-launched ballistic missile(s)
SLCM	sea-launched cruise missile(s)

SLEP	service life extension programme
some	up to
Sov	Soviet
Sp	Spain
SP	self-propelled
spt	support
sqn	squadron(s)
SRAM	short-range attack missile(s)
SRBM	short-range ballistic missile(s)
SS(C/I)	submarine(s) (coastal/inshore)
SSB	ballistic-missile submarine(s)
SSBN	nuclear-fuelled SSB
SSGN	SSN with dedicated non-ballistic missile launchers
SSM	surface-to-surface missile(s)
SSN	nuclear-fuelled submarine(s)
START	Strategic Arms Reduction Talks
STOL	short take-off and landing
STOVL	short take-off, vertical landing
SUGW	surface-to-underwater GW
Sw	Sweden
Switz	Switzerland
sy	security
t	tonnes
TA	Territorial Army (UK)
tac	tactical
TD	tank division
tk	tank(s)
tkr	tanker(s)
TLE	treaty-limited equipment
tps	troop(s)
tpt	transport(s)
tr	trillion
trg	training
TT	torpedo tube(s)
Tu	Turkey
UN	United Nations
(See pp. 247–50 for peacekeeping forces)	
URG	underway replenishment group(s)
USGW	underwater-to-surface GW
USMC	US Marine Corps
UUGW	underwater-to-underwater GW
veh	vehicle(s)
VIP	very important person(s)
VLS	vertical launch system(s)
V/(S)TOL	vertical(/short) take-off and landing
wg	wing(s)
WGF	Western Group of Forces (Rus)
wpn	weapon
Yug	Yugoslavia

Type	Name/designation	Origin	Maker
Orao	IAR-93		
Ouragan		France	Dassault
OV-1	*Mohawk*	US	Rockwell
OV-10	*Bronco*	US	Rockwell
P-2J	[SP-2]	Japan	Kawasaki
P-3		Switz	Pilatus
P-3	*Orion*	US	Lockheed
P-95	EMB-110		
P-149		Italy	Piaggio
P-166		Italy	Piaggio
PA-18	*Super Cub*	US	Piper
PA-23	*Aztec*		
PA-24	*Comanche*	US	Piper
PA-28	*Cherokee*	US	Piper
PA-31	*Navajo*	US	Piper
PA-34	*Seneca*	US	Piper
PA-44	*Seminole*	US	Piper
PBY-5	*Catalina*	US	Consolidated
PC-6	*Porter*	Switz	Pilatus
PC-6A/B	*Turbo Porter*	Switz	Pilatus
PC-7	*Turbo Trainer*	Switz	Pilatus
PC-9		Switz	Pilatus
PD-808		Italy	Piaggio
Pembroke		UK	BAe
Pillán	T-35		
PL-1	*Chien Shou*	Taiwan	AIDC
Porter	PC-6		
PZL-104	*Wilga*	Poland	PZL
PZL-130	*Orlik*	Poland	PZL
Q-5	'Fantan' [MiG-19]	China	Nanchang
Queen Air	(U-8)		
R-160		France	Socata
R-235	*Guerrier*	France	Socata
RC-21	(C-21)		
RC-47	(C-47)		
RC-95	(EMB-110)		
RC-135	[Boeing 707]		
RF-4	(F-4)		
RF-5	(F-5)		
RF-35	(F-35)		
RF-84	(F-84)		
RF-104	(F-104)		
RF-172	(Cessna 172)	France	Reims-Cessna
RG-8A		US	Schweizer
RT-26	(EMB-326)		
RT-33	(T-33)		
RU-21	(King Air)		
RV-1	(OV-1)		
S-2	*Tracker*	US	Grumman
S-3	*Viking*	US	Lockheed
S-208		Italy	SIAI
S-211		Italy	SIAI
Sabreliner	(CT-39)	US	Rockwell
Safari	MFI-15		
Safir	SAAB-91 (SK-50)	Sweden	SAAB
SC-7	*Skyvan*	UK	Short
SE-210	*Caravelle*		
Sea Harrier	(*Harrier*)		
Seascan	IAI-1124		
Searchmaster B/L	N-24		
Seneca	PA-34	US	Piper
	(EMB-810)		
Sentry	(O-2)	US	Summit
SF-37	(J-37)		
SF-260	(SF-260W *Warrior*)	Italy	SIAI
SH-37	(J-37)		
Shackleton		UK	BAe

Type	Name/designation	Origin	Maker
Sherpa	Short 330, C-23		
Short 330		UK	Short
Sierra 200	(*Musketeer*)		
SK-35	(J-35)	Sweden	SAAB
SK-37	(J-37)		
SK-50	(*Safir*)		
SK-60	(SAAB-105)	Sweden	SAAB
SK-61	(*Bulldog*)		
Skyvan		UK	Short
SM-1019		Italy	SIAI
SN-601	*Corvette*		
SNJ	T-6 (Navy)		
SP-2H	*Neptune*	US	Lockheed
SR-71	*Blackbird*	US	Lockheed
Su-7	'Fitter A'	Russia	Sukhoi
Su-15	'Flagon'	Russia	Sukhoi
Su-17/-20/-22	'Fitter'	Russia	Sukhoi
Su-24	'Fencer'	Russia	Sukhoi
Su-25	'Frogfoot'	Russia	Sukhoi
Su-27	'Flanker'	Russia	Sukhoi
Super Etendard		France	Dassault
Super Galeb		Yug	SOKO
Super Mystère		France	Dassault
T-1		Japan	Fuji
T-1A	*Jayhawk*	US	Beech
T-2	*Buckeye*	US	Rockwell
T-2		Japan	Mitsubishi
T-3		Japan	Fuji
T-6	*Texan*	US	N. American
T-17	(*Supporter*, MFI-17)	Sweden	SAAB
T-23	*Uirapurú*	Brazil	Aerotec
T-25	Neiva *Universal*	Brazil	Embraer
T-26	EMB-326		
T-27	*Tucano*	Brazil	Embraer
T-28	*Trojan*	US	N. American
T-33	*Shooting Star*	US	Lockheed
T-34	*Mentor*	US	Beech
T-35	*Pillán* [PA-28]	Chile	Enaer
T-36	(C-101)		
T-37	(A-37)		
T-38	*Talon*	US	Northrop
T-39	(*Sabreliner*)	US	Rockwell
T-41	*Mescalero* (Cessna 172)	US	Cessna
T-42	*Cochise* (*Baron*)	US	Beech
T-43	(Boeing 737)		
T-44	(*King Air*)		
T-47	(*Citation*)		
TB-20	*Trinidad*	France	Aérospatiale
TB-30	*Epsilon*	France	Aérospatiale
TC-45	(C-45, trg)		
T-CH-1		Taiwan	AIDC
Texan	T-6		
TL-1	(KM-2)	Japan	Fuji
Tornado		UK/Ge/It	Panavia
TR-1	[U-2]	US	Lockheed
Travel Air	Beech 95		
Trident		UK	BAe
Trislander	BN-2		
Tristar	L-1011		
TS-8	*Bies*	Poland	PZL
TS-11	*Iskra*	Poland	PZL
Tu-16	'Badger'	Russia	Tupolev
Tu-22	'Blinder'	Russia	Tupolev
Tu-26 (Tu-22M)	'Backfire'	Russia	Tupolev

Type	Name/designation	Origin	Maker
Hkp-4	KV-107		
Hkp-5	Hughes 300		
Hkp-6	AB-206		
Hkp-9	Bo-105		
Hkp-10	AS-332		
HR-12	OH-58		
HSS-1	(S-58)		
HSS-2	(SH-3)		
HT-17	CH-47		
HT-21	AS-332		
HU-1	(UH-1)	Japan/US	Fuji/Bell
HU-8	UH-1B		
HU-10	UH-1H		
HU-18	AB-212		
Hughes 269		US	MD
Hughes 300		US	MD
Hughes 369		US	MD
Hughes 500/520	*Defender*	US	MD
IAR-316/-330	(SA-316/-330)	Ro/France	IAR/Aérospatiale
Ka-25	'Hormone'	Russia	Kamov
Ka-27	'Helix'	Russia	Kamov
KH-4	(Bell 47)	Japan/US	Kawasaki/Bell
KH-300	(Hughes 269)	Japan/US	Kawasaki/MD
KH-500	(Hughes 369)	Japan/US	Kawasaki/MD
Kiowa	OH-58		
KV-107	[CH-46]	Japan/US	Kawasaki/Vertol
Lynx		UK	Westland
MH-6	(AH-6)		
MH-53	(CH-53)		
Mi-1	'Hare'	Russia	Mil
Mi-2	'Hoplite'	Russia	Mil
Mi-4	'Hound'	Russia	Mil
Mi-6	'Hook'	Russia	Mil
Mi-8	'Hip'	Russia	Mil
Mi-14	'Haze'	Russia	Mil
Mi-17	'Hip'	Russia	Mil
Mi-24	'Hind'	Russia	Mil
Mi-25	'Hind'	Russia	Mil
Mi-26	'Halo'	Russia	Mil
Mi-28	'Havoc'	Russia	Mil
Mi-35	(Mi-25)		
NAS-332	AS-332	Indon/France	Nurtanio/Aérospatiale
NB-412	Bell 412	Indon/US	Nurtanio/Bell
NBo-105	Bo-105	Indon/Ge	Nurtanio/MBB
NH-300	(Hughes 300)	Italy/US	Nardi/MD
NSA-330	(SA-330)	Indon/France	Nurtanio/Aérospatiale
OH-6	*Cayuse* (Hughes 369)	US	MD
OH-13	(Bell 47G)		
OH-23	*Raven*	US	Hiller
OH-58	*Kiowa* (Bell 206)		
OH-58D	(Bell 406)		
PAH-1	(Bo-105)		
Partizan	(*Gazela*, armed)		
PZL-W3	*Sokol*	Poland	Swidnik
RH-53	(CH-53)		
S-55	(*Whirlwind*)	US	Sikorsky
S-58	(*Wessex*)	US	Sikorsky
S-61	SH-3		
S-65	CH-53		
S-70	UH-60		
S-76		US	Sikorsky
S-80	CH-53		
SA-315	*Lama* [*Alouette* II]	France	Aérospatiale
SA-316	*Alouette* III (SA-319)	France	Aérospatiale
SA-318	*Alouette* II (SE-3130)	France	Aérospatiale
SA-319	*Alouette* III (SA-316)	France	Aérospatiale
SA-321	*Super Frelon*	France	Aérospatiale
SA-330	*Puma*	France	Aérospatiale
SA-341/-342	*Gazelle*	France	Aérospatiale
SA-360	*Dauphin*	France	Aérospatiale
SA-365	*Dauphin* II (SA-360)		
Scout	(*Wasp*)	UK	Westland
SE-3130	(SA-318)		
SE-316	(SA-316)		
Sea King	[SH-3]	UK	Westland
SH-2	*Sea Sprite*	US	Kaman
SH-3	(*Sea King*)	US	Sikorsky
SH-34	(S-58)		
SH-57	Bell 206		
SH-60	*Sea Hawk* (UH-60)		
Sioux	(Bell 47)	UK	Westland
TH-55	Hughes 269		
TH-57	*SeaRanger* (Bell 206)		
UH-1	*Iroquois* (Bell 204/205)		
UH-12	(OH-23)	US	Hiller
UH-13	(Bell 47J)		
UH-19	(S-55)		
UH-34T	(S-58T)		
UH-46	(CH-46)		
UH-60	*Black Hawk* (SH-60)	US	Sikorsky
VH-4	(Bell 206)		
Wasp	(*Scout*)	UK	Westland
Wessex	(S-58)	US/UK	Sikorsky/Westland
Whirlwind	(S-55)	US/UK	Sikorsky/Westland
Z-5	[Mi-4]	China	Harbin
Z-6	[Z-5]	China	Harbin
Z-8	[SA-321]	China	Changhe
Z-9	[SA-365]	China	Harbin

Type	Name/ designation	Origin	Maker	Type	Name/ designation	Origin	Maker
Halcón	[C-101]			L-21	*Super Cub*	US	Piper
Harrier	(AV-8)	UK	BAe	L-29	*Delfin*	Cz	Aero
Harvard	(T-6)			L-39	*Albatros*	Cz	Aero
Hawk		UK	BAe	L-70	*Vinka*	Finland	Valmet
HC-130	(C-130)			L-100	C-130		
HF-24	*Marut*	India	HAL		(civil version)		
HFB-320	*Hansajet*	Ge	Hamburger FB	L-188	*Electra* (P-3 *Orion*)	US	Lockheed
				L-410	*Turbolet*	Cz	LET
HJ-5	(H-5)			L-1011	*Tristar*	US	Lockheed
HJT-16	*Kiran*	India	HAL	*Learjet*	(C-21)	US	Gates
HPT-32	*Deepak*	India	HAL	Li-2	[DC-3]	Russia	Lisunov
HS-125	(*Dominie*)	UK	BAe	LR-1	(MU-2)		
HS-748	[*Andover*]	UK	BAe	*Magister*	CM-170		
HT-2		India	HAL	*Marut*	HF-24		
HU-16	*Albatross*	US	Grumman	*Mashshaq*	MFI-17	Pakistan/ Sweden	PAC/ SAAB
HU-25	(*Falcon 20*)						
Hunter		UK	BAe	*Matador*	(AV-8)		
HZ-5	(H-5)			MB-326		Italy	Aermacchi
IA-35	*Huanquero*	Arg	FMA	MB-339	(*Veltro*)	Italy	Aermacchi
IA-50	*Guaraní*	Arg	FMA	MBB-233	*Flamingo*		
IA-58	*Pucará*	Arg	FMA	MC-130	(C-130)		
IA-63	*Pampa*	Arg	FMA	*Mercurius*	(HS-125)		
IAI-201/-202	*Arava*	Israel	IAI	*Merlin*		US	Fairchild
IAI-1124	*Westwind, Seascan*	Israel	IAI	*Mescalero*	T-41		
IAR-28		Ro	IAR	*Metro*		US	Fairchild
IAR-93	*Orao*	Yug/Ro	SOKO/IAR	MFI-15	*Safari*	Sweden	SAAB
Il-14	'Crate'	Russia	Ilyushin	MFI-17	*Supporter*, (T-17)	Sweden	SAAB
Il-18	'Coot'	Russia	Ilyushin	MH-1521	*Broussard*	France	Max Holste
Il-20	(Il-18)			MiG-15	'Midget' trg	Russia	MiG
Il-28	'Beagle'	Russia	Ilyushin	MiG-17	'Fresco'	Russia	MiG
Il-38	'May'	Russia	Ilyushin	MiG-19	'Farmer'	Russia	MiG
Il-62	'Classic'	Russia	Ilyushin	MiG-21	'Fishbed'	Russia	MiG
Il-76	'Candid' (tpt)	Russia	Ilyushin	MiG-23	'Flogger'	Russia	MiG
	'Mainstay' (AEW)			MiG-25	'Foxbat'	Russia	MiG
	'Midas' (tkr)			MiG-27	'Flogger D'	Russia	MiG
Impala	[MB-326]	S. Africa	Atlas	MiG-29	'Fulcrum'	Russia	MiG
Islander	BN-2			MiG-31	'Foxhound'	Russia	MiG
J-2	[MiG-15]	China		*Mirage*		France	Dassault
J-5	[MiG-17F]	China	Shenyang	*Mission-master*	N-22		
J-6	[MiG-19]	China	Shenyang				
J-7	[MiG-21]	China	Xian	*Mohawk*	OV-1		
J-8	[Sov Ye-142]	China	Shenyang	MS-760	*Paris*	France	Aérospatiale
J-32	*Lansen*	Sweden	SAAB	MS-893	*Commodore*		
J-35	*Draken*	Sweden	SAAB	MU-2		Japan	Mitsubishi
J-37	*Viggen*	Sweden	SAAB	*Musketeer*	Beech 24	US	Beech
JA-37	(J-37)			Mya-4	'Bison'	Russia	Myasishchev
Jaguar		Fr/UK	SEPECAT	*Mystère-Falcon*		France	Dassault
JAS-39	*Gripen*	Sweden	SAAB	N-22	*Floatmaster,*	Aust	GAF
Jastreb		Yug	SOKO		*Missionmaster*		
Jet Provost		UK	BAe	N-24	*Searchmaster* B/L	Aust	GAF
Jetstream		UK	BAe				
JJ-6	(J-6)			N-262	*Frégate*	France	Aérospatiale
JZ-6	(J-6)			N-2501	*Noratlas*	France	Aérospatiale
KA-3	[A-3]			*Navajo*	PA-31	US	Piper
KA-6	[A-6]			NC-212	C-212	Sp/Indon	CASA/ Nurtanio
KC-10	*Extender* [DC-10]	US	MD				
KC-130	[C-130]			NC-235	C-235	Sp/Indon	CASA/ Nurtanio
KC-135	[Boeing 707]						
KE-3	[E-3]			*Nesher*	[*Mirage* III]	Israel	IAI
Kfir		Israel	IAI	NF-5	(F-5)		
King Air		US	Beech	*Nightingale*	(DC-9)		
Kiran	HJT-16			*Nimrod*		UK	BAe
Kraguj		Yug	SOKO	O-1	*Bird Dog*	US	Cessna
Kudu	C-4M			O-2	(Cessna 337, *Skymaster*)	US	Cessna
LIM-6	[MiG-17]	Poland					
L-4	*Cub*			OA-4	(A-4)		
L-18	*Super Cub*	US	Piper	OA-37	*Dragonfly*		
L-19	O-1						

ABBREVIATIONS

(	under 100 tons
–	part of unit is detached/ less than
+	unit reinforced/more than
*	training aircraft considered as combat capable
†	equipment where serviceability is in doubt
ε	estimated
' '	unit with overstated title/ ship class nickname
AA	anti-aircraft
AAM	air-to-air missile(s)
AAV	amphibious armoured vehicle
AAW	anti-air warfare
AB	airborne
ABD	airborne division
ABM	anti-ballistic missile(s)
about	the total could be higher
ac	aircraft
ACC	Air Combat Command (US)
ACM	advanced cruise missile
ACV	air cushion vehicle/vessel
AD	air defence
adj	adjusted
AE	auxiliary(ies), ammunition carrier
AEF	auxiliary(ies) explosives and stores
AEW	airborne early warning
AF	stores ship(s) with RAS capability
AFB/S	Air Force Base/Station
AFR	Air Force Reserve (US)
AGHS	hydrographic survey vessel(s)
AGI	intelligence collection vessel(s)
AGOR	oceanographic research vessel(s)
AGOS	ocean surveillance vessel(s)
AH	hospital ship(s)
AIFV	armoured infantry fighting vehicle
AIP	air-independent propulsion
AK	cargo ship(s)
ALARM	air-launched anti-radiation missile
ALCM	air-launched cruise missile(s)
AMC	Air Mobility Command (US)
amph	amphibious/amphibian(s)
ANG	Air National Guard (US)
AO	tanker(s) with RAS capability
AOE	auxiliary(ies), fuel and ammunition, RAS capability
AOT	tanker(s) without RAS capability
AP	passenger ship(s)
APC	armoured personnel carrier(s)
AR	repair ship(s)
AR	Army Reserve (US)
Arg	Argentina
ARM	anti-radiation (anti-radar) missile
armd	armoured
ARNG	Army National Guard (US)

arty	artillery
AS	submarine depot ship(s)
aslt	assault
ASM	air-to-surface missile(s)
ASTT	anti-submarine TT
ASUW	anti-surface-unit warfare
ASW	anti-submarine warfare
AT	tug(s)
ATBM	anti-tactical ballistic missile
ATGW	anti-tank guided weapon(s)
ATK	anti-tank
ATTU	Atlantic to the Urals
Aust	Australia
avn	aviation
AVT	aviation training ship
AWACS	airborne warning and control system
BA	Budget Authority
BB	battleship(s)
bbr	bomber(s)
bde	brigade(s)
bdgt	budget(s)
Be	Belgium
bn	battalion(s)/billion(s)
BSAG	battleship surface attack group
bty	battery(ies)
Bu	Bulgaria
cal	calibration
CAS	close air support
Cat	Category
cav	cavalry
cbt	combat
CBW	chemical and biological warfare
CC	cruiser(s)
Cdn	Canada
cdo	commando
CG	SAM cruiser(s)
CGH	CG with helicopters
CGN	nuclear-fuelled CG
cgo	freight aircraft
Ch	China (PRC)
CIS	Commonwealth of Independent States
COIN	counter-insurgency
comb	combined/combination
comd	command
comms	communications
CONUS	Continental United States
coy	company(ies)
CSCE	Conference on Security and Cooperation in Europe
CV	aircraft carrier(s)
CVBG	carrier battle group
CVN	nuclear-fuelled CV
CVV	V/STOL and hel CV
CW	chemical warfare
Cz	Czechoslovakia
DD	destroyer(s)
DDG	destroyer(s) with area SAM
DDH	destroyer(s) with hel
def	defence
defn	definition
det	detachment(s)
div	division(s)
Dk	Denmark

ECM	electronic countermeasures
ECR	electronic combat and reconnaissance
ELINT	electronic intelligence
elm	element(s)
engr	engineer(s)
EOD	explosive ordnance disposal
eqpt	equipment
ESM	electronic support measures
est	estimate(d)
EW	electronic warfare
excl	excludes/excluding
exp	expenditure
FAC	forward air control
fd	field
FF	frigate(s)
FFG	frigate(s) with area SAM
FFH	frigate(s) with helicopter
FGA	fighter(s), ground-attack
flt	flight(s)
FMA	foreign military assistance
Fr	France
ftr	fighter(s) (aircraft)
FW	fixed-wing
FY	fiscal year
GA	Chinese Integrated Group Army
GDP	gross domestic product
Ge	Germany
GNP	gross national product
gp	group(s)
Gr	Greece
GW	guided weapon(s)
hel	helicopter(s)
HWT	heavy-weight torpedo(es)
Hu	Hungary
hy	heavy
ICBM	intercontinental ballistic missile(s)
imp	improved
incl	includes/including
indep	independent
Indon	Indonesia
inf	infantry
INF	intermediate-range nuclear forces
IRBM	intermediate-range ballistic missile(s)
Is	Israel
It	Italy
kg	kilogram(s)
km	kilometre(s)
KT	kiloton(s)
LAMPS	light airborne multi-purpose system
LANTIRN	low altitude navigation and targeting infra-red system night
LCA	landing craft, assault
LCAC	landing craft, air cushion
LCM	landing craft, mechanized
LCT	landing craft, tank
LCU	landing craft, utility
LCVP	landing craft, vehicles and personnel
LHA	landing ship(s), assault
LKA	assault cargo ship(s)
log	logistic

Type	Name/designation	Origin	Maker
Tu-28	*'Fiddler'*	Russia	Tupolev
Tu-95	*'Bear'*	Russia	Tupolev
Tu-126	*'Moss'*	Russia	Tupolev
Tu-134	*'Crusty'*	Russia	Tupolev
Tu-142	*'Bear F'*	Russia	Tupolev
Tu-154	*'Careless'*	Russia	Tupolev
Tu-160	*'Blackjack'*	Russia	Tupolev
Turbo Porter	PC-6A/B		
Twin Bonanza	Beech 50		
Twin Otter	DHC-6		
Tzukit	[CM-170]	Israel	IAI
U-2		US	Lockheed
U-3	(Cessna 310)	US	Cessna
U-7	(L-18)		
U-8	(Twin Bonanza/ Queen Air)	US	Beech
U-9	(EMB-121)		
U-10	*Super Courier*	US	Helio
U-17	(Cessna 180, 185)	US	Cessna
U-21	(King Air)		
U-36	(Learjet)		
U-42	(C-42)		
U-93	(HS-125)		
UC-12	(King Air)		
UP-2J	(P-2J)		
US-1		Japan	Shin Meiwa
US-2A	(S-2A, tpt)		
US-3	(S-3, tpt)		
UTVA-66		Yug	UTVA
UTVA-75		Yug	UTVA
UV-18	(DHC-6)		
V-400	*Fantrainer* 400	Ge	VFW
V-600	*Fantrainer* 600	Ge	VFW
Vampire	DH-100		
VC-4	*Gulfstream* I		
VC-10		UK	BAe
VC-11	*Gulfstream* II		
VC-91	(HS-748)		
VC-93	(HS-125)		
VC-97	(EMB-120)		
VC-130	(C-130)		
VFW-614		Ge	VFW
Victor		UK	BAe
Vinka	L-70		
Viscount		UK	BAe
VU-9	(EMB-121)		
VU-93	(HS-125)		
WC-130	[C-130]		
WC-135	[Boeing 707]	US	Boeing
Westwind	IAI-1124		
Winjeel	CA-25		
Xavante	EMB-326		
Xingu	EMB-121		
Y-5	[An-2]	China	Hua Bei
Y-7	[An-24]	China	Xian
Y-8	[An-12]	China	Shaanxi
Y-12		China	Harbin
Yak-11	*'Moose'*	Russia	Yakovlev
Yak-18	*'Max'*	Russia	Yakovlev
Yak-28	*'Firebar'* (*'Brewer'*)	Russia	Yakovlev
Yak-38	*'Forger'*	Russia	Yakovlev
Yak-40	*'Codling'*	Russia	Yakovlev
YS-11		Japan	Nihon
Z-43		Cz	Zlin
Z-226		Cz	Zlin
Z-326		Cz	Zlin
Z-526		Cz	Zlin
Zéphyr	CM-175		

HELICOPTERS

Type	Name/designation	Origin	Maker
A-109	*Hirundo*	Italy	Agusta
A-129	*Mangusta*	Italy	Agusta
AB-. . .	(Bell 204/205/206/ 212/214, etc.)	Italy/ US	Agusta/ Bell
AH-1	*Cobra/ Sea Cobra*	US	Bell
AH-6	(Hughes 500/530)	US	MD
AH-64	*Apache*	US	Hughes
Alouette II	SE-3130, SA-318	France	Aérospatiale
Alouette III	SA-316, SA-319	France	Aérospatiale
AS-61	(SH-3)	US/Italy	Sikorsky/Agusta
AS-332	*Super Puma*	France	Aérospatiale
AS-350	*Ecureuil*	France	Aérospatiale
AS-355	*Ecureuil II*		
AS-550	*Fennec*	France	Aérospatiale
ASH-3	(*Sea King*)	Italy/US	Agusta/Sikorsky
AUH-76	(S-76)		
Bell 47		US	Bell
Bell 204		US	Bell
Bell 205		US	Bell
Bell 206		US	Bell
Bell 212		US	Bell
Bell 214		US	Bell
Bell 406		US	Bell
Bell 412		US	Bell
Bo-105	(NBo-105)	Ge	MBB
CH-3	(SH-3)		
CH-34	*Choctaw*	US	Sikorsky
CH-46	*Sea Knight*	US	Boeing-Vertol
CH-47	*Chinook*	US	Boeing-Vertol
CH-53	*Stallion (Sea Stallion)*	US	Sikorsky
CH-54	*Tarhe*	US	Sikorsky
CH-113	(CH-46)		
CH-118	Bell 205		
CH-124	SH-3		
CH-135	Bell 212		
CH-136	OH-58		
CH-139	Bell 206		
CH-147	CH-47		
Cheetah	[SA-315]	India	HAL
Chetak	[SA-319]	India	HAL
Commando	(SH-3)	UK/US	Westland/ Sikorsky
EH-60	(UH-60)		
EH-101		UK/ Italy	Westland/ Agusta
FH-1100	(OH-5)	US	Fairchild- Hiller
Gazela	(SA-342)	France/ Yug	Aérospatiale/ SOKO
Gazelle	SA-341/-342		
H-34	(S-58)		
H-76	S-76		
HA-15	Bo-105		
HB-315	*Gavião* (SA-315)	Brazil/ France	Helibras/ Aérospatiale
HB-350	*Esquilo* (AS-350)	Brazil/ France	Helibras/ Aérospatiale
HD-16	SA-319		
HH-3	(SH-3)		
HH-34	(CH-34)		
HH-53	(CH-53)		
Hkp-2	*Alouette* II/ SE-3130		
Hkp-3	AB-204		

1993 SUBSCRIPTIONS ORDER FORM

(for single copy sales see over)

Please tick appropriate box to order

Please enter me a **Military Balance** Subscription for:

☐ 1993 at £35.00/$58.00

Please enter me a **Strategic Survey** Subscription for:

☐ 1993 at £18.00/$29.00

Please enter me a **Survival** Subscription for:

☐ 1993 at £36.00/$50.00

Please enter me an **Adelphi Papers** Subscription for:

☐ 1993 at £83.00/$135.00

Please enter me a **Combined** Subscription for:

☐ 1993 at £166.00/$259.00

(Combined Subscription includes a copy of The Military Balance and Strategic Survey, plus four issues of Survival and approximately ten Adelphi Papers)

PAYMENT:

☐ Payment enclosed £/$ . . . .   ☐ Bill me

Payment Method: ☐ Cheque   ☐ Postal Order   ☐ International Money Order
(Please make cheques, etc., payable to **Brassey's (UK) Ltd.**)

Credit Cards ☐ Access ☐ Mastercard ☐ Visa

Card No. ☐☐☐☐☐☐☐☐☐☐☐☐☐☐☐☐

Expiry date _____

Signature *(obligatory for credit card orders)*: . . . .

Name _____

Address _____

City _____

Country _____

PLEASE PRINT NAME AND ADDRESS CLEARLY

Please return this card, in an envelope, to the appropriate address below:

(residents of North America):

IISS Subscriptions
Turpin Transactions
P.O. Box 9931
McLean, VA 22102
Fax: (703) 790 9063

(residents of ALL other countries):

Turpin Distribution Services Ltd
Blackhorse Road
Letchworth, Herts.
SG6 1HN UK
Phone: (+44) 462 672555
Fax: (+44) 462 480947

SINGLE COPY SALES ORDER FORM

Please tick appropriate box to order. All orders must be prepaid.

☐ *Military Balance 1992–1993* (Flexicover) 1-85753-027-6 £35.00/$55.00

☐ *Military Balance 1991–1992* (Hardback) 0-08 041324 2 £39.95/$67.95

☐ *Strategic Survey 1991–1992* (Flexicover) 0-08-041784-1 £20.00/$30.00

☐ *Strategic Survey 1990–1991* (Hardback) 0-08-040975-X £24.95/$42.95

Please send .... copies of *The Military Balance 1992–1993*
at £35.00/$55.00 (Flexicover) (ISBN 1-85753-027-6)

Please send .... copies of *Strategic Survey 1991–1992*
at £20.00/$30.00 (Flexicover) (ISBN 0-08-041784-1)

PAYMENT:

☐ Payment enclosed £/$ .... ☐ Bill me

Payment Method: ☐ Cheque ☐ Postal Order ☐ International Money Order
(Please make cheques, etc., payable to **Brassey's (UK) Ltd.**)

Credit Cards ☐ Access ☐ Mastercard ☐ Visa ☐ Amex ☐ Diners

Card No. ☐☐☐☐☐☐☐☐☐☐☐☐☐☐☐☐

Expiry date _____

Signature (*obligatory for credit card orders*): ....

Name _____

Address _____

City _____

Country _____

PLEASE
PRINT
NAME AND
ADDRESS
CLEARLY

Please return this card, in an envelope, to the appropriate address below:

Marston Book Services
P.O. Box 87
Oxford OX2 0DT
Tel: 0865 791155
Fax: 0865 791927

Post & Packaging Charges
        1 book Per Extra Book
UK   £1.50   £1.00
Europe £2.50   £1.50

North America only:
Macmillan Distribution Center
Book Order Department
100 Front and Brown Street
Box 500
Riverside, NJ 08075-7500
TOLL FREE TEL: 1-800-257-5755
TOLL FREE FAX: 1-800-562-1272
Please add state or local tax and
$2.50 for Shipping/Handling